Second Edition

Basic Construction Materials

CHARLES A. HERUBIN, P.E.
Associate Professor of Civil Engineering Technology
Hudson Valley Community College

THEODORE W. MAROTTA
Associate Professor of Civil Engineering Technology
Hudson Valley Community College

Reston Publishing Company, Inc.
Reston, Virginia
A Prentice-Hall Company

Library of Congress Cataloging in Publication Data

Herubin, Charles A. 1931–
  Basic construction materials.

  Includes index.
  1. Building materials. I. Marotta, Theodore W.,
joint author. II. Title.
TA403.H43 1981   624.1′8   80-28984
ISBN 0-8359-0362-1

© 1981 by
Reston Publishing Company, Inc.
A Prentice-Hall Company
Reston, Virginia 22090

10 9 8 7 6 5 4 3 2 1

Printed in the United States of America.

CHAPTER 5   IRON AND STEEL   201

CHAPTER 6   WOOD   235

CHAPTER 4   PORTLAND CEMENT CONCRETE   145

CHAPTER 3   ASPHALT   83

Contents

Preface

This book is intended to help the reader to prepare for work in the construction industry whether in designing, supplying materials, selecting materials, building, or inspecting a builder's operations. It covers a few basic materials of the many used in construction. These are covered thoroughly in order to provide a solid preparation for further courses in construction methods, specification writing, or design methods, or for entering the construction field.

The materials selected for the book are aggregates, asphalt, portland cement concrete, iron, steel, and wood. These are the materials most widely used in construction and, with the exception of the metals, are the ones over which people in the construction industry have the most control. Shaping to final size, protecting from the elements, and fitting together are accomplished in the field to a greater extent with these materials than with most of the others, which are prepared in a factory and simply set in place at the construction site.

We appreciate the assistance of all the technical organizations and manufacturers' associations whose publications provided much valuable information for this book. Comments from our teaching colleagues and students have also been very helpful and are gratefully acknowledged.

Charles A. Herubin
Theodore W. Marotta

1

Introduction

Every construction project is intended to result in a finished product which will perform certain functions in conformance with, and sometimes in spite of, the effects of nature. Whether or not satisfactory results are achieved depends upon the materials selected and how they are used. They must perform under specific conditions of usage. The designer, the builder, and the user must all understand construction materials to produce the finished facility and to use it to best advantage. Knowledge of design procedures, construction methods, and maintenance practices is needed. Underlying all these qualifications is a knowledge of materials. In order to be completely satisfactory, each material used must perform its function well over a sufficiently long time, and both original cost and maintenance expense must be reasonable.

THE CONSTRUCTION PROCESS

The construction process begins when a person or organization, hereafter called the *owner*, decides to improve the land with permanent or semi-permanent additions. The next step is to hire a *designer*, either an engineer or an architect, to design the finished construction project. The designer's organization prepares *plans* consisting of drawings showing how the finished construction will look. The plans explain briefly what materials are to be used. *Specifications* are prepared explaining in greater detail what materials to use, the characteristics the materials must have, and what methods of inspection and testing the owner's representative will use to check those characteristics.

Basic materials, such as wood, iron, and stone, and manufactured products, such as plywood sheets, cast iron pipe, and concrete blocks, must all be specified. Combinations of materials are commonplace, such as trusses consisting of glued laminated timber members in combination with steel members, cast iron pipe with portland cement lining, concrete beams reinforced with prestressed steel wire, or window and frame units containing glass, several kinds of metal, and plastic all in one *assembly*.

1

An assembly is either fully built at the factory (*shop assembled*) or partially completed in the factory and assembled in the field (*jobsite assembled*). Some of the types of work performed in the field are also manufacturing processes. The mixing and placing of concrete and the cutting and welding of steel are in this category.

A *builder* is chosen to perform the construction and enters into a contract with the owner to provide a finished product completed in accordance with the plans and specifications. The owner is represented during the construction stage by an agent, usually the designer, who *supervises construction* by administering the contract impartially, by approving or rejecting materials and workmanship, by approving final construction, and by determining the amount of payment due. *Inspectors* are present at the jobsite to inspect the work in progress and perform field tests as part of construction supervision. Laboratory testing may be performed by an *independent testing laboratory*. The testing laboratory reports whether or not materials comply with specifications.

The builder uses materials in his operation which do not become part of the finished construction and are not controlled by the designer. Examples are temporary sheeting to hold back the sides of an excavation, and removable forms to hold concrete in the desired shape until it cures. The builder, like the designer, must select, inspect, and test materials best suited for his purpose from among those available.

Those who supply materials and partially or fully assembled components to be used in construction are called *suppliers*. Included are manufacturers, quarries, saw mills, and others.

NEED FOR MATERIALS WITH VARIOUS QUALITIES

The construction industry requires materials for a vast range of uses. The qualities these materials possess are as varied as the strength and flexibility required of an elevator cable or the warm, wood grain appearance and smooth finish of a birch or maple cabinet. (See Fig. 1-1.)

The construction of a building requires selection of materials to perform the following tasks:

1. Footing

    a. Distribute the weight of the building to the soil

    b. Resist cracking despite uneven soil settlement

    c. Resist corrosive attack from soil and water

2. Basement floor

    a. Provide a smooth surface

    b. Resist wear

    c. Resist cracking despite upward water pressure or uneven soil settlement

    d. Keep moisture out

    e. Resist corrosive attack from soil and water

3. Basement walls

    a. Support the rest of the building

    b. Resist lateral side pressure from the earth

    c. Keep moisture out

    d. Resist corrosive attack from soil and water

4. Other floors and ceilings

    a. Provide a smooth surface

    b. Resist wear

    c. Support furniture and people without sagging excessively or breaking

    d. Provide a satisfactory appearance

    e. Clean easily

    f. Insulate against noise transmission

5. Outside walls

    a. Support floors and roof

    b. Resist lateral wind pressure

    c. Provide a satisfactory appearance inside and out

    d. Insulate against noise and heat transmission

    e. Keep moisture out

6. Partitions

    a. Support floors and roof

    b. Provide a satisfactory appearance

    c. Insulate against noise transmission

7. Roof

    a. Keep moisture out

    b. Support snow and other weights

    c. Resist wind pressure and wind uplift

    d. Provide a satisfactory appearance

    e. Insulate against noise and heat transmission

(a)

(c)

(b)

4

(e)

(d)

FIGURE 1-1. Materials for various types of construction: (A) asphalt concrete pavement; (B) concrete bridge (Courtesy Portland Cement Association); (C) steel towers; (D) wood floor pattern (Courtesy Wood Mosaic); (E) wood framing (Courtesy Weyerhaeuser)

The types of materials used in smaller buildings have become somewhat standardized. However, new materials are constantly being proposed, and the use of the better ones results in lowered costs or improved living conditions. Their development and proper use require an understanding of materials.

A building is used to illustrate the point that a construction project includes many components that must perform various functions and that new materials must be constantly analyzed. However, the same is true of any other construction project. A project such as paving a street or laying a pipeline requires more kinds of material to perform more differing functions than the casual observer would ever guess. New materials are continually available in these fields also.

As man's desires expand, the need is created for materials with new qualities. In order to explore space, lightweight materials were needed that could resist heat of a higher degree than ever before. Necessary qualities may be obtained by developing special treatments for common materials or by developing entirely new materials. For example, treatments have been developed to make wood highly fire resistant. The development of steel allowed the construction of bridges with longer spans than had been possible when wood was the only available material.

SELECTING MATERIALS

We constantly encounter man-made objects built of materials carefully selected to be the most satisfactory ones for that particular use. Any satisfactory choice always requires a knowledge of construction materials and an adequate selection procedure.

A construction project originates in the mind of the owner. The owner may be a city administrator determined to build a sewer system and a plant for treating sewage; a landowner who wants to build an office building and lease office space; or a government body planning to build a dam or bridge. The owner is concerned with the cost of the project and the service it will provide.

A designer is selected who, among other things, is responsible for selection of all construction materials to achieve the desired performance within the budget cost. He considers the service each component must perform, appearance, original cost, maintenance expense, and useful life expectancy. Maintenance includes such operations as cleaning, preventing and repairing corrosion damage, and repairing or replacing damaged material.

Original cost and maintenance expense must be weighed together against useful life expectancy. Original cost and maintenance expense must also be balanced against each other. Often a low first cost means high maintenance expense and vice versa. However, this is not always so. Expensive material may be expensive to maintain. Even though it is the total cost that must be considered, it is important to remember that the original cost must be paid during construction and immediately thereafter, while the maintenance expense is paid through the life of the facility.

The designer may then select the material or assembly he wants, or prepare specifications describing the performance required and let the builder do the selecting within the requirements of the specifications subject to the approval of the person supervising construction.

If the designer specifies exactly what materials and assemblies are to be incorporated into the project, he knows, either from past experience or from investigation, that they will be satisfactory. He avoids the risk of using something new or unfamiliar. He also misses the opportunity of using something that is more economical or performs better. Specifications prepared this way are called *material specifications*.

If the designer specifies performance in terms of appearance, strength, corrosion resistance, and other features, he has the benefit of the builder's experience in selecting the most economical materials. Specifications prepared this way are called *performance specifications*. They must be very carefully written to prevent any inferior products from satisfying the specification requirements; and the builder's selections must be carefully investigated to be sure they are acceptable according to the specifications. Both types of specification and various combinations of the two types are used. Each type is suitable for certain cases.

The process of selection includes the following steps:

1. Analysis of the problem (performance required, useful life required, allowable cost and maintenance expense);

2. Comparison of available materials or products with the criteria of step 1;

3. Design or selection of type of material, size, shape, finish, method of preserving, and method of fastening in place.

PROPERTIES OF MATERIALS

The properties most often considered when selecting building materials are discussed here.

Thermal Expansion

All building materials change size with a change in temperature, becoming smaller when colder and larger when hotter. A long piece of material, if heated uniformly, expands with each unit length becoming a certain percentage longer. This elongation takes place in all directions and is somewhat different for each material. In order to define the amount of expansion to be expected, a *coefficient of expansion* is determined for each material. It is a decimal representing the increase in length per unit length per degree increase in temperature. The coefficient varies somewhat at different temperatures but is nearly constant for the range of temperatures involved in most cases so that one coefficient can be used for each material.

The coefficient of expansion for iron is 0.0000067 in. per in. per °F or 0.0000121 cm per cm per °C. Each in. of length, width, or thickness becomes 1.0000067 in. if the temperature is increased 1 °F and increased an additional 0.0000067 in. for each additional °F increase. As the temperature decreases, the dimensions decrease at the same rate. Figure 1-2 shows the coefficients of expansion for some common building materials.

Materials to be used together in an assembly must have approximately the same coefficients of expansion or else some provision must be made for

Material	Coefficient of Linear Expansion	
	per °F	per °C
Asphalt	0.00034*	0.00061*
Portland cement concrete	Assumed to be 0.0000055 but varies from 0.000004 to 0.000007	Assumed to be 0.0000099 but varies from 0.000007 to 0.000013
Gray cast iron	0.0000059	0.0000106
Wrought iron	0.0000067	0.0000121
Structural steel	0.0000065	0.0000117
Stainless steel	0.0000055 to 0.0000096	0.0000099 to 0.0000173
	parallel to grain	
Wood	0.000001 to 0.000003	0.000002 to 0.000005
	perpendicular to grain	
	0.000015 to 0.000035	0.000027 to 0.000063
Mineral aggregate	0.000003 to 0.000007	0.000005 to 0.000013

*Coefficient of volumetric expansion.
Coefficient of linear expansion is not useful.

FIGURE 1-2. Coefficients of expansion

their different expansions. Long structural members may expand and contract so much that expansion room must be provided at the ends.

Thermal Conductivity

A building used by people must be kept warmer than the surrounding air in cold climates and cooler than the surrounding air in hot climates. Heat flows to a cooler area much like water flows to a lower level. The flow continues until outside and inside temperatures are equal. Heat movement takes place by conduction through any solid object separating areas of different temperatures. It costs money to heat or cool a building, and the movement of heat in the wrong direction is expensive. The rate at which it takes place varies with the material through which the heat passes. For large areas such as walls and roofs this rate is an important consideration. The rate is measured as thermal conductivity (U) in British thermal units (Btu) of heat transmitted per square foot of cross section per hour per °F difference in temperature between the two sides of the material. *Insulation,* which is material with a very low U, is used to line large surfaces to lessen the rate of heat flow. The U of a material varies directly with its density. Dead air spaces in a material are effective in reducing the U factor. The best insulation, expanded plastic foam, consists of bubbles with the proportion of solid material less than 1 percent of the volume and the rest consisting of air or gas. Insulation is also made of fibers, ground particles, or other porous material. However, some structural materials have a low U factor and therefore serve as insulation also. Wood and certain types of lightweight concrete are two such materials that are covered in this book.

Sound Absorption

Loud sound is objectionable in most buildings and is reduced by the use of acoustic material to absorb it, whether originating in the building or outside. Sound is absorbed by air spaces in the material. Porous material is used, or material is fabricated with a pattern of openings to absorb sound. Among the materials discussed in this book, wood and rough-surfaced, porous concrete are effective in absorbing sound.

Strength and Stress

All construction materials must resist force. A *force* is a push or pull that has a value and a direction. The pull of gravity is responsible for most of the forces dealt with in construction. However, there are other causes such as wind and water currents. *Unit stress,* also referred to as *stress,* is force per unit area over which the force acts. It is obtained by dividing the force by the area on which it acts and is expressed as pounds per square inch, or psi.

Strength of a material, in general terms, is the ability to resist a force.

That ability depends on the size and shape of the object as well as on the material of which it is made. A large object can resist more force than a small object of the same material.

In order that strength may be considered as a property of the material, it is necessary to relate strength to the material itself regardless of its size or shape. Therefore, the *strength* of a material in technical terms is equal to the unit stress that the material can resist. Strength has the same units as unit stress.

The useful strength of a material is equal to the unit stress at failure. Failure takes place when an object can no longer serve its purpose. The material may fail by breaking or by excessive deformation. *Deformation* means a change in the outside dimensions of an object caused by a force.

The amount of deformation depends on the size and shape of the object as well as on the material of which it is made. As in the case of strength it is desirable to relate deformation to the material itself regardless of its size or shape. The term *unit strain,* also referred to as *strain,* means the total change in dimension divided by the original dimension. Unit strain is the effect caused by unit stress.

Unit strain is a ratio and therefore has no units. The amount of deformation and the original length must be measured in the same units to provide a correct ratio. They are usually measured in inches.

Unit strain can be shown by stretching a rubber band or compressing or twisting a piece of rubber hose. A sample of rubber subjected to a compressive force becomes substantially shorter and a little wider. One subjected to a tensile stress becomes substantially longer and a little narrower. The deformation and original length considered in computing unit strain are the ones in the direction of the unit stress.

If a metal bar with a square cross section 2 in. by 2 in. breaks when pulled with a force of 200,000 lb, its breaking strength equals the unit stress or:

$$\text{Breaking strength} = \frac{P}{A}$$

$$= \frac{200,000 \text{ lb}}{2 \times 2 \text{ sq in.}}$$

$$= 50,000 \text{ lb per sq in.}$$

If a lower force stretches the bar so far that it is no longer useful, its failure strength equals the unit stress found by dividing the lower force by the area of the original cross section. The deformation that can be allowed in the bar depends on what it is used for. Therefore, failure depends upon the purpose for which the material is used. Failure could conceivably take place at a lower unit stress in one case with a particular material than in another case with the same material. Beams supporting a warehouse roof where appearance is not important can withstand any unit stress that does not break them; but if the beams support a plaster ceiling, they fail at a unit stress that causes sufficient deflection to crack the plaster.

Through experience and the performance of tests, the unit stress that causes failure can be determined for various materials and uses. A knowledge of this unit stress is useful for designing purposes. However, nothing is designed to be stressed to the point where it is ready to fail. Instead, a lower unit stress called the *allowable unit stress* is selected, and this is the maximum allowed.

There are several reasons for not designing a material to be stressed close to the failure stress.

1. Actual failure unit stress may be somewhat less than that determined experimentally.

2. The actual force on a structure may exceed expectations.

3. The simplified procedures used in design predict approximate unit stresses which may be somewhat exceeded in actuality.

4. Materials may be weakened by rusting (steel), rotting (wood), or spalling (concrete).

The failure unit stress is greater than the allowable unit stress by a factor called the *safety factor*. If failure unit stress is twice the value of the allowable unit stress, the safety factor is two. The safety factor equals the failure unit stress divided by the allowable unit stress.

Usually failure unit stress is determined experimentally. A safety factor and an allowable unit stress are selected by a committee of experts and the allowable unit stresses are published. Some organizations that publish allowable unit stresses are the American Institute of Steel Construction, the American Concrete Institute, and the National Forest Products Association. Designers select kinds of material and sizes and shapes of members to support loads that subject the member to unit stresses that are equal to or less than the allowable. Economy requires that the actual unit stress be near the allowable; if it is not, the material is being used inefficiently because less material would be adequate. The actual unit stress is called the *working unit stress*.

Important factors considered in deciding on a safety factor are listed here.

1. How exactly loads can be calculated,

2. How exactly unit stresses can be calculated,

3. How consistently the material conforms to the experimental strength,

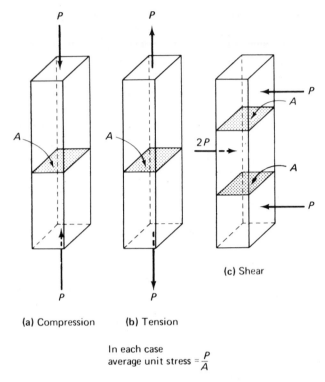

(a) Compression   (b) Tension

In each case
average unit stress $= \dfrac{P}{A}$

FIGURE 1-3. Illustration of stresses

4. How serious the consequences of a failure are, and

5. How much warning the material gives before failing.

There are three kinds of unit stresses and corresponding strengths—compressive, tensile, and shearing. They depend on the position of the forces with respect to the object. The three are illustrated in Fig. 1-3.

Unit stress is determined by dividing the acting force by the original area upon which it acts. This is the area that resists displacement. Tensile and compressive unit stresses act on the cross-sectional area perpendicular to the direction of the force. Shear unit stresses act on the cross-sectional area parallel to the direction of the force. Usually the force is not uniformly distributed across the area, but in computing tensile and compressive unit stresses it is assumed to be uniform with satisfactory accuracy.

Shearing unit stress acts unequally over an area, and the unit stress at the location of highest unit stress must be considered. The action of shearing unit stresses is complex compared to that of the axial unit stresses, tension and compression.

Since the cross sections are changed in size by forces, they influence the unit stresses. If a force remains constant, the actual unit stress changes when the cross section changes. It is customary to compute unit stress on the basis of the area as it is before any force is applied. Computations are easier this way and in all practical applications the area of interest is the original area, since any problem relating size to strength will be solved on the basis of original size, not a size distorted by a force.

Materials differ in their response to unit stress. A *ductile* material can be drawn into a thin, long wire by a tensile force. A *malleable* material can be flattened into a thin, wide sheet by a compressive force. A *brittle* material breaks with very little deformation. It appears to fail suddenly because there is no noticeable deformation to serve as a warning.

In this discussion, forces have been assumed to be applied once for a brief period of time. Ordinary tests made to determine strength consist of subjecting a sample of the material to a force that increases steadily until the material breaks. These tests take a few minutes. However, in a structure, forces may be applied for extended periods of time, they may be applied, removed, and applied many times, and they may be applied suddenly with impact or shock.

A material, even if brittle, deforms slowly when a force is applied to it for an extended period of years, even though the force is too small to cause failure in a short time. This deformation is called *creep*. The creep may be great enough to constitute failure.

Although a force of a certain amount cannot cause breaking no matter how long it is applied, it can cause breaking if it is applied and removed many times (hundreds of thousands of times) even if over a shorter time. Structural members of a bridge are subjected to application and removal of unit stress each time a vehicle crosses. Failure from this cause is called *fatigue,* and it occurs with very little deformation.

Because there is so little deformation, there is no warning and the break seems to be sudden. However, it begins as a tiny crack and becomes larger over many cycles until it fails by breaking. The smaller the unit stress, the more times it must be repeated to cause failure. There is a unit stress below which the material will not fail at any number of cycles, called the *endurance limit*.

Specimens tested for endurance are generally subjected to bending first one way and then the opposite way. This reversal of unit stress produces failure at fewer cycles than the simple application and removal of force. The endurance limit found this way may be less than half the static unit stress at failure.

Toughness is the capacity of a material to absorb energy while a force is applied to it. Energy is expended by a force acting over a distance and is absorbed by a material being forced to deform through a distance. Toughness

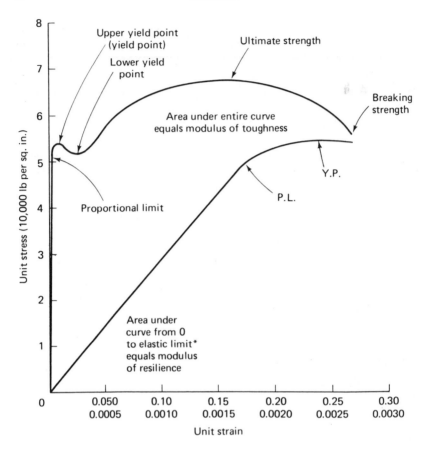

*Elastic limit is difficult to determine and is usually assumed to be at the proportional limit. This is very nearly correct and is accurate enough for ordinary use.

(a) Stress-strain diagram for ductile steel: upper curve (upper scale) shows relationship up to breaking point; lower curve (lower scale) shows curve with greater accuracy up to the yield point.

FIGURE 1-4. Stress-strain diagrams

is the product of unit stress and unit strain up to the point of fracture. It is computed by determining the area under the stress–strain curve (see Fig. 1-4) which is equivalent to multiplying the average unit stress by the total unit strain (force times distance). The result is called the *modulus of toughness*. Strength and ductility are both involved. The toughness of a material indicates its ability to withstand a sudden force known as an *impact load* or *shock load*.

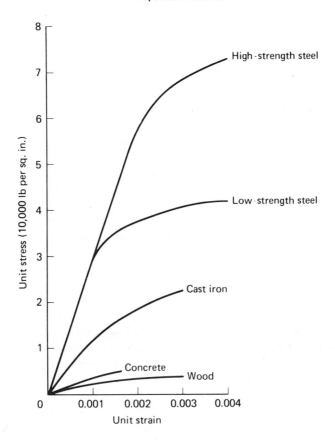

(b) Relative shapes of stress-strain diagrams for different materials

FIGURE 1-4. Stress–strain diagrams (continued)

Resilience is the ability of a material to recover its original size and shape after being deformed by an impact load. The *modulus of resilience* is the product of unit stress and unit strain up to the elastic limit. It is a measure of the useful toughness because beyond the elastic limit permanent deformation ordinarily renders the material unfit for further use. It is computed by determining the area under the stress–strain curve from zero to the elastic limit.

Modulus of Elasticity

Unit strain is directly proportional to unit stress over a considerable range for many materials. At unit stresses higher than this range, the additional unit strain is increasingly greater for each additional amount of unit stress. The unit stress at which unit strain just begins to increase at a rate greater than in the proportional range is the *proportional limit*. An example is shown in Fig. 1-4. Unit stress in lb per sq in. is a very large number compared to the resulting unit strain for almost all construction materials.

The constant value of unit stress divided by unit strain is called the *modulus of elasticity*. The relationship is expressed as modulus of elasticity equals unit stress divided by unit strain or $E = s/\epsilon$. Since ϵ is a ratio with no units, E has units of lb per sq in. the same as s although E is not a unit stress. The modulus of elasticity indicates the stiffness or resistance to movement of a material. A stiff material deforms less under a given unit stress than does a material of less stiffness. A metal wire is very stiff compared to a rubber band of the same size and the E of the metal wire is a much higher value. The modulus of elasticity is a characteristic which is different for each material.

Some materials do not have a range of constant relationship between unit stress and unit strain. The unit stress–unit strain relationship for this type of material is shown in Fig. 1-4. As unit stress is increased in a test specimen of this type of material, the unit strain increases at a greater rate. There is no modulus of elasticity for such materials because there is no range of constant relationship between unit stress and unit strain. However, an E value is so convenient for design that an approximate value is sometimes used. Any ratio of unit-stress–unit-strain selected as the E value is correct at only one unit stress or possibly two. However, a ratio may be chosen which is reasonably close throughout the range of unit stresses that is encountered in use. This ratio is used for design. Methods used to determine approximate E ratios are shown in Fig. 1-5.

Any of the values in the equation $E = s/\epsilon$ can be determined if the other two are known. The modulus of elasticity has been determined by extensive testing for all commonly used construction materials, and the usual design problem is to find either unit stress or unit strain. In experimental work a sample is tested under increasing unit stress with the unit strain being measured. Both are recorded at suitable intervals and the values used to plot their relationship.

The modulus E applies to compressive or tensile forces and for most materials is very nearly the same in compression and tension. The relationship of shearing unit stress to shearing unit strain is designated E_s (the modulus of rigidity) and is a lower value.

Elastic and Plastic Properties

Elasticity is the property of a material that enables it to return to its original size and shape after a force is removed. Elasticity is not judged by the amount of unit strain caused by a given unit stress, but by the completeness with which the material returns to its original size and shape when the force is removed. A metal wire does not stretch nearly as far as the same size rubber

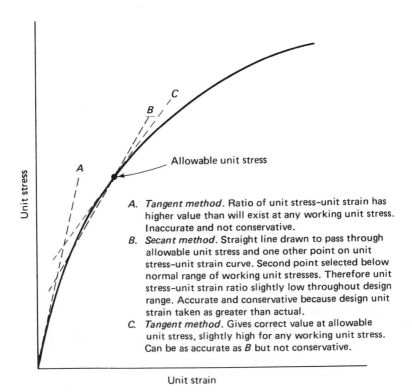

A. *Tangent method*. Ratio of unit stress–unit strain has higher value than will exist at any working unit stress. Inaccurate and not conservative.

B. *Secant method*. Straight line drawn to pass through allowable unit stress and one other point on unit stress–unit strain curve. Second point selected below normal range of working unit stresses. Therefore unit stress–unit strain ratio slightly low throughout design range. Accurate and conservative because design unit strain taken as greater than actual.

C. *Tangent method*. Gives correct value at allowable unit stress, slightly high for any working unit stress. Can be as accurate as *B* but not conservative.

FIGURE 1-5. Typical stress-strain diagram for material without a range of constant s/ϵ values, showing methods of determining a usable modulus of elasticity

band under the same force. However, it is just as elastic within its elastic range because it returns to its original size and shape when the force is removed as truly as the rubber band does.

Plasticity is the property that enables a material changed in size or shape by a force to retain the new size and shape when the force is removed. Many materials are completely elastic (i.e. return exactly to original size and shape upon removal of a force) throughout a range of unit stress from zero to a unit stress called the *elastic limit*. At unit stresses greater than the elastic limit, the material takes a *permanent set* or a plastic deformation which remains when the force is removed. When a material is stressed beyond the elastic limit, the total unit strain is made up of recoverable elastic unit strain and permanent plastic unit strain.

Elastic unit strain takes place first, followed by the plastic unit strain; that is, as unit stress is increased starting from zero, the unit strain is entirely elastic until the elastic limit is reached, and then any additional unit strain is entirely plastic as unit stress greater than the elastic limit is imposed. For an elastic material, the total unit strain may be elastic or it may be elastic plus plastic, but it may not be plastic only. For each type of material, the elastic limit has a value in lb per sq in. It is the unit stress above which plastic deformation takes place and below which elastic deformation takes place.

Materials of construction behave differently at high and low temperatures. Like many familiar objects, they are stronger and more brittle at low temperatures and weaker and more pliable (ductile) at high temperatures. Ice, plastic or rubber garden hose, and spaghetti exhibit similar behavior. The transformation is not noticeable in materials such as steel, wood, and concrete unless the change in temperature is quite large.

SOURCES OF INFORMATION

To use materials properly, it is necessary to understand the natural characteristics of the basic materials, the variations in these characteristics made possible through special techniques, and the ways in which materials can be used in combination with one another. This information is obtained from past performance of materials in use and from experimental investigation and tests performed on materials. Much of the information is published in technical reports or in advertising material prepared by suppliers. Some sources of information are described here.

Sweets Catalog File is a compilation of technical advertising literature published by suppliers. The file includes approximately a dozen categories, with each supplier's literature included in the appropriate category. Literature from about 2000 suppliers describing many thousands of products is included. Each supplier pays the publisher of *Sweets Catalog File,* the F. W. Dodge Company, a fee for the inclusion of his literature, and the file is available free to designers who have a sufficient volume of business to justify receiving it.

Groups of suppliers producing the same product often set up *manufacturers associations* to promote the use of their product. The association, which is financed by the suppliers, is a separate organization functioning to increase the usage of the product. The association does not sell anything or represent any one of the associated suppliers.

The association seeks to increase sales by finding new and better ways to use the product and by utilizing advertising campaigns. It conducts research and provides the latest findings to designers and builders, often at no charge. It provides technical assistance to designers and builders by means of published material including standard specifications and by personal visits from staff members to the office or jobsite to assist in solving unusual problems. It is to the association's advantage that its product be used successfully so that it will be used again. Some well-known manufacturers associations are the Portland Cement Association (PCA), National Clay Pipe Institute (NCPI),

American Iron and Steel Institute (ASI), The Asphalt Institute, National Sand and Gravel Association (NSGA), American Plywood Association (APA), and National Ready Mix Concrete Association (NRMCA).

The *American Society for Testing and Materials* (ASTM) is an organization engaged in the standardization of specifications and testing methods and in the improvement of materials. It is made up of suppliers, designers, builders, and others interested in engineering materials. The organization publishes the ASTM Standards containing more than 400 standard specifications and testing methods covering design, manufacture, construction, and maintenance for practically every type of construction material. The ASTM Standards consist of 48 separate parts, each covering one field of interest and each under the jurisdiction of a standing committee which continually reviews and improves standards.

Each committee has members representing suppliers and users. New standards and revised standards are published as tentative for a time so that criticisms can be considered before adoption of them is final. The ASTM Standards may be purchased one standard at a time; by the individual volume, each of which includes several related parts of the 48 parts; or as a complete set.

The *American Standards Association* (ASA) develops national industrial standards through the work of committees representing manufacturers, technical organizations, and government departments. The final standards are determined in much the same way as standards of ASTM. The ASA also adopts the standards of other organizations and has adopted many of the ASTM standards. There are many other national organizations with memberships and purposes similar to those of ASTM or ASA, but with narrower interests. These organizations develop standard specifications, inspection methods, and test procedures and also adopt ASTM or ASA standards. Some of these organizations are the American Association of State Highway and Transportation Officials (AASHTO), American Institute of Steel Construction (AISC), and American Concrete Institute (ACI).

Underwriters Laboratories (UL) is a nonprofit organization which investigates and tests materials, products, equipment, construction methods, and construction systems in its laboratories. A supplier may have his product tested for a fee, and, if approved, it will be included in the UL approved list and the UL seal of approval may be displayed on the product. This approval is widely recognized as a safeguard against hazards to life and property, and specifications often require UL approval. The UL is particularly well known for evaluation of fire resistance of building components.

Professional organizations such as the American Society of Civil Engineers (ASCE) and the American Institute of Architects (AIA) devote much of their effort to improving design and construction practices. Valuable information concerning materials is published in their magazines and technical reports.

INSPECTION AND TESTING

Inspection means examining a product or observing an operation to determine whether or not it is satisfactory. The inspection may include scaling the dimensions, weighing, tapping with a hammer, sifting through the fingers, or scratching with a knife, as well as many other operations, some of which could conceivably be called tests. However, the results of the inspection and minor tests are not generally measurable. Often an inspection raises questions which are then resolved by testing.

A *test* consists of applying some measurable influence to the material and measuring the effect on the material. A common type of test consists of subjecting a sample of material to a measured force which is increased steadily until the material breaks or is deformed beyond a specified amount. This type of test measures the strength of the material directly by determining how strong the test specimen is. Some tests predict one characteristic by measuring another. For example, the resistance of aggregate to the destructive influence of freezing and thawing weather is predicted by soaking the aggregate in sodium sulfate or magnesium sulfate, drying in an oven, and determining the weight loss.

Inspection and tests can be categorized according to purpose as:

1. *Acceptance*—Inspection and tests performed to determine whether or not a material or product meets specific requirements in order to decide whether or not to accept or reject the material or product. A manufacturer performs such inspections and tests on raw materials he intends to use. A builder performs these inspections and tests on manufactured products and raw materials that he intends to use; and the owner's representative performs them on the builder's finished product.

2. *Control*—Inspection and tests performed periodically on selected samples to ensure that the product is acceptable. A supplier or manufacturer monitors his own operation by periodic checks of his product. The builder may check his product similarly. If control measures show the product to be below standards, the reason is determined and corrective measures taken.

3. *Research and development*—Inspection and tests performed to determine the characteristics of new products and also to determine the usefulness of particular inspection procedures and tests to judge characteristics or predict behavior of materials. A reputable manufacturing company tests a new product extensively before putting it on the market. Before adopting a new, simpler type of inspection or test procedure for acceptance or control, a highway department compares results obtained from the new procedure with results from the old procedure over a large range of conditions and over an extended period of time.

Tests for acceptance or control must usually be quickly performed. For reasons of economy, the tests cannot interfere with the manufacturing process. At a construction site, tests cannot unduly delay the construction work for the same reason. Since these tests are performed so many times, their cost is an important factor. Therefore, quick, inexpensive tests proven to be good indicators of actual performance are used extensively for these purposes. The type of test used in development of a product must give more exact results and is generally more time consuming and requires more expensive equipment.

An example will illustrate inspection and testing for the different purposes. A company making building blocks of concrete tries to reduce cost by using an industrial waste material as an aggregate. The proposed aggregate is examined and tested extensively before being used. It is then used in various combinations to make batches of concrete blocks which are compared with each other by inspection and testing. The combination that proves to be most satisfactory is used to manufacture blocks.

While blocks are in production, a continuous program is carried on to check the finished blocks by inspection and tests. A certain percentage of the blocks are checked as a matter of routine to determine whether or not the quality changes. If there are indications of a change in quality the cause of the change is determined and action taken to return to production of uniform quality.

The builder who purchases the block or the owner's representative then inspects and tests a certain percentage of the blocks before accepting them. Each block is inspected for damage before being put into place in the structure. A final inspection is given to the entire project as a whole when it is completed.

Tests performed on samples of material from the same source do not yield exactly the same results for each sample. There are two reasons for this:

1. No material is perfectly homogeneous. There are slight differences in the composition of any substance from one point to another. In addition, there are always minute flaws which, though unimportant in a large mass of material, have a great effect if one is included in a small sample to be tested. Thus, one sample is not completely representative of the whole.

2. The testing methods, although performed according to standard procedures, cannot be duplicated exactly each time.

Some tests give very nearly the same results when performed by different operators. These tests are said to have a high degree of *repeatability*. Tests have varying degrees of repeatability which should be taken into account when interpreting the results. An indication of degree of repeatability is included in some test procedures. A supplier can be required to meet very exacting specifications if a test method is available that provides very accurate results. If there is no such method, more accuracy can be obtained by taking the average of several tests. If it is not feasible to do this, the specifications must be written to permit more variation in the product.

Variations in test results can be kept small by selecting large enough samples, by employing proper procedures for their random selection, and by running enough tests to get a meaningful average and by eliminating those results that are erroneous because of a faulty sample or faulty test performance.

A certain minimum size sample or minimum number of samples is needed to be truly representative of the whole. The more variable a material is, the larger or more numerous the samples must be. The less precise the test methods are, or the lower the correlation between test results and the property actually being investigated, the greater the number of times the test must be run.

The size and number of samples should be determined on a statistical basis. Size and number must be large enough to include all the characteristics to be tested, the least common characteristic once and the more common ones in their proper proportion. Many testing procedures include minimum sizes or numbers of samples to accomplish this.

STANDARDS

The designer or builder may desire any number of properties in the material he is going to use. He must be able to specify the degree of each property in terms that he and the supplier understand, and he and the supplier must have some mutually acceptable means of determining whether or not the materials possess each property in sufficient amount. The supplier must be able to prove to the buyer that the material possesses the properties desired to the degree desired.

In unusual cases a measurement or test may be devised for one specific application. Fortunately, this is not usually necessary. Standard measuring and testing methods are available and so are standard definitions of terms. Both buyer and supplier understand what is meant when standard terminology is used or reference is made to standard specifications, and both can use the same reproducible methods to determine whether or not the materials possess the required properties in sufficient quantity.

When standard specifications and standard testing methods are available, it makes no more sense to devise special, nonstandard specifications or test methods than it does to measure lengths with a yardstick or meter stick of nonstandard size. Material specifications consist largely of explanations of what properties a material must possess and the allowable limits for those properties.

A *testing method* is a specification explaining how to perform a test and how to measure the results. When the material is tested, if it possesses all the required properties to a sufficient degree, it is said to meet the standards or meet the specifications.

Inspections often require measurements. A measurement may be as simple as determining the diameter of a piece of pipe by measuring it with a 6-foot rule to be sure it is of the size specified, or it may involve a more time-consuming and accurate measurement such as the determination of the percentage of air entrained in portland cement concrete.

A measurement may consist of determining the size of a crack in the end of a piece of wood by measuring it with a carpenter's rule. The piece of wood is considered to lose a certain percentage of its strength according to the size of the crack, and it must be discarded if it has a crack larger than a certain size.

However, there are three types of cracks and each is measured in a different way. Therefore, the cracks must be measured according to standard specifications if all pieces are to be graded on an equitable basis. Tests can be effective only if they measure the appropriate characteristic the same way each time so that the results can be evaluated according to their relationship to past results. Inspection should be performed in an identical way each time as much as possible for the same reason.

Review Questions

1. Explain the functions of independent testing laboratories in the construction industry.

2. Why must a builder understand materials?

3. Explain how the material used for a basement floor and the material used for a roof must be different.

4. As a research project, make a list of the kinds of materials used in (a) a water distribution system; (b) a city street pavement; (c) a sewage collection system.

5. Discuss the advantages of material specifications versus performance specifications.

6. A mechanical device rests in a level position on two supports, each 3 feet long, at 60°F. The support at one end is gray cast iron; at the other end, portland cement concrete. What is the greatest amount the device can be out of level due to differences in expansion if the temperature rises to 120°F? Use Fig. 1-2.

7. What is the unit stress in a steel rod with cross section of 2.8 sq in.

if it is subjected to a tension of 100,000 lb? In a concrete cylinder 6 in. in diameter subjected to a compressive force of 53,000 lb?

8. A material is expected to fail at 5000 psi. A safety factor of 2.2 is to be used. What is the allowable unit stress?

9. A material may fail by breaking or deforming excessively. Which is the case for creep? For fatigue? For impact failure?

10. What is the purpose of manufacturers' associations and how do they accomplish it?

11. What is the difference between inspection and testing?

$$\text{UNIT STRESS} = \frac{\text{FORCE}}{\text{AREA}}$$

$$\text{Safety Factor} = \frac{\text{Failure Unit Stress}}{\text{Allowable Unit Stress}}$$

$$BSG = \frac{OD}{SSD - SUB} \qquad ASG = \frac{OD}{OD - Sub} \qquad ABS = \frac{SSD - OD}{OD} \cdot 100$$

$$SG = \frac{W_{OD}}{\left[\left(W_w + W_c\right) - W_c\right] - \left[\left(W_w + W_A + W_c\right) - W_c - W_{ssd}\right]}{W_w}$$

$$SG = \frac{W_{OD}}{\left[\left(W_w + W_c\right) - W_c\right] - \left[\left(W_w + W_A + W_c\right) - W_c - W_{OD}\right]}{W_w}$$

2

Aggregates

Aggregates are particles of random shape. They are found in nature as sand, gravel, stones, or rock that can be crushed into particles. They may also be byproducts or waste material from an industrial process or mining operation. The term *aggregates* generally refers to mineral particles which have rock as their origin unless otherwise specified. These include sand, gravel, field stone, boulders, and crushed rock, since all are derived from rock by the forces of nature or, in the case of crushed rock, by a manufacturing process. *Rock* includes any large solid mass of mineral matter which is part of the earth's crust. Some other materials used as aggregates are blast-furnace slag, boiler slag, building rubble, refuse incinerator residue, and mine refuse.

Aggregate sizes vary from several inches to the size of the smallest grain of sand. In special cases aggregate larger than several inches may be used. Particles smaller than the size of a grain of sand are considered as impurities even if they are of mineral composition. Depending on the amount of impurities and the use to be made of the aggregate, these impurities may be tolerated or removed. In some cases these small particles are deliberately mixed with aggregate and are then considered as an additive.

The roadbuilding industry is the greatest consumer of aggregates. Aggregates are used as bases or cushions between the soil and traffic wheels or between the soil and pavement, and are also used in bituminous pavement and portland cement concrete pavement. They are used extensively in the portland cement manufacturing industry. They are used as leveling and supporting bases between the soil and all types of structures. They are used as *ballast* which is the base for railroad tracks. They are used as protective and decorative coatings on roofs and floors. Another major use of aggregates is to filter water, which requires holding back suspended solids while allowing water to pass through. Aggregates are also used to provide easy drainage of water without filtering.

There is not always a clear distinction between aggregate and the engineering material, soil, which also comes originally from rock. Some naturally occurring sand and gravel soils are usable as aggregate without processing. Most aggregate is soil that has been processed. Soil which remains in place and serves as the ultimate foundation of all construction is not considered as aggregate, no matter what its composition.

DEFINITIONS

Terms related to concrete aggregates are defined in ASTM C125, Terms
Relating to Concrete and Concrete Aggregates. Many of the definitions are
applicable to any type of aggregate and are given here to facilitate the dis-
cussions in this chapter.

Coarse Aggregate*: (1) Aggregate predominantly retained on the No. 4
(4.76-mm) sieve; or (2) that portion of an aggregate retained on the No.
4 (4.76-mm) sieve.

Fine Aggregate*: (1) Aggregate passing the ⅜-in. sieve and almost entirely
passing the No. 4 (4.76-mm) sieve and predominantly retained on the
No. 200 (74-micron) sieve; or (2) that portion of an aggregate passing
the No. 4 (4.76-mm) sieve and retained on the No. 200 (74-micron)
sieve.

Gravel*: (1) Granular material predominantly retained on the No. 4
(4.76-mm) sieve and resulting from natural disintegration and abrasion
of rock or processing of weakly bound conglomerate; or (2) that portion
of an aggregate retained on the No. 4 (4.76-mm) sieve and resulting
from natural disintegration and abrasion of rock or processing of weakly
bound conglomerate.

Sand*: (1) Granular material passing the ⅜-in. sieve and almost entirely
passing the No. 4 (4.76-mm) sieve and predominantly retained on the
No. 200 (74-micron) sieve, and resulting from natural disintegration
and abrasion of rock or processing of completely friable sandstone; or
(2) that portion of an aggregate passing the No. 4 (4.76-mm) sieve and
predominantly retained on the No. 200 (74-micron) sieve, and resulting
from natural disintegration and abrasion of rock or processing of completely friable sandstone.

Bank Gravel**: Gravel found in natural deposits, usually more or less
intermixed with fine material, such as sand or clay, or combinations
thereof; gravelly clay, gravelly sand, clayey gravel, and sandy gravel
indicate the varying proportions of the materials in the mixture.

Crushed Gravel: The product resulting from the artificial crushing of
gravel with substantially all fragments having at least one face resulting
from fracture.

Note: The definitions are alternatives to be applied under differing circumstances.
Definition (1) is applied to an entire aggregate, either in a natural condition or after processing.
Definition (2) is applied to a portion of an aggregate. Requirements for properties and grading
should be stated in the specification.
**Definition from ASTM D8.

Crushed Stone: The product resulting from the artificial crushing of rocks, boulders, or large cobblestones, substantially all faces of which have resulted from the crushing operation.

Crushed Rock***:   The product resulting from the artificial crushing of all rock, all faces of which have resulted from the crushing operation or from blasting.

Blast-Furnace Slag: The nonmetallic product, consisting essentially of silicates and alumino-silicates of lime and of other bases, which is developed in a molten condition simultaneously with iron in a blast furnace.

SOURCES

The earth's crust is solid rock called _bedrock,_ and much of the crust is covered with soil particles originally derived from the bedrock. This soil is classified, according to size, as gravel, sand, silt, and clay with gravel being the largest and clay the smallest. Natural aggregates include sand, gravel or larger stones, and bedrock reduced to particle size by manufacturing methods.

The sand and gravel occurring in nature were at one time broken from massive parent rock, transported by nature, and left in various types of deposits called sand or gravel banks. The processes that cause breaking, transporting, and depositing have operated continuously throughout the past and continue to operate now.

Cracking of rock and eventual fracturing occurs mainly through expansion and contraction of the rock due to changing temperatures. The process is hastened if temperatures are sometimes low enough so that water within the cracks freezes and expands. The broken particles fall or roll short distances downhill under the force of gravity and may be carried farther by flowing water or the slowly flowing ice of a glacier. Many particles are broken loose originally by flowing water or glacial ice.

A freshly broken particle has a rough surface and an angular shape. The more it travels, the smoother its surface becomes and the more rounded its shape becomes. Rolling down a mountainside has a rounding effect. Sliding farther along, helped by rain water runoff, and eventually tumbling along in a stream cause further rounding and smoothing. Being scraped along the ground first on one side and then on another while being carried in glacial ice has a particular effect on the shape and texture of aggregate particles. Glacial deposits consist of particles of widely varying sizes with some of the coarseness and angularity worn away. Many of the glacier-carried particles reach the streams of melt water at the melting end of the glacier. They are then carried

---

***Definition used in this book.

the same way with the same results as in any other stream. The deposits simply dropped by a glacier are called *till* and those carried farther by meltwater are called *outwash*. Outwash deposits are smoother, rounder, and more uniform in size than till.

The most perfectly rounded particles are those that are carried to the edge of a large body of water where they are washed back and forth incessantly by ocean or lake waves and become smooth and nearly spherical.

Rock particles, especially in dry climates or flat areas, may lie where they fall—next to a steep cliff, for example. Centuries of such deposition may provide sufficient quantities for commercial extraction and use of the aggregate which is rough-surfaced and of angular shape.

Many particles fall or roll into flowing water, and many deposits of sand and gravel are found in the beds of streams and rivers or where streams and rivers formerly were. The size of particles a stream carries is approximately proportional to the sixth power of the velocity of flow. The velocity depends on the slope, being greater with a greater slope, and on the quantity of water, being greater with a greater quantity. Greater quantities of water flow at certain times of the year and steeper slopes in some sections of a flowing stream cause faster flow in those sections regardless of the quantity of flow. These variations in quantity of flow and in stream slope result in a wide variety of carrying capacities throughout a stream over a period of time. The result is a separation of aggregates into various size ranges along the length of the stream. In some cases gravel with remarkable uniformity of size is found in one location.

An example is a level, slow-flowing section of river following a steep section with swift current. The swift current carries large and small particles. When the water reaches the slow-flowing section, the large particles settle and the smaller ones are carried past. The result is a deposit of clean gravel of a fairly uniform size, containing no silt, clay, or trash. If the current continues to flow slower and slower, smaller and smaller particles will gradually be dropped in succession as the water flows downstream. The entire reach of the river is then an aggregate deposit graded from larger particles upstream to smaller particles downstream. (See Fig. 2-1.) The very finest particles are carried to a lake or ocean and settle there where the movement of water is negligible. Lake deposits often contain too many fine particles to be good aggregate sources.

Glaciers are formed in high altitudes and pushed slowly down valleys by the weight of ice and snow piled up behind them. They scrape and gouge pieces of rock, large and small, from the sides of the valley and carry them slowly to the lower, melting edge of the glacier, where the larger particles are dropped and the smaller ones are carried away by the stream of melt water. The melting edge moves downhill in winter and recedes uphill in the heat of summer. The flow of water is greater in the daytime than at night and greater

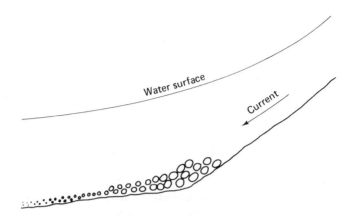

FIGURE 2-1. Section through river showing aggregates deposited because of reduction in water velocity due to flatter slope

in the summer than in winter. The variation in flow causes a wide variety of particle sizes deposited helter skelter as the stream changes channels and cuts through previous deposits. This area about the variable melting edge, which is known as a *moraine,* contains many large boulders, and the area downstream has the aggregate deposits expected in a stream.

Aggregates are obtained from beds of lakes and streams, but more often are obtained from deposits where there were formerly lakes or streams. Movements in the earth's crust result in relocation of streams and lakes, so that some former stream and lake beds are now on high ground with their aggregate deposits intact.

At several periods of time much of the northern hemisphere was covered by glaciers. These glaciers, behaving similarly to the valley glaciers described previously, but covering the width of a continent, left huge deposits of aggregate, and the streams of melt water flowing from their southern extremities also deposited huge quantities. The glaciers have receded and the streams and rivers they caused have disappeared. The deposits they left provide many of the best gravel banks now to be found.

METHODS OF EXTRACTION AND PROCESSING

Aggregate is recovered from deposits laid down in geologic times and from deposits still being laid down. The deposits are found on the ground surface and below the surface of the ground or water. Some aggregate is suitable for a specific use just as extracted, and some must be processed before being used.

Underwater Sources

Aggregate is brought up from lake and river bottoms by barge-mounted dredges with a single scoop or an endless chain of scoops and by dragline. The disturbance to the bottom and the motion of the scoop or bucket through the water cause some of the undesirable fine particles and lightweight material to be washed away as the load is being brought up. Barges are loaded and transported to shore, where their cargoes of aggregate are unloaded and stockpiled (see Fig. 2-2).

Aggregate is also pumped with pumps similar to those used for pumping concrete described in Chap. 4. Aggregate of sizes up to 6 in. and larger can be pumped and forced through a pipe to a barge or directly to the shore.

A knowledge of the characteristics of stream flow and deposition is required to locate the most likely places to find worthwhile aggregates. Samples of aggregates are brought to the surface and examined for desired characteristics before equipment is moved to a site to begin recovering them. Unsuitable material may have to be removed first to reach the kind of aggregate that is wanted.

The operating area is generally controlled by government regulations to prevent interference with the natural flow of water and to preserve navigation channels. Many times when channels or harbors must be deepened for ships, the aggregate brought up from the bottom has commercial value.

Land Sources

Aggregates are excavated from natural banks on land by bucket loaders, power shovels, draglines, and power scrapers. Unsuitable soil and vegetation, called *overburden,* must be removed to reach the deposits. Removal, which is accomplished with bulldozers and power scrapers, is called *stripping.* (See Fig. 2-3.)

The landform indicates what type of deposit is below the surface. Landforms are studied by means of aerial photographs or field trips, and the best locations are pinpointed. Holes are bored or test pits dug, samples are brought up, and examinations and tests are made to determine the suitability of the aggregates for the intended purpose.

The landforms containing natural deposits can be recognized by one who understands the processes of nature by which they were formed. Certain types of glacial deposits consist of much silt and clay or particles of a wide range of sizes, including large boulders. Neither type is as valuable as glacial outwash, which contains cleaner aggregates of more uniform size.

If crushed rock is to be used as aggregate, it must be blasted loose with explosives and then crushed by machinery to the size desired. Crushing provides a finished product of uniform size, and by proper blasting, crushing, and screening, the size can be controlled to suit the market. (See Fig. 2-4.)

(b)

(a)

FIGURE 2-2. Obtaining aggregate from underwater deposits: (A) dragline excavating from the bottom of a bay; (B) dredging from a river bottom (Courtesy Dravo Corporation)

31

FIGURE 2-3. Aggregate being loaded with bucket loader (Courtesy Dravo Corporation)

FIGURE 2-4. Blasting bedrock (Courtesy Dravo Corporation)

Particles of crushed rock have angular shapes and rough surfaces which are better suited for some uses than the more rounded shapes and smoother surfaces of naturally formed particles. These characteristics will be discussed later in this chapter. A rock formation has similar characteristics throughout so that when a good formation is found, a large supply of consistently good-quality aggregate is likely. This is usually not true of sand and gravel deposits which are likely to have inferior particles mixed with acceptable ones. A mixture is inevitable if particles were transported through a geological time period from many rock formations to form the sand or gravel deposit. As a result, bank sand and gravel are often of poorer quality than crushed rock, and additional processing is needed to remove unacceptable particles.

Bank run aggregate is of a particular size range in any one deposit, and the finished product is normally screened to obtain separation of sizes and may be crushed to a smaller size. However, if a size larger than most of the available bank run aggregate is needed, then crushed rock must be used. Generally, a crushed rock source has more versatility, and a natural bank is likely to be more economical for one particular type of aggregate.

ROCK TYPES

The constituents of the more common, or more important, natural mineral aggregates derived from rock are described in ASTM C 294 and briefly summarized here. Rock, from which most aggregate is derived, is of three types according to origin—igneous, sedimentary, and metamorphic. *Igneous rock* was at one time molten and cooled to its present form. *Sedimentary rock* at one time consisted of particles deposited as sediment by water, wind, or glacier. Most were deposited at the bottom of lakes or seas. The pressure of overlying deposits together with the presence of cementing materials combined to form rock. *Metamorphic rock* is either igneous or sedimentary rock that has been changed in texture, structure, and mineral composition, or in one or two of these characteristics, by intense geologic heat or pressure or both. The natural mineral aggregates of whatever sizes and wherever found came from one of the three types of rock. Any given particle of aggregate may have been through the cycle of rock formation, breaking, transporting, and depositing more than one time.

Igneous rock varies in texture from coarse grains to glasslike smoothness, depending on how quickly it cooled. Slower cooling creates a coarser texture. Some volcanic rock cooled as foam resulting in very light weight because of the hollow bubbles.

Granite is a common, coarse-grained, light-colored igneous rock. *Gabbro* is a common, coarse-grained, dark-colored igneous rock. Both are much used in the construction industry. *Basalt* is a fine-grained equivalent of gabbro. *Diabase* is intermediate in grain size between gabbro and basalt. Diabase and basalt are known as *trap rock*. Trap rock provides excellent aggregate. Light-colored *pumice* and dark-colored *scoria* are two types of igneous rock filled with bubbles. They are used to produce lightweight aggregate.

Sedimentary rock generally shows stratification indicating the way it was laid down; and it generally breaks more easily along the lines of stratification. Rock formed of gravel is called *conglomerate* and, if formed of sand, is either *sandstone* or *quartzite*. *Siltstone* and *claystone* are soft rock formed of silt or clay. *Shale* is hard claystone. All three break along planes or stratification to form flat particles. Therefore, they do not make the best aggregate, although shale is better because of its greater hardness.

Limestone (mainly calcium carbonate) and *dolomite* (mainly magnesium carbonate and calcium carbonate) were formed under salt water and are largely the remains of sea creatures. They do not break into flat particles. They are both rather soft but generally make satisfactory aggregates. *Chert,* which is formed from fine sand, is hard but often is not resistant to weathering.

It is difficult to generalize about metamorphic rock since the change, or metamorphosis, takes so many different forms. Metamorphic rock is dense but often forms platy particles. Generally, aggregate is hard and strong, but its platy shape is undesirable. *Marble* is a recrystalized limestone or dolomite. *Slate* is a harder form of shale. *Gneiss* is a very common metamorphic rock often derived from granite, but also derived from other rock. It is laminated but does not necessarily break along the laminations. *Schist* is more finely laminated than gneiss but of similar character. Granite, schist, and gneiss are often found together, separated from one another by gradual gradations.

It should be noted that gradations from one type of rock to another are common, and much rock does not fit into any definite category. Aggregate from a natural aggregate deposit may be of various kinds, and it is not then necessary to identify the parent rock types. Even when aggregate is to be obtained from a rock formation, identifying the rock types gives only a general indication of its characteristics which must be checked by testing samples. However, once characteristics are known for part of a geologic formation, only spot checks are necessary to verify characteristics of the entire formation since it was all formed over the same time by the same processes.

PROPERTIES AND USES

The usefulness of aggregates to the engineering and construction fields depends on a variety of properties. Performance can be predicted from these properties, and, therefore, the selection of aggregate for a particular task is based on examination and tests. Rather than writing rigid specifications defining properties absolutely required, the specification writer must take into account the types of aggregate readily available and design his specifications to obtain the most suitable aggregate from local sources. A comparison of the specifications devised by various states for highway construction aggregate shows this to be the practice. States containing an abundance of high quality natural aggregate have more demanding specifications.

Qualities that indicate the usefulness of aggregate particles to the construction industry are

1. Weight,

2. Strength of the particles to resist weathering, especially repetitive freezing and thawing,

3. Strength as demonstrated by the ability of the mass to transmit a compressive force,

4. Strength as demonstrated by the ability of the individual particles to resist being broken, crushed, or pulled apart,

5. Strength of the particles to resist wear by rubbing or abrasion,

6. Adhesion or the ability to stick to a cementing agent, and

7. Permeability of the mass, or the ability to allow water to flow through, without the loss of strength or the displacement of particles.

Weight is of primary importance for large-size stone called *rip rap* placed along the edge of a body of water to protect the bank or shore from eroding; for a *blanket* of stones placed to prevent erosion of sloping gound; and for stone retaining walls held in place by wire baskets called *gabions*.

Resistance to weathering is necessary for long life of any aggregate unless it is used only indoors. The quality of resisting weathering is called *soundness*.

Strength of the mass is needed if the aggregate is to be used as a base to support the weight of a building, pipeline, or road, or if it is to be used in portland cement concrete or bituminous concrete. The strength of individual particles to resist being broken, crushed, or pulled apart is important when the aggregate is to be subjected to a load. Pressure on a particle can crush or break it, allowing movement of adjacent particles. Failure of too many particles causes enough movement to constitute failure. Aggregate particles embedded in portland cement are often subject to tension. Concrete pavement and other concrete structures are subject to tension, although not as severe as the compression they receive. The tension and compression must be carried through the aggregate particles as well as the cement paste.

Aggregate may be subject to rubbing and abrasion during processing and handling, and also in service. Aggregate may be chipped or ground by loading equipment, screening equipment, or conveyor belts. Aggregate having insufficient resistance to abrasion produces some additional small broken particles, and the original particles become somewhat smaller and more rounded. The result is that size, gradation, and shape are all changed from what was originally intended. Aggregate particles in bituminous pavement and aggregate particles in the wearing surface of any pavement are subject to abrasion from vehicle wheels or from movement relative to each other.

If the aggregate is to be used in concrete, adhesion between the particles and the cementing agent (either portland cement or asphalt cement) is necessary. Although most aggregate adheres well enough, some requires removal of unsatisfactory material before use, and some is definitely not suitable for use in concrete.

A high degree of permeability is needed if the aggregate is used as a filter or drain, and a low permeability is necessary if the aggregate is used for anything else. *Permeability* is a measure of the ability of aggregate to allow water to flow through.

Miscellaneous Uses

Various sizes of stone are used for rip rap to protect natural or man-made earthwork. The individual pieces must be large enough so that the force of the water will not move them. Along a reservoir shore or the water's edge at a dam, protective aggregate consisting of particles from baseball size to basketball size might be dumped in a belt extending from low water to high water along the waterline location. On the banks of swiftly flowing streams, it may be considered necessary to place much larger sizes with each one being fitted

FIGURE 2-5. Rip rap on stream bank (Photo by Richard S. Williams, Jr., U.S. Geological Survey)

into place much like a stone wall, but lying against the bank in a belt extending from low water to high water level. Broken rock of irregular slablike shapes is often used and put into place with a crane. The chief requirements for rip rap are high weight and low cost. (See Fig. 2-5.)

When the bank is too steep or the current too violent for rip rap, gabions may be used to hold stones in place. A *gabion* is a basketlike container for stones that is made of heavy steel mesh, forming the shape of a block with level top and bottom and four vertical sides. Gabions are set in place and filled with stones the size of a fist or larger to act as rip rap or to form a retaining wall to hold back an earth bank. They may be piled one on top of another as shown in Fig. 2-6. Stones are placed by hand or with machinery. The gabions are wired to each other to form a continuous structure. However, the structure is flexible and adjusts without breaking to uneven soil settlement or undermin-

FIGURE 2-6. Bekaert gabions partially in place in Northern California (Courtesy Terra Aqua Conservation)

ing by water current. The stone-filled gabions are permeable so that soil water flows through readily without building up pressure behind a gabion wall. If stones are available nearby, there is little cost for production or transportation of materials. Most of the work can be performed by unskilled workers. The finished gabion structure looks rustic, making it more suitable for some settings than concrete or steel work.

River and lake currents and tide movement are often diverted from their natural paths to control the deposition of water-borne particles—in order to fill a beach or to keep a ship docking area from being filled, for example. This is done by building long, narrow obstructions to guide the flow of water in a new direction that will deposit suspended material where it is wanted or remove deposits from where they are not wanted. These low wall-like structures are called *training walls, breakwaters, groins,* or *jetties.* They are built of loose stones piled into the shape of a low, wide wall or of gabion construction where greater forces must be resisted.

High unit weight and reasonably good resistance to weathering are all that are required of the material for the uses described so far. Even though some substances are heavier and more weather resistant than natural stones, no other material approaches the advantages in low cost and ready availability in nearly every possible location. The useful life of the stones in any of these structures is very long, although in some cases abrasion, breakage, or washing away of stones can be expected to shorten life. Wire gabions should be inspected regularly for corrosion or wear. When replacement is needed, the entire structure is replaced, or a new one is built right over the original one.

Aggregates and Strength

Aggregate obviously cannot transmit a tensile force from one particle to another. Cementing agents, which are considered later in this chapter and in Chapters 3 and 4, combine with the particles to form a mass which can resist a small amount of tension. It may appear that particles transmit compressive forces from one to another. However, they do not. If particles with flat surfaces were piled vertically, as shown in Fig. 2-7a, a comprehensive force could be transmitted through the pile just as it is in a structural column made of stone.

Aggregate cannot be piled in this way. It appears as shown in Fig. 2-7b when in use. Figure 2-7b illustrates a cross section through a container of aggregate with a concentrated weight or force acting downward on one particle of aggregate. Because of the random arrangement of particles, the concentrated load is necessarily transmitted to more particles as the force is transmitted deeper into the container and thereby is spread over most of the bottom of the container.

In order for the load to spread horizontally, there must be a horizontal force. The vertical load from the top is transmitted through the points of contact, as indicated in Fig. 2-7c, over an ever larger area with ever smaller

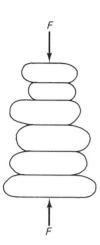

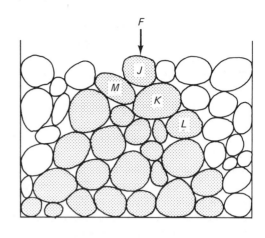

(a) Aggregate piled to transmit a compressive force. This is not a practical arrangement.

(b) Aggregate in a container. A compressive force on particle J is transmitted by shear through the shaded particles.

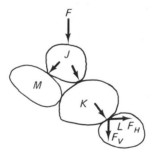

(c) Particle J pushes down and out on K and M like a wedge. Particle K transmits part of the force to L with horizontal and vertical components.

FIGURE 2-7. An "aggregate column" contrasted with a container of aggregate which transmits force by shear

forces. The originally vertical force has a horizontal component at each point of contact below the point of original application. At the points of contact, if the surfaces are not perpendicular to the line of force, there is a tendency for the upper particle to slide across the lower particle or push the lower particle aside so that the lower one slides across the particle below it. The tendency to slide transversely is a shearing stress, and the strength to resist the sliding is the shearing strength of the aggregate. This strength is the result of friction and interlocking between adjacent particles. Failure to resist the shearing stress results in the particles' being forced closer together.

The surface of aggregate settles when particles are pushed closer together. The settlement could be considered as a strain caused by the imposed stress. Aggregate should be compacted so that all the significant settlement takes place before the aggregate is put to use and harmful settlement is eliminated. The only other way in which aggregate can settle is for particles to be crushed. They will not be crushed unless they are soft or very brittle. Particles with such defects should not be used.

Although aggregate particles can be crushed if a great enough force is exerted on them, in use, good aggregate will not hold still to be crushed. Horizontal displacement takes place under a smaller force than is needed to crush or break the aggregate. Therefore, the controlling strength is shearing strength which is indicated by the load that can be carried without horizontal movement sufficient to be considered failure.

The tendency to move horizontally is resisted by friction and interlocking between particles. Both are illustrated in Fig. 2-8. The friction that can be developed between two particles depends on the roughness or smoothness of the particle surfaces. The rougher the surface is, the more resistance there is to sliding. The resistance developed by interlocking depends on the shape of the particles and is greatest for angular particles such as crushed rock, and least for well-rounded particles such as beach sand.

In Fig. 2-8, particle A pushes down and to the right on particle B. Particle A cannot move downward without pushing particle B down or to the right. To go down or to the right, B must push C down or slide across it. In this example, C can't be pushed down because it is held by particles under it. Particle B must overcome friction to slide over C. The force exerted by A on B may be enough to push B right over C. Theoretically, C could also push

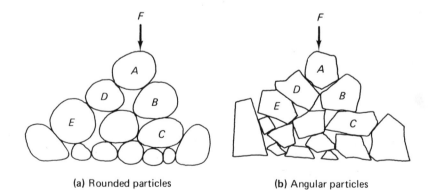

(a) Rounded particles   (b) Angular particles

Particles labeled B resist horizontal movement by friction.
Particles labeled C, D, and E resist by friction and interlocking.

FIGURE 2-8. Friction and interlocking

lower particles aside, but such a progression cannot continue without particles sliding over particles at some level.

Particle D is in a situation similar to particle B, but must move upward to overcome interlocking in order to move horizontally. A greater force is needed on D to push it up and over E. If the forces are great enough to cause horizontal movement at enough points of contact, the aggregate fails.

No force acts on a single particle, but some loads, such as the forces from the wheels of a vehicle, act on a small area at a time. Even wheel loads, however, act over a number of particles, which causes the actual transmittal of forces from particle to particle to be more complicated than indicated in Fig. 2-7. Figure 2-7 shows a partial sketch of forces in one plane. The load is actually transmitted outward in all directions, forming an ever larger circle as it proceeds downward.

Figure 2-9 shows what an aggregate road looks like after failure. Overloading causes particles to be pushed aside and forced to ride up over adjacent particles.

Because of the way in which a concentrated force is spread out through a thickness of aggregate and converted to a lower pressure distributed over a larger area, aggregate is often used as a *base* to support a weight which is too heavy to be applied directly to the soil. The aggregate base spreads the weight over a larger area of soil at a lower pressure. Generally, soil is not as strong as aggregate, but it consists of separate particles as aggregate does and so behaves in much the same way under a load. It fails in shear if overloaded. It is capable of settling more than aggregate and may also fail by settling excessively. Aggregate is obtained from the best source and brought to the construction site, but the construction takes place on whatever soil is there. Therefore, the soil may be much weaker than available aggregate. Figure 2-10a shows how a concentrated wheel load is spread out over the soil by an aggregate base. Stress on the soil is reduced in proportion to the square of the depth of the aggregate base because the area of the circle over which stress is spread is proportional to the square of the depth.

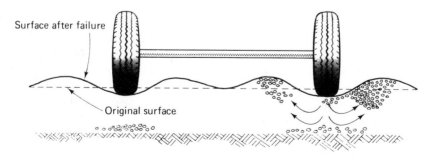

FIGURE 2-9. Aggregate failure under wheel loads

The radius of the circle of pressure equals the depth of aggregate multiplied by the tangent of the angle θ shown in Fig. 2-10a. The area of the circle equals the radius squared multiplied by π. The mathematical equation ranges from $R = h \tan 30°$ to $R = h \tan 45°$, depending on the strength of the aggregate. Aggregate with greater shearing strength spreads the load over a greater area, and the angle θ in Fig. 2-10a is greater. With the load applied over an area small enough to be considered a point, the forces are distributed to the soil over a circular area with a radius of $h \tan \theta$. The forces are not distributed uniformly within this circle, but for ordinary cases the pressure may be considered uniform.

Example

A wheel load of 3000 lb is applied directly to a crushed rock base 8 in. deep as illustrated in Fig. 2-10a. Compute the pressure transmitted to the soil if the base material is of high quality, and angle θ can be considered to be 45°.

$$\text{Pressure} = \frac{\text{Force}}{\text{Area}} = \frac{\text{Force}}{\pi R^2}$$

$$\text{Area} = \pi(h \tan \theta)^2 = 3.14 \, (^8/_{12} \times 1)^2$$

$$\text{Area} = 1.4 \text{ sq ft}$$

$$\text{Pressure} = \frac{3,000 \text{ lb}}{1.4 \text{ sq ft}} = 2,100 \text{ PSF}$$

Figure 2-9b shows a concrete spread footing transmitting a structural column load through a crushed stone base to the soil. The pressure from the bottom of the footing spreads in all directions as it passes through the base to the soil. It may be assumed to spread in the shape of the footing (normally square or rectangular), becoming wider in all directions as the depth increases.

The highly concentrated load carried by the column is spread out within the footing until it is transmitted to the base over the entire bottom of the footing. The footing is one solid unit and does not transmit force in the same way as the aggregate particles. However, its purpose is the same. It reduces the pressure on the base as the base reduces the pressure on the soil. The footing could be built directly on soil. Whether or not to use a cushion of aggregate is decided by comparing the cost of a larger footing with the cost of the smaller footing plus the aggregate.

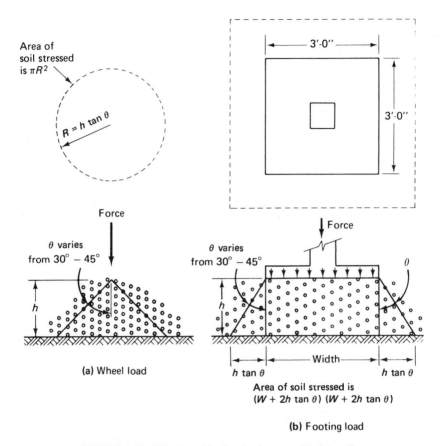

FIGURE 2-10. Wheel and footing loads transmitted to soil

Example

Using Fig. 2-9b, calculate the pressure on the soil if the depth of aggregate base is 8 in., and determine what depth of base is needed to reduce the pressure on the soil to 1.0 Kip per sq ft. Assume angle θ is 40°. What is the maximum pressure on the aggregate?

$$\frac{\text{Pressure 8 in.}}{\text{below footing}} = \frac{\text{Force}}{\text{Area}} = \frac{\text{Force}}{(W + 2h \tan \theta)^2}$$

$$\text{Area} = (3 + 2 \times {}^{8}/_{12} \times 0.839)^2$$

$$\text{Area} = 16.9 \text{ sq ft}$$

$$\text{Pressure} = \frac{33 \text{ Kips}}{16.9 \text{ sq ft}} = 1.95 \text{ KSF}$$

$$\frac{\text{Area required for}}{\text{1 KSF pressure}} = \frac{\text{Force}}{\text{Pressure}}$$

$$\text{Area} = \frac{33K}{1 \text{ KSF}} = 33 \text{ sq ft}$$

$$\text{Area} = (W + 2h \tan \theta)^2$$

$$33 = (3 + 2h \times 0.839)^2 = (1.678h + 3)^2$$

$$2.81 \ h^2 + 10.07 \ h - 24 = 0$$

$$h = \frac{-10.07 + \sqrt{10.07^2 - 4 \times 2.81 \ (-24)}}{2 \times 2.81}$$

$$h = 1.63 \text{ or, say, 1 ft 8 in.}$$

$$\frac{\text{Maximum pressure}}{\text{(at bottom of footing)}} = \frac{\text{Force}}{\text{Area}}$$

$$\text{Pressure} = \frac{33}{(3 \times 3)} = 3.67 \text{ KSF}$$

Loosely piled aggregate particles may be easily pushed aside. In other words, they lack shearing strength. (See Fig. 2-11.) Aggregates have a loose arrangement or structure somewhat like Fig. 2-11a after handling. They are normally compacted into a tighter structure to increase friction and interlocking before a permanent load is placed on them. The reasons for compacting aggregate base material are to reduce its compressibility and to increase its shear strength. Vibrations jar the particles into a close structure more effectively than simply rolling with a heavy weight. This can be demonstrated by filling a box with sand or gravel and compacting it by applying weight with a roller or some other means which does not jar or vibrate the material. A small amount of compaction takes place. Then shake the box lightly or rap it on the sides, and a substantial lowering of the level of the material takes place caused by compaction due to vibration.

Compaction results in an increase in density, and the density or unit weight can be used as an indication of the strength of an aggregate base. In Fig. 2-11, example *b* is denser than example *a*. Another way to increase density is to mix a variety of sizes. The smaller particles will occupy spaces that would be voids if all the particles were large. (See Fig. 2-12.) If the sizes

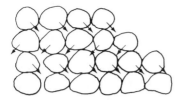 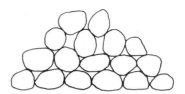

(a) Aggregate dumped and spread.
Strength due to friction only.
Particles readily move downward
and horizontally under a vertical
load as indicated by arrows.

(b) Compacted aggregate.
Strength due to friction and
interlocking.
Particles are pushed downward
and horizontally as far as they
can go and are now stable.

FIGURE 2-11. Increased shear strength due to compaction

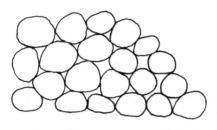

(a) Uniform size aggregate:
1. Friction at few points
of contact
2. Poor interlocking
3. High percentage of voids

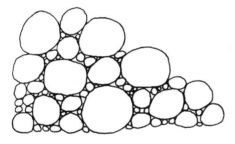

(b) Well-graded aggregate:
1. Friction at many points
of contact
2. Excellent interlocking
3. Very few voids

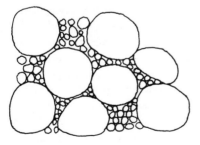

(c) Mixture of coarse and fine
aggregate:
1. Friction at many points
of contact
2. Good interlocking
3. Few voids
4. Economical preparation

FIGURE 2-12. Increased density (and shearing strength) of well-graded
aggregate

are equally represented throughout the entire range of sizes, the aggregate is *well graded*. The aggregate must be well graded to achieve the highest shearing strength. A very strong base can be built with aggregate having a wide range of sizes of proportions designed to achieve the greatest density, as in Fig. 2-12b. It is customary to obtain a high strength with a mixture of coarse and fine aggregates which achieves a strength close to that of the ideal mixture with substantial economy in the cost of handling and mixing materials. Aggregates are separated into standard sizes by screening, and each size is stockpiled. A desirable mixture is obtained by mixing two, and sometimes more, sizes of aggregate.

Factors which increase the shearing strength of aggregates are summarized here. All the factors, with the exception of the roughness of the particle surfaces, increase density, and the amount of increase in density is an indication of the amount of strength gain to be expected.

1. A well-graded aggregate is stronger than one not well graded.

2. The larger the maximum size of aggregate is, the greater its strength is. Larger particles provide greater interlocking, because particles must move upward for greater distances to override them.

3. The more flat, broken faces the particles have, the greater the strength developed through interlocking. Flat faces fit together more compactly with more contact between faces than if the particles are rounded. This does not mean the particles themselves should be flat. Flat particles slide readily over each other and result in lack of strength.

4. Compaction, especially by vibration, increases the shearing strength of aggregate of any size, shape, and gradation.

5. Rough particle surfaces increase strength because of greater friction between them.

Pavement Base

Typical pavement construction consists of several layers or *courses* which reduce the pressure of concentrated wheel loads so that the underlying soil or *foundation* is not overloaded. (See Fig. 2-13.) Wearing surfaces of asphalt mixtures and portland cement concrete are discussed in Chapters 3 and 4. The underlying soil may be that which is there naturally or may be hauled in to build a fill or embankment. It is not considered to be aggregate. It is strengthened by compaction with heavy construction equipment before a base or subbase is placed on it. Subbase material is usually unprocessed, run of bank material selected to meet specifications which have proven through performance to provide satisfactory material. Base material is more carefully selected.

In typical asphalt pavement, called *flexible* pavement, the base and

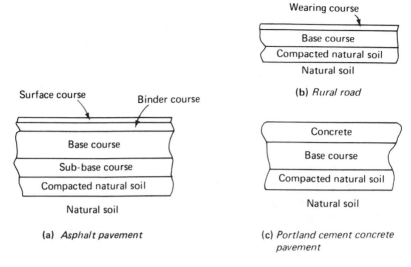

FIGURE 2-13. Typical pavement cross sections

The load spreads over an area that increases with depth. Therefore the unit stress is less at greater depths. The material is arranged to be weaker and less expensive at greater depths.

subbase carry the load and distribute it to the soil under two thin layers of asphalt concrete. The concrete slab is the chief load-bearing element of portland cement concrete pavement, which is known as *rigid* pavement. (See Fig. 2-13.)

The base under the rigid pavement slab spreads the load somewhat over the foundation, but is designed mainly to protect the pavement from the detrimental effects of too much moisture. These effects are frost action (heaving up against the slab when freezing and losing support by liquifying when thawing); standing water which lowers the strength of the base; and *pumping* which occurs when the pressure of passing traffic forces water out through pavement joints or at pavement edges carrying small particles out with it. Eventually, a hollow space is formed under the pavement by the removal of particles.

Water does not accumulate if voids are large enough so the base drains freely and capillary water cannot rise into the base. A well-graded coarse aggregate with no appreciable amount of fines is needed. Water may also be kept out if the aggregate has all voids filled to make it watertight. A well-graded aggregate with sufficient fine material to fill the voids is needed for watertightness.

The base under the wearing surface is the chief load-bearing element of rural or secondary roads. (See Fig. 2-13.) The asphalt surface course is there to resist traffic abrasion and protect the base from rain. Therefore, strength of the base aggregate to transfer the load to the foundation is of utmost importance. With a tight, water-repellant surface, aggregate must be well graded and compacted for strength but have enough open voids so that capillary water will not rise to be trapped under the surface course. Often the base is strengthened by mixing in just enough asphalt cement to coat the particles but leave the voids open.

A base course with no surfacing must resist traffic and rain as well as support the load and transfer it satisfactorily to the foundation. The aggregate must be tightly bound for strength and watertightness, but should allow the rise of capillary moisture to replace moisture lost to the air. A lightly traveled road does not need a protective covering over a properly constructed base.

Freezing of water in the base or subbase does not cause much expansion. If water is drawn up by capillary action to replace the water removed by freezing and it in turn freezes, larger masses of ice called *ice lenses* are formed. These cause disruptive heaving of the surface. Coarse soils have such large voids that water cannot rise by capillarity. Fine soils with sufficient clay allow capillary water to rise very high, but movement is so slow that the quantity of water rising is insufficient to form ice lenses. The voids of silt-sized particles are small enough to permit a capillary rise of several feet in quantities sufficient to form ice lenses. Aggregate sizes must be such that voids are either too large or too small to form ice lenses.

Thawing of ice lenses results in a quantity of water being held under the surface course by frozen soil below it which keeps it from draining. This removes the solid support of the base causing the surface to break up under traffic.

The seepage of rain water through the base carries fine particles out of the base suspended in the water. The more the particles are carried out, the faster the water flows and the larger the particles it carries are, weakening the base more and more.

Water rises by capillarity in all aggregate unless the voids are too large. Since a small amount of moisture gives added strength in cohesion to the base, it is desirable for capillary water to rise in sufficient quantity to replace evaporated water. If there is no surface over the base, capillarity should be encouraged. If the base is sealed by a watertight surface, the capillary water will accumulate under the surface course, weakening it by depriving it of solid support from the base.

Road and airplane runway bases, whether covered with pavement or not, are subject to moving loads and are exposed to weather and running water—conditions which do not ordinarily affect aggregate bases for pipelines or footings. The moving traffic loads push horizontally. When accelerating or decelerating, tires change the vehicle velocity by pushing (backward to accelerate, forward to decelerate) against the surface below them. (See Fig. 2-14.)

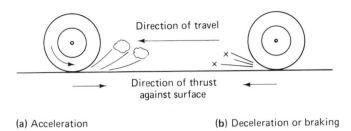

(a) Acceleration   (b) Deceleration or braking

FIGURE 2-14. Horizontal traffic loads on pavement

The vibration of traffic movement assists in loosening the bond and pushing particles to the sides. Freezing and thawing of the moisture in the aggregate, rain water seepage downward, and movement of capillary water upward all tend to loosen the aggregate bond and remove fine particles, which further loosens and weakens the bond between particles.

Aggregate bases subject only to static loads and protected from weather and moving water need not meet the rigid standards required of pavement bases. Often the gradation of such bases is not critical. The gradation of base material for roads and airplane runways is more important in order to achieve maximum contact between particles and maximum watertightness.

Sufficient fine material must be used to ensure filling the voids without separating the larger particles from contact with each other. The larger particles are the load-bearing structure, and the fine particles hold or bind the coarser ones by preventing movement between them. The fine material is called *binder*. Base material may be a mixture of several sizes of processed aggregate or a mixture of soil and aggregate. The most efficient procedure is to mix the proper quantity and sizes of aggregate with the natural soil occurring on the site of the road or runway to produce suitable base material. Sometimes only a small percentage of aggregate is needed, and sometimes the soil is not usable at all so that the entire base must be aggregate. However, it is desirable to use the maximum amount of soil from as close to the finished construction as possible.

Stabilizing Aggregate

Strength can be improved by the addition of clay, which is a very fine soil having properties unlike any of the larger soil particles. One of these properties is *cohesion* or the tendency to stick together. The strength due to cohesion is added to the shearing strength possessed by the aggregate. The clay, therefore, acts as a cement or paste. Other substances are also used for the same purpose. These include salts, lime, portland cement, and bituminous cement. The use of these other substances to increase strength is called *stabilization*.

Calcium chloride and sodium chloride are the two salts mixed with aggregate to increase it strength. Coarse aggregate, fine aggregate, and binder must all be in the proper proportion, and the salt is mixed with them in quantities of 1 to 2½ lb per sq yd of surface or 2 percent of the weight of aggregate. The salt, either calcium chloride or sodium chloride, is well mixed with the aggregate and the proper amount of moisture. The salt forms a brine with the water. This brine forms a film around each particle which increases the strength of the aggregate in two ways.

The brine film is stronger in surface tension than ordinary moisture, and because of this it increases the cohesion of the particles. The brine film allows the particles to be forced closer together under compaction than they could be with ordinary moisture. It may be thought of as a better lubricant than plain water. Increased cohesion and increased density each cause an increase in strength.

Stabilizing with salt improves the roadway in two additional ways. These improvements result in greater strength, although in themselves they do not increase strength. Abrasion of the roadway surface by traffic causes fine particles to be lost as dust. The loss of these particles leaves voids which loosen larger particles, with the result that much of the aggregate is thrown to the sides of the road. In addition to damaging the road, the loss of the dust causes dust clouds, which are a nuisance and even a health hazard.

Brine does not evaporate as readily as untreated water, and therefore it holds fine particles in place much better despite abrasion by traffic, thereby lessening damage to the road and to nearby properties. Calcium chloride, in addition, is a hygroscopic substance, meaning that it absorbs moisture from the air. It therefore maintains a damp surface that prevents dusting.

Water percolating through aggregate removes some of the fine particles as it flows. The result is damage to the roadway similar to that caused by wheel abrasion on a dry roadway. Salt stabilization fills the voids with stationary moisture, closing the voids to the passage of water and preventing the washing through of fine particles.

Lime is also used to stabilize aggregate base material. The lime used is burned limestone in either of two forms—quicklime, which is calcium oxide containing magnesium oxide in an amount as high as 40 percent or as low as 0.5 percent ($CaO \cdot MgO$); or hydrated lime, which is quicklime combined with enough water to produce $Ca(OH)_2 \cdot MgO$ or $Ca(OH)_2 \cdot Mg(OH)_2$. Unburned limestone cannot be used. Hydrated lime is more stable and therefore easier to store than quicklime, which hardens upon contact with air.

Lime is mixed with the aggregate in quantities of 2 percent to 4 percent of the aggregate weight. Water is used to accomplish thorough mixing and to combine chemically with the lime to form the final product, which is limestone.

Lime stabilizes aggregate in two ways. It reacts with clay, causing the particles to combine to form larger particles, giving a better gradation to aggregate containing too much clay. The new, larger particles will not swell excessively when moist as some clay does. Lime also causes a solidifying of the mass by reacting chemically with silica and alumina in the clay and aggregate. Calcium silicates and calcium aluminates are formed. These are cementing agents which act to hold the particles together. These cementing agents are also contained in portland cement and cause its cementing ability. A pozzolan may be added to provide silica and alumina when the aggregate does not contain enough. These readily combine with the lime to form a cement. Pozzolans are discussed in Chapter 4.

Portland cement or asphalt may be added to aggregate base to increase its strength. Stabilization with these two materials is covered in Chapters 3 and 4. Stabilization is not the same as manufacturing portland cement or asphalt concrete. It refers to the addition and mixing of a small amount of cement to improve the strength of aggregate.

Concrete is aggregate stabilized with portland cement paste or asphalt cement so that a different material is formed which is no longer made up of particles. The material formed is continuous and rigid in the case of portland cement concrete, and semi-rigid in the case of asphalt concrete. Concrete strength depends on the strength of the aggregates, the strength of the cementing agent, and the strength of the adhesion between the two.

Permeability and Filters

The best permeability is obtained by using aggregate as large as possible and as uniform in size as possible. Both properties cause large voids with the result that water flows through easily. These voids would have to be filled with smaller particles for the aggregate to achieve its highest strength. Therefore, good permeability and high strength cannot be obtained together.

A filter consists of aggregate designed and installed for the purpose of holding back particles larger than a certain size while letting water flow through with a minimum of interference. A filter works as shown in Fig. 2-15 with each layer being held in place by larger particles and in turn holding back smaller particles. Size and gradation are of primary importance for a filter.

Size must be such that the voids, which are smaller than the filter particles, are also smaller than the particles to be held back. However, they must be as large as feasible to permit water to flow through readily.

The filter catches all particles larger than the voids. If the filter particles are of uniform gradation, the void size is also uniform and all particles above the void size will be caught. Because of this fact, a filter can be designed to hold particles larger than a certain size.

If the filter material is not uniform, some areas will allow particles of a certain size to go through and other areas will hold the same size particles. Where filter particles are too small, the filter becomes plugged, and where filter particles are too large, particles that should be caught are allowed to pass through.

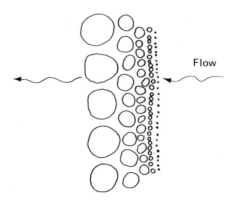

FIGURE 2-15. Filter particles positioned by flowing water

In a properly designed filter, the filter material originally lets all particles below the void size flow through, gradually forming a layer of particles smaller than the filter particles and just too large to flow through the voids. This layer of particles, having smaller voids, catches smaller particles, and a layer of these smaller particles is formed. Layer after layer builds up until voids become so small that no particles flow through and water flow is somewhat restricted. Eventually the filter is plugged. Several important types of filter are shown in Fig. 2-16.

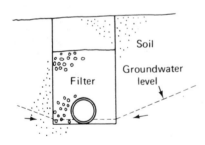

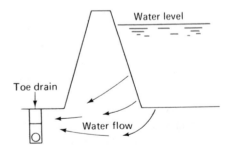

(a) *Underdrain* — lowers groundwater by carrying it away through a perforated pipe. The pipe is surrounded by a filter to prevent small particles from entering the pipe through the perforations, settling in the pipe, and restricting pipe flow.

(b) *Toe drain* — underdrain that intercepts water seeping through and under an earth dam. Its purpose is to prevent undermining by piping which is the removal of soil particles by the flowing water until the dam is undermined. The filter prevents piping by holding the soil in place while allowing water to pass.

FIGURE 2-16. Five types of filter

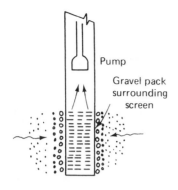

(c) *Gravel pack* — filter that prevents particles from entering the well as water flows through the soil, through the screen, through the pump, and to a water system at the surface.

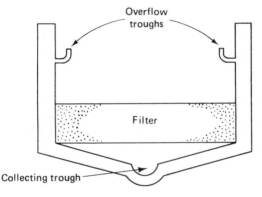

(d) *Water filter* — holds particles as water seeps downward through filter to collecting trough. When filter becomes nearly plugged, a small amount of water is pumped rapidly upward through the filter, overflowing into the troughs and carrying the filtered particles out with it. The particles that collect over many hours are removed in a few minutes.

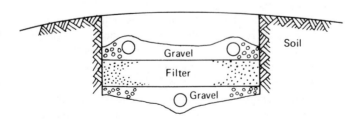

(e) *Sand filter* — sewage, with most of the solids removed by settling, flows through the upper pipes, into the filter through perforations, through the filter, and through perforations into the lower pipes which carry it to a stream or lake. The particles caught in the filter are organic and are consumed by bacteria. If properly designed, the filter will last indefinitely without cleaning.

FIGURE 2-16. (Continued)

An underdrain system must be removed and replaced before it becomes completely plugged. A water well filter preventing sand from entering the well must be cleaned periodically by surging water back and forth through the filter. This removes fine particles by jarring them loose. They enter the well and are removed by pumping. This process is a major operation. A filter for cleaning a drinking water supply requires cleaning daily or several times a day. It is a routine operation and is performed by forcing water backward rapidly through the filter forcing out the finer layers which have built up. These are collected and disposed of as waste material. A sewage filter requires occasional removal of a thin layer from the top as it becomes plugged and eventual replacement after a sufficient thickness is removed. If the filter is below the ground surface as shown in Fig. 2-16e, and the sewage filtered is not excessive, the filter operates indefinitely without maintenance because the sewage particles are consumed by microbes.

Filters may be divided into two categories. One type holds a mass of soil in place so that water can flow through the soil and then through the filter without carrying particles of soil with it. Mineral aggregates are always used for this type. The first three examples in Fig. 2-16 are of this type. Another type of filter removes suspended particles from water as it flows through. Drinking water is cleaned this way before use, and waste water is cleaned this way before being returned to the ground or to a body of water. The last two examples in Fig. 2-16 are of this type. Sand is used for this type filter but so are many other materials including coal, charcoal, and diatomaceous earth.

TESTS

The behavior of aggregates in use depends on the interrelationship of many properties. Many of these properties have been identified and defined. Standard tests have been devised to evaluate the properties. Performance can be predicted from test results based on past performances.

Cost is of great importance when large quantities of aggregates are being selected. Aggregate is always available at low cost; but the cost rises significantly if the aggregate must be handled one additional time or transported a great distance. It is often preferable to use the best aggregate available nearby rather than to improve it by processing or to obtain better aggregate from a greater distance. It must sometimes be decided whether to accept aggregate of a satisfactory quality or to pay for more processing to obtain aggregate of a better quality. The worth of a particular property is often a matter for individual judgment. Aggregate routinely used in some areas might not be acceptable where better aggregate is readily available. Because of this there is no absolute value required for many of the properties and even ASTM standards do not specify exact requirements for acceptability.

Size and Gradation

Particle sizes are important for all applications. The concept of aggregate size is difficult to express since the particles have odd shapes that can't be easily measured, and the shapes and sizes vary greatly in any one sample. The important features are *range of sizes,* or smallest and largest particles, and *gradation,* or distribution of sizes within the range covered. A few very large particles or a few very small particles do not ordinarily affect the performance of the mass of aggregate. Therefore, what is usually important is the range from the smallest particles that are contained in a significant amount to the largest particles that are contained in a significant amount.

A set of sieves fitting tightly one on top of the other is used to determine size and gradation of aggregate. A sample of the aggregate to be analyzed is placed in the top sieve which has the largest holes. The second sieve has smaller holes, and each succeeding sieve has holes smaller than the sieve above it. At the bottom is a solid pan. The pan collects all particles smaller than the openings in the finest sieve which is chosen to collect particles of the smallest significant size.

The *nest* of sieves is shaken, and each particle settles as far as it can. If no particle remains on the top sieve, then the top sieve size represents one kind of maximum size for the sample. The absolute maximum particle size is somewhere between this top sieve size and the size of the next sieve. If even a few particles remain on the top sieve, it is not known how large the maximum size particles are. Usually it is not significant if only a small percentage remains on the top sieve.

Some particles fall through to the pan, and their size is not known either. If the lowest sieve has small enough holes to catch the smallest significant size, the size of particles in the pan is not important. However, an excessive quantity of material fine enough to reach the pan is of interest, just as an excessive quantity of aggregate larger than the largest sieve is of interest.

A sieve consists of a circular frame holding wires strung in such a way as to form square holes of a designated size. Particles are considered to be the size of the holes in the sieve on which they are caught. Whether or not flat particles and long, narrow ones go through a screen may depend on how they land on the screen while being shaken. Thus chance may play a minor part in the number of particles retained on or passing a sieve. Statistically, results are the same over a large number of tests of the same material. Extremely flat or elongated particles, which could cause the greatest variations, are unacceptable in nearly all cases and so are not ordinarily tested by sieve analysis.

Some standard sieve sizes commonly used for aggregates in construction and actual dimensions of the sides of the square openings are listed in Fig. 2-17. Nominal dimensions and permissible variations for openings in all

Aggregates

Sieve Designation		Nominal Opening (in.)
75 mm	3 in.	3.0
37.5 mm	1½ in.	1.5
19.0 mm	¾ in.	0.75
12.5 mm	½ in.	0.5
6.3 mm	¼ in.	0.25
4.76 mm	No. 4	0.187
2.36 mm	No. 8	0.0937
1.18 mm	No. 16	0.0469
0.6 mm	No. 30	0.0234
0.3 mm	No. 50	0.0117
0.15 mm	No. 100	0.0059
0.074 mm	No. 200	0.0029

FIGURE 2-17. Sieve sizes commonly used in construction

standard sieves, as well as other specifications for their construction, are listed in ASTM E11, Standard Specifications for Wire-Cloth Sieves for Testing Purposes.

Sizes designated in millimeters and inches or fractions of an inch indicate that clear openings between wires are squares with the given dimension as the length of the sides of the square. When the size is a number such as No. 50, it means there are that number of holes in a lineal inch. The No. 50 sieve has a total of 50 openings per lineal inch or 2500 openings in a square inch. The openings are not 1/50 of an inch in width because wire takes up much of the space. Therefore, these openings are smaller. Figure 2-17 shows the length of the sides of each square opening.

The results of a sieve analysis are tabulated and percentages computed as shown in Fig. 2-18. All relationships are by weight. The title "percent retained" refers to the percentage of the total that is retained on each sieve. The title "cumulative percent retained" refers to the percentage of the total that is larger than each sieve. It is, therefore, the sum of the percentage retained on the sieve being considered plus the percentage retained on each sieve coarser than the one being considered. The title "percent passing" means the percentage of the total weight that passes through the sieve under consideration. It is, therefore, the difference between 100 percent and the cumulative percentage retained for that sieve. A small error should be expected. Usually some dust is lost when the sieves are shaken. There is a gain in weight if particles left in the sieves from previous tests are shaken loose.

ASTM C136, Sieve or Screen Analysis of Fine and Coarse Aggregates, describes standard procedures for performing a sieve analysis and specifies the amount of error allowed. A brief description of the proper procedure

Sieve Size	Weight Retained (Grams)	Percent Retained	Cumulative Percent Retained	Percent Passing
3 in.	540	10.5	10.5	89.5
1½ in.	1090	21.2	31.7	68.3
¾ in.	1908	37.2	68.9	31.1
½ in.	892	17.4	86.3	13.7
¼ in.	495	9.6	95.9	4.1
Pan	211	4.1	100.0	0.0
Total	5136	100.0		

FIGURE 2-18. Sieve analysis results (coarse aggregate)

follows. A representative sample is placed in the top sieve after the entire nest including the pan has been put together. The cover is placed on top. The nest of sieves is shaken by hand or a mechanical shaker long enough so that additional shaking cannot appreciably change the quantities retained on each sieve. The quantity retained on each sieve is removed from the sieve, using a brush to collect particles caught in the wire mesh, and weighed. Each quantity weighed should be kept on a separate sheet of paper until the sum of individual weights has been compared with the total weight of the sample.

It is customary in the aggregate industry to process and stockpile aggregates in several size ranges, designated either as fine and coarse or by the size of the largest sieve retaining an appreciable percentage of the total particles. There are several advantages in this type of handling rather than stockpiling aggregate of the entire range of sizes in one pile. Segregation is more difficult to prevent in a quantity with a wide range of sizes. Also, a mixture of any desired range and gradation can be prepared with the proper proportions from several stockpiles. Therefore, the supplier with aggregate separated according to size is prepared to supply whatever the market requires. The mixture proportions can even be adjusted slightly during a project when conditions require it.

Other ASTM standards deal with specialized types of sieve analysis. ASTM C117, Standard Method of Test for Materials Finer than No. 200 Sieve in Mineral Aggregate by Washing, provides a method for washing clay particles through the sieves when the clay is stuck together in chunks or adheres to larger particles. ASTM D451, Sieve Analysis of Granular Mineral Surfacing for Asphalt Roofing and Shingles; ASTM D452, Sieve Analysis of Nongranular Mineral Surfacing for Asphalt Roofing and Shingles; and ASTM D546, Sieve Analysis of Mineral Filler, set forth other specialized sieve analysis procedures. Mineral filler is very fine, dustlike, aggregate used in bituminous concrete to fill voids between fine aggregate particles.

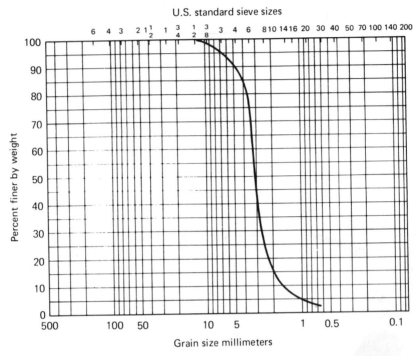

FIGURE 2-19. Typical gradation curve—uniform aggregate

The results of a sieve analysis are often plotted on graph paper with sieve sizes on the horizontal axis as the abscissa and percent coarser (retained) and finer (passing) on the vertical axis or as the ordinates. A sample plot is shown in Fig. 2-19. The horizontal axis is divided according to a logarithmic scale because of the wide range of sizes to be plotted. The largest sieve openings may be several hundred times the size of the smallest sieve openings. The smaller sizes must be spaced far enough apart for clarity; but, if the same scale is used for the larger sizes, an excessively long sheet of paper is needed. Linear scales are therefore not used. The semi-logarithmic scale is much more satisfactory.

A graph of percent by weight versus sieve sizes is called a *gradation chart*. It is a better presentation in some ways than a tabulation. Size, range, and gradation can be seen on the graph. The range of sizes can be obtained from graph or tabulation with equal ease. However, finding the size and gradation may require the use of a gradation chart. There are several ways in which the size of aggregate is defined.

It has been found that the filtering performance of an aggregate can be predicted by the particle size that has a certain percentage by weight finer than its own size. This size is designated by the letter D with a subscript denoting the percentage finer. In Fig. 2-19, D_{15} is 2 mm and D_{85} is 4 mm.

The *effective size,* used to designate size of aggregate to be used as a filter for sewage or drinking water, is that diameter or size on the graph which has 10 percent of the total finer than its size. It is not necessarily a sieve size and cannot be found accurately without a gradation curve. It is convenient to plot percentage finer versus sieve sizes in descending order to obtain this value. Figure 2-19 is plotted in this way. In Figs. 2-20 and 2-21 the sieve sizes are in ascending order.

The *maximum size* of aggregate, when used in the design of portland cement concrete mixes, is taken for that purpose to be the size of the sieve next above the largest sieve that has 15 percent of the total sample coarser than it (cumulative percentage retained).

Fineness modulus is a value used in the design of portland cement concrete mixes to indicate the average size of fine aggregate. It may also be used to indicate the average size of coarse aggregate. It is found by adding the cumulative percentages retained on specified sieves and dividing by 100. Specified sieves include 6 in., 3 in., 1½ in., ¾ in., ⅜ in., No. 4, No. 8, No. 16, No. 30, No. 50, and No. 100. The sample must be run through all these sieves, omitting only those too large to retain any aggregate.

The fineness modulus should be determined to two decimal places. The whole number indicates the sieve in which an average size particle would be retained. To locate this sieve, count upward from the pan a number of sieves corresponding to the whole number of the fineness modulus. The average size is further defined by considering it to be located between the designated sieve and the sieve above it a portion of the distance upward, as indicated by the decimal. The decimal .75 would locate the average size at 75 percent of the way up from the lower sieve toward the upper one.

Gradation, meaning the distribution of particle sizes within the total range of sizes, can be identified on a graph as well graded, uniform, or gap graded (sometimes called skip graded). *Well graded* means all sizes, within the entire range, are in approximately equal amounts. *Uniform* gradation means that a large percentage of the particles are of approximately the same size. *Gap graded* or *skip graded* means that most particles are of a large size or a small size with very few particles of an intermediate size. Typical curves for the three types of gradation are shown in Fig. 2-20.

The shape of the curve aids in identifying the type of gradation. A line nearly vertical indicates that a large quantity of material is retained on one or possibly two sieves. In Fig. 2-20a, 85 percent of the particles are finer than the ⅜-in. sieve, and only 10 percent are finer than the No. 4 sieve. Therefore, 75 percent of the material is caught on the No. 4 sieve. In other words, much of the aggregate is the same size, and the material is uniform.

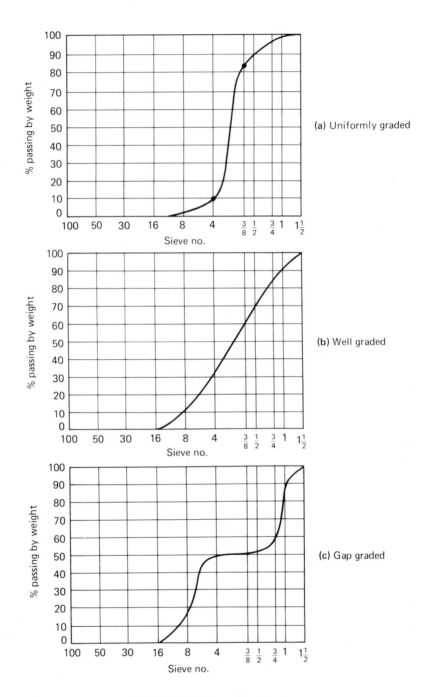

FIGURE 2-20. Three gradation types

A line with a constant slope, as in Fig. 2-20b, changes the same amount in the vertical direction with each equal increment in the horizontal direction. This indicates that the same quantity of material is retained on each successive sieve and therefore that the aggregate being tested is well graded.

A horizontal or nearly horizontal line, as in Fig. 2-20c, indicates there is no change or little change in percent finer through several successive sieves. Therefore, no material or very little material is retained on these sieves, and there is a gap in the gradation. Aggregate can be processed or mixed to provide any of these gradations if desired. In nature aggregate seldom occurs this way, and gradation charts usually take less idealized shapes.

The gradation curve does not give a precise indication of uniformity, although if curves for two aggregates are plotted at the same scale, one could tell which is more uniform. The *uniformity coefficient* is a mathematical indication of how uniform the aggregate is. It is determined by dividing the diameter or size of the D_{60} by the diameter or size of the D_{10}. The smaller the quotient, the more uniform in size the aggregate. The uniformity coefficient cannot be determined from a tabulation of sieve analysis results because the D_{60} and D_{10} are usually between sieve sizes, and a plot must be made to locate them.

Aggregate size and gradation are often specified by listing sieve sizes and a range of "percent passing" for each size. The sample being tested is sieved with the specified sieves and is acceptable if, for each sieve, the

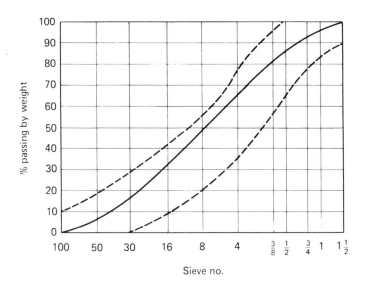

FIGURE 2-21. Gradation curve that fits within an envelope, thereby meeting the specification

sample's percentage falls within the specified range. A plot of the upper and lower specified limits is called an *envelope*. An aggregate meets the specifications if its gradation curve plots entirely within the envelope. (See Fig. 2-21.) A gradation curve is not needed but it shows the aggregate's relationship to the envelope in detail that cannot be obtained from a tabulation.

Another way to specify size and gradation is with a range for the effective size and a range for the uniformity coefficient.

Surface Area

The surface area of a quantity of aggregate is sometimes important. A ratio of surface area to volume or surface area to weight is determined and used for computations dealing with surface area. Of all possible particle shapes, a sphere has the lowest ratio of surface area to volume or weight. Particles that roughly approximate spheres in shape also have roughly the same surface to volume ratio as spheres, and all other shapes have greater ratios, with the ratio being greater as the particle differs more from a spherical shape. The following calculation shows the ratio of surface area to volume for a sphere.

$$\text{Surface area} = 4 \pi r^2$$

$$\text{Volume} = \left(\frac{4 \pi r^3}{3} \right)$$

$$\text{Ratio} \qquad \frac{\text{Surface area}}{\text{Volume}} = \frac{4 \pi r^2}{\left(\dfrac{4 \pi r^3}{3} \right)} = \frac{3}{r}$$

The ratio is therefore 3 divided by the radius of the sphere. The ratio is greater for small particles than for large particles because the ratio becomes greater as the radius becomes smaller.

In waste water filters, organic matter is consumed by bacteria that live on aggregate surfaces. Consumption, and therefore the quantity of waste water that can be treated, is proportional to the numbers of bacteria which are proportional to the total surface of the particles. It is, therefore, advantageous to have a large total surface per volume of aggregate to support more bacteria.

It is also of importance if aggregate particles are to be bound together for strength. The design of an asphalt paving mixture requires enough liquid asphalt to form a coat of a certain thickness completely over each particle. An estimate is made of the square feet of surface per pound of aggregate, and the proportion by weight of asphalt material to aggregate is determined according to the amount of surface to be coated. The particles are always bulky in shape for strength so that the surface area is small (slightly larger than for spheres), and the result is that a small quantity of asphalt material is sufficient to coat the particles.

Weight–Volume Relationships

The total volume of an aggregate consists of solid particles and the voids between the particles. The total volume is important because aggregate must be ordered to fill a certain volume. Aggregate for a filter must cover a certain number of square feet to a particular depth. Aggregate for a roadbed must be placed in a certain width and thickness for a specified number of miles. However, the volume of solid matter is also of importance.

The volume of one aggregate particle consists of a mass of solid material. However, all particles used as aggregates contain some holes or pores. The pores range in size from a large open crack that can hold small particles to holes that can't be seen, but can absorb water. For some uses the volume of these pores is important and for some uses it is not.

In asphalt concrete, a percentage of the volume of the pores is filled with liquid asphalt material. Therefore, the correct quantity of asphalt cement for the mix includes enough to coat the particles plus enough to partially fill the pores.

In portland cement concrete, the mixing water completely fills the pores in the aggregate. Lightweight aggregate, because of its very porous structure, may absorb so much water that there is not enough remaining to combine with the cement satisfactorily.

The volume of the pores in aggregate used as a base or as a filter is of little importance except that freezing and thawing cause the breaking of porous particles, more so than of more solid particles. A few fine particles may enter the larger pores in coarse aggregate, but their total volume is negligible. In base material the voids between coarse aggregate particles are filled with fine aggregate. The volume of voids must be known to obtain the correct volume of fine aggregate but not the volume of pores.

It is usually desirable to know the volume of aggregate in relationship to its weight. This is so because the quantity needed is determined according to the volume it must occupy; but that quantity is ordered and measured for payment by weight.

Various combinations are used to relate weight and volume depending on how the aggregate is to be used. The possibilities include using total volume (solids and voids), volume of solids including pores, or volume of solids less volume of pores; and using wet weight, air-dry weight, or oven-dry weight. These alternatives are illustrated in Fig. 2-22.

1. The volume of aggregate may include solid matter, plus pores in the particles, plus voids. This is called *bulk volume* of aggregate.

2. The volume may include solid matter, plus pores in the particles but not voids. This is called the *saturated, surface-dry volume*.

3. The volume may include solid matter only, not pores or voids. This is called *solid volume*.

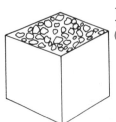

1 cu. ft. box holds
1 cu. ft. of aggregate
(bulk volume)

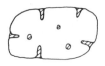

(a) *Bulk volume* – volume
of solid particles including
their pores plus volume of
voids.

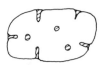

(b) *Saturated surface – dry
volume* – volume of
solids including pores.

(c) *Solid volume* –
volume of solid
material not
including pores.

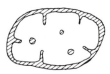

(d) *Wet weight* – weight
of solid material plus
absorbed water filling
the pores plus some
free water on the
particle surfaces. The
amount of free water
is variable.

(e) *Air dry weight* –
weight of solid
material plus some
absorbed water in
the pores. The
amount of absorbed
water is variable.
The weight in a
saturated surface-
dry condition is
more consistent
and is called the
saturated surface-
dry weight.

(f) *Oven dry weight* – weight
of solid material only. This
is the most consistent weight
because no water is included.

FIGURE 2-22. Kinds of volume and weight for aggregate particles

If aggregate particles are soaked in water until all pores are filled and
then removed and wiped dry, the pores will remain filled with water for a
time. If that aggregate is placed into a calibrated container of water, the rise in
water level indicates the saturated, surface-dry volume of aggregate because
the volume added to the container of water consists of solids plus pores
saturated with water.

If aggregate is dried in an oven until all moisture is driven from the
particle pores and then placed into a calibrated container of water, the rise in
water level indicates the solid volume because the volume added to the container of water consists only of solid material. Some time is needed for the
water to enter the pores, and the solid volume cannot be determined at once.

In soaking particles to fill their pores with water, a 24-hour soaking period is considered sufficient.

The simplest weight–volume relationship is expressed as unit weight of aggregate. The procedure for determining it is contained in ASTM C29, Unit Weight of Aggregate. The sample of aggregate is oven dried, and a cylindrical metal container of known volume is filled with it and weighed. The procedure for filling the container is specified in detail to ensure consistent results. The container is filled in three equal layers, and each layer is compacted with 25 strokes of a rod of standard dimensions. The oven-dry weight of aggregate divided by its bulk volume is its unit weight.

Specific gravity (SG) of a substance is the ratio of the unit weight of that substance to the unit weight of water. The specific gravity of aggregate particles is useful in calculations, particularly those to convert weight of the irregularly shaped particles to saturated, surface-dry volume or to solid volume. There are two kinds of specific gravity used with aggregate particles. *Bulk specific gravity* depends on saturated, surface-dry volume. Pores in the particles are considered as part of the volume. *Apparent specific gravity* depends on solid volume. Both depend on oven-dry weight, and both are calculated as the unit weight of aggregate particles divided by the unit weight of water. Either one of these can be considered as a true specific gravity, and each has its own use. Note that unit weight of aggregate particles is not the same as unit weight of aggregate which is described in the previous paragraph.

A type of specific gravity called *effective specific gravity* is used in the design of asphalt concrete. It is derived by dividing oven-dry weight by the weight of a volume of water equal to the solid volume plus the volume of pores that is not filled with asphalt cement when aggregate and cement are mixed.

Dividing the weight of a certain volume of any substance by the weight of the same volume of water is equivalent to dividing unit weight of the substance by unit weight of water, and so the result is specific gravity of the substance. Methods for determining bulk and apparent specific gravity and absorption for aggregate are contained in ASTM C127, Specific Gravity and Absorption of Coarse Aggregate, and ASTM C128, Specific Gravity and Absorption of Fine Aggregate. Bulk specific gravity is sometimes determined using saturated, surface-dry weight, and that method is included in these two ASTM standards.

The methods are briefly described here.

Specific Gravity of Coarse Aggregate

1. A representative sample of coarse aggregate weighing about 5 kilograms is dried by heating and weighed at intervals until two successive weighings show no loss of weight. The final weight is recorded as the oven-dry weight.

2. The oven-dried sample is soaked in water for 24 hours.

3. The aggregate is removed from the water and dried with a cloth until no film of water remains, but the particle surfaces are damp.

4. The aggregate is then weighed. The result is saturated, surface-dry weight in air.

5. The aggregate is submerged in water in a wire basket, and the submerged weight is obtained. The submerged weight of the basket must be deducted. The submerged particles displace a volume of water equal to their own volume including all pores because the pores are filled with water before being submerged. There is a weight loss when submerged which is equal to the weight of water displaced.

6. Oven-dry weight of aggregate in air divided by the difference between saturated, surface-dry weight in air and weight submerged equals bulk specific gravity. The weight loss in water is the weight of a quantity of water equal to the saturated, surface-dry volume of aggregate. Therefore, this calculation determines the ratio of weight of a volume of aggregate (solid matter plus pores) to the weight of an equal volume of water.

7. Oven-dry weight of aggregate in air divided by the difference between oven-dry weight of aggregate in air and weight submerged equals apparent specific gravity. In this case the weight loss in water is the weight of a quantity of water equal to the volume of solid matter of aggregate. Therefore, this calculation determines the ratio of weight of aggregate solid matter without pores to weight of an equal volume of water. It should be understood that oven-dry weight of solid matter alone is the same as oven-dry weight of solid matter plus pores since the empty pores have no weight. The only difference between calculating bulk specific gravity and apparent specific gravity is that the saturated, surface-dry volume is used for bulk specific gravity and the volume of solid matter alone is used for apparent specific gravity. Using the weight of saturated, surface-dry particles in air to determine weight loss in water means that saturated, surface-dry volume is the basis for determining the weight of an equal volume of water to find bulk specific gravity. Using the weight of oven-dry particles in air to determine weight loss in water means that the solid volume is the basis for determining the weight of an equal volume of water to find apparent specific gravity.

8. Bulk specific gravity is based on oven-dry weight unless specified otherwise. It may be determined on a saturated, surface-dry basis by using the saturated, surface-dry (SSD) weight in air as aggregate weight rather than oven-dry (OD) weight. This variation is covered in ASTM C127.

9. *Absorption,* which is the percentage of the weight of water needed to fill the pores compared to the oven-dry weight of aggregate, is computed by

dividing the difference between SSD weight and OD weight in air by the OD weight in air.

Example

Given: SSD weight in air   5480 g

Submerged weight 3450 g
OD weight 5290 g

$$\text{Bulk SG} = \frac{\text{OD weight}}{\text{SSD weight} - \text{submerged weight}} = \frac{5290}{5480 - 3450} = 2.61$$

$$\text{Apparent SG} = \frac{\text{OD weight}}{\text{OD weight} - \text{submerged weight}} = \frac{5290}{5290 - 3450} = 2.88$$

$$\text{Absorption} = \frac{\text{SSD weight} - \text{OD weight}}{\text{OD weight}} \cdot 100 = \frac{5480 - 5290}{5290} = 3.6\%$$

Specific Gravity of Fine Aggregate

1. A representative sample of fine aggregate weighing about 1000 g is dried to a constant weight, the oven-dry weight.

2. The oven-dried sample is soaked in water for 24 hours.

3. The wet aggregate is dried until it reaches a saturated, surface-dry condition. This condition cannot be easily recognized with small-sized aggregate. To determine the point at which it reaches this condition, the drying must be interrupted frequently to test it. The test consists of putting the aggregate into a standard metal mold shaped as the frustum of a cone and tamping it 25 times with a standard tamper. The cone is removed vertically and the fine aggregate retains the mold shape if sufficient moisture is on the particle surfaces to cause cohesion. The aggregate is considered saturated, surface-dry the first time the molded shape slumps upon removal of the mold.

4. A representative sample consisting of 500 g of aggregate (saturated, surface-dry weight) is put into a 500 cm^3 container, and the container is filled with water at 23°C.

5. The full container is weighed. The total weight consists of the sum of:

    a. known weight of flask,

    b. known weight of aggregate (SSD), and

    c. unknown weight of water.

The weight of water can be determined by subtracting flask and aggregate weights from the total weight.

6. The entire contents is removed from the container, with additional rinsing as required to remove all particles, and the oven-dry weight of aggregate is determined.

7. The container is weighed full of water.

8. The foregoing procedures provide all the data needed to compute SG and absorption. Saturated, surface-dry volume of aggregate is used for bulk SG, and solid volume is used for apparent SG. Oven-dry weight of aggregate is used for either type of SG, and SSD weight may be used for bulk SG if so stated. Either SG equals oven-dry weight of aggregate divided by weight of container filled with water plus weight of aggregate in air, minus weight of container filled with water and aggregate. For bulk SG, the SSD weight of aggregate in air is used in the denominator, and for apparent SG the oven-dry weight of aggregate in air is used in the denominator. The procedure is illustrated in Fig. 2-23.

9. Absorption is the weight of water needed to fill the particle holes, divided by the weight of solid matter and expressed as a percentage. It is computed by dividing SSD weight minus oven-dry weight by oven-dry weight.

Deleterious Matter

Excessive amounts of foreign material are detrimental in aggregate used for any purpose. What constitutes an excessive amount depends on the usage of the aggregate. Very little foreign matter can be permitted in aggregate for portland cement concrete, asphalt concrete, or filters. Permissible amounts are greater for aggregate used as a base.

ASTM C33 contains allowable limits for seven types of deleterious substances which must be controlled in aggregates to be used for portland cement concrete. Maximum permissible quantities are listed according to a percentage of the weight of the entire sample for fine aggregates and coarse aggregates. The seven categories are friable particles, material finer than No. 200 sieve, soft particles, coal and lignite, chert, organic impurities, and materials reactive with the alkalis in cement.

Friable particles are those which are easily crumbled such as clay lumps, weak sandstone, or oxidized ores. An excessive amount of these causes a change to a gradation with more fine particles when the friable ones are broken in use. The end result is similar to using an aggregate with excessive fine material in it. The method of testing for friable particles is described in ASTM C142, Test for Friable Particles in Aggregates. Friable particles are described as those that can be crushed between thumb and forefinger without using fingernails. Material is separated on sieves before the test, and after all friable particles are broken, each fraction is sieved on a sieve finer than the one it was retained on. The weight of crushed particles that goes through the

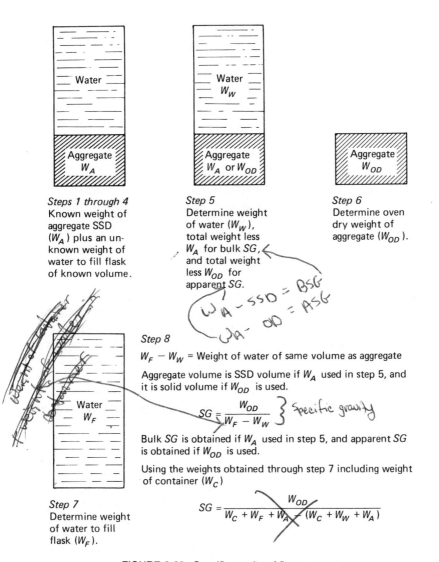

FIGURE 2-23. Specific gravity of fine aggregate

finer sieves divided by the total weight of the test sample gives the percentage of friable particles. ASTM C33 limits friable particles to 1 percent for fine aggregates and 0.25 percent for coarse aggregates when either is to be used for portland cement concrete.

Material finer than No. 200 sieve is that material which passes through the No. 200 sieve in a washed sieve analysis performed according to ASTM C117, Test for Materials Finer than No. 200 Sieve in Mineral Aggregates by

Washing. The material must be washed through the sieves because much of it may be stuck to larger particles. One reason the fine material is objectionable is that it coats larger particles. The coating is a hindrance to the adherence of portland cement paste or asphalt cement to the aggregates. In portland cement concrete, the fine material, whether loose or coating a particle, absorbs water before the water can combine with cement to form a paste. ASTM C33 limits material finer than the No. 200 sieve in fine aggregate to 3 percent for portland cement concrete subject to abrasion and 5 percent for other portland cement concrete, and in coarse aggregate to 1 percent for all concrete. If the finer material is stone dust which has a bulky shape, it is not as harmful as clay particles which have a flat shape, and 1.5 percent is permitted. Fine material may be objectionable in filter material because it will either be washed through the filter or partially plug the filter, depending on the relative sizes of the fine material and the filter material. Plugging to any extent is always undesirable as it lowers the quantity of water that can pass through the filter. Fine material flowing through is objectionable if it settles to the bottom and impedes the flow of water in a conduit following the filter or if the filter's purpose is to provide clear water.

Soft particles are those that are marked with a groove after being scratched on a freshly broken surface by a pointed brass rod under a force of 2 lb in accordance with ASTM C235, Test for Scratch Hardness of Coarse Aggregate Particles. The test is simple and suitable for field investigation of a possible aggregate source. Soft particles are detrimental when the aggregate is to be subject to abrasion, such as in a gravel road, bituminous concrete road, or portland cement concrete floor subject to steel wheel traffic. The main concern is that soft particles will be crushed or rubbed into powder, thereby interrupting the continuity of the aggregate structure by removing some of the aggregate particles that are needed either to transmit shear or to maintain a continuous surface. Therefore, soft particles are of little concern in fine aggregate. ASTM C33 limits soft particles in coarse aggregate to 5 percent for concrete in which surface hardness is important and has no limit for soft particles in fine aggregate.

Lightweight pieces are particles in coarse or fine aggregate that have a SG substantially less than that of the aggregate as a whole. They are objectionable for several reasons. They are often soft or weak. If they consist of coal or lignite, they cause unsightly pitting and black staining at the surface of a portland cement concrete structure and have a SG of about 2.0. Chert particles with a SG of 2.35 expand because of their porous particle structure and cause pitting in concrete.

The test for determining the percentage of lightweight pieces in aggregate is described in ASTM C123, Lightweight Pieces in Aggregate. It consists in placing the aggregate sample into a mixture of liquids proportioned to have a SG between that of the acceptable aggregate and that of the lightweight pieces. The SG of the liquid is designed according to the SG's of particles to be separated. The lightweight particles float and are skimmed or poured out. Zinc chloride in water may be used, or carbon tetrachloride or kerosene may be blended with a heavy liquid to produce the desired SG. ASTM C33 limits coal and lignite in fine and coarse aggregate to 0.5 percent when surface appearance of concrete is important and to 1 percent when it isn't. Chert is limited in coarse aggregate to 1 percent for concrete exposed to severe weather and 5 percent for concrete with mild exposure.

Organic impurities are nonmineral material of an organic type, mainly tannic acid, sometimes found in fine aggregate. Organic material hinders the hardening of portland cement paste and so must be limited in fine aggregate to be used in portland cement concrete. A simple method of testing for excessive organic impurities is contained in ASTM C40, Organic Impurities in Sands for Concrete. The principal value of the test is to furnish a warning that further tests are necessary before the aggregate can be approved.

The method consists of preparing a reference solution of standard brown color and comparing it with a solution containing a sample of the aggregate being tested. A measured quantity of the fine aggregate is mixed with a specified solution of sodium hydroxide in water. After 24 hours the solution containing aggregate is compared to the standard color solution. The more organic material there is in the aggregate, the darker the solution is. If it is darker than the standard color, it presumably contains excessive organic material.

It should not be used for portland cement concrete unless it can be proven that mortar made from it is as strong or nearly as strong as mortar made from the same aggregate with the organic impurities washed out. The method for making this comparison is described in ASTM C87, Effect of Organic Impurities in Fine Aggregate on Strength of Mortar. Cubes of mortar are made from both washed and unwashed aggregate, and the average crushing strengths compared. The mortar made from the unwashed aggregate should be at least 95 percent as strong as the mortar made with clean aggregate. This test takes one week for the mortar cubes to cure compared to one day for the simpler presumptive test.

Reactive aggregates are those which contain minerals which react with alkalies in portland cement, causing excessive expansion of mortar or concrete. The expansion causes disintegration which may not be apparent in use for several years. The reaction is either alkali-silica or alkali-carbonate, depending on the type of aggregate. The reaction takes place when mortar or concrete is subject to wetting, extended exposure to humid atmosphere, or contact with moist ground. It can be prevented by using cement with a low alkali content or with an additive which has been proven to prevent the harmful expansion. The additives either combine with alkalies while the cement paste is still in a semi-liquid state, thus removing the alkalies, or prevent the reaction between the deleterious substance and the alkali. The alternative is to check aggregates for reactivity whenever it is suspected. The tests are difficult and usually time consuming, and no one test is entirely satisfactory for all cases. Often aggregates are accepted based on past experience in similar cases and in doubtful cases the aggregate is tested.

A standardized microscopic examination which is useful to determine the quantity of reactive material in aggregate is described in ASTM C295, Petrographic Examination of Aggregates for Concrete. However, the actual results caused by the reactive substance are a better criterion than the quantity of reactive substance in the aggregate.

A chemical method, described in ASTM C289, Test for Potential Reactivity of Aggregates (Chemical Method), indicates the potential reactivity by the amount of reaction between a sodium hydroxide solution and the aggregate submerged in it. This test is not completely reliable but serves as an indicator before undertaking a longer test.

Another method, described in ASTM 227, Test for Potential Alkali Reactivity of Cement–Aggregate Combination (Mortar Bar Method), is to make mortar specimens and measure them for possible expansion while stored at uniform temperature and moisture over a period of at least 3 months and preferably 6 months. This method is recommended to detect only alkali-silica reactions because carbonate aggregates of substantial reaction potential give very little indication of it during this test.

ASTM C342, Test for Potential Volume Change of Cement–Aggregate Combinations, describes a similar test to determine volume change of reactive aggregates in mortar specimens exposed to wide variations in temperature and moisture over a period of 1 year. This test applies particularly to certain cement–aggregate combinations found in parts of the central United States.

ASTM C586, Potential Alkali Reactivity of Carbonate Rocks for Concrete Aggregates (Rock Cylinder Method), indicates the potential alkali-carbonate reactivity between cement and limestone or dolomite. Small cylinders cut from aggregate are immersed in a sodium hydroxide solution, and change in length is determined over a period of about a year. The method is meant for research or screening of a possible source rather than to check conformance to specifications.

Miscellaneous Properties

Toughness, which means resistance to abrasion and impact is indicated either by the Deval test described in ASTM D2, Abrasion of Rock by Use of the Deval Machine, and ASTM D289, Abrasion of Coarse Aggregate by Use of the Deval Machine; or by the Los Angeles abrasion test described in ASTM C131, Resistance to Abrasion of Small Size Coarse Aggregate by Use of the Los Angeles Machine, and in ASTM C535, Resistance to Abrasion of Large Size Coarse Aggregate by Use of the Los Angeles Machine. ASTM D2 describes the Deval test for crushed rock, and ASTM D289 describes the Deval test for other aggregate. The two Los Angeles tests are for any coarse aggregate, one for smaller and one for larger sizes. The Los Angeles tests are of more recent origin. They can be run in less time and provide a greater range of results so that differences in toughness are more apparent.

Toughness is an important quality for aggregate subjected to mixing in a portland cement concrete mixer or an asphalt concrete pugmill (actions similar to that of the Deval and Los Angeles tests); to compaction with heavyweight or vibratory compaction equipment as roadbeds and asphalt pavement are; or to steel-wheeled or hard-rubber-tired traffic as some industrial floors are. In addition, the particles in gravel roads and asphalt concrete roads rub against each other throughout the lifetime of the road each time traffic passes by. All these processes can break and abrade particles, thus changing the design gradation and opening holes in the surface.

In the Deval test, aggregate is rotated 10,000 times in a cylinder with six steel spheres for ASTM D289 and no spheres for ASTM D2. Coarse aggregate of various sizes may be tested but none smaller than the No. 4 sieve. Material broken fine enough to pass the No. 12 sieve is expressed as a percentage of the total sample weight to indicate the susceptibility to abrasion and breakage.

In the Los Angeles test, aggregate of the type to be used is combined with 12 steel spheres or fewer for smaller aggregates and rotated in a cylinder 500 times for small-size coarse aggregate and 1000 times for large-size coarse aggregate. A shelf inside the cylinder carries the aggregate and steel balls to a point near the top where they fall once each revolution. This fall plus the addition of more spheres for larger aggregates causes greater abrasion and breakage than in the Deval tests. Material broken fine enough to pass the No. 12 sieve is expressed as a percentage of the total sample weight to indicate the susceptibility to abrasion and breakage.

If the aggregate particles are all of equal toughness, the loss of weight in fine particles increases in direct proportion to the number of revolutions. If there are some very weak particles, they will be completely crushed in the early part of the test while the tougher particles will continue to lose weight at a constant rate throughout the test. In this case there will be a rapid loss of weight at first, tapering off to a uniform rate of loss near the end. A very tough aggregate with a small but significant percentage of very weak particles is not as valuable as an aggregate that is consistently moderately tough. Yet each type could produce the same results at the end of a test. A method of checking on the uniformity of toughness throughout the sample consists of comparing the weight of material passing the No. 12 sieve after one-fifth of the revolutions with the weight passing after all the revolutions. The ratio should be approximately one-fifth if the sample is of uniform toughness, and will be higher if the sample is not uniform.

Soundness of aggregates means resistance to disintegration under weathering including alternate heating and cooling, wetting and drying, and freezing and thawing. Expansion and contraction strains caused by temperature changes impose a stress on aggregate (as well as on any other material) which may eventually cause breaking. Chemical changes which slowly disintegrate some types of aggregate are brought about by atmospheric moisture which contains dissolved gases. Drying and rewetting renews the chemical attack which is generally the dissolving of a constituent of the aggregate. By far the most destructive effect of weathering is caused by freezing and thawing. Pores in the particles become filled with water which freezes, expanding within the pores and exerting great pressure tending to break the particle open at the pores.

ASTM C88, Soundness of Aggregates by Use of Sodium Sulfate or Magnesium Sulfate, provides a method for measuring soundness by immersing aggregate in a sodium sulfate or magnesium sulfate solution and removing and oven-drying it. Each cycle requires a day's time. This procedure causes an effect similar to weathering in that particles are broken away from the aggregate but at an accelerated rate. It is believed that salt crystals accumulating in the aggregate pores exert an expanding pressure similar to that caused by the formation of ice. After the specified number of cycles, which varies with the intensity of weathering that must be resisted, the weight in material that passes a sieve is determined as an indication of the soundness of the aggregate. The sieve is slightly smaller than the size that retained all the aggregate originally for coarse aggregate and the same size as the one that retained all the aggregate for fine aggregate. The procedure is designed to test resistance to the freeze–thaw cycle because this is the most destructive type of weathering, and aggregate with high resistance to freezing and thawing can resist any weather. An alternative test may be made by freezing and thawing the wet aggregate; but many cycles and a long period of time are necessary if the freezing and thawing during the useful life of the aggregate are to be simulated.

Hydrophilic aggregate is that aggregate which does not maintain adhesion to asphalt when it becomes wet. The word *hydrophilic* means "loves water." The implication is that hydrophilic aggregate prefers water to asphalt. Some silicious aggregates, e.g. quartzite, are hydrophilic and therefore cannot be used satisfactorily with asphalt cement without special preparation of the asphalt cement. ASTM D1664, Coating and Stripping of Bitumen–Aggregate Mixtures, provides a method for testing aggregates for adhesion to asphalt. Aggregate is completely coated with the asphalt and submerged in water for 16 to 18 hours. The amount of asphalt coating that strips away from the aggregate is determined by a visual estimate of whether the aggregate surface left coated is more or less than 95 percent of the total surface.

Sampling

Aggregate tests and inspection must be performed on representative samples. Ideally, a representative sample is a small quantity with exactly the same characteristics as the entire quantity. Expressed practically, a representative sample closely reproduces those characteristics of the entire mass that is to be tested. Methods of taking samples must avoid *segregation* which is any separation of particles on the basis of some property. The most common segregation is by particle size with smaller particles tending to become separated from larger ones. ASTM D75, Sampling Stone, Slag, Gravel, Sand and Stone Block for Use as Highway Materials, provides methods for proper sampling of aggregate.

Samples are required for:

1. Preliminary investigation of a possible source of supply, whether a rock formation, an aggregate deposit, or an industrial byproduct. The supplier makes this investigation before investing the money to extract and process aggregate.

2. Acceptance or rejection of a source of supply by the buyer. This is a preliminary determination. An inspection and tests are made for this purpose by a prospective buyer who intends to buy large quantities for one project or a series of projects. An example is a state public works department which approves or disapproves gravel or sand pits for state projects for the coming year or other period of time.

3. Acceptance or rejection by the buyer of specified material from the supplier. Inspection and tests are performed as a final check for conformance to the agreement at the time of delivery.

4. Control of removal and processing operations. The supplier assures himself that his product remains of consistent quality by testing it.

A natural deposit is investigated by making test holes and examining or testing their entire contents. A layered deposit with somewhat different characteristics in each layer requires a sample cutting through a large number of layers. Aggregate sources frequently include pockets or areas of nontypical aggregate. Separate samples may be needed from each of these pockets or areas whenever they are observed.

A representative sample from a stockpile that may be segregated requires one large sample made up of samples from top, middle, and bottom of the pile. A representative sample from a bin should be taken in several increments while aggregate is being discharged by intercepting the entire cross section of the stream of particles each time but not the very first or very last particles being discharged. A representative sample from a railroad car,

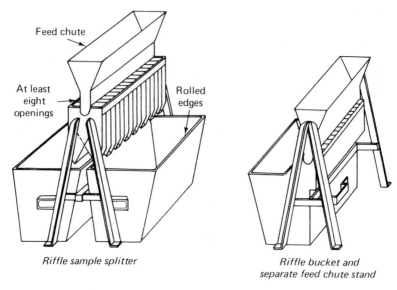

Feed chute

At least eight openings

Rolled edges

Riffle sample splitter

Riffle bucket and separate feed chute stand

(a) Large riffle samplers for coarse aggregate

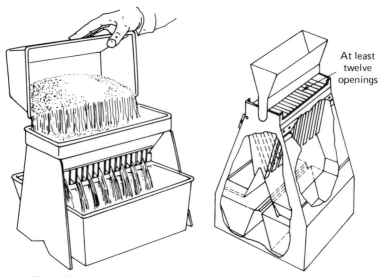

At least twelve openings

Note – May be constructed as either closed or open type. Closed type is preferred.

(b) Small riffle sampler for fine aggregate

FIGURE 2-24. Reducing sample size (Courtesy American Society for Testing and Materials) .

Cone sample on hard clean surface   Mix by forming new cone   Quarter after flattening cone

Sample divided into quarters   Retain opposite quarters reject the other two quarters

(c) Quartering on a hard, clean, level surface

Mix by rolling on blanket   Form cone after mixing   Quarter after flattening cone

Sample divided into quarters   Retain opposite quarters, reject the other two quarters

(d) Quartering on a canvas blanket

FIGURE 2-24. (Continued)

truck, or barge should be taken from an appropriate number of flat-bottomed trenches dug completely across the width of the contained aggregate.

The samples collected in any of the ways noted are generally combined in appropriate proportions to make one large sample representing the entire quantity of aggregate. That is, the size of each separate sample has the same relationship to the size of the combined sample as the quantity of aggregate represented by each separate sample has to the entire quantity of aggregate. When variations in characteristics or amount of segregation are of importance, each uncombined sample is inspected and tested separately.

The combined samples are often too large to use and must be reduced in size for handling and testing without changing characteristics that are to be investigated. Sample size is reduced by quartering or by dividing in a sample splitter. Either method provides a representative sample. The two methods are illustrated in Fig. 2-24.

SPECIAL AGGREGATES

Lightweight aggregates are those that have a unit weight of no more than 70 lb per cu ft (1120 kg per m^3) for the fine aggregate, 55 lb per cu ft (880 kg per m^3) for coarse aggregate, and 65 lb per cu ft (1040 kg per m^3) for combined fine and coarse aggregate. These weight limitations and other specifications for lightweight aggregate for structural use are found in ASTM C330, Lightweight Aggregates for Structural Concrete, and ASTM C331, Lightweight Aggregates for Concrete Masonry Units. The purpose of using lightweight aggregate in concrete structures is usually to reduce the weight of upper parts of a structure so that the lower supporting parts (foundations, walls, columns, and beams) may be smaller and therefore cost less. Lightweight aggregates are also used in insulating concrete. Transportation costs are less for lightweight aggregates and for lightweight concrete or masonry products than for their traditional, heavier counterparts.

Three types of lightweight aggregate are used for concrete in which strength is of major importance. Volcanic rock such as pumice, scoria, or tuff—all of which contain numerous air bubbles or man-made particles prepared by expanding blast-furnace slag, clay, diatomite, fly ash, perlite, shale, slate, or vermiculite—are used in portland cement concrete structural members or for concrete masonry units. In addition, cinders from the combustion of coal or coke are used for masonry units only.

As slag flows from a blast furnace in a molten stream at temperatures of 1400–1600°C, it is chilled with high-pressure water spray forced into the molten mass where it becomes steam as it cools the slag. The expanding steam causes bubbles so that the slag is frothy by the time it cools. The operation, which is completed in a few minutes, results in a hard mass of lightweight material called *expanded slag* or *foamed slag* which must be crushed into aggregate size.

Certain slags, shales, and slates when heated sufficiently expand to as much as seven times their original size because of the expansion of gas formed within them. The gas may be formed from minerals occurring naturally in the clay or rock or from a chemical that is added. The heating process, which usually takes place in a rotary kiln, must be rapid so that the gas expands with explosive force sufficient to expand the particle. The expansion must take place when the particle is soft enough from the heat to be expanded by the gas rather than shattered. The aggregate may be reduced to proper size before heating to produce particles of the desired size or may be crushed to the desired size after expansion and cooling.

Diatomite, which consists of the skeletons of tiny aquatic plants called diatoms, can be heated to the melting point to be used as a cinderlike, lightweight aggregate.

Fly ash consists of fine mineral particles produced by the burning of coal. It is useful in portland cement concrete as a substitute for cement. This use is discussed in Chapter 4. Fly ash to be used as an aggregate may be pelletized to form coarse aggregate or used as fine aggregate. It may be mixed with coal mine wastes for aggregate manufacture. In fact, the production of aggregates made of fly ash in combination with other materials for road bases, railroad ballast, and asphalt or portland cement concrete occupies many large industries.

Perlite is volcanic glass in spherical particles of concentric layers. It contains water which, if heated rapidly enough, becomes steam with enough force to shatter the spheres into particles and expand the particles.

Vermiculite includes a variety of water-bearing minerals derived from mica. These expand perpendicularly to the layers when steam is formed by rapid heating.

Cinders used as aggregates are fused into lumps by combustion of coal or coke and are not the softer ashes formed by lower temperature combustion. Cinders contain some unburned material which is undesirable. Sulfur compounds found in cinders corrode steel, and cinders or concrete containing cinders should not be placed in contact with steel.

Lightweight aggregate is incorporated into concrete installed primarily for heat insulation. Any of the aggregates used for lightweight concrete designed primarily for strength except cinders may also be used for insulating concrete. However, aggregates prepared by expanding natural minerals such as perlite and vermiculite are the lightest and generally the best insulators of all these. ASTM C332, Lightweight Aggregates for Insulating Concrete, specifies a maximum weight of 12 lb per cu ft (dry loose weight) for perlite and 10 lb per cu ft for vermiculite.

Lightweight aggregate may have a tendency to stain concrete surfaces because of iron compounds that are washed out by rain. ASTM C641, Staining Materials in Lightweight Concrete Aggregates, describes procedures for testing this tendency.

Heavy aggregates are those with higher specific gravities than that of aggregates in general use although there is no definite line separating them from ordinary aggregates. They are used primarily to make heavy concrete. Heavy concrete is needed in special cases to resist the force of flowing water or to counterbalance a large weight, on a bascule bridge, for instance. Heavy aggregate is also used in nuclear-radiation–shielding concrete where greater density provides greater shielding. Natural minerals used are iron minerals and ores with specific gravities as high as 4 to 5.5 and barium minerals with specific gravities up to 4.5. Steel punchings, iron shot, and a byproduct of the production of phosphorus called ferrophosphorus (SG of 5.7 to 6.5) are used as heavy aggregates.

Natural heavy mineral aggregates and ferrophosphorus are described in ASTM C638, Constituents of Aggregates for Radiation-Shielding Concrete, and general requirements are specified in ASTM C637, Aggregates for Radiation-Shielding Concrete.

Radiation shielding is also accomplished by the inclusion of natural boron minerals, or boron minerals heated to partial fusion, as aggregates in the concrete shield. These are also described in ASTM C638.

Review Questions

1. How is bedrock reduced to aggregate particles in nature?
2. How could you differentiate between a gravel deposit of glacial till and one of glacial outwash?
3. A 2000-lb wheel load is to be supported by aggregate over soil that can withstand a pressure of 1000 lb per sq ft. What depth of aggregate is needed if $\theta = 40°$?
4. A pipe is to be installed under the ground on a bed of aggregate 6 in. thick. The entire weight on the aggregate from pipe and soil above the pipe is 1800 lb per lineal ft of pipe. What is the pressure on the soil if $\theta = 45°$? Assume the pipe load on the aggregate acts on a line.
5. What is the way in which all stabilizing techniques increase the strength of aggregate?
6. Explain why a filter should be made of uniformly graded aggregate.
7. Using the following data, determine percent retained, cumulative percent retained, and percent passing for each sieve. Plot the gradation curve.

Determine the effective size and uniformity coefficient. Determine the fineness modulus.

Sieve Size (in.)	Wt. Retained (gm)	Sieve Size	Wt. Retained (g)
3	736	No. 4	238
2	984	No. 8	346
1½	1642	No. 16	552
¾	1030	No. 30	511
⅜	625	No. 50	388
Pan	96	No. 100	267
		Pan	40

8. How many cubic yards of aggregate must be ordered for a road base 10 in. deep and 2½ miles long with a top width of 24 ft, if the side slopes are one on one or 45°?

9. A sample of coarse aggregate weighs 5360 g when oven dry, 5455 g when saturated surface-dry, and 3338 g submerged. What is bulk specific gravity? What is apparent specific gravity? What is absorption?

10. A sample of fine aggregate weighs 500.0 g when SSD and 492.6 g when OD. A flask weighing 35.3 g empty weighs 537.6 g when filled with water and 846.2 g when filled with the aggregate sample and water. What are the bulk specific gravity, apparent specific gravity and absorption?

11. What is the difference in detrimental effects of clay lumps and clay particles in aggregate to be used for portland cement concrete?

12. Explain why a comparison is made between the percent of the sample passing the No. 12 sieve after one-fifth of the Los Angeles Abrasion test and the percent passing at the completion of the test.

13. What are the four situations in which aggregate must be sampled and tested?

14. Describe the structure of lightweight aggregate.

3

Asphalt

Bituminous materials are important construction materials. They are strong cements, durable, highly waterproof, and readily adhesive. Bituminous materials are also highly resistant to the action of most acids, alkalies, and salts. They will be found on all types of construction projects from buildings to highway and heavy construction. They are used in roofing systems, sealants, and coatings and in pavements. Asphalt and tar are bituminous materials. Asphalt is produced by the distillation of petroleum crude oil, and tar is produced by the destruction distillation of organic materials.

HISTORY

The use of asphalt by man can be traced back to approximately 3800 B.C. Asphalts were used as cements to hold stonework together and as waterproofing in pools and baths. Some asphalt was mixed with sand and used to pave streets and palace floors.

The Egyptians made use of asphalt in the mummification process and as a building material. The Greeks and Romans not only used asphalt as a building material but also used burning asphalt as a military weapon.

The asphalt used by these ancient civilizations was *natural asphalt* formed when crude petroleum oils rose to the earth's surface and formed pools. The action of the sun and wind drove off the lighter oils and gases leaving a heavy residue. The residue was asphalt with impurities such as water and soil present. Using crude distillation processes, cementing and waterproofing materials were obtained.

NATURAL ASPHALT

Many pools of natural asphalt still exist; the largest are the Bermudez deposit in Venezuela and the asphalt lake on the island of Trinidad. Sir Walter Raleigh obtained Trinidad asphalt to caulk his ships during a voyage to the

FIGURE 3-1. Formation of natural asphalt (Courtesy Barber-Greene Co.)

New World. Until the development of distillation processes to produce asphalt from crude petroleum, the deposits were a major source of asphalt. In the United States the LaBrea pits in Los Angeles, California, are of interest because of the fossil remains and skeletons of prehistoric animals found in the pits.

Rock asphalt is another natural asphalt of limited commercial value because of its low asphalt content. As early as 1802 crushed rock asphalt was being used in France to pave floor, bridge, and sidewalk surfaces. Rock asphalt was imported in 1838 to pave sidewalks in Philadelphia, Pennsylvania. *Rock asphalt* is asphalt impregnated in porous rock while another form called gilsonite is found in veins. *Gilsonite* is a hard, brittle, and relatively pure asphalt which can be economically extracted from the earth for commercial purposes.

Even though natural asphalt does occur, the majority of asphalt used in construction today is obtained from petroleum crude. Depending upon its use, the asphalt can be produced in a variety of types and grades ranging from a hard, brittle material to a thin liquid. Approximately 70 percent of the asphalt produced is used in paving and related industries, 20 percent is used in the manufacture of roofing materials and systems such as built-up roofs, and the remaining 10 percent is used in miscellaneous areas such as metal coatings and waterproofing.

BITUMINOUS MATERIALS

The American Society for Testing and Materials defines bituminous asphalt and tar as follows:

Bitumens: mixtures of hydrocarbons of natural or pyrogenous origin or combinations of both, frequently accompanied by their nonmetallic derivatives, which may be gaseous, liquid, semi-solid, or solid, and which are completely soluble in carbon disulfide.

Asphalt: a dark brown to black cementitious material. Solid or semi-solid in consistency, in which the predominating constituents are bitumens which occur in nature as such or are obtained as residue in refining petroleum.

Tar: brown or black bituminous material, liquid or semi-solid in consistency, in which the predominating constituents are bitumens obtained as condensates in the destructive distillation of coal, petroleum, oil shale, wood, or other organic materials, and which yields substantial quantities of pitch when distilled.

Tar

Asphalt should not be confused with coal tar because their properties differ greatly. Asphalt is composed almost entirely of bitumens while tar has a low bitumen content.

Tar is generally produced as a byproduct during the production of coke.

While the coal is being heated, the gases generated are refined to produce road tars, roofing tars, waterproofing pitches, creosote oils and various tar chemicals. The amount of coal tar produced by this distillation process will vary depending upon the coal, equipment, and temperature used. Coal tars generally have high specific gravities, viscosities, and good adhesive properties.

Asphalt

Petroleum asphalt is the basic paving material in use today, even though some countries still use relatively small amounts of natural asphalt and tars.

Petroleum crude oils are generally classified on the basis of their crude oil content.

1. Asphaltic base crude (almost entirely asphalt)
2. Paraffin base crude (contains paraffin but no asphalt)
3. Mixed base crude (contains both paraffin and asphalt)

The amount of asphalt obtained from a crude oil is based upon its American Petroleum Institute (API) gravity; the higher the gravity, the lower the asphalt content, and the lower the API crude gravity, the higher the asphalt content. A crude with an API gravity of 30 may produce about 20–26 percent asphalt, while a crude with an API gravity of 17 may produce 50 percent asphalt. The remaining products would be gasoline, kerosene, fuel oil, and lubricating oils.

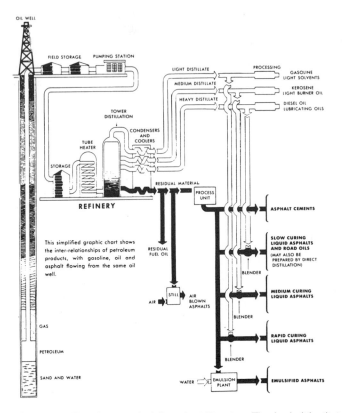

FIGURE 3-2. Petroleum asphalt flow chart (Courtesy The Asphalt Institute)

ASPHALT PRODUCTION

Asphalt Cements

Asphalt is produced from crude oil by distillation. The method preferred for the production of asphalt for paving construction is *fractional distillation*. The crude oil is heated and the lighter oils vaporize and are drawn off at their condensation temperature, leaving a residual material—asphalt cement.

To increase the production of the lighter constituents of crude oil such as fuels and lubricating oils, *destructive distillation* is employed. The crude oil is heated under pressure to higher temperatures than used in fractional distillation. The resulting asphalt from this system is called "cracked" asphalt. The *cracked asphalts* are usually less durable and weather resistant and are not used in highway surface construction, but they are used in base construction where they are protected from weathering by the surface course.

In both processes the distillation may be stopped while the residue is still liquid or semi-solid. The material is then called residual oil. When the resulting product is solid or semi-solid, it is called *asphalt cement*.

Special properties may be imparted to asphalt by blowing air through the residual oil. The oil is at an elevated temperature, and the asphalt is oxidized. The asphalts produced are called *blown asphalts*.

One of the significant property changes is the raising of the asphalts softening point. Since asphalt is a *thermoplastic* material, it softens as it is heated and hardens as it is cooled. The raising of the asphalt's softening point becomes an important property change. The degree of blowing will determine the changes in the asphalt's properties. Blown asphalts are generally not used as paving materials.

Blown asphalts are used mainly for roofing materials, automobile undercoatings, pipe coatings, and crack and joint sealers, and as sealing asphalts to fill cavities under portland cement concrete pavements.

With the addition of catalysts during the blowing process, a material results which will remain soft at temperatures far below those at which asphalt becomes brittle. These *catalytically* blown asphalts have uses as canal liners because of their elasticity.

Liquid Asphalts

The asphalt cement produced by distillation will require heating to a liquid state before it can be used in construction. To eliminate the need to heat the asphalt to a liquid state, the cement can be modified into a cutback asphalt or emulsified asphalt. The *cutback asphalt* is produced by dissolving the cement in a solvent. The solvents are sometimes called distillate, diluent, or cutter stock. The solvent will evaporate after the completion of construction, leaving the asphalt cement to perform its function. If the asphalt is an *emulsion*—that is, suspended in water—when the water evaporates or the emulsion breaks, the asphalt cement will remain.

Asphalt Cutbacks. The cutback liquid asphalts are produced by cutting the asphalt cement with a petroleum solvent. The cutbacks are classified according to the relative speed of evaporation of the solvent and are split into three groups.

1. Rapid-curing (RC): asphalt cement and a volatile solvent in the gasoline or naptha boiling point range.

2. Medium-curing (MC): asphalt cement and a solvent in the kerosene boiling point range.

3. Slow-curing (SC): asphalt cement and an oily solvent which has low volatility.

The liquid asphalt obtained by the addition of a solvent will vary in fluidity depending upon the asphalt cement, the volatility of the solvent, and the proportion of solvent to cement. Therefore, several grades of a cutback will be found in each classification.

The RC, MC, and SC designations define the cutbacks by class. Within each class the minimum kinematic viscosity in centistokes at 140°F denote the grades of cutback asphalts. For example, the MC 3000 cutback has a minimum viscosity of 3000 centistokes and a maximum viscosity of 6000 centistokes. The *viscosity* of a fluid or semi-fluid is a measure of the material's resistance to continuous flow; therefore, the higher grade numbers designate the more viscous cutbacks.

To produce an RC 70 the refiner would blend approximately 40 percent solvent with 60 percent asphalt; to produce a more viscous grade, the RC 3000, a blend of approximately 15 percent solvent to 85 percent asphalt would be required.

Asphalt Emulsions. Emulsified asphalts are produced by separating the hot asphalt cement into minute globules and dispersing them in water that has been treated with an *emulsifying agent*. The asphalt is called the discontinuous phase and the water the continuous phase. The asphalt emulsion is processed in a *colloidal mill* which applies shearing stress to the asphalt and water as it passes between a stationary plate and a rotating plate. Emulsions may also be classified as *inverted* emulsions with the asphalt as the continuous phase and the water in minute globule size as the discontinuous phase. This inverted emulsion is usually produced with asphalt cement that has been cut with a small amount of an MC type solvent.

If the asphalt globule has a negative charge, the emulsion produced is classified as *anionic*. When the asphalt globule has a positive charge, the emulsion is classified as *cationic*. Since anionic emulsified asphalts carry a negative charge, they work best with positive-charged aggregates such as limestone and dolomite. The cationic asphalt emulsion with its positive charge works best with silicious aggregates and with wet aggregates. The two types of emulsions cannot be mixed together.

By varying the materials and manufacturing processes, three emulsion grades are produced in either the anionic or the cationic state.

Grade	Anionic	Cationic
Rapid setting	RS	CRS
Medium setting	MS	CMS
Slow setting	SS	CSS

Since like charges repel, the asphalt globules are kept apart until the material comes in contact with aggregate particles and the charges are neutralized or the water evaporates. The process of the asphalt globules coming together in rapid- and medium-curing emulsions is called the *break* or *set*. The slow-setting emulsions depend primarily upon the evaporation of water to set.

The production of liquid asphalt products is based upon the cutting back or emulsifying of asphalt cement with the exception of slow-curing cutbacks. The slow-curing cutback may be produced by direct distillation if the residual material is of good quality and can be refined to meet an SC standard grade.

With the increasing realization that the world supply of petroleum is limited, highway engineers have begun research into using other materials that are plentiful and economical as substitutes for asphalt.

Sulfur has been used experimentally as a pavement binder because it is plentiful and economical, and it exhibits certain desirable properties when mixed with other engineering materials.

Sulfur extended asphalt (SEA) is a binder in which up to 50 percent of the asphalt is replaced with elemental sulfur. Between 15 and 20 percent of the sulfur is dissolved by the asphalt, and the remaining sulfur is dispersed as micron-sized particles in the binder. The blending of the sulfur into the asphalt requires high shear energy, such as that supplied by a colloidal mill.

The resulting SEA binder when combined with aggregates can be used as a road paving material. Current research indicates no detrimental effects upon the test pavements now in service.

Sand asphalt sulfur (SAS) is a blend of sand, asphalt, and sulfur, with the sulfur comprising 8–14 percent of the mix weight. SAS is used as a paving material. While hot, it can be cast in place like portland cement concrete or it can be placed by utilizing asphalt paving equipment. As the material cools, it develops strength, with the sulfur filling the voids and locking the sand particles together. This locking or keying of the sand particles allows the use of aggregates that would be unsuitable for a normal asphaltic concrete.

Plasticized sulfur (PS) is elemental sulfur combined with one or more chemical modifers. The Federal Highway Administration (FHWA) is currently supporting research in the area of plasticized sulfurs with the ultimate goal of producing a pavement binder which will replace asphalt cements and possibly portland cements. The plasticized sulfur paving mixes are mixed and handled with conventional paving techniques and equipment. The material costs are about the same as asphalt pavements, but as material prices continue to rise, plasticized sulfurs may become the paving materials of the future.

ASPHALT TESTING

Thermoplastic materials such as asphalt are classified by their consistency at different temperatures. *Consistency* describes the fluidity or plasticity of an asphalt at a particular temperature. Since the characteristics and behaviors of thermoplastics vary with temperature, it is important that all tests be performed at standard test temperatures. If the test temperatures were different, it would be possible to evaluate two different asphalts and have the test results indicate that the asphalts tested were the same materials.

Various tests have been developed to predict asphalt's suitability to perform certain functions. Generally the tests performed on asphalt will measure consistency, durability, rate of hardening, serviceability, and ability to be effective in hostile environments.

Some of the tests are common to both solid and liquid asphalts while others are suitable for only solid or only liquid asphalts.

The appendix indicates the current asphalt specifications with reference to detailed AASHTO (American Association of State Highway and Transportation Officials) and ASTM (American Society for Testing and Materials).

Asphalt Cements

Penetration Test. *Empirical tests* are those tests based upon experience over long periods of time with a particular test procedure. An empirical measure of asphalt consistency is the penetration test. The penetration test determines the relative hardness or consistency of an asphalt cement.

Based upon penetration ranges at 77°F, the 40–50 range is the hardest asphalt cement, and at room temperature a faint thumbprint may be left in a sample's surface. Cements harder than the 40–50 range can be produced for special uses. The softest cements are in the 200–300 range, and gentle finger pressure will indent the surface of a sample.

A sample of asphalt cement is placed in a sample tin which is immersed in a constant temperature bath at 77°F (25°C). The sample is placed on the penetrometer base where a needle weighted to 100 g is brought into contact with the sample surface. The needle is allowed to penetrate the sample for 5 s.

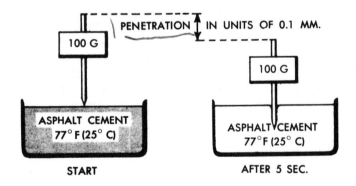

FIGURE 3-3. Standard penetration test (Courtesy The Asphalt Institute)

The distance the needle penetrates into the sample is measured in units of 0.1 mm and is called the penetration. The penetration ranges listed in the appendix are therefore the distances the needle could penetrate a sample in millimeters for it to be classified as a particular asphalt cement. The standard conditions for this test may be found in ASTM D5 and AASHTO T49.

Viscosity Test. The *viscosity* of a material is a measure of its resistance to flow. To provide control of asphalt cement consistencies at temperature ranges more closely associated with construction uses, the viscosity of asphalt cements is tested at 275°F and 135°F. The viscosity of asphalt cements can be determined by either the Kinematic Viscosity test at 275°F, or the Saybolt Furol Viscosity test at 135°F.

The Saybolt Furol Viscosity test requires the heating of a given sample of asphalt in a standard tube. The tube has a standard *orifice* or opening of prescribed shape and dimensions. The orifice has a stopper in place until the material reaches test temperature. When the material reaches test temperature, the stopper is removed and the material is allowed to flow into a flask. The time required in seconds for 60 ml of asphalt cement to flow through the

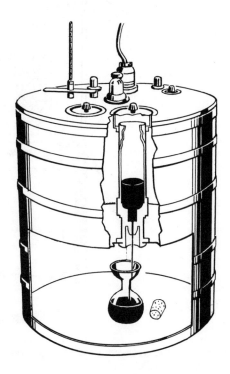

FIGURE 3-4. Saybolt furol viscosity test (Courtesy The Asphalt Institute)

orifice into the flask is determined. The time in seconds is the Saybolt Furol viscosity of the asphalt cement—(SSF) Seconds–Saybolt Furol.

The thicker or more viscous the material, the longer the time required for 60 ml of material to pass through the orifice and the higher the Saybolt Furol viscosity (SSF).

The viscosity of an asphalt cement may also be determined by using the kinematic viscosity apparatus shown in Fig. 3-5. A thermostatically controlled constant temperature bath is used. The bath is filled with a suitable clear oil when tests are made at 275°F. The Zeitfuchs cross-arm viscometer tubes are suspended in the heated oil. The asphalt cement sample is poured into the large opening of the tube until it reaches the filling line, being careful

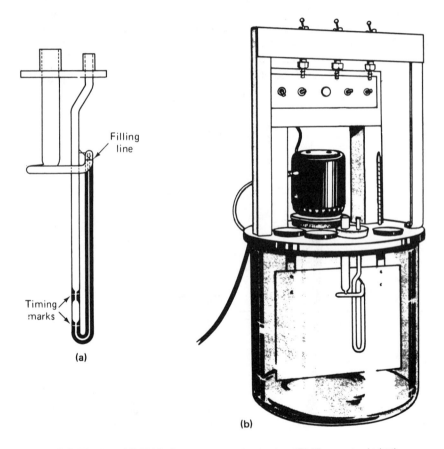

FIGURE 3-5. (A) Zeitfuchs cross-arm viscometer; (B) Viscometer in bath (Courtesy The Asphalt Institute)

not to exceed the line limit or the sample will pass through the tube before it has reached the proper test temperature. After the sample has been in the tube for the required time, a slight pressure is applied to the large opening or a vacuum to the small opening to start the sample flowing over the fill line. Once the sample passes over the siphon section of the tub, gravity causes the material to flow down the vertical section of the tube. The timer is started when the sample reaches the first mark and stopped when the material reaches the second mark. The tubes have previously been calibrated using standard oils of known viscosity characteristics. The calibration factor of the tube times the number of seconds required for the material to pass through the timing marks is the kinematic viscosity of the material in units of centistokes.

The numerical results of the Saybolt Furol Viscosity test are approximately one-half the results of the Kinematic Viscosity test. Care must be taken when cleaning the cross-arm tubes that have been calibrated since they are expensive.

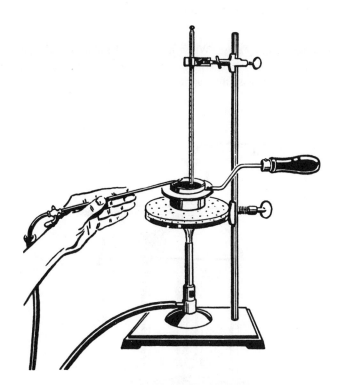

FIGURE 3-6. Cleveland open cup flash point test (Courtesy The Asphalt Institute)

Flash Point Test. The *Flash Point test* is a safety test. Since asphalt cements must be heated to be used in construction, the flash point of an asphalt tells the user the maximum temperature the material may be heated to before an instantaneous flash will occur in the presence of an open flame. The flash point is usually well above the normal heating ranges of asphaltic cements. While usually not specified, the fire point of an asphalt cement is the higher temperature at which the material will support combustion.

The Cleveland Open Cup (COC) Flash Point test is usually used to determine the flash point of an asphalt cement. The brass cup is filled with the proper sample amount of asphalt cement and heated at a specified temperature gain rate. A small flame is passed over the surface of the asphalt cement being heated, and the temperature at which an instantaneous flash occurs is called the flash point.

Another test used to determine the flash points of asphalt cements is the Pensky–Martens (PM) Point test. The PM test is a little different in that the sample is stirred continuously in the closed container. The PM method often gives lower values for the flash point of an asphalt cement than the COC method.

Thin Film Oven Test. When asphalt is heated and then cooled, its consistency tends to increase. When asphalt is heated and exposed to air, as during the mixing process, the asphalt hardens. Since the material must be

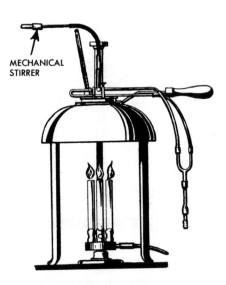

FIGURE 3-7. Pensky–Martens flash point test (Courtesy The Asphalt Institute)

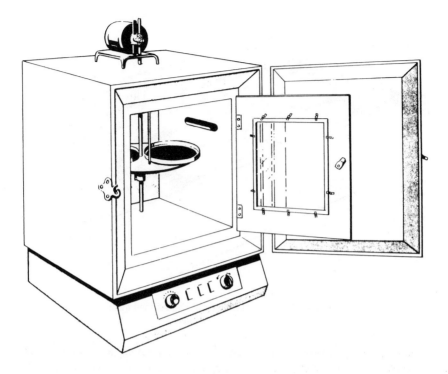

FIGURE 3-8. Thin film oven test (Courtesy The Asphalt Institute)

heated before it can be used, the *Thin Film Oven (TFO) test* is a procedure used to expose the asphalt to conditions which occur in heating operations. There should be no appreciable difference in consistency when the material is heated to 325°F and then cooled. Since asphalt coating thicknesses vary and temperature will vary, the test is only used as an indicator of probable behavior.

The test requires that a 50 cc sample of cement be placed in a 5.5-in. diameter flat bottom pan with a ⅜-in. depth. The film thickness is about ⅛-in. The pan is placed on a shelf in a ventilated oven at 325°F for 5 hours. The shelf rotates the sample 5 revolutions per minute. After 5 hours have elapsed, the sample is then placed in a penetration sample tin. The penetration loss of the sample after the oven test is expressed as a percentage of the penetration of the material before being heated in the oven.

Ductility Test. In many applications, ductility is considered an important property of asphalt cements. The presence or absence of ductility is usually considered more significant than the degree of ductility. Asphalt cements possessing *ductility* are normally more adhesive than asphalt cements

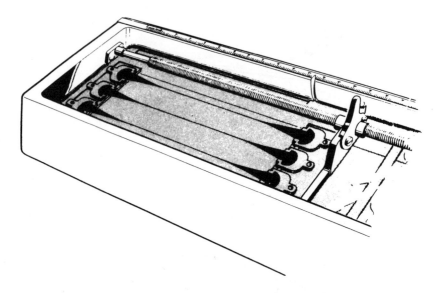

FIGURE 3-9. Ductility test (Courtesy The Asphalt Institute)

lacking ductility. However, some asphalt cements having a high degree of ductility are also more temperature susceptible. That is, their consistency will change more for a temperature change. In paving mixes, ductility and adhesion are important properties, while in crack filling and pavement undersealing, temperature susceptibility is the more important property.

Asphalt cement ductility is measured by an "extension" type test. Standard briquettes of asphalt are molded and brought to the standard test temperature of 77°F. One part of the specimen is pulled away from the other at 5 cm per minute until the thread connecting the two parts of the sample breaks. The ductility of the asphalt is the elongation in centimeters.

Solubility Test. The *Solubility test* determines the purity of an asphalt cement. The active cementing portion of the sample is represented by that portion of the sample that is soluble in carbon disulfide. The inert matter such as salts, free carbon, or nonorganic materials is insoluble. Since asphalt cements are about as soluble in trichlorethylene, carbon tetrachloride, and other solvents as they are in carbon disulfide, they are often used because they are less hazardous.

The test is simple to perform. A 2 g sample of asphalt is dissolved in 100 ml of solvent and the solution filtered through an asbestos mat in a porcelain (Gooch) crucible. The residue on the mat is weighed and expressed as a percentage of the original sample.

Liquid Asphalts

Specifications for rapid curing (RC), medium curing (MC) and slow curing (SC) are given in the appendix. The three types are produced in comparable grades based on kinematic viscosity ranges at 140°F. In the medium-curing (MC) specification, an extra grade appears—the MC30. It is used as a priming grade in some sections of the United States. Each grade of cutback is categorized by the *kinematic viscosity* or resistance to flow while in motion in centistokes and is designated by the lowest viscosity of that grade. Each grade includes a range from the designating value to a value of twice that amount. The most viscous grades of the three asphalts (RS-3000, MC-3000, SC-3000) are only moderately less viscous than the highest penetration grade (200–300) of asphalt cement. The least viscous grades (RC-70, MC-30, MC-70, SC-70) may be poured at room temperature. The consistency of these grades is approximately the same as heavy dairy cream.

Kinematic Viscosity Test. RC, MC, and SC liquid asphalts are classified into standard grades by the *Kinematic Viscosity test*. The basic test procedures are the same as for asphalt cements. Since the kinematic viscosity is determined at 140°F, water can be used as the medium in the constant temperature bath instead of oil. To prevent the volatiles from escaping, sample preparations are different. The full test particulars will be found in ASTM D2170 and AASHTO T201.

Flash Point Test. The purpose and significance of the *Flash Point test* on asphalt cutbacks is the same as asphalt cements. The Cleveland Open Cup test is used to determine the flash point of SC materials. Indirect heating is used to test for the flash point of RC and MC grades because of the volatile nature of the diluent in these grades. The Tag Open Cup apparatus is used for this test. The cup is glass instead of metal, and the material is heated in a water bath rather than by direct flame.

Liquid asphalts are commonly used at temperatures above their flash points. The more volatile the diluent in the liquid asphalt, the more hazardous its use. Some rapid-curing cutbacks may flash at temperatures as low as 80°F. All of the cutbacks present some danger in use and should be handled properly.

Distillation test. Since RC, MC, and, in some instances, SC grades of liquid asphalt are blends of asphalt cement and suitable diluents, properties of these materials are of importance in their application and performance.

The *Distillation test* separates the asphalt cement and diluents to determine their quantities and for other testing. Two hundred ml of liquid asphalt is placed in a distillation flash connected to a water-cooled condenser tube. As the flask is heated, the diluent vaporizes and is liquified in the condenser tube

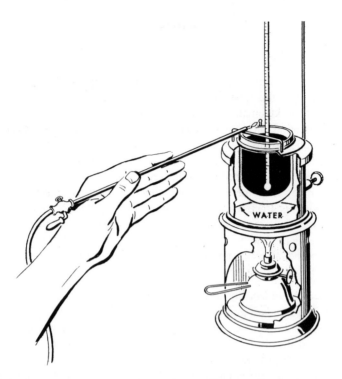

FIGURE 3-10. Tag open cup flash point test (Courtesy The Asphalt Institute)

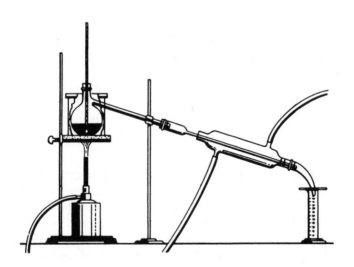

FIGURE 3-11. Distillation test for cutback asphalts (Courtesy The Asphalt Institute)

which drains into a graduated cylinder. The volatility characteristics of the diluent are indicated by the quantity of condensate driven off at several specified temperatures. When 680°F is reached, the material remaining in the distillation flask is considered asphalt cement. For RC and MC cutbacks, penetration, ductility, and solubility properties of the residue are determined as described for asphalt cements.

For SC cutbacks, the amounts of distillate at various temperatures is of little importance; since they are mainly oily in nature, their rate of evaporation in service is quite slow. Therefore, only the total quantity of distillate driven off up to 680°F is measured. The residue is considered to be representative of the asphalt portion of the cutback, and its consistency is determined by the Kinematic Viscosity test.

Solubility of an SC cutback is determined using the material itself and not the residue from distillation.

Water Test. Asphaltic materials, except emulsified asphalts, are usually specified to be *water free,* or substantially so. Water present in the asphalt materials creates a hazardous condition by causing foaming when the materials are heated. To determine the amount of water present, if any, in liquid asphalt, a sample of the material is mixed with xyol or high boiling-range petroleum naptha in a glass or metal still. A reflux condenser is attached to the still with its discharge into a graduated trap. When heat is applied to the still, any water in the liquid asphalt will collect in the trap. The percentage of water by volume is then determined.

Asphalt Emulsions

Specifications for emulsified asphalts are given in the appendix. Asphalt emulsions, which have a variety of viscosities, asphalt cement bases, and setting properties are available.

Saybolt Furol Viscosity Test. The consistency properties of anionic and cationic emulsions are measured by the Saybolt Furol Viscosity test. As a matter of testing convenience and to achieve suitable testing accuracy, two testing temperatures are used (77°F and 122°F) depending on the viscosity characteristics of the specific type and grade of asphalt emulsion. The test procedure is basically the same as that used to test asphalt cements. The unit of measure is poises.

Distillation Test. The *Distillation test* is used to determine the relative proportions of asphalt cement and water in the asphalt emulsion. Some grades of emulsified asphalt also contain an oil distillate. The Distillation test provides information on the amount of this material in the emulsion. Also, the Distillation test provides an asphalt cement residue, on which additional tests

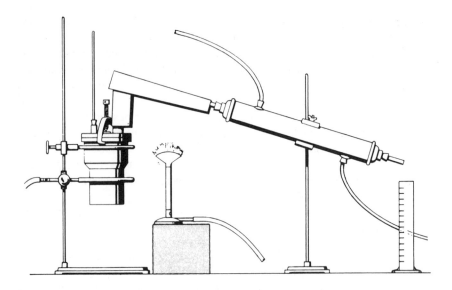

FIGURE 3-12. Distillation test for emulsified asphalts (Courtesy The Asphalt Institute)

(penetration, solubility, and dutility) may be made as previously described for asphalt cement.

The test procedure is substantially the same as that described for liquid asphalt. A 200 g sample of emulsion is distilled to 500°F. The principal difference in the emulsion distillation test is that the end point of distillation is 500°F rather than 680°F, and an iron or aluminum alloy still and ring burners are used instead of a glass flask and Bunsen burner. This equipment is designed to prevent trouble that may result from foaming of emulsified asphalt as it is being heated. The end point of distillation is carried to 500°F, and this temperature is held for 15 minutes in order to produce a smooth, homogeneous residue.

Settlement Test. The *Settlement test* detects the tendency of asphalt globules to "settle out" during storage of emulsified asphalt. It provides the user with an element of protection against separation of asphalt and water in unstable emulsions that may be stored for a period of time.

A 500 ml sample is placed in each of two graduated cylinders, stoppered, and allowed to stand undisturbed for 5 days. Small samples are taken from the top and bottom parts of each cylinder. Each sample is placed in a beaker and weighed. The samples are then heated until water evaporates; residues are then weighed. The weights obtained provide the basis for determining the difference, if any, between asphalt cement content in this upper and lower portions of the graduated cylinder, thus providing a measure of settlement.

Sieve Test. The *Sieve test* complements the settlement test and has a somewhat similar purpose. It is used to determine quantitatively the percent of asphalt cement present in the form of pieces, strings, or relatively large globules. Such non-dispersed particles of asphalt might clog equipment and would tend to provide nonuniform coatings of asphalt on aggregate particles. This nonuniformity might not be detected by the Settlement test, which is of value in this regard only when there is a sufficient difference in the specific gravities of asphalt and water to allow settlement.

In the Sieve test, 1,000 g of asphalt emulsion are poured through a U.S. standard No. 20 sieve. For anionic emulsified asphalts, the sieve and retained asphalt are then rinsed with a mild sodium oleate solution. For cationic emulsified asphalts, rinsing is with distilled water. After rinsing, the sieve and asphalt are dried in an oven, and the relative amount of asphalt retained on the sieve is determined.

Demulsibility Test. The *Demulsibility test* is used only for rapid- and medium-setting grades of anionic asphalt emulsions. It indicates the relative rate at which colloidal asphalt globules coalesce (or break) when spread in thin films on soil or aggregate particles.

Calcium chloride coagulates or flocculates the minute globules present in anionic emulsified asphalts. To make the test, a 100 g sample is thoroughly mixed with a calcium chloride solution. The mixture is then poured over a No. 14 sieve and washed. The degree of coalescence is determined from the amount of asphalt residue remaining on the sieve.

A high degree of demulsibility is required for the rapid-setting grade of anionic emulsified asphalt because it is expected to break almost immediately on contact with the aggregate surface. Therefore, a very weak calcium chloride solution is used for the demulsibility test on these products. A somewhat more concentrated solution is used when testing medium-setting grades, as they are formulated to break more slowly.

Slow-setting grades often are used in mixes containing fine aggregates or in other applications where rapid coalescence of asphalt particles is undesirable. The Cement Mixing test is therefore used in lieu of the Demulsibility test as a control for the setting rate of these products.

Cement Mixing Text. The *Cement Mixing test* is performed by adding 100 ml of emulsion diluted to 55 percent residue with water to 50 g of high, early strength portland cement with stirring for thorough mixing. Additional water is stirred in. The mixture is then washed over a No. 14 sieve, and the percent of coagulated material retained on the sieve is determined.

As noted, the Cement Mixing test is used instead of the Demulsibility test for slow-setting grades of emulsified asphalt. It is specified for both the anionic and cationic types to assure products substantially immune from rapid coalescence of asphalt particles in contact with fine-grained soils or aggregates.

Coating Ability and Water Resistance Test.   This test determines the ability of an emulsified asphalt to:

1. coat an aggregate thoroughly,

2. withstand mixing action while remaining as a film on the aggregate, and

3. resist the washing action of water after mixing is completed.

The test is primarily intended to aid in identifying asphalt emulsions that are suitable for mixing with coarse-graded aggregate intended for job use. For specification purposes, the test is required only for cationic, medium-setting asphalt emulsions.

A 465-g air-dried sample of aggregate that is to be used on a project is mixed with 35 g of emulsified asphalt for 5 minutes. One-half of the mixture is removed from the pan and placed on absorbent paper, and the percentage of coated particles determined.

The remaining mixture in the pan is carefully washed with a gentle spray of tap water and drained until the water runs clear. This mixture is then placed on absorbent paper and the percentage of coated aggregate particles determined.

This procedure is repeated for wet aggregate (9.3 ml of water mixed with the air-dried aggregate) before mixing with emulsified asphalt.

Particle Charge Test.   This is an identification test for rapid- and medium-setting grades of cationic asphalt emulsions.

A positive electrode (anode) and a negative electrode (cathode) are immersed in a sample of emulsified asphalt and connected to a controlled direct-current electrical source. After 30 minutes, or after the current has dropped to 2 milliamperes, the two electrodes are examined to determine which one has an asphalt deposit. An asphalt depsosit on the cathode identifies a cationic emulsified asphalt.

pH Test.   The *Acidity–Alkalinity (pH) test* is used only to determine and specify the degree of acidity for slow-setting grades of cationic asphalt emulsions. It is used in place of the Particle Charge test, which is used for rapid- and medium-setting grades of cationic asphalt emulsions.

A potentiometer, or pH meter, is used to make the test. A small sample of asphalt emulsion is placed in a beaker, and glass electrodes are inserted in the sample. The difference in potential is then measured in pH or millivolt units, which is an indication of the acidity of the sample.

Oil Distillate Test.   Rapid- and medium-setting grades of cationic asphalt emulsion, and some anionic asphalt emulsions, may include an oily distillate fraction, the maximum amount of which usually is limited by specifications. The amount of distillate is determined in the Distillation test (for

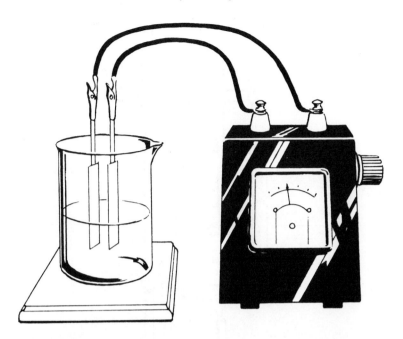

FIGURE 3-13. Particle charge test (Courtesy The Asphalt Institute)

emulsified asphalts) previously described. Distillate collected in the graduated cylinder includes both oil and water from the asphalt emulsion. Because these two materials separate in the graduated cylinder, the amounts of each can be determined.

Air-Blown Asphalts

Although similar in many respects to the normal paving grades of asphalt cement previously discussed, the blowing process provides materials that soften at higher temperatures than asphalt cements. Because the higher softening point is a most important and desirable property of blown asphalts, they are usually classified in terms of the Ring and Ball Softening Point test, rather than in terms of the Penetration test used for asphalt cements.

Specifications for blown asphalts used in undersealing portland cement concrete pavements are given in the appendix.

While blown asphalts are graded on the basis of the softening point, there are still Penetration test requirements at three temperatures. These requirements provide a degree of control over the temperature susceptibility, or the rate of consistency change with temperature, for these materials.

Tests included in the specifications will be discussed, except where they are the same as those discussed for asphalt cement.

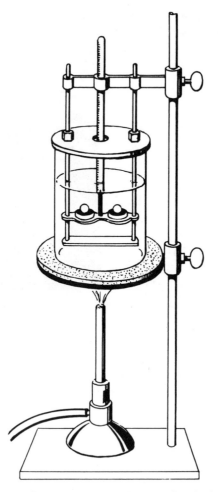

FIGURE 3-14. Softening point test (Courtesy The Asphalt Institute)

Softening Point Test. The *Softening Point test* is used as the basic measurement of consistency for grading blown asphalts.

Samples of asphalt loaded with steel balls are confined in brass rings suspended in a beaker of water or glycerine, 1 inch above a metal plate. The water, or glycerine, is then heated at a prescribed rate. As the asphalt softens, the balls and the asphalt gradually sink toward the plate. At the moment the asphalt touches the plate, the temperature of the water is determined, and this is designated as Ring and Ball (RB) Softening Point of asphalt.

Penetration Test. The specifications indicate penetration requirements at temperatures of 32°F, 77°F, and 115°F. The Penetration test as made at 77°F was described and illustrated for asphalt cements; and, at this temperature, the test is the same for the blown asphalts. At 32°F and 115°F, the differences are in the needle weight and the length of time the needle is permitted to bear on the surface of the asphalt. These differences are indicated in the specification tables.

Loss on Heating Test. The *Loss on Heating test* is generally similar to the Thin Film Oven test as described for asphalt cements. The only differences are in the dimensions of the asphalt sample. Whereas the asphalt sample in the TFO test is about 5½ in. in diameter and ⅛ in. deep, the sample for the loss on heating test is approximately 2¼ in. in diameter and 1 in. deep. In both tests the asphalt and container are placed on a rotating shelf in a ventilated oven and maintained at 325°F for a period of 5 hours. The shelf rotates at approximately five to six revolutions per minute.

As with the TFO test, the Loss on Heating test actually is not a test within itself. It is a procedure that is intended to subject the asphalt to hardening conditions similar to those expected in the application processes. A Penetration test usually is made on the asphalt after the Loss on Heating test for comparison with the penetration of the asphalt prior to the test.

EFFECTS OF TEMPERATURE AND VISCOSITY

As discussed previously, asphalt is a thermoplastic material that changes viscosity with changes in temperature. However, the precise relationship between temperature and viscosity (called temperature–viscosity curves or graphs) for a particular penetration grade and type of asphalt from one refinery may not be identical with the same type and grade of asphalt from another refinery.

Assume for a given mix that asphalt at a viscosity of 100 seconds–Saybolt Furol (SSF) will provide ideal mixing conditions. To obtain this viscosity, asphalt *A* must be mixed at 315°F, and asphalt *C* at 275°F. The difference in temperatures between asphalts *A* and *C* required to produce equal viscosity is 40°F. Therefore, unless temperatures were regulated to have the asphalt mixes at a temperature providing substantially equal viscosity for the asphalt cements, mixing and handling characteristics of mixes with these two asphalts would be different. This does not mean that there is a difference in quality of the two asphalts, only a difference in a physical property that must be taken into account when the asphalts are used.

Viscosity of asphalt during construction operations such as mixing and spraying is of prime importance. Therefore, the temperature–viscosity rela-

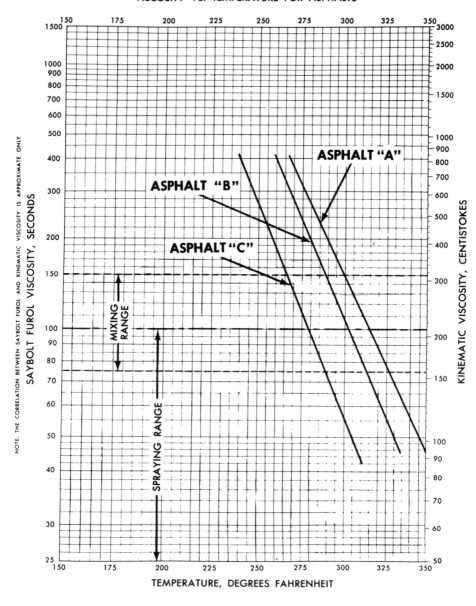

FIGURE 3-15. Viscosity vs. temperature for asphalts (Courtesy The Asphalt Institute)

106

tionship for the asphalt being used should be known so the mixing and spraying temperatures can be regulated.

ASPHALT PAVEMENTS

The basic idea in building a road or parking area for all-weather use by vehicles is to prepare a suitable subgrade or foundation, provide necessary drainage, and construct a pavement that will:

1. Have sufficient total thickness and internal strength to carry expected traffic loads;

2. Prevent the penetration or internal accumulation of moisture; and

3. Have a top surface that is smooth and resistant to wear, distortion, skidding, and deterioration by weather and de-icing chemicals.

The subgrade ultimately carries all traffic loads. Therefore, the structural function of a pavement is to support a wheel load on the pavement surface and transfer and spread that load to the subgrade without overtaxing either the strength of the subgrade or the internal strength of the pavement itself.

Figure 3-16 shows wheel load, W, being transmitted to the pavement surface through the tire at an approximately uniform vertical pressure, P_0. The

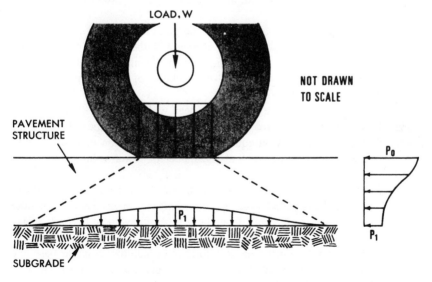

FIGURE 3-16. Spread of wheel load through pavement structure (Courtesy The Asphalt Institute)

pavement then spreads the wheel load to the subgrade so that the maximum pressure on the subgrade is only P_1. By proper selection of pavement materials and with adequate pavement thickness, P_1 will be small enough to be easily supported by the subgrade.

Asphalt pavement is a general term applied to any pavement that has a surface constructed with asphalt. Normally, it consists of a surface course (layer) of mineral aggregate coated and cemented with asphalt and one or more supporting courses, which may be of the following types:

1. Asphalt base, consisting of asphalt–aggregate mixtures;

2. Crushed stone (rock), slag, or gravel;

3. Portland cement concrete; and

4. Old brick or stone block pavements.

Asphalt pavement structure consists of all courses above the prepared subgrade or foundation. The upper or top layer is the asphalt wearing surface. It may range from less than 1 inch to several inches in thickness, depending on a variety of design factors.

While a variety of bases and subbases may be used in asphalt pavement structures, more commonly they consist of compacted granular materials (such as crushed rock, slag, gravel, sand, or a combination of these) or stabilized soil. One of the main advantages of asphalt pavements is that a variety of materials may be used; thus, economy is achieved by using locally available materials.

Generally, it is preferable to treat the granular material used in bases. The most common treatment is to mix asphalt with the granular material, thus producing an asphalt base. A 1-in. thickness of asphalt base is about equal in load-carrying performance to a 2- or 3-in. thickness of granular base materials not treated with asphalt.

Untreated bases and subbases have been widely used in the past. However, as modern traffic increases in weight and volume, these bases show performance limitations. Consequently, it is now common practice to limit use of untreated bases to pavements designed for lower volumes of lighter traffic.

When the entire pavement structure above the subgrade consists of asphalt mixtures, it is called a *full-depth asphalt pavement*. This is generally considered the most modern and dependable type of pavement for present-day traffic.

Other materials sometimes used to treat or stabilize granular base and subbase materials or selected soils are portland cement, lime, coal, tar, calcium chloride, or salt (sodium chloride).

PAVEMENT THICKNESS FOR DRIVEWAYS FOR PASSENGER CARS

THICKNESS REQUIREMENTS IN INCHES

	FULL DEPTH ASPHALT CONCRETE		ASPHALT CONCRETE SURFACE		PLANT-MIX SURFACE USING LIQUID ASPHALT		ASPHALT SURFACE TREATMENT	
	Asphalt Concrete Surface	Asphalt Concrete Base [1]	Asphalt Concrete Surface	Crushed Rock Base [2]	Asphalt Plant-Mix Surface	Crushed Rock Base [2]	Asphalt Surface Treatment	Crushed Rock Base [2]
Gravelly or sandy soils, well drained	1	2–3	3	2	4.5*	2	1**	6–8
Average clay loam soils, not plastic	1	3–4	3	2–4	4.5*	2–4	1**	8–10
Soft clay soils, plastic when wet	1	4–5	3	4–6***	4.5*	4–6***	1**	10–12***

[1] *Prime required on subgrade.*
[2] *Prime required on base.*
* *Must be spread and compacted in layers not exceeding 1½ inches in depth and the volatiles (petroleum solvents or water) allowed to evaporate before the next layer is placed. Also, a seal coat may be required as a final surfacing.*
** *Economical but relatively limited service life. Usually less than 1 inch thick.*
*** *Two inches of coarse sand or stone screenings recommended between subgrade and base as an insulation course.*

FIGURE 3-17. Suggested pavement thickness for parking areas and driveways (Courtesy The Asphalt Institute)

PAVEMENT THICKNESS FOR PARKING AREAS FOR PASSENGER CARS

THICKNESS REQUIREMENTS IN INCHES

	FULL DEPTH ASPHALT CONCRETE		ASPHALT CONCRETE SURFACE		PLANT-MIX SURFACE USING LIQUID ASPHALT		ASPHALT SURFACE TREATMENT	
	Asphalt Concrete Surface	Asphalt Concrete Base[1]	Asphalt Concrete Surface	Crushed Rock Base[2]	Asphalt Plant-Mix Surface	Crushed Rock Base[2]	Asphalt Surface Treatment	Crushed Rock Base[2]
Gravelly or sandy soils, well drained	1	2–3	3	2	4.5*	2	1**	6–8
Average clay loam soils, not plastic	1	3–4	3	2–4	4.5*	2–4	1**	8–10
Soft clay soils, plastic when wet	1	4–5	3	4–6***	4.5*	4–6***	1**	10–12***

[1] Prime required on subgrade.
[2] Prime required on base.
* Must be spread and compacted in layers not exceeding 1½ inches in depth and the volatiles (petroleum solvents or water) allowed to evaporate before the next layer is placed. Also, a seal coat may be required as a final surfacing.
** Economical but relatively limited service life. Usually less than 1 inch thick.
*** Two inches of coarse sand or stone screenings recommended between subgrade and base as an insulation course.

FIGURE 3-17 (continued). Suggested pavement thickness for parking areas and driveways (Courtesy The Asphalt Institute)

PAVEMENT THICKNESS FOR PARKING AREAS FOR HEAVY TRUCKS

THICKNESS REQUIREMENTS IN INCHES

	FULL DEPTH ASPHALT CONCRETE	ASPHALT CONCRETE SURFACE			SURFACE TREATMENT ON PENTRATION MACADAM		PLANT-MIX SURFACE USING LIQUID ASPHALT	
	Asphalt Concrete Surface	Asphalt Concrete Base[1]	Asphalt Concrete Surface	Crushed Rock Base[2]	Asphalt Surface Treatment	Asphalt Penetration Macadam Base[1]	Asphalt Plant-Mix Surface	Crushed Rock Base[2]
Gravelly or sandy soils, well drained	1.5	3–5	4.5	0–4	1*	7–10	7**	2–4
Average clay loam soils, not plastic	1.5	5–6	4.5	4–6	1*	10–11.5	7**	4–6
Soft clay soils, plastic when wet	1.5	6–8	4.5	6–10***	1*	11.5–14.5	7**	6–10***

[1] Prime required on subgrade.
[2] Prime required on base.
* Usually less than 1 inch thick.
** Must be spread and compacted in layers not exceeding 1½ inches in depth and the volatiles (petroleum solvents or water) allowed to evaporate before the next layer is placed. Also, seal coat may be required as a final surfacing.
*** Two inches of coarse sand or stone screenings recommended between subgrade and base as an insulation course.

FIGURE 3-17. (Continued)

DETERMINING REQUIRED PAVEMENT THICKNESS

A significant advance in highway engineering is the realization and demonstration that structural design of asphalt pavements is similar to the problem of designing any other complex engineering structure. When asphalt pavement was first being introduced, determining the proper thickness was a matter of guesswork, rule of thumb, and opinion based on experience. Almost the same situation once prevailed in determining the dimensions of masonry arches and iron and steel structures. However, these early techniques have long since yielded to engineering analysis. Similarly, based on comprehensive analysis of vast volumes of accumulated data, the structural design of asphalt pavements has now been developed into a reliable engineering procedure. Research aimed at further refinements and a fully rational design procedure is continuing.

There is no standard thickness for a pavement. However, the Asphalt Institute has published general guidelines to be used for parking areas and driveways. Required total thickness is determined by engineering design procedure. Factors considered in the procedure are:

1. Traffic to be served initially and over the design service life of the pavement;

2. Strength and other pertinent properties of the prepared subgrade;

3. Strength and other influencing characteristics of the materials available or chosen for the layers or courses in the total asphalt pavement structure; and

4. Any special factors peculiar to the road being designed.

Traffic Analysis

The weight and volume of traffic a road is expected to carry initially and throughout its design service life influences the required thickness of asphalt pavement structure. Several methods have been developed to determine present and future traffic volumes. The information obtained is used for pavement design purposes. Necessary factors have been derived from road test data and from elaborate traffic counts on roads in service. However, in special situations, such as logging roads where the weight and frequency of the actual trucks are known, the designed pavement thickness is based specifically on the known factors.

Subgrade Evaluation

There are several methods for evaluation or estimating the strength and supporting power of a subgrade, including:

1. Loading tests in the field on the subgrade itself; for example, the Plate Bearing test uses large circular plates loaded to produce critical amounts of deformation on the subgrade in place.

2. Loading tests in a laboratory using representative samples of the subgrade soil. Some commonly used tests are (a) California Bearing Ratio (CBR) test, which is sometimes used on the subgrade in place in the field; (b) Hveem Stabilometer test; and (c) Triaxial test.

3. Evaluations based on classification of soil by identifying and testing the constituent particles of the soil. Four well-known classification systems are (a) American Association of State Highway and Transportation Officials (AASHTO) Classification System; (b) United Soil Classification System; (c) Corps of Engineers, U.S. Army; and (d) U.S. Federal Aviation Administration (FAA) method.

Asphalt Paving-Mix Design

The design of asphalt paving mixes, as with other engineering materials designs, is largely a matter of selecting and proportioning materials to obtain the desired qualities and properties in the finished construction. The overall objective for the design of asphalt paving mixes is to determine an economical blend and gradation of aggregates and asphalt that yields a mix having:

1. Sufficient asphalt to ensure a durable pavement;

2. Sufficient mix stability to satisfy the demands of traffic without distortion or displacement;

3. Sufficient voids in the total comparted mix to allow for a slight amount of additional compaction under traffic loading without flushing, bleeding, and loss of stability, yet low enough to keep out harmful air and moisture; and

4. Sufficient workability to permit efficient placement of the mix.

There are currently three methods used to design asphalt paving mixes and the selection and use of any of these three mix design methods is principally a matter of engineering preference. Each of the methods has unique features and advantages for particular design problems.

The three methods are

1. The Marshall method

2. The Hubbard-Field method

3. The Hveem method

The complete test methods will be found in the Asphalt Institute Manual MS-2, *Mix Design Methods for Asphalt Concrete and Other Hot-Mix Types.*

TYPES OF ASPHALT PAVEMENT CONSTRUCTION

Plant Mix

Asphalt paving mixtures prepared in a central mixing plant are known as *plant mixes*. Asphalt concrete is considered the highest-quality type of plant mix. It consists of well-graded, high-quality aggregate and asphalt cement. The asphalt and aggregate are heated separately from 250°F to 325°F, carefully measured and proportioned, and then mixed until the aggregate particles are coated with asphalt. Mixing is done in the pugmill unit of the mixing plant. The hot mixture, kept hot during transit, is hauled to the construction site, where it is spread on the roadway by an asphalt paving machine. The smooth layer from the paver is compacted by rollers to proper density before the asphalt cools.

Asphalt concrete is but one of a variety of hot-asphalt plant mixes. Other mixes, such as sand asphalt, sheet asphalt, and coarse-graded mixes, are prepared and placed in a similar manner. However, each has one common ingredient—asphalt cement.

Asphalt mixes containing liquid asphalt also may be prepared in central mixing plants. The aggregate may be partially dried and heated or mixed as it is withdrawn from the stockpile. These mixes are usually referred to as *cold mixes,* even though heated aggregate may have been used in the mixing process.

Asphalt mixtures made with emulsified asphalt and some cutback asphalts can be spread and compacted on the roadway while quite cool. Such mixtures are called *cold-laid asphalt plant mixes.* They are hauled and placed in normal warm-weather temperatures. To hasten evaporation of emulsification water or cutback solvents, these mixtures, after being placed on the roadway, are sometimes processed or worked back and forth laterally with a motor grader before being spread and compacted.

Mixed-in-Place (Road Mix)

Emulsified asphalt and many cutback asphalts are fluid enough to be sprayed onto and mixed into aggregate at moderate- to warm-weather temperatures. When this is done on the area to be paved, it is called *mixed-in-place construction.* Although *mixed-in-place* is the more general term, and is applicable whether the construction is on a roadway, parking area, or airfield, the term *road mix* is often used when construction is on a roadway.

Mixed-in-place construction can be used for surface, base, or subbase courses. As a surface or wearing course, it usually is satisfactory for light and medium traffic rather than heavy traffic. However, mixed-in-place layers covered by a high-quality asphalt plant-mix surface course make a pavement suitable for heavy traffic service. Advantages of mixing in place include:

1. Utilization of aggregate already on the roadbed or available from nearby sources and usable without extensive processing, and

2. Elimination of the need for a central mixing plant. Construction can be accomplished with a variety of machinery often more readily available, such as motor graders, rotary mixers with revolving tines, and traveling mixing plants.

Slurry Seal

A *slurry seal* is a thin asphalt overlay applied by a continuous process machine to worn pavements to seal them and provide a new wearing surface. Slurry seals are produced with emulsified asphalts. Aggregates used for slurry seals must be hard, angular, free of expansive clays, and uniformly graded from a particle size about the thickness of the finished overlay down to No. 200. Crushed limestone or granite, slag, expanded clays, and other light-weight materials are typical aggregates used for slurry seals. The truck-mounted equipment transports, proportions, mixes, and applies the slurry seal.

FIGURE 3-18. Continuous process slurry seal machine (Courtesy Slurry Seal Inc.)

ASPHALT SPRAY APPLICATIONS

Many necessary and useful purposes are served when paving asphalt, temporarily in a fluid condition, can be sprayed in uniform and controlled amounts onto a surface.

Surface Treatments and Seal Coats

A sprayed-on application of asphalt to a wearing surface, with or without a thin layer of covering aggregate, is called an *asphalt surface treatment*. By definition, such surface treatments are 1 inch or less in thickness. Sometimes these surface treatments are included in original construction. More often they are applied to old pavements after a period of service and before surface deterioration from traffic wear and weathering proceeds too far.

The sprayed-on asphalt serves to improve or restore the waterproof condition of the old pavement surface. Also, it serves to arrest any scuffing or raveling of the wearing surface. The addition of a cover of aggregate over the sprayed-on asphalt restores and improves the skid resistance of the wearing surface.

Multiple surface treatments consist of two or more alternate layers of sprayed-on asphalt and aggregate cover.

Surface treatments that have waterproofing or texture improvement, or both, as their main purpose are called *seal coats*.

Single- or multiple-surface treatments with aggregate cover also may be placed on granular-surfaced roads to upgrade them for traffic. The treatment eliminates dust, protects the road by shedding water, and provides a smoother riding surface. It is a useful, low-cost, all-weather improvement of a granular-surfaced road, but it has limited traffic capacity and should be used only where traffic is light or where the period of expected service is limited.

Tack Coats and Prime Coats

Each layer in an asphalt pavement should be bonded to the layer beneath. This is accomplished by spraying onto the surface of the underlying layer a thin coating of asphalt to bind the layers together. This thin spread of asphalt is called a *tack coat*. Tack coats are used to bond asphalt layers to a portland cement concrete base or old brick and stone pavements.

When an asphalt pavement or asphalt surface treatment is to be placed on a granular base, it is desirable to treat the top surface of the base by spraying on a liquid asphalt that will seep into or penetrate the base. This is called *priming*, and the treatment is called *prime coat*. Its purpose is to serve as a transition from the granular material to the asphalt layer and bind them together. A prime coat is different from a tack coat as to type and quantity of asphalt used. However, both are spray applications.

Penetration Macadam

Asphalt penetration macadam pavement consists of one or more layers of large-sized broken stone and rock chips interlocked by rolling. Fluid asphalt is sprayed onto each layer, and it seeps into or penetrates the layer to bind the stones together.

An asphalt surface treatment or asphalt mixture of some kind is usually put on the top of a penetration macadam pavement to serve as a wearing surface.

ASPHALT PLANTS

Asphalt paving mixes made with asphalt cement are prepared at an asphalt mixing plant. Here aggregates are blended, heated and dried, and mixed with asphalt cement to produce a hot-asphalt paving mixture. The mixing plant may be small and simple, or it may be large and complex, depending on the type and quantity of asphalt mixture being produced.

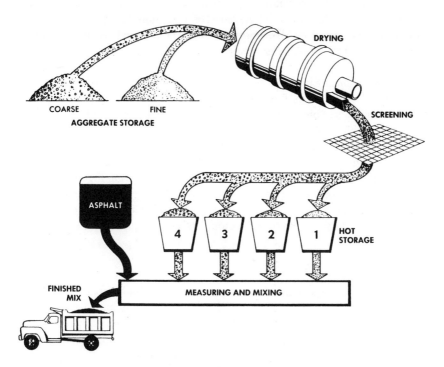

FIGURE 3-19. Typical diagram of asphalt plant (Courtesy The Asphalt Institute)

Components of an asphalt plant are

1. cold aggregate storage
2. drying
3. screening
4. hot storage
5. measuring and mixing

Aggregate is removed from storage, or stockpiles, in controlled amounts and passed through a dryer where it is dried and heated. The aggregate then passes over a screening unit that separates the material into different size fractions and deposits them into bins for hot storage. The aggregate and mineral filler, when used, are then withdrawn in controlled amounts, combined with asphalt, and thoroughly mixed. This mix is hauled to the paving site.

During the production of asphaltic concrete, various tests are utilized to measure the quality of the hot mix being manufactured.

A *hot bin analysis* is the test used to verify that the aggregates in the hot bins meet the grading requirements for the asphaltic concrete mix. Individual hot bin samples are drawn and sieved. The gradation data is then combined and evaluated, the Job Mix Formula (JMF) being used as the evaluation criteria. The JMF is the mix design used for the asphalt concrete being produced.

The *bitumen extraction test* is used to measure the asphalt content and percentages of materials finer than the No. 80 sieve of the hot mix during production. A sample of the mix is obtained, weighed, and placed in a centrifuge with a solvent. After repeated wash cycles, the sample is removed from the centrifuge, dried, and reweighed. The weight loss divided by the dry weight will give the percentage of asphalt in the original sample.

The quality control technician will also be monitoring the temperatures of the asphalt cement and aggregates going into the pugmill as well as the mix temperature as it leaves the plant in trucks. The technician will also be checking scale accuracy and recording equipment and maintaining the daily records.

Types of Asphalt Plants

Asphalt plants are classified as *stationary* or *portable*—both *batch* and *continuous-mix type*. The stationary plant is permanently situated and is not normally dismantled and moved. The portable plant can be easily disassembled, moved by rail or highway, and reassembled with a minimum of time and energy.

In the batch-type mixing plant, different size fractions of hot aggregate in storage bins are withdrawn in desired amounts to make up one batch for

HOT BIN ANALYSIS

PLANT **Vaughn Asphalt Products** INSPECTOR **David Wemple** DATE **5 / 12 / 80**

ITEM NO. **403.11** MIX TYPE **1** AGGREGATE TEMP. **250** °F BITUMEN TEMP. **325** °F

Project NYS Thruway TAA80-4B

BIN BREAKDOWN

Sieve Sizes	No. 2 Wt.	% ret.	% pass	No. 1 Wt.	% ret.	% pass	No. 1A Wt.	% ret.	% pass	No. 1B Wt.	% ret.	% pass	FINES Wt.	% ret.	% pass	MINERAL FILLER Wt.	% ret.	% pass
2"	.00	0	100															
1½"	.70	2.4	97.6															
1"	3.75	12.8	84.8	0	0	100												
½"	23.99	81.8	3.0	3.31	15.2	84.8	0	0	100									
¼"	.65	2.2	.8	17.58	80.6	4.2	2.77	13.6	86.4				0	0	100			
1/8"				.63	2.9	1.3	16.87	82.9	3.5				2.7	.4	99.6			
20													327.2	53.9	45.7			
40													102.3	16.8	28.9			
80													79.0	13.0	15.9			
200													57.2	9.4	6.5			
PAN	.25	.8		.30	1.3		.70	3.5					38.9	6.5				
Totals	29.34			21.82			20.34						607.3					

COMBINED GRADATION

BIN	lbs batched	% batched	2"	1-1/2"	1"	1/2"	1/4"	1/8"	20	40	80	200
2		30.5	30.5	29.8	25.9	.9	.2					
1		15.8	15.8	15.8	15.8	13.4	.7	.2				
1A		14.8	14.8	14.8	14.8	14.8	12.8	.5				
1B												
FINES		38.9	38.9	38.9	38.9	38.9	38.9	38.7	17.8	11.2	6.2	2.5
Min. Filler												
TOTAL		100%	100	99.3	95.4	68.0	52.6	39.4	17.8	11.2	6.2	2.5
JOB MIX LIMITS			100	92/100	81/96	65/77	49/63	35/49	17/31	9/23	6/14	4/8

Lbs. Bitumen Batched **300**

% BITUMEN **5.0**

JOB MIX LIMITS **4.6-5.4**

FIGURE 3-20. Sample data sheet—hot bin analysis (Courtesy Soil and Material Testing, Inc.)

SOIL & MATERIAL TESTING

MATERIALS BUREAU

BITUMINOUS CONCRETE PLANT EXTRACTION RESULTS

Region _____6_____   Sample No. _____

Plant __Vaughn Asphalt Products__   Location __Saratoga, N. Y.__

This test represents ____1____ days production of Item No. ___403.13_____

Mix type ____3_____ Job Mix Formula No. _____

Type of sample; Plant ___X___ ,   Paving _____.

Date sampled __5/12/80_____   By _____David Wemple_____

Weight of Sample __614.4_____ grams

Weight of Aggregate ___555.9_____ grams   % Bitumen Content ___4.86%_____

Weight of Bitumen _____28.5_____ grams   Job Mix Limits ___4.5-5.3_____

SIEVE ANALYSIS				
Sieve	Grams Retained	% Retained	Cumulative % Passing	Job Mix Limits
2"				
1½"		.0	100	100
1"	17.6	3.0	97	95-100
½"	116.3	19.8	77.2	74-86
¼"	126.8	21.6	55.6	51-65
1/8"	94.0	16.0	39.6	32-46
#20	146.4	25.0	14.6	15-29
#40	30.4	5.2	9.4	8-22
#80	19.8	3.4	6.0	4-12
#200	16.1	2.7	3.3	2-6
Pan	3.9+14.6=18.5	3.3		
Totals	585.9			

29.4 - 25.5# = 3.9

Computed By _____D. Wample__

FIGURE 3-21. Sample data sheet—bituminous concrete plant extraction results (Courtesy Soil and Material Testing, Inc.)

120

FIGURE 3-22. Asphalt batch plant (Courtesy *Constructioneer*)

mixing. The entire combination of aggregate is then dumped into a mixing chamber called a *pugmill*. The asphalt, which has also been weighed, is thoroughly mixed with the aggregate. After mixing, the material is emptied from the pugmill in one batch.

In the continuous-type mix plant, aggregate and asphalt are withdrawn, combined, mixed, and discharged in one uninterrupted flow. The combining of materials is generally done by volumetric measurements, based on unit weight. Interlocked devices, feeding the aggregate and asphalt to one end of the pugmill mixer, automatically maintain the correct proportions. While being mixed, the materials are propelled by stirring paddles to the discharge end.

Storage of Hot-Mix Asphalt

Should paving operations be temporarily interrupted, rather than stop production at the plant, a *surge bin* may be installed and used for temporarily storing the hot mix. This is usually a round, silo-type structure, the lower end of which is cone shaped. Hot mix is dumped into the top of the silo so as to fall vertically along the vertical axis of the structure. The bin is designed so that segregation of the mix is held to a minimum. As it is withdrawn from the bottom, its uniformity is maintained.

Surge bins also speed the loading of trucks with hot mix. They can be filled in a matter of seconds, while a truck at the plant has to wait for the production of several batches before it is loaded.

Surge bins are insulated and can store 50 to 100 tons of mix. They can usually store hot mix up to 12 hours with no significant loss of heat or quality.

Where paving operations can lay the hot mix at a rate faster than the plant can produce it, full surge bins at the beginning of the day will increase the plant's effective daily output.

Sometimes it is necessary or desirable to store hot-asphalt mixes for more than 12 hours. Storage silos, similar to surge bins, are used for this purpose. The capacity of these heated silos may be as much as 350 tons. They can store hot paving mixes up to 28 days with no damage to the mix. Hot-mix asphalt ages quite rapidly during exposure to air. The oxidizing process hardens the asphalt. For long-term storage, an atmosphere free of oxygen is used to fill the silo to prevent age-hardening of the hot mix.

Storage silos may be remotely located. This makes it possible for the asphalt plant to serve a larger area and provide paving mix at times when the plant would normally not be operating.

ESTIMATING ASPHALTIC CONCRETE

The unit of measure for the purchase of asphalt concrete is the ton (2000 lb). Therefore, the number of tons of asphalt concrete required to complete a paving job must be determined. Some paving contractors utilize quantity charts or slide rule type paving calculators to determine required quantities of material while others produce their own tables based upon local materials.

On small paving jobs the quantities are usually determined using a rule of thumb which states that 1 ton of asphaltic concrete will cover 80 sq ft, 2 in. thick.

Example

$$\text{Area to be paved} = 2600 \text{ sq ft}$$
$$\text{Thickness} = 2 \text{ in.}$$
$$\frac{2600 \text{ sq ft}}{80 \text{ sq ft/ton}} = 32.5 \text{ tons}$$

Larger paving estimates are based upon the unit weight of the asphaltic concrete. Asphaltic concrete's unit weight will range from 140 lb/cu ft to 150 lb/cu ft. The formula used is:

$$T = \frac{A \times t \times uw}{2000 \text{ lb}}$$

T = Tons of asphaltic concrete required
A = Area to be paved in sq ft
t = Thickness of pavement in ft
uw = Unit weight of asphaltic concrete

Example

Area to be paved = 180,000 sq ft
Thickness = 3 in. = 0.25 ft
Unit weight of asphaltic concrete = 150 lb/cu ft

$$T = \frac{180{,}000 \text{ sq ft} \times 0.25 \text{ ft} \times 150 \text{ lb/cu ft}}{2000 \text{ lb/ton}}$$

$$T = 3{,}375 \text{ tons}$$

PREPARATION OF UNPAVED SURFACES

The following roadway surfaces are generally considered unpaved surfaces:

1. Compacted subgrade,
2. Improved subgrade,
3. Untreated base, and
4. Nonsurfaced aggregate roadway.

Certain treated or stabilized granular bases are considered unpaved surfaces when being prepared for asphalt paving. Bases that have been treated or stabilized with either asphalt or portland cement are considered paved surfaces and are excluded from this classification.

Prepared Subgrade

A *prepared subgrade* is one that has been worked and compacted. This may be the foundation soil or a layer of stabilized soil, select soil, or otherwise improved subgrade material.

The riding quality of the pavement surface depends largely on proper construction and preparation of the foundation material. The roadway should be shaped and proof-rolled so that the paving equipment has no difficulty in placing the material at a uniform thickness to a smooth grade.

Weather conditions should be suitable and the roadway surface should

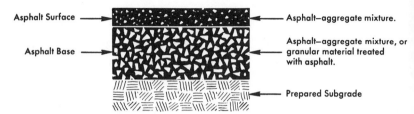

Asphalt Surface ⟶ ◄— Asphalt–aggregate mixture.

Asphalt Base ⟶ ◄— Asphalt–aggregate mixture, or granular material treated with asphalt.

◄— Prepared Subgrade

FULL DEPTH ASPHALT PAVEMENT

◄— Asphalt Surface (asphalt-aggregate mixture)

◄— Base, Granular material — normally untreated but sometimes treated with something other than asphalt.

◄— Subbase, Granular material or selected soil. Normally not treated.

◄— Prepared Subgrade

ASPHALT PAVEMENT WITH UNTREATED BASE (AND SUBBASE)

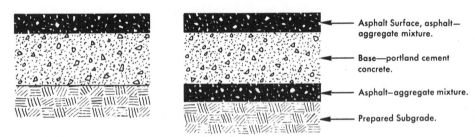

◄— Asphalt Surface, asphalt–aggregate mixture.

◄— Base—portland cement concrete.

◄— Asphalt–aggregate mixture.

◄— Prepared Subgrade.

ASPHALT PAVEMENT WITH PORTLAND CEMENT CONCRETE OR COMBINED PORTLAND CEMENT CONCRETE AND ASPHALT BASE

FIGURE 3-23. Asphalt pavement cross sections showing typical asphalt pavement structures (Courtesy The Asphalt Institute)

be firm, dust-free, and dry, or just slightly damp when paving operations are started.

Untreated Base

Untreated aggregate bases and some chemically stabilized bases other than portland cement and asphalt-treated bases should be properly shaped and proof-rolled.

When asphalt pavement courses are to be placed on an untreated aggregate base, loose aggregate particles should be swept from the surface of the roadway using power brooms. Care should be taken, however, not to dislodge or otherwise disturb the bond of the aggregate in the surface of the base. When the loose material has been properly removed, only the tops of the aggregate in the surface will be exposed, and the pieces solidly embedded in the base. When the surface has been cleaned, it is ready to be primed with asphalt.

For priming, an asphalt distributor sprays about 0.2 to 0.5 gal per sq yd liquid asphalt, usually MC-30 or MC-70, over the surface. The asphalt then penetrates or soaks into the surface. If it is not absorbed within 24 hours after application, too much prime has been used. To correct this condition, sand should be spread over the surface to blot the excess asphalt. Care should be taken to prevent overpriming. The prime should be fully set and cured before placing the asphalt mixture on the base.

Asphalt sometimes is mixed into the top 2 or 3 in. of base material in lieu of priming when it is difficult to obtain uniform and thorough penetration. This provides a tough working surface for equipment, a waterproof protective layer, and a bond to the superimposed construction.

Nonsurfaced Granular Roadways

Nonsurfaced aggregate roadways are similar to untreated aggregate bases. They differ primarily in that they have been used as a roadway by traffic and, typically, have been in use for a considerable time.

Again, it cannot be stressed too strongly that the riding quality of the surface depends to a great degree on conditioning and preparing the underlying pavement structure. It is advisable, where the aggregate-surfaced roadway is rough and uneven, to bring the surface to grade by scarifying the top few inches of material, blending in more aggregate as may be necessary, compacting, and priming with asphalt. If the aggregate roadway has had a previous asphalt treatment and is rough and uneven, it is advisable to place a *leveling course* of hot-asphalt plant-mix ahead of the first layer of the surface course.

Placing a leveling course is an operation employed when the road surface is so irregular that it exceeds the leveling capabilities of the paver. The paver is usually effective on irregularities of lengths not longer than 1½ to 2 times the wheel base of the machine. Beyond these lengths, outside help is needed. Generally, irregularities no longer than 40 or 50 feet can be handled with a traveling stringline device and automatic screed control on the paver.

PAVED SURFACES

Flexible-Type Pavements

Structural distress occurring in old asphalt pavements is usually the result of inadequate design, inadequate execution of the design including compaction, or both. Poor mix design can also cause several types of distress, and excess asphalt may cause corrugation or rutting. Cracking may be caused by excessive pavement deflection under traffic due to an inadequate pavement structure or a spongy foundation. Insufficient or oxidized asphalt may also cause cracking because the mix may be brittle.

Before the old pavement receives an overlaying course of asphalt, it should first be inspected. The remedy for whatever failures exist depends on the type and extent of the distress. If failure is extensive, reconstruction will probably be necessary. In any case, all needed repairs to the old surface should be made before paving.

A slick surface on an old pavement may be caused by aggregate polishing under traffic or by too much asphalt in the mix. If the cause is excess asphalt, it should be either burned off or removed with a *heater–planer* before placing the overlay.

Old pavements having small cracks should be given a fog seal before overlaying. A *fog seal* is a light application of emulsified asphalt diluted with water and sprayed over the surface. Larger cracks warrant having the surface treated with an emulsion slurry seal. The *slurry seal* is a mixture of emulsified asphalt, fine aggregate, and mineral filler, with water added to produce a slurry consistency.

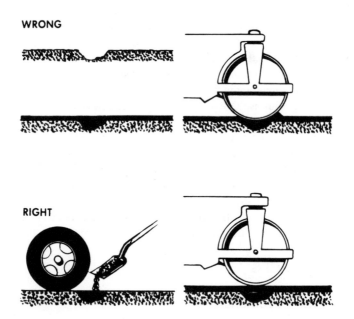

FIGURE 3-24. Potholes should be filled and compacted before spreading the first course (Courtesy The Asphalt Institute)

Potholes in an old pavement that is otherwise strong should be filled with asphalt concrete and compacted before the roadway surface is paved. If the base beneath the old pavement has failed, the damaged areas will eventually show in the new paved surface. Patching, of course, must be done before paving, and the patch should be deep enough to strengthen the base.

All bleeding and unsuitable patches, excess asphaltic crack or joint filler, loose scale, and any surplus bituminous material should be removed from the surface of the existing pavement.

All depressions of 1 inch or more should be overlaid with a leveling course and compacted ahead of the surfacing operation. All surfaces, both

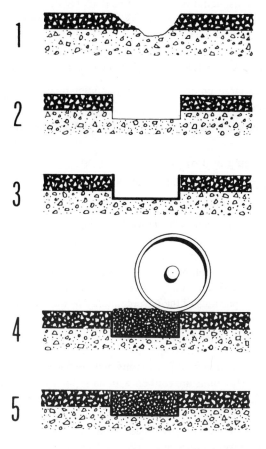

FIGURE 3-25. Pothole permanent repair: (1) untreated pothole; (2) surface and base removed to firm support; (3) tack coat applied; (4) full-depth asphalt mixture placed and being compacted; (5) finish patch compacted to level of surrounding pavement (Courtesy The Asphalt Institute)

horizontal and vertical, that will be in contact with the new asphalt surface must be thoroughly cleaned. Cleaning flat surfaces is usually done with rotary brooms, but washing or flushing may be necessary to remove clay or dirt. A tack coat should be applied to the existing pavement and to all vertical faces. These include curbs, gutters, drainage gratings, manholes, and other contact surfaces. A uniform coating of liquid asphalt or asphalt emulsion will provide a closely bonded waterproof joint. For repairs to pavements that will not be resurfaced, the procedure illustrated in Fig. 3-25 should be used.

Rigid-Type Pavements

Distress in rigid-type pavements also must be corrected before resurfacing. Additional layers of asphalt mixtures must be thick enough not only to provide required additional strength but also to minimize the reflection of cracks from old pavement in the new surface.

Preparation of damaged or distressed rigid pavements differs from that for asphalt pavements. Preparation may include one or more of the following:

1. Breaking large cracked slabs into smaller pieces and seating them firmly with heavy rollers,

2. Cracking slabs that rock under traffic and seating them with heavy rollers,

3. Undersealing to provide uniform support,

4. Patching disintegrated and spalled areas,

5. Sealing cracks to prevent the intrusion of water from below.

Pumping at the joints is caused by the rocking of slabs under traffic. The wet subgrade is removed from beneath the slab, and this causes cracking and breaking in the joint area. Usually a pavement can be stabilized by undersealing with asphalt specially prepared for this purpose. Otherwise, the rocking slabs should be cracked into smaller pieces and seated.

In some cases portions of the pavement may be disintegrated or so badly broken up that the pavement fragments should be removed. In such cases, these areas should be prepared and patched with asphalt concrete prior to the resurfacing operation.

Filler material is removed from joints and cracks in the slabs to a depth of at least ¼ inch. The joints are refilled with an asphalt joint filling material. Any asphalt patches having excess asphalt, as well as any excess crack filler that may have accumulated next to cracks and joints, are removed.

As a final step, before any asphalt paving is placed, the pavement surface should be swept clean and given a tack coat. Where preparation measures have caused settlement or pavement roughness, a leveling course of asphalt concrete should be placed prior to the resurfacing operation.

INSPECTION OF MIX

Close cooperation between the paving crew and the asphalt plant is essential in securing a satisfactory and uniform job. A fast means of communication should be established between the paving operation and the asphalt plant so that any change in the mixture can be made promptly. When possible, the paving inspector and the plant inspector should frequently exchange visits. When the paving inspector is familiar with plant operations, he can easily determine if changes at the plant are necessary to improve the mix. The plant inspector, on the other hand, by being familiar with the paving operation can better understand problems attendant to it.

Every truckload of material should be observed as it arrives. The mix temperature should be checked regularly. If it is not within specified tolerance, the mix should not be used.

Mistakes in batching, mixing, and temperature control can and do occur, and these errors may sometimes go unnoticed by the plant inspector. Consequently, loads arriving at the spreader may be unsatisfactory. When the paving inspector rejects a load, he should record his action, with the reason for rejection, both on the ticket and in his diary so that the proper deduction can be made from the pay quantities. If appropriate, a sample should be obtained for laboratory analysis. A record should also be kept of the loads accepted and placed. These records should be checked daily, or more frequently, with those of the plant inspector so no discrepancies exist when work is completed.

Mix Deficiencies

Some mix deficiencies that may justify discarding the mix are as follows:

1. *Too Hot:* Blue smoke rising from the mix usually indicates an overheated batch. The temperature should be checked immediately. If the batch exceeds maximum specification limits, it should be discarded. If it exceeds optimum placing temperature but does not exceed the specification limit, the batch is usually not discarded, but immediate steps should be taken to correct the condition.

2. *Too Cold:* A generally stiff appearance, or improper coating of the larger aggregate particles, indicates a cold mixture. Again, the temperature should be checked immediately. If it is below the specification limit, it should be discarded. If it is within the specification limit but below optimum placing temperature, steps should be taken immediately to correct the situation.

3. *Too Much Asphalt:* When loads have been arriving at the spreader with the material domed up or peaked and suddenly a load appears lying flat,

it may contain too much asphalt. Excessive asphalt may be detected under the screed by the way the mix slicks off.

4. *Too Little Asphalt:*   A mix containing too little asphalt generally can be detected immediately if the asphalt deficiency is severe. It has a lean, granular appearance and improper coating, and lacks the typical shiny, black luster. The pavement surface has a dull, brown appearance, and the roller does not compact it satisfactorily. A less severe deficiency is difficult to detect by appearance; suspicions should be checked by testing.

5. *Non-uniform Mixing:*   Non-uniform mixing shows up as spots of lean, brown, dull-appearing material within areas having a rich, shiny appearance.

6. *Excess Coarse Aggregate:*   A mix with excess coarse aggregate can be detected by the poor workability of the mix and by its coarse appearance when it is on the road. Otherwise, it resembles an overrich mix.

7. *Excess Fine Aggregate:*   A mix with an excess of fine aggregate has a different texture from a properly graded mix after it has been rolled. Otherwise, it resembles a lean mix.

8. *Excess Moisture:*   Steam rising from the mix as it is dumped into the hopper of the spreader indicates moisture in the mix. It may be bubbling or popping as if it were boiling. The mix may also foam so that it appears to have too much asphalt.

9. *Miscellaneous:*   Segregation of the aggregates in the mix may occur because of improper handling and may be serious enough to warrant rejection. Loads that have become contaminated because of spilled gasoline, kerosene, oil, and the like should not be used in the roadway.

THE PAVING OPERATION

Spreading and compacting asphalt mixture is the operation to which all the other processes are directed. Aggregates have been selected and combined; the mix designed; the plant and its auxiliary equipment set up, calibrated, and inspected; and the materials mixed together and delivered to the paver.

Asphalt mix is brought to the paving site in trucks and deposited directly into the paver or in windrows in front of the paver. The paver then spreads the mix at a set width and thickness as it moves forward. In doing so, the paver partially compacts the material. Immediately or shortly thereafter and while the mix is still hot, steel-wheeled and rubber-tired rollers are driven over the freshly paved strip, further compacting the mix. Rolling is usually continued until the pavement is compacted to the required density, or until the temperature has dropped to a point where further compaction may produce detrimental results.

FIGURE 3-26. Paver and steel wheel roller placing and compacting asphalt pavement (Courtesy *Constructioneer*)

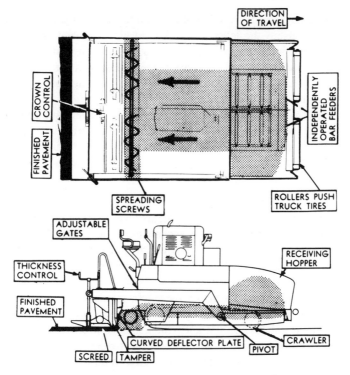

FIGURE 3-27. Flow of materials through a typical asphalt paver (Courtesy Barber-Greene Co.)

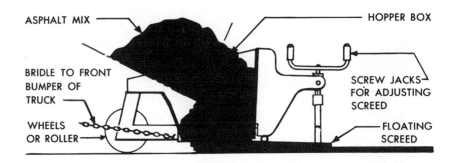

FIGURE 3-28. Flow of material through a tow-type paver (Courtesy The Asphalt Institute)

After the pavement course has been compacted and allowed to cool, it is ready for additional paving courses or ready to support traffic loads.

The Asphalt Paver

The *asphalt paver* spreads the mixture in a uniform layer of desired thickness and shape, or finishes the layer to the desired elevation and cross section, ready for compaction. Modern pavers are supported on crawler treads or wheels. These machines can place a paved layer of less than 1 inch to about 10 inches in thickness over a width of 6 to 32 feet. Working speeds generally range from 10 to 70 feet per minute.

On small paving jobs it is sometimes more convenient and economical to use a towed-type paver than to use the larger, self-powered pavers. Towed-type pavers are attached to the rear of the dump truck that hauls the asphalt mix from the plant.

Hand-Spreading Operations

The increasing use of asphalt in construction has resulted in an increased number of related projects in which asphalt mixes are used. For example, asphalt paving mixes are used for constructing driveways, parking areas, shoulders, and sidewalks. Such incidental construction is becoming more and more a part of the paving contract.

Normally, mix requirements for these jobs are the same as for roadway mixes. However, where it is anticipated that the major portion of placing will be by hand, mixes should be designed for good workability. This is easily achieved by decreasing the amount of coarse aggregate in the mix. Placing and compaction methods for hand-placed asphalt mixes are the same as for machine-spread paving.

Certain differences in construction methods are required, especially

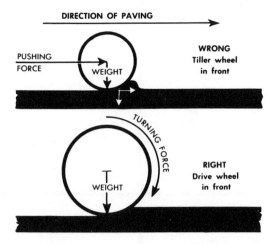

FIGURE 3-29. Rolling direction is important (Courtesy The Asphalt Institute)

where special equipment such as sidewalk pavers is not available. In addition, there are apt to be places on a regular road-paving job where spreading with a paver is either impractical or impossible. In these cases, hand spreading may be permitted.

Placing and spreading by hand should be done very carefully and the material distributed uniformly to avoid segregation.

Material should not be broadcast or spread from shovels since this causes segregation. Rather, it should be deposited from shovels or wheelbarrows into small piles and spread with asphalt rakes or wide-blade lutes. Any part of the mix that has formed into lumps and does not break down easily should be discarded.

The Roller Operation

Rolling should start as soon as possible after material has been spread. Rolling consists of three consecutive phases: *breakdown or initial rolling, intermediate rolling,* and *finish rolling.*

Breakdown rolling compacts the material beyond that imparted by the paver, to obtain practically all of the density it needs. Intermediate rolling densifies and seals the surface. Finish rolling removes roller marks and other blemishes left from previous rolling. Rollers available for these operations are:

1. steel-wheeled,

2. pneumatic-tired,

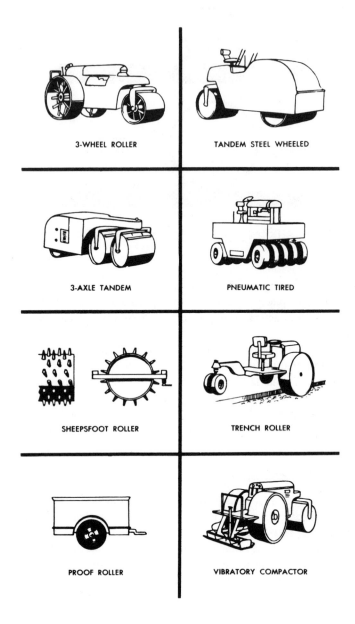

FIGURE 3-30. Types of compactors (Courtesy The Asphalt Institute)

FIGURE 3-31. Vibratory roller compacting asphalt overlay (Courtesy *Constructioneer*)

3. vibrating, and

4. combination steel-wheeled and pneumatic-tired.

Steel-wheeled rollers have been and may be used for all three rolling phases. A pneumatic-tired roller sometimes is used for breakdown rolling, but is generally preferred for intermediate rolling. Vibrating rollers are also used primarily for intermediate rolling. During rolling, the roller wheels should be kept moist with only enough water to avoid picking up material. Rollers should move at a slow, uniform speed with the drive roll nearest the paver. Rollers should be in good mechanical condition. The line of rolling should not change suddenly, nor should the roller be reversed quickly, thereby displacing the mix. Any major change in roller direction should be done on stable material. If rolling causes displacement of the material, the area affected should be loosened and restored to original grade with loose new material before being rolled again.

Two important areas of rolling are the transverse and longitudinal joints. The transverse joints are perpendicular to the center line of the pavement, and the longitudinal joints are parallel to the center line.

The roller should be placed on the previously compacted material with about 6 inches of the roller wheel on the uncompacted mix. The roller should work successive passes, each covering 6 to 8 inches, until the entire width of the drive roll is on the new mix.

If the specified density of asphalt pavement mix is not obtained during construction, subsequent traffic will further consolidate the pavement. This consolidation occurs principally in the wheel paths and appears as channels in the pavement surface.

Most mixtures compact quite readily if spread and rolled at temperatures that assure proper asphalt density.

Pavement Density

The degree or amount of compaction obtained by rolling is determined by *Density tests*. Ordinarily, specifications require that a pavement be compacted to a minimum percentage of either maximum theoretical density or density obtained by laboratory compaction. Density determinations of the finished pavement are necessary to check this requirement. These are made in the laboratory in accordance with the test method, Specific Gravity of Compressed Bituminous Mixtures (AASHTO T166), on samples submitted by the paving inspector.

Care should be exercised in obtaining and transporting these samples to the field laboratory to ensure a minimum of disturbance. Sampling of compacted mixes from the roadway should be done in accordance with AASHTO T168, Sampling Bituminous Paving Mixtures. A pavement power saw or coring machine used for taking samples provides the least disturbance of samples and compacted pavement.

Currently Air Permeability tests and Nuclear Density tests have progressed to the point where compaction may be controlled without having to obtain a sample of compacted pavement. These non-destructive tests also make possible the rapid determination of density so that additional compaction may be given, if required, while the pavement is still hot.

AUXILIARY EQUIPMENT

Asphalt Distributor

The asphalt distributor is used to apply either a prime coat or a tack coat to the surface to be paved. Prime coats are applications of liquid asphalt to an absorbent surface such as granular base. Tack coats are very light applications of liquid asphalt to an existing paved surface.

The *distributor* consists of a truck or trailer on which is mounted an insulated tank with a heating system, usually oil burning. The distributor has a power-driven pump and a system of spray bars and nozzles through which the asphalt is forced, under pressure, onto the construction surface.

It is important that asphalt sprayed from a distributor be spread over the surface uniformly at the desired rate of application. This requires a pump in good working order and free-flowing spray bars and nozzles.

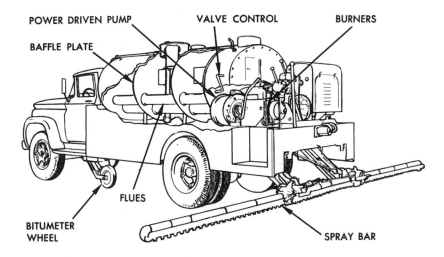

FIGURE 3-32. Bituminous distributor truck (Courtesy The Asphalt Institute)

To obtain a desired rate of application, the speed of the distributor must be determined for a given pumping rate and coverage width. Distributors usually have a bitumeter which indicates the forward speed of the distributor in feet per minute. This speed must be held constant if the asphalt coverage is to be uniform and in a longitudinal direction.

Motor Grader

In some situations the *motor grader* may be used to spread asphalt plant-mixes. For example, in the placement of leveling courses. A leveling course is a thin layer of asphalt plant-mix placed under a pavement's wearing surface. The leveling course helps the paver lay a smooth, uniform-wearing course by removing irregularities in the old pavement.

Windrowing Equipment

Windrows of asphalt plant mixes are sometimes placed in the roadway and in front of the asphalt paver. An elevator attachment fixed to the front end of the paver picks up the asphalt mix and discharges it into the hopper. This eliminates the necessity of having trucks backing up and discharging their loads as the paver moves forward.

Windrowing equipment may also be used for controlling the amount of material for leveling courses spread by a motor grader.

Incidental Tools

Adequate hand tools and proper equipment for cleaning and heating them should be available for the paving operation. Incidental tools include:

1. Rakes;
2. Shovels;
3. Lutes;
4. Tool heating torch;
5. Cleaning equipment;
6. Hand tampers;
7. Small mechanical virbrating compactors;
8. Blocks and shims for supporting the screed of the paver when beginning operations;
9. Rope, canvas, or timbers for construction of joints at ends of runs;
10. Joint cutting and painting tools; and
11. Straightedge.

Not all of these tools are necessarily used on every paving project or every day of a particular job. Rakes, shovels, and lutes are frequently used by personnel around the paver. While the paver is operating, the laborers work or rework a portion of the mix to fit the paving around objects or fill in areas that the paver does not pave adequately or cannot reach during the paving operation. Ramps, intersections, and areas broken up by bridge columns and piers are typical areas where hand paving will be required.

ASPHALT ROOFING PRODUCTS

The preservative and waterproofing characteristics of asphalt make it an ideal material for roofing systems.

Asphalts used in the production of roofing products include *saturant* or oil-rich asphalts, and a harder, more viscous asphalt known as a "*coating asphalt.*" The softening point of saturants varies from 100°F to 160°F, and the softening point of coating asphalt may run as high as 260°F.

The sheet material used in the production of roofing products may be either an *organic felt sheet* or an *inorganic glass fiber mat.* Cellulose fibers from rags, paper, and wood are processed into a dry felt which must have certain characteristics of strength, absorptive capacity, and flexibility. The glass fiber mat is composed of continuous or random thin glass fibers bonded with plastic binders. Glass mats are coated and impregnated with asphalt in

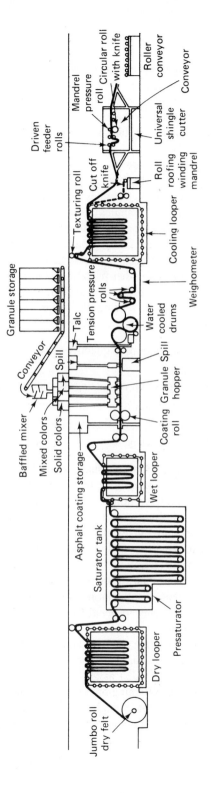

FIGURE 3-33. Flow diagram of a typical roofing plant (Courtesy Asphalt Roofing Manufacturers Association)

139

one operation, while the felt sheets are impregnated with the saturant first and then coated with the coating asphalt. Coating asphalts generally contain a finely ground mineral stabilizer, giving the coating increased weathering resistance and increased resistance to shattering in cold weather. Some mineral stabilizers used are silica, slate dust, talc, micaceous materials, dolomite, and trap-rock.

Certain asphalt roofing products are coated with mineral aggregate granules. The granules protect the coating asphalt from light and offer a weathering protection. The mineral granules also increase the fire resistance of asphalt roofing. The mineral granules also impart the various colors or color blends that are available in roofing products.

The manufacturer distributes finely ground talc or mica powder on the surfaces of rolled roofing and shingles to prevent their sticking together before they are used. The powder has no other purpose and usually disappears from exposed surfaces soon after the roofing is installed.

During production of asphalt roofing, the materials are rigidly inspected to ensure conformance with standards. Some important items checked are:

1. Saturation of felt to determine quantity of saturant and efficiency of saturation,

2. Thickness and distribution of coating asphalt,

3. Adhesion and distribution of mineral granules,

4. Weight, count, size, coloration, and other characteristics of finished product before and after it is packaged.

The installation of asphalt roofing usually will require small amounts of accessory asphaltic materials. *Flashing cements* are used as part of a flashing system at points of vertical intersection such as where the roof meets a wall, chimney, or vent pipes. Flashing cements are processed to remain elastic through the normal temperature ranges of summer to winter. They are elastic after setting, and normal expansion and contraction of the roof deck should not cause separation to occur.

Lap cements are thinner than flashing cements and are used to make a water-tight bond between laps of roll roofing. *Roof coatings* are thin liquids applied with brush or by spraying to resurface old roofs and may be either emulsified or cutback asphalts.

Manufactured asphalt roofing products are produced to American Society for Testing and Materials Standards. Asphalt roofing that is listed by the Underwriters Laboratories, Inc. (UL) as *A, B,* or *C* will not ignite easily, readily spread flames, or create flaming brands to endanger nearby buildings. Underwriters Laboratories also rate shingles for wind resistance. They must withstand a 60-mph wind for 2 hours to carry the UL label.

Prepared roofing products are those products which are manufactured and packaged ready to apply to the roof deck, usually by nailing. Asphalt shingles and certain roll roofings are considered prepared roofing products.

Another asphalt roofing system is the built-up roof. The *built-up roof* is used on flat or almost flat roofs and consists of alternate layers of roofing felt and asphalt covered with an aggregate coating.

Roofing asphalt is heated in an asphalt kettle, and is raised to the roof by pulley or pumped directly from the kettle to the roof. The hot asphalt is mopped or distributed by hot-asphalt applicators and covered with roofing felt in layers until the last coat of asphalt is applied, depending upon the number of plys specified. The last asphalt application is a flood coat which is immediately covered with mineral aggregates before it cools. The aggregate is generally spread mechanically, but can be done by hand.

Asphalts used for built-up roofs are softer asphalts and have greater temperature susceptibility so that they soften and flow slightly during warm weather. This softening enables the asphalt to "heal" small cracks which may develop from contraction, expansion, or minor movements due to settlement of the building.

There is a roofing asphalt available for use in any climate and on any slope on which built-up roofing can be used. Refer to ASTM D312–71 Section 4 in the Appendix for the types and general applications.

ASPHALT PIPE COATINGS

There are three major systems for protecting pipe with asphalt coating:

1. Wrapped system
2. Mastic systems
3. Interior coating systems

Asphalt-wrapped systems for pipe lines consist of a prime coat followed by either one or two applications of asphalt enamel in conjunction with one or more layers of reinforcing and protective wrapping. The wrapping material is asphalt-saturated felt or asphalt-saturated glass wrap.

Mastic systems for pipe lines consist of a prime coat followed by a coating of a dense, impervious, essentially voidless mixture of asphalt, mineral aggregate, and mineral filler which may include asbestos fiber. The minimum thickness is usually ¼ inch. The finished mastic coating is usually coated with whitewash.

Interior coating systems consist of a prime coat followed by a centrifugally cast layer of asphalt enamel about $1/_{32}$ in. to $3/_{32}$ in. thick.

ASPHALT MULCH TREATMENTS

Stabilizing slopes and flat areas on construction projects is a chronic problem. Soil erosion caused by wind and water can be prevented by the establishment of vegetation which anchors the soil in place.

However, during the germination of seed and early plant growth, mulch must be used to prevent erosion. There are two acceptable methods for using asphalt in the mulching process:

1. Asphalt spray mulch

2. Asphalt mulch tie-down

The *asphalt spray mulch* is usually an emulsified asphalt sprayed on the newly seeded area. The thin film of asphalt has three beneficial effects. First, it holds the seed in place against erosion. Secondly, by virtue of its dark color, it absorbs and conserves solar heat during the germination period. Finally, it holds moisture in the soil promoting speedy plant growth. The asphalt film shrinks and cracks permitting plant growth. Eventually, after it has served its purpose, the asphalt film disintegrates.

An *asphalt mulch tie-down* can be done using either of two acceptable methods. The first method is to spread the straw or hay on the graded slope. When the mulch is in place, a mixture of seed, fertilizer, and water is sprayed over the mulch. The liquid passes through the mulch to the soil. The liquid asphalt is then sprayed over the mulch to lock it in place.

The second method requires the spreading of the seed and fertilizer upon the prepared soil, followed by the spraying of the asphalt and mulching material simultaneously.

ASPHALT JOINT MATERIALS

Asphalt is used as a *joint* and *crack filler* in pavements and other structures. The joint between two concrete pavement slabs may be filled with hot asphalt. The asphalt's properties of adhesion and flexibility allow the two separate slabs to expand and contract without permitting moisture to penetrate the joint. The asphalt material used may also be premolded in strips. The strips are composed of asphalt mixed with fine mineral substances, fibrous materials, cork, or sawdust, manufactured in dimensions suitable for use in joints. The premolded strips are inserted at joint locations before placement of the portland cement concrete and eliminate the filling of the joint openings after the slabs have cured.

Asphalt is a widely used construction material with many diverse applications. To ensure that asphalt and its products are used properly, organizations such as the Asphalt Institute, Asphalt Roofing Manufacturers Association, and others produce technical literature concerning asphalt uses. For an indepth treatment of the material this technical literature is recommended.

Review Questions

1. How are natural asphalts formed?
2. What are the differences between asphalt and tar?
3. What are bituminous materials?
4. What are the classifications of petroleum crude oil based upon their asphalt content?
5. How is the percentage of asphalt in a crude oil determined?
6. What distillation processes are used to produce asphalt?
7. What are blown asphalts, and what are they used for?
8. How are asphalt cements liquified other than by heat?
9. What do the basic tests on asphaltic materials measure?
10. What are the basic requirements for an asphaltic pavement?
11. What factors must be considered when designing an asphalt pavement?
12. What objectives must the design of an asphalt pavement meet?
13. What are tack coats and prime coats?
14. What is surge-storage, and how is it used in asphalt concrete production?
15. Calculate the number of tons of asphalt concrete required to pave a 300-sq ft area 3 in. thick. The asphaltic concrete has a density of 150 lb per cu ft.
16. Briefly detail the paving operation utilizing mechanized equipment.
17. What is an asphalt distributor?
18. Describe briefly how asphaltic roofing materials are produced.
19. How is asphalt used for slope stabilization in highway construction?

4

Portland Cement Concrete

Concrete has many characteristics that make it a widely used construction material. Among them are raw material availability, the ability of concrete to take the shape of the form it is placed in, and the ease with which its properties can be modified. The ability to modify such properties as its strength, durability, economy, watertightness, and abrasion resistance are most important. The ease with which concrete can be modified by its variables can often work to the disadvantage of the user if quality control is not maintained from the first to the last operations in concrete work.

Basically, *concrete* is 60–80 percent aggregates (i.e., sand, stone), which are considered "inert" ingredients, and 20–40 percent "paste" (i.e., water, portland cement), considered the active ingredients. These materials are combined or mixed, and cured to develop the hardened properties of concrete.

During this production sequence, concrete is very often produced by one firm with products supplied by three or four other firms and sold in an unfinished state to a contractor who will place, finish, and cure it. During this process it will be subject to the weather and other variables. Therefore, in order to ensure that the concrete initially designed for a specific function is the same concrete that ends up in service, careful consideration must be given to all of the variables which may affect it.

HISTORY

The development of cementing materials can be traced back to the Egyptians and Romans, and their use of masonry construction. The Egyptians used a cement produced by a heating process, and this may have been the start of the technology. Roman engineering upgraded simple lime mortars with the addition of volcanic ash which increased their durability, as evidenced by the sound structures which still stand.

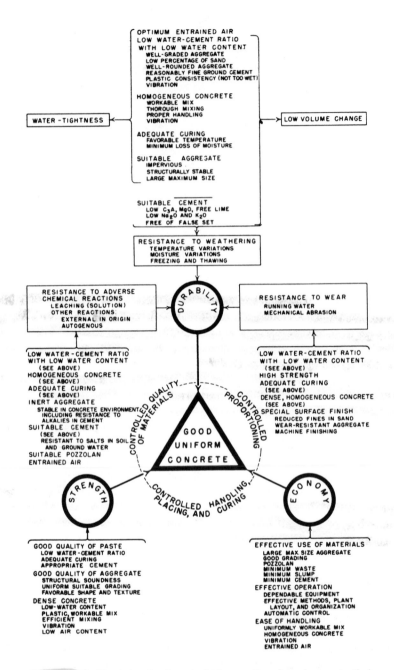

FIGURE 4-1. Chart showing the principal properties of good concrete, their relationship, and the elements which control them. Many factors are involved in the production of good, uniform concrete. 288–D–795. (Courtesy U.S. Department of the Interior, Water and Power Resources Service)

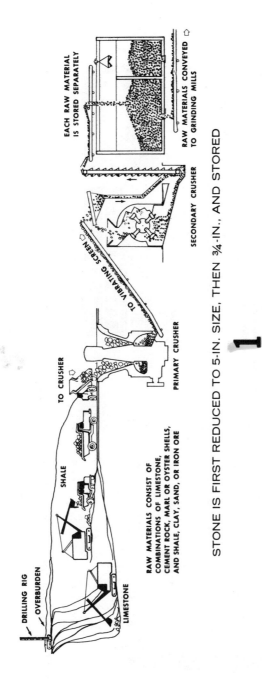

FIGURE 4-2. Flowchart of manufacture of Portland Cement (Courtesy Portland Cement Association)

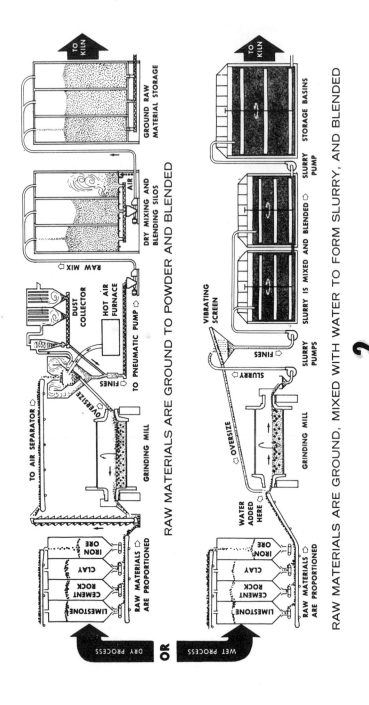

RAW MATERIALS ARE GROUND TO POWDER AND BLENDED

RAW MATERIALS ARE GROUND, MIXED WITH WATER TO FORM SLURRY, AND BLENDED

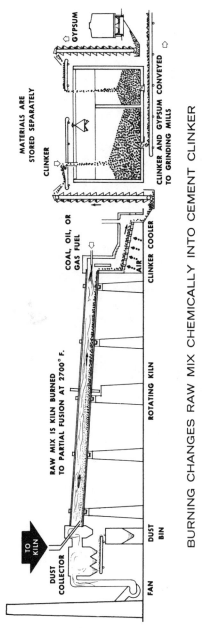

BURNING CHANGES RAW MIX CHEMICALLY INTO CEMENT CLINKER

FIGURE 4-2 (continued). Flowchart of manufacture of Portland Cement
(Courtesy Portland Cement Association)

149

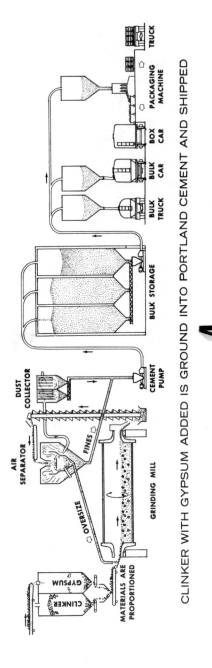

CLINKER WITH GYPSUM ADDED IS GROUND INTO PORTLAND CEMENT AND SHIPPED

FIGURE 4-2 (continued). Flowchart of manufacture of Portland Cement
(Courtesy Portland Cement Association)

The development of a concrete or cement technology as we know it probably can be traced back to England, where in 1824 Joseph Aspdin produced a portland cement from a heated mixture of limestone and clay. He was awarded a British patent and the name portland cement was used because when the material hardened, it resembled a stone from the quarries of Portland, England. There is evidence that several of Joseph Aspdin's contemporaries were involved in the same research, but evidence shows that he fired his product above the clinkering temperature, thus producing a superior product.

The production of portland cement in the United States dates back to 1872, when the first portland cement plant was opened at Coplay, Pennsylvania.

Today, the industry is considered a basic industry, and the production of portland cement occurs in all regions of the world.

MANUFACTURE OF PORTLAND CEMENT

The manufacture of portland cement requires raw materials which contain lime, silica, alumina, and iron. The sources of these elements vary from one manufacturing location to another, but once these materials are obtained, the process is rather uniform.

The process begins with the acquisition of raw materials such as limestone, clay, and sand. The limestone is reduced to an approximately 5-inch size in the primary crusher and further reduced to ¾ inch in the secondary crusher. All of the raw materials are stored in the bins and proportioned prior to delivery to the grinding mill.

Most portland cement is made utilizing the wet process. The wet process results in a slurry, which is mixed and pumped to storage basins. The dry process produces a fine ground powder which is stored in bins.

Both systems feed rotary kilns where the actual chemical changes will take place. The material is fed into the upper end of the kiln, and as the kiln rotates, the material passes slowly from the upper to the lower end at a rate controlled by the slope and speed of rotation of the kiln. As the material passes through the kiln, its temperature is raised to the point of *incipient fusion* or clinkering temperature where the chemical reactions take place. Depending upon the raw materials, this temperature is usually between 2400°F (1316°C) and 2700°F (1482°C). Chemical recombinations of the raw ingredients take place in this temperature range to produce the basic chemical components of portland cement.

The *clinker* produced is black or greenish black in color and rough textured. Its size makes it relatively inert in the presence of moisture. From clinker storage the material is transported to final grinding where approximately 2 to 3 percent gypsum will be added to control the setting time of the portland cement when it is mixed with water.

The portland cement produced is either distributed in bulk by rail, barge, or truck, or packaged in bags. Bulk cement is sold by the barrel which is the equivalent of four bags or 376 lb, or by the ton. Bag cement weighs 94 lb and is considered to be 1 bulk cubic foot of cement.

The manufacture of portland cement involves the use of many technical skills to ensure a uniform product. Engineers, chemists, and technicians are all employed in the process of determining and controlling the various chemical and physical properties of the cements produced. For practical purposes, Type I portland cement will contain the oxides illustrated in Fig. 4-3.

Oxide	Range (Percent)
Lime, CaO	60–66
Silica, SiO_2	19–25
Alumina, Al_2O_3	3–8
Iron, Fe_2O_3	1–5
Magnesia, MgO	0–5
Sulfur trioxide, SO_3	1–3

FIGURE 4-3. Oxide composition of Type I Portland Cement (Courtesy Portland Cement Association)

CHEMICAL COMPOSITION OF PORTLAND CEMENT

Portland cements are composed of the four basic chemical compounds shown with their names, chemical formulas, and abbreviations.

1. Tricalcium silicate $3CaO\ S_1O_2 = C_3S$

2. Dicalcium silicate $2CaO\ S_1O_2 = C_2S$

3. Tricalcium aluminate $3CaO\ Al_2O_3 = C_3A$

4. Tetracalcium aluminoferrite $4CaO\ Al_2O_3F_2O_3 = C_4AF$

The relative percentages of these compounds can be determined by chemical analysis. Each of the compounds exhibits a particular behaviorism, and it can be shown that by modifying the relative percentages of these compounds, the behavior of the cement can be altered.

Tricalcium silicate hardens rapidly and is largely responsible for initial set and early strength. In general, the early strength of portland cement concretes will be higher with increased percentages of C_3S. However, if moist curing is continued, the later strength after about 6 months will be greater for cements with a higher percentage of C_2S.

Dicalcium silicate hardens slowly, and its effect on strength increases occurs at ages beyond 1 week.

Tricalcium aluminate contributes to strength development in the first few days because it is the first compound to hydrate. It is, however, the least desirable component because of its high heat generation and its reactiveness with soils and water containing moderate to high sulphate concentrations. Cements made with low C_3A contents usually generate less heat, develop higher strengths, and show greater resistance to sulfate attacks.

The tetracalcium aluminoferrite compound assists in the manufacture of portland cement by allowing lower clinkering temperatures. C_4AF contributes very little to the strength of concrete even though it hydrates very rapidly.

Most specifications for portland cements place limits on certain physical properties and chemical composition of the cements. Therefore, the study of this material requires an understanding of some of these basic properties.

PHYSICAL PROPERTIES OF PORTLAND CEMENT

One factor which affects the hydration of cement, regardless of its chemical composition, is its *fineness*. The finer a cement is ground, the higher the heat of hydration and resulting accelerated strength gain. The strength gain due to fineness is evident during the first 7 days. For a given weight of cement, the surface area of the grains of a coarse-ground cement is less than for a fine-ground cement. Since the water is in contact with more surface area in a

Type of Portland Cement		Compound Composition (Percent)*				Fineness, (Sq cm per g)**
ASTM	CSA	C_3S	C_2S	C_3A	C_4AF	
I	Normal	50	24	11	8	1800
II		42	33	5	13	1800
III	High-Early-Strength	60	13	9	8	2600
IV		26	50	5	12	1900
V	Sulfate-Resisting	40	40	4	9	1900

*The compound compositions shown are typical. Deviations from these values do not indicate unsatisfactory performance. For specification limits see ASTM C150 or CSA A5.

**Fineness as determined by Wagner turbidimeter test.

FIGURE 4-4. Typical calculated compound composition and fineness of Portland Cements (Courtesy Portland Cement Association)

fine-ground cement, the hydration process occurs more rapidly in a fine-ground cement. If the cement is ground too fine, however, there is a possibility of prehydration due to moisture vapor during manufacturing and storage with the resulting loss in cementing properties of the material. There is evidence to show that in some cases very coarse-ground particles may never completely hydrate.

Currently the fineness of cement is stated as *specific surface* (i.e., the calculated surface area of the particles in square centimeters) per gram of cement. Even though the specific surface is only an approximation of the true area, good correlations have been obtained between specific surfaces and those properties influenced by particle fineness. Higher specific surfaces indicate finer-ground cements and usually a more active cement.

Soundness is the ability of a cement to maintain a stable volume after setting. An unsound cement will exhibit cracking, disruption, and eventual disintegration of the material mass. This delayed-destruction expansion is caused by excessive amounts of free lime or magnesium.

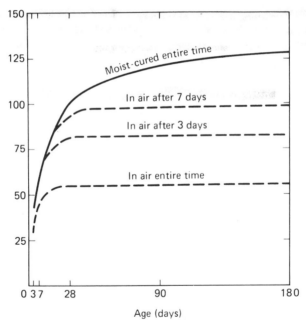

FIGURE 4-5. Strength of concrete continues to increase as long as moisture is present for hydration of cement (Courtesy Portland Cement Association)

The free lime is enclosed in cement particles, and eventually the moisture reaches the lime after the cement has set. At that time the lime expands with considerable force, disrupting the set cement.

The current test for soundness in cement is the ASTM Autoclave test. Standard specimens of neat cement paste are subjected to high pressure and temperature for 3 hours. After cooling, the length of bars is compared with the length before testing and cements which exhibit an expansion of not more than 0.50 percent are considered to be sound. Since the introduction of the Autoclave test, there have been almost no cases of delayed expansion due to unsound cements.

WATER–CEMENT REACTION

Hydration is the chemical reaction that takes place when portland cement and water are mixed together.

When cement is mixed with water to form a fluid paste, the mixture will eventually become stiff and then hard. This process is called *setting*. A cement used in concrete must not set too fast for then it would be unworkable, that is, it would stiffen and become hard before it could be placed or finished. When it sets too slowly, valuable construction time would be lost. Most portland cements exhibit initial set in about 3 hours and final set in about 7 hours. If gypsum were not added during final grinding of normal portland cement, the set would be very rapid and the material unworkable.

False set of portland cement is a stiffening of a concrete mixture with little evidence of significant heat generation. To restore plasticity, all that is required is further mixing without additional water. There are cases where a *flash set* is exhibited by a cement, and in this case the cement has *hydrated* and further remixing will do no good. The actual setting time of the concrete will vary from job to job depending upon the temperature of the concrete and wind velocity, humidity, placing conditions, and other variables.

The ability of a cement to develop compressive strength in a concrete is an important property. The compressive strengths of cements are usually determined on standard 2-in. cubes. The results of these tests are useful in comparing strengths of various cements in neat paste conditions. *Neat paste* is water, cement, and a standard laboratory sand used to standardize this test. They will not predict concrete strength values due to the variables in concrete mixtures that also influence strength.

The heat generated when water and cement chemically react is called the *heat of hydration,* and it can be a critical factor in concrete use. The total amount of heat generated is dependent upon the chemical composition of the cement and the rate is affected by the fineness, chemical composition, and curing temperatures.

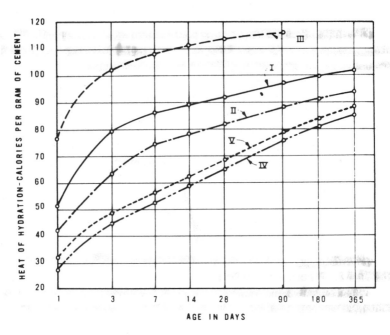

HEAT OF HYDRATION FOR VARIOUS TYPES OF CEMENT

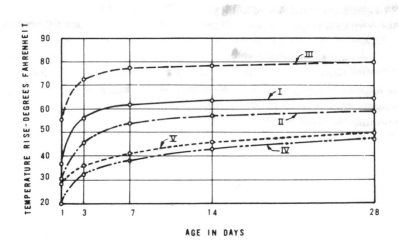

TEMPERATURE RISE OF CONCRETE

Tests of mass concrete with $4\frac{1}{2}$-in. maximum aggregate,
containing 376 pounds of cement per cubic yard in
17-by 17-in. cylinders, sealed and cured in adiabatic
calorimeter rooms

FIGURE 4-6. Heat of hydration and temperature rise for concretes made
with various types of cement. 288–D–118. (Courtesy U.S. Department of the
Interior, Water and Power Resources Service)

Approximate amounts of heat generation during the first 7 days of curing using Type I cement as the base are as follows:

Type I	100%
Type II	80–85%
Type III	150%
Type IV	40–60%
Type V	60–75%

Concrete has a low tensile strength; it is approximately 11 percent of concrete's compressive strength. To allow the use of concrete in locations where tensile strength is important or increased compressive strength is required, steel is used to reinforce the concrete. Steel used for reinforcing concrete can be welded wire mesh, deformed reinforcing bars, or cable tendons. Steel has a high strength-to-weight ratio, and its coefficient of thermal expansion is almost the same as concrete's.

Plain reinforced concrete can be used for most construction. The steel is positioned in the form and the concrete placed around it. When the concrete has cured, the materials will be bonded together and act as one.

Pre-stressed concrete requires the application of a load to the steel before concrete placement. When the concrete has cured, the load is removed from the steel and the concrete is placed in compression. Post-tensioned concrete involves the application of a load to the steel after the concrete has cured. Open ducts are left in the concrete through which steel tendons are placed. When the concrete has cured, loads are applied to the steel. Post-tensioned concrete is versatile because the loads applied to the steel can be changed according to actual conditions of structure loading.

TYPES OF PORTLAND CEMENT

ASTM Type I (Normal)

This type is a general concrete construction cement utilized when the special properties of the other types are not required. It is used where the concrete will not be subjected to sulfate attack from soil or water or be exposed to severe weathering conditions. It is generally not used in large masses because of the heat of hydration generated. Its uses include pavements and sidewalks, reinforced concrete buildings, bridges, railway structures, tanks, and reservoirs, culverts, water pipes, and masonry units.

ASTM Type II (Moderate Heat or Modified)

Type II cement is used where resistance to moderate sulfate attack is important, as in areas where sulfate concentration in groundwater is higher than normal but not severe. Type II cements produce less heat of hydration than

	Type of Portland Cement		Compressive Strength (Percent of Strength of Type I or Normal Portland Cement Concrete)			
ASTM	CSA	1 day	7 days	28 days	3 mos.
I	Normal	100	100	100	100
II		75	85	90	100
III	High-Early-Strength	190	120	110	100
IV		55	55	75	100
V	Sulfate-Resisting	65	75	85	100

FIGURE 4-7. Approximate relative strength of concrete as affected by type of cement (Courtesy Portland Cement Association)

Type I, thus their use in structures of mass such as piers, abutments, and retaining walls. They are used in warm-weather concreting because of their lower temperature rise than Type I. The use of Type II for highway pavements will give the contractor more time to saw control joints because of the lower heat generation and resulting slower setting and hardening.

ASTM Type III (High-Early-Strength)

Type III cements are used where an early strength gain is important and heat generation is not a critical factor. When forms have to be removed for reuse as soon as possible, Type III supplies the strength required in shorter periods of time than the other types. In cold-weather concreting, Type III allows a reduction in the heated curing-time with no loss in strength.

ASTM Type IV (Low Heat)

Type IV cement is used where the rate and amount of heat generated must be minimized. The strength development for Type IV is at a slower rate than Type I. It is primarily used in large mass placements such as gravity dams where the amount of concrete at any given time is so large that the temperature rise resulting from heat generation during hardening becomes a critical factor.

ASTM Type V (Sulfate-Resisting)

Type V is primarily used where the soil or groundwater contains high sulfate concentrations and the structure would be exposed to severe sulfate attack.

Air-Entraining Portland Cements

ASTM C175 governs the air-entraining cements, Types IA, IIA, and IIIA. The three cements correspond to Types I, II, and III, with the addition of small quantities of air-entraining materials integrated with the clinker during the manufacturing process. These cements provide the concrete with improved resistance to freeze–thaw action and to scaling caused by chemicals and salts used for ice and snow removal. Concrete made with these cements contains microscopic air bubbles, separated, uniformly distributed, and so small that there are many billions in a cubic foot.

White Portland Cement

White portland cement is a true portland cement, its color being the principal difference between it and normal portland cement. The cement is manufactured to meet ASTM C150 and C175 specifications. The selected raw materials used in the manufacture of white cement have negligible amounts of iron and manganese oxide, and the process of manufacture is controlled to produce the white color. Its primary use is for architectural concrete products, cement paints, tile grouts, and decorative concrete. Its use is recommended wherever white or colored concrete or mortar is desired. Colored concretes are produced by using a coloring additive, and the white cement allows for more accurate control of colors desired.

Portland Blast-Furnace Slag Cements

In these cements granulated blast-furnace slag of selected quality is interground with portland cement. The slag is obtained by rapidly chilling or quenching molten slag in water, steam, or air. Portland blast-furnace slag cements include two types Type IS and Type IS-A, conforming to ASTM C595. These cements can be used in general concrete construction wherever the specific properties of the other types are not required. However, moderate heat of hydration (MH), moderate sulfate resistance (MS), or both are optional provisions. Type IS has about the same rate of strength development as Type I cement, and both have the same compressive strength requirements.

Portland-Pozzolan Cements

IP, IP-A,P, and P-A designate the Portland-Pozzolan cements with the A denoting air-entraining additives as specified in C595. They are used principally for large hydraulic structures such as bridge piers and dams. These cements are manufactured by intergrinding portland cement clinker with a suitable pozzolan such as volcanic ash, fly ash from power plants, or diatomaceous earth, or by blending the portland cement or portland blast-furnace slag cement and a pozzolan.

Masonry Cements

Type I and Type II masonry cements are manufactured to conform to ASTM C91 and contain portland cement, air-entraining additives, and materials selected for their ability to impart workability, plasticity, and water-retention properties to the masonry mortars.

Special Portland Cements

Oil Well Cement. Oil well cement is used for sealing oil wells. It is usually slow setting and resistant to high pressures and temperatures. The American Petroleum Institute Specifications for Oil Well Cements (API standard 10A) cover requirements for six classes of cements. Each class is applicable for use at a certain range of well depths. Conventional portland cements are also used with suitable set modifying admixtures.

Waterproofed Portland Cements. Waterproofed portland cement is manufactured by the addition of a small amount of calcium, aluminum, or other stearate to the clinker during final grinding. It is manufactured in either white or grey color, and is used to reduce water penetration through the concrete.

MIXING WATER

In the production of concrete, water plays an important role. It is used to wash aggregates, as mixing water, and during the curing process.

The use of an impure water for aggregate washing may result in aggregate particles coated with silt, salts, or organic materials. Aggregates that have been contaminated by such impure water may produce distressed concrete due to chemical reactions with the cement paste or poor aggregate bonding. In most cases comparative tests should be run on possible contaminated aggregates.

It is generally accepted that any potable water can be used as mixing water in the manufacture of concrete. Duff Abrams found sea water having a 3.5-percent salt content adequate in producing concrete so that some waters used in concrete making are not potable.

Questionable water may be used for concrete if mortar cubes made with this water have 7- and 28-day strengths equal to at least 90 percent of the strength of cubes made with a known water supply. Impurities in water may also affect setting time and volume stability, and may cause *efflorescence* (the leaching of free lime), discoloration, and excessive reinforcement corrosion.

A water source similar in analysis to any of the water in Fig. 4-8 is probably satisfactory for use in concrete. The waters represent the approximate compositions of water supplies for most cities with populations over 20,000 in the United States and Canada. The units used to designate foreign matter in water are ppm (parts per million) and designate the weight of foreign matter to the weight of water.

The upper limit of total dissolved solids is usually 2000 parts per million (ppm). Although higher concentrations are not always harmful, certain cements may react adversely. Therefore, possible higher concentrations should be avoided.

Analysis No.	1	2	3	4	5	6
Silica (SiO₂)	2.4	0.0	6.5	9.4	22.0	3.0
Iron (Fe)	0.1	0.0	0.0	0.2	0.1	0.0
Calcium (Ca)	5.8	15.3	29.5	96.0	3.0	1.3
Magnesium (Mg)	1.4	5.5	7.6	27.0	2.4	0.3
Sodium (Na)	1.7	16.1	2.3	183.0	215.0	1.4
Potassium (K)	0.7	0.0	1.6	18.0	9.8	0.2
Bicarbonate (HCO₃)	14.0	35.8	122.0	334.0	549.0	4.1
Sulfate (SO₄)	9.7	59.9	5.3	121.0	11.0	2.6
Chloride (Cl)	2.0	3.0	1.4	280.0	22.0	1.0
Nitrate (NO₃)	0.5	0.0	1.6	0.2	0.5	0.0
Total dissolved solids	31.0	250.0	125.0	983.0	564.0	19.0

FIGURE 4-8. Typical analyses of city water supplies (parts per million)
(Courtesy Portland Cement Association)

The effects of many common impurities have been well documented in technical literature.

Carbonates and bicarbonates of sodium and potassium affect the setting times of concrete. Sodium carbonate may cause very rapid setting; bicarbonates may either accelerate or retard the set. In large concentrations these salts can materially reduce concrete strength. When the sum of these dissolved salts exceed 1000 ppm (0.1 percent), tests for setting time and 28-day strength should be made.

Sodium chloride or sodium sulfate can be tolerated in large quantities; waters having concentrations of 20,000 ppm of sodium chloride and 10,000 ppm of sodium sulfate have been used successfully. Carbonates of calcium and magnesium are not very soluble in water and are seldom found in high enough concentrations to affect concrete properties. Bicarbonates of calcium and magnesium are present in some municipal water supplies, and concentrations of the bicarbonate ion up to 400 ppm are not considered harmful.

Concentrations of magnesium sulfate and magnesium chloride up to 40,000 ppm have been used without harmful effects on concrete strength. Calcium chloride is often used as an accelerator in concrete in quantities up to 2 percent by weight of the cement. It cannot be used in prestrengthened concrete or in concrete containing aluminum conduit or pipe.

Iron salts in concentrations of up to 40,000 ppm have been used successfully; however, natural groundwater usually contains no more than 20 to 30 ppm.

The salts of manganese, tin, zinc, copper, and lead may cause reductions in strength and variations in setting times. Salts that act as retarders include sodium iodate, sodium phosphate, sodium arsenate, and sodium borate, and when present in amounts as little as a few tenths of 1 percent by weight of cement, they can greatly retard set and strength development. Concentrations of sodium sulfide as low as 100 ppm warrant testing.

Generally sea water containing 35,000 ppm of salt can be used in nonreinforced concrete which will exhibit higher early strength with a slight reduction in 28-day strength. The reduction in 28-day strength is usually compensated for in the mix design. Sea water has been used in reinforced concrete; however, if the steel does not have sufficient cover or if the concrete is not watertight, the risk of corrosion is increased greatly. Sea water should never be used in prestressed concrete.

Aggregates from the sea may be used with fresh mixing water since the salt coating would amount to about 1 percent by weight of the mixing water.

Generally, mixing waters having common inorganic acid concentrations as high as 10,000 ppm have no adverse effects on concrete strength. The acceptance of mixing waters containing acid should be based on concentrations of acids in ppm rather than the pH value since the latter is an intensity index.

Sodium hydroxide concentrations of 0.5 percent by weight of cement do not greatly affect the concrete strength, providing quick set does not occur. Potassium hydroxide in concentrations up to 1.2 percent by weight of cement can reduce strengths of certain cements while not materially affecting strengths of others.

Industrial waste water and sanitary sewage can be used in concretes. After sewage passes through a good disposal system, the concentration of solids is usually too low to have any significant effect on concrete. Waste waters from tanneries, paint factories, coke plants, chemical plants, and galvanizing plants, etc., may contain harmful impurities. As with all questionable water sources, it pays to run the comparative strength tests before using such waters in concrete manufacturing.

Sugar in concentrations of as little as 0.03 to 0.15 percent by weight of cement will usually retard the setting time of cement. There may be a reduction in 7-day strength and an increase in 28-day strength. When the amount of sugar is raised to 0.20 percent by weight of cement, the set is accelerated. When the sugar exceeds 0.25 percent, there may be rapid setting and a reduction in 28-day strength. Water containing an excess of 500 ppm of sugar should be tested.

Clay or fine particles can be tolerated in concentrations of up to 2000 ppm. Though the clay may affect other properties of cement, the strength shouldn't be affected at higher concentrations.

Silty water should settle in basins before use to reduce the suspended silts and clays.

Mineral oils have less effect on strength development than vegetable or animal oils; however, when concentrations are greater than 2 percent by weight of cement, a strength loss of approximately 20 percent or more will occur.

Organic impurities such as algae in mixing water may cause excessive strength reductions by affecting bond or by excessive air entrainment. As with all of the ingredients used in concrete production, if the water available is questionable, the comparative property tests should be run. Sometimes the concrete mix can be modified to compensate for water which produces low strength or exhibits other adverse characteristics.

The use of water containing acids or organic substances should be questioned because of the possibility of surface reactions or retardation. The other concern with curing water is the possibility of staining or discoloration due to impurities in the water.

AGGREGATES

The aggregate component of a concrete mix occupies 60–80 percent of the volume of concrete, and their characteristics influence the properties of the concrete. The selection of aggregates will determine the mix design proportion and the economy of the resulting concrete. It is therefore necessary to understand the importance of aggregate selection, testing, and handling as discussed in Chapter 2.

Aggregates selected for use should be clean, hard, strong, and durable particles, free of chemicals, coatings of clay, or other materials that will affect the bond of the cement paste. Aggregates containing shale or other soft and porous organic particles should be avoided because they have poor resistance to weathering. Coarse aggregates can usually be inspected visually for weaknesses. Any aggregates that do not have adequate service records should be tested for compliance with requirements. Most concrete aggregate sources are periodically checked to ensure that the aggregates being produced meet the concrete specifications.

The commonly used aggregates such as sand, gravel, and crushed stone produce normal weight concrete weighing 135 to 160 lb per cubic foot. Various expanded shales and clays produce structural lightweight concrete having unit weights ranging from 85 to 115 lb per cubic foot. Much lighter concretes weighing 15 to 90 lb per cubic foot, using vermiculite, pumice, and perlite as aggregates, are called insulating concretes. The use of materials such as barites, limonite, magnetite iron, and iron particles produces heavyweight concretes with weights going as high as 400 lb per cubic foot.

Aggregates must possess certain characteristics to produce a workable, strong, durable, and economical concrete. These basic characteristics are shown in Fig. 4-9 with their significant ASTM or CSA test or practice designation and specification requirement.

The most common test used to measure abrasion resistance of an aggregate is the Los Angeles rattler. A quantity of aggregate is placed in a steel drum with steel balls, the drum is rotated for a preset number of revolutions,

CHARACTERISTIC	SIGNIFICANCE OR IMPORTANCE	TEST OR PRACTICE, ASTM AND CSA DESIGNATION	SPECIFICATION REQUIREMENT
Resistance to abrasion	Index of aggregate quality Warehouse floors, loading platforms, pavements	C131	Max. percent loss*
Resistance to freezing and thawing	Structures subjected to weathering	C290, C291	Max. number of cycles
Chemical stability	Strength and durability of all types of structures	C227 (mortar bar)	Max. expansion of mortar bar*
		C289 (chemical) C586 (aggregate prism) C295 (petrographic)	Aggregates must not be reactive with cement alkalies*
Particle shape and surface texture	Workability of fresh concrete		Max. percent flat and elongated pieces
Grading	Workability of fresh concrete Economy	C136 A23.2.2	Max. and min. percent passing standard sieves
Bulk unit weight	Mix design calculations Classification	C29 A23.2.10	Max. or min. unit weight (special concretes)
Specific gravity	Mix design calculations	C127 (coarse aggregate) C128 (fine aggregate) A23.2.6 (fine aggregate)	
Absorption and surface moisture	Control of concrete quality	C70, C127, C128 A23.2.6, A23.2.11	

FIGURE 4-9. Characteristics of aggregates (Courtesy Portland Cement Association)

* Aggregates not conforming to specification requirements may be used if service records or performance tests indicate they produce concrete having the desired properties.

and the percentage of material worn away is determined. While the test is a general index of aggregate quality, there is no direct correlation generally with concrete abrasion using the same aggregate. If wear resistance is critical, it is more accurate to run abrasion tests on the concrete itself.

Porosity, absorption and pore structure determine the freeze–thaw resistance of an aggregate. If an aggregate particle absorbs too much water, when it is exposed to freezing there will be little room for water expansion. At any freezing rate there may be a critical particle size above which the particle will fail if completely saturated.

There are two ways used to determine the resistance to freezing–thawing of an aggregate: past performance records, if available, and the freezing–thaw test on concrete specimens containing the aggregates. Specimens are cast and cyclically exposed to freezing and thawing temperatures with the deterioration measured by the reduction in the dynamic modulus of elasticity of the specimens.

While aggregates are generally considered to be the "inert" component of a concrete mix, alkali–aggregate reactions do occur. Past performance records are usually adequate, but if no records are available or if a new aggregate source is being used, laboratory tests should be performed to determine the aggregate's alkali-reactiveness.

Fresh concrete is affected by particle texture and shape more than hardened concrete. Rough-textured or flat aggregates require more water to produce a workable concrete than rounded or cubical, well-shaped aggregates. The National Ready Mix Concrete Association, based upon the use of well-shaped cubical aggregate as the standard, suggests that flat, elongated, or sharply angular aggregates will require 25 lb of water more per cubic yard, thus requiring more cement to maintain the same water–cement ratio. The use of rounded gravel aggregates will usually allow a 15-lb reduction in mixing water, with the resulting reduction in cement thus producing a savings to the concrete producer. It is recommended that long, flat particles not exceed 15 percent by weight of the total aggregate. This requirement is important when using manufactured sand because it contains more flat, elongated particles than natural sand.

As described in Chapter 2, the method of determining aggregate gradation and maximum aggregate size is by sieve analysis. The grading and maximum size of aggregates affect relative aggregate proportion as well as cement and water requirements, workability, economy, porosity, and shrinkage of concrete. Variations in grading may seriously affect the uniformity of concrete from one batch to another. Harsh sands often produce unworkable mixes and very fine sands often produce uneconomical concretes. Generally, aggregates that have smooth grading curves, that is, no excesses or deficiencies, produce the most satisfactory results. For workability in leaner mixes, a grading that approaches the maximum recommended percentage passing each sieve is desirable. Coarse grading is required for economy in richer mixes. Generally, if the water–cement ratio is held constant and if the proper ratio of coarse to fine aggregate is chosen, a wide range in grading may be used with no effect on strength.

Usually more water is required for smaller aggregates than for larger maximum sizes. Conversely, the larger sizes require less water, and therefore less cement, to maintain a constant ratio with its resulting economy. The higher cost of obtaining or handling aggregates in the 2-in.-plus range usually offsets the saving in cement.

Generally, in higher strength ranges, smaller aggregates will produce higher strengths than larger aggregates.

In certain cases, aggregates that have been gap graded may be used to produce higher strengths in stiff concrete mixes. Close control of gap-graded mixes is required because the variations may produce segregation.

The maximum sizes for coarse aggregates are usually based on the following recommendations:

1. One-fifth the minimum dimension of nonreinforced members. Assume a minimum dimension of 15 in.

$$1/5 \times 15 \text{ in.} = 3\text{-in. maximum aggregate size}$$

2. Three-fourths the clear spacing between reinforcing bars or between reinforcing bars and forms.

Subtract the distance occupied by stirrups, bars, and covers from the total dimension.

Width of member	14 in.
Two ¼-in. stirrups	−½ in.
Two 1½-in. covers	−3 in.
Four ¾-in. bars	−3 in.
Clear space	7½ in.

7½ in. divided into 3 spaces = 3 2½-in. spaces

¾ × 2½ in. = 1.875 in. = 1⅞ in.

Check cover

$$¾ \times 1½ \text{ in.} = 1⅛ \text{ in.}$$

In this example cover governs. Select the next lower commercially available aggregate, 1 in.

3. One-third the depth of nonreinforced slabs on grade. Assume a 6-in. slab on grade.

$$6 \text{ in.} \times ⅓ = 2\text{-in. maximum aggregate size}$$

Bar Size	Diameter In Inches	Pounds Per Foot
#3	.375	.376
#4	.500	.668
#5	.625	1.043
#6	.750	1.502
#7	.875	2.044
#8	1.000	2.670
#9	1.128	3.400
#10	1.270	4.303
#11	1.410	5.313
#14	1.693	7.65
#18	2.257	13.60

FIGURE 4-10. Standard rebar sizes and weights.

If, in the judgment of the engineer, the concrete is workable and can be placed without honeycomb or excessive voids, these requirements may be modified.

The weight of an aggregate per unit volume is called its bulk unit weight because the volume is occupied by aggregates and voids. A known container is filled with aggregate following ASTM C29 and then weighed to find the aggregate's bulk unit weight.

Insulating lightweight aggregates   6–70 lb/cu ft
Structural lightweight aggregates   30–70 lb/cu ft
Normal weight concrete aggregates   75–110 lb/cu ft
Heavyweight concrete aggregates   110–290 lb/cu ft

The specific gravity is not a measure of aggregate quality, but is used to design and control mixes. The specific gravity is defined as the ratio of the weight of a substance to the weight of an equal volume of water. In the metric system under standard conditions the unit weight of water may be taken as unity; therefore, the weight of a substance in grams per cubic centimeters is equal to its specific gravity. In the English system the unit weight of water,

62.4 lb/cu ft, is divided into the solid unit weight of the substance to find its specific gravity.

For use in concrete design the bulk specific gravity is determined on aggregates in a saturated, surface-dry state. The bulk specific gravity is not the true specific gravity. It is defined as the ratio of the weight of volume of material in air including its normal pore structure to the weight of an equal volume of water in air at standard temperatures.

The moisture content of the aggregate is separated into internal moisture called absorbed moisture and external or surface moisture.

The moisture content of an aggregate must be known so that the batch weights and water content' of concrete may be controlled. Some concrete production facilities have automatic equipment to measure moisture conditions of the aggregates and make adjustments in batch weights.

ADMIXTURES

The basic concrete mix design can be modified by the addition of an admixture. *Admixtures* are defined as any material other than portland cement, aggregates, and water added to a concrete or mortar mix before or during mixing. Usually good concrete-mixing practice will impart the qualities that will be required of the concrete when it is placed into service. Very often by using a different type of cement or modifying the mix design desired, property changes can be obtained for special concrete service.

There are times, however, where it is important to modify the design, and the only way of making a change is through the use of an admixture. Admixtures are generally used for one or more of the following reasons.

1. To improve workability of the fresh concrete;

2. To reduce water content—thereby increasing strength for a given water–cement ratio;

3. To increase durability of hardened cement;

4. To retard setting time or increase it;

5. To impart color to concrete;

6. To maintain volume stability by reducing or offsetting shrinkage during curing;

7. To increase concrete resistance to freezing and thawing.

Most admixtures perform more than one function; for example, when an air-entraining admixture is used, increased resistance to freeze–thaw cycles in the hardened concrete, a reduction in bleedwater, and increased workability in the fresh concrete can be expected. Sometimes the admixture produces an adverse reaction in conjunction with the desired one such as some finely powdered workability admixtures which tend to increase drying shrinkage.

Since the effectiveness of an admixture varies with the type and amount of cement, aggregate shape, gradation, proportion, mixing time, water content, concrete, and air temperature, it is usually advisable to make trial mixes before using an admixture.

Trial mixes or small sample batches duplicate job conditions as close as possible so that the admixture dosages and results will be close to job expectations. Trial mixes also will allow study of admixtures compatibility if more than one admixture is to be used in the concrete.

When deciding whether to use a certain admixture or not, the designer should consider a mix design modification, a comparison of costs between the modification, and the admixture cost including purchase, storage, and batching costs and any adverse reactions that can be expected.

It is advised that any admixture being considered meet or exceed ASTM, state, or federal specifications and that the manufacturer's recommendations be followed.

The most commonly used admixtures today are air-entraining agents, accelerators, retarders, and water reducers. The air-entraining admixtures are covered by ASTM C260; the others are covered by ASTM C494. Although both of the specifications set no limits on chemical composition and are based more upon performance, they require the producer of the admixture to state the chloride content of the product.

The air-entraining admixture is used to increase the durability of concrete by protecting it against freeze–thaw cycle damage. When a concrete has been placed in service and it is subjected to water saturation followed by freezing temperatures, the resulting expansion of the water into ice usually will damage the concrete. By entraining air in concrete to form a microscopic air-void system, the expansion is provided a relief valve system. The air-void system in the hardened concrete paste allows water to freeze, with the empty air-voids providing room for the expansion that occurs as water changes to ice.

The normal mixing of concrete will entrap a certain percentage of air depending upon aggregate size, temperature, and other variables, but this air is usually in the form of widely spaced large bubbles and under a microscope can be distinguished from entrained air. The ability to handle the expansion of the water is a function of the spacing factor or average distance from any point in the paste to the nearest air void. The recommended spacing factor is 0.008 in.

The size of the effective air voids is in the range of 50 to 500 microns, the largest and smallest voids having little effect in protecting the paste.

The actual dosages required to produce a given air content will vary. If excess fines are present, for example, a higher dose of admixture would be required to produce the required air content.

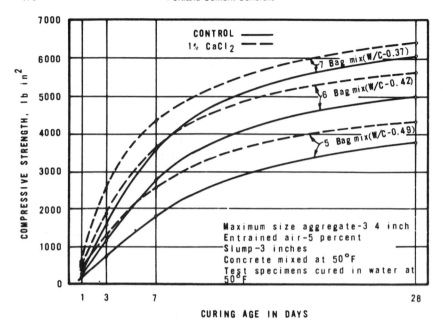

FIGURE 4-11. The effects of calcium chloride on the strength of concrete of different cement contents and at different ages with Type II cement. 288–D-1530. (Courtesy U.S. Department of the Interior, Water and Power Resources Service)

Generally, if air-entraining admixtures are used, the water content may be decreased 0.3 to 4 lb per 1 percent of air with the same workability due to the ball bearing action of the air voids. If no reduction in water content is made and cement content is maintained, a decrease in compressive strength of 3 to 4 percent for each 1 percent of air entrained will result.

To accelerate the setting time of concrete, the admixtures used are usually soluble chlorides, carbonates, and silicates, the most widely used being calcium chloride. The general dosage of calcium chloride should not exceed 2 percent by weight of cement, and it should not be used in prestressed concrete because of corrosion. Calcium chloride may be used during the winter to speed up initial setting time to allow earlier finishing. Calcium chloride is not an antifreeze and does not substantially lower freezing temperatures of the concrete. It does, however, get the concrete through its early setting stage faster, and it is during these early stages when freezing will damage the concrete.

For concrete placements during warm weather, a retarder is generally used. The retarders are primarily organic compounds such as lignosulfonic acid salts or hydroxylated carboxylic acid salts.

Table 4-1. Typical properties of polymer-impregnated concrete.

Property	Unimpregnated Concrete	Polymer-Impregnated Concrete [1]
Compressive strength, lb/in^2	5,300	18,200
Modulus of elasticity, 10^6 lb/in^2	3.5	6.2
Tensile strength, lb/in^2	400	1,500
Modulus of rupture, lb/in^2	700	2,300
Flexural elasticity modulus, 10^6 lb/in^2	4.3	7.1
Hardness, "L"-type impact hammer	32	52
Abrasion loss,		
inches	0.050	0.015
weight loss, grams	14	4
Cavitation loss, inches	0.32	0.02
Water absorption, percent	6.4	0.3
Water permeability, 10^3 ft/yr	53	14
Thermal conductivity, 73° F Btu/ft-hr $-$° F	1.33	1.27
Coefficient of expansion, 10^6 in/in	4.02	5.25
Diffusivity at 73° F, ft^2/hr	0.0387	0.0385
Specific heat, 73° F, Btu/lb/°F	0.241	0.220
Specific gravity	2.317	2.386
Freeze-thaw durability,		
cycles	490	3,650
percent weight loss	>25	2
Sulfate attack resistance (accelerated test),		
days exposure	480	1,436
percent expansion	0.50	0.017
Resistance to 15 percent HCl,		
days exposure	105	1,395
percent weight loss	>25	10
Resistance to 5 percent H$_2$SO$_4$,		
days exposure	49	133
percent weight loss	>25	25

[1] Conventional concrete impregnated with methyl methacrylate
Thermal-catalytic polymerization
Specimens contain 4.6 to 6.7 percent polymer by weight

For normal conditions the setting time of concrete can be reduced 30 to 50 percent for normal dosages. The use of a retarder during warm weather helps to offset the decreased setting time due to higher placement temperatures. Retarders can also be used to reduce cold joints, allow smaller crews to finish flat work, and permit later control joint sawing. Water reducers are usually retarders that have been modified to suppress or modify the retarding effect.

Polymer-impregnated concrete has become a major step forward in concrete technology. *Polymer-impregnated concrete* (PIC) consists of pre-formed, cured concrete that is impregnated with a liquid monomer or resin system and subsequently polymerized. The process requires completely dry concrete, a pressure impregnation system, except for surface treatments, and a heating system such as electric blankets or commercial ovens.

Polymer-cement concrete (PCC) consists of portland cement concrete to which a monomer or resin system has been added during mixing. The concrete can be polymerized in the form or after form removal.

Polymer-concrete (PC) is a system utilizing only graded aggregates and a monomer or resin system. The concrete can be produced with conventional equipment. The concrete is polymerized and in about three hours will attain full strength.

Although the polymerization process is not difficult, it is quite costly. Polymer-impregnated concretes may exhibit economic advantages over plain concrete in situations that require exceptional strength or durability and in areas where maintenance or repair is expensive or impractical. Research is currently being performed on bridge decks, prefabricated concrete structural systems, and concrete pipe that will be subjected to corrosive environments.

PROPORTIONING CONCRETE INGREDIENTS

Since concrete strength is inversely proportional to the water–cement ratio, a reduction in water while maintaining cement content will give an increase in strength. A rule of thumb for good concrete of 0.45 to 0.58 water–cement ratio says that each 0.01 reduction in the water–cement will increase 28-day strength by 100 psi. It also follows that for a given strength, if the water is reduced, then the cement may be reduced with resulting economy.

In higher strength concretes, the use of a water reducer is required because of the low water–cement ratio being used, 0.30 to 0.35. If concrete of this water–cement ratio is to be workable, a water reducer is required to raise the workability of such a mix.

The determination of the relative amounts of materials required to produce a concrete that will be economical and workable in the plastic state and that will have the required properties in the hardened state is called mix design or proportioning. Proportioning may vary from the simple—as the 1 : 2 : 3 formula which means 1 part cement, 2 parts fine aggregate, 3 parts coarse aggregate—to the ACI mix design procedure which is included in the appendix. Some of the proportioning is based on empirical information and some on tests and calculations. What is important is that the concrete to be produced from the initial proportioning satisfies its service requirements. When proportioning concrete, the technician or engineer must look at the entire job. Factors such as mixing apparatus, concrete handling and transportation, finishing, curing, and strength requirements must be considered since strength is often used as an indicator of concretes as well as other properties such as weather resistance.

Concrete economy is bascially a matter of reducing cement content, since it is usually the most expensive ingredient, without sacrificing the service requirements.

Admixtures such as water reducers have played a part in reducing cement contents while still maintaining required strengths. Cement reductions are also possible by utilizing the stiffest mix placeable, the largest maximum aggregate size, and the proper ratio of fine to coarse aggregates. Generally, labor, handling, and forming costs are the same for varying concretes so that basic saving can only be recognized in the initial design.

The workability of the fresh concrete is an important factor during mix design. Maximum aggregate sizes, water contents, method of transporting, and finishing must be considered here. Concrete that can be placed in slabs on grade with little reinforcing may not be easily placed in heavily reinforced walls or beams. A very stiff concrete that is to be machine finished would be useless to a contractor who must hand trowel a concrete slab.

The service requirements such as strength and exposure must also be considered. All concretes do not have the same strength requirement; mix designs may range from 2000 psi to 10,000 psi. Exposure conditions may vary from sulfate groundwater conditions to freezing and thawing conditions, but whatever the exposure condition, the mix design must produce concrete to meet the service needs.

Trial batches are usually produced and tested before actual production of concrete begins. A materials testing laboratory usually performs this operation. The laboratory is supplied the mix requirements and samples of materials to be used on the job. Their job is to design the most economical concrete mix that will satisfy the job requirements. One of the problems inherent in this system is the size of the trial mixes, and usually when production begins, adjustments are made in the design.

Concrete proportioning can be performed by trial batching. If the cement ratio is given, the technician can produce a paste (water and cement) for that water–concrete ratio, and vary the fine aggregate and coarse aggregate to produce different aggregate ratios. The batches are usually produced based on past trial batches so that it does not require the analysis of all possible combinations. The trial batch that meets the design requirement is then enlarged to job batch sizes, and if it requires further refinement, it can be made when production starts.

Another method used is to base designs on past experience. If the concrete producer has good records, it could possibly supply concrete based on past performance.

A widely used method for mix designs is the ACI 211.1-77, Recommended Practice for Designing Normal and Heavyweight Concrete. The complete procedure will be found in the appendix.

The proportioning of concrete mixes is not an exact science, and human judgment is an important factor to be considered. The technician or engineer will not find all of the mix design solutions in charts and tables, but in a blend of his skill and judgment and the technical information available.

CONCRETE MANUFACTURING

The production of concrete for the job covers a wide range of methods. Concrete can be mixed by hand in small portable mixers, in transit mix trucks, and in large stationary mixers. But no matter how the concrete is mixed, the end result desired is the same—a quality concrete meeting the design requirements. To produce quality concrete, the batching and measuring of ingredients must be done accurately. Therefore, most specifications require that materials be weighed and combined rather than combined by volume. Water is the one ingredient that is usually measured out either way, by weight or by volume. Weighing materials allows for adjustments in moisture conditions, especially in the fine aggregates where bulking can occur due to moisture.

ASTM C94-71a specifies weight measurements be made to the following tolerances:

1. Cement: when the quantity of cement in a batch exceeds 30 percent of scale capacity, the quantity indicated by scale shall be within 1 percent of the required weight. For small batches [1 yd³ (1 m³)] the quantity of cement shall be not less than required nor more than 4 percent in excess.

2. Aggregates: Batch weights based on dry weights plus total weight of absorbed and surface moisture when aggregates are weighed separately: 2 percent in a cumulative aggregate batch; 1 percent when scale is used in excess of 30 percent of its capacity. For cumulative weights less than 30-percent scale capacity, the tolerance shall be 0.3 percent of scale capacity or 3 percent of the required cumulative weight.

3. Water: Mixing water shall consist of added water, ice, surface moisture on aggregates, and water added in the form of admixtures; and shall be measured by weight or volume to an accuracy of 1 percent of total mixing water required.

4. Admixtures: Powdered admixtures shall be measured by weight, paste or liquid admixtures by volume or weight. Accuracy for weighing shall be 3 percent; volumetric measurement shall be within an accuracy of 0.3 percent of the total amount required, or plus and minus the volume of dose required for one sack of cement, whichever is greater.

All weighing equipment should be checked periodically and adjustments made when required. Admixture equipment should be checked daily since overdoses can be very detrimental to quality concrete production. From the discussion on air-entraining admixtures, it can be seen that an overdose here could possibly reduce the concrete strength considerably.

Concrete Mixing

The actual mixing of concrete is performed for the most part by mixing equipment. The mixing equipment is usually rated for two functions: first, the actual mixing of the ingredients to produce concrete, and second, the agitating of already mixed concrete. The agitating capacity is higher than the mixing capacity. The mixing equipment can be stationary, mounted on wheels and towable, mounted on a truck for transit mix, or mounted on crawlers for paving operations.

Stationary mixing equipment can be found on jobs which require large amounts of concrete at steady rates. A good example is a large concrete dam; the amount of concrete required and the steady placement scheduled permit the semipermanent installation. Large highway paving jobs also may utilize stationary mixers. The concrete is produced at one central location and transported to the paving equipment by special agitator trucks or in ordinary dump trucks if conditions permit. The economy of such a system should be evident when comparing the cost of transit mix trucks to dump or agitator trucks. The actual mixing drums may vary from 2 cu yd to 12 cu yd and may be placed in tandem so that while one drum is discharging, the other drum is mixing a batch.

The required mixing time of a stationary mixer may vary but generally 1 minute is required for the first cubic yard and 15 seconds for each additional cubic yard or fraction of a cubic yard. The mixing time is measured from the time all of the solid ingredients are in the drum, provided that all of the water has been added before one-fourth the mixing time has elapsed. Many of the stationary mixes have timing devices which can be set and locked to prevent the discharge of the concrete before proper mixing time has elapsed.

ASTM C94 specifies mixing time based on drum revolutions. Generally 70 to 100 revolutions at rotation rate designated by manufacturer of the mixer is required to produce uniform concrete. No more than 100 revolutions at mixing speed can be made. All revolutions over 100 must be made at agitating speed. ASTM C-94 also specifies that discharge of the concrete shall be completed within 1½ hours or before the drum has revolved 300 revolutions—whichever comes first—after the introduction of the mixing water to the cement and aggregates, or after the introduction of cement to the aggregates.

Concrete Mixing Methods

Stationary mixers are also used by some ready mix producers. The concrete is mixed at the central yard and delivered to various job sites in transit mix trucks. The trucks are able to deliver more concrete per trip because they are operating at agitating capacity which is higher than mixing capacity.

Many of the stationary mixers in use today are actually portable in that the components are maintained on trailers, and after the job's completion, the plant can be disassembled easily and transported to the next site.

For smaller concrete jobs many contractors will rely on the portable mixer or construction mixer. The capacities of these mixers are generally in cubic feet, and they are used for small concrete placement or where time of placement must be controlled. The biggest problem with concrete produced with construction mixers is quality control. Most contractors do not bother to weigh batch ingredients but instead use volumetric batching. While the total cubic yards placed by this method today is rather small, the same care should be exercised by those contractors who still use it as is used in a modern concrete producer's plant.

Paving mixers are concrete mixers mounted on crawler treads. The materials are fed into the mixer from dry batch trucks, and the machine travels along the finish grade and deposits fresh concrete behind itself to be screened and finished by the rest of the paving train.

Shotcrete is a nonproprietary term used to describe mortar or concrete placed by high-velocity compressed air that adheres to the surface on which it is projected. In the dry-mix process, the dry materials are thoroughly mixed with enough water to prevent dusting. The dry mixture is forced through the delivery hose by compressed air, and the water is added at the mixing nozzle. The wet-mix utilizes wet mortar or concrete forced through the delivery hose to the nozzle, where compressed air is introduced to increase the velocity of

FIGURE 4-12. Transit mixer (Courtesy T. L. Smith Co.)

the material. Because of the velocity at impact, a certain amount of material bounces off the surface of the structure; this material is called *rebound*. With dry-mix shotcrete, rebound may average 30 percent on overhanging surfaces or squaring corners, about 25 percent for vertical surfaces, and on nearly level surfaces about 20 percent. The rebound material must be cleared away from the application area, since it is mostly the sand and coarse particles rather than cement that make up rebound. In fact, the cement content of the shotcrete in place is higher than the cement content of the rebound.

Either sand or coarse aggregate shotcrete can be applied to the surfaces of various materials. The primary uses of shotcrete are in repairing and strengthening existing structures, as protective coatings for structural steel and masonry, in tunnel and canal construction, and in the building of free-form swimming pools.

Shotcrete's strength is usually evaluated by cores removed from sample panels or from the application itself, if the shotcrete is thick enough.

The most familiar concrete production system is ready mix. Ready mix is concrete delivered to the job site ready for placement. Ready mix concrete is produced by one of three methods: central mix, transit mix, and shrink mix. Central mix concrete is mixed in a stationary mixer at the producer's yard and delivered to the job site in a transit mixer operating at agitating speeds, in an agitator truck, or in dump trucks. Transit mixed concrete is completely mixed in the truck. The ingredients are batched, water is added, and the concrete is mixed in the drum mounted on a truck. Shrink mixed concrete is a combination of central mix and transit mix with mixing requirements split between the central plant and the transit truck.

Concrete mixing equipment loads should not exeed rated capacities. When capacities are exceeded to increase production, the quality of the concrete produced is lowered. The interior of the mixing drum should be periodically checked for worn blades and hardened concrete buildup, both factors decreasing mixing efficiency.

The final quality of the concrete produced by a ready mix supplier is determined by the contractor's operations. which include forming, placement, and curing. This joint involvement in material production can cause problems. If the contractor's placing and curing operations are faulty, concrete which should have met all requirements may not meet job service requirements.

This division of responsibilities generally requires a third party, the materials testing laboratory, to become involved in concrete construction. The materials laboratory will monitor the concrete production, placement, and curing operations by performing ASTM or other specified tests during these operations. Most ready mix firms have quality control programs to monitor their products' performance. When concrete is produced by any method, job site or ready mixed, several basic tests are performed to measure quality. It is advised that the technician read the specification carefully and note the who, what, when, and where of the tests.

TESTING CONCRETE

It is important that the samples of concrete to be tested be representative samples. If they are not, then the results obtained by testing will not represent the concrete placed. ASTM makes provision for sampling fresh concrete in C172-71. It spells out procedures for sampling various production systems and specifies a sample size of 1 cu ft except for routine Slump and Air-Content tests. The sample must be tested within 15 minutes and during testing must be protected from the weather.

A major requirement of fresh concrete is *workability,* a composite term used to denote the ease with which concrete can be mixed, transported, placed, and finished without segregation. Workability is a relative term because concrete which satisfies its requirements under one set of conditions may not satisfy its requirements under different conditions. A concrete used in a nonreinforced footing may not be usable in a reinforced wall or column.

A major requirement of fresh concrete is *consistency,* denoted by the fluidity of the concrete as measured by the slump test. If the slump of a concrete mix is controlled, the consistency and workability necessary for proper placement and indirectly the water cement ratio can be controlled. Changes in water content have a pronounced effect on slump. A 3 percent change in water content will increase the slump about 1 in. If the surface moisture on the sand changes by about 1 percent, the slump may increase 1 to 1½ in.

In conjunction with slump, the term *workability* is often used to denote the ease with which concrete can be mixed, transported, placed, and finished without segregation. The workability of a concrete mix can be estimated by the Slump test and by observations of the concrete for stickiness and harshness. Wet concretes are usually more workable than dry concretes. but concretes of the same slump may vary in workability depending on the paste and aggregates involved.

ASTM C143-71 test for slump of portland cement concrete details the procedure for performing Slump tests on fresh concrete. A slump cone is filled in three layers of equal volume so the first layer is about 2-⅝ in. (76 mm) high, and the second layer is 6-⅛ in. (155 mm) high. Each layer is rodded 25 times with a tamping rod 24 in. (600 mm) long and ⅝ in. (16 mm) in diameter, with a hemispherical tip with a ⅝-in. diameter. The rodding is uniformly distributed and is full depth for the first layer and just penetrating previous layers for the second and third layers. If the level of concrete falls below the top of cone during the last rodding, add additional concrete as required to keep an excess above the top of the mold. Strike off the surface of concrete by a screeding motion and rolling the rod across the top of the cone. In 5 ± 2 seconds, raise the cone straight up. Set the slump cone next to the

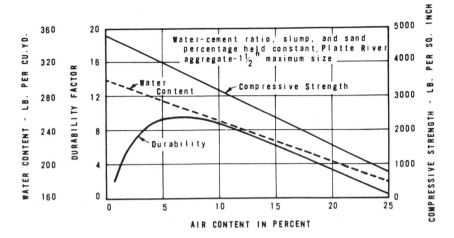

FIGURE 4-13. Effects of air content on durability, compressive strength, and required water content of concrete. Durability increases rapidly to a maximum and then decreases as the air content is increased. Compressive strength and water content decrease as the air content is increased. 288–D–1520. (Courtesy U.S. Department of the Interior, Water and Power Resources Service)

concrete, and measure the difference in height between the slump cone and the original center of the specimen. With the rod set on the cone, this slump measurement can be read to the nearest ¼ in. (6 mm). The test from filling of the slump cone to measuring the slump should take no longer than 2½ minutes. If two consecutive tests on a sample show a falling away of a portion of the sample, the concrete probably lacks the cohesiveness for the Slump test to be applicable.

The *air content* of fresh concrete is a very important value. If a mix design for a certain air content is to meet exposure requirements, that air content must be maintained. If it decreases, durability decreases; if it increases, strength decreases about 3 percent for each 1 percent of air. There are two field procedures in use today: the ASTM C173-73 test for air content of freshly mixed concrete by the volumetric system, and the ASTM C231-72T test for air content of freshly mixed concrete by the pressure method.

The volumetric method can be used with all types of aggregates and is recommended for lightweight or porous aggregates. A sample of concrete is placed in the bowl in three layers, each layer is rodded 25 times, and the side of the bowl is tapped with a mallet 10 to 15 times after each rodding. After filling and rodding, strike off the excess concrete, clean the bowl flange, and clamp the top section onto bowl. Using the special funnel, fill the top section, remove the funnel, and adjust the water level with a syringe until the bottom of the meniscus is at zero. Attach and tighten the screw cap. Invert and agitate until the concrete settles from the base; then rock and roll the apparatus until no further drops in water level occur. Dispel the foam by removing the cap and adding isopropyl alcohol in 1-cup increments. Make a direct reading of the liquid in the neck, reading to the bottom of the meniscus and estimating to the nearest 0.1 percent. The air content is that reading plus the number of cupfuls of alcohol used.

The pressure method cannot be used with lightweight or porous aggregates since the water will be forced into the aggregates pore structure and erroneous results will be obtained. Correction factors are relatively constant for normal weight aggregates and, even though small, should be determined and applied when air contents are determined by the pressure method. The pressure method of determining air content is based on Boyle's Law which relates pressure to volume. When the pressure is applied, the air in the concrete sample compresses. ASTM C231-72T recognizes two types of apparatus designed Meter Type A and Meter Type B.

Operation of the Type A meter involves the introduction of water in a glass tube to a predetermined height above a sample of concrete of known volume and the application of a predetermined air pressure over the water. By observing the reduction in the water level, the percentage of air in the concrete can be read from the glass tube.

The Type B meter involves the equalizing of a known volume of air at a known pressure in a sealed air chamber with the unknown volume of air in the concrete sample, the dial and the pressure gauge being calibrated in terms of percentage of air for the pressure at which equalization takes place.

The *unit weight* of fresh concrete and yield determinations are covered by ASTM C138-73. The unit weight of fresh concrete is determined in pounds per cubic foot or kilograms per cubic meter, and yield is the number of cubic feet of concrete produced from a mixture of known quantities of materials.

The unit weight determination is made with a standard cylindrical measure which is filled in three equal layers with each layer rodded 25 times. The sides of the container must be rapped 10 or more times until no large air bubbles appear and the holes left from rodding have closed. The surface of the concrete must be struck off the sides of the container, the container cleaned, and the container full of concrete weighed. Subtract the weight of the container from the weight of the container full of concrete and multiply the resulting number by the calibration factor as determined by ASTM C29. The resulting number is the weight of the concrete per cubic foot or cubic meter. The unit weight of concrete is often used as a guide for air contents. If the unit weight falls, it usually indicates that the air content is rising. It is also an indicator of strength for a given class of concrete.

Yield determinations are important in that the volume of concrete being produced for a given batch can be checked. If the total weight of all of the ingredients batched is divided by the unit weight of concrete, the result is the yield in cubic feet.

Example

Batch Weights

Water	265 lb
Cement	510
C/A	1917
F/A	1350
	4042 lb total

Unit weight $= 149.2$ lb/cu ft

$$\text{Yield} = \frac{4042 \text{ lb}}{149.2 \text{ lb/cu ft}} = 27.1 \text{ cu ft}$$

The volume of concrete produced as determined by yield calculations enables a ready mix producer to check his production, and the contractor can check that he is getting the material he is paying for. The yield calculation can be used to solve disputes concerning the cubic yards of concrete required to fill a set of forms. If the forms move during placement, the yardage required to fill them will increase and the contractor may claim he was shortchanged. If the yield determinations are available, then some problems can be easily solved.

While the tests are being completed on a sample of concrete, the temperature of the concrete should also be taken and recorded, since placement temperature may govern setting times, curing, and strength development. In hot weather, the maximum placement temperature is often limited to 90°F; in cold weather, a minimum temperature of 55°F or 60°F is sometimes specified. The armored thermometer used should be accurate to ±2°F, and the recorded value should be the average of three readings taken over the concrete sample.

COMPRESSIVE STRENGTH TESTS

ASTM C31-69 is the test procedure for making compressive test cylinders. The standard test cylinder is 6 inches in diameter by 12 inches high for aggregates up to 2 inches. For larger aggregates the diameter should be at least three times the aggregate size and the height at least twice the diameter. The molds used are generally waxed cardboard or plastic, and ASTM C470-73T is the governing specification.

The test cylinders are filled in three equal layers and each layer rodded 25 times. Concretes of 1- to 3-inch slump may be rodded or vibrated; concretes under 1-inch slump must be vibrated, while concretes over 3-inch slump must be rodded. After the cylinders have been filled, they are struck off level and covered with a glass or steel plate or damp burlap and allowed to set for 24 hours. During the first 24 hours the specimen can be affected by movement, temperature changes, or drying. The cylinders are then moved to proper curing facilities where moist curing will take place for the required time. The strengths of cylinders are generally taken at 7 and 28 days.

The speed with which construction takes place has cast some doubt on the usefulness of the 7- and 28-day concrete strength tests. If concrete strengths are not adequate in the footings of a building, the engineer may not receive the information until walls have already been cast on the questionable footing concrete.

Accelerated tests are being developed to allow earlier acquisition of strength information. Systems currently being tested or approved include 2-day breaks of cylinders that have been cured in boiling water or in autogenous curing boxes, 5-hour breaks of cylinders cured under heat and pressure, and a system that will chemically analyze plastic concrete before placement for its potential strength. These systems will require extensive correlation testing with 28-day cylinders before they gain wide acceptance. The compressive strength of the concrete is determined by loading the cylinders to failure.

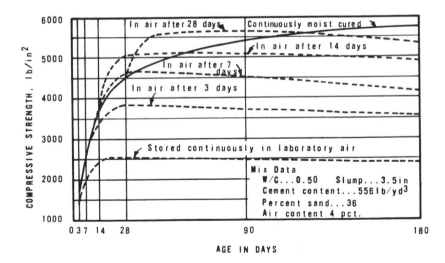

FIGURE 4-14. Compressive strength of concrete dried in laboratory air after preliminary moist curing. 288–D–2644. (Courtesy U.S. Department of the Interior, Water and Power Resources Service)

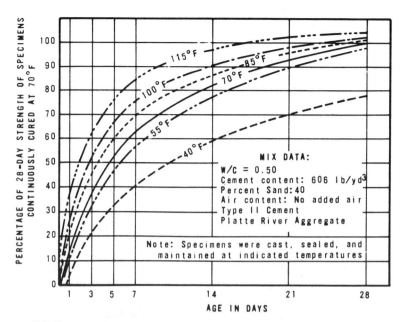

FIGURE 4-15. Effect of curing temperature on compressive strength of concrete. 288-D-2645. (Courtesy U.S. Department of the Interior, Water and Power Resources Service)

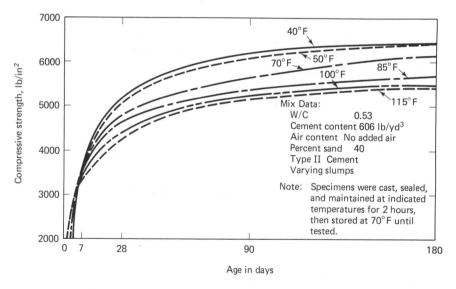

FIGURE 4-16. Effect of initial temperature on compressive strength of concrete. 288-D-2646. (Courtesy U.S. Department of the Interior, Water and Power Resources Service)

183

Cylinder diameter = 6 in.
Load at failure = 115,000 lb

$$S = P/A$$

S = compressive strength
P = load in lb
A = area in sq in.

$$S = \frac{115,000 \text{ lb}}{28.26 \text{ sq in.}}$$

$$S = 4070 \text{ lb/sq in.}$$

The specimens made under controlled curing conditions are generally the specimens used to judge the quality of the concrete for the job and are called *record cylinders.*

The contractor may have cylinders made and cured under jobsite conditions to determine when forms may be stripped or the structure may be put into service.

The evaluation of compressive strength test results is usually based on

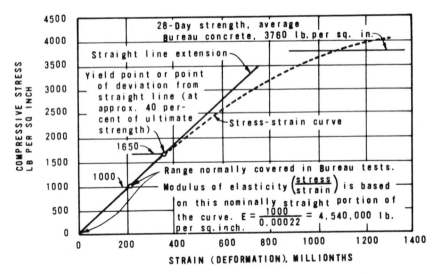

FIGURE 4-17. Typical stress–strain diagram for thoroughly hardened concrete that has been moderately preloaded. The stress–strain curve is very nearly a straight line within the range of usual working stresses. 288-D-799. (Courtesy U.S. Department of the Interior, Water and Power Resources Service)

ASTM C94-73a or ACI 214 criteria. The evaluations use statistical methods
to determine the adequacy of concrete strengths.

Statistical computations used to control the quality of concrete can be
performed manually or by using simple calculators. The results of concrete
strength tests will, if plotted, assume the "normal distribution"—that is, the
familiar bell-shaped curve. The curve can be described by two characteristics:
the mean or average denoted by the letter $\bar{x}$ and the standard deviation
denoted by the Greek letter sigma σ.

$$\text{Mean } \bar{x} = \frac{\Sigma x}{n}$$

$$\text{Standard deviation } \sigma = \sqrt{\frac{\Sigma (x - \bar{x})^2}{n}}$$

$\bar{x}$ = mean
x = test strength
n = number of tests
σ = standard deviation

The smaller the standard deviation, the steeper the curve, indicating
results grouped tightly around the mean; the higher the standard deviation, the
shallower the normal distribution curve, indicating widespread test results.

Whatever the value of the standard deviation, vertical lines drawn at
one, two, and three standard deviations on either side of the mean always
include the same proportion of area under the curve. For example, if $\bar{x}$ =
3500 psi and σ = 250 psi, approximately 68 percent of the test results would
fall between 3750 psi and 3250 psi, 94 percent between 4000 psi and 3000
psi, and almost 100 percent (99.73 percent) between 4250 psi and 2750 psi.

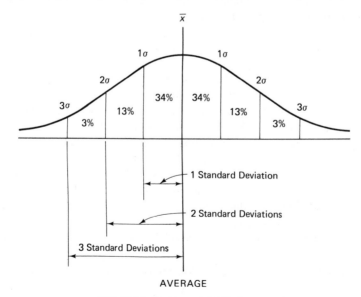

FIGURE 4-18. Normal distribution curve

To measure the degree of uniformity of concrete production at a given concrete plant the coefficient of variation is usually determined.

$$V = \frac{\sigma}{\bar{x}} \times 100$$

V = coefficient of variation
σ = standard deviation
$\bar{x}$ = mean

The coefficient of variation is used as a rating for the degree of control the concrete plant has over production variables. If the value of V is low, it indicates a fairly uniform product; conversely, if the value of V is high, the product will not be very uniform.

The coefficient of variation is used to determine overdesign requirements for concrete mix designs. Example: A concrete producer has a coefficient of variation of 10, and another producer has a coefficient of variation of 25. The specification limits the probability of tests' falling below specified strength (f'_c) to one out of every ten tests. The producers would check ASTM C94, Table 1; the first producer would have to overdesign by a factor of 1.15, while the second producer by a factor of 1.47, indicating the obvious economic advantages to maintaining good quality control.

To test compressive strength of in-place concrete, various destructive and nondestructive methods can be used.

Coring with diamond drills can be used to remove a specimen for strength testing. Nondestructive testing can be done with ultrasonics by correlating density to strength. The impact hammer measures the rebound of a spring-loaded plunger after hitting a smooth concrete surface. The hammer must be calibrated with test cylinders from the particular concrete before they are tested in compression and a calibration curve developed. The hammer is not considered a substitute for compressive strength tests, but if used properly, it can detect wide variations in strengths in the concrete of a structure.

Direct tests for tensile strength of concrete are seldom made, but a convenient, reliable test to determine indirectly the tensile strength of concrete is in use today. Developed in Brazil and standardized by ASTM, the test gives a splitting tensile strength value which is about 15 percent higher than values obtained through direct tensile tests.

The method utilizes standard 6-by-12-inch cylinders which are loaded along the length of the cylinder. (See Fig. 4-19.)

The splitting tensile strength is determined by using a formula based on the theory of elasticity.

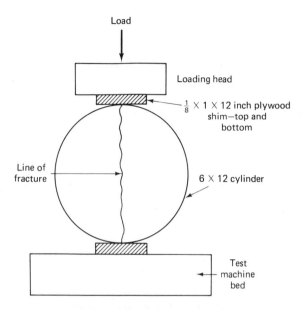

FIGURE 4-19. Spitting tensile test

$$\sigma = \frac{2P}{\pi l d}$$

where σ = splitting tensile strength, psi
  P = maximum load, lb.
  l = length of cylinder, in.
  d = diameter of cylinder, in.

Concrete used for pavement slabs is subjected to bending loads, and the flexure strength or modulus of rupture of the concrete is usually determined with 6 by 6 concrete beam specimens. The test procedure is ASTM C78-64 and utilizes simple beams with third point loading. When the full ASTM procedure is not used, an adequate estimate of flexure strength using the compressive strength of the concrete can be determined.

$$R = k \sqrt{f'_c}$$

where R = modulus of rupture, psi
  f'_c = compressive strength, psi
  k = a constant value between 8 and 10

PLACEMENT OF CONCRETE

During the testing of the fresh concrete. the contractor's crews will be placing the concrete in the forms. Depending upon the job conditions, various methods of concrete placement are utilized. Equipment will vary from simple chutes, wheelbarrows, and buggies to sophisticated conveyor or pump systems. Regardless of how the concrete is placed, extreme care must be taken to ensure that the concrete is not changed by transporting it and that it does not become segregated during placement. *Segregation* or the separation of coarse aggregate from the mortar or the water from the ingredients can be very detrimental to quality in service concrete.

One versatile method of handling plastic concrete on many construction sites is the concrete pump. The concrete pump transports plastic concrete thru a pipeline system from the ready-mix truck to the point of placement without changing the basic characteristics of the concrete mix.

The normal pumping distances will range from 300 to 1000 feet horizontally or 100 to 300 feet vertically. In some instances, concrete has been successfully pumped over 2000 feet horizontally and 900 feet vertically. Curves, vertical lifts, and harsh mixes tend to reduce maximum pumping distances. A 90-deg bend in the pipe is the equivalent of about 40 feet of straight horizontal line, and each 1 foot of vertical lift is the equivalent of about 8 feet of horizontal line.

The pipe used to carry the concrete is generally steel; however, on smaller pump systems heavy rubber hose has been found satisfactory. Aluminum pipe, which originally was introduced as a labor-saving device, because of its light weight is no longer permitted for most federal and state construction work. (The concrete passing through the pipe grinds aluminum particles from the pipe wall. These aluminum particles, reacting with lime from the concrete, creates hydrogen gas, which increases the voids in the concrete and substantially reduces concrete strengths.)

Normal pump capacities range from 10 to 125 cubic yards per hour, with special pumps having capacities of 200 cubic yards per hour. Aggregate sizes are important; generally the maximum size aggregate should not exceed 40 percent of the diameter of the pipe if the aggregate has a well-rounded shape. Since ideally shaped aggregates are not always available, further reductions in maximum aggregate size may be required for flat and elongated aggregates. Pumping lightweight aggregate concrete presents no problem, provided that the lightweight aggregate has been presoaked. Without the presoak, pump pressures tend to force water into the aggregate during pumping, and the concrete discharge becomes dry and unworkable. Slump ranges for lightweight concretes run between 2 to 5 inches. Most pumps will handle concretes with slumps of 3 to 4 inches. In this slump range the concrete discharge will exhibit no segregation. In fact, any concrete that does not

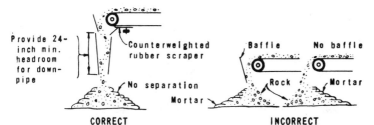

Provide 24-inch min. headroom for down-pipe

Counterweighted rubber scraper

No separation

Mortar

Baffle   No baffle

Rock   Mortar

CORRECT

The above arrangement prevents separation of concrete whether it is being discharged into hoppers, buckets, cars, trucks, or forms.

INCORRECT

Improper or complete lack of control at end of belt

Usually a baffle or shallow hopper merely changes the direction of separation.

CONTROL OF SEPARATION OF CONCRETE AT THE END OF CONVEYOR BELT

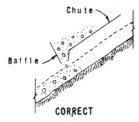

Chute

Baffle

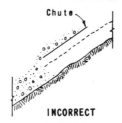

Chute

CORRECT

Place baffle and drop at end of chute so that separation is avoided and concrete remains on slope.

INCORRECT

Concrete discharged from a free end chute on a slope to be paved. Rock is separated and goes to bottom of slope. Velocity tends to carry concrete down slope.

PLACING CONCRETE ON A SLOPING SURFACE

No separation

Provide 24-inch minimum headroom for downpipe

Mortar

Baffle

Rock   Mortar

CORRECT

The above arrangement prevents separation, no matter how short the chute, whether concrete is being discharged into hoppers, buckets, cars, trucks, or forms.

INCORRECT

Improper or lack of control at end of any concrete chute, no matter how short.

Usually a baffle merely changes direction of separation.

CONTROL OF SEPARATION AT THE END OF CONCRETE CHUTES

This applies to sloping discharges from mixers, truck mixers, etc. as well as to longer chutes, but not when concrete is discharged into another chute or onto a conveyor belt.

FIGURE 4-20. Correct and incorrect methods of concrete placement using conveyor belts and chutes. Proper procedures must be used if separation at the ends of conveyors and chutes is to be controlled. 288–D–854. (Courtesy U.S. Department of the Interior, Water and Power Resources Service)

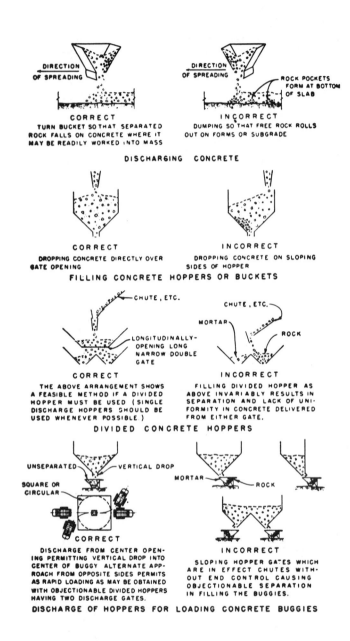

FIGURE 4-21. Correct and incorrect methods for loading and discharging concrete buckets, hoppers, and buggies. Use of proper procedures avoids separation of the coarse aggregate from the mortar. 288–D–3276. (Courtesy U.S. Department of the Interior, Water and Power Resources Service)

segregate before pumping will not tend to segregate during pumping. If a concrete exhibits segregation before pumping, it usually is not a pumpable mix.

Before actual pumping begins, the pump lines are lubricated with a concrete mix that contains no coarse aggregate. The amount of mortar used will depend on the length of run. A cubic yard of mortar will lubricate approximately 1000 feet of pipe. If delays occur during the pumping process, the pump operator will have to move some concrete through the system at regular intervals to prevent plugs from forming in the system.

After completion of the concrete placement the pump and lines can be washed out with water. Some lines may require the use of a *go-devil*, a dumbbell-shaped insert placed in the pipe which will push out the concrete, leaving clean interior walls in the pipe system.

Conveyor belts have been used by the concrete industry to move plastic concrete for a number of years. The first successful use of a belt conveyor appears to be a 1929 concrete placement utilizing a 600-foot conveyor to transport concrete on a bridge job. Early belt conveyors had capacities of 30 to 40 cubic yards per hour, while today equipment with capacities of up to 300 cubic yards per hour is available for massive concrete placements. The volume of concrete transported by a conveyor is determined by the belt width, conveyor speed, angle of incline or decline, and the properties of the concrete mix itself, such as aggregate size and shape, mix proportions, and slump. Conveyors, charging hoppers, transfer devices, and belt wipers generally do not modify any of the important characteristics of the concrete being carried to the placement area. However, if placement is delayed excessively or weather conditions are not optimum, some provision may have to be made to cover the conveyor system.

The conveying system must be properly designed with enough power to start and stop with fully loaded belts during placement delays. The individual sections are designed for high mobility because the delivery of fresh concrete must be continuous over the placement area without excessive construction joints. Figure 4-24 illustrates a feeder-type belt system which operates in series with end discharge transfer points and a radial discharge conveyor at the point of placement. The radial discharge allows placement thru a 360-deg arc. This type of system has an appreciable setup time and cost; therefore it is only used on large-volume placements.

On construction projects utilizing pumps or conveyors there tends to be some discussion as to the proper location for concrete testing. Should the tests be performed on the concrete as discharged from the truck into the transporting system, or after the concrete has traveled through the system to the placement area? The general recommendation is to make tests at both locations; if satisfactory correlation can be made, tests may be performed at the most accessible location as long as placement conditions do not change.

Like all materials used in construction, concrete expands and contracts under different conditions of moisture and temperature. To control random cracking, joints must be placed in the concrete to allow cracking to occur at the proper location. A *control joint* is a cut made into the surface of the concrete one-fifth the slab's thickness. The slab is weakened at that point and cracks should develop in the joint rather than randomly. The joint may be sawed, made with a groover, or formed with divider strips.

The *isolation joint* is designed to physically separate areas of concrete from one another or from columns, poles, and walls; this separation allows for differential settlement. The joint is usually formed with a premolded filler which is left in place just slightly below the concrete surface's tooled edges.

Construction joints are the result of not being able to place concrete continuously, i.e., one day's concrete placement from the next day's concrete placement. Construction joints should be located in the concrete so that they

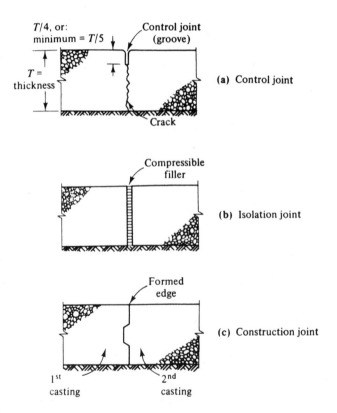

FIGURE 4-22. Basic types of joints used in concrete construction. (Courtesy of the Canadian Portland Cement Association)

may act as control joints. Some load-transfer device must be used to carry loads across the joint. Dowels or keyways can be used.

After the concrete has been properly placed and consolidated by rodding or vibration and the final screeding operations have been completed, the contractor must apply the proper surface finish and curing system.

During concrete placement the contractor must consolidate the plastic concrete. The consolidation must eliminate as far as practical the voids in the concrete. Well-consolidated concrete is free of rock pockets or honeycomb or bubbles of entrapped air and is in close contact with forms, reinforcement, and other embedded items such as anchor bolts and pipe sleeves.

Vibrators may be either immersion or external form-mounted systems powered by air or electricity. The contractor must determine a vibrator pattern and the amplitude and frequency of vibration, as well as the depth of the

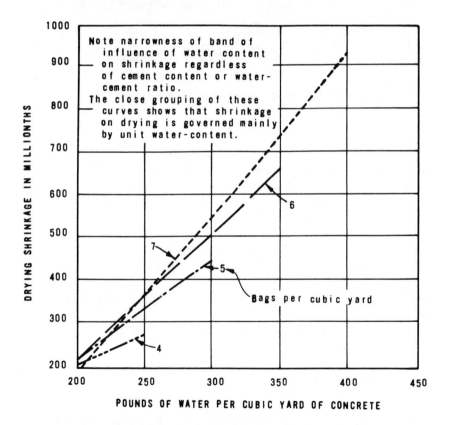

FIGURE 4-23. The interrelation of shrinkage, cement content, and water content. The chart indicates that shrinkage is a direct function of the unit water content of fresh concrete. 288-D-2647. (Courtesy U.S. Department of the Interior, Water and Power Resources Service)

FIGURE 4-24. Concrete placement using a conveyor system (Courtesy Morgen Manufacturing Co.)

vibrator into the concrete to ensure good consolidation. Care must be taken so as not to overvibrate fresh concrete, which will cause the coarse aggregate to settle and leave a wet mortar film at the surface of the concrete placement.

There is considerable evidence to indicate that revibration is beneficial to concrete, provided that the concrete is brought back to a plastic condition. The revibrated concrete exhibits a higher strength and less settlement cracking, and the effects of internal bleeding are reduced.

The finish of a concrete surface may vary from a wood float, broomed finish up to a hard troweled finish. Wood float and broom finishes are usually used on exterior flatwork while the trowel finish is an interior finish. Contractors may choose to finish small areas by hand trowels and larger areas by power trowels. The power trowels are usually gasoline powered and have three or four steel blades which rotate on the surface of the concrete.

CURING CONCRETE

Proper curing must begin after surfaces have been worked to proper finish for concrete to adequately gain its design strength, increase its resistance to freeze–thaw, improve its watertightness and wear resistance. This requires that hydration of the cement be continued. The continued hydration of the

FIGURE 4-25. Concrete placement using a concrete pump (Courtesy Morgen Manufacturing Co.)

cement requires moisture and favorable temperatures to be maintained for an adequate time. The time required will depend upon type of cement, mix proportions, design strength, size and shape of the concrete structure, and future exposure conditions.

The optimum concrete temperature at placement will vary with conditions, but generally 90°F (32.2°C) is set as the upper limit. To obtain the specified placement temperature in hot weather often requires the use of prechilled aggregates and possibly the substitution of shaved ice for mix water. During cold weather the aggregates and mixing water may be heated to raise the concrete temperature.

During hot-weather concreting, the loss of moisture after placement is critical, and various methods can be used to prevent the moisture loss or to add additional curing water to the concrete.

Methods used to prevent moisture loss may include the use of waterproof papers, plastic film, and liquid curing compounds which form a membrane and the leaving of forms in place. During hot weather, dark coverings should not be used as they will absorb the sun's rays.

The additional water methods are by ponding, sprinkling, and using wet coverings such as burlap, sand, and straw. The methods utilized will vary, but care should be taken so that the entire concrete surface is protected, especially corners and edges, and that the material used as a curing system will not stain the concrete.

Table 4–2   Effects of various substances on hardened concrete
(Courtesy U.S. Department of the Interior, Water and Power Resources Service)

Substance	Effect on unprotected concrete
Petroleum oils, heavy, light, and volatile	None.
Coal-tar distillates	None, or very slight.
Inorganic acids	Disintegration.
Organic materials:	
Acetic acid	Slow disintegration.
Oxalic and dry carbonic acids	None.
Carbonic acid in water	Slow attack.
Lactic and tannic acids	Do.
Vegetable oils	Slight or very slight attack.
Inorganic salts:	
Sulfates of calcium, sodium, magnesium, potassium, aluminum, iron.	Active attack.
Chlorides of sodium, potassium	None.
Chlorides of magnesium, calcium	Slight attack.
Miscellaneous:	
Milk	Slow attack.
Silage juices	Do.
Molasses, corn syrup, and glucose	Slight attack.
Hot distilled water	Rapid disintegration.

Cold-weather concreting requires the maintenance of internal heat or the use of additional heat to provide the proper curing temperatures. To maintain internal heat, insulating blankets and straw may be used. The external heat may be supplied by salamanders, space heaters, or live steam. If fuel-burning heaters are used, care must be taken to see that they are properly vented to prevent *carbonation*. The carbon dixoide produced by the combustion of fossil fuels reacts with the calcium hydroxide in the fresh concrete to form a calcium carbonate layer on the surface of the concrete. This surface weakness will cause the floor to dust when put into service.

No two concrete jobs are alike, and the specifications must be checked carefully to determine what will be required for hot- or cold-weather concrete placement and what methods of curing will be allowed.

PRECAST CONCRETE PRODUCTS

Precast concrete products are construction items usually manufactured off site and delivered to the construction site ready for installation into the structure. During the manufacturing process the same quality control measures applied to site-cast concrete are used to ensure the use of quality materials in the production of precast items. Precast concrete pipe, catch basins, septic systems, and structural elements such as beams, columns, and floor units are concrete items that can be precast in standard sizes and shapes and marketed as products ready for installation at the construction site.

Precast concrete pipe is classified by the production method utilized to manufacture the pipe. Cast concrete pipe is usually 48 inches in diameter or larger, with varying lengths. The split steel forms stand upright, and the concrete is placed between the inner and outer steel form. The pipe is reinforced with steel rebar and wiremesh. The concrete usually has a 3-inch or less slump and is consolidated by external form-mounted vibrators. Special care must be taken to ensure tight form connections; otherwise, as the concrete is vibrated, objectionable mortar leaks will occur at the joints. The concrete pipe will be removed from the mold and cured, steam or moist curing being used.

The centrifugally spun system is used to produce reinforced pipe 42 inches in diameter or less. The system utilizes a single outside form which can be rotated at high speeds. The concrete is deposited inside the spinning mold by a conveyor belt and compacted by centrifugal force. Variations used to aid compaction are vibration and steel rollers in direct contact with the concrete being placed. The concrete used has a slump of 0 to 2 inches and is deposited in the form to ensure a specified wall thickness with minimum variations. The duration and speed must be sufficient to prevent the concrete from sagging when the rotation stops. The pipe is cured with the same methods as cast pipe.

Tamped and packerhead pipe are usually nonreinforced concrete pipe made by compacting very dry concrete into steel molds. The mold is split and can be removed as soon as the pipe section is completed without damaging the pipe. The packerhead system utilizes a stationary mold, with the packerhead placing and shaping the interior surface. The tamped system uses a fixed interior cylinder with the outside mold rotating while the concrete is compacted by vertical tampers. When the pipe unit is completed, the form is removed and moist or steam curing is used to produce required concrete strengths.

Prestressed concrete pipe is used for high-pressure water distribution systems. Prestressed pipe is made in stages. The core of the pipe is produced by means of the centrifugal system. When the core has cured, it is wrapped with reinforcement steel in tension. Some systems utilize longitudinal steel in tension also. The wrapped core is then coated with mortar and cured to complete the pipe assembly.

Precast structural elements such as beams and columns are produced in casting beds of varying shapes and lengths. The forms or casting beds are usually set with the top of the form at grade; external vibrators are mounted on them. The forms are adjusted to the required dimensions of the finished beam;

all required reinforcement is set, and the concrete is deposited in the form. Generally precast operations attempt a 24-hour turnover or cycle for form use. To aid the initial set of the concrete, external heat is applied to the mold with electric heaters or a pipe system containing heated oil.

Using high-early strength cements, water-reducers, and heated curing, precast plants attain concrete strengths of 3000 psi or more within a 24-hour cycle. The concrete beams cast are removed from the molds and stored on the plant site ready for delivery when needed, and the casting cycle is repeated.

Whether site cast or precast, the concrete structure or product must be constructed with careful attention and quality control to ensure a long service life with a minimum of maintenance and repairs.

Concrete as a construction material is a complex subject. In order to deal with it, many organizations have been formed which share technical information with the users of concrete. The serious student of concrete should study the literature of organizations such as the American Concrete Institute, the Portland Cement Institute, the National Ready Mixed Concrete Association, and others to keep abreast of new developments and to help understand the behavior of concrete as a construction material.

Review Questions

1. List the basic types of portland cement, and describe their characteristics and uses.

2. What is the heat of hydration? What factors affect the rate of heat generation?

3. What factors influence the air content of concrete in the plastic state?

4. What are the four basic chemical compounds which make up portland cement, and what effect do they have on portland cement concrete?

5. If water from an untested source is to be used for concrete manufacturing, what test must be made for strength?

6. Determine the yield for the following concrete batch (the fresh unit weight of the concrete is 148 lb per cu ft):

Water	285 lb
Cement	520 lb
Coarse aggregate	1900 lb
Fine aggregate	1350 lb

7. Determine the compressive strength of a 6-in. diameter concrete cylinder which failed at a test load of 122,000 lb.

8. Design a concrete mix to satisfy the following requirements:

f'_c = 3000 psi
Non–air-entrained   Interior slab on grade
Nonreinforced   Max. aggregate size = 1"

	Sp. Gr.	F.M.	Aggregate Data: Bulk Unit Wt.	Moisture ABS.	Free
CA	2.68	6.00	95	0.5	1
FA	2.59	2.70	105	1	3

9. Design a concrete mix to satisfy the following requirements:

$f'_c = 4000$ psi
Air entrained   Exterior slab on grade
Nonreinforced   Max. aggregate size $= 1\frac{1}{2}''$

	Sp. Gr.	F.M.	Aggregate Data: Bulk (loose) Unit Wt.	Moisture ABS.	Free
CA	2.71	6.10	98	0.4	0.7
FA	2.65	2.80	112	0.9	2.1

total v
1, 1
3·0

10. What is the maximum aggregate size which can be used in concrete for the following conditions:

a. Nonreinforced wall

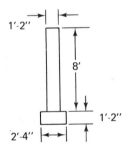

b. Slab on grade

c. Reinforced beam

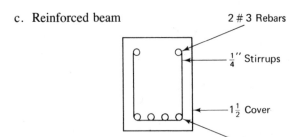

11. What is the difference between the types of air meters used to measure air content of fresh concrete, and why is the difference important?

12. Do the results of the following test breaks satisfy ASTM C94? The original concrete design utilized the working stress method and $f'_c = 4000$ psi.

4000 psi
3950 psi
4200 psi
3825 psi
3900 psi

13. What are admixtures, and what are they used for?

14. What modification is made to concrete to increase its resistance to freeze–thaw damage?

15. Why is concrete such a widely used construction material?

16. What factors are important during hot- and cold-weather concrete placement?

17. Determine the approximate modulus of rupture for a concrete with a compressive strength of 4000 psi. Assume $K = 9$.

18. A splitting tensile test was performed on a standard 6-by-12-inch cylinder; the load indicator registered 49,200 lb when the cylinder fractured. Calculate the splitting tensile strength and the approximate direct tensile strength of the concrete.

5

Iron and Steel

Iron in its various forms, including steel, is by far the most important of the metals used in the construction industry. All forms of iron and steel are included in the term *ferrous metals*. They are manufactured to meet a wide variety of specifications for various uses. Chemical composition and internal structure are accurately controlled during manufacturing. Therefore, strength and other mechanical properties can be determined with a high degree of reliability.

Ferrous products are fabricated in shops to desired size and shape. The finished products are ordinarily delivered to a construction site ready to be installed with inspection and testing completed. Ferrous metals are seldom damaged during transportation because of their strength and hardness. Therefore, people in the construction field have little opportunity to control the quality of iron or steel. Compared to aggregates, asphalt concrete, or portland cement concrete, all of which are partially "manufactured" during installation at the construction site, there is little that can be done to improve or harm a ferrous metal product once it leaves the fabrication shop.

STRUCTURE AND COMPOSITION

Iron and steel appear to be smooth and uniform, yet they consist of particles called *grains* or *crystals* that can be distinguished under a microscope. The grains are formed as the metal passes from the liquid to the solid state. This internal crystalline structure called the *constitution* determines to a great extent what mechanical properties the metal has. Each grain consists of a symmetrical pattern of atoms which is the same in all iron and steel. The grains are not all similar because they press on each other as they form, causing variations in size, shape, and arrangement. The size, shape, and arrangement of grains account for many of the differences in the behavior of various irons and steels.

Some types of iron and steel also contain a different kind of grain interspersed among the typical grains. These have an influence on the material's behavior. The internal structure is determined by the way the metal is cooled and by the way the metal is given its final shape. Grain size, shape, and arrangement are generally the same throughout a finished piece of metal; but special procedures can be used to make them different in different areas of the same piece.

The strength of the metal depends on the cohesion of the atoms in each crystal and the cohesion between adjacent crystals. In this respect the structure is somewhat like that of aggregate surrounded by adhesive to make concrete. Instead of adhesion holding the crystals or grains together, an atomic bond which is much stronger holds them. Iron and steel therefore have a higher tensile strength than any aggregate–adhesive combination.

Strain of any kind consists of movement of the atoms, closer together in compression or farther apart in tension. Atoms arranged close together allow more stretching or, in other words, more ductility than less-concentrated atomic arrangements. As long as the atoms retain their spatial relationships, even in a distorted way, they return to their original positions when stress is removed. The extent to which the atoms can move and still return to their original positions is the limit of elastic deformation. Beyond this extent, the pattern cannot be distorted without slippage along a plane or parallel planes through the grains. Any distortion in this range is plastic or permanent.

The final temperature and rate of heating do not affect the internal structure at the time materials are melted to make pig iron or when pig iron is melted to make iron or steel. However, the rate of cooling is important. Rapid cooling causes large crystals. Metal with large crystals is more brittle and does not have the strength, ductility, or shock resistance of metal with the smaller crystals caused by slower cooling. However, large crystals produce better machinability. Any elongation and alignment of grains in one direction increase the strength of the metal to resist stresses in that direction. The means of producing ferrous metals, both the refining with heat and the working into final shape, affect the mechanical properties of the material.

No ferrous metal is pure iron. All include the elements shown in Fig. 5-1 which have great effect on the properties of the metal, even if present in very small amounts. Phosphorus occasionally may not be included. Chemical content is determined by the composition of the iron ore, the way in which the metal is heated, and the elements added. Iron ore contains varying percentages of manganese, silicon, and sulfur, and may or may not contain some phosphorus. Carbon comes from the burning coke, and additional carbon may be added to the molten metal. Excess sulfur may be removed by the addition of manganese.

Generally speaking, longer or hotter treatment in a furnace decreases the percentages of carbon, manganese, phosphorus, silicon, and sulfur. Increases are made by adding the desired element to the liquid metal. Other elements also may be added to the liquid metal. These are shown in Fig. 5-7.

ELEMENT	COMMON CONTENT	EFFECTS
Carbon	Up to 0.90%	Increases hardness, tensile strength, and responsiveness to heat treatment with corresponding increases in strength and hardness.
	Over 0.90%	Increases hardness and brittleness; over 1.2%, causes loss of malleability.
Manganese	0.50% to 2.0%	Imparts strength and responsiveness to heat treatment; promotes hardness, uniformity of internal grain structure.
Silicon	Up to 2.50%	Same general effects as manganese.
Sulfur	Up to 0.050%	Maintained below this content to retain malleability at high temperatures, which is reduced with increased content.
	0.05% to 3.0%	Improves machinability.
Phosphorus	Up to 0.05%	Increases strength and corrosion resistance, but is maintained below this content to retain malleability and weldability at room temperature.

FIGURE 5-1. Ferrous metal properties (From "Construction Lending Guide," Courtesy U.S. League of Savings Associations)

PRODUCTION OF FERROUS METALS

The first step in the manufacture of iron or steel is to produce a low grade of iron in a continuously operating furnace called a *blast furnace*. These furnaces are about 200 feet high and about 50 feet in diameter. (See Fig. 5-2.) Iron ore, coke, and limestone are loaded continuously at the top. Iron ore is an oxide of iron found in nature mixed with rock or soil called *gangue*. Coke is

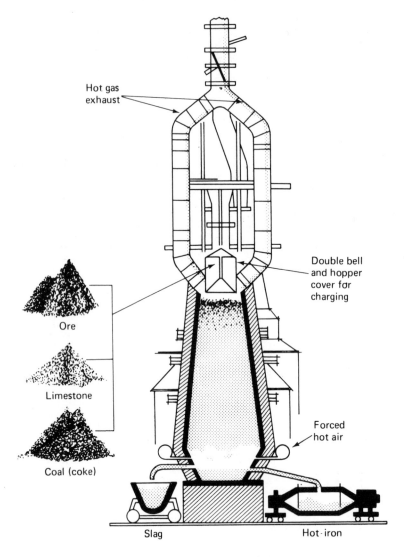

Hot gas exhaust

Double bell and hopper cover for charging

Ore

Limestone

Forced hot air

Coal (coke)

Slag   Hot-iron

FIGURE 5-2. Typical blast furnace

produced by heating coal to drive the impurities out. It then burns with greater heat than coal. Limestone is a type of rock that occurs in nature. Burning the coke and supporting the combustion with a strong blast of hot air melt the iron ore and limestone at a temperature of about 1500°F (815°C). The heat melts the iron, frees it of oxygen, and forms carbon monoxide gas which imparts carbon to the liquid iron.

Melting permits separation of iron from the gangue which combines with the molten limestone to form slag. Iron is much heavier than slag so there is a natural separation of the two as they melt. Iron flows to the bottom of the furnace and molten slag floats on the iron. Iron is removed from a tap near the bottom and slag from a tap slightly higher. These are removed a half dozen times per 24 hours of operation. Use of the slag as an aggregate is discussed in Chapter 2. The iron flows into molds and is allowed to solidify into shapes called *pigs,* or it is taken in a ladle while still liquid to be refined into steel or a better grade of iron. In either case, the product of the blast furnace is called *pig iron.*

The makeup of the iron resulting from this process is not accurately controlled. It contains about 4 percent carbon, about 2 percent silicon, about 1 percent manganese, and about 0.05 percent sulfur. It may contain up to 2 percent phosphorus depending on the type of ore used.

Pig iron is not useful for construction because it is weak and brittle, although it is very hard. The general term *iron* refers to a ferrous metal that is of a higher quality than pig iron. To produce useful iron or steel, a second melting is needed for further purification. In the future, iron and steel will be produced in one operation, but it is not yet economically feasible.

Iron

It is possible to refine pig iron until it is nearly pure iron containing little more than traces of impurities. In this form, iron is suitable for construction. It is highly resistant to corrosion, highly ductile, and readily machined. It is drawn into wires and rolled into sheets for roofing, siding, and corrugated pipe. Vitreous enamel coatings adhere well to this type of iron. Despite these qualities, the high cost of refining prevents this type of iron from being one of the major construction materials.

The types of iron more common to the construction industry are gray and white cast iron, malleable cast iron, and wrought iron. *Cast iron* is a general term denoting ferrous metals composed primarily of iron, carbon, and silicon, and shaped by being cast in a mold. They are too brittle to be shaped any other way. The brittleness is caused by the large amount of carbon which also increases strength. *Wrought iron* is highly refined iron with slag deliberately incorporated but not in chemical union with the iron. The slag forms one-directional fibers uniformly distributed throughout the metal. Chemical compositions of various types of iron are shown with cast steel in Fig. 5-3.

Metal	C	Typical Composition (Percent)			
		Si	Mn	P	S
Cast steel	0.5–0.9	0.2–0.7	0.5–1.0	0.05	0.05
Gray cast iron	2.5–3.8	1.1–2.8	0.4–1.0	0.15	0.10
White cast iron	1.8–3.6	0.5–2.0	0.2–0.8	0.18	0.10
Malleable cast iron	2.0–3.0	0.6–1.3	0.2–0.6	0.15	0.10
Wrought iron	<0.035	0.075–0.15	<0.06	0.10–0.15	0.006–0.015
Pure iron	0.015	Trace	0.025	0.005	0.025
Pig iron	3–5	1–4	0.2–1.5	0.1–2.0	0.04–0.10

FIGURE 5-3. Typical composition of ferrous metals

Pig iron is remelted before casting. Its chemical composition is controlled by the addition of scrap iron or steel of various kinds and of silicon and manganese as needed.

The molten metal flows from the furnace to a ladle from which it is poured into molds to be formed into useful shapes. This operation is called *casting*. The materials of which molds are made are listed here:

Molding Sand: a cohesive mixture of sand and clay

Loam: a cohesive mixture of sand, silt, and clay

Shell Mold: a mold consisting of a mixture of sand and resin that hardens when heated prior to the casting

Metal Dies: molds machined to the proper mold shape

The first three types of mold are used once and broken to remove the casting. The dies may be used thousands of times. The first two types are formed around a *pattern* which is usually made of wood. For a shell mold the pattern is made of metal which is heated to solidify the mold material. The size of the pattern in all cases must allow for cooling shrinkage of the casting. Patterns may be reused, whether wood or metal.

The mold material is packed around the pattern, which has been heated in the case of a shell mold. Removal of the pattern leaves a mold of the desired shape. The molds, except a few very simple ones, are made in two parts and placed together for the casting. Sometimes more than two parts are needed and intermediate sections are placed between the upper and lower molds. Cores are inserted to supplement the mold when necessary. A typical mold is shown in Fig. 5-4. Manhole frames and covers, storm water inlet grates,

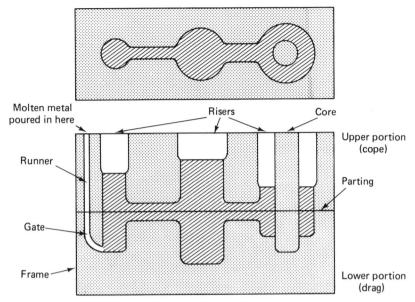

Molten metal poured in here

Runner

Gate

Frame

Risers

Core

Upper portion (cope)

Parting

Lower portion (drag)

Molten metal in the risers fills the mold as cooling contraction takes place.

FIGURE 5-4. Mold and casting

pump casings, fire hydrants, sinks, and bathtubs are made of iron castings.

Iron is also cast in centrifugal molds which are of cylindrical shape with metal or sand linings. They are spun rapidly as the molten iron is poured, forcing the metal to the outside by centrifugal force and causing it to solidify as a hollow cylinder. Iron pipe for water and gas is made this way.

The projections shown in Fig. 5-4 must be broken off and machined smooth. After casting, the metal surface has the roughness of the mold material. Even if die cast, the surface is not smooth because of cooling shrinkage. Certain areas of a casting may be required to fit tightly against another surface. These areas must be machined to a smooth finish. Often castings are made in two parts and bolted together. The contact surfaces are machined for a tight fit, and bolt holes are drilled through the flanges of the two castings. (See Fig. 5-5.)

Gray cast iron, the most widely used type of iron, has a high carbon content and contains large numbers of graphite flakes. The flakes give a gray appearance to a fractured surface. Properties of gray iron include low viscosity when molten (so that fairly intricate castings can be made), excellent machinability, high resistance to abrasion, and rather poor ductility and toughness. ASTM A48, Gray Iron Castings, contains specifications for gray cast iron.

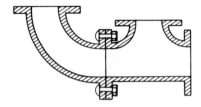

FIGURE 5-5. Cast iron pipe fittings bolted together

White cast iron contains its carbon completely combined with the iron. A fractured surface appears bright white. The advantages of white iron over gray iron are that it is harder and more resistant to wear from abrasion. However, it is more difficult to machine, less resistant to corrosion, more brittle, and more difficult to cast. By controlling chemical composition and cooling rate, castings with cores of gray iron and surfaces of white iron can be made. These are called *chilled iron* castings. White iron is used in machinery such as crushers, grinders, chutes, and mixers where resistance to abrasion is critical.

Cast iron with the carbon reformed from flakes into tiny spheroids by the addition of magnesium to the molten iron is known as *ductile iron*. The basic nature of the iron is not changed, except that tensile strength, ductility, and the ability to withstand shock loads are greatly increased.

Malleable cast iron consists of white iron made tough and ductile by *annealing* which consists of heating to about 1600°F (870°C), holding that temperature for a time, and cooling very slowly to about 1275°F (710°C). This process requires several days. During the entire process, carbon is precipitated from the solution as small lumps in the metal until there is no combined carbon. Some carbon may be allowed to remain combined to increase hardness, strength, and resistance to abrasion. There is then a loss of ductility and toughness. Brittleness is eliminated by removal of carbon from solution, and machinability is improved by the carbon lumps. Malleable iron is used for pipe fittings, guard rail fittings, and other items which require machining and which are subject to shock loads.

Wrought iron is made by refining pig iron in a furnace in a way similar to the refining of steel. The iron silicate slag is melted, and the relatively pure molten iron is poured into the slag. A pasty mixture of the two is formed with the slag evenly distributed as individual particles. The mixture forms a semi-solid ball which is dumped out and pressed into a rectangular block, squeezing the excess slag out in the process. The block is rolled to the desired shape, aligning the slag as strings or ribbons in the direction of rolling. It is then readily shaped further by drawing, bending, or forging, and can be made into thin, intricate shapes. It is easily welded and machined.

The fibrous structure of wrought iron results in a material with different mechanical properties parallel and perpendicular to the fibers or the axis of the grains. Tensile strength is 10 to 15 percent lower across the fibers than parallel to them, and ductility is only about 20 percent as much. Shearing strength across the fibers is much greater than shearing strength along the fibers. A rod, twisted until it fails in torsion, comes apart along the axis, separating between fibers.

Wrought iron has excellent corrosion resistance which is greater on faces that have been rolled than on sheared or machined faces. Wrought iron pipe is used extensively where corrosion resistance is needed. This type of pipe has threaded joints because wrought iron is easily machined. Cast iron pipe joints must be of another kind. Wrought iron is also used extensively for ornamental iron work, as well as for miscellaneous iron work where corrosion resistance, machinability, or ductility and malleability are needed. (See Fig. 5-6.)

FIGURE 5-6. Ornamental wrought iron grille

Steel

Pig iron is further oxidized in another furnace at about 3000°F (1650°C) to produce steel. Most steel is made by the basic oxygen process, electric-arc process, open hearth process, or vacuum process. Each has unique features, but in all cases, pig iron, scrap steel, and sometimes iron ore are melted together with a flux of limestone or lime. The process is a repetition of the blast-furnace operation with variations. The purpose is the same—to remove impurities. Impurities are removed as gases and in the slag.

Phosphorus and sulfur are each reduced to less than 0.05 percent of the steel. Manganese content is reduced to an amount from 0.2 to 2.0 percent; silicon from 0.01 percent to 0.35 percent. The final amounts depend on the specifications for the steel. Carbon is the key element in controlling the properties of ordinary steel called *carbon steel*. Strength and hardness increase with an increase in carbon up to about 1.2 percent. Brittleness increases and ductility decreases as carbon increases. Usually an amount less than 1.2 percent is specified in order to obtain a product satisfactory in all respects.

Carbon in an amount up to 2 percent is completely soluble in molten iron, and when cooled, the mixture forms a solid chemical solution. Carbon in greater amounts forms separate grains of graphite or iron carbide throughout the metal.

Steel is defined as a chemical union of iron and carbon (carbon is, therefore, less than 2 percent by weight) plus other elements. This definition does not exclude every kind of iron. However, almost all iron contains carbon in excess of 2 percent and steel usually contains less than 1.2 percent carbon. Therefore, it is usually obvious whether a ferrous metal is iron or steel. Customary terminology should be used for borderline cases. The term *iron* is used to refer to cast iron, malleable cast iron, ductile iron, wrought iron, or pure iron. As can be seen in Fig. 5-3, some of these metals may have less than 2 percent carbon.

Carbon, manganese, silicon, phosphorus, and sulfur are considered impurities because generally they must all be reduced below the amount found in iron ore. However, each one improves the final product when present in the correct amount. In some cases, due to the characteristics of the iron ore, there is a deficiency of one or more of these elements, and they must be added to the molten steel.

Any added element is considered an *alloying element,* but when only these five elements are involved, the steel is not considered an alloy steel. Other elements may be added to impart certain properties to steel. These are also called alloying elements, and the steel that results is called *alloy steel*. See Fig. 5-7 for the effects of alloying elements.

Steels are identified according to a classification system of the Society of Automotive Engineers (SAE). Each type of steel is designated by a group of numbers. The first digit indicates the class of steel. For example, carbon steel is designated by No. 1 and nickel steel by No. 2. The next one or two digits indicate the approximate percentage of the major alloying element for alloy steels. The last two or three digits indicate the carbon content in hundredths of a percent. The classification system is outlined in Fig. 5-8.

Besides the key information shown directly by the classification number, percentage ranges for all impurities and alloying elements are also designated indirectly when the system is used. The system provides a simplified way to specify steel. For example a 1018 steel is a carbon steel

ELEMENT	AMOUNT	EFFECT
Aluminum	Variable	Promotes small grain size and uniformity of internal grain structure in the as-cast metal or during heat treatment.
Copper	Up to 0.25%	Increases strength and corrosion resistance.
Lead	0.15% to 0.35%	Improves machinability without detrimental effect on mechanical properties.
Chromium	0.50% to 1.50%	In alloy steels, increases responsiveness to heat treatment and hardenability.
	4.0% to 12%	In heat-resisting steels, causes retention of mechanical properties at high temperatures.
	Over 12%	Increases corrosion resistance and hardness.
Nickel	1.0% to 4.0%	In alloy steels, increases strength, toughness, and impact resistance.
	Up to 27.0%	In stainless steels, improves performance at elevated temperatures and prevents work-hardening.
Molybdenum	0.10% to 0.40%	In alloy steels, increases toughness and hardenability.
	Up to 4.0%	In stainless steels, increases corrosion resistance and strength retention at high temperatures.
Tungsten	17% to 20%	In tool steels, promotes hardness at high cutting temperatures; in stainless steels, smaller amounts assure strength retention at high temperatures.
Vanadium	0.15% to 0.20%	Promotes small grain size and uniformity of internal grain structure in the as-cast metal or during heat treatment; improves resistance to thermal fatigue and shock.
Tellurium	Up to 0.05%	Improves machinability when added to leaded steels.
Titanium	Variable	Prevents loss of effective chromium through carbide precipitation in "18-8" stainless steels.
Cobalt	17.0% to 36.0%	Increases magnetic properties of alloy steels. In smaller amounts, promotes strength at high temperatures in heat resisting steels.

FIGURE 5-7. Effects of alloying elements (From "Construction Lending Guide," Courtesy U.S. League of Savings Associations)

containing 0.15 to 0.20 percent carbon, 0.60 to 0.90 percent manganese, 0.040 maximum percent phosphorus, and 0.050 maximum percent sulfur; and 4320 steel is a molybdenum steel containing 0.17 to 0.22 percent carbon, 0.45 to 0.65 percent manganese, 0.040 percent phosphorus, 0.040 percent sulfur, 0.20 to 0.35 percent silicon, 1.65 to 2.00 percent nickel, 0.40 to 0.60 percent chromium, and 0.20 to 0.30 percent molybdenum.

The American Iron and Steel Institute has adopted the SAE system with some variations and has added letter prefixes to designate the steel making process used and other letters to designate special conditions. These designations are shown in Fig. 5-8.

The chemical composition of steel is determined by the composition of the materials used, the temperature, the length of time in the furnace, the medium surrounding the steel (whether air, oxygen, or vacuum), and whether open flame or heat. The surrounding medium depends on the process used, and the other variables can be controlled for each process. The steel is tested

SAE CLASSIFICATION SYSTEM

Carbon steels	1xxx
Plain carbon	10xx
Free-cutting (screw stock)	11xx
Free-cutting, manganese	X13xx*
High-manganese	T13xx**
Nickel steels	2xxx
0.50% nickel	20xx
1.50% nickel	21xx
3.50% nickel	23xx
5.00% nickel	25xx
Nickel–chromium steels	3xxx
1.25% nickel, 0.60% chromium	31xx
1.75% nickel, 1.00% chromium	32xx
3.50% nickel, 1.50% chromium	33xx
3.00% nickel, 0.80% chromium	34xx
Corrosion- and heat-resisting steels	30xxx
Molybdenum steels	4xxx
Chromium	41xx
Chromium–nickel	43xx
Nickel	46xx and 48xx
Chromium steels	5xxx
Low-chromium	51xx
Medium-chromium	52xxx
Chromium–vanadium steels	6xxx
Tungsten steels	7xxx and 7xxxx
Triple alloy steels	8xxx
Silicon–manganese steels	9xxx

* X indicates manganese or sulfur content has been varied from the standard for that number.
** T indicates manganese content has been varied in 1300 range steels.

ADDITIONAL SYMBOLS USED IN AISI SYSTEM

10xx   Basic open hearth and acid Bessemer carbon steel grades, non-sulphurized and nonphosphorized.

11xx   Basic open hearth and acid Bessemer carbon steel grades, sulphurized but not phosphorized.

12xx   Basic open hearth carbon steel grades, phosphorized.

Prefix

B   Acid Bessemer carbon steel.

C   Basic open hearth carbon steel.

CB   Either acid Bessemer or basic open hearth carbon steel at the option of the manufacturer.

D   Acid open hearth carbon steel.

E   Electric furnace alloy steel.

FIGURE 5-8. Classification of steels

at intervals during the process, and adjustments are made. Alloying elements are added just before the melt is tapped to flow from the furnace to a ladle. The steel may be poured directly from the ladle into molds to make castings. Steel castings are made the same way and used for the same purposes as iron castings. Steel is stronger and tougher, but more expensive.

Most of the steel is poured into ingot molds prior to further shaping. The ingots are of various sizes and shapes depending on future plans for them. Their weight ranges from hundreds of pounds to many tons. They are tall compared to their cross sections, which are square or rectangular. A common size is about 6 feet tall with a cross section 2 feet by 2 feet and a weight over 4 tons. An ingot is cooled to a uniform temperature throughout in a *soaking pit* which is a furnace where the steel temperature is allowed to decrease to about 2300°F (1260°C). It is then taken to a mill to be given its final shape.

Steel properties are influenced to a great extent by the mechanical operations that change an ingot of steel into a useful shape. The operations are rolling, extruding, drawing, forging, and casting. All except casting may be performed while the steel is in a plastic condition at a temperature of about 2000°F (1090°C), or as low as room temperature. The operations are called *hot working* or *cold working*.

Hot working breaks up coarse grains and increases density by closing tiny airholes and forcing the grains closer together. Cold working elongates grains in the direction of the steel elongation, increases strength and hardness, and decreases ductility. Cold working results in more accurately finished products because there is no cooling shrinkage to be estimated. The surfaces are smoother because oxide scale does not form as it does during hot working. Overworking, whether hot or cold, causes brittleness.

For all but very large objects, working to final shape is done in two stages. The first stage consists of squeezing the ingot into a smaller cross section between two rollers, called *blooming rolls,* which exert a very high pressure. This operation is always performed while the steel is hot. The ingot is rolled into a much longer piece with a square or rectangular cross section closer to its final size. The desired cross section is obtained by turning the ingot 90° to be rolled on the sides as it is passed back and forth through the rolls. If it is approximately square in cross section, it is called a *bloom* if large (over 36 sq in.), and a *billet* if smaller. It is called a *slab* if the width is twice the thickness or more. The appropriate shape is used to manufacture beams, rails, plate, sheets, wire, pipe, bolts, or other items by one of the following methods.

Rolling consists of compressing and shaping an ingot into a useful shape by squeezing it through a succession of rollers, each succeeding set of rollers squeezing the material smaller in cross section and closer to the final shape. The piece being rolled becomes longer and wider as it is compressed. It may be made narrower by cutting or by rolling after turning 90° so that the rolling

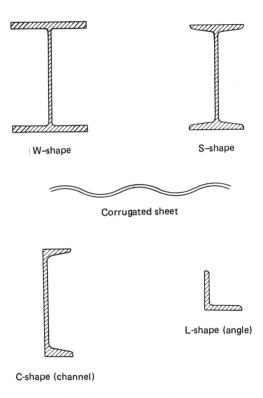

W–shape   S–shape

Corrugated sheet

L-shape (angle)

C-shape (channel)

FIGURE 5-9. Typical rolled sections

reduces the width. A wide variety of cross sections can be rolled in long
pieces by means of specially shaped rollers. (See Fig. 5-9.) Flat sheets can be
rolled by rollers of a constant diameter. Corrugated sheets can be rolled from
flat sheets with corrugated rollers. Corrugated steel roof deck can be seen in
Fig. 5-19. Hot rolling usually precedes cold rolling until the steel is close to its
final shape. Hot rolling is usually the first step in reducing the size of an ingot
prior to extruding, drawing, or forging.

   Extrusion consists of forcing a billet of hot, plastic steel through a die of
the desired shape to produce a continuous length of material of reduced cross
section in the shape of the die. The resulting product has the shape of a rolled
product. That is, it is long with a constant cross section. However, more
intricate shapes can be formed by extrusion than by rolling, and the surface is
of higher quality. An extrusion is made in one operation rather than repetitive
operations as in the case of rolling. An extruded section can sometimes be
used in place of a section that requires several operations if formed any other
way. (See Fig. 5-10.) Extrusions can be made with cross sections having a
maximum dimension of nearly 2 feet.

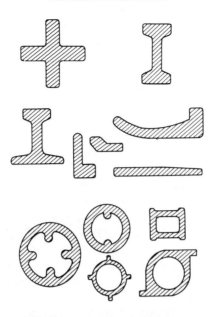

FIGURE 5-10. Typical extruded sections

Drawing consists of pulling steel through a small die to form wire or a small rod of round, square, oval, or other cross section. Steel is hot rolled to form a rod with size not much larger than the shape to be drawn. It is then finished by cold drawing. Seamless steel pipe may also be finished by cold drawing over a round, bullet-shaped mandrel to form a hollow center and through a die to form the outside. The advantages of cold drawing are a smoother finish, more accurate size, more strength, and better machinability.

Forging consists of deforming steel by pressure or blows into a desired shape. The forging may be made from an ingot or from a rolled shape. The steel is usually heated to a semi-solid state at a temperature over 2000°F (1090°C). In some cases it is forged cold. It is forced to fill the shape between dies by pressure or blows of the upper die upon the lower one. The shape may be formed more accurately by successive forgings, each succeeding operation performed with smaller dies closer to the desired final shape. Instead, the final shape may be achieved by machining. Many shapes can be either cast or forged. Economics often determine which method is used. However, forging is preferred if strength of the part is important. Forging improves the mechanical properties of the metal, as does other hot working or cold working, and produces a stronger, more ductile, more uniform product with smaller grain size than is produced by casting.

After steel cools and is given its final shape, further heating and cooling processes can change the internal structure and thereby impart certain properties. Heat treatment consists of heating, holding the metal at the high temperature, and cooling. Even here the rate of heating is not important except for high carbon alloyed steels. The metal is held at the upper temperature so that it can be heated to a uniform temperature throughout. The rate of cooling is very important.

Normalizing consists of heating the steel to a temperature of about 1500°F (815°C) or higher, depending on the type of metal, and cooling several hundred degrees slowly in air. This process increases uniformity of structure.

Annealing consists of heating the steel to a temperature slightly lower than for normalizing and cooling it several hundred degrees very slowly, usually in a furnace. Methods vary somewhat depending on the purpose, which may be to soften the metal, produce special structure, facilitate machining, facilitate cold shaping, or reduce stresses.

Quenching consists of cooling steel very rapidly in oil, water, or brine from a temperature of about 1500°F (815°C). Quenching increases hardness and strength, but reduces ductility and toughness. Residual stresses are introduced by quenching and should be relieved by tempering.

Tempering consists of reheating the quenched steel to a temperature of 300 to 1200°F (150 to 650°C) and cooling in air to reduce the residual stresses and increase ductility. Heating to the lower temperature range produces greater hardness, strength, and wear resistance, while higher heat produces greater toughness.

STRUCTURAL STEEL

Figure 5-11 shows a typical structural steel frame building under construction. Plain carbon steel is commonly used for structural purposes and has performed satisfactorily for many years. The type of carbon steel most commonly used for structural purposes is described in ASTM A36 and is known as A36 steel. It has high strength, high ductility, and great stiffness, and is highly resistant to wear or abrasion. It also rusts very readily and loses its strength and stiffness at high temperatures. Structural carbon steel is low in carbon, usually below 0.3 percent. Carbon steel is made according to the requirements of ASTM Specification A36, or in a stronger type with 142,000-psi-minimum yield point strength according to ASTM Specification A529. This steel is known as A529 steel.

Rusting is oxidation or combining of the iron with oxygen which occurs in the presence of moisture. It proceeds more rapidly where there is noticeable dampness, but it occurs in any air with a relative humidity higher than 70 percent. It progresses more rapidly in salt air and in an industrial atmosphere. The thickness of metal lost by rusting is ½ mil (a mil is 0.001 in.) or less per year in average conditions. It may be much higher in the presence of industrial air pollution. The rust is formed from the solid metal, reducing its size so that

FIGURE 5-11. Steel frame building under construction

the member becomes weaker and loses any decorative finish it might have. The rust penetrates deeper as time goes on. A coating over the steel prevents rust. However, this coating is expensive and must be replaced periodically at additional cost. Carbon steel may be made more rust resistant by the addition of copper as an alloying element.

Ordinary steel cannot be used where it is exposed to high temperatures. At a very high temperature it melts to the liquid state, and it begins the process of liquifying at moderately high temperatures. Steel weakens at 800–900°F (430–480°C) and cannot support any load at 1200°F (650°C). Steel may be used economically for structural support of industrial furnaces, incinerators, and other heat-producing devices, but it must be insulated from the heat.

Structural steel that is ordinarily subjected to normal temperatures may be subjected to great heat during an accidental fire. The steel will then melt or at least become soft from the heat unless protected by insulation. Usually the steel is encased in concrete to insulate it.

A fire must always be considered a possibility. However, if the possibility is remote and the cost of insulating is high compared to the cost of failure from heat, it may be decided to leave the steel unprotected. A steel highway bridge, for example, is protected from the burning of an automobile by the concrete pavement; and the possibility of a damaging fire under the bridge is usually very slight. Adding the weight of a heat-protective covering over all the steel would greatly increase the required bridge size and cost. Therefore, the steel is not insulated for fire protection.

Special steels are available with much higher mechanical properties, much greater resistance to rust, or greater heat resistance than plain carbon steels.

Alloying elements added to steel can impart properties impossible to impart by heating and cooling or by working. (See Fig. 5-7.) An important reason for adding alloys is to improve mechanical properties. High-strength, low-alloy steels contain alloying elements that improve mechanical properties and resistance to rust. The total amount of alloying elements added is 2 or 3 percent. Specifications for these steels require that they meet certain performance standards rather than certain chemical formulas. Each supplier has his own method of producing a product that meets the standards.

Each steel is known by the number of its ASTM designation, although the manufacturer may also call it by a trade name. The types used for structural members are shown in Fig. 5-12. The high strength steel A440 has four times as much resistance to rust as carbon steel, but it cannot be successfully welded. Of the high-strength, low-alloy steels, A441 has twice the rust resistance of carbon steels, and A242 and A588 are so resistant to rust that they are used with no protective coating in all but the most corrosive environments. A588 steel is available with greater strength in the larger sizes and thicknesses.

Both types of steel form a thin, rust-colored, protective coating of iron oxide which eventually becomes blue-gray and which prevents any further corrosion. Two or three years are required for the coating to form completely. The coating does not protect against corrosion from concentrated corrosive industrial fumes, from wetting with salt water, or from being submerged in water or buried in the ground. Steel of these types is called *weathering steel.* During the early stages of weathering, rain water dripping from the steel carries corroded materials which stains concrete, brick, and other light-colored, porous materials.

The protection of ordinary steel in a moderately corrosive atmosphere requires thorough cleansing of the steel followed by the application of three coats of various types of oil base paint with a total thickness of 4 mils (0.004 in.). The prevention of rust can be made easier by careful design to avoid pockets or crevices that hold water, spots that are inaccessible for repainting, and sharp edges that are difficult to coat with the required thickness of paint.

Another type of protection commonly used is *galvanizing,* or coating with zinc or with zinc-pigmental paints. Zinc adheres readily to iron or steel to

METAL	SPECIFIC GRAVITY	COEFFICIENT OF THERMAL EXPANSION[1] (in/in/°F)	MODULUS OF ELASTICITY (psi)	YIELD POINT[2,3,5] (psi)	ULTIMATE STRENGTH[3,4,5] (psi)	DUCTILITY (ELONGATION IN 2")[4,5]
Irons						
Gray cast iron	7.2	5.9×10^{-6}	15×10^6	22,000	30,000	(not ductile)
Malleable cast iron	7.4	6.6×10^{-6}	25×10^6	30,000	54,000	18%
Wrought iron	7.8	6.7×10^{-6}	27×10^6	27,000	48,000	25%
Carbon steels						
ASTM A373				32,000	58,000 to 75,000	24%
ASTM A7	7.85	6.5×10^{-6}	29×10^6	33,000	60,000 to 72,000	24%
ASTM A36				36,000	58,000 to 80,000	23%
High-strength steels						
ASTM A440	7.85	6.5×10^{-6}	29×10^6	42,000 to 50,000	63,000 to 70,000	24%
ASTM A441						
ASTM A242						
Stainless steels						
AISI 410 (martensitic)	7.75	5.5×10^{-6}	29×10^6	45,000	70,000	25%
AISI 430 (ferritic)	7.75	5.8×10^{-6}	29×10^6	50,000	75,000	25%
AISI 302 (austenitic)	8.0	9.6×10^{-6}	28×10^6	40,000	90,000	50%

[1] Within temperature range of 32 to 212°F for stainless steels.
[2] Yield strength or yield point is measure of usable strength (i.e., maximum stress which produces deformation without increase in load).
[3] These mechanical properties of ASTM steels are specified minimums which vary according to shape and thickness of the material.
[4] Ultimate strength is measure of total reserve strength (i.e., maximum stress which produces rupture in a test specimen).
[5] Values given for stainless steels are for annealed sheet and strip only. Higher strength values are common for products and alloys hardened by cold working or heat treating.

FIGURE 5-12. Selected physical and mechanical properties of representative iron and steel types (From "Construction Lending Guide," Courtesy U.S. League of Savings Associations)

form a tight seal against the atmosphere. It prolongs the life of iron and steel because it corrodes much more slowly than they do. Zinc continues to protect the iron or steel even after it has been eaten through in spots because corrosion will take place in the zinc in preference to the ferrous metal. The zinc coating has a shiny, silvery appearance which is not suitable for all uses.

Bituminous coatings are used to protect iron and steel from the effects of atmosphere, water, or soil. The usefulness of bitumens as protective coatings is discussed in Chapter 3. The appearance and odor of bitumens make them unsuitable for many applications.

Judging by the high strengths of the alloy steels of Fig. 5-12, one might wonder why carbon steel is still used. Carbon steel is so much cheaper by the pound that a member made of it may be cheaper than a smaller member of the same strength made of stronger, more expensive steel. In addition to this, the size of many members is dictated by considerations other than strength, and they cannot be smaller, no matter how strong the material is. In these cases, the least expensive material is used unless corrosion resistance or heat resistance is of great importance.

Stainless steels, which are known as high alloy steels, have chromium and nickel as their chief alloying elements. They contain 12 to 20 percent chromium and may contain up to 10 percent nickel. They have high resistance to corrosion, retaining a bright, shiny surface indefinitely. They are used where appearance or sanitation is important, as in kitchens, laboratories, and exterior building trim. They are also used for mechanisms in wet or corrosive atmospheres, such as rockers and rocker plates for bridges, water valves and gates, and smokestack controls. Corrosion resistance is due to the forming of a thin, transparent coating of chromium oxide over the surface. Stainless steel may be made harder at a sacrifice of some of the corrosion resistance.

Stainless steels are available with various characteristics, such as good corrosion resistance at high temperatures, no magnetic property, good weldability, and a low coefficient of thermal expansion. The tendency toward galvanic corrosion when in contact with other metals and a higher than normal coefficient of thermal expansion for some kinds of stainless steel can lead to trouble unless precautions are taken in design.

Heat-resisting steel contains chromium in quantities of less than 12 percent as the primary alloying element. This steel does not lose a significant amount of strength at temperatures up to 1100°F (590°C). It can be hardened by heat treatment.

Steel is produced in mills to standard shapes: plate of standard thicknesses, pipe, tubing, plain rods, deformed rods and wire of standard diameters, and various rolled shapes of standard dimensions. These products are listed in Fig. 5-13. Designers ordinarily select standard shapes that best suit their purposes and adapt their designs to conform to what is available. In some cases they modify standard shapes to conform to their design requirements. Some examples of modified standard shapes are Tee shapes cut from W or S

Designation	Type of Shape
W 24 × 76	W shape
W 14 × 26	
S 24 × 100	S shape
M 8 × 18.5	M shape
M 10 × 9	
M 8 × 34.3	
C 12 × 20.7	American standard channel
MC 12 × 45	Miscellaneous channel
MC 12 × 10.6	
HP 14 × 73	HP shape
L 6 × 6 × ¾	Equal leg angle
L 6 × 4 × ⅝	Unequal leg angle
WT 12 × 38	Structural Tee cut from W shape
WT 7 × 13	
ST 12 × 50	Structural Tee cut from S shape
MT 4 × 9.25	Structural Tee cut from M shape
MT 5 × 4.5	
MT 4 × 17.15	
PL ½ × 18	Plate
Bar 1 ⯐	Square bar
Bar 1¼ ϕ	Round bar
Bar 2½ × ½	Flat bar
Pipe 4 Std.	Pipe
Pipe 4 X—Strong	
Pipe 4 XX—Strong	
TS 4 × 4 × 0.375	Structural tubing: square
TS 5 × 3 × 0.375	Structural tubing: rectangular
TS 3 OD × 0.250	Structural tubing: circular

FIGURE 5-13. Designations of rolled steel shapes

shapes, L's cut from C shapes, and tapered members fabricated from various shapes.

Steel produced in a mill is not sent directly to a construction project. It goes next to a fabricating shop where the final operations of the manufacturing process take place. Detail drawings that show exactly how separate parts fit together to form a structure are used to determine the finished lengths and any variations in shape needed to facilitate the assembly of the parts at the jobsite. These variations are fabricated in the shop as much as possible to make field work simpler.

The operations performed in the fabricating shop include cutting or shearing to the correct length. Steel is cut with an oxygen torch machine or sheared with a mechanical cutting device with a large blade that drops onto the steel to shear it to the correct length. When smoother ends are needed, the cut or sheared surfaces are finished by planing or grinding to a smooth surface. Holes for rivets or bolts are drilled through thick sections and punched through thinner ones. Holes may also be punched and reamed smooth. If connections are to be made by welding, the work is partially done in the fabricating shop. As a general rule, the less riveting, bolting, or welding left for the field, the more efficient the entire operation is. Examples of fabrication are shown in Fig. 5-14.

Open web steel joists are fabricated of angles and rods and are stocked in standard lengths grouped according to the roof load or floor load they are able to support. They are Warren trusses with a top chord fabricated to support a roof deck or floor. They are designed to be spaced close together and are available in lengths from 4 feet to 96 feet. See Fig. 5-14. Open web steel joists can be seen in Fig. 5-19.

Steel, especially the more complicated shapes, may cool unevenly while being rolled. The final cooling then causes a variation in the amount of shrinkage of various areas, which results in curved or twisted members. These must be straightened to specified tolerances in the fabricating shop.

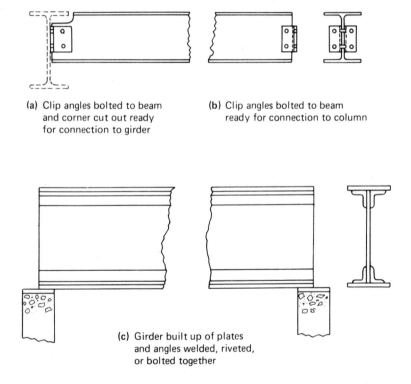

(a) Clip angles bolted to beam
and corner cut out ready
for connection to girder

(b) Clip angles bolted to beam
ready for connection to column

(c) Girder built up of plates
and angles welded, riveted,
or bolted together

FIGURE 5-14. Examples of fabricated steel

Straightening is done by forcing the member back into a straight alignment with or without softening the steel with heat. Steel is normally cleaned and painted with one coat of paint in the shop. This is considered sufficient protection from rust until the steel is installed and given a finish painting.

STRUCTURAL CONNECTIONS

Steel members must be connected to form a structure. They may be connected by riveting, welding, or bolting. A connection is not designed on a rational basis as the structural members are. Stresses at connections are so complex that the connections are designed according to empirical methods based on successful experience. A connection includes a group of rivets or bolts or a predetermined length of weld.

Riveting

Riveting was once the most common method of making connections. It is now used only for shop connections and seldom used even there. Holes are punched or drilled through the members to be connected, and a steel rivet (shown in Fig. 5-15) slightly smaller than the holes is heated to a cherry red color (1000°–1950°F) and inserted through the holes. The head is braced and the shank end is hammered until it flattens to a head, compressing the members between the two rivet heads, as shown in Fig. 5-15. Cooling of the rivet causes the rivet to shorten, compressing the members still further.

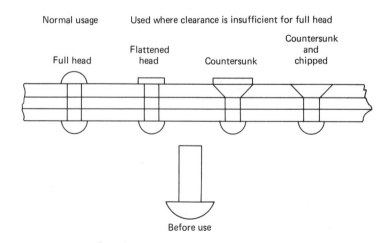

FIGURE 5-15. Rivets

Welding

A welded connection is neat in appearance and the metal of a weld is stronger than the metal being connected. Weld metal is manufactured to more demanding specifications than structural steel and is protected from the atmosphere while cooling. The weld metal also benefits somewhat by combining with constituents of the welding rod coating. The result is a steel with better crystalline structure and higher mechanical properties.

Chemical and mechanical properties of weld metal must be matched to the metal being welded. Therefore, a wide variety of welding electrodes is available. The American Welding Society and ASTM have established a numbering system for electrodes. All designations begin with the letter E, which is followed by a four- or five-digit number. The first two or three digits indicate the minimum tensile strength in kips per square inch. The next digit indicates the recommended welding positions. Digit 3 is for flat only; 2 is for flat and horizontal, and 1 is for all positions including also vertical and overhead. The next digit indicates current supply and recommended welding techniques. The four welding positions are shown in Fig. 5-16.

Welding consists of heating the two pieces to be joined until they melt enough to fuse. The heat comes from an electric arc that is formed between a welding rod and the two pieces to be welded. A portable electric generator is connected to the structural steel and to the welding rod, and either an alternating or direct current is passed through the rod and the structural members when the rod touches or nearly touches the members. The tip of the rod and some depth of the base metal called *penetration* are melted. The two metals combine and harden upon cooling. The liquid metal rapidly absorbs oxygen and nitrogen, which causes it to be brittle and lose its resistance to corrosion unless it is protected from the atmosphere.

Four welding methods are allowed by the American Institute of Steel Construction for structural work. In the *shielded metal-arc method*, the metal

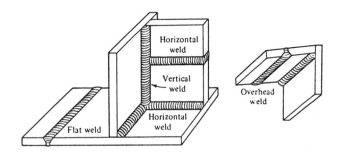

FIGURE 5-16. The four welding positions (Courtesy U.S. Department of the Interior, Bureau of Reclamation)

welding rod is coated with a *flux,* which melts as the weld metal melts and covers the molten metal, shielding it from the atmosphere. The flux is partially converted to gas, which surrounds the working area, helping to protect the weld from oxygen and nitrogen. Shielded metal-arc welding is a manual method suited for field use. The three other methods discussed here are suitable for semi-automatic or automatic use.

In the *submerged-arc method,* powdered flux is automatically spread ahead of the electrode and completely covers the welding arc and also protects the new weld metal.

In *gas metal-arc welding,* a coil of electrode wire is constantly fed to a holder as the electrode melts. The new weld metal is protected from the air by CO_2 or other gas constantly fed to the location as the welding proceeds.

In *flux-cored arc welding,* the welding rod consists of a core of flux surrounded by weld metal. This is used to facilitate continuous feeding of the electrode as welding takes place.

The fillet weld is the most frequently used type. Other types commonly used are the butt or groove weld and the plug or slot weld. All are shown in Fig. 5-17. The *fillet weld* is triangular in cross section and is placed at a right angle joint formed by the pieces to be connected.

For a *butt* or *groove weld,* the ends to be connected are butted together and welded. The abutting edges may be smooth, flat surfaces, or they may be shaped to form a groove. Grooves of several shapes are used. Flat edges and the two most common grooves are shown in Fig. 5-17. Most butt welding is done to join plates edge to edge. Butt welding requires that the pieces to be

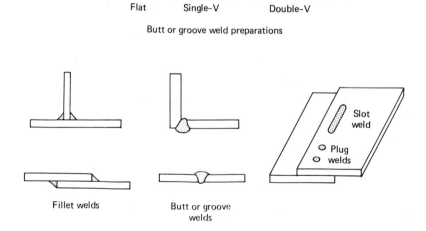

Butt or groove weld preparations

FIGURE 5-17. Weld types

welded be cut precisely to size or they will not meet properly. This expensive, precise cutting is avoided if the pieces are lapped and welded with fillet welds. This economy accounts for the greater popularity of fillet welds even though butt welds are stronger.

A *plug* or *slot weld* consists of filling with weld metal a circular or oblong hole in one piece, which is positioned on top of the piece to which it is to be connected. This type of weld is useful for joining pieces that must act together over an area too large to be satisfactorily connected at the edges, such as elements of the flange of a plate girder. They are also used on plate joints that are overlapped to avoid overhead welding in the field. Fillet welds may be used inside the plugged or slotted holes.

Bolts

A *bolt* is manufactured with a head at one end and threads at the other end to which a nut can be threaded. Washers may be used. They fit loosely on the shank of the bolt at either or both ends and increase the area that bears on the member when the nut is tightened. When the bolt is in position to hold two members together, a tightening of the nut pulls the bolt with a tensile force and presses inward on the two members, causing friction between them to resist movement. (See Fig. 5-18.)

A bolted joint is subject to two types of loading from the structure. Tension tends to pull the plates apart in a line parallel with the bolt axis, and shear tends to make the plates slip against the friction between their surfaces in a direction perpendicular to the bolt axis. The friction available to resist shear is proportional to the bolt tension. Movement perpendicular to the bolt axis cannot occur until the friction between the members is overcome. If the friction is overcome, there is slight movement, and both members bear on the bolt. A bearing connection is satisfactory, provided slight movement is permissible and the load is static. If the joint is subject to load changes, stress reversal, impact, or vibration, a bearing connection is unsatisfactory, because it may loosen. The joint must then be designed so that sufficient friction is developed between the members to resist any load perpendicular to the bolt axis and so that the load parallel with the bolt is not sufficient to stretch it and thereby reduce that friction.

Like rivets, common bolts have an uncertain tension, and therefore the friction caused between members cannot be accurately determined. Nevertheless, common bolts and rivets have been and still are used successfully. In many connections where little strength is required and there are no vibrations, impact loads, or stress cycles, common bolts should be used because they are less expensive and easier to install than high-strength bolts. However, common bolts are much weaker than high-strength bolts; they loosen under vibration, impact loads, or cyclic loads, especially if there is stress reversal.

The load (T) is resisted by the bolt in tension. The
load (S) is resisted by friction between the two
members. The friction is caused by compression of
the members between the bolt head and the nut.

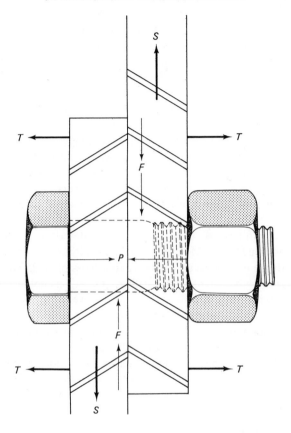

FIGURE 5-18. Principie of high strength bolting

High-strength Bolts

High-strength steel bolts can be installed to produce a predetermined tension
greater than that of a common bolt. Because of the great friction developed
between members, there is very little movement between them when loads are
applied to the members. High-strength bolts are several times as strong in
tension as common bolts. They are the most recently developed fastening
device, but have become the most popular by far, especially for field connections.

Each nut in a group of high-strength bolts must be tightened until bolt tension is equal to or greater than that specified for the bolt size by the American Institute of Steel Construction. Two methods of obtaining the required bolt tension are approved.

Tightening may be done with a calibrated wrench. In this case at least three bolts of those to be used on that job are tightened in a calibrating device that indicates the tension in each bolt. The wrench is set to stall at whatever load produces the correct tension. Each bolt is then turned until the wrench stalls.

The turn-of-nut method depends on the fact that tightening of the nut elongates the bolt and induces tension in the bolt, and therefore friction between the members, in proportion to the bolt elongation. All nuts are first tightened as tight as they can be by one man using an ordinary spud wrench. Any turning of the nut beyond this original tightening draws one end of the bolt into the nut, thereby stretching the bolt. All nuts are then rotated the prescribed additional part of a turn (½ to ¾) to obtain correct elongation and tension.

High-strength bolts are of two types: A325, described in ASTM-A325, and A490, described in ASTM-A490. The A325 bolts are of carbon steel, and the A490 bolts are of alloy steel. There are four types of A325 bolts: medium carbon steel, low carbon martensite, weathering steel, and hot dip galvanized. There are two types of A490 bolts: alloy steel and weathering steel. An A325 bolt has the strength of one and one-half rivets of the same size, and an A490 bolt has the strength of one and one-half A325 bolts of the same size. Figure 5-19 shows a typical connection made with high-strength bolts. Clip angles were shop welded to the beams, and the angles were bolted to the column in the field. Also shown are open web steel joists and corrugated sheet steel roof decking.

REINFORCING STEEL

Steel is used as the reinforcing in combination with portland cement concrete for reinforced concrete structural members. Members are constructed so that steel resists all tension and compression is resisted by concrete or by concrete and steel together. Reinforcing steel is shown tied in place for a concrete column in Fig. 5-20. Rods are bent outward to join those of the beams that will be supported by the column.

Reinforcing bars are made either plain or deformed. Figure 5-21 shows a deformed rebar. Deformed bars create a better bond between concrete and steel. They are designated by the number of eighths of an inch in their diameter and are available in sizes from number 2, or ¼ in. diameter, to number 18, or 2¼ in. diameter. A table of rebar sizes and weights is in Chapter 4.

FIGURE 5-19. Steel framing with bolted column to beam connection

FIGURE 5-20. Reinforcing steel for a reinforced concrete column

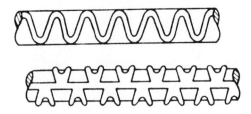

FIGURE 5-21. Deformed reinforcing bars (Courtesy U.S. Department of
the Interior, Bureau of Reclamation)

Rebars are made from Bessemer or open-hearth carbon steel with 0.40
percent to 0.70 percent carbon; from scrap carbon steel axles of railroad cars;
and from standard section T rails. The bars are hot rolled and furnished in the
grades shown in Fig. 5-22.

Grade	Ultimate Tensile Strength (psi)	Yield Point (psi)
structural	55,000–75,000	35,000 min.
intermediate	70,000–90,000	40,000
hard	80,000 min.	50,000

FIGURE 5-22. Reinforcing bar grades

FERROUS METAL PIPE

Both gray cast iron and ductile iron have been used extensively for pipe
installed underground. Ductile iron has all but replaced cast iron for this
purpose because of its greater ability to withstand the stresses of handling and
underground installation. It is used to carry liquids or gas under pressure and
also to carry nonpressure flows of liquid. Water, sewage, and natural gas are
frequently transported through iron pipe.

Pipe is cast in a cylindrical water-cooled steel mold, with or without
resin lining, and with no core. The mold is nearly horizontal but is inclined
slightly so that liquid metal flows toward one end. At the other end, molten
metal is poured into a trough that is suspended inside the mold and extends
to the opposite, lower end. As the molten iron flows out the lower end of
the trough into the mold, the mold spins rapidly, forming a uniform layer
on the inside surface of the mold. The mold is withdrawn horizontally from the
trough at a rate matched to the rate of flow so that the desired pipe wall
thickness is obtained.

FIGURE 5-23. Corrugated steel pipe construction (Courtesy of Republic
Steel Manufacturing Group)

Unequal settling and shifting of the earth may subject buried pipes to
tensile stresses under beam or arch loading conditions. See Fig. 5-23. Handling pipe between the manufacturing plant and the jobsite often causes impact or shock loads due to bumping and jarring the pipe. The ability of ductile
iron to withstand these stresses is very high compared to its cost.

Corrosion resistance is important for any material to be buried underground. Ductile iron and gray cast iron are much more resistant to corrosion
than steel, though not as resistant as clay and plastics that are also used for
pipes. The two are about equal in corrosion resistance, with ductile iron
possibly a little more resistant. It is, nevertheless, standard manufacturing
procedure to coat the outside of both types of pipe with a one-mil (one
thousandth of an inch)-thick coat of bituminous material.

A loose tube of polyethylene has proven to be an effective deterrent to
all types of corrosion in gray cast iron or ductile iron pipe. The tube is inserted
over the pipe at the time of installation. The covering need not be watertight,
although contact between soil and pipe must be prevented. Groundwater that
seeps between the polyethylene sheet and the pipe surface does not cause a
measurable amount of corrosion. Sheets of polyethylene may be wrapped
around the pipe and secured with tape. However, use of the tubes is usually

more economical. Standards for protection with loose polyethylene encasement are contained in American Water Works Association Standard C105.

Steel pipe is also used as an underground conduit for liquids and gases under pressure. Narrow, rolled sheets of steel are wound spirally and are butt welded at the spiral joint to form a tube. Steel pipe is also fabricated with one straight longitudinal joint butt welded. Steel has greater tensile strength, toughness, and ductility than ductile iron, but is not as resistant to corrosion as gray cast iron or ductile iron. However, all these characteristics in a pipeline depend on wall thickness, bedding and backfill conditions, and corrosion protection. All must be properly designed to suit the installation conditions.

That is, the pipe wall must be thick enough not to be overstressed by the external load or the internal pressure of the liquid or gas; the soil must be arranged under, around, and over the pipe so that it does not concentrate forces on the pipe; and the material must be protected from external and internal corrosion.

Steel pipe is protected from external corrosion by a coating of coal tar enamel. The coal tar enamel is protected from scratches or abrasion by tough paper or fabric wrapped tightly around the enamel.

Coal tar is also used as a lining for iron and steel pipe. However, cement–mortar made of portland cement and sand is much more popular for coating pipe interiors. A lining is necessary to protect the ferrous metal from being corroded by some of the many substances that are transported through pipes.

Many natural waters contain dissolved iron on which iron bacteria feed and multiply, forming solid deposits on iron or steel pipe walls. These deposits, called *tubercles,* look somewhat like rust and grow nearly large enough to fill the pipe so that flow is inadequate. *Tuberculation* does not take place if the metal is protected from contact with the water. Most water and sewer pipe is cement–mortar lined to prevent tuberculation and corrosion.

A tube full of mortar is inserted into a rapidly spinning horizontal length of pipe, and the mortar is dumped uniformly along the pipe length. The pipe continues to spin, compacting the mortar to a uniform thickness by centrifugal force. The finished thickness is 3/16 in. or thinner, depending on the pipe size.

The mortar may instead be discharged from the end of the tube and spread with a trowel attached to the tube as the pipe spins; the tube is withdrawn at a rate matched to the rate of discharge of mortar so that the desired thickness of mortar is applied. Centrifugal force and vibration combine to form a dense lining of uniform thickness with the entrapped air and excess water driven out.

A wide variety of materials can be used to line iron and steel pipe when special protection is needed. Polypropylene, polyethylene, and glass linings are among those available.

FIGURE 5-24. Open web steel joists on a steel frame (Photo: G. Lim-brunner)

Steel, usually a copper or other rust-resisting alloy, is also used for corrugated pipe up to 10 ft in diameter for storm drains, sanitary sewers, and other nonpressure flows. This pipe is made of thin metal sheets (from 0.05 in. to 0.17 in. thick) which have been corrugated between rollers. They are made of rectangles curved to circular shape and riveted together or of long, narrow strips wound spirally and joined with one long spiral lock seam. (See Fig. 5-24.)

The strength of corrugated steel pipe comes partly from the deep section given to it by the corrugations. The corrugations cause the pipe to be much stronger than a noncorrugated pipe of the same wall thickness. However, most of its strength is due to the fact that it is flexible. The thin metal deflects extensively under load before it breaks. To achieve its potential strength, it must be confined all around by soil. A heavy weight on flexible, corrugated pipe flattens the top and bottom and bulges the sides outward unless they are restrained. A properly constructed pipeline is surrounded by solidly tamped soil so that the sides cannot bulge and, therefore, the top cannot deflect.

Nonflexible pipe cracks before it deflects noticeably, and therefore soil pressure from the sides causes very little increase in its resistance to loading.

Corrugated steel pipe is protected from corrosion by galvanizing as a standard procedure for ordinary usage. It is coated inside and out by dipping in hot asphalt in addition to the galvanizing for protection from corrosive soil or corrosive water. Asbestos fibers may be used to join the zinc and asphalt, thereby improving the bond between them.

The interior may be paved with asphalt thick enough to cover the corrugations with a smooth surface to decrease resistance to flow and to protect the inside of the pipe from corrosion or erosion by solid particles carried in the liquid. The paving may cover the entire circumference or just the lower part, depending on where flow improvement and protection are needed.

Elliptical cross sections and cross sections approximating a circle with the bottom flattened are popular for special uses and are easily fabricated of corrugated steel. Very large sizes of all the cross sections are shipped as curved plates completely fabricated for erection by bolting the plates together at the jobsite.

Review Questions

1. What two treatments determine the internal structure of ferrous metals?
2. Describe the raw materials and the product of a blast furnace.
3. What conditions of use would require a chilled iron casting?
4. What is the difference between steel and iron, chemically and in physical properties?
5. How is steel improved by cold-working?
6. What are the advantages of extrusion compared to rolling?
7. How does forging improve steel compared to casting?
8. What improvements can be made in steel by heat treatment?
9. How does steel fail in a fire?
10. In what environments does weathering steel need protection from corrosion?
11. What is the chief characteristic of stainless steel?
12. Sketch the three most common types of weld.
13. Describe the two methods of installing high-strength bolts.

6

Wood

Wood has universal appeal. It is generally pleasant in appearance, no matter how it is cut or finished. Certain types can be extremely beautiful if properly cut and finished.

Most wood has a pleasant odor for a long time after it is removed from the forest. Because of its poor heat conducting properties, wood does not remove heat from the hand and so feels warm to the touch. Metals, plastics, stone, and concrete conduct heat rapidly from the hand whenever they are lower in temperature than the human body. Because normal room temperature is lower than body temperature, these materials feel unpleasantly cold to the touch when compared to wood.

Wood is an excellent material for doors, door and window frames, flooring, trim, and other items where appearance is of primary importance. Wood is used extensively in dwellings where feelings of comfort and well being are especially desired. Some uses of wood are shown in Fig. 6-1.

GROWTH OF TREES

Trees are either *deciduous,* having broad leaves and usually shedding them in the fall, or *coniferous,* having needles and cones containing seeds. In the wood industry the deciduous trees are called *hardwoods* and the conifers are called *softwoods*. Hardwoods are generally harder than softwoods, but this is not true of all species. As examples, douglas fir and southern pine are harder than some hardwoods, and basswood and poplar are softer than many softwoods.

The way a tree grows explains much about the characteristics of lumber. (See Fig. 6-2.) Wood consists of long, narrow, hollow cells called *fibers*. New fibers grow at the outside of the tree, increasing the diameter layer by layer. The thin, growing layer is called the *cambium layer*. The *sapwood* is within the cambium layer, and its fibers are active in the life processes of the tree, but they do not grow. The *heartwood* at the center of the tree consists of dead fibers. Heartwood and sapwood do not differ in mechanical properties. However, heartwood is a darker shade because of the resins, gums, and

(a)

(b)

(c)

FIGURE 6-1. Uses of wood: (A) flooring (Courtesy Memphis Hardwood Flooring Co.); (B) chapel ceiling (Courtesy American Institute of Timber Construction); (C) railroad bridge (Courtesy American Institute of Timber Construction)

236

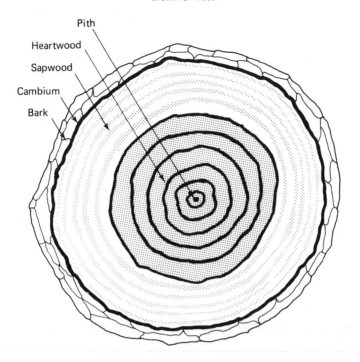

FIGURE 6-2. Cross section of tree

minerals it contains. At the center is a thin vein ot soft tissue called *pith* extending the length of the tree and having no strength. Outside the cambium layer is the *bark* which protects the growing cells from insects, but is useless as a structural material.

The fibers of all wood species consist of a structurally sound material called *cellulose* (approximately 70 percent of the volume) cemented with *lignin* (approximately 25 percent), plus miscellaneous substances that are of less importance. Paper is made of the cellulose from wood.

Forming of new fibers and growth of fibers proceed rapidly in the spring and early summer, forming large, thin-walled fibers with a small percentage of wall material in their cross section. In the summer and autumn, growth is slower with a greater percentage of fiber wall material. In cold weather, there is no growth. Springwood and summerwood form alternating concentric bands around the tree. This circular pattern is easily seen when the tree is sawed transversely. Summerwood is heavier, darker, harder, and stronger than springwood.

The age of the tree can be determined by the number of rings. Something about the weather during the tree's lifetime can be told by the width of the individual rings of springwood and summerwood. They indicate whether or not conditions were favorable for growth. The strength of a piece of wood can be judged by the percentage of summerwood compared to springwood showing in cross section. The strength can also be judged by the unit weight or specific gravity. A higher proportion of summerwood results in greater strength and greater weight.

Some fibers grow transversely, forming radial lines from the center. These lines are called *rays* and are useful in the life processes of the tree. They do not affect strength, but they do have an influence on the appearance of finished lumber.

The hollow fiber structure of wood makes it an excellent insulator against the passage of heat and sound. Generally, wood is not used primarily as an insulator, but the insulation is an added benefit when wood is selected for the siding or roofing of a building. However, fiber boards intended primarily as insulation are manufactured of pressed wood chips and sawdust.

The solid matter in wood is heavier than water. Wood floats because it consists of hollow fibers containing air that cause its overall unit weight to be less than that of water. Wood with the fibers saturated with water is heavier than water and will sink in it.

The hollow fibers are easily crushed or pulled apart in a transverse direction. They have a great deal more strength longitudinally because fiber walls make up a greater percentage of the cross section in this direction than in a transverse direction. Figure 6–3 shows how there is more cell wall material to resist stresses along the axis of a tree or the axis of a piece of wood sawed from a tree. Notice how lateral forces can collapse the long, narrow fibers without crushing any fiber walls. This is not true in the longitudinal direction where the resisting walls are too long and close together.

If stress is applied in any direction between longitudinal and transverse, the resisting strength varies from maximum in the longitudinal direction to minimum in the transverse direction.

The coefficient of thermal expansion of wood varies from 0.000001 to 0.000003 per °F (0.0000005 to 0.000002 per °C) parallel to the grain, and from 0.000015 to 0.000035 per °F (0.000008 to 0.000019 per °C) perpendicular to the grain. It varies with the species and is seldom important because expansion and contraction due to moisture changes are greater unless the humidity is nearly constant and the temperature varies greatly.

The hollow cells of a tree contain water both within the hollow space and within the cell walls. The total weight of water often exceeds the weight of solid material. Moisture evaporates from the wood after the tree is dead until an equilibrium moisture is reached that depends on air temperature and humidity. The *free water* in the hollow space evaporates first with no change in the volume of the wood. When the free water is gone, *absorbed water*

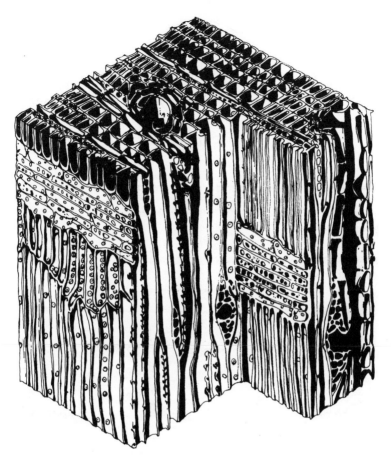

FIGURE 6-3. Wood cells (Courtesy U.S. Forest Products Laboratory)

evaporates from the cell walls causing shrinkage of the wood. This shrinkage is the cause of cracks in the wood called *checks*.

When wood is sawed parallel to the length of the tree, the light and dark annual rings appear as stripes called *grain*. The width of the grain is determined by the angle between the rings and the sawed surface. The stripes are the same width as the annual rings if the cut is perpendicular to the rings and become wider as the cut varies more from the perpendicular. (See Fig. 6-4.)

The grain (and therefore the fibers) may be inclined to the axis of the piece of wood because of a branch nearby or because of a bend in the tree. This deviation in direction of grain is called *slope of grain*. Figure 6-5 shows how a branch causes slope of grain. A bend in a tree trunk or a fork in a tree obviously causes the grain to slope in a piece of wood sawed straight. Because

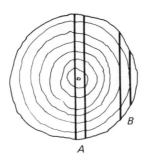

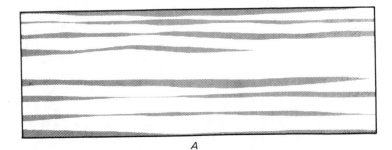

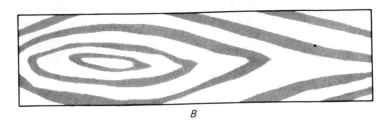

FIGURE 6-4. Pattern of grain depends on how wood is cut from log

nearly all major stresses on a piece of wood are parallel to the long axis, a slope in grain away from the axis weakens the wood for normal usage. The greater the angle is between axis and grain, the weaker the wood is. (See the discussion of the Hankinson formula and the Scholten nomographs later in the chapter.)

The outward growth of new cells partially encloses branches that have started to grow and forms a discontinuity in the annual ring pattern. The discontinuity appears as a knot in a piece of lumber. (See Fig. 6-6.) The branch may die and the branch stub become completely enclosed within the trunk forming a loose knot. The branch may continue to grow by adding cells the same way the trunk does and form a solid knot.

The knot causes weakness, whether loose or tight. The center of a loose knot has no more strength than a hole. If the knot is solid, the center is still

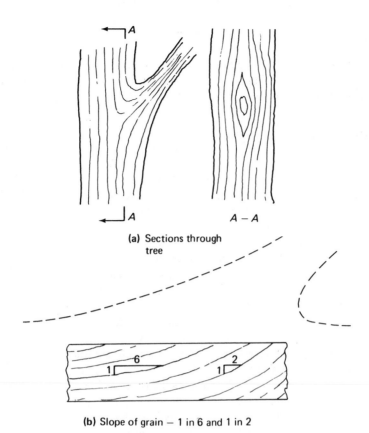

(a) Sections through tree

A – A

(b) Slope of grain — 1 in 6 and 1 in 2

FIGURE 6-5. Slope of grain caused by a branch

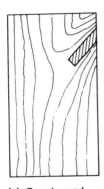

(a) Board sawed on axis of branch showing spike knot

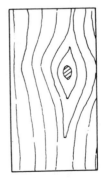

(b) Board sawed perpendicular to axis of branch

FIGURE 6-6. Knots in lumber

weak, because its cells are approximately perpendicular to the long axis of the wood. The nearby cells are at various angles caused by the spreading of the new growth around the branch, and they therefore have varying strengths.

LUMBER PRODUCTION

Trees are felled and cut and trimmed into logs with portable, power-driven chain saws and hauled to a saw mill for sawing into lumber. The logs are kept moist while stored at the mill to prevent shrinkage cracks, unless they will be stored only a short time.

Blades remove bark before the log is sawed. The sawyer decides how to saw the log for maximum production on the basis of its size, shape, and irregularities. The log is then sawed lengthwise into large rectangular and semi-round shapes for further sawing into lumber sizes, or it may be cut directly into lumber thickness by gang saws cutting the log into many slices at once. Saws called *edgers* trim the rough-edged slabs longitudinally to the desired lumber width and cut off the rounded edges. Saws called *trimmers* then saw the lumber tranversely into desired lengths and trim away defective portions.

Figure 6–7 shows the two basic methods of sawing a log into lumber and also a combination method. The slash cut lumber is called *plain sawed* in the terminology of the hardwood industry and *flat grain* in softwood terminology. The rift cut lumber is called *quarter sawed* when referring to hardwood and *edge grain* when referring to softwoods.

Lumber is finished in one of several ways. *Rough lumber* remains as sawed on all four sides with no further finishing. *Dressed lumber* or *surfaced lumber* is planed or surfaced on at least one face. It is designated as S1S if surfaced on one side, S1E if surfaced on one edge, and S1S1E if surfaced on one side and one edge. The abbreviations S2S, S2E, S1S2E, S2S1E, and S4S are used for other combinations of sides and edges that are surfaced. *Worked lumber* is dressed and also worked to provide tongue-and-groove or shiplap joints and/or to change the cross section in some other way. See Fig. 6–8 for typical cross sections of worked lumber.

Lumber to be finished may be planed while green, or it may be seasoned first and planed later. *Seasoning* is the process of reducing the moisture until a suitable moisture level is reached. The cross section of the wood becomes smaller during seasoning. If lumber is planed to the proper size after seasoning, it will remain the proper size. If it is planed first, it must be left larger than the proper size to allow for shrinkage to the proper size.

Lumber is sawed to nominal sizes (usually to the whole inch), but the width of the saw blade reduces the size somewhat. Planing reduces the size

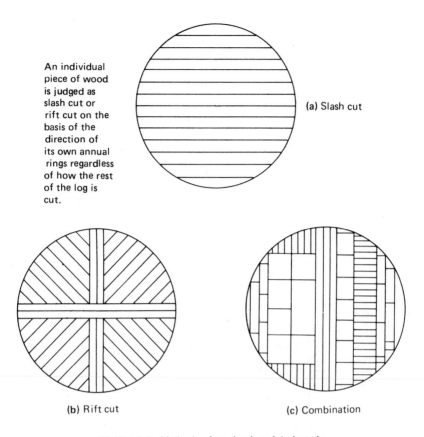

An individual piece of wood is judged as slash cut or rift cut on the basis of the direction of its own annual rings regardless of how the rest of the log is cut.

(a) Slash cut

(b) Rift cut

(c) Combination

FIGURE 6-7. Methods of sawing logs into boards

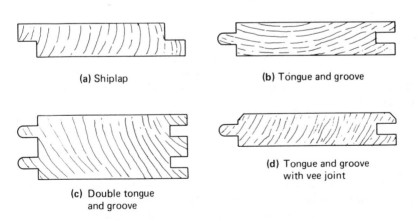

(a) Shiplap

(b) Tongue and groove

(c) Double tongue and groove

(d) Tongue and groove with vee joint

FIGURE 6-8. Typical cross sections of worked lumber

NOMINAL AND MINIMUM-DRESSED SIZES OF BOARDS, DIMENSION, AND TIMBERS

(The thicknesses apply to all widths and all widths to all thicknesses.)

Item	Thicknesses			Face widths		
	Nominal	Minimum dressed		Nominal	Minimum dressed	
		Dry[1]	Green[1]		Dry[1]	Green[1]
		Inches	Inches		Inches	Inches
Boards ------------	1	3/4	25/32	2	1-1/2	1-9/16
	1-1/4	1	1-1/32	3	2-1/2	2-9/16
	1-1/2	1-1/4	1-9/32	4	3-1/2	3-9/16
				5	4-1/2	4-5/8
				6	5-1/2	5-5/8
				7	6-1/2	6-5/8
				8	7-1/4	7-1/2
				9	8-1/4	8-1/2
				10	9-1/4	9-1/2
				11	10-1/4	10-1/2
				12	11-1/4	11-1/2
				14	13-1/4	13-1/2
				16	15-1/4	15-1/2
Dimension ---------	2	1-1/2	1-9/16	2	1-1/2	1-9/16
	2-1/2	2	2-1/16	3	2-1/2	2-9/16
	3	2-1/2	2-9/16	4	3-1/2	3-9/16
	3-1/2	3	3-1/16	5	4-1/2	4-5/8
				6	5-1/2	5-5/8
				8	7-1/4	7-1/2
				10	9-1/4	9-1/2
				12	11-1/4	11-1/2
				14	13-1/4	13-1/2
				16	15-1/4	15-1/2
Dimension ---------	4	3-1/2	3-9/16	2	1-1/2	1-9/16
	4-1/2	4	4-1/16	3	2-1/2	2-9/16
				4	3-1/2	3-9/16
				5	4-1/2	4-5/8
				6	5-1/2	5-5/8
				8	7-1/4	7-1/2
				10	9-1/4	9-1/2
				12	11-1/4	11-1/2
				14	------	13-1/2
				16	------	15-1/2
Timbers -----------	5 and thicker	------	1/2 off	5 and wider	------	1/2 off

1.   Dry lumber is defined as lumber which has been seasoned to a moisture content of 19 per cent or less. Green lumber is defined as lumber having a moisture content in excess of 19 per cent.

FIGURE 6-9. Standard sizes of yard lumber and timbers (Courtesy National Forest Products Association)

further to the correct net or finished size at which the lumber is sold. Nominal sizes and net sizes before and after seasoning are shown in Fig. 6-9.

Quantities of lumber are measured and sold by the *foot board measure* (*fbm*). One *board foot* is a quantity 1 ft square by 1 in. thick. When fbm of finished lumber is calculated, nominal dimensions are used so width and

Species	Average Moisture Content (Percent of Dry Weight)	
	Heartwood	Sapwood
Hardwoods		
Ash, white	38	40
Beech	53	78
Birch, yellow	68	71
Elm, American	95	92
Gum, black	50	61
Maple, silver	60	88
Maple, sugar	58	67
Softwoods		
Douglas fir	36	117
Fir, lowland white	91	136
Hemlock, eastern	58	119
Hemlock, western	42	170
Pine, loblolly	34	94
Pine, lodgepole	36	113
Pine, longleaf	34	99
Pine, Norway	31	135
Pine, ponderosa	40	148
Pine, shortleaf	34	108
Redwood	100	210
Spruce, Engelmann	54	167
Spruce, Sitka	33	146

FIGURE 6-10. Average moisture content of green heartwood and sapwood of 20 species of American trees (Courtesy U.S. Forest Products Laboratory)

thickness are always in full inches. Finished lumber less than an inch thick is considered 1 in. thick when computing board feet. Lumber length is taken to the next lower foot if its length is a number of whole feet plus a fraction. For example, a 12 ft 3 in. length of 2 × 4 lumber contains $12 \times 2 \times 4/12 = 8$ board ft. Multiply the length in feet by the thickness in inches by the width in feet or fraction of a foot.

SEASONING

Although the moisture of green wood is very high, it will eventually reach equilibrium with the surrounding atmosphere by losing moisture to the atmosphere. (See Figs. 6–10, 6–11, and 6–12.)

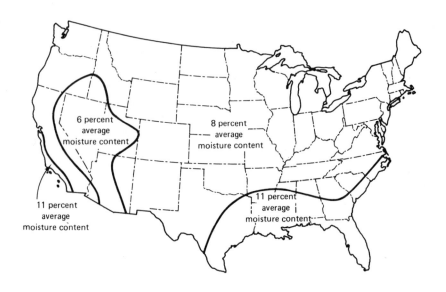

FIGURE 6-11. Recommended moisture content averages for interior finish woodwork in various parts of the United States (Courtesy U.S. Forest Products Laboratory)

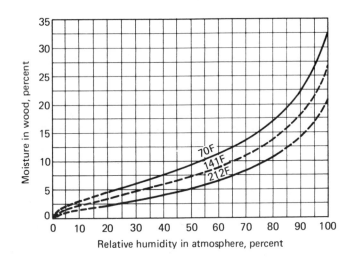

FIGURE 6-12. Relation of the equilibrium moisture content of wood to the relative humidity of the surrounding atmosphere at three temperatures (Courtesy U.S. Forest Products Laboratory)

Moisture in wood is expressed as *moisture content* (*m.c.*) which is the weight of water in the wood expressed as a percentage of the weight of the oven-dry wood. Moisture content can be determined by weighing a piece of wood including the water, and then driving all water out by drying in an oven and weighing the same piece of wood in the oven-dry condition. The difference between weight with water and weight without water is the weight of the water. Dividing this weight by the oven-dry weight gives a ratio of weight of water to oven-dry weight of wood. This ratio expressed as a percentage is the moisture content.

Reaching equilibrium takes months or years for green wood. Wood may be seasoned in the air, or much time may be saved by seasoning it in a kiln. Wood being dried in a kiln is subjected to warm, moist air or steam and loses sufficient moisture in a period of several days to several months. This is far less than the 4 years sometimes needed for air drying some hardwoods.

Seasoning can take place through the use of hygroscopic chemicals applied to the wood. This method reduces shrinkage cracks (checks) because the chemical keeps the surface of the wood moist and partially replaces moisture lost from the cell walls with the chemical. After the chemical is applied, the wood is dried in a solution of the chemical, in a kiln, or in the air.

Seasoning is continued until a moisture content is reached that approximates the average equilibrium m.c. for the conditions in which the lumber will be used. This varies, depending on the geographical area in which the lumber will be used and on whether it is to be used indoors or outdoors. See Fig. 6-11. The m.c. of wood does not exceed 19 per cent in normal outdoor usage.

In use wood never ceases to change its moisture content with the seasons or other influencing factors. It takes moisture from the atmosphere or releases its moisture to the atmosphere continuously in response to changing atmospheric conditions. However, it never again approaches the high moisture content it had while living. Figure 6-12 shows how wood m.c. varies with temperature and humidity of the surrounding air.

The strength of a given piece of wood increases as the moisture content decreases. This fact is acknowledged by allowing higher stresses in seasoned wood. (See Fig. 6-18.) This is sufficient reason for drying wood before using it, and also sufficient reason for specifying maximum allowable moisture contents when ordering wood to be used where strength is important.

Another reason for drying wood before use is that it shrinks in size when dried, but it does not shrink uniformly. Longitudinal size change is negligible. Transverse shrinkage is greatest in the curved direction of the annual rings and varies to a minimum of one-half to one-third this amount radially or in a direction perpendicular to the annual rings. For this reason a log develops large radial cracks (*checks*) if dried too rapidly. Checks are shown in Fig. 6-13. Because the direction of maximum shrinkage is along the annual

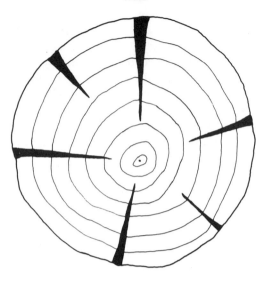

FIGURE 6-13. Checks in a log

growth rings, shrinkage is greater as the circumference is greater. Thus, the cracks are open wider at the outside, becoming narrower toward the center.

The splitting or checking is increased by the fact that drying takes place at the outside of the log before the inside dries. The outer portion is restrained from shrinking inward by the unyielding center and the cracks are larger as a result. It is therefore advantageous to saw wood into smaller sizes before seasoning to minimize checking. After seasoning, when there will be very little additional change in size, the wood is finished to its final cross section size.

Differential shrinkage results in distortion as the wood dries. In many cases the distortion is insignificant, but it is sometimes sufficient to cause construction difficulties. If the wood is too distorted, it cannot be used for construction. However, if green wood is fastened in place, it pulls fastenings loose and distorts the structure as it dries. The various distortions caused by differential shrinkage are shown in Fig. 6-14.

Seasoned wood also changes shape with changes in moisture content. Doors that swell and stick in damp weather and shrink, leaving open cracks, when the weather is dry are common evidence of volume change with change in moisture content. The shrinkage is most noticeable indoors when wintertime heating causes the air to be very dry.

Joints in wooden door and window frames open during a period when the air is dry and close again when moisture is normal. Figure 6-15 shows how a joint opens. The shrinkage is a certain percentage of the original width

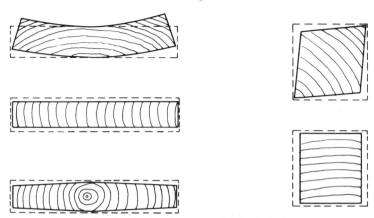

(a) Typical unequal shrinkage determined by direction of annual rings

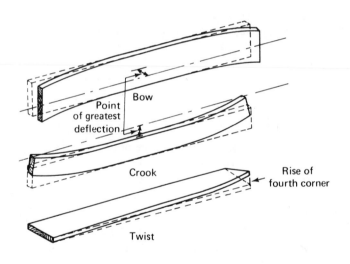

Bow

Point
of greatest
deflection

Crook

Rise of
fourth corner

Twist

(b) Warping caused by various combinations of shrinkage

FIGURE 6-14. Shrinkage and distortion

for a given moisture loss, and therefore the total shrinkage is greater where the wood is wider. This explains why the joint opening is greater where the wood is wider in the direction of shrinkage.

If the wood is cut so that the wide dimension is radial to the annual rings (rift cut), there is less change in width than if wood is cut tangential to the annual rings (slash cut). See Fig. 6-14 for illustration.

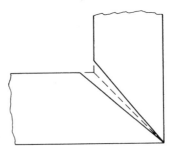

FIGURE 6-15. Open joint due to shrinkage

If the wood gains moisture greatly in excess of the amount it contained when it was installed, the resulting expansion can cause damage. For example, if the wood at the joint in Fig. 6–15 expanded instead of contracting, the corner of the frame would be pushed apart, cracking the wood or loosening the nails. Shrinkage may be unsightly, but damage from it is less likely. For this reason the m.c. at the time of construction should approximate the upper level the wood is expected to have during ordinary usage.

STRENGTH

The important stresses and corresponding strengths of wood are divided into the following six types:

Modulus of Elasticity (E): This is a measure of the stiffness or resistance to deflection. It is not usually considered a measure of strength, but is a measure of the ability to resist failure due to excessive deformation. It is used to predict movement under load and avoid failure due to excessive movement.

Extreme Fiber Stress in Bending (F_b): This is the unit stress (compression at the top, tension at the bottom) that must be resisted in a beam undergoing bending.

Tension Parallel to Grain (F_t): This is the unit stress induced by pulling apart in a longitudinal direction. Resistance to tension perpendicular to grain is so weak that it is usually considered negligible.

Compression Parallel to Grain (F_c): This is the unit stress induced by pressing together longitudinally.

Compression Perpendicular to Grain ($F_{c\perp}$): This is the unit stress induced by pressing together in a transverse direction. There is no appreciable difference in strength to resist this compression perpendicular to the annual rings or parallel to them.

Horizontal Shear (F_v): This is the unit stress induced by the tendency for upper fibers to slide over lower fibers as a beam bends.

The first step in obtaining useful allowable unit stresses and an accurate modulus of elasticity is to test small, perfect samples of wood to determine the unit stresses at failure and the modulus of elasticity for each species. This testing is done in accordance with ASTM D2555, Methods for Establishing Clear Wood Strength Values. The samples tested have no defects to reduce their strength or stiffness.

Allowable unit stresses for lumber are determined by reducing the unit stresses in the samples at failure to provide a safety factor of approximately 2.5. By this means basic allowable unit stresses and modulus of elasticity are established for each species of tree. These are published in ASTM D245, Methods for Establishing Structural Grades for Visually Graded Lumber, as Basic Stresses for Clear Lumber Under Long-Time Service at Full Design Load.

Because individual pieces of lumber contain defects that reduce strength and stiffness, studies and tests are conducted to determine the reduction in strength and stiffness caused by the various kinds of defects. The allowable unit stresses and correct modulus of elasticity are determined by reducing the values for clear wood using the procedures of ASTM D245.

The method requires determination of the location, magnitude, and condition of defects that reduce strength and stiffness in order to determine the total amount of that reduction. Each defect reduces the strength somewhat, and the total effect of these reductions is expressed as a ratio that represents the unit strength of the piece of lumber being graded compared to the unit strength of clear wood. This ratio is used to establish usable allowable unit stresses by multiplying the allowable unit stresses for clear wood and the modulus of elasticity for clear wood by the ratio.

National Design Specification for Stress-Grade Lumber and Its Fastenings includes grades established for each species of wood with usable allowable unit stresses for each grade and also design procedures. The unit stresses are derived by multiplying the basic allowable unit stresses by ratios. A sample of allowable stresses from the National Design Specification is shown in Fig. 6–16.

Each manufacturers' association then establishes grading rules to categorize its lumber products according to the various grades. Each piece of lumber is assigned to the correct grade according to the association's rules and may be used with the specified allowable unit stresses for that grade.

Lumber may be stress graded by machine with a supplementary visual inspection. Lumber so graded is called *machine stress-rated* (*MSR*). Each piece is subjected to beam loading, and the modulus of elasticity is determined from the resulting deflection without damaging the piece. The piece is then

Allowable unit stresses in pounds per square inch

DOUGLAS FIR-LARCH (Surfaced dry or surfaced green. Used at 19% max. m.c.)

Species and commercial grade	Size classification	Extreme fiber in bending "F_b" Single-member uses	Extreme fiber in bending "F_b" Repetitive-member uses	Tension parallel to grain "F_t"	Horizontal shear "F_v"	Compression perpendicular to grain "$F_{c\perp}$"	Compression parallel to grain "F_c"	Modulus of elasticity "E"	Grading rules agency
Dense Select Structural	2" to 4" thick 2" to 4" wide	2450	2800	1400	95	455	1850	1,900,000	West Coast Lumber Inspection Bureau and Western Wood Products Association
Select Structural		2100	2400	1200	95	385	1600	1,800,000	
Dense No. 1		2050	2400	1200	95	455	1450	1,900,000	
No. 1		1750	2050	1050	95	385	1250	1,800,000	
Dense No. 2		1700	1950	1000	95	455	1150	1,700,000	
No. 2		1450	1650	850	95	385	1000	1,700,000	
No. 3		800	925	475	95	385	600	1,500,000	
Appearance		1750	2050	1050	95	385	1500	1,800,000	
Stud		800	925	475	95	385	600	1,500,000	
Construction	2" to 4" thick 4" wide	1050	1200	625	95	385	1150	1,500,000	
Standard		600	675	350	95	385	925	1,500,000	
Utility		275	325	175	95	385	600	1,500,000	
Dense Select Structural	2" to 4" thick 6" and wider	2100	2400	1400	95	455	1650	1,900,000	
Select Structural		1800	2050	1200	95	385	1400	1,900,000	
No. 1		1500	1750	1000	95	455	1450	1,800,000	
No. 2		1460	1700	1000	95	455	1250	1,800,000	
No. 3		1250	1450	950	95	385	1050	1,700,000	
Appearance		725	850	475	95	385	675	1,700,000	
		1500	1750	1000	95	385	1500	1,800,000	
Dense Select Structural	Beams and Stringers	1900	—	1100	85	455	1300	1,700,000	West Coast Lumber Inspection Bureau
Select Structural		1600	—	950	85	385	1100	1,600,000	
Dense No. 1		1550	—	775	85	455	1100	1,700,000	
No. 1		1300	—	675	85	385	925	1,600,000	
Dense Select Structural	Posts and Timbers	1750	—	1150	85	455	1400	1,700,000	
Select Structural		1500	—	1000	85	385	1200	1,600,000	
Dense No. 1		1400	—	950	85	455	1200	1,700,000	
No. 1		1200	—	825	85	385	1000	1,600,000	
Select Dex	Decking	1750	2000	—	—	385	—	1,800,000	
Commercial Dex		1450	1650	—	—	385	—	1,700,000	
Dense Select Structural	Beams and Stringers	1900	—	1250	85	455	1300	1,700,000	Western Wood Products Association
Select Structural		1600	—	1050	85	385	1100	1,600,000	
Dense No. 1		1550	—	1050	85	455	1100	1,700,000	
No. 1		1350	—	900	85	385	925	1,600,000	
Dense Select Structural	Posts and Timbers	1750	—	1150	85	455	1350	1,700,000	
Select Structural		1500	—	1000	85	385	1150	1,600,000	
Dense No. 1		1400	—	950	85	455	1200	1,700,000	
No. 1		1200	—	825	85	385	1000	1,600,000	
Selected Decking	Decking	—	2000	—	—	—	—	1,800,000	
Commercial Decking		—	1650	—	—	—	—	1,700,000	
Selected Decking	Decking	—	2150	(Surfaced at 15% max. m.c. and used at 15% max. m.c.)				1,900,000	
Commercial Decking		—	1800					1,700,000	

PONDEROSA PINE (Surfaced dry or surfaced green. Used at 19% max. m.c.)

Select Structural	2" to 4" thick	1400	1650	825	70	250	1050	1,200,000
No. 1	2" to 4" thick	1200	1400	700	70	250	850	1,200,000
No. 2		1000	1150	575	70	250	675	1,100,000
No. 3		550	625	325	70	250	400	1,000,000
Appearance	2" to 4" wide	1200	1400	700	70	250	850	1,200,000
Stud		550	625	325	70	250	400	1,000,000
Construction	2" to 4" thick	725	825	425	70	250	775	1,000,000
Standard		400	450	225	70	250	625	1,000,000
Utility	4" wide	200	225	100	70	250	400	1,000,000
Select Structural	2" to 4" thick	1200	1400	825	70	250	950	1,200,000
No. 1		1050	1200	700	70	250	850	1,200,000
No. 2	6" and wider	850	975	550	70	250	700	1,100,000
No. 3		500	575	325	70	250	450	1,000,000
Appearance		1050	1200	700	70	250	850	1,200,000
Select Structural	Beams and Stringers	1100	--	725	65	250	750	1,100,000
No. 1		925	--	500	65	250	625	1,100,000
Select Structural	Posts and Timbers	1000	--	675	65	250	800	1,100,000
No. 1		825	--	550	65	250	700	1,100,000
Select	Decking	--	1450	--	--	250	--	1,300,000
Commercial		--	1250	--	--	250	--	1,100,000

National Lumber Grades Authority. A Canadian Agency.

PONDEROSA PINE—SUGAR PINE (PONDEROSA PINE—LODGEPOLE PINE) (Surfaced dry or surfaced green. Used at 19% max. m.c.)

Select Structural	2" to 4" thick	1400	1650	825	70	235	1050	1,200,000
No. 1	2" to 4" thick	1200	1400	700	70	235	850	1,200,000
No. 2		1000	1150	575	70	235	675	1,100,000
No. 3		550	625	325	70	235	400	1,000,000
Appearance	2" to 4" wide	1200	1400	700	70	235	1000	1,200,000
Stud		550	625	325	70	235	400	1,000,000
Construction	2" to 4" thick	725	825	425	70	235	775	1,000,000
Standard		400	450	225	70	235	625	1,000,000
Utility	4" wide	200	225	100	70	235	400	1,000,000
Select Structural	2" to 4" thick	1200	1400	825	70	235	950	1,200,000
No. 1		1050	1200	700	70	235	850	1,200,000
No. 2	6" and wider	850	975	550	70	235	700	1,100,000
No. 3		500	575	325	70	235	450	1,000,000
Appearance		1050	1200	700	70	235	1000	1,200,000
Select Structural	Beams and Stringers	1100	--	725	65	235	750	1,100,000
No. 1		925	--	625	65	235	625	1,100,000

Western Wood Products Association

FIGURE 6-16. Allowable unit stresses—visual grading (Courtesy National Forest Products Association)

Allowable unit stresses in pounds per square inch

Species and commercial grade	Size classification	Extreme fiber in bending "F_b" Single-member uses	Extreme fiber in bending "F_b" Repetitive-member uses	Tension parallel to grain "F_t"	Horizontal shear "F_v"	Compression perpendicular to grain "$F_{c\perp}$"	Compression parallel to grain "F_c"	Modulus of elasticity "E"	Grading rules agency
PONDEROSA PINE—SUGAR PINE (PONDEROSA PINE—LODGEPOLE PINE) (Surfaced dry or surfaced green. Used at 19% max. m.c.)									
Select Structural	Posts and Timbers	1000	—	675	65	235	800	1,100,000	
No. 1		825	—	550	65	235	700	1,100,000	
Selected Decking	Decking	—	1350	—	—	—	—	1,200,000	
Commercial Decking		—	1150	—	—	—	—	1,100,000	
	(Surfaced at 15% max. m.c. and used at 15% max. m.c.)								
Selected Decking	Decking	—	1450	—	—	—	—	1,300,000	
Commercial Decking		—	1250	—	—	—	—	1,100,000	
RED PINE (Surfaced dry or surfaced green. Used at 19% max. m.c.)									National Lumber Grades Authority.
Select Structural	2" to 4" thick 2" to 4" wide	1400	1600	800	70	280	1050	1,300,000	
No. 2		1200	1350	700	70	280	825	1,300,000	
No. 3		975	1100	575	70	280	650	1,200,000	
Appearance		1200	1350	675	70	280	925	1,300,000	
Stud		525	625	325	70	280	400	1,000,000	
Construction	2" to 4" thick 4" wide	700	800	400	70	280	750	1,000,000	
Standard		400	450	225	70	280	600	1,000,000	
Utility		175	225	100	70	280	400	1,000,000	
Select Structural	2" to 4" thick 6" and wider	1200	1350	800	70	280	900	1,300,000	A Canadian Agency.
No. 1		1000	1150	675	70	280	825	1,300,000	
No. 2		825	960	550	70	280	675	1,200,000	
No. 3		500	550	325	70	280	425	1,000,000	
Appearance		1000	1150	675	70	280	925	1,300,000	
Select Structural	Beams and Stringers	1050	—	625	65	280	725	1,100,000	
No. 1		875	—	450	65	280	600	1,100,000	
Select Structural	Posts and Timbers	1000	—	675	65	280	775	1,100,000	
No. 1		800	—	550	65	280	675	1,100,000	
Select	Decking	1150	1350	—	—	280	—	1,300,000	
Commercial		975	1100	—	—	280	—	1,300,000	

FIGURE 6-16 (continued). Allowable unit stresses—visual grading (Courtesy National Forest Products Association)

The allowable unit stresses listed are for normal loading conditions.

Grading rules agency Grade designation	Size classification	Allowable unit stresses in pounds per square inch		Tension parallel to grain "F_t"	Compression parallel to grain "F_c"	Modulus of elasticity "E"
		Extreme fiber in bending "F_b" (4)				
		Single-member uses	Repetitive-member uses			
WESTERN WOOD PRODUCTS ASSOCIATION						
1200f-1.2E	Machine Rated Lumber 2" thick or less All widths	1200	1400	600	950	1,200,000
1500f-1.4E		1500	1750	900	1200	1,400,000
1650f-1.5E		1650	1900	1020	1320	1,500,000
1800f-1.6E		1800	2050	1175	1450	1,600,000
2100f-1.8E		2100	2400	1575	1700	1,800,000
2400f-2.0E		2400	2750	1925	1925	2,000,000
2700f-2.2E		2700	3100	2150	2150	2,200,000
3000f-2.4E		3000	3450	2400	2400	2,400,000
3300f-2.6E		3300	3800	2650	2650	2,600,000
900f-1.0E	Machine Rated Joists 2" thick or less All widths	900	1050	350	725	1,000,000
900f-1.2E		900	1050	350	725	1,200,000
1200f-1.5E		1200	1400	600	950	1,500,000
1350f-1.8E		1350	1550	750	1075	1,800,000
1800f-2.1E		1800	2050	1175	1450	2,100,000
WEST COAST LUMBER INSPECTION BUREAU						
900f-1.0E	Machine Rated Lumber 2" thick or less All widths	900	1050	350	725	1,000,000
1200f-1.2E		1200	1400	600	950	1,200,000
1450f-1.3E		1450	1650	800	1150	1,300,000
1500f-1.4E		1500	1750	900	1200	1,400,000
1650f-1.5E		1650	1900	1020	1320	1,500,000
1800f-1.6E		1800	2050	1175	1450	1,600,000
2100f-1.8E		2100	2400	1575	1700	1,800,000
2400f-2.0E		2400	2750	1925	1925	2,000,000
2700f-2.2E		2700	3100	2150	2150	2,200,000
900f-1.0E	Machine Rated Joists 2" thick or less 6" and wider	900	1050	350	725	1,000,000
900f-1.2E		900	1050	350	725	1,200,000
1200f-1.5E		1200	1400	600	950	1,500,000
1500f-1.8E		1500	1750	900	1200	1,800,000
1800f-2.1E		1800	2050	1175	1450	2,100,000
SOUTHERN PINE INSPECTION BUREAU						
1200f-1.2E	Machine Rated Lumber 2" thick or less All widths	1200	1400	600	950	1,200,000
1500f-1.4E		1500	1750	900	1200	1,400,000
1650f-1.5E		1650	1900	1020	1320	1,500,000
1800f-1.6E		1800	2050	1175	1450	1,600,000
2100f-1.8E		2100	2400	1575	1700	1,800,000
2400f-2.0E		2400	2750	1925	1925	2,000,000
2700f-2.2E		2700	3100	2150	2150	2,200,000
3000f-2.4E		3000	3450	2400	2400	2,400,000
3300f-2.6E		3300	3800	2650	2650	2,600,000
900f-1.0E	Machine Rated Lumber 2" thick or less All widths	900	1050	350	725	1,000,000
900f-1.2E		900	1050	350	725	1,200,000
1200f-1.5E		1200	1400	600	950	1,500,000
1350f-1.8E		1350	1550	750	1075	1,800,000
1800f-2.1E		1800	2050	1175	1450	2,100,000

Footnotes Applicable to MACHINE STRESS-RATED LUMBER

1. Allowable unit stresses for horizontal shear "F_v" (DRY) and compression perpendicular to grain "$F_{c\perp}$" (DRY) are:

Douglas Fir–Larch (WWPA/WCLIB)	Douglas Fir–S (WWPA)	Hem–Fir (WWPA/WCLIB)	Western Hemlock (WWPA/WCLIB)	Pine(2) (WWPA)	Engelmann Spruce (WWPA)	Cedars(3) (WWPA/WCLIB)	Southern Pine (SPIB)
Horizontal Shear "F_v" (DRY)							
95	90	75	90	70	70	75	90
						For Southern Pine KD	95
Compression perpendicular to Grain "$F_{c\perp}$" (DRY)							
385	335	245	280	190	195	265	405

2. Pine includes Idaho White, Lodgepole, Ponderosa or Sugar Pine.

3. Cedar includes Incense or Western Red Cedar.

4. Tabulated Extreme Fiber in Bending values "F_b" are applicable to lumber loaded on edge. When loaded flatwise, these values may be increased by multiplying by the following factors:

Nominal Width (in)	3"	4"	6"	8"	10"	12"	14"
Factor	1.06	1.10	1.15	1.19	1.22	1.25	1.28

FIGURE 6-17. Allowable unit stresses—machine stress-rated lumber (Courtesy National Forest Products Association)

examined for characteristics and manufacturing imperfections that fall below standards. If it is acceptable, it is stamped with the value of modulus of elasticity and allowable fiber stress in bending. The fiber stress and the tension and compression parallel to grain are inferred from the modulus of elasticity and verified by the visual inspection. The "f—E" values recognized by the Western Wood Products Association are shown in Fig. 6–17. Note that the allowable compression perpendicular to grain and horizontal shear are constant for each species, regardless of the modulus of elasticity.

Allowance is made for the fact that strength increases as wood becomes drier by modifying allowable unit stresses according to moisture content.

When 2″ to 4″ thick lumber is manufactured at a maximum moisture content of 15 percent and used in a condition where the moisture content does not exceed 15 percent, the design values for surfaced dry or surfaced green lumber shown in Fig. 6–16 may be multiplied by the following factors:

Extreme Fiber in Bending (F_b)	Tension Parallel to Grain (F_t)	Horizontal Shear (F_v)	Compression Perpendicular to Grain ($F_{c\perp}$)	Compression Parallel to Grain (F_c)	Modulus of Elasticity (E)
1.08	1.08	1.05	1.00	1.17	1.05

When 2″ to 4″ thick lumber is designed for use where the moisture content will exceed 19 percent for an extended period of time, the values shown in Fig. 6–16 should be multiplied by the following factors:

Extreme Fiber in Bending (F_b)	Tension Parallel to Grain (F_t)	Horizontal Shear (F_v)	Compression Perpendicular to Grain ($F_{c\perp}$)	Compression Parallel to Grain (F_c)	Modulus of Elasticity (E)
0.86	0.84	0.97	0.67	0.70	0.97

When lumber 5″ and thicker is designed for use where the moisture content will exceed 19 percent for an extended period of time, the values shown in Fig. 6–16 should be multiplied by the following factors:

Extreme Fiber in Bending (F_b)	Tension Parallel to Grain (F_t)	Horizontal Shear (F_v)	Compression Perpendicular to Grain ($F_{c\perp}$)	Compression Parallel to Grain (F_c)	Modulus of Elasticity (E)
1.00	1.00	1.00	0.67	0.91	1.00

FIGURE 6-18. Variations in allowable unit stresses because of moisture content (Courtesy National Forest Products Association)

Allowable unit stresses listed are for lumber that is to be used at an m.c. not exceeding 19 percent, whether surfaced at this m.c. or surfaced green and left oversize to allow for shrinkage. Adjustment factors for more or less moisture are shown in Fig. 6-18. The increased allowable unit stress applies only if lumber is surfaced and used at 15 percent m.c. or less. The decreased allowable unit stress applies if the wood is to be used with m.c. greater than 19 percent for any extended period of time.

Allowable unit stresses are for normal duration of loading and must be decreased for longer loading. Wood can withstand substantially greater loads for a short period of time, and allowable unit stresses of greater value are permitted for a short duration. *Normal load duration* means approximately 10 years of full allowable unit stress and approximately 90 percent of allowable unit stress continuously throughout the rest of the life of the members. The 10 years at full load may be over a continuous period or an accumulation of shorter periods of time. Figure 6-19 shows the variation of allowable unit stress with duration of load. The National Design Specification allows the following increases in allowable unit stress for loads of short duration:

1. 15 percent for 2 months' duration, as for snow;
2. 25 percent for 7 days' duration;

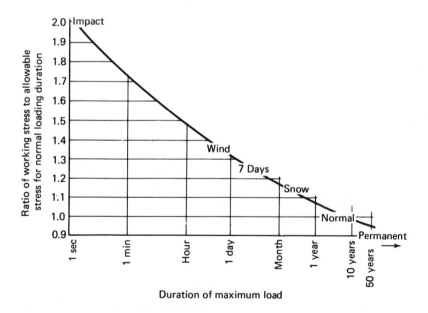

FIGURE 6-19. Adjustment of allowable unit stresses for various durations of load (Courtesy National Forest Products Association)

3. 331/3 percent for wind or earthquake;

4. 100 percent for impact (this is due to wood's toughness or ability to withstand shock).

When the full design load is applied permanently or for many years, the allowable unit stress is 90 percent of the allowable for normal loading.

Allowable compression is much greater parallel to grain than perpendicular to grain (see Fig. 6-16) and is intermediate in value for any other direction. The Hankinson formula is used to compute the allowable compression or bearing at other angles. The formula follows:

$$F_n = \frac{F_c \times F_{c\perp}}{F_c \sin^2 \theta + F_{c\perp} \cos^2 \theta}$$

where

F_c = Allowable unit stress in compression parallel to grain
$F_{c\perp}$ = Allowable unit stress in compression perpendicular to grain
θ = Angle between direction of grain and direction of load
F_n = Allowable unit compressive stress at angle θ with the direction of grain

The Scholten nomographs in Fig. 6-20 are used to solve the equation. The equation or nomograph is used with allowable unit stresses F_c and $F_{c\perp}$ to find the allowable unit stress at any angle desired.

LUMBER CLASSIFICATION

Standards have been established for the classification of lumber according to appearance, strength, shape, and use. Each piece of lumber is assigned to a grade according to certain rules. Softwoods come mainly from the southeastern area of the United States, the western part of the United States, or Canada where they are graded to meet widely recognized standards and are used throughout the world. Hardwoods are produced throughout a greater area, although total production is much less and distribution from any one mill is usually not so extensive.

Organizations

Grading standards for softwoods are published by the U.S. Department of Commerce in Product Standard PS 20 (American Softwood Lumber Standard) which is recognized by the associations that issue grading rules throughout the United States and Canada. Grading rules for each region are established by

Bearing strength of wood at angles to the grain (Hankinson formula)
The compressive strength of wood depends on the direction of the grain with respect to the direction of the applied load. It is highest parallel to the grain, and lowest perpendicular to the grain. The variation in strength, at angles between parallel and perpendicular, is determined by the Hankinson formula. The Scholten nomographs, shown here, are a graphical solution of this formula which is —

$$F_n = \frac{F_c F_{c\perp}}{F_c \sin^2 \theta + F_{c\perp} \cos^2 \theta}$$

F_c Unit stress in compression parallel to the grain.

$F_{c\perp}$ Unit stress in compression perpendicular to the grain.

θ Angle between the direction of grain and direction of load normal to the face considered.

F_n Unit compressive stress at inclination θ with the direction of grain.

The difference between the two charts is in scale, the one on the right to units of 1000 pounds, and the one on the left to units of 100 pounds. These units may be applied to allowable lumber stresses in pounds per square inch, or to total loads in the case of bolts, timber connectors, or lag screws.

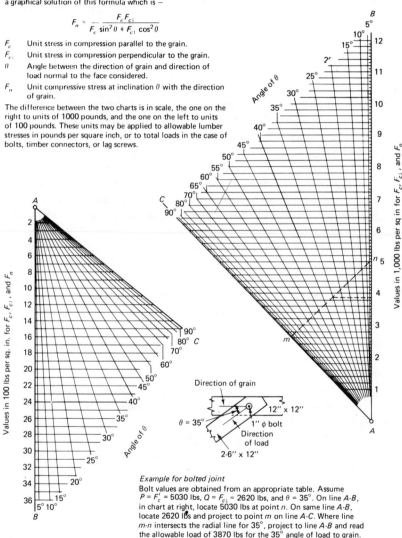

Example for bolted joint
Bolt values are obtained from an appropriate table. Assume $P = F_c' = 5030$ lbs, $Q = F_{c\perp} = 2620$ lbs, and $\theta = 35°$. On line *A-B*, in chart at right, locate 5030 lbs at point *n*. On same line *A-B*, locate 2620 lbs and project to point *m* on line *A-C*. Where line *m-n* intersects the radial line for 35°, project to line *A-B* and read the allowable load of 3870 lbs for the 35° angle of load to grain.

FIGURE 6-20. Scholten nomographs (Courtesy National Forest Products Association)

organizations whose rules conform to PS 20 with additions for special conditions of each region.

The Western Wood Products Association, consisting of lumber producers within the states of Arizona, California, Colorado, Idaho, Montana, Nevada, New Mexico, Oregon, South Dakota, Utah, Washington, and Wyoming, provides grading rules for the following: douglas fir, engelmann spruce, mountain hemlock, western hemlock, Idaho white pine, incense cedar, larch, lodgepole pine, ponderosa pine, sugar pine, the true firs, and western red cedar.

The California Redwood Association is similar, but covers only 12 northern California counties and provides rules for redwood and some other softwood species.

The Southern Forest Products Association, consisting of lumber producers within the states of Alabama, Arkansas, Florida, Georgia, Louisiana, Maryland, Mississippi, Missouri, North Carolina, Oklahoma, South Carolina, Texas, and Virginia, provides grading rules for shortleaf, longleaf, loblolly, slash, Virginia, and pond pine.

The National Lumber Grades Authority, a Canadian government agency, provides grading rules effective throughout Canada for Sitka spruce, douglas fir, western larch, eastern hemlock, tamarack, eastern white pine, western hemlock, amabilis fir, ponderosa pine, red pine, white spruce, red spruce, black spruce, engelmann spruce, lodgepole pine, jack pine, alpine fir, balsam fir, western red cedar, Pacific coast yellow cedar, western white pine, and several hardwoods.

The Northeastern Lumber Manufacturers' Association, consisting of lumber producers within the states of Connecticut, Maine, Massachusetts, New Hampshire, New York, Pennsylvania, Rhode Island, and Vermont, provides grading rules for red spruce, white spruce, black spruce, balsam fir, white pine, jack pine, Norway pine, pitch pine, hemlock, tamarack, white cedar, and several hardwoods.

The National Hardwood Lumber Association, consisting of lumber producers throughout the United States, provides grading rules for hardwoods. The lumber produced to meet these rules is used to manufacture products such as furniture, paneling, tool handles, flooring, and a wide variety of other products. Hardwood used directly in construction is usually purchased from local mills according to specifications agreed on between producer and user.

Grading

Lumber is a term including all finished or semi-finished wood shaped with parallel longitudinal surfaces. Those pieces 1½ in. or less in thickness and 2 in. or more in width are *boards*. Pieces at least 2 in. thick and less than 5 in. thick and 2 in. or more wide are *dimension* lumber. Pieces 5 in. or more in thickness and width are *timbers*. These are nominal dimensions and finished sizes are smaller.

Each piece of lumber is assigned on the basis of expected use to the category of *factory and shop lumber* or *yard lumber*. Factory and shop lumber includes pieces to be used in making sash, doors, jambs, sills, and other millwork items. This lumber is graded on the basis of how much is usable and how much must be wasted because of defects. Yard lumber is that which is used structurally and includes most of that used in construction. Figure 6–21 illustrates the categories into which it is divided.

Yard lumber is divided according to size and shape into boards, dimension lumber, and timbers as shown in Fig. 6–21. Boards are used for roofs, floors, siding, paneling, and trim. Dimension lumber is used for joists, studs, and rafters. Timbers are used infrequently as part of a structure. They are used more often for shoring earthwork or mine tunnels, or as bracing for concrete forms.

Dimensions and timbers are almost always *stress graded,* which means each piece is assigned to a grade depending on its strength. Allowable stresses are specified for each grade and the design stresses cannot exceed these. A structure is designed by selecting members of cross section sizes and stress grades in the most appropriate combinations to perform the required functions. Each piece may have design unit stresses up to the allowable unit stresses for its grade. See Fig. 6–16 for an example of commercial grades with their allowable stresses. The lumber for the structure must be of the correct grade. A lower grade is too weak and a higher grade is unnecessarily expensive.

Wood frame construction consists of studs, joists, and rafters which act in unison to support loads on the structure. (See Fig. 6–22 for illustration.) If one member is weaker and sags or moves out of line more than adjacent members, those adjacent members receive a greater load and the sagging one is relieved of part of its load. If the added load on the adjacent members causes them to move excessively, they are helped out by the next members. Therefore, these members, called *repetitive members,* are not required to support the design load independently. If most of them can bear a slightly greater load, the occasional weaker one is supported by them. Therefore, a smaller safety factor is justified.

Figure 6–16 shows that the National Design Specification's allowable unit stresses provide a lower safety factor for repetitive members by specifying a higher allowable unit stress for the extreme fiber in bending. This means that lumber of any particular commercial grade can be designed with a higher unit stress when used for repetitive members subjected only to beam loading.

The grade for each piece of lumber depends on its appearance and strength. The two are related. Often a flaw that is considered to mar the appearance is also a weakness. Standards are established for each grade. The

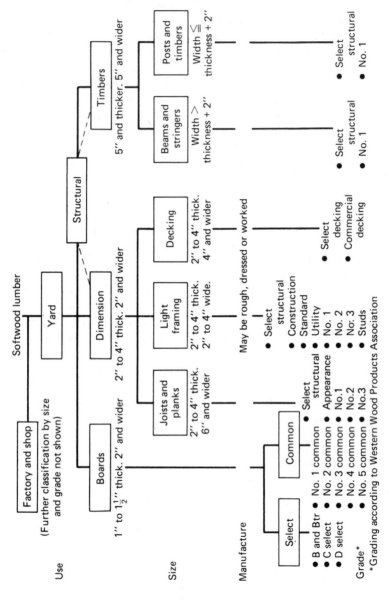

FIGURE 6-21. Softwood lumber classification (Courtesy Western Wood Products Association)

FIGURE 6-22. Wood frame building under construction (Courtesy National Forest Products Association)

standards consist of the maximum size or degree of each characteristic and manufacturing imperfection allowed for each grade. *Characteristics* are natural marks resulting from the tree's growth or from seasoning, and manufacturing imperfections are imperfections resulting from sawing, planing, or other manufacturing operations. Some of the characteristics affect appearance, others affect strength, and still others affect both appearance and strength. Manufacturing imperfections affect only appearance.

Each piece of lumber is visually inspected to compare its natural characteristics and manufacturing imperfections with the standards. It is then assigned to the correct grade which is stamped onto the piece. Some grade stamps are shown in Fig. 6-23.

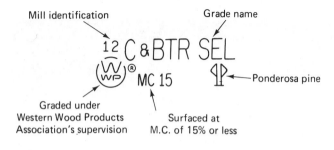

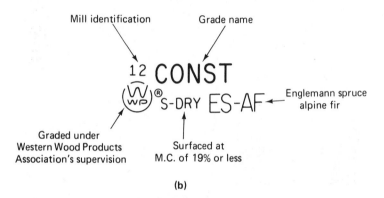

FIGURE 6-23. Typical grade stamps (Courtesy Western Wood Products Association)

If a graded piece is cut into parts, each part must be regraded since the parts do not necessarily rate the same grade as the original.

__Boards__. Boards are ordinarily graded strictly on the basis of appearance. Factors considered in grading boards are listed here:

Stains: Discolorations that affect appearance but not strength. They are allowed to some extent in all grades.

Checks: Lengthwise separations of the wood normally occurring across the annual growth rings and caused by seasoning or by the flattening of a piece of cupped lumber between rollers. They affect appearance and strength. Some are allowed in all grades.

Shakes: Lengthwise separations caused by slippage occurring between the annual growth rings and sometimes outward from the pith through the rings. Shakes are caused while the tree is growing. They affect appearance and strength, and are permitted only in the lower grades.

Cup and Crook: Distortions caused by unequal shrinkage during seasoning. They affect appearance and are permitted to some extent in all grades. (See Fig. 6-14 for description.)

Wane: Bark or missing wood on an edge or corner of a piece of lumber. It affects appearance and strength, and is permitted to some extent in all grades.

Splits: Separation of the wood due to the tearing apart of wood cells. They affect appearance and strength, and are permitted to some extent in all but the highest grades.

Pitch: An accumulation of resinous material. It affects appearance and is permitted to some extent in all grades.

Pockets: Well-defined openings between the annual growth rings which develop during the growth of the tree and usually contain pitch or bark. They affect appearance and strength, and are permitted to some extent in all grades.

Pith: The small, soft core in the structural center of a log. It affects appearance and strength, and is permitted to some extent in most grades.

Holes: These may occur and extend partly or completely through the wood. They affect appearance and strength, and are permitted to some extent in most grades.

Knots: Portions of branches over which the tree has grown. They affect appearance and strength, and are permitted to some extent in all grades. They may be desirable for appearance. The sizes and condition of knots are important. A knot may be decayed or sound, have a hole in it, be loose or tight, and be intergrown with the growth rings of the surrounding wood or "encased" with no intergrowth.

Unsound Wood: The result of disintegration of the wood substance due to action of wood-destroying fungi. It is also known as rotten or decayed wood. There are several kinds of unsound wood caused by fungi that cease activity when the tree is felled. Additional decay is no more likely to take place in this kind of lumber than in lumber with no decay. Unsound wood affects appearance and strength, and is permitted only in lower grades.

Torn Grain: An irregularity in the surface of a piece where wood has been torn or broken out by surfacing. It affects appearance and is permitted to some extent in all grades. It could affect strength only if very severe, in which case it would not be acceptable from an appearance standpoint either.

Raised Grain: An unevenness between springwood and summerwood on the surface of dressed lumber. It affects appearance and is permitted to some extent in nearly all grades.

Skips: Areas that did not surface cleanly. They affect appearance and are permitted to some extent in all grades.

These characteristics and manufacturing imperfections do not detract from a good appearance if they are on the side of the lumber that does not show. Most pieces have one side with a better appearance than the other, and because only one side shows in normal usage, the grading rules allow the grade to be determined by judging the better side for many of the grading factors.

Rules for each of the grades shown in Fig. 6–21 describe the maximum extent to which each characteristic or imperfection is permitted. Some are not permitted at all in the higher grades. Requirements become more lenient for each succeeding grade from Select B and better to No. 5 common. Stress-rated boards are available for trusses, box beams, structural bracing, and other engineered construction.

Dimension Lumber.   Dimension lumber is graded for use as joists and planks, light framing, or decking according to the same characteristics and manufacturing imperfections as boards. Some additional characteristics are also considered. Because of the greater thickness of dimension lumber, bow and twist (see Figure 6–14) are subject to limits. They are not considered for boards because a board is flexible enough to be forced into a flat, untwisted position and nailed into place.

Two other characteristics are considered because strength is a major consideration. The direction of grain is not permitted to vary by too great an angle from the axis of the piece of lumber, and a minimum density of wood is required. *Slope* of grain is the deviation between the general grain direction and the axis of the lumber. It is determined by measuring a unit length of offset between grain and axis, and measuring the length along the axis in which the deviation takes place. It is the tangent of the angle between grain and axis expressed as a fraction with 1 as the numerator. As an example, the slope of grain may be expressed as 1 in 8. Determining the density is a way of determining the proportion of summerwoood compared to the total amount of wood. It is determined by measuring the thickness of summerwood and springwood annual rings or by determining the specific gravity.

For dimension joists and planks and light framing, checks, shakes, and splits are limited only at the ends of the lumber pieces, and larger knots are allowed along the longitudinal centerline than near the edges. See the discussion on timber stress grading below for an explanation.

Timbers.   Timbers are graded as beams and stringers or as posts and timbers. Beams and stringers are pieces with a width more than 2 in. greater than the thickness, and posts and timbers have a width not more than 2 in. greater than the thickness. The grading rules for each take into account the proposed usage. A piece graded under beams and stringers rules can be used most efficiently by being stressed to its allowable unit stress under beam loading. If graded under posts and timbers rules, it can be used most efficiently by being stressed to its allowable unit stress under column loading. However, any member can sustain any of the allowable unit stresses listed for its grade, and therefore it may be used in any way as long as it is not stressed beyond the allowable unit stresses.

The chief difference in grading requirements between the two categories is in the allowed locations for characteristics that lower the strength of the member. The greatest tension and compression fiber stresses (due to bending) under beam loading are at the center of the beam's length at the top and bottom edges of the beam. The greatest tendency for the fibers of a beam to move relative to each other (fail in shear) under beam loading is at both ends along the centerline between top and bottom. A column is stressed more uniformly throughout its entire length and cross section.

This difference is reflected in the grading requirements. Larger knots are allowed near the longitudinal centerline than near the top and bottom edges of beams and stringers where they have more effect in lessening the resistance to fiber stress. Checks, shakes, and splits are limited only near the ends of beams and stringers and, even there, not in the vicinity of the top and bottom edges where unit shearing stress is negligible.

For posts and timbers, the knot location is not considered. Checks, shakes, and splits are measured at the ends for posts and timbers. The shorter of the two projections of a shake onto the faces of the member is considered in grading posts and timbers; and for beams and stringers, the horizontal projection of the shake while the member is in use is considered.

Special Use Wood

Wood meets the requirements for several special construction items so perfectly that entire industries are in operation, producing these items.

Wood *shingles* and *shakes* are used for roofing and siding. Most are made of western red cedar, a species with high resistance to decay and weathering and highly impermeable to water. This wood has a high strength-to-weight ratio. This is advantageous for any roofing material because it means that the structural frame has only a lightweight roof to support. The close, straight grain of the cedar allows the wood to be sawed into thin shingles parallel to the grain with very little cutting across the grain. This is an advantage over most other woods because each shingle has its flexure loading parallel to grain or nearly so.

The grain permits thin shakes to be split from a block of wood either by hand or with a machine. Shakes are thicker than shingles and have a hand-hewn look. Shingles and shakes can be treated with fire-resistant chemicals so that they do not support combustion.

Wood is frequently used for *flooring*. Both hardwoods and softwoods of many kinds are used, and both rift cut and slash cut lumber are used. Abrasion resistance is important for any floor, and close-grained species are preferred. The wood is installed in strips or blocks with side grain showing where appearance is important, or in blocks with end grain showing where appearance is not important. Wear resistance is greater on end grain.

The pieces of wood are usually of tongue-and-groove construction or interlocked in some way to prevent uneven warping. Wood is highly valued as flooring where appearance (in homes) or proper resilience (for basketball courts) is important. Wood is difficult to maintain under heavy usage if appearance is important, but easy to maintain even under heavy industrial usage if appearance is not important. It is valued for industrial floors in certain cases because of its resistance to acids, petroleum products, and salts. It is also nonsparking and is less tiring to the feet and legs of workers than harder floors.

DETERIORATION OF WOOD

Wood has four major enemies: insects, marine borers, fungi, and fire. Any of the four can destroy the usefulness of wood. However, wood can be protected to a great extent from any of them by the use of chemicals. Certain woods, such as cedar, cypress, locust, and redwood, are more resistant to fungi (decay) than other wood, and have long been used for fence posts and foundations of small buildings. The heartwood of all trees is more resistant to decay and insect attack than the sapwood because some of the substances that give the heartwood its color are poisonous to fungi and insects. However, sapwood absorbs preservative chemicals better because its cells are not occupied by these poisonous substances. The sapwood can be made more resistant with chemicals than the untreated heartwood.

Insects of various types damage wood by chewing it. Termites are the best known. They are antlike creatures that consume cellulose as food, digesting the cellulose content of cardboard, paper and cloth, as well as wood. They do not fly ordinarily, but do fly in swarms to form new colonies in the spring and lose their wings thereafter. They are most easily seen before a new colony is established and therefore are often seen with wings. Once they establish a colony, they do not venture out into daylight, and in fact cannot survive long in the sun's rays. Once they enter a piece of lumber, they are capable of consuming most of it without ever eating their way to the outside. A structural member that appears sound may be eaten hollow and may fail before the termites are discovered.

Subterranean termites, which are found throughout the United States, eat wood but live in the earth. They cannot live without the moisture they find there. Since they die quickly by drying out in sunlight, they construct passageways from their dwelling place in the moist soil to the food supply. These passageways may be tunnels underground directly to wood in contact with the ground. If the wood is not in contact with the ground, they construct a mud tube attached to a wall, pier, or whatever provides a route to the wood. The tube may even be built from ground to wood across a vertical gap. The termites are protected from the sun as long as they use the passageway for their travels. The tube passageway, which can easily be seen, gives away the presence of these termites.

Nonsubterranean termites are found in the southern part of the United States and are far fewer in number than the subterranean kind. They can live in wood, whether damp or dry, without returning to the ground for moisture. They therefore do not give themselves away by building passageways and are not as easily discovered as the subterranean variety. The termites' excrement of very tiny pellets resembling sawdust and their discarded wings are signs that indicate their presence inside wood structural members. Wings are found when the termites have just moved in, usually in late spring or early summer. These termites may be within lumber that is delivered to the construction site, and lumber should be inspected for evidence of infestation before it is used.

Two methods of protecting wood structures from termites are to provide either a physical barrier or a chemical barrier to keep them from reaching the wood. The physical barrier consists of concrete or steel supports that provide a space between the ground and all wood. A projecting metal shield may be installed around the supports. A physical barrier is not guaranteed to keep termites out, but makes it possible to discover their passagways through regular inspections. A chemical barrier consists of saturating the soil adjacent to the structure with poison. This method is used against subterranean termites when their passageways are found. The termites cannot pass the poison barrier. Therefore, those that are in the wood will dry out and die, and those in the soil will have to leave or starve to death. The wood adjacent to the soil may be saturated with poison to get rid of either type of termite. It is better to treat the wood before construction and prevent the entrance of termites. A coat of paint prevents nonsubterranean termites from entering wood; but repainting is required and may be difficult to do in the areas under a building where termites are likely to enter.

Carpenter ants are a problem in some parts of the United States. They excavate hollows for shelter within wood, although they do not eat wood.

They can be as destructive as termites, but do not attack the harder woods.

Marine borers, which include several kinds of mollusks and crustaceans, attack wood from its outer surface, eating it much more rapidly than termites would. They are found occasionally in fresh water, but are much more numerous in salt water and are particularly active in warm climates. Docks and other structures are often supported over water on wood piles, and their protection is a major problem. Heavy impregnation of the wood fibers with creosote oil or creosote–coal tar solution slows the attack of borers, but does not prevent it completely. The only complete protection available is complete encasement of the wood within concrete.

Fungi, which are microscopic, plantlike organisms, feed on wood fibers, leaving a greatly weakened residue of rotten wood. All forms of rot or decay are caused by some type of this microorganism which is carried on air currents and deposited on the wood. Fungi require air, moisture, and a temperature above 40°F (4°C) to be active. They are most active at temperatures around 80°F (27°C). Wood with a moisture content of 19 percent or below, which is normal outdoors, is not subject to decay. Wood which is indoors is normally drier.

Wood kept below water does not decay because there is no air for the fungi. Logs that have been at the bottom of lakes or rivers since the earliest logging days have been recovered and found to be completely sound. Wood continuously below the groundwater table does not decay because it lacks air. Wood marine piles in water and foundation piles in soil remain sound below water. They do not decay above water either because of the lack of moisture.

The length of pile between high and low water elevations is alternately above water and below water. If in tidal water, it never dries completely when out of water, and when submerged, it is seldom, if ever, so saturated that there is no air. Even underground, with a fluctuating water table, moisture and air are both available much of the time. Fungi thrive in this zone, and the wood is completely rotten there while the dry wood above and the saturated wood below are still sound. Wood is often used for the lower part of a pile with concrete or steel for the part above low water level. Various chemicals are used to protect wood from fungi when the wood must survive conditions favorable to the fungi.

FIRE

Fire is the obvious enemy of wood, yet buildings of wood construction can be as fire-safe as buildings of any other type of construction. Large timbers do not support combustion except where there are corners or narrow openings next to them, and when they do burn, the square edges burn first. This is demonstrated by the way logs burn in a fireplace. One log alone does not burn unless the fire is constantly fed by other fuel, but two or three logs close together support combustion in the spaces between them with no additional fuel. The sharp edges of a split log burn better than a rounded natural log.

The charred exterior caused by fire is a partially protective coating for the inner wood, cutting the rate of consumption by fire to less than half the rate for unburned wood. A large timber may have enough sound wood remaining to be effective after a protective covering is built up.

A construction method called *heavy timber construction* has been devised to take advantage of these observations. It consists of using large structural members with their exposed edges trimmed to remove the square shape and with corners blocked in to remove "pockets" of heat concentration. Siding, decking, and flooring are thick with tight joints that permit no cracks to support combustion and allow no heat or flames to burst through. A building of this type does not burn unless the contents maintain a very hot fire for an extended period of time. In that case no other kind of building can resist the fire either. Even though other building materials do not burn, they fail by melting, expanding excessively, or simply losing strength.

Protected construction consists of ordinary wood frame construction with a protective coating of plaster, gypsum board, or acoustical tile protecting the joists and with plywood used for walls, floors, and roof. With joists having some protection, structural failure is delayed so that there is time for people within the building to escape. The plywood is a barrier to the passage of flames and heat from the source of the fire to other parts of the building.

Wood can be impregnated with fire-retardant chemicals which decrease flame spread and smoke generation. Burning occurs when wood becomes heated sufficiently (300°F, 149°C) and escaping gases burst into flame. The absorbed chemicals prevent this from happening by changing these combustible gases to water plus noncombustible gases.

Fire-retardant paints which have an appearance satisfactory for a finish coat can also provide reduction in flame spread and smoke generation through their insulating properties. Impregnation is more effective than painting and is not detrimental to appearance or strength. However, if wood is to be impregnated with a chemical, it must be done before the wood is part of a structure.

Therefore, paint is usually used to increase the fire resistance of existing buildings, and impregnation is used for new construction. It is done by saturating the wood cells with a fire-retardant chemical dissolved in water. Wood swells when it absorbs the water and shrinks when it dries again. These size changes can cause problems if no allowance is made for them.

Because of the way a fire is fueled, the rapidity with which it causes damage, and the ways in which it causes damage, there is much more involved in fire protection than the selection of materials. Building contents in many cases include trash, cleaning supplies which often burn readily, flammable waxes and polishes applied to floors and furniture, drapes, spilled liquids which may be flammable, and many kinds of flammable stored materials.

People cannot survive in a room with a fire for more than a few minutes, even if the space is large. They are killed by heat, smoke, or lack of oxygen in less than 10 minutes and sometimes in a minute or two. The contents of a room are very quickly damaged by smoke and heat, even if not actually burned. Water damage may also be extensive. The material that burns and the damage done by the burning are largely beyond the control of the designer of the building.

Therefore, the strategy employed by designers and by fire fighters is to delay collapse of any part of a building so that all occupants can get out, to provide safe passageways for them to get out, and to prevent the spread of the fire to other spaces. It is not feasible to accomplish more than this unless the contents of the building do not burn. The fire safety of a building depends on the contents and how they are stored, good housekeeping, sprinkler and fire alarm systems, fire fighting methods, and the type of construction more than on building materials.

PRESERVATION OF WOOD

Preserving wood involves treating it with a poison so that fungi and insects do not consume it. Strength is not affected by the poisonous preservative. The preservative may be brushed onto the surface of the wood. This provides a small amount of protection. More protection is obtained by dipping the wood into a solution containing the preservative. These two methods are used only for small projects or for wood requiring little protection.

The best protection is obtained by forcing the preservative into the fibers of the wood. A certain retention of preservative in lb per cu ft is specified depending on the type of preservative, species of wood, and conditions under which the wood is to be used. Some woods must be punctured with sharp points (*incised*) before the operation to retain the specified amount of preservative. All wood must have the bark removed before being treated because the preservatives do not penetrate bark well. If at all possible, wood is cut to final size before treatment to avoid wasting preservative on excess wood and to avoid later cutting into parts of the wood not penetrated by the preservative. If later cutting exposes any untreated wood, it should be painted with a heavy coat of the preservative.

Preservatives commonly used are of three kinds. Water-soluble salts with such chemicals as sodium fluoride, copper sulfate, or zinc chloride as their primary ingredient are injected into wood in weak solutions (less than 5 percent). The water evaporates, leaving the salts within the wood in the required amounts which vary but are about 1 lb per cu ft for protection against fungi and insects. Salts containing zinc chloride are retained in quantities up to 5 lb per cu ft for protection against fire in addition to fungi and insects.

These preservatives, which are suitable for indoor use, are inoffensive in appearance and odor, and the wood can be painted after it is treated. There are some disadvantages, however. The wood expands and increases in weight when water is injected, and some time is required to dry the wood to an acceptable m.c. for use. Because these preservatives are soluble in water, the wood treated with them cannot be used in water or exposed to rain without the loss of some of the salts by leaching. Therefore, they are not suitable for outdoor use.

Poisonous organic materials such as pentachlorophenol or copper napthenate dissolved in petroleum oil are used to protect wood from fungi and insects. Since these poisonous materials are not soluble in water, they are effective on wood used in wet places. The oil evaporates rapidly after treatment so that the wood is ready for use sooner than that treated with water-borne salts. The wood cannot be painted after treatment, but does not have an unpleasant appearance. Required retention is in the range of ½ lb per cu ft.

Creosote, a liquid byproduct of the refining of tar, is the most effective preservative against fungi and insects and the only one effective at all against marine borers. It is used alone, mixed with coal tar, or mixed with petroleum. Railroad ties and utility poles are treated with one of the three. Mixing with petroleum is an economy measure to increase the quantity of preservative for uses where less effective preservation is satisfactory. Creosote and creosote–coal tar mixtures are used for more demanding conditions and are the only types used in salt water.

Creosote is a black or dark brown, foul smelling, sticky substance and is therefore not satisfactory for all uses. Wood treated with creosote is very difficult to paint. Creosote after application burns very readily until it cures by drying. Generally, it is not a fire hazard by the time the wood is put to use. Creosote must be used in larger quantities than the other preservatives. However, it is so much cheaper that it is more economical to use it wherever its unpleasant appearance and odor are not objectionable.

Typical retention requirements are 8 lb per cu ft for installation above ground, 10 lb per cu ft for wood in contact with the ground, and 25 lb per cu ft for piling in salt water.

Foundations built of wood, pressure treated with water-borne preservatives, are practical for wood frame buildings. The foundation walls are built like any stud wall with plywood sheeting on the outside and are supported on a footing of dimension lumber of a 2 in. nominal thickness resting on a gravel base. The wood is shielded from contact with the earth by sheets of plastic sealed at the joints. All wood to a height of 6 to 8 in. (15 to 20 cm) above the ground is treated.

Pressure treatment of wood includes placing seasoned wood into a pressure vessel, flooding it with the preservative, and forcing the preservative into the cells of the wood with air pressure. The full-cell method results in the cell walls being completely coated and hollow cells being nearly filled with preservative. The empty-cell method results in the cells being nearly empty but with the cell walls completely coated. The weight of preservative retained is greater after the full-cell operation. It is more costly, but it is necessary to achieve the high retention needed for the most severe conditions.

Wood exposed to the weather becomes eroded, often turns gray, and develops checks. It may be protected from the weather by a surface coating of paint, enamel, varnish, or sealer. All should be applied with the wood at the moisture content it will have in use so that there will be a minimum of shrinkage or swelling to loosen the coating. Satisfactory performance requires the finish to be hard enough for protection, to be flexible enough not to crack when the wood shrinks and swells, and to adhere strongly to the wood.

These same finishes may be used primarily for appearance rather than protection. They may be designed for interior use solely to improve appearance by providing a desired color, enhancing the natural wood appearance, hiding blemishes, making the surface smooth, or improving lighting with a more reflective surface.

Paint consists of finely divided solids suspended in a liquid vehicle to allow it to spread over a surface where it dries to a solid protective film covering the wood from view. It is normally applied in two coats: the first (prime coat) to bond to the wood, and the second (cover coat) to provide protection.

Enamel is similar to paint and provides a smoother, harder, and more brittle surface. Because of the brittleness, it is not suitable for exterior use in wet or cold climates because swelling and shrinking or expansion and contraction cause it to crack and chip.

Varnish consists of resins dissolved in a liquid vehicle. It provides a clear coat through which the wood grain shows.

A sealer consists of a water-repellant substance dissolved in a solvent and used to seal and moistureproof the wood by penetration into the pores while allowing the grain to show.

GLUED LAMINATED WOOD

Construction with sawn wood is limited by the size, shape, and characteristics of readily available trees. Lumber longer than 24 ft (7.2 m) or with a cross section dimension greater than 12 in. × 12 in. is difficult to obtain in large quantities. When lumber of these sizes is sawed, each piece is more likely to have some characteristic that seriously reduces strength or lowers the quality of its appearance than is likely with smaller pieces. Even if there are no serious weaknesses at the time of sawing, it is difficult and time consuming to season large timbers without producing serious checks, and difficult to season long pieces without serious warping. Heavy timber construction and long spans are not feasible with sawn lumber. Sawn lumber cannot be bent into curves except in small cross sections and is ordinarily used straight.

However, structural members of any length and cross section and with just about any desired curve can be made by gluing smaller pieces together. The smaller pieces, which are of standard lumber cross section, are glued one over the other, wide face to wide face, as laminations. No one lamination need be as long as the member. They are glued end to end to reach the full length. A structural member made this way is called a *glu-lam member* (short for glued and laminated), and construction with members of this kind is called *glu-lam construction*. The supporting members for heavy timber construction are glu-lam timbers. Almost all glu-lam members are made of douglas fir or southern pine.

Lumber of 2 in. nominal thickness is ordinarily used for laminations. These laminations can be used straight in columns or beams and can be bent to form arches or for desired architectural effects. For sharper curves, thinner laminations are used. Bending lumber introduces deformation as shown in Fig. 6-24. Deformation causes stresses just as stresses cause deformation,

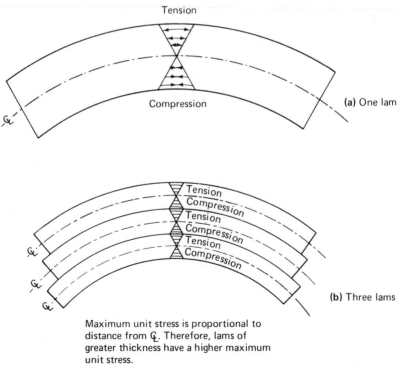

Maximum unit stress is proportional to distance from ₵. Therefore, lams of greater thickness have a higher maximum unit stress.

FIGURE 6-24. Unit stress due to bending laminations

FIGURE 6-25. Manufacturing of Glu-Lam Arches (Courtesy Weyerhaeuser)

both in accordance with the modulus of elasticity of the material. Figure 6-24 demonstrates how the same curvature introduces greater stress in a thicker lamination. Sharper curves can be made using thinner lams as long as the allowable F_b is not exceeded. Horizontal shear is also induced by bending, and the allowable F_v must not be exceeded in the wood. The glue holding the lams together must also resist horizontal shear.

Preparation of wood to fabricate a glu-lam structural member is shown in Fig. 6-25, and a finished product is shown in Fig. 6-26. The individual laminations are placed so that:

1. Weak spots are separated from each other to avoid a concentration of weaknesses.

2. Disfiguring characteristics are hidden within the member.

3. End joints between lams are separated from each other to avoid a plane of weakness.

4. The strongest wood is placed where stresses are the highest.

5. The wood with best appearance is placed where it can be seen.

Usually the lamination width is the full width of the member. If laminations must be placed side by side to equal the proper width, their side joints must be glued and not be located one over another. End joints and side joints are shown in Fig. 6-27.

FIGURE 6-26. Finished curved roof beam (Courtesy Weyerhaeuser)

(a) Staggered end joints

(b) Staggered side joints

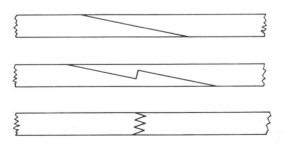

(c) Types of scarf joint

FIGURE 6-27. Joints in glu-lam members

The use of glu-lam construction allows wood to be used in large projects for which only concrete or steel would have been considered previously. Glu-lam members can be made stronger than the strongest sawn lumber of the same size. Large members can be made entirely from small trees or from the small pieces left after the weak parts are cut out of large trees. Glu-lam has proven particularly popular for roof arches such as those for churches, auditoriums, and supermarkets.

PLYWOOD

Plywood is another type of glued laminated wood. The laminations are thin and are arranged with the grain of each one running perpendicular to the grain of the laminations adjacent to it. The laminations are called *veneers*. The center veneer is called the *core*, the outside veneers are the *face* and *back*, and the inner veneers with grain perpendicular to the face and back are called *cross bands*. There is always an odd number of veneers, usually three or five.

Alternating the grain direction tends to equalize the strength in both directions, although the strength is less parallel to grain than it would be if the grain of all veneers were in the same direction. The advantages far outweigh this disadvantage, however.

The advantages of plywood over sawn lumber of comparable thickness are listed here:

1. Plywood's greater transverse strength stiffens or braces the entire structure to a greater degree than lumber sheathing when plywood is used over studs, joists, and rafters for wood frame construction.

2. Plywood's greater stiffness allows it to bridge wider spaces between beams without excessive deflection, thus reducing the number of beams required.

3. Plywood resists concentrated loads better because its mutually perpendicular grain structure spreads the loads over a larger area.

4. Plywood can be worked closer to the edges without splitting, allowing it to be bolted, screwed, or nailed with less excess material.

5. Desired appearance can be obtained by using thin veneers of high-quality wood only where they show. A matching repetitive pattern can be obtained by using one log for all the face veneer and wood with less desirable appearance for the other veneers.

6. Length change and warping due to moisture change are much less in plywood than in sawn lumber because shrinkage parallel to grain is negligible, and wood grain running both ways prevents excessive shrinkage either way. Using an odd number of veneers results in the grain on top and bottom running

in the same direction so that shrinkage and expansion are equalized in both directions on the two faces and warping is prevented.

7. Plywood can be more easily bent to form curves for concrete forms or for curved wood construction.

8. Plywood is fabricated in large sheets that can be handled more efficiently at the construction site than sawn lumber. One sheet covers the same area as half a dozen boards and, therefore, requires less handling and fitting into place.

9. Plywood has demonstrated greater fire resistance than boards of the same thickness.

Plywood does not have equal strength in both directions. If there is an equal thickness of veneers in each direction, the tensile and compressive strengths are equal. However, bending strength is greater parallel to the grain of the face and back, unless there is a much greater thickness of cross bands with their grain in the other direction. If cross bands are thick enough to provide equal bending strength perpendicular to face grain, tensile and compressive strengths are much greater perpendicular to the face grain.

Plywood is usually made in 4 ft by 8 ft sheets with the face grain in the long direction. If the panel is subjected to bending across a 4 ft by 8 ft opening, the bending unit stress (F_b) is less in the 4 ft dimension. The unit stresses resulting from a uniform load are balanced. This means they have roughly the same percentage of allowable unit stress in each direction, since the direction of greater allowable unit stress is also the direction of greater actual unit stress.

Veneers of plywood are manufactured by being cut from logs slightly longer than the 8 ft length of a finished plywood veneer. The cutting is done with a knife blade held in place while the log rotates against it. A thin, continuous layer is peeled from the ever-decreasing circumference and cut into sheet size veneers.

The veneers cannot always be made 4 ft wide and must sometimes be made from more than one piece and neatly joined side by side. The desired combination of these veneers is dried in an oven, glued together, and pressed into plywood sheets. Sometimes veneers are cut in slices across the log parallel to the axis of the log in the same direction as slash cut lumber to obtain a special appearance. The veneers are usually $1/16$ in. to $3/16$ in. thick.

Softwood Plywood

The types and grades of softwood plywood are described in the U.S. Department of Commerce's Product Standard PS1 for Softwood Plywood— Construction and Industrial. Softwood plywood sheet thicknesses in common

GROUP 1	GROUP 2	GROUP 3	GROUP 4	GROUP 5
Apitong[a,b]	Cedar, Port Orford	Alder, red	Aspen	Basswood
Beech, American	Cypress	Birch, paper	bigtooth	Fir, balsam
Birch	Douglas fir 2[c]	Cedar, Alaska	quaking	Poplar, balsam
sweet	Fir	Fir, subalpine	Cativo	
yellow	California red	Hemlock, eastern	Cedar	
Douglas fir 1[c]	grand	Maple, bigleaf	incense	
Kapur[a]	noble	Pine	western red	
Keruing[a,b]	Pacific silver	jack	Cottonwood	
Larch, western	white	lodgepole	eastern	
Maple, sugar	Hemlock, western	ponderosa	black (western poplar)	
Pine	Lauan	spruce	Pine	
Caribbean	almon	Redwood	eastern white	
ocote	bagtikan	Spruce	sugar	
Pine, southern	mayapis	black		
loblolly	red lauan	engelmann		
longleaf	tangile	white		
shortleaf	white lauan			
slash	Maple, black			
Tanoak	Mengkulang[a]			
	Meranti, red[a,d]			
	Mersawa[a]			
	Pine			
	pond			
	red			
	Virginia			
	western white			
	Spruce			
	red			
	Sitka			
	Sweetgum			
	Tamarack			
	Yellow poplar			

[a] Each of these names represents a trade group of woods consisting of a number of closely related species.

[b] Species from the genus Dipterocarpus are marketed collectively: Apitong if originating in the Philippines; Keruing if originating in Malaysia or Indonesia.

[c] Douglas fir from trees grown in the states of Washington, Oregon, California, Idaho, Montana, and Wyoming, and the Canadian Provinces of Alberta and British Columbia shall be classed as Douglas fir No. 1. Douglas fir from trees grown in the states of Nevada, Utah, Colorado, Arizona, and New Mexico shall be classed as Douglas fir No. 2.

[d] Red Meranti shall be limited to species having a specific gravity of 0.41 or more based on green volume and oven dry weight.

FIGURE 6-28. Classification of species (Courtesy American Plywood Association)

use are ¼, ⁵/₁₆, ⅜, ½, ⅝, ¾, ⅞, 1⅛, and 1¼ in. Veneers are classified into five *grades* based on finished appearance as judged by knots, pitch pockets, discoloration, and other characteristics similar to those used in grading lumber. The grades, starting with the best, are N, A, B, C, and D. Only the face and back veneers are judged. These may be repaired by cutting out defects and replacing them with patches that match so well in grain and color and fit so tightly in the hole that they are difficult to see.

Plywood is classified into five *species groups* according to strength and stiffness with Group 1 the strongest and stiffest. The species of wood included in each group are shown in Fig. 6–28. The sheet is considered to be in a group if the face and back are of a species from that group although the inner veneers may be of another group. This is logical because the stiffness and bending strength depend almost entirely on the outer veneers. Although more than 50 species are listed, most plywood is made from douglas fir.

Two general *types* of plywood are manufactured: interior and exterior. *Interior type plywood* is made with glue that is adequate for service indoors, and *exterior type plywood* is made with hot, phenolic resin glue that is unaffected by water and resists weathering as well as wood does. Exterior type plywood does not include any veneers, outer or inner, below C grade. It is intended for permanent outdoor installation. Interior plywood may be made in any grade.

The interior type is available in three categories. Interior glue is used for plywood intended for use where it may be exposed briefly to weather. Intermediate glue is used for plywood intended for use in high humidity or for exposure to the weather for a short time. Exterior glue is used for plywood expected to be exposed to weather for an extended period during construction.

Plywood is graded for strength although not in the same way as lumber. Based on the thickness and classification of species, strength is indicated by stamping two *identification index* numbers on the plywood sheet. The first number gives the maximum span if the sheet is used for a roof, and the second gives the maximum span if the sheet is used for a subfloor.

Plywood is specified and graded primarily either for appearance or for strength, depending on how it is to be used. Descriptions of the appearance veneer grades are listed in Fig. 6–29. If an appearance grade is desired, the grade, number of veneers, species group, type, and thickness are specified. If an engineered grade is desired for strength, the grade, identification index, number of veneers, and thickness are specified. These specified requirements are verified by a certification of quality stamped on the back or edge of each piece of plywood. Examples of such grade stamps are shown in Fig. 6–30.

Structural members can be fabricated of plywood, or of plywood in combination with sawn lumber or glu-lam lumber. The plywood is fastened to the lumber by nailing or gluing. Glue may be held under pressure by specialized equipment while drying, or the pressure may be applied by nailing tightly immediately after gluing in a procedure called *nail gluing*.

N	Smooth surface "natural finish" veneer. Select, all heartwood or all sapwood. Free of open defects. Allows not more than 6 repairs, wood only, per 4 × 8 panel, made parallel to grain and well matched for grain and color.
A	Smooth, paintable. Not more than 18 neatly made repairs, boat, sled, or router type, and parallel to grain, permitted. May be used for natural finish in less demanding applications.
B	Solid surface. Shims, circular repair plugs and tight knots to 1 inch permitted. Wood or synthetic patching material may be used. Some minor splits permitted.
C (plugged)	Improved C veneer with splits limited to ⅛ inch width and knotholes and borer holes limited to ¼ × ½ inch. Admits some broken grain. Synthetic repairs permitted.
C	Tight knots to 1½ inch. Knotholes to 1 inch and some to 1½ inch if total width of knots and knotholes is within specified limits. Synthetic or wood repairs. Discoloration and sanding defects that do not impair strength permitted. Limited splits allowed.
D	Knots and knotholes to 2½ inch width and ½ inch larger within specified limits. Limited splits are permitted.

FIGURE 6-29. Veneer grades used in plywood (Courtesy American Plywood Association)

Plywood is used for the gusset plates and splices of sawn wood trusses. It is also used for *box beams* where it serves as the web with sawn or glu-lam lumber as the flanges. *Stressed-skin panels* are made with the materials reversed. The upper and lower flanges (panel covers) are made of plywood with webs of sawn lumber. The assembly is very wide compared to its depth, but is stressed like a beam while having the shape of a panel.

Sandwich panels consist of plywood panel covers separated by a comparatively weak material with no need for sawn lumber except at the edges of the panels in some cases. The material between panel faces may be plastic foam or resin-impregnated paper in a honeycomb pattern. The material need only be strong enough to unite the load-bearing upper and lower panel faces which act structurally like the upper and lower chords of a truss. Truss chords are held apart by a thin network of web members, and the panel faces are also held apart by a thin network of material. See Fig. 6–31 for illustration of the various types of structural components.

Plywood siding is manufactured with face materials of various kinds to provide a particular effect while retaining the desirable properties of plywood. *Overlaid plywood* has a resin-treated surface, hot-bonded to the plywood sheet. The surface is smooth and intended for paint finish of the best quality. It is also used for concrete forms because its smooth surface makes a better

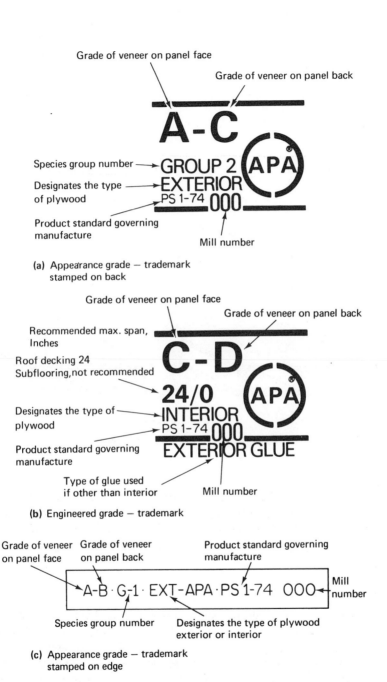

Grade of veneer on panel face

Grade of veneer on panel back

Species group number → GROUP 2

Designates the type → EXTERIOR

of plywood — PS 1-74

A-C

APA

000

Product standard governing
manufacture

Mill number

(a) Appearance grade — trademark
stamped on back

Grade of veneer on panel face

Grade of veneer on panel back

Recommended max. span,
Inches

Roof decking 24
Subflooring, not recommended

C-D

24/0

APA

Designates the type of —
plywood

INTERIOR
PS 1-74 000

Product standard governing
manufacture

EXTERIOR GLUE

Type of glue used
if other than interior

Mill number

(b) Engineered grade — trademark

Grade of veneer   Grade of veneer   Product standard governing
on panel face   on panel back   manufacture

A-B · G-1 · EXT-APA · PS 1-74 000

Mill
number

Species group number   Designates the type of plywood
                        exterior or interior

(c) Appearance grade — trademark
stamped on edge

FIGURE 6-30. Plywood grade (Courtesy American Plywood Association)

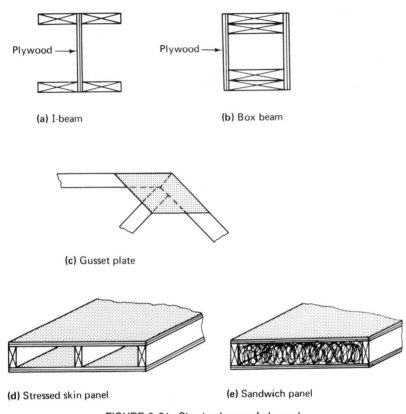

(a) I-beam   (b) Box beam

(c) Gusset plate

(d) Stressed skin panel   (e) Sandwich panel

FIGURE 6-31. Structural uses of plywood

concrete surface and allows forms to be removed easily. *Coated plywood* is surfaced with metal or plastic designed to produce a special effect. Coatings that simulate stucco or exposed aggregate are available as well as metal coatings of various textures and colors and clear plastic coating for protection only.

Hardwood Plywood

The types and grades of hardwood plywood are described in the U.S. Department of Commerce's Product Standard PS51 for Hardwood and Decorative Plywood. Hardwood plywood is usually selected for its appearance to be used as the face of cabinets, furniture, doors, flooring, and wall paneling. Many special effects can be obtained in wood pattern by the way the veneer is cut from the log. Knots, crooked grain, and other characteristics that indicate weakness are valued for their appearance.

Wall paneling is made with a face veneer selected for its appearance and then stained or treated for special effects. It may be sand blasted, antiqued, striated, or grooved to give the appearance of individual boards. It is made in sheets as thin as ⅛ in. with little strength and little care for the appearance of the back.

The core material behind hardwood veneers may be sawn lumber with a thin veneer on one or both faces for cabinets or furniture. It may be made from sawdust, shavings, and other scraps of wood mixed with glue and pressed into flat sheets called particle boards. It may also be made of noncombustible material for fire resistant construction.

GLUE

Glues commonly used in the manufacturing of plywood and in other wood fabrication are listed here.

Animal glues have traditionally been used for gluing wood. They are made from hides, hoofs, and other animal parts. They are heated before application and pressed cold, set quickly, show little stain, develop high strength, do not dull tools excessively, are not moisture resistant, and are low priced. They are used mostly for furniture, millwork, and cabinet work.

Casein glues are made from milk. They are used cold, set quickly, stain some woods excessively, develop high strength, cause tools to become dull, and perform well in damp conditions. They are used for structural joining and glu-lam and plywood manufacturing.

Melamine resin, phenol resin, resorcinol resin, and *resorcinol resin-phenol resin* combinations are used when waterproof glues are needed. All except resorcinol require high temperatures for curing, although some resorcinol–phenol combinations may use temperatures as low as 100°F (38°C). All of them show little stain, develop very high strength, and are expensive. They are used for structural joining and glu-lam and plywood manufacturing.

Some *vegetable glues* are made from starch. They are used cold, set at various rates, stain some woods slightly, develop high strength, cause some dulling of tools, and have low resistance to moisture. They are used in manufacturing plywood.

MECHANICAL FASTENERS

Wood members are fastened together and to other materials with metal fasteners of various kinds. The traditional nails made of steel and sometimes aluminum, copper, zinc, or brass are widely used. The standard lengths of nails are made in three diameters called box nails, common nails, and spikes, with box nails being the thinnest and spikes the thickest. Spikes are also made in longer sizes than the others. The tendency of wood to split when nailed is proportional to its specific gravity, and it is necessary to use several thinner nails rather than one thick one in heavy wood. The three diameters allow flexibility in the design of nailed joints.

Unseasoned wood that is nailed causes the nails to loosen as it shrinks during seasoning. Wood must be nailed dry if it is to be dry in use. However, wet wood may be nailed if it is going to stay wet.

A nail may be subjected to an axial force tending to pull it out of the wood. The nail is said to be subjected to withdrawal loading. The resistance to withdrawal depends on the nail diameter and the length driven into the wood and on the specific gravity of the wood, being much greater for heavier wood. Wood is much better able to resist withdrawal from side grain than from end grain. Nails subjected to withdrawal from end grain have half the resistance of those in side grain and are not permitted by the National Design Specification. Nails are sometimes coated with cement or rosin to make them more resistant to withdrawal.

The most common load on the wood of a nailed joint is a lateral load in side grain. The load that can be resisted depends on the specific gravity of the wood and on the length and diameter of the nail embedded in the wood. It does not depend on the direction of load. The nails connecting flanges and webs of box beams and the nails connecting truss joints are loaded laterally. Resistance to lateral loads in end grain is two-thirds of the side grain resistance. Wood offers more resistance to lateral loads than to withdrawal, and nails should be loaded laterally in preference to withdrawal whenever possible. See Fig. 6–32 for illustrations of nailed joints.

Wood screws are used for the same purpose as nails and transmit withdrawal or lateral loads to the wood in much the same way. Strength depends on the length and width of the screw and on specific gravity of the wood. It is independent of direction for lateral loads. Screws can resist stronger forces than nails of comparable size because of the grip of the threads in the wood. Resistance to lateral loads is greater, and the design should require them rather than withdrawal loads if at all possible. Resistance to withdrawal from end grain is low, and screws are not permitted by the National Design Specification to be loaded this way. Lateral resistance in end grain is two-thirds of the resistance in side grain.

Bolts are used to transmit lateral forces from one wood member to another and are not loaded in withdrawal. A bolt is inserted into a predrilled hole and held in place between the bolt head and a nut. The load transmitted by a laterally loaded bolt is different from the load transmitted by a laterally

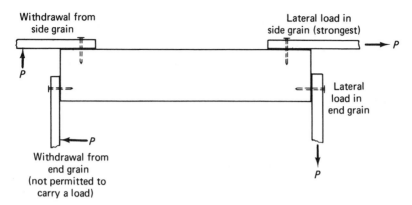

FIGURE 6-32. Loads on nails

loaded nail or screw. The resistance is a function of the compressive strength of the wood and the area (length × width of bolt) bearing against the wood. Just as wood is strongest in compression parallel to grain and weakest in compression perpendicular to grain, so the bolted joint is strongest when the load is parallel to grain and weakest when the load is perpendicular to grain, and has an intermediate strength at any other angle. The allowable load at other angles is determined by using the Hankinson formula or Scholten nomographs and the allowable loads parallel and perpendicular to grain.

Lag screws, which are threaded at the pointed end for one-half to three-quarters of the length and unthreaded toward the head, provide good withdrawal resistance like a screw and strong lateral resistance like a bolt.

Two types of connectors are used in combination with bolts to increase the area of wood in compression. One split ring or a pair of shear plates is used for wood to wood connections and one shear plate for metal to wood connections. Several may be used in one joint. Both types are inserted into tight-fitting prefabricated holes. They may be used in side grain or end grain at any angle. Their strength depends on the area of wood in contact with the connector and the compressive strength of the wood at that angle as determined by the Hankinson formula or Scholten nomographs. Split rings transfer the load from wood to wood through the ring, and the bolt takes no load, but only holds the joint together. Shear connectors fit tightly over the bolt, and the load is transferred from one member to another through the bolt. Many other specialized fasteners are designed for connecting wood rapidly and securely. See Fig. 6-33 for illustration of some of the types in use.

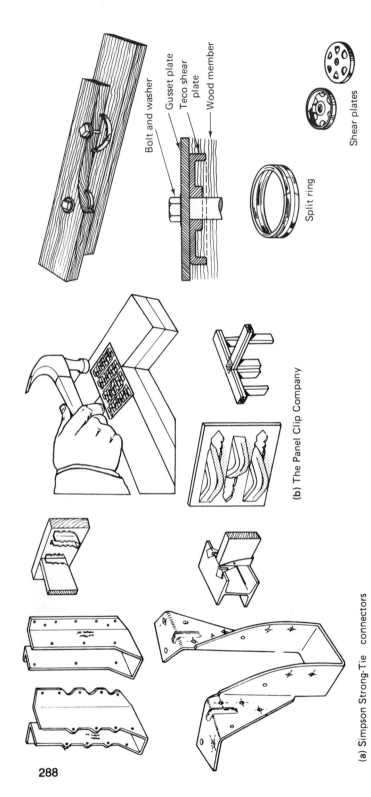

(a) Simpson Strong-Tie connectors

(b) The Panel Clip Company

Bolt and washer

Gusset plate
Teco shear plate
Wood member

Split ring

Shear plates

(c) Timber Engineering Company

FIGURE 6-33 Typical connectors used with wood: (A) Simpson Strong-Tie® Connectors (Courtesy Simpson Co.); (B) top plate tie with truss clip (Courtesy Panel Clip Co.); (C) split rings and shear plates (Courtesy Timber Engineering Co.)

Review Questions

1. At what time of year was the tree in Fig. 6–2 cut down? Explain your answer.

2. Indicate in a sketch the pattern of grain in a straight board sawed from a tree with a bend in it. Show boards sawed parallel to the plane of the bend and perpendicular to the plane of the bend.

3. Give the fbm of the following quantities of wood: (a) 800 lineal feet of ¾″ × 8″; (b) 15 pieces of 2 × 4 from 12′0″ to 12′11″ in length; (c) one post 10′ long, 14″ × 14″ in cross section.

4. Should a window frame as shown in Fig. 6–15 be slash cut or rift cut to keep joint opening to a minimum? Explain your answer.

5. In what ways do springwood and summerwood differ?

6. Define equilibrium moisture content.

7. Describe three methods of seasoning wood.

8. If the unit stress at failure in bending is 7200 psi for small, perfect samples of a certain species of wood, what is the allowable bending unit stress for a piece of lumber with defects that are judged to reduce the strength by 40%?

9. Determine the allowable compressive unit stress at an angle of 18° with the grain for select structural ponderosa pine posts and timbers (by formula or nomograph).

10. Explain the difference between single member and repetitive member.

11. What is the difference between a characteristic and a manufacturing imperfection?

12. If other factors are equal, which piece of lumber is weaker—one with a slope of grain of one in five or one with a slope of grain of one in six?

13. How do preservatives protect wood from rotting, insects, and marine borers?

14. Discuss the advantages and disadvantages of creosote as a preservative.

15. Why can glu-lam timbers be stronger than sawn timbers?

16. What characteristic of plywood is indicated by the veneer grade? By the species group?

17. What does the designation 24/16 mean on a plywood grade-trade-mark?

Appendix

ASTM Standards Relating to Aggregates*

 **Designation: C 29 – 71**

American National Standard A37.16
American National Standards Institute

American Association State
Highway Officials Standard
AASHO No.: T 19

Standard Method of Test for
UNIT WEIGHT OF AGGREGATE[1]

This Standard is issued under the fixed designation C 29; the number immediately following the designation indicates the year of original adoption or, in the case of revision, the year of last revision. A number in parentheses indicates the year of last reapproval.

1. Scope

1.1 This method covers the determination of the unit weight of fine, coarse, or mixed aggregates.

NOTE 1—The values stated in U.S. customary units are to be regarded as the standard. The metric equivalents of U.S. customary units may be approximate.

2. Apparatus

2.1 *Balance*—A balance or scale accurate within 0.1 percent of the test load at any point within the range of use. The range of use shall be considered to extend from the weight of the measure empty to the weight of the measure plus its contents at 100 lb/ft³ (1600 kg/m³).

2.2 *Tamping Rod*—A round, straight steel rod, ⅝ in. (16 mm) in diameter and approximately 24 in. (600 mm) in length, having one end rounded to a hemispherical tip of the same diameter as the rod.

2.3 *Measure*—A cylindrical metal measure, preferably provided with handles. It shall be watertight, with the top and bottom true and even, preferably machined to accurate dimensions on the inside, and sufficiently rigid to retain its form under rough usage. The top rim shall be smooth and plane within 0.01 in (0.25 mm) and shall be parallel to the bottom within 0.5 deg (Note 2). Measures of the two larger sizes listed in Table 1 shall be reinforced around the top with a metal band, to provide an over-all wall thickness of not less than 0.20 in. (5 mm) in the upper 1½ in. (38 mm). The capacity and dimensions of the measure shall conform to the limits in Table 1 or 2 (Note 3).

NOTE 2—The top rim is satisfactorily plane if a 0.01-in. (0.25-mm) feeler gage cannot be inserted between the rim and a piece of ¼-in. (6-mm) or thicker plate glass laid over the measure. The top and bottom are satisfactorily parallel if the slope between pieces of plate glass in contact with the top and bottom does not exceed 1 percent in any direction.

NOTE 3—Dimensional tolerances and thicknesses of metal prescribed here are intended to be applied to measures acquired after January 1, 1968. Measures acquired before that date may conform either to this standard or to Section 2(c) of Method C 29 – 60.[2]

3. Sample

3.1 The sample of aggregate shall be dried to essentially constant weight, preferably in an oven, at 220 to 230 F (105 to 110 C) and thoroughly mixed.

4. Calibration of Measure

4.1 Fill the measure with water at room temperature and cover with a piece of plate glass in such a way as to eliminate bubbles and excess water.

4.2 Determine the net weight of water in the measure to an accuracy of ± 0.1 percent.

4.3 Measure the temperature of the water and determine its unit weight, from Table 3, interpolating if necessary.

4.4 Calculate the factor for the measure by dividing the unit weight of the water by the weight required to fill the measure.

COMPACT WEIGHT DETERMINATION

5. Rodding Procedure

5.1 The rodding procedure is applicable to

---

[1] This method is under the jurisdiction of ASTM Committee C-9 on Concrete and Concrete Aggregates and is the direct responsibility of Subcommittee C09.03.05 on Methods of Testing and Specifications for Physical Characteristics of Concrete Aggregates.
Current edition effective Jan. 8, 1971. Originally issued 1920. Replaces C 29 – 69.
[2] Discontinued, see *1966 Book of ASTM Standards*, Part 10.

* Reprinted by permission of the American Society for Testing and Materials from copyright material.

aggregates having a maximum size of 1½ in. (40 mm) or less.

5.1.1 Fill the measure one-third full and level the surface with the fingers. Rod the layer of aggregate with 25 strokes of the tamping rod evenly distributed over the surface. Fill the measure two-thirds full and again level and rod as above. Finally, fill the measure to overflowing and again rod as above. Level the surface of the aggregate with the fingers or a straightedge in such a way that any slight projections of the larger pieces of the coarse aggregate approximately balance the larger voids in the surface below the top of the measure.

5.1.2 In rodding the first layer, do not allow the rod to strike the bottom of the measure forcibly. In rodding the second and third layers, use only enough force to cause the tamping rod to penetrate the previous layer of aggregate.

5.1.3 Weigh the measure and its contents and record the net weight of the aggregate to the nearest 0.1 percent. Multiply this weight by the factor calculated as described in 4.4. The product is the compact unit weight of the aggregate.

6. Jigging Procedure

6.1 The jigging procedure is applicable to aggregates having a maximum size greater than 1½ in. (40 mm) and not to exceed 4 in. (100 mm).

6.1.1 Fill the measure in three approximately equal layers as described in 5.1.1, compacting each layer by placing the measure on a firm base, such as a cement-concrete floor, raising the opposite sides alternately about 2 in. (50 mm), and allowing the measure to drop in such a manner as to hit with a sharp, slapping blow. The aggregate particles, by this procedure, will arrange themselves in a densely compacted condition. Compact each layer by dropping the measure 50 times in the

manner described, 25 times on each side. Level the surface of the aggregate with the fingers or a straightedge in such a way that any slight projections of the larger pieces of the coarse aggregate approximately balance the larger voids in the surface below the top of the measure.

6.1.2 Weigh the measure and its contents and record the net weight of the aggregate to the nearest 0.1 percent. Multiply this weight by the factor calculated as described in 4.4. The product is the compact unit weight of the aggregate.

LOOSE WEIGHT DETERMINATION

7. Shoveling Procedure

7.1 The shoveling procedure is applicable to aggregates having a maximum size of 4 in. (100 mm) or less.

7.1.1 Fill the measure to overflowing by means of a shovel or scoop, discharging the aggregate from a height not to exceed 2 in. (50 mm) above the top of the measure. Exercise care to prevent, so far as possible, segregation of the particle sizes of which the sample is composed. Level the surface of the aggregate with the fingers or a straightedge in such a way that any slight projections of the larger pieces of the coarse aggregate approximately balance the larger voids in the surface below the top of the measure.

7.1.2 Weigh the measure and its contents and record the net weight of the aggregate to the nearest 0.1 percent. Multiply this weight by the factor calculated as described in 4.4. The product is the loose unit weight of the aggregate.

8. Reproducibility of Results

8.1 Results by an operator using the same sample and procedure should check within 1 percent.

TABLE 1 Dimensions of Measures, U.S. Customary System[a]

Capacity, ft³	Inside Diameter, in.	Inside Height, in.	Thicknesses of metal, min, in.		Size of Aggregate, max, in.[b]
			Bottom	Wall	
¹/₁₀	6.0 ± 0.1	6.1 ± 0.1	0.20	0.10	½
⅓	8.0 ± 0.1	11.5 ± 0.1	0.20	0.10	1
½	10.0 ± 0.1	11.0 ± 0.1	0.20	0.12	1½
1	14.0 ± 0.1	11.2 ± 0.1	0.20	0.12	4

[a] The indicated size of container may be used to test aggregates of a maximum nominal size equal to or smaller than that listed.

[b] Based on sieves with square openings.

TABLE 2 Dimensions of Measures, Metric System[a]

Capacity, liters	Inside Diameter, mm	Inside Height, mm	Thicknesses of metal, min, mm		Size of Aggregate, max, mm[b]
			Bottom	Wall	
3	155 ± 2	160 ± 2	5.0	2.5	12.5
10	205 ± 2	305 ± 2	5.0	2.5	25
15	255 ± 2	295 ± 2	5.0	3.0	40
30	355 ± 2	305 ± 2	5.0	3.0	100

[a] The indicated size of container may be used to test aggregates of a maximum nominal size equal to or smaller than that listed.

[b] Based on sieves with square openings.

TABLE 3 Unit Weight of Water

Temperature		lb/ft³	kg/m³
deg F	deg C		
60	15.6	62.366	999.01
65	18.3	62.336	998.54
70	21.1	62.301	997.97
(73.4)	(23.0)	(62.274)	(997.54)
75	23.9	62.261	997.32
80	26.7	62.216	996.59
85	29.4	62.166	995.83

 **Designation: C 33 – 74 a**

American National Standard A37.124
American National Standards Institute

Standard Specification for
CONCRETE AGGREGATES[1]

This Standard is issued under the fixed designation C 33; the number immediately following the designation indicates the year of original adoption or, in the case of revision, the year of last revision. A number in parentheses indicates the year of last reapproval.

1. Scope

1.1 This specification covers fine and coarse aggregate, other than leightweight aggregate, for use in concrete.[2]

NOTE 1—This specification is regarded as adequate to ensure satisfactory materials for most concrete. It is recognized that, for certain work or in certain regions, it may be either more or less restrictive than needed.

NOTE 2—Definitions of terms used in this specification may be found in Definitions C 125.

2. Applicable Documents

2.1 The following documents form a part of this specification to the extent referenced herein:

2.1.1 *ASTM Standards:*

C 29 Test for Unit Weight of Aggregate[3]

C 39 Test for Compressive Strength of Cylindrical Concrete Specimens[3]

C 40 Test for Organic Impurities in Sands for Concrete[3]

C 78 Test for Flexural Strength of Concrete (Using Simple Beam with Third-Point Loading)[3]

C 87 Test for Effect of Organic Impurities in Fine Aggregate on Strength of Mortar[3]

C 88 Test for Soundness of Aggregates by Use of Sodium Sulfate or Magnesium Sulfate[3]

C 117 Test for Materials Finer than No. 200 (75-μm) Sieve in Mineral Aggregates by Washing[3]

C 123 Test for Lightweight Pieces in Aggregate[3]

C 125 Definitions of Terms Relating to Concrete and Concrete Aggregates[3]

C 131 Test for Resistance to Abrasion of

Small Size Coarse Aggregate by Use of the Los Angeles Machine[3]

C 136 Test for Sieve or Screen Analysis of Fine and Coarse Aggregates[3]

C 142 Test for Clay Lumps and Friable Particles in Aggregates[3]

C 227 Test for Potential Alkali Reactivity of Cement-Aggregate Combinations (Mortar-Bar Method)[3]

C 235 Test for Scratch Hardness of Coarse Aggregate Particles[3]

C 289 Test for Potential Reactivity of Aggregates (Chemical Method)[3]

C 295 Recommended Practice for Petrographic Examination of Aggregates for Concrete[3]

C 342 Test for Potential Volume Change of Cement-Aggregate Combinations[3]

C 535 Test for Resistance to Abrasion of Large Size Coarse Aggregate by Use. of the Los Angeles Machine[3]

C 586 Test for Potential Alkali Reactivity of Carbonate Rocks for Concrete Aggregates (Rock Cylinder Method)[3]

C 666 Test for Resistance of Concrete to

---

[1] This specification is under the jurisdiction of ASTM Committee C-9 on Concrete and Concrete Aggregates and is the direct responsibility of Subcommittee C09.03.05 on Methods of Testing and Specifications for Physical Characteristics of Concrete Aggregates.

Current edition approved Oct. 25, 1974. Published December 1974. Originally published as C 33 – 21 T. Last previous edition C 33 – 74.

[2] For lightweight aggregates, see ASTM Specification C 331, for Lightweight Aggregates for Concrete Masonry Units, ASTM Specification C 332, for Lightweight Aggregates for Insulating Concrete, and ASTM Specification C 330, for Lightweight Aggregates for Structural Concrete, which appear in the *Annual Book of ASTM Standards*, Part 14.

[3] *Annual Book of ASTM Standards*, Part 14.

Rapid Freezing and Thawing[2]
D 75 Sampling Aggregates[3]

FINE AGGREGATE

3. General Characteristics

3.1 Fine aggregate shall consist of natural sand, manufactured sand, or a combination thereof. Certain manufactured sands produce slippery pavement surfaces and should be investigated for acceptance before use.

4. Grading

4.1 *Sieve Analysis*—Fine aggregate, except as provided in 4.2, shall be graded within the following limits:

Sieve	Percent Passing
⅜-in. (9.5-mm)	100
No. 4 (4.75-mm)	95 to 100
No. 8 (2.36-mm)	80 to 100
No. 16 (1.18-mm)	50 to 85
No. 30 (600-μm)	25 to 60
No. 50 (300-μm)	10 to 30
No. 100 (150-μm)	2 to 10

4.2 The minimum percent shown above for material passing the No. 50 and No. 100 sieves may be reduced to 5 and 0, respectively, if the aggregate is to be used in air-entrained concrete containing more than 4½ bags of cement per cubic yard (251 kg/m³) or in nonair-entrained concrete containing more than 5½ bags of cement per cubic yard (307 kg/m³) or if an approved mineral admixture is used to supply the deficiency in percent passing these sieves. Air-entrained concrete is here considered to be concrete containing air-entraining cement or an air-entraining agent and having an air content of more than 3 %.

4.3 The fine aggregate shall have not more than 45 % retained between any two consecutive sieves of those shown in 4.1, and its fineness modulus shall be not less than 2.3 nor more than 3.1.

4.4 Fine aggregate failing to meet the sieve analysis and fineness modulus requirements of 4.1, 4.2, or 4.3, may be acceped provided that it is demonstrated that concrete of the class specified, made with the fine aggregate under consideration, will have relevant properties at least equal to those of concrete made with the same ingredients, with the exception that a reference fine aggregate be used which conforms to 4.1, 4.2, and 4.3 and which is selected

from a source having an acceptable performance record in similar concrete construction.

NOTE 3—Relevant properties are those properties of the concrete which are important to the particular application being considered. ASTM Special Technical Publication 169 A, *Significance of Tests and Properties of Concrete and Concrete-Making Materials*, provides a discussion of important concrete properties.

4.5 If the fineness modulus varies by more than 0.20 from the value assumed in selecting proportions for the concrete, the fine aggregate shall be rejected unless suitable adjustments are made in concrete proportions to compensate for the difference in grading.

5. Deleterious Substances

5.1 The amount of deleterious substances in fine aggregate shall not exceed the limits prescribed in Table 1.

5.2 *Organic Impurities:*

5.2.1 Fine aggregate shall be free of injurious amounts of organic impurities. Except as herein provided, aggregates subjected to the test for organic impurities and producing a color darker than the standard shall be rejected.

5.2.2 A fine aggregate failing in the test may be used, provided that the discoloration is due principally to the presence of small quantities of coal, lignite, or similar discrete particles.

5.2.3 A fine aggregate failing in the test may be used, provided that, when tested for the effect of organic impurities on strength of mortar, the relative strength at 7 days calculated in accordance with Method C 87, is not less than 95 %.

5.3 Fine aggregate for use in concrete that will be subject to wetting, extended exposure to humid atmosphere, or contact with moist ground shall not contain any materials that are deleteriously reactive with the alkalies in the cement in an amount sufficient to cause excessive expansion of mortar or concrete, except that if such materials are present in injurious amounts, the fine aggregate may be used with a cement containing less than 0.6 % alkalies calculated as sodium oxide or with the addition of a material that has been shown to prevent harmful expansion due to the alkali-aggregate reaction. (See Appendix X1.)

6. Soundness

6.1 Except as provided in 6.2 and 6.3, fine aggregate subjected to five cycles of the soundness test, shall show a loss, weighted in accordance with the grading of a sample complying with the limitations set forth in Section 4, not greater than 10 % when sodium sulfate is used or 15 % when magnesium sulfate is used.

NOTE 4—The specifier should designate which of the two salts is to be used. If the salt is not designated, the aggregate will be acceptable if it meets the indicated limit for either sodium sulfate or magnesium sulfate.

6.2 Fine aggregate failing to meet the requirements of 6.1 may be accepted, provided that concrete of comparable properties, made from similar aggregate from the same source, has given satisfactory service when exposed to weathering similar to that to be encountered.

6.3 Fine aggregate not having a demonstrable service record and failing to meet the requirements of 6.1 may be accepted, provided it gives satisfactory results in concrete subjected to freezing and thawing tests.

COARSE AGGREGATE

7. General Characteristics

7.1 Coarse aggregate shall consist of gravel, crushed gravel, crushed stone, or air-cooled blast furnace slag, or a combination thereof, conforming to the requirements of this specification.

8. Grading

8.1 Coarse aggregates shall be graded between the limits specified and shall conform to the requirements prescribed in Table 2.

9. Deleterious Substances

9.1 Except for the provisions of 9.3 and for the special case of gravels consisting predominantly of chert, the limits given in Table 3 shall apply to all coarse aggregates for the respective weathering regions shown in Fig. 1 (Note 5). The map is intended to serve only as a guide to probable weathering severity. Those undertaking construction, especially near the boundaries of the weathering regions, should consult local Weather Bureau records for amount of winter precipitation and number of freeze-thaw cycles to be expected. These data should be used to assign the weathering severity degree for establishing test requirements of the coarse aggregate.

NOTE 5—It is expected that the limits for coarse aggregates corresponding to each class designation are sufficient to ensure satisfactory performance in concrete for the respective type and location of construction. In many localities, aggregates exceeding the most restrictive quality requirements listed are readily procurable. Where this is not the case, available aggregates are often of adequate quality to satisfy at least some of the listed uses or can be made so by appropriate processing. Aggregates purchased to meet a given class designation often have properties qualifying them for a type or location of construction for which more restrictive limits are prescribed in Table 3. In the latter case, they are eligible for reclassification at once to the more restrictive class.

9.2 Coarse aggregate for use in concrete that will be subject to wetting, extended exposure to humid atmosphere, or contact with moist ground shall not contain any materials that are deleteriously reactive with the alkalies in the cement in an amount sufficient to cause excessive expansion of mortar or concrete, except that if such materials are present in injurious amounts, the coarse aggregate may be used with a cement containing less than 0.6 % alkalies calculated as sodium oxide or with the addition of a material that has been shown to prevent harmful expansion due to the alkali-aggregate reaction (see Appendix X1).

9.3 Coarse aggregate having test results exceeding the limits specified in Table 3 may be accepted provided that concrete made with similar aggregate from the same source has given satisfactory service when exposed in a similar manner to that to be encountered; or, in the absence of a demonstrable service record, provided that the aggregate produces concrete having satisfactory characteristics when tested in the laboratory.

METHODS OF SAMPLING AND TESTING

10. Methods of Sampling and Testing

10.1 Sample and test the aggregates in accordance with the following methods, except as otherwise provided in this specification. Make the required tests on test samples that comply with requirements of the designated test methods and are representative of the grading that will be used in the concrete. The same test sample may be used for sieve analysis and for determination of material finer than the No. 200 (75-μm) sieve. Separated sizes from the sieve analysis may be used in preparation of samples for soundness or abrasion tests. For determination of all other tests and for evaluation of potential alkali reactivity where' required, use independent test samples (Note 4).

10.1.1 *Sampling*—Methods D 75.

10.1.2 *Grading*—Method C 136.

10.1.3 *Amount of Material Finer than No. 200 (75-μm) Sieve*—Method C 117.

10.1.4 *Organic Impurities*—Method C 40.

10.1.5 *Effect of Organic Impurities on Strength*—Method C 87.

10.1.6 *Compressive Strength*—Method C 39.

10.1.7 *Flexural Strength*—Method C 78.

10.1.8 *Soundness*—Method C 88.

10.1.9 *Clay Lumps and Friable Particles*—Method C 142.

10.1.10 *Coal and Lignite*—Method C 123, using a liquid of 2.0 sp gr to remove the particles of coal and lignite. Only material that is brownish-black, or black, shall be considered coal or lignite. Coke shall not be classed as coal or lignite.

10.1.11 *Weight of Slag*—Method C 29.

10.1.12 *Abrasion of Coarse Aggregate*—Method C 131 or Method C 535.

10.1.13 *Fineness Modulus*—The fineness modulus, as defined in Definitions C 125, is obtained by adding the total percentages shown by the sieve analysis to be retained on each of the following sieves, and dividing the sum by 100: No. 100 (150-μm), No. 50 (300-μm), No. 30 (600-μm), No. 16 (1.18-mm), No. 8 (2.36-mm), No. 4 (4.75-mm), ⅜-in. (9.5-mm), ¾-in. (19.0-mm), 1½-in. (37.5-mm), and larger, increasing in the ratio of 2 to 1.

10.1.14 *Soft Particles*—Method C 235.

10.1.15 *Reactive Aggregates*—Method C 227, Method C 289, Recommended Practice C 295, Method C 342, and Method C 586.

10.1.16 *Freezing and Thawing*—Procedures for making freezing and thawing tests of concrete are described in Method C 666.

TABLE 1 Limits for Deleterious Substances in Fine Aggregate for Concrete

Item	Weight Percent of Total Sample, max
Clay lumps and friable particles	3.0
Material finer than No. 200 (75-μm) sieve:	
Concrete subject to abrasion	3.0[a]
All other concrete	5.0[a]
Coal and lignite:	
Where surface appearance of concrete is of importance	0.5
All other concrete	1.0

[a] In the case of manufactured sand, if the material finer than the No. 200 (75-μm) sieve consists of the dust of fracture, essentially free from clay or shale, these limits may be increased to 5 and 7 %, respectively.

TABLE 2 Grading Requirements for Coarse Aggregates

Size Number	Nominal Size (Sieves with Square Openings)	Amounts Finer than Each Laboratory Sieve (Square Openings), Weight Percent												
		4 in. (100 mm)	3½ in. (90 mm)	3 in. (75 mm)	2½ in. (63 mm)	2 in. (50 mm)	1½ in. (37.5 mm)	1 in. (25.0 mm)	¾ in. (19.0 mm)	½ in. (12.5 mm)	⅜ in. (9.5 mm)	No. 4 (4.75-mm)	No. 8 (2.36-mm)	No. 16 (1.18-mm)
1	3½ to 1½ in. (90 to 37.5 mm)	100	90 to 100	...	25 to 60	...	0 to 15	...	0 to 5	...	...	...	...	...
2	2½ to 1½ in. (63 to 37.5 mm)	...	...	100	90 to 100	35 to 70	0 to 15	...	0 to 5	...	...	...	...	...
357	2 in. to No. 4 (50 to 4.75 mm)	...	...	...	100	95 to 100	...	35 to 70	...	10 to 30	...	0 to 5	...	...
467	1½ in. to No. 4 (37.5 to 4.75 mm)	...	...	...	...	100	95 to 100	...	35 to 70	...	10 to 30	0 to 5	0 to 5	...
57	1 in. to No. 4 (25.0 to 4.75 mm)	...	...	...	...	...	100	95 to 100	...	25 to 60	...	0 to 10	0 to 5	...
67	¾ in. to No. 4 (19.0 to 4.75 mm)	...	...	...	...	...	...	100	90 to 100	...	20 to 55	0 to 10	0 to 5	...
7	½ in. to No. 4 (12.5 to 4.75 mm)	...	...	...	...	...	...	...	100	90 to 100	40 to 70	0 to 15	0 to 5	...
8	⅜ in. to No. 8 (9.5 to 2.36 mm)	...	...	...	...	...	...	...	...	100	85 to 100	10 to 30	0 to 10	0 to 5
3	2 to 1 in. (50 to 25.0 mm)	...	...	...	100	90 to 100	35 to 70	0 to 15	...	0 to 5	...	...	...	...
4	1½ to ¾ in. (37.5 to 19.0 mm)	...	...	...	...	100	90 to 100	20 to 55	0 to 15	...	0 to 5	...	...	...

TABLE 3 Limits for Deleterious Substances and Physical Property Requirements of Coarse Aggregate for Concrete

NOTE—See Fig. 1 for location of weathering regions

Class Design-nation-	Type or Location of Concrete Construction	Maximum Allowable, %						
		Clay Lumps and Friable Particles	Chert (Less than 2.40 sp gr SSD)[c]	Sum of Clay Lumps, Friable Particles and Chert (Less Than 2.40 sp gr SSD)[c]	Material Finer Than No. 200 (75-μm) Sieve	Coal and Lignite	Abrasion[a]	Magnesium Sulfate Soundness (5-cycles)[b]
		Severe Weathering Regions						
1S	Footings, foundations, columns and beams not exposed to the weather, interior floor slabs to be given coverings	10.0	--	--	1.0[d]	1.0	50	--
2S	Interior floors without coverings	5.0	--	--	1.0[d]	0.5	50	--
3S	Foundation walls above grade, retaining walls, abutments, piers, girders, and beams exposed to the weather	5.0	5.0	7.0	1.0[d]	0.5	50	18
4S	Pavements, bridge decks, driveways and curbs, walks, patios, garage floors, exposed floors and porches, or waterfront structures subject to frequent wetting	3.0	5.0	5.0	1.0[d]	0.5	50	18
5S	Exposed architectural concrete	2.0	3.0	3.0	1.0[d]	0.5	50	18
		Moderate Weathering Regions						
1M	Footings, foundations, columns, and beams not exposed to the weather, interior floor slabs to be given coverings	10.0	--	--	1.0[d]	1.0	50	--
2M	Interior floors without coverings	5.0	--	--	1.0[d]	0.5	50	--
3M	Foundation walls above grade, retaining walls, abutments, piers, girders, and beams exposed to the weather[e]	5.0	8.0	10.0	1.0[d]	0.5	50	18
4M	Pavements, bridge decks, driveways and curbs, walks, patios, garage floors, exposed floors and porches, or waterfront structures subject to frequent wetting[e]	5.0	5.0	7.0	1.0[d]	0.5	50	18

[a] Crushed air-cooled blast-furnace slag is excluded from the abrasion requirements. The compact unit weight of crushed air-cooled blast-furnace slag shall be not less than 70 lb/ft³ (1120 kg/m³). The grading of slag used in the unit weight test shall conform to the grading to be used in the concrete. Abrasion loss of gravel, crushed gravel, or crushed stone shall be determined on the test size or sizes most nearly corresponding to the grading or gradings to be used in the concrete. When more than one grading is to be used, the limit on abrasion loss shall apply to each.

[b] The allowable limits for soundness shall be 12 % if sodium sulfate is used.

[c] These limitations apply only to aggregates in which chert appears as an impurity. They are not applicable to gravels that are predominantly chert. Limitations on soundness of such aggregates must be based on service records in the environment in which they are used.

[d] In the case of crushed aggregates, if the material finer than the No. 200 (75-μm) sieve consists of the dust of fracture, essentially free of clay or shale, this percentage may be increased to 1.5.

[e] For construction at altitudes exceeding 5000 ft above sea level, the requirements of the "Severe Weathering Region" shall apply.

TABLE 3 *continued*

Class Desig-nation	Type or Location of Concrete Construction	Maximum Allowable, %						
		Clay Lumps and Friable Particles	Chert (Less than 2.40 sp gr SSD)[c]	Sum of Clay Lumps, Friable Particles and Chert (Less Than 2.40 sp gr SSD)[c]	Material Finer Than No. 200 (75-μm) Sieve	Coal and Lignite	Abra-sion[a]	Magne-sium Sulfate Soundness (5-cycles)[b]
5M	Exposed architectural concrete[e]	3.0	3.0	5.0	1.0[d]	0.5	50	18
	Negligible Weathering Regions							
1N	Slabs subject to traffic abrasion, bridge decks, floors, sidewalks, pavements[e]	5.0	--	--	1.0[d]	0.5	50	--
2N	All other classes of concrete[e]	10.0	--	--	1.0[d]	1.0	50	--

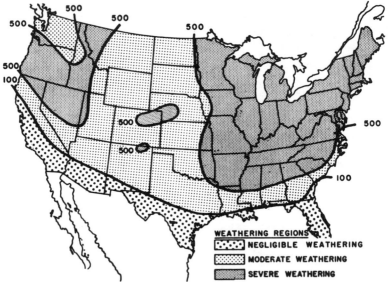

NOTE—Derivation of the weathering regions is given in ASTM Specification C 62, for Building Brick (Solid Masonry Units Made from Clay or Shale), which appears in the *Annual Book of ASTM Standards*, Part 16.

FIG. 1 Location of Weathering Regions.

APPENDIX

X1. METHODS FOR EVALUATING POTENTIAL REACTIVITY OF AN AGGREGATE

X1.1 A number of methods for detecting potential reactivity have been proposed. However, they do not provide quantitative information on the degree of reactivity to be expected or tolerated in service. Therefore, evaluation of potential reactivity of an aggregate should be based upon judgment and on the interpretation of test data and examination of concrete structures containing a combination of fine and coarse aggregates and cements for use in the new work. Results of the following tests will assist in making the evaluation:

X1.1.1 *Recommended Practice C 295*—Certain materials are known to be reactive with the alkalies in cements. These include the following forms of silica: opal, chalcedony; tridymite, and cristobalite; intermediate to acid (silica-rich) volcanic glass such as is likely to occur in rhyolite, andesite, or dacite; certain zeolites such as heulandite; and certain constituents of some phyllites. Determination of the presence and quantities of these materials by petrographic examination is helpful in evaluating potential alkali reactivity. Some of these materials render an aggregate deleteriously reactive when present in quantities as little as 1.0 % or even less.

X1.1.2 *Method C 289*—In this test, aggregates represented by points lying to the right of the solid line of Fig. 2 of Method C 289 usually should be considered potentially reactive.

X1.1.2.1 If R_c exceeds 70, the aggregate is considered potentially reactive if S_c is greater than R_c.

X1.1.2.2 If R_c is less than 70, the aggregate is considered potentially reactive if S_c is greater than 35 + $(R_c/2)$.

X1.2.2.3 These criteria conform to the solid line curve given in Fig. 2 of Method C 289. The test can be made quickly and, while not completely reliable in all cases, provides helpful information, especially where results of the more time-consuming tests are not available.

X1.1.3 *Method C 227*—The results of this test when made with a high-alkali cement, furnish information on the likelihood of harmful reactions occur-

ring. The alkali content of the cement should be substantially above 0.6 %, and preferably above 0.8 %, expressed as sodium oxide. Combinations of aggregate and cement which have produced excessive expansions in this test usually should be considered potentially reactive. While the line of demarcation between nonreactive and reactive combinations is not clearly defined, expansion is generally considered to be excessive if it exceeds 0.05 % at 3 months or 0.10 % at 6 months. Expansions greater than 0.05 % at 3 months should not be considered excessive where the 6-month expansion remains below 0.10 %. Data for the 3-month tests should be considered only when 6-month results are not avilable.

X1.1.4 *Method C 342*—Cement aggregate combinations tested by this procedure whose expansion equals or exceeds 0.200 % at an age of 1 year may be considered unsatisfactory for use in concrete exposed to wide variations of temperature and degree of saturation with water.

X1.1.5 *Potential Reactivity of Carbonate Aggregates*—The reaction of the dolomite in certain carbonate rocks with alkalies in portland cement paste has been found to be associated with deleterious expansion of concrete containing such rocks as coarse aggregate. Carbonate rocks capable of such reaction possess a characteristic texture and composition. The characteristic texture is that in which large crystals of dolomite are scattered in a fine-grained matrix of calcite and clay. The characteristic composition is that in which the carbonate portion consists of substantial amounts of both dolomite and calcite, and the acid-insoluble residue contains a significant amount of clay. Except in certain areas, such rocks are of relatively infrequent occurrence and seldom make up a significant proportion of the material present in a deposit of rock being considered for use in making aggregate for concrete. Method C 586 has been successfully used in (*1*) research and (*2*) preliminary screening of aggregate sources to indicate the presence of material with a potential for deleterious expansions when used in concrete.

American National Standard A37.19-1973(R-1967
Reaffirmed July 20, 1973
By American National Standards Institute
American Association State
Highway Officials Standard
AASHO No.: T 21

Standard Method of Test for
ORGANIC IMPURITIES IN SANDS FOR CONCRETE[1]

This Standard is issued under the fixed designation C 40; the number immediately following the designation indicates the year of original adoption or, in the case of revision, the year of last revision. A number in parentheses indicates the year of last reapproval.

1. Scope

1.1 This method covers an approximate determination of the presence of injurious organic compounds in natural sands which are to be used in cement mortar or concrete. The principal value of the test is to furnish a warning that further tests of the sands are necessary before they are approved for use.

2. Applicable Documents

2.1 *ASTM Standards:*
D 1544 Test for Color of Transparent Liquids (Gardner Color Scale)[2]

3. Apparatus

3.1 *Glass Bottles*—12-fluid oz (approximately 350-ml) colorless glass, graduated bottles of oval cross section, equipped with watertight stoppers or caps.

4. Reagent and Reference Standard Color Solution

4.1 *Reagent Sodium Hydroxide Solution (3 percent)*—Dissolve 3 parts by weight of sodium hydroxide (NaOH) in 97 parts of water.

4.2 *Reference Standard Color Solution*—Dissolve reagent grade potassium dichromate ($K_2Cr_2O_7$) in concentrated sulfuric acid (sp gr 1.84) at the rate of 0.250 g/100 ml of acid. The solution must be freshly made for the color comparison using gentle heat if necessary to effect solution.

5. Sample

5.1 A representative test sample of sand weighing about 1 lb (approximately 450 g) shall be obtained by quartering or by the use of a sampler.

6. Procedure

6.1 Fill a glass bottle to the 4½-fluid oz (approximately 130-ml) level with the sample of the sand to be tested.

6.2 Add a 3 percent NaOH solution in water until the volume of the sand and liquid, indicated after shaking, is 7 fluid ounces (approximately 200 ml).

6.3 Stopper the bottle, shake vigorously, and then allow to stand for 24 h.

7. Determination of Color Value

7.1 *Preferred Procedure*—At the end of the 24-h standing period, fill a glass bottle to the 2½-fluid oz (approximately 75-ml) level with the fresh reference standard color solution, prepared not longer than 2 h previously, as prescribed in 4.2. Then compare the color of the supernatant liquid above the test sample with that of the reference standard color solution and record whether it is lighter or darker or of equal color to that of the reference standard. Make the color comparison by holding the two bottles close together and looking through them.

7.2 *Alternative Procedure A*—To define more precisely the color of the liquid of the test sample, five color solutions may be used as prescribed in Table 1 of Method D 1544, using the following colors:

[1] This method is under the jurisdiction of ASTM Committee C-9 on Concrete and Concrete Aggregates and is the direct responsibility of Subcommittee C09.03.05 on Methods of Testing and Specifications for Physical Characteristics of Concrete Aggregates.
Current edition approved March 29, 1973. Published May 1973. Originally published as C 40 – 21 T. Last previous edition C 40 – 66 (1973).
[2] *1974 Annual Book of ASTM Standards*, Parts 27, 28, and 29.

Gardner Color Standard No.	Organic Plate No.
5	1
8	2
11	3 (standard)
14	4
16	5

The preparation and comparison procedure described in 7.1 shall be used, except that the organic plate number which is nearest the color of one of the five prepared solutions shall be reported.

7.3 *Alternative Procedure B*—Instead of the procedures described in 7.1 or 7.2, the color of the supernatant liquid above the test sample may be compared with a glass having a color equivalent to the color of the reference standard color specified in 4.2.

NOTE—A suitable instrument consists of the glass color standard mounted in a plastic holder. For the benefit of users of the alternative procedure, the instrument is provided with all five organic plate number colors.

8. Interpretation of Results

8.1 If the color of the supernatant liquid is darker than that of the reference standard color solution, the sand under test shall be considered to possibly contain injurious organic compounds, and further tests should be made before approving the sand for use in concrete.

Standard Method of Test for
SPECIFIC GRAVITY AND ABSORPTION OF COARSE AGGREGATE[1]

This Standard is issued under the fixed designation C 127; the number immediately following the designation indicates the year of original adoption or, in the case of revision, the year of last revision. A number in parentheses indicates the year of last reapproval.

1. Scope

1.1 This method covers the determination of bulk and apparent specific gravity, 73.4/73.4 F (23/23 C), and absorption of coarse aggregate. Bulk specific gravity is the characteristic generally used for calculations of the volume occupied by the aggregate in portland-cement concrete.

1.2 This method determines (after 24 h in water) the bulk specific gravity and the apparent specific gravity as defined in Definitions E 12, the bulk specific gravity on the basis of weight of saturated surface-dry aggregate, and the absorption as defined in Definitions C 125.

2. Applicable Documents

2.1 *ASTM Standards:*

C 125 Definitions of Terms Relating to Concrete and Concrete Aggregates[2]
C 702 Reduction of Field Samples to Testing Size[3]
E 12 Definitions of Terms Relating to Density and Specific Gravity of Solids, Liquids, and Gases[3]
Manual of Concrete Testing[3]

3. Apparatus

3.1 *Balance*—A weighing device having a capacity of 5 kg or more, as required for the sample size selected; sensitive and readable to 0.5 g or 0.0001 times the sample weight, whichever is greater; and accurate within 0.1 percent of the test load at any point within the range used for this test. Within any 500-g range of test load, a difference between readings shall be accurate within 0.5 g or 0.0001 times the sample weight, whichever is greater.

3.2 *Sample Container*—A wire basket of No. 6 (3-mm), or finer mesh, or a bucket, of approximately equal breadth and height, with a capacity of 4000 to 7000 cm³ for 1½ in. (38.1 mm) nominal maximum size aggregate or smaller, and a larger capacity container in the range from 8000 to 16000 cm³ for the testing of large maximum size aggregate.

3.3 Suitable apparatus for suspending the sample container in water from the center of the scale pan or balance.

4. Test Specimen

4.1 Thoroughly mix the sample of aggregate to be tested and reduce it to the approximate quantity needed by use of a sample splitter or by quartering (Note 1). Reject all material passing a No. 4 (4.75-mm) sieve. In many instances it may be desirable to test a coarse aggregate in several separate size fractions; and if the sample contains more than 15 percent retained on the 1½-in. (38.1-mm) sieve, test the plus 1½ in. fraction or fractions separately from the smaller size fractions. The minimum weight of sample to be used is given below; when an aggregate is tested in separate size fractions, use the sample size corresponding to the nominal maximum size of each fraction:

[1] This method is under the jurisdiction of ASTM Committee C-9 on Concrete and Concrete Aggregates and is the direct responsibility of Subcommittee C09.03.05 on Methods of Testing and Specifications for Physical Characteristics of Concrete.
Current edition approved March 29, 1973. Published May 1973. Originally published as C 127 – 36 T. Last previous edition C 127 – 68.
[2] 1974 Annual Book of ASTM Standards, Parts 14 and 15.
[3] 1974 Annual Book of ASTM Standards, Part 14.

Nominal Maximum Size, in. (mm)	Minimum Weight of Sample, kg
½ (12.5) or less	2
¾ (19.0)	3
1 (25.0)	4
1½ (37.5)	5
2 (50)	8
2½ (63)	12
3 (75)	18
3½ (90)	25

NOTE 1—The process of quartering and the correct use of a sample splitter are discussed in the Manual of Concrete Testing and in Method C 702.

5. Procedure

5.1 After thoroughly washing to remove dust or other coatings from the surface of the particles, dry the sample to constant weight at a temperature of 212 to 230 F (100 to 110 C), cool in air at room temperature for 1 to 3 h, and then immerse in water at room temperature for a period of 24 ± 4h.

NOTE 2—Where the absorption and specific gravity values are to be used in proportioning concrete mixtures in which the aggregates will be in their naturally moist condition, the requirement for initial drying to constant weight may be eliminated, and, if the surfaces of the particles in the sample have been kept continuously wet until test, the 24-h soaking may also be eliminated. Values for absorption and for specific gravity in the saturated-surface-dry condition may be significantly higher for aggregate not oven dried before soaking than for the same aggregate treated in accordance with 5.1. Therefore, any exceptions to the procedure of 5.1 should be noted on reporting the results.

5.2 Remove the specimen from the water and roll it in a large absorbent cloth until all visible films of water are removed. Wipe the larger particles individually. Take care to avoid evaporation of water from aggregate pores during the operation of surface-drying. Weigh the specimen in the saturated surface-dry condition. Record this and all subsequent weights to the nearest 0.5 g or 0.0001 times the sample weight, whichever is greater.

5.3 After weighing, immediately place the saturated-surface-dry specimen in the sample container and determine its weight in water at 73.4 ± 3 F (23 ± 1.7 C), having a density of 0.997 ± 0.002 g/cm³. Take care to remove all entrapped air before weighing by shaking the container while immersed.

NOTE 3—The container should be immersed to a depth sufficient to cover it and the test specimen during weighing. Wire suspending the container should be of the smallest practical size to minimize any possible effects of a variable immersed length.

5.4 Dry the specimen to constant weight at a temperature of 212 to 230 F (100 to 110 C), cool in air at room temperature 1 to 3 h, and weigh.

6. Bulk Specific Gravity

6.1 Calculate the bulk specific gravity, 73.4/73.4 F (23/23 C), as defined in Definitions E 12, as follows:

$$\text{Bulk sp gr} = A/(B - C)$$

where:

A = weight of oven-dry specimen in air, g,
B = weight of saturated-surface-dry specimen in air, g, and
C = weight of saturated specimen in water, g.

7. Bulk Specific Gravity (Saturated-Surface-Dry Basis)

7.1 Calculate the bulk specific gravity, 73.4/73.4 F (23/23 C), on the basis of weight of saturated-surface-dry aggregate as follows:

$$\text{Bulk sp gr (saturated-surface-dry basis)} = B/(B - C)$$

8. Apparent Specific Gravity

8.1 Calculate the apparent specific gravity, 73.4/73.4 F (23/23 C), as defined in ASTM Definitions E 12, as follows:

$$\text{Apparent sp gr} = A/(A - C)$$

9. Absorption

9.1 Calculate the percentage of absorption, as defined in ASTM Definitions C 125, as follows:

$$\text{Absorption, percent} = [(B - A)/A] \times 100$$

10. Calculation of Average Values

10.1 When the sample is tested in separate size fractions the average value for bulk specific gravity, bulk specific gravity (saturated-surface-dry basis), or apparent specific gravity can be computed as the weighted average of the values as computed in accordance with Section 6, 7, or 8 using the following equation:

$$G = \cfrac{1}{\cfrac{P_1}{100\,G_1} + \cfrac{P_2}{100\,G_2} + \ldots \cfrac{P_n}{100\,G_n}}$$

(see Appendix X1)

where:

G = average specific gravity. Either bulk-dry, saturated-surface-dry, or apparent specific gravities can be averaged in this manner.

$G_1, G_2, \ldots G_n$ = appropriate specific gravity values for each size fraction depending on the type of specific gravity being averaged.

$P_1, P_2, \ldots P_n$ = weight percentages of each size fraction present in the original sample.

10.2 For absorption the average value is the weighted average of the values as computed in Section 9, weighted in proportion to the weight percentages of the size fractions in the original fraction as follows:

$$A = (P_1 A_1/100) + (P_2 A_2/100) + \ldots (P_n A_n/100)$$

where:

A = average absorption, percent,

$A_1, A_2, \ldots A_n$ = absorption percentages for each size fraction, and

$P_1, P_2, \ldots P_n$ = weight percentages of each size fraction present in the original sample.

11. Precision

11.1 Data from carefully conducted tests on normal weight aggregate at one laboratory yielded the following for tests on the same specimen. Different specimens from the same source may vary more.

11.1.1 For specific gravity, single-operator and multi-operator precision (2S limits) less than ±0.01 from the average specific gravity. Differences greater than 0.01 between duplicate tests on the same specimen by the same or different operators should occur by chance less than 5 percent of the time (D2S limit less than 0.01).

11.1.2 For absorption, single-operator and multi-operator precision ±0.09 from the average percent absorption 95 percent of the time (2S limits). The difference between single tests by the same or different operators on the same specimen should not exceed 0.13 more than 5 percent of the time (D2S limit).

APPENDIX

X1. DEVELOPMENT OF EQUATIONS

X1.1 The derivation of the equation is apparent from the following simplified cases using two solids. Solid 1 has a weight W_1 in grams and a volume V_1 in millilitres; its specific gravity (G_1) is therefore W_1/V_1.

Solid 2 has a weight W_2 and volume V_2, and $G_2 = W_2/V_2$. If the two solids are considered together, the specific gravity of the combination is the total weight in grams divided by the total volume in millilitres:

$$G = (W_1 + W_2)/(V_1 + V_2)$$

Manipulation of this equation yields the following:

$$G = \cfrac{1}{\cfrac{V_1 + V_2}{W_1 + W_2}} = \cfrac{1}{\cfrac{V_1}{W_1 + W_2} + \cfrac{V_2}{W_1 + W_2}}$$

$$G = \cfrac{1}{\cfrac{W_1}{W_1 + W_2}\left(\cfrac{V_1}{W_1}\right) + \cfrac{W_2}{W_1 + W_2}\left(\cfrac{V_2}{W_2}\right)}$$

However, the weight fractions of the two solids are:

$$W_1/(W_1 + W_2) = P_1/100 \text{ and } W_2/(W_1 + W_2) = P_2/100$$

and,

$$1/G_1 = V_1/W_1 \text{ and } 1/G_2 = V_2/W_2$$

Therefore,

$$G = 1/[(P_1/100)(1/G_1) + (P_2/100)(1/G_2)]$$

An example of the computation is given in Table X1.

TABLE X1 Example of Calculation of Average Values of
Specific Gravity and Absorption for a Coarse Aggregate
Tested in Separate Sizes

Size Fraction, in. (mm)	Percent in Original Sample	Sample Weight Used in Test, g	Bulk Specific Gravity (SSD)	Absorption, percent
No. 4 to 1_2 (12.5)	44	2213.0	2.72	0.4
1_2 to $1 1_2$ (37.5)	˙35	5462.5	2.56	2.5
$1 1_2$ to $2 1_2$ (63)	21	12593.0	2.54	3.0

Average Specific Gravity (SSD)

$$G_{SSD} = \frac{1}{\dfrac{0.44}{2.72} + \dfrac{0.35}{2.56} + \dfrac{0.21}{2.54}} = 2.62$$

Average Absorption

$$A = (0.44)(0.4) + (0.35)(2.5) + (0.21)(3.0)$$
$$= 1.7 \text{ percent}$$

Standard Method of Test for
SPECIFIC GRAVITY AND ABSORPTION OF FINE AGGREGATE[1]

This Standard is issued under the fixed designation C 128; the number immediately following the designation indicates the year of original adoption or, in the case of revision, the year of last revision. A number in parentheses indicates the year of last reapproval.

1. Scope

1.1 This method covers the determination of bulk and apparent specific gravity, 73.4/73.4 F (23/23 C), and absorption of fine aggregate. Bulk specific gravity is the characteristic generally used for calculations of the volume occupied by the aggregate in portland-cement concrete.

1.2 This method determines (after 24 h in water) the bulk specific gravity and the apparent specific gravity as defined in the ASTM Definitions E 12, Terms Relating to Density and Specific Gravity of Solids, Liquids and Gases,[2] the bulk specific gravity on the basis of weight of saturated surface-dry aggregate, and the absorption as defined in ASTM Definitions C 125, for Terms Relating to Concrete and Concrete Aggregates.[3]

NOTE 1—The values stated in U.S. customary units are to be regarded as the standard.

2. Apparatus

2.1 *Balance*—A balance or scale having a capacity of 1 kg or more, sensitive to 0.1 g or less, and accurate within 0.1 percent of the test load at any point within the range of use for this test. Within any 100-g range of test load, a difference between readings shall be accurate within 0.1 g.

2.2 *Pycnometer*—A flask or other suitable container into which the fine aggregate test sample can be readily introduced and in which the volume content can be reproduced within ±0.1 cm³. The volume of the container filled to mark shall be at least 50 percent greater than the space required to accommodate the test sample. A volumetric flask of 500 cm³ capacity or a fruit jar fitted with a pycnometer top is satisfactory for a 500-g test sample of most fine aggregates.

2.3 *Mold*—A metal mold in the form of a frustum of a cone with dimensions as follows: 40 ± 3 mm inside diameter at the top, 90 ± 3 mm inside diameter at the bottom, and 75 ± 3 mm in height, with the metal having a minimum thickness of 0.8 mm.

2.4 *Tamper*—A metal tamper weighing 12 ± ½ oz (340 ± 15 g) and having a flat circular tamping face 1 ± ⅛ in. (25 ± 3 mm) in diameter.

3. Preparation of Test Specimen

3.1 Obtain approximately 1000 g of the fine aggregate from the sample by use of a sample splitter or by quartering (Note 2). Dry it in a suitable pan or vessel to constant weight at a temperature of 212 to 230 F (100 to 110 C). Allow it to cool to comfortable handling temperature, cover with water, and permit it to stand for 24 ± 4 h (Note 3). Decant excess water with care to avoid loss of fines, spread the sample on a flat surface exposed to a gently moving current of warm air, and stir

---

[1] This method is under the jurisdiction of ASTM Committee C-9 on Concrete and Concrete Aggregates and is the direct responsibility of Subcommittee C09.03.05 on Methods of Testing and Specifications for Physical Characteristics of Concrete Aggregates.
Current edition approved Oct. 29, 1973. Published December 1973. Originally published as C 128 – 36. Last previous edition C 128 – 68.
[2] *1974 Annual Book of ASTM Standards*, Part 14.
[3] *1974 Annual Book of ASTM Standards*, Parts 14 and 15.

frequently to secure uniform drying. Continue this operation until the test specimen approaches a free-flowing condition. Then place a portion of the partially dried fine aggregate loosely into the mold, held firmly on a smooth nonabsorbent surface with the large diameter down, lightly tamp the surface 25 times with the tamper, and lift the mold vertically. If surface moisture is still present, the fine aggregate will retain the molded shape. Continue drying with constant stirring and test at frequent intervals until the tamped fine aggregate slumps slightly upon removal of the mold. This indicates that it has reached a surface-dry condition (Note 4). If desired, mechanical aids such as tumbling or stirring may be employed to assist in achieving the saturated surface-dry condition.

Note 2—The process of quartering and the correct use of a sample splitter are discussed in the Manual of Concrete Testing.[2]

Note 3—Where the absorption and specific gravity values are to be used in proportioning concrete mixtures with aggregates used in their naturally moist condition, the requirement for initial drying to constant weight may be eliminated and, if the surfaces of the particles have been kept wet, the 24-h soaking may also be eliminated. Values for absorption and for specific gravity in the saturated-surface-dry condition may be significantly higher for aggregate not oven dried before soaking than for the same aggregate treated in accordance with 3.1.

Note 4—The procedure described in Section 3 is intended to ensure that the first cone test trial will be made with some surface water in the specimen. If the fine aggregate slumps on the first trial, it has been dried past the saturated and surface-dry condition. In this case thoroughly mix a few cubic centimeters of water with the fine aggregate and permit the specimen to stand in a covered container for 30 min. The process of drying and testing for the free-flowing condition shall then be resumed.

4. Procedure

4.1 Immediately introduce into the pycnometer 500.0 g (Note 5) of the fine aggregate, prepared as described in Section 3, and fill with water to approximately 90 percent of capacity. Roll, invert, and agitate the pycnometer to eliminate all air bubbles. Adjust its temperature to 73.4 ± 3 F (23 ± 1.7 C), if necessary, by immersion in circulating water and bring the water level in the pycnometer to its calibrated capacity. Determine total weight of the pycnometer, specimen, and water (Note 6). Record this and all other weights to the nearest 0.1 g.

Note 5—An amount other than 500 g, but not less than 50 g, may be used provided that the actual weight is inserted in place of the figure "500" wherever it appears in the formulas of 5.1, 6.1, 7.1 and 8.1. If the weight used is less than 500 g, limits on accuracy of weighing and measuring must be scaled down in proportion.

Note 6—As an alternative, the quantity of water necessary to fill the pycnometer may be determined volumetrically using a buret accurate to 0.15 cm³. The total weight of the pycnometer, specimen, and water is then computed as follows:

$$C = 0.9976 V_a + 500 + W$$

where:
C = weight of pycnometer filled with the specimen plus water, g,
V_a = volume of water added to pycnometer, cm³, and
W = weight of the pycnometer empty, g.

4.2 Remove the fine aggregate from the pycnometer, dry to constant weight at a temperature of 212 to 230 F (100 to 110 C), cool in air at room temperature for ½ to 1½ h, and weigh.

4.3 Determine the weight of the pycnometer filled to its calibration capacity with water at 73.4 ± 3 F (23 ± 1.7 C).

Note 7—If a volumetric flask is used and is calibrated to an accuracy of 0.15 cm³ at 20 C, the weight of the flask filled with water may be calculated as follows:

$$B = 0.9976 V + W$$

where:
B = weight of flask filled with water, g,
V = volume of flask, cm³, and
W = weight of the flask empty, g.

5. Bulk Specific Gravity

5.1 Calculate the bulk specific gravity, 73.4/73.4 F (23/23 C), as defined in ASTM Definitions E 12, as follows:

$$\text{Bulk sp gr} = A/(B + 500 - C)$$

where:
A = weight of oven-dry specimen in air, g,
B = weight of pycnometer filled with water, g, and
C = weight of pycnometer with specimen and water to calibration mark, g.

6. Bulk Specific Gravity (Saturated Surface-Dry Basis)

6.1 Calculate the bulk specific gravity, 73.4/73.4 F (23/23 C), on the basis of weight of saturated surface-dry aggregate as follows:

Bulk sp gr (saturated surface-dry basis)
$$= 500/(B + 500 - C)$$

7. Apparent Specific Gravity

7.1 Calculate the apparent specific gravity, 73.4/73.4 F (23/23 C), as defined in Definitions E 12, as follows:

$$\text{Apparent sp gr} = A/(B + A - C)$$

8. Absorption

8.1 Calculate the percentage of absorption, as defined in Definitions C 125, as follows:

$$\text{Absorption, percent} = [(500 - A)/A] \times 100$$

9. Precision

9.1 Data from carefully conducted tests on normal weight aggregate at one laboratory yielded the following for tests on the same specimen. Different specimens from the same source may vary more.

9.1.1 For specific gravity, single-operator and multi-operator precision (2S limits) less than ±0.02 from the average specific gravity. Differences greater than 0.03 between duplicate tests on the same specimen by the same or different operators should occur by chance less than 5 percent of the time (D2S limit less than 0.03).

9.1.2 For absorption, single-operator precision ±0.31 from the average percent absorption 95 percent of the time (2S limits). Multi-operator tests are probably less precise. The difference between tests by the same operator on the same specimen should not exceed 0.45 more than 5 percent of the time (D2S limit).

Standard Method of Test for

RESISTANCE TO ABRASION OF SMALL SIZE COARSE AGGREGATE BY USE OF THE LOS ANGELES MACHINE[1]

This Standard is issued under the fixed designation C 131: the number immediately following the designation indicates the year of original adoption or, in the case of revision, the year of last revision. A number in parentheses indicates the year of last reapproval.

1. Scope

1.1 This method covers a procedure for testing sizes of coarse aggregate smaller than $1\frac{1}{2}$ in. (37.5 mm) for resistance to abrasion using the Los Angeles testing machine.

NOTE 1—A procedure for testing coarse aggregate larger than $\frac{3}{4}$ in. (19 mm) is covered in ASTM Method C 535, Test for Resistance to Abrasion of Large Size Coarse Aggregate by Use of the Los Angeles Machine.[2]

2. Apparatus

2.1 *Los Angeles Machine*—The Los Angeles abrasion testing machine, conforming in all its essential characteristics to the design shown in Fig. 1, shall be used. The machine shall consist of a hollow steel cylinder, closed at both ends, having an inside diameter of 28 ± 0.2 in. (711 ± 5 mm), and an inside length of 20 ± 0.2 in. (508 ± 5 mm). The cylinder shall be mounted on stub shafts attached to the ends of the cylinder but not entering it, and shall be mounted in such a manner that it may be rotated with the axis in a horizontal position within a tolerance in slope of 1 in 100. An opening in the cylinder shall be provided for the introduction of the test sample. A suitable, dust-tight cover shall be provided for the opening with means for bolting the cover in place. The cover shall be so designed as to maintain the cylindrical contour of the interior surface unless the shelf is so located that the charge will not fall on the cover, or come in contact with it during the test. A removable steel shelf extending the full length of the cylinder and projecting inward 3.5 ± 0.1 in. (89 ± 2 mm) shall be mounted on the interior cylindrical surface of the cylinder, or on the inside surface of the cover, in such a way that a plane centered between the large faces coincides with an axial plane. The shelf shall be of such thickness and so mounted, by bolts or other suitable means, as to be firm and rigid. The position of the shelf shall be such that the distance from the shelf to the opening, measured along the outside circumference of the cylinder in the direction of rotation, shall be not less than 50 in. (1.27 m).

NOTE 2—The use of a shelf of wear-resistant steel, rectangular in cross section and mounted independently of the cover, is preferred. However, a shelf consisting of a section of rolled angle, properly mounted on the inside of the cover plate, may be used provided the direction of rotation is such that the charge will be caught on the outside face of the angle. If the shelf becomes distorted from its original shape to such an extent that the requirements given in X1.2 of the Appendix to this method are not met, the shelf shall either be repaired or replaced before additional abrasion tests are made.

2.2 *Sieves*, conforming to ASTM Specification E 11, for Wire-Cloth Sieves for Testing Purposes.[2]

2.3 *Balance*—A balance or scale accurate within 0.1 percent of test load over the range required for this test.

3. Abrasive Charge

3.1 The abrasive charge shall consist of

[1] This method is under the jurisdiction of ASTM Committee C-9 on Concrete and Concrete Aggregates and is the direct responsibility of Subcommittee C09.03.05 on Methods of Testing and Specifications for Physical Characteristics of Concrete Aggregates.
Current edition effective Oct. 3, 1969. Originally issued 1937. Replaces C 113 - 66.
[2] *Annual Book of ASTM Standards*, Parts 14 and 15.

steel spheres averaging approximately 1²⁷⁄₃₂ in. (46.8 mm) in diameter and each weighing between 390 and 445 g.

3.2 The abrasive charge, depending upon the grading of the test sample as described in Section 4, shall be as follows:

Grading	Number of Spheres	Weight of Charge, g
A	12	5000 ± 25
B	11	4584 ± 25
C	8	3330 ± 20
D	6	2500 ± 15

NOTE 3—Steel ball bearings 1¹³⁄₁₆ in. (46.0 mm) and 1⅞ in. (47.6 mm) in diameter, weighing approximately 400 and 440 g each, respectively, are readily available. Steel spheres 1²⁷⁄₃₂ in. (46.8 mm) in diameter weighing approximately 420 g may also be obtainable. The abrasive charge may consist of a mixture of these sizes conforming to the weight tolerances of 3.1 and 3.2.

4. Test Sample

4.1 The test sample shall be prepared from aggregate representative of that being furnished. The aggregate shall be washed and oven-dried at 221 to 230 F (105 to 110 C) to substantially constant weight (Note 5), separated into individual size fractions, and recombined to the grading of Table 1 most nearly corresponding to the range of sizes in the aggregate as furnished for the work. The weight of the sample prior to test shall be recorded to the nearest 1 g.

5. Procedure

5.1 Place the test sample and the abrasive charge in the Los Angeles abrasion testing machine and rotate the machine at a speed of 30 to 33 rpm for 500 revolutions. The machine shall be so driven and so counterbalanced as to maintain a substantially uniform peripheral speed (Note 4). After the prescribed number of revolutions, discharge the material from the machine and make a preliminary separation of the sample on a sieve coarser than the No. 12 (1.70-mm). Sieve the finer portion on a No. 12 sieve in a manner conforming to Section 5.2 of ASTM Method C 136, Test for Sieve or Screen Analysis of Fine and Coarse Aggregates.[2] Wash the material coarser than the No. 12 sieve (Note 5), oven-dry at 221 to 230 F (105 to 110 C) to substantially constant weight, and weigh to the nearest 1 g (Note 6).

NOTE 4—Back-lash or slip in the driving mechanism is very likely to furnish test results which are not duplicated by other Los Angeles abrasion machines producing constant peripheral speed.

NOTE 5—If the aggregate is essentially free from adherent coatings and dust, the requirement for washing before and after test may be waived. Elimination of washing after test will seldom reduce the measured loss by more than about 0.2 percent of the original sample weight.

NOTE 6—Valuable information concerning the uniformity of the sample under test may be obtained by determining the loss after 100 revolutions. This loss should be determined without washing the material coarser than the No. 12 sieve. The ratio of the loss after 100 revolutions to the loss after 500 revolutions should not greatly exceed 0.20 for material of uniform hardness. When this determination is made, care should be taken to avoid losing any part of the sample; the entire sample, including the dust of abrasion, shall be returned to the testing machine for the final 400 revolutions required to complete the test.

6. Calculation

6.1 Express the difference between the original weight and the final weight of the test sample as a percentage of the original weight of the test sample. Report this value as the percentage of wear.

NOTE 7—The percentage of wear determined by this method has no known consistent relationship to the percentage of wear for the same material when tested by Method C 535.

TABLE 1 Gradings of Test Samples

Sieve Size (Square Openings)		Weight of Indicated Sizes, g			
		Grading			
Passing	Retained on	A	B	C	D
1½ in. (37.5 mm)	1 in. (25.0 mm)	1 250 ± 25	...	...	...
1 in. (25.0 mm)	¾ in. (19.0 mm)	1 250 ± 25	...	...	...
¾ in. (19.0 mm)	½ in. (12.5 mm)	1 250 ± 10	2 500 ± 10	...	...
½ in. (12.5 mm)	⅜ in. (9.5 mm)	1 250 ± 10	2 500 ± 10	...	...
⅜ in. (9.5 mm)	¼ in. (6.3 mm)	...	...	2 500 ± 10	...
¼ in. (6.3 mm)	No. 4 (4.75-mm)	...	...	2 500 ± 10	...
No. 4 (4.75-mm)	No. 8 (2.36-mm)	...	...	...	5 000 ± 10
Total		5 000 ± 10	5 000 ± 10	5 000 ± 10	5 000 ± 10

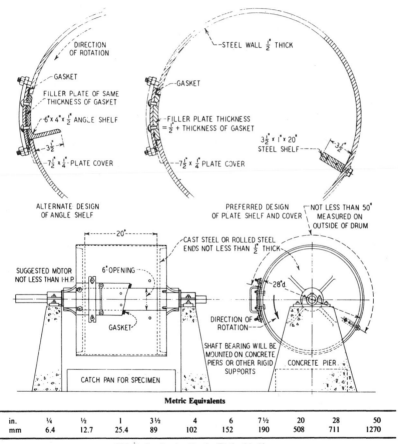

Metric Equivalents

in.	¼	½	1	3½	4	6	7½	20	28	50
mm	6.4	12.7	25.4	89	102	152	190	508	711	1270

FIG. 1 Los Angeles Abrasion Testing Machine.

APPENDIX

A1. MAINTENANCE OF SHELF

A1.1 The shelf of the Los Angeles Machine is subject to severe surface wear and impact. With use, the working surface of the shelf is peened by the balls and tends to develop a ridge of metal parallel to and about 1¼ in. (32 mm) from the junction of the shelf and the inner surface of the cylinder. If the shelf is made from a section of rolled angle, not only may this ridge develop but the shelf itself may be bent longitudinally or transversely from its proper position.

A1.2 The shelf should be inspected periodically to determine that it is not bent either lengthwise or from its normal radial position with respect to the cylinder. If either condition is found, the shelf should be repaired or replaced before further abrasion tests are made. The influence on the test result of the ridge developed by peening of the working face of the shelf is not known. However, for uniform test conditions, it is recommended that the ridge be ground off if its height exceeds 0.1 in. (2 mm).

ASTM Designation: C 136 – 71

American National Standard A37.8-1973
Approved March 7, 1973
By American National Standards Institute
American Association State
Highway Officials Standard
AASHO No. T 27

Standard Method of Test for
SIEVE OR SCREEN ANALYSIS OF FINE AND COARSE AGGREGATES[1]

This Standard is issued under the fixed designation C 136: the number immediately following the designation indicates the year of original adoption or. in the case of revision. the year of last revision. A number in parentheses indicates the year of last reapproval.

1. Scope

1.1 This method covers the determination of the particle size distribution of fine and coarse aggregates by sieving or screening.

2. Summary of Method

2.1 A weighed sample of dry aggregate is separated through a series of sieves or screens of progressively smaller openings for determination of particle size distribution.

3. Apparatus

3.1 *Balance*—A balance or scale accurate within 0.1 percent of the test load at any point within the range of use.

3.2 *Sieves or Screens*—The sieves or screens shall be mounted on substantial frames constructed in a manner that will prevent loss of material during sieving. Suitable sieve sizes shall be selected to furnish the information required by the specifications covering the material to be tested. The sieves shall conform to ASTM Specification E 11, for Wire-Cloth Sieves for Testing Purposes.[2]

3.3 *Oven*—An oven of appropriate size capable of maintaining a uniform temperature of 230 ± 9 F (110 ± 5 C).

4. Test Sample

4.1 The sample of aggregate to be tested for sieve analysis shall be thoroughly mixed and reduced by use of a sample splitter or by quartering (Note 1) to an amount suitable for testing. Fine aggregate shall be moistened before reduction to minimize segregation and loss of dust. The sample for test shall be approximately of the weight desired when dry and shall be the end result of the reduction method. Reduction to an exact predetermined weight shall not be permitted.

NOTE 1—The process of quartering and the correct use of a sample splitter are described in the "Manual of Concrete Testing."[3]

4.2 *Fine Aggregate*—The test sample of fine aggregate shall weigh, after drying, approximately the following amount:

Aggregate with at least 95 percent passing a No. 8 (2.36-mm) sieve	100 g
Aggregate with at least 85 percent passing a No. 4 (4.75-mm) sieve and more than 5 percent retained on a No. 8 sieve	500 g

In no case, however, shall the fraction retained on any sieve at the completion of the sieving operation weigh more than 4 g/in.² of sieving surface.

NOTE 2—This amounts to 200 g for the usual 8-in. (203-mm) diameter sieve. The amount of material retained on the critical sieve may be regulated by (*1*) the introduction of a larger-opening sieve immediately above the critical sieve, or (*2*) selection of a sample of proper size.

4.3 *Coarse Aggregate*—The weight of the test sample of coarse aggregate shall conform with the following:

Maximum Nominal Size, Square Openings, in. (mm)	Minimum Weight of Sample, kg
⅜ (9.5)	2
½ (12.5)	4
¾ (19.0)	8

---

[1] This method is under the jurisdiction of ASTM Committee C-9 on Concrete and Concrete Aggregates and is the direct responsibility of Subcommittee C 09.03.05 on Methods of Testing and Specifications for Physical Characteristics of Concrete Aggregates.
Current edition effective Sept. 17, 1971. Originally issued 1938. Replaces C 136 – 67.
[2] *1974 Annual Book of ASTM Standards*, Parts 14 and 15.
[3] *1974 Annual Book of ASTM Standards*, Part 14.

Maximum Nominal Size, Square Openings, in. (mm)	Minimum Weight of Sample, kg
1 (25.0)	12
1½ (37.5)	16
2 (50)	20
2½ (63)	25
3 (75)	45
3½ (90)	70

NOTE 3—It is recommended that sieves mounted in frames of 16-in. (406-mm) diameter or larger be used for testing coarse aggregate.

4.4 In the case of mixtures of fine and coarse aggregates, the material shall be separated into two sizes on the No. 4 (4.75-mm) sieve. The samples of fine and coarse aggregate shall be prepared in accordance with 4.2 and 4.3.

5. Procedure

5.1 Dry the sample to constant weight at a temperature of 230 ± 9 F (110 ± 5 C).

5.2 Nest the sieves in order of decreasing size of opening from top to bottom and place the sample on the top sieve. Agitate the sieves by hand or by mechanical apparatus for a sufficient period, established by trial or checked by measurement on the actual test sample, to meet the criterion for adequacy of sieving described in 5.3.

5.3 Continue sieving for a sufficient period and in such manner that, after completion, not more than 1 weight percent of the residue on any individual sieve will pass that sieve during 1 min of continuous hand sieving performed as follows: Hold the individual sieve, provided with a snug-fitting pan and cover, in a slightly inclined position in one hand. Strike the side of the sieve sharply and with an upward motion against the heel of the other hand at the rate of about 150 times/min, turn the sieve about one sixth of a revolution at intervals of about 25 strokes. In determining sufficiency of sieving for sizes larger than the No. 4 (4.75-mm) sieve, limit the material on the sieve to a single layer of particles. If the size of the mounted testing sieves makes the described sieving motion impractical, use 8-in. (203-mm) diameter sieves to verify the sufficiency of sieving.

5.4 Dry sieving alone is usually satisfactory for routine testing of normally graded aggregates. However, when accurate determination of the total amount passing the No. 200 (75-μm) sieve is desired, first test the sample in accordance with ASTM Method C 117, Test for Materials Finer than No. 200 (75-μm) Sieve in Mineral Aggregates by Washing.[2] Add the percentage finer than the No. 200 sieve determined by that method to the percentage passing the No. 200 sieve by dry sieving of the same sample. After the final drying operation in Method C 117, dry-sieve the sample in accordance with 5.2 and 5.3.

5.5 Determine the weight of each size increment by weighing on a scale or balance conforming to the requirements specified in 3.1, to the nearest 0.1 percent of the weight of the sample

6. Calculation

6.1 Calculate percentages on the basis of the total weight of the sample, including any material finer than the No. 200 sieve determined in accordance with Method C 117.

7. Report

7.1 The report shall include the following:

7.1.1 Total percentage of material passing each sieve, or

7.1.2 Total percentage of material retained on each sieve, or

7.1.3 Percentage of material retained between consecutive sieves, depending upon the form of the specifications for use of the material under test. Report percentages to the nearest whole number, except for the percentage passing the No. 200 (75-μm) sieve. which shall be reported to the nearest 0.1 percent.

Designation: C 702 – 75

Standard Methods for
REDUCING FIELD SAMPLES OF AGGREGATE TO TESTING SIZE[1]

This Standard is issued under the fixed designation C 702; the number immediately following the designation indicates the year of original adoption or, in the case of revision, the year of last revision. A number in parentheses indicates the year of last reapproval.

1. Scope

1.1 These methods cover the reduction of field samples of aggregate to the appropriate size for testing employing techniques that are intended to minimize variations in measured characteristics between the test samples so selected and the field sample.

NOTE 1—Under certain circumstances, reduction in size of the field sample prior to testing is not recommended. Substantial differences between the selected test samples sometimes cannot be avoided, as for example, in the case of an aggregate having relatively few large size particles in the field sample. The laws of chance dictate that these few particles may be unequally distributed among the reduced size test samples. Similarly, if the test sample is being examined for certain contaminants occurring as a few discrete fragments in only small percentages, caution should be used in interpreting results from the reduced size test sample. Chance inclusion or exclusion of only one or two particles in the selected sample may importantly influence interpretation of the characteristics of the field sample. In these cases, the entire field sample should be tested.

2. Applicable Documents

2.1 *ASTM Standards:*
C 128 Test for Specific Gravity and Absorption of Fine Aggregate[2]
D 75 Sampling Aggregates[2]

3. Selection of Method

3.1 *Fine Aggregate*—Field samples of fine aggregate that are drier than the saturated-surface-dry condition (Note 2) shall be reduced in size by a mechanical splitter according to Method A. Field samples having free moisture on the particle surfaces may be reduced in size by quartering according to Method B, or the entire field sample may be

dried to at least the surface-dry condition, using temperatures that do not exceed those permitted for any of the tests contemplated, and then reduced to test sample size using Method A.

3.1.1 If the moist field sample is very large, a preliminary split may be made using a mechanical splitter having wide chute openings (1½ in. (38 mm) or more) to reduce the sample to not less than 5000 g, the portion so obtained is then dried, and reduction to test sample size is completed using Method A.

NOTE 2—The method of determining the saturated-surface-dry condition is described in Section 3.1 of Method C 128. As a quick approximation, if the fine aggregate will retain its shape when molded in the hand, it may be considered to be wetter than saturated-surface-dry.

3.2 *Coarse Aggregate*—Use of a mechanical splitter in accordance with Method A is preferred; otherwise the field sample shall be reduced by quartering in accordance with Method B.

4. Field Sample Size

4.1 When gradation tests only are contemplated, the size of the field sample shall conform to the requirements of Method D 75. When additional tests are to be conducted,

---

[1] These methods are under the jurisdiction of ASTM Committee C-9 on Concrete and Concrete Aggregates and are the direct responsibility of Subcommittee C09.03.05 on Methods of Testing and Specifications for Physical Characteristics of Concrete Aggregates.
Current edition approved March 28, 1975. Published May 1975. Originally published as C 702 – 71 T. Last previous edition C 702 – 71 T.
[2] *Annual Book of ASTM Standards*, Part 14.

the user shall satisfy himself that the initial size of the field sample is adequate to accomplish all intended tests.

METHOD A—MECHANICAL SPLITTER

5. Apparatus

5.1 *Sample Splitter*—Sample splitters shall have an even number of equal width chutes, but not less than a total of eight for coarse aggregate, or twelve for fine aggregate, which discharge alternately to each side of the splitter. The minimum width of the individual chutes shall be approximately 50 percent larger than the largest particles in the sample to be split (Note 3). The splitter shall be equipped with two receptacles to hold the two halves of the sample following splitting. It shall also be equipped with a hopper or straightedged pan which has a width equal to or slightly less than the over-all width of the assembly of chutes, by which the sample may be fed at a controlled rate to the chutes. The splitter and accessory equipment shall be so designed that the sample will flow smoothly without restriction or loss of material (Fig. 1)

NOTE 3—Mechanical splitters are commonly available in sizes adequate for coarse aggregate having the largest particle not over 1½ in. (37.5 mm). For fine aggregate, a splitter having chutes ½ in. (13 mm) wide will be satisfactory when the entire sample will pass a ⅜-in. (9.5-mm) sieve.

6. Procedure

6.1 Place the field sample in the hopper or pan and uniformly distribute it from edge to edge, so that when it is introduced into the chutes, approximately equal amounts will flow through each chute. The rate at which the sample is introduced shall be such as to allow free flowing through the chutes into the receptacles below. Reintroduce the portion of the sample in one of the receptacles into the splitter as many times as necessary to reduce the sample to the size specified for the intended test. The portion of the material collected in the other receptacle may be reserved for reduction in size for other tests.

METHOD B—QUARTERING

7. Apparatus

7.1 Apparatus shall consist of a straight-edged scoop, shovel, or trowel; a broom or brush; and a canvas blanket approximately 6 by 8 ft (2 by 2.5 m).

8. Procedure

8.1 Use either the procedure described in 8.1.1 or 8.1.2 or a combination of both.

8.1.1 Place the field sample on a hard, clean, level surface where there will be neither loss of material nor the accidental addition of foreign material. Mix the material thoroughly by turning the entire sample over three times. With the last turning, shovel the entire sample into a conical pile by depositing each shovelful on top of the preceding one. Carefully flatten the conical pile to a uniform thickness and diameter by pressing down the apex with a shovel so that each quarter sector of the resulting pile will contain the material originally in it. The diameter should be approximately four to eight times the thickness. Divide the flattened mass into four equal quarters with a shovel or trowel and remove two diagonally opposite quarters, including all fine material, and brush the cleared spaces clean. Successively mix and quarter the remaining material until the sample is reduced to the desired size (Fig. 2).

8.1.2 As an alternative to the procedure described in 8.1.1, when the floor surface is uneven, the field sample may be placed on a canvas blanket and mixed with a shovel as described in 8.1.1, or by alternately lifting each corner of the canvas and pulling it over the sample toward the diagonally opposite corner causing the material to be rolled. Flatten the pile as described in 8.1.1. Divide the sample as described in 8.1.1, or if the surface beneath the blanket is uneven, insert a stick or pipe beneath the blanket and under the center of the pile, then lift both ends of the stick, dividing the sample into two equal parts. Remove the stick leaving a fold of the blanket between the divided portions. Insert the stick under the center of the pile at right angles to the first division and again lift both ends of the stick, dividing the sample into four equal parts. Remove two diagonally opposite quarters, being careful to clean the fines from the blanket. Successively mix and quarter the remaining material until the sample is reduced to the desired size (Fig. 3).

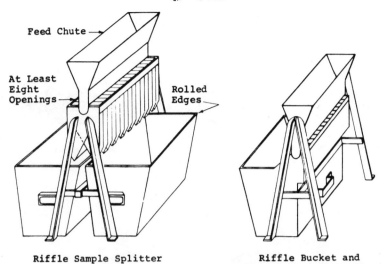

(a) Large Riffle Samplers for Coarse Aggregate.

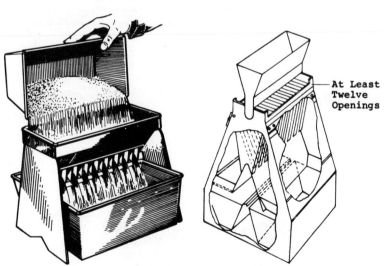

NOTE—May be constructed as either closed or open type. Closed type is preferred.

(b) Small Riffle Sampler for Fine Aggregate.

FIG. 1 Sample Dividers (Riffles).

Cone Sample on Hard Clean Surface   Mix by Forming New Cone   Quarter After Flattening Cone

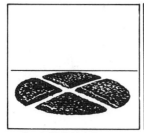 

Sample Divided into Quarters   Retain Opposite Quarters
Reject the Other Two Quarters

FIG. 2   Quartering on a Hard, Clean, Level Surface.

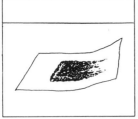  

Mix by Rolling on Blanket   Form Cone after Mixing   Quarter After Flattening Cone

  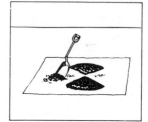

Sample Divided into Quarters   Retain Opposite Quarters
Reject the Other Two
Quarters

FIG. 3   Quartering on a Canvas Blanket.

Designation: D 75 – 71

American National Standard A37.75
American National Standards Institute
American Association State
Highway Officials Standard
AHSHO No.: T 2

Standard Methods of
SAMPLING AGGREGATES[1]

This Standard is issued under the fixed designation D 75; the number immediately following the designation indicates the year of original adoption or, in the case of revision, the year of last revision. A number in parentheses indicates the year of last reapproval.

1. Scope

1.1 These methods cover sampling of coarse and fine aggregates for the following purposes (Note 1):

1.1.1 Preliminary investigation of the potential source of supply,

1.1.2 Control of the product at the source of supply,

1.1.3 Control of the operations at the site of use, and

1.1.4 Acceptance or rejection of the materials.

NOTE 1—Sampling plans and acceptance and control tests vary with the type of construction in which the material is used. The preliminary investigation and sampling of potential aggregate sources and types occupies a very important place in determining the availability and suitability of the largest single constituent entering into the construction. It influences the type of construction from the standpoint of economics and governs the necessary material control to ensure durability of the resulting structure, from the aggregate standpoint.

2. Applicable Documents

2.1 *ASTM Standards:*

D 2234 Sampling of Coal[2]

E 105 Recommended Practice for Probability Sampling of Materials[3]

E 122 Recommended Practice for Choice of Sample Size to Estimate the Average Quality of a Lot or Process[3]

E 141 Recommended Practice for Acceptance of Evidence Based on the Results of Probability Sampling[3]

3. Securing Samples

3.1 *General*:

3.1.1 Sampling is equally as important as the testing, and the sampler shall use every precaution to obtain samples that will show the true nature and condition of the materials which they represent.

3.1.2 Samples for preliminary investigation tests are obtained by the party responsible for development of the potential source. Samples of materials for control of the production at the source or control of the work at the site of use are obtained by the manufacturer, contractor, or other parties responsible for accomplishing the work. Samples for tests to be used in acceptance or rejection decisions by the purchaser are obtained by the purchaser or his authorized representative.

3.1.3 Where practicable, samples to be tested for quality shall be obtained from the finished product. Samples from the finished product to be tested for abrasion loss shall not be subject to further crushing or manual reduction in particle size in preparation for the abrasion test unless the size of the finished product is such that it requires further reduction for testing purposes.

3.2 *Inspection:*

3.2.1 The material shall be inspected to determine discernible variations. The seller shall provide suitable equipment needed for proper inspection and sampling.

3.3 *Sampling*:

3.3.1 *Sampling from the Conveyor Belt*— Select units to be sampled by a random method from the production. Obtain at least three approximately equal increments, selected at random, from the unit being sampled and combine to form a field sample whose mass equals or exceeds the minimum recommended in 3.4.2. Stop the conveyor belt

[1] This specification is under the jurisdiction of ASTM Committee D-4 on Road and Paving Materials.
Current edition effective Nov. 22, 1971. Originally issued 1920. Replaces D 75 – 59 (1968).
[2] *1974 Annual Book of ASTM Standards*, Part 26.
[3] *1974 Annual Book of ASTM Standards*, Part 41.

while the sample increments are being obtained. Insert two templates, the shape of which conforms to the shape of the belt in the aggregate stream on the belt, and space them such that the material contained between them will yield an increment of the required weight. Carefully scoop all material between the templates into a suitable container and collect the fines on the belt with a brush and dust pan and add to the container.

3.3.2 *Sampling from a Flowing Aggregate Stream (Bins or Belt Discharge)*—Select units to be sampled by a random method from the production. Obtain at least three approximately equal increments, selected at random from the unit being sampled, and combine to form a field sample whose mass equals or exceeds the minimum recommended in 3.4.2. Take each increment from the entire cross section of the material as it is being discharged. It is usually necessary to have a special device constructed for use at each particular plant. This device consists of a pan of sufficient size to intercept the entire cross section of the discharge stream and hold the required quantity of material without overflowing. A set of rails may be necessary to support the pan as it is passed under the discharge stream. Take samples only from bins that are full, or nearly so, to minimize the chance of obtaining segregated material.

NOTE 2—The unit selected for sampling should not include the initial discharge from a conveyor or newly filled bin.

3.3.3 *Sampling from Stockpiles*—Avoid sampling from stockpiles whenever possible, particularly when the sampling is done for the purpose of determining aggregate properties that may be dependent upon the grading of the sample. If, on the other hand, circumstances make it mandatory to obtain samples from a stockpile of coarse aggregate or a stockpile of combined coarse and fine aggregate, design a sampling plan for the specific case under consideration. This approach will allow the sampling agency to use a sampling plan that will give a confidence in results obtained therefrom that is agreed upon by all parties concerned to be acceptable for the particular situation.

3.3.4 *Sampling from Roadway (Bases and Subbases)*—Sample units selected by a random method from the construction. Obtain at least three approximately equal increments, selected at random from the unit being sampled, and combine to form a field sample whose mass equals or exceeds the minimum recommended in 3.4.2. Take all increments from the roadway for the full depth of the material, taking care to exclude any underlying material. Clearly mark the specific areas from which each increment is to be removed; a metal template placed over the area is a definite aid in securing approximately equal increment weights.

3.4 *Number and Masses of Field Samples:*

3.4.1 The number of field samples (obtained by one of the methods described in 3.3) required depends on the criticality of, and variation in, the properties to be measured. Designate each unit from which a field sample is to be obtained prior to sampling. The number of field samples from the production should be sufficient to give the desired confidence in test results.

NOTE 3—Guidance for determining the number of samples required to obtain the desired level of confidence in test results may be found in Method D 2234, Recommended Practice E 105, Recommended Practice E 122, and Recommended Practice E 141.

3.4.2 The field sample masses cited are tentative. The masses must be predicated on the type and number of tests to which the material is to be subjected and sufficient material obtained to provide for the proper execution of these tests. Standard acceptance and control tests are covered by ASTM standards and specify the portion of the field sample required for each specific test. Generally speaking, the amounts specified in Table 1 will provide adequate material for routine grading and quality analysis. Extract test portions from the field sample by splitting or other appropriate methods.

4. Shipping Samples

4.1 Transport aggregates in bags or other containers so constructed as to preclude loss or contamination of any part of the sample, or damage to the contents from mishandling during shipment.

4.2 Shipping containers for aggregate samples shall have suitable individual identification attached and enclosed so that field reporting, laboratory logging, and test reporting may be facilitated.

TABLE 1 Size of Samples

Maximum Nominal Size of Aggregates[a]	Approximate Minimum Mass of Field Samples, lb (kg)[b]
Fine Aggregate	
No. 8 (2.36 mm)	25 (10)
No. 4 (4.75 mm)	25 (10)
Coarse Aggregate	
⅜ in. (9.5 mm)	25 (10)
½ in. (12.5 mm)	35 (15)
¾ in. (19.0 mm)	55 (25)
1 in. (25.0 mm)	110 (50)
1½ in. (37.5 mm)	165 (75)
2 in. (50 mm)	220 (100)
2½ in. (63 mm)	275 (125)
3 in. (75 mm)	330 (150)
3½ in. (90 mm)	385 (175)

[a] For processed aggregate the maximum nominal size of particles is the largest sieve size listed in the applicable specification, upon which any material is permitted to be retained.

[b] For combined coarse and fine aggregates (for example, base or subbase) minimum weight shall be coarse aggregate minimums plus 25 lb (10 kg).

AASHTO Standards Relating to Asphalts*

Standard Specification for
Cut-Back Asphalt
(Medium Curing Type)
AASHTO DESIGNATION: M 82-73

1. SCOPE

1.1 This specification covers liquid petroleum products, produced by fluxing an asphaltic base with suitable petroleum distallates, to be used in the treatment of road surfaces.

2. GENERAL REQUIREMENTS

2.1 The cut-back ashpalt shall show no separation or curdling prior to use and shall not foam when heated to the application temperature.

3. PROPERTIES

3.1 Cut-back asphalt of the grade designated shall conform to the requirements shown in Table 1.

4. METHODS OF SAMPLING AND TESTING

4.1 Sampling and testing cut-back asphalt (medium curing type) shall be in accordance with the following standard methods of the American Association of State Highway and Transportation Officials:

Sampling	T 40
Water	T 55
Flash point	T 79
Kinematic viscosity	T 201
Saybolt Furol viscosity	T 72
Distillation	T 78
Penetration	T 49
Ductility	T 51
Solubility in trichloroethylene	T 44
Spot test	T 102

* Reprinted by permission of the American Association of State Highway and Transportation Officials.

M82
TABLE 1

	MC-30		MC-70		MC-250		MC-800		MC-3000	
	Min.	Max.	Min.	Max.	Min.	Max.	Min.	Max.	Min.	Max.
Kinematic Viscosity at 60 C (140 F) (See Note 1) centistokes	30	60	70	140	250	500	800	1600	3000	6000
Flash point (Tab. open-cup). degrees C (F)	38 (100)	…	38 (100)	…	66 (150)	…	66 (150)	…	66 (150)	…
Water percent	…	0.2	…	0.2	…	0.2	…	0.2	…	0.2
Distillation test: Distillate percentage by volume of total distillate to 360 C (680 F)										
to 225 C (437 F)	…	25	0	20	0	10	…	…	…	…
to 260 C (500 F)	40	70	20	60	15	55	0	35	0	15
to 315 C (600 F)	75	93	65	90	60	87	45	45	15	75
Residue from distillation to 360 C (680 F) Volume percentage of sample by difference	50	…	55	…	67	…	75	…	80	…
Tests on residue from distillation: Penetration, 100 g; 5 sec., at 25 C (77 F)	120	250	120	250	120	250	120	250	120	250
Ductility, 5 cm/cm., cm. at 25 C (77 F) (See Note 2)	100	…	100	…	100	…	100	…	100	…
Solubility in Trichloroethylene, percent	99.0	…	99.0	…	99.0	…	99.0	…	99.0	…
Spot test (See Note 3) with: Standard naptha					Negative for all grades					
Naphtha - xylene solvent, - percent xylene					Negative for all grades					
Heptane - xylene solvent, - percent xylene					Negative for all grades					

NOTE 1. As an alternate, Saybolt Furol viscosities may be specified as follows:
  Grade MC-70—Furol viscosity at 50C (122 F)—60 to 120 sec.
  Grade MC-30—Furol viscosity at 25 C (77 F)—75 to 150 sec.
  Grade MC-250—Furol viscosity at 60 C (140 F)—125 to 250 sec.
  Grade MC-800—Furol viscosity at 82.2 C (180 F)—100 to 200 sec.
  Grade MC-3000—Furol viscosity at 82.2 C (180 F)—300 to 600 sec.

NOTE 2. If the ductility at 25 C (77 F) is less than 100, the material will be acceptable if its ductility at 15.5 C (60 F) is more than 100.

NOTE 3. The use of the spot test is optional. When specified, the Engineer shall indicate whether the standard naphtha solvent, the naphtha xylene solvent, or the heptane xylene solvent will be used in determining compliance with the requirement, and also, in the case of the xylene solvents, the percentage of xylene to be used.

Standard Specification for

Emulsified Asphalt

AASHTO Designation: M 140-70[1]

(ASTM Designation: D 977-69)

1. SCOPE

1.1 This specification covers seven grades of emulsified asphalt for use in pavement construction in the manner designated.

2. REQUIREMENTS

2.1 The emulsified asphalt shall be homogeneous. Within 30 days after delivery and provided separation has not been caused by freezing, the emulsified asphalt shall be homogeneous after thorough mixing.

2.2 Emulsified asphalt shall conform to the requirements prescribed in Table 1.

3. SAMPLING

3.1 Samples of emulsified asphalt shall be taken in accordance with AASHTO T 40, Sampling Bituminous Materials.

3.2 Samples shall be stored in clean, airtight sealed containers as specified in paragraph 4.1.2 of T 40 at a temperature of not less than 4.5 C (40 F) until tested.

4. METHODS OF TEST

4.1 The properties of the emulsified asphalts given in Table 1 shall be determined in accordance with AASHO T 59, Testing Emulsified Asphalts.

[1] See AASHTO: M 208 for cationic emulsions.

TABLE 1
Requirements for Emulsified Asphalt

Type	Rapid-Setting				Medium-Setting						Slow-Setting			
Grade	RS-1		RS-2		MS-1		MS-2		MS-2h		SS-1		SS-1h	
	min	max	min	max	min	max	min	max	min	max	min	max	min	max
Tests on emulsions:														
Viscosity, Saybolt Furol at 77 F (25 C) s	20	100									20	100	20	100
Viscosity, Saybolt Furol at 122 F (50 C) s			75	400	100		100		100					
Settlement,[a] 5 days, percent		5		5		5		5		5		5		5
Storage stability test,[b] 1 day		1		1		1		1		1		1		1
Demulsibility,[c] 35 ml, 0.02 N CaCl₂, percent	60		60											
Coating ability and water resistance:														
Coating, dry aggregate					good		good		good					
Coating, after spraying					fair		fair		fair					
Coating, wet aggregate					fair		fair		fair					
Coating, after spraying					fair		fair		fair					
Cement mixing test, percent												2.0		2.0
Sieve test, percent		0.10		0.10		0.10		0.10		0.10		0.10		0.10
Tests on Residue from Distillation Test:														
Residue by distillation, percent	55		63		55		65		65		57		57	
Penetration, 77 F (25 C), 100 g, 5 s	100	200	100	200	100	200	100	200	40	90	100	200	40	90
Ductility, 77 F (25 C), 5 cm/min, cm	40		40		40		40		40		40		40	
Solubility in trichloroethylene, percent	97.5		97.5		97.5		97.5		97.5		97.5		97.5	
Suggested uses	surface treatment, penetration macadam and tuck coat		surface treatment and penetration macadum		plant or road mixture with coarse aggregate substantially all of which is retained on a No. 8 (2.36-mm) sieve and practically none of which passes a No. 200 (0.075 mm) sieve; tack coat		plant or road mixture with coarse aggregate substantially all of which is retained on a No. 8 (2.36-mm) sieve and practically none of which passes a No. 200 (0.075-mm) sieve				plant or road mixture with graded and fine aggregates, a substantial quantity of which passes a No. 8 (2.36-mm) sieve and a portion of which may pass a No. 200 (0.075-mm) sieve; slurry seal treatments			

[a] The test requirement for settlement may be waived when the emulsified asphalt is used in less than 5 days time; or the purchaser may require that the settlement test be run from the time the sample is received until it is used, if the elapsed time is less than 5 days.

[b] The 24-h (1-day) storage stability test may be used instead of the 5-day settlement test.

[c] The demulsibility test shall be made within 30 days from date of shipment.

Standard Specification for

Viscosity Graded Asphalt Cement

AASHTO Designation: M 226-73

1. SCOPE.

1.1   This specification covers asphalt cements graded by viscosity at 60 C (140 F) for use in pavement construction. Three sets of limits are offered in this specification. The purchaser shall specify the applicable table of limits. In the event the purchaser does not specify limits. Table 1 shall apply. For asphalt cements graded by penetration at 25 C (77 F), see AASHTO M 20 for Asphalt Cement.

2. MANUFACTURE

2.1   The asphalt cement shall be prepared from crude petroleum by suitable methods.

3. REQUIREMENTS

3.1   The asphalt cement shall be homogeneous, free from water, and shall not foam when heated to 175 C (347 F).

3.2   The asphalt cements shall conform to the requirements given in Tables 1, 2 or 3, as specified by the purchaser.

4. METHODS OF SAMPLING AND TESTING

4.1   Sampling and Testing of asphalt cements shall be in accordance with the following standard methods of the American Association of State Highway and Transportation Officials:

Sampling	T 40
Viscosity at 60 C (140 F)	T 202
Viscosity at 135 C (275 F)	T 201
Penetration	T 49
Flash Point (COC)	T 48
Flash Point (P.M.C.T.)	T 73
Solubility in trichloroethylene	T 44
Thin-film oven test	T 179
Ductility	T 51
Spot test	T 102
Rolling Thin film oven test	T 240
Water	T 55

TABLE 1
Requirements for Asphalt Cement Graded by Viscosity at 60 C (140 F)
(Grading based on original asphalt)

TEST	VISCOSITY GRADE				
	AC-2.5	AC-5	AC-10	AC-20	AC-40
Viscosity, 60 C (140 F), poises	250 ± 50	500 ± 100	1000 ± 200	2000 ± 400	4000 ± 800
Viscosity, 135 C (275 F), Cs-minimum	80	110	150	210	300
Penetration, 25 C (77 F), 100 g., 5 sec.-minimum	200	120	70	40	20
Flash Point, COC, C (F)-minimum	163(325)	177(350)	219(425)	232(450)	232(450)
Solubility in trichloroethylene, percent-minimum	99.0	99.0	99.0	99.0	99.0
Tests on residue from Thin-Film Oven Test:					
Viscosity, 60 C (140 F), poises-maximum	1000	2000	4000	8000	16000
Ductility, 25 C (77 F), 5 cm per minute cm-minimum	100 [1]	100	50	20	10
Spot test (when and as specified) [2] with:					
Standard naphtha solvent	Negative for all grades				
Naphtha-Xylene-solvent, % Xylene	Negative for all grades				
Heptane-Xylene-solvent, % Xylene	Negative for all grades				

[1] If ductility is less than 100, material will be accepted if ductility at 15.6 C (60 F) is 100 minimum.

[2] The use of the spot test is optional. When it is specified, the Engineer shall indicate whether the standard naphtha solvent, the naphtha-xylene solvent, or the heptane-xylene solvent will be used in determining compliance with the requirement, and also, in the case of xylene solvents, the percentage of xylene to be used.

TABLE 2
Requirements for Asphalt Cement Graded by Viscosity at 60 C (140 F)
(Grading based on original asphalt)

TEST	VISCOSITY GRADE				
	AC-2.5	AC-5	AC-10	AC-20	AC-40
Viscosity, 60 C (140 F), poises	250 ± 50	500 ± 100	1000 ± 200	2000 ± 400	4000 ± 800
Viscosity, 135 C (275 F), Cs-minimum	125	200	250	300	400
Penetration, 25 C (77 F), 100 g, 5 sec.-minimum	220	140	80	60	40
Flash Point, COC, C (F)-minimum	163(325)	177(350)	219(425)	232(450)	232(450)
Solubility in trichloroethylene, percent-minimum	99.0	99.0	99.0	99.0	99.0
Tests on residue from Thin-Film Oven Test:					
Loss on heating, percent-maximum		1.0	0.5	0.5	0.5
Viscosity, 60 C (140 F), poises-maximum	1000	2000	4000	8000	16000
Ductility 25 C (77 F), 5 cm per minute, cm-minimum	100 [1]	100	75	50	25
Spot test (when and as specified) [2] with:					
Standard naphtha solvent	Negative for all grades				
Naphtha-Xylene-solvent, % Xylene	Negative for all grades				
Heptane-Xylene-solvent, % Xylene	Negative for all grades				

[1] If ductility is less than 100, material will be accepted if ductility at 15.6C (60 F) is 100 minimum.
[2] The use of the spot test is optional. When it is specified, the Engineer shall indicate whether the standard naphtha solvent, the naphtha-xylene solvent, or the heptane-xylene solvent will be used in determining compliance with the requirement, and also, in the case of xylene solvent, the percentage of xylene to be used.

TABLE 3
Requirements for Asphalt Cement Graded by Viscosity at 60 C (140 F)
(Grading based on residue from Rolling Thin Film Oven Test)

TESTS ON RESIDUE FROM AASHTO TEST METHOD T 240 [1]	VISCOSITY GRADE				
	AR-10	AR-20	AR-40	AR-80	AR-160
Viscosity, 60 C (140 F), poise	1000 ± 250	2000 ± 500	4000 ± 1000	8000 ± 2000	16000 ± 4000
Viscosity, 135 C (275 F), Cs-minimum	140	200	275	400	550
Penetration, 25 C (77 F), 100 g, 5 sec.-minimum	65	40	25	20	20
Percent of original Pen., 25 C (77 F)-minimum	—	40	45	50	52
Ductility, 25 C (77 F), 5 cm per min., cm-minimum	100 [2]	100 [2]	75	75	75
TESTS ON ORIGINAL ASPHALT					
Flash Point, P.M.C.T., C (F)-minimum	205(400)	219(425)	227(440)	232(450)	238(460)
Solubility in Trichloroethylene, percent-minimum	99.0	99.0	99.0	99.0	99.0

[1] AASHTO T 179 (Thin-Film Oven Test) may be used, but AASHTO T 240 shall be the referee method.
[2] If ductility is less than 100, material will be accepted if ductility at 15.6 C (60 F) is 100 minimum.

ASTM Standards Relating to Asphalts*

 **Designation: D 312 – 71**

American National Standard A109.24-1973
Approved January 18, 1973
By American National Standards Institute

Standard Specification for
ASPHALT FOR USE IN CONSTRUCTING BUILT-UP ROOF COVERINGS[1]

This Standard is issued under the fixed designation D 312; the number immediately following the designation indicates the year of original adoption or, in the case of revision, the year of last revision. A number in parentheses indicates the year of last reapproval.

1. Scope

1.1 This specification covers asphalt intended for use as hot-cement and mopping coat in the construction of built-up roof coverings for roofs surfaced in various manners, laid either over boards or concrete on various inclines.

2. Primer

2.1 The material used as a primer when this asphalt is used over concrete and gypsum roof slabs shall be asphalt primer conforming to ASTM Specification D 41, for Primer for Use with Asphalt in Dampproofing and Waterproofing.[2]

3. Membrane Materials

3.1 The felts for use in constructing built-up roof coverings with this asphalt shall be of the type covered by any of the following specifications:

3.1.1 ASTM Specification D 226, for Asphalt-Saturated Roofing Felt for Use in Waterproofing and in Constructing Built-Up Roofs,[2]

3.1.2 ASTM Specification D 250, for Asphalt-Saturated Asbestos Felts for Use in Waterproofing and in Constructing Built-Up Roofs,[2] and

3.1.3 ASTM Specification D 655, for Asphalt-Saturated and Coated Asbestos Felts for Use in Constructing Built-Up Roofs.[3]

4. Types

4.1 The asphalts covered by this specification include four types as defined below. The specifications are for general classification purposes with no restrictions on the slope at which the asphalt must be used. These requirements may be used for purchasing specifications or serve as guides for the preparation of purchasing specifications requiring narrower limits because of the conditions to which the asphalt will be subjected. The suggested uses for each grade are not absolute, and overlapping of the fields of use may occur between adjoining grades, depending upon the type and occupancy of the building involved, the type of roof employed, the presence, absence, or thickness of any insulation, the specific materials and construction used in the roofing membrane itself, and the temperatures and other climatic conditions to which the roofing may be subjected in service.

4.1.1 *Type I* includes asphalts relatively susceptible to temperature, with good adhesive and "self-healing" properties for use in smooth and slag- or gravel-surfaced roofing, on inclines generally not exceeding 1 in./ft.

4.1.2 *Type II* includes asphalts moderately susceptible to temperature, for roofing laid on inclines generally greater than ½ in. up to and including 3 in./ft, and may be either smooth or surfaced with slag or gravel.

4.1.3 *Type III* includes asphalts relatively nonsusceptible to temperature, for use on inclines generally in the range of more than ½

---

[1] This specification is under the jurisdiction of ASTM Committee D-8 on Bituminous and Other Organic Materials for Roofing, Waterproofing, and Related Building or Industrial Uses.
Current edition approved July 25, 1971. Originally issued 1929. Replaces D 312 – 64 (1970).
[2] *1974 Annual Book of ASTM Standards*, Part 15.
[3] Discontinued, see *1970 Annual Book of ASTM Standards*, Part 11.

---

* Reprinted by permission of the American Society for Testing and Materials from copyright material.

in. up to and including 6 in./ft, and may be either smooth or surfaced with slag or gravel.

4.1.4 *Type IV* includes harder grades of asphalt suited for use for roofing with relatively steep slopes, generally in areas with relatively high year-round temperatures.

5. Physical Requirements

5.1 The asphalt shall be homogeneous and free from water. It shall conform to the requirements prescribed in Table 1.

6. Sampling and Methods of Test

6.1 The asphalt shall be sampled and the properties enumerated in this specification shall be determined in accordance with the following methods of the American Society for Testing and Materials:

6.1.1 *Sampling*—ASTM Method D 140, Sampling Bituminous Materials.[2]

6.1.2 *Softening Point*—ASTM Method D 2398, Test for Softening Point of Asphalt (Bitumen) and Tar in Ethylene Glycol (Ring-and-Ball).[2]

6.1.3 *Flash Point*—ASTM Method D 92, Test for Flash and Fire Points by Cleveland Open Cup.[2]

6.1.4 *Penetration*—ASTM Method D 5, Test for Penetration of Bituminous Materials.[2]

6.1.5 *Ductility*—ASTM Method D 113, Test for Ductility of Bituminous Materials.[2]

6.1.6 *Loss on Heating*—ASTM Method D 6, Test Loss on Heating of Oil and Asphaltic Compounds.[2]

6.1.7 *Soluble in Carbon Disulfide*—ASTM Method D 4, Test for Bitumen.[2]

6.1.8 *Bitumen Soluble in Organic Solvents* —ASTM Method D 2042 Test for Solubility of Bituminous Materials in Organic Solvents.[2]

6.1.9 *Ash*—ASTM Method D 271, Laboratory Sampling and Analysis of Coal and Coke.[4]

6.1.10 *Coarse Particles*—ASTM Method D 313, Test for Coarse Particles in Mixtures of Asphalt and Mineral Matter.[2]

[4] *1973 Annual Book of ASTM Standards*, Part 19.

TABLE 1   Requirements for Asphalt for Constructing Built-up Roof Coverings

	Type of Roofing							
	Type I		Type II		Type III		Type IV	
	Min	Max	Min	Max	Min	Max	Min	Max
Softening point (ring- and ball-method), deg F	135	150	160	175	180	200	205	225
Flash point (Cleveland open cup), deg F	437	...	437	...	437	...	437	...
Penetration:								
32 F (0 C) 200 g, 60 s	3	...	6	...	6	...	6	...
77 F (25 C) 100 g, 5 s	18	60	18	40	15	35	12	25
115 F (46 C) 50 g, 5 s	90	180	...	100	...	90	...	75
Ductility at 77 F (25 C) (5 cm/min), cm	10	...	3	...	3	...	1.5	...
Loss on heating at 325 F (163 C) 50 g, 5 h, percent	...	1	...	1	...	1	...	1
Penetration of residue, percent of original	60	...	60	...	60	...	75	...
Total bitumen (soluble in CS$_2$), percent:								
Mineral stabilized asphalt	65	...	65	...	65	...	65	...
Asphalt without mineral stabilizer	99	...	99	...	99	...	99	...
Proportion of bitumen soluble in CCl$_4$, percent	99.5	...	99.5	...	99.5	...	99.5	...
Ash, percent:								
Mineral stabilized asphalt	10	35	10	35	10	35	10	35
Asphalt without mineral stabilizer	...	1	...	1	...	1	...	1
Coarse particles retained on 200-mesh sieve as percentage of matter insoluble in CS$_2$, percent[a]	...	12	...	12	...	12	...	12

[a] This limit applies only on mineral-stabilized or native asphalt.

By publication of this standard no position is taken with respect to the validity of any patent rights in connection therewith, and the American Society for Testing and Materials does not undertake to insure anyone utilizing the standard against liability for infringement of any Letters Patent nor assume any such liability.

ASTM **Designation: D 449 - 73**

American National Standard A109.16-1973
Approved January 18, 1973
By American National Standards Institute

American Association State
Highway Officials Standard
AASHO No.: M 115

Standard Specification for

ASPHALT FOR DAMPPROOFING AND WATERPROOFING[1]

This Standard is issued under the fixed designation D 449; the number immediately following the designation indicates the year of original adoption or, in the case of revision, the year of last revision. A number in parentheses indicates the year of last reapproval.

1. Scope

1.1 This specification covers three types of asphalt suitable for use as a mopping coat in dampproofing, or as a plying or mopping cement in the construction of a membrane system of waterproofing.

2. Primer

2.1 The material used as a primer shall conform to ASTM Specification D 41, for Primer for Use with Asphalt in Dampproofing and Waterproofing.[2]

3. Membrane Materials

3.1 For the construction of a membrane system of waterproofing, any or all of the following felts or fabrics conforming to the specifications may be used alone or in various combinations:

3.1.1 *Felt*—ASTM Specification D 226, for Asphalt-Saturated Roofing Felt for Use in Waterproofing and in Constructing Built-Up Roofs.[2]

3.1.2 *Asbestos Felt*—ASTM Specification D 250, for Asphalt-Saturated Asbestos Felts for Use in Waterproofing and in Constructing Built-Up Roofs.[2]

3.1.3 *Cotton Fabrics*—ASTM Specification D 173, for Woven Cotton Fabrics Saturated with Bituminous Substances for Use in Waterproofing,[2] asphalt type.

4. Types

4.1 The asphalts covered by this specification are of three types, as follows:

4.1.1 *Type A*—A soft, adhesive "self-healing" asphalt which flows easily under the

mop and which is suitable for use below ground level under uniformly moderate temperature conditions both during the process of installation and during service.

NOTE 1—This type of asphalt is suitable for foundations, tunnels, subways, etc.

4.1.2 *Type B*—A somewhat less susceptible asphalt with good adhesive and "self-healing" properties for use above ground level where not exposed to temperatures exceeding 125 F (50 C).

NOTE 2—This type of asphalt is suitable for railroad bridges, culverts, retaining walls, tanks, dams, conduits, spray decks, etc.

4.1.3 *Type C*—An asphalt less susceptible to temperature than Type B, with good adhesive properties for use above ground level where exposed on vertical surfaces in direct sunlight or at temperatures above 125 F (50 C).

5. Properties

5.1 The asphalt shall be homogeneous and free from water, and shall conform to the requirements prescribed in Table 1.

6. Methods of Sampling and Testing

6.1 The asphalt shall be sampled and the properties enumerated in this specification shall be determined in accordance with the following methods:

[1] This specification is under the jurisdiction of ASTM Committee D-8 on Bituminous and Other Organic Materials for Roofing, Waterproofing, and Related Building or Industrial Uses.
Current edition approved Nov. 27, 1973. Published January 1974. Originally published as D 449 – 37. Last previous edition D 449 – 71.
[2] *1974 Annual Book of ASTM Standards*, Part 15.

D 449

6.1.1 *Sampling*—ASTM Methods D 140, Sampling Bituminous Materials.[2]

6.1.2 *Softening Point*—ASTM Method D 2398, Test for Softening Point of Asphalt (Bitumen) and Tar in Ethylene Glycol (Ring-and-Ball).[2]

6.1.3 *Flash Point*—ASTM Method D 92, Test for Flash and Fire Points by Cleveland Open Cup.[2]

6.1.4 *Penetration*—ASTM Method D 5, Test for Penetration of Bituminous Materials.[2]

6.1.5 *Ductility*—ASTM Method D 113, Test for Ductility of Bituminous Materials.[2]

6.1.6 *Loss on Heating*—ASTM Method D 6, Test for Loss on Heating of Oil and Asphaltic Compounds.[2]

6.1.7 *Bitumen Soluble in Carbon Disulfide* —ASTM Method D 4, Test for Bitumen.[2]

6.1.8 *Bitumen Soluble in Carbon Tetrachloride*—ASTM Method D 2042, Test for Solubility of Bituminous Materials in Organic Solvents.[2]

6.1.9 *Ash*—ASTM Methods D 271, Laboratory Sampling and Analysis of Coal and Coke.[3]

6.1.10 *Coarse Particles*—ASTM Method D 313, Test for Coarse Particles in Mixtures of Asphalt and Mineral Matter.[2]

---

[3] *1973 Annual Book of ASTM Standards*, Part 19.

TABLE 1 **Requirements for Asphalt for Dampproofing and Waterproofing**

	Type A		Type B		Type C	
	Min	Max	Min	Max	Min	Max
Softening point (ring-and-ball method)	115 F (46 C)	145 F (63 C)	145 F (63 C)	170 F (77 C)	180 F (82 C)	200 F (93 C)
Flash point (Cleveland open cup)	350 F (175 C)	...	400 F (205 C)	...	400 F (205 C)	...
Penetration:						
32 F (0 C), 200 g, 60 s	5	...	10	...	10	...
77 F (25 C), 100 g, 5 s	50	100	25	50	20	40
115 F (46 C), 50 g, 5 s	100	...	...	115	...	100
Ductility at 77 F (25 C), (5 cm/min), cm	30	...	10	...	2	...
Loss on heating at 325 F (163 C), 50 g, 5 h, percent	...	2	...	1	...	1
Penetration of residue, percent of original	60	...	60	...	60	...
Total bitumen soluble in carbon disulfide, percent:						
Filled or native asphalt	95	...	...	...	...	....
Unfilled asphalt	99	...	99	...	99	...
Proportion of bitumen soluble in carbon tetrachloride, percent	99	...	99	...	99	...
Ash, percent:						
Filled or native asphalt	...	5	...	...	...	...
Unfilled asphalt	...	1	...	1	...	1
Coarse particles retained on No. 200 (75-µm) sieve as percentage of bitumen insoluble in carbon disulfide, percent	...	12	...	...	...	...

Standard Specification for
ASPHALT CEMENT FOR USE IN PAVEMENT CONSTRUCTION[1]

This Standard is issued under the fixed designation D 946; the number immediately following the designation indicates the year of original adoption or, in the case of revision, the year of last revision. A number in parentheses indicates the year of last reapproval.

1. Scope

1.1 This specification covers asphalt cement for use in the construction of pavements.

1.2 This specification covers the following penetration grades:

40–50,	120–150, and
60–70,	200–300.
85–100,	

2. Manufacture

2.1 Asphalt cement shall be prepared by the refining of crude petroleum by suitable methods.

3. Properties

3.1 The asphalt cement shall be homogeneous and shall not foam when heated to 347°F (174°C).

3.2 The various grades of asphalt cement shall conform to the requirements prescribed in Table 1.

4. Methods of Sampling and Testing

4.1 The material shall be sampled and the properties enumerated in this specification shall be determined in accordance with the following ASTM methods:

4.1.1 *Sampling*—Method D 140, Sampling Bituminous Materials.[2]

4.1.2 *Penetration*—Method D 5, Test for Penetration of Bituminous Materials.[2]

4.1.3 *Flash Point*—Method D 92, Test for Flash and Fire Points by Cleveland Open Cup.[2]

4.1.4 *Ductility*—Method D 113, Test for Ductility of Bituminous Materials.[2]

4.1.5 *Thin Film Oven Test*—Method D 1754, Test for Effect of Heat and Air on Asphaltic Materials (Thin-Film Oven Test).[2]

4.1.6 *Solubility in Trichloroethylene*—Method D 2042, Test for Solubility of Bituminous Materials in Organic Solvents.[2]

---

[1] This specification is under the jurisdiction of ASTM Committee D-4 on Road and Paving Materials.
Current edition approved Oct. 25, 1974. Published December 1974. Originally published as D 946 – 47 T. Last previous edition D 946 – 69a.
[2] *Annual Book of ASTM Standards*, Part 15.

TABLE 1 Requirements for Asphalt Cement for Use in Pavement Construction

	Penetration Grade									
	40–50		60–70		85–100		120–150		200 300	
	Min	Max	Min	Max	Min	Max	Min	Max	Min	Max
Penetration at 77°F (25°C) 100 g, 5 s	40	50	60	70	85	100	120	150	200	300
Flash point, °F (Cleveland open cup)	450	...	450	...	450	...	425	...	350	...
Ductility at 77°F (25°C) 5 cm/min, cm	100	...	100	...	100	...	100	...	100	...
Retained penetration after thin-film oven test, %	55+	...	52+	...	47+	...	42+	...	37+	...
Ductility at 77°F (25°C) 5 cm/min, cm after thin-film oven test.	...	...	50	...	75	...	100	...	100	...
Solubility in trichloroethylene, %	99.0	...	99.0	...	99.0	...	99.0	...	99.0	...

Standard Specification for
LIQUID ASPHALT (SLOW-CURING TYPE)[1]

This Standard is issued under the fixed designation D 2026; the number immediately following the designation indicates the year of original adoption or, in the case of revision, the year of last revision. A number in parentheses indicates the year of last reapproval.

1. Scope

1.1 This specification covers liquid petroleum asphalts of the slow-curing type for use in the construction and treatment of pavements.

2. Applicable Documents

2.1 *ASTM Standards:*

D 92 Test for Flash and Fire Points by Cleveland Open Cup[2]

D 95 Test for Water in Petroleum Products and Bituminous Materials by Distillation[2]

D 113 Test for Ductility of Bituminous Materials[2]

D 140 Sampling Bituminous Materials[2]

D 243 Test for Residue of Specified Penetration[2]

D 402 Test for Distillation of Cut-Back Asphaltic Products[2]

D 2042 Test for Solubility of Bituminous Materials in Organic Solvents[2]

D 2170 Test for Kinematic Viscosity of Asphalts[2]

D 2171 Test for Absolute Viscosity of Asphalts[2]

3. Properties

3.1 The liquid asphalt shall not foam when heated to application temperature and shall conform to the requirements prescribed in Table 1.

4. Methods of Test

4.1 The material shall be sampled in accordance with Method D 140, and the properties enumerated in this specification shall be determined in accordance with the following ASTM methods:

4.1.1 *Flash Point (Cleveland Open Cup)*— Method D 92.

4.1.2 *Viscosity, Kinematic*—Method D 2170 and Method D 2171.

4.1.3 *Distillation*—Method D 402.

NOTE—If a 100-ml graduate does not permit sufficiently close readings to determine conformity to this specification, receivers graduated in 0.1-ml divisions shall be used.

4.1.4 *Asphalt Residue*—Method D 243.

4.1.5 *Ductility*—Method D 113.

4.1.6 *Solubility in Trichloroethylene*— Method D 2042.

4.1.7 *Water*—Method D 95.

---

[1] This specification is under the jurisdiction of ASTM Committee D-4 on Road and Paving Materials.
Current edition approved Dec. 29, 1972. Published March 1973. Originally published as D 2026 – 63 T. Last previous edition D 2026 – 69.
[2] *Annual Book of ASTM Standards*, Part 11.

TABLE 1 Requirements for Liquid Asphalt (Slow-Curing Type)

NOTE 1—Kinematic Viscosity Method D 2170 covers the range from 30 to 6000 cSt while Absolute Viscosity Method D 2171 covers the range from 42 to 200 000 P.

NOTE 2—If the ductility at 77 F (25 C) is less than 100, the material will be acceptable if its ductility at 60 F (15.5 C) is more than 100.

Designation	SC-70		SC-250		SC-800		SC-3000	
	Min	Max	Min	Max	Min	Max	Min	Max
Kinematic viscosity at 140 F (60 C), cSt.	70	140	250	500	800	1600	3000	6000
Flash point (Cleveland open cup), deg F (deg C)	150 (66)	...	175 (79)	...	200 (93)	...	225 (107)	...
Distillation test:								
Total distillate to 680 F (360 C), volume percent	10	30	4	20	2	12	...	5
Kinematic viscosity on distillation residue at 140 F (60 C), St	4	70	8	100	20	160	40	350
Asphalt residue:								
Residue of 100 penetration, percent	50	...	60	...	70	...	80	...
Ductility of 100 penetration residue at 77 F (25 C), cm	100	...	100	...	100	...	*100	...
Solubility in trichloroethylene, percent	99.0	...	99.0	...	99.0	...	99.0	...
Water, percent	...	0.5	...	0.5	...	0.5	...	0.5

Standard Specification for
LIQUID ASPHALT (RAPID-CURING TYPE)[1]

This Standard is issued under the fixed designation D 2028; the number immediately following the designation indicates the year of original adoption or, in the case of revision, the year of last revision. A number in parentheses indicates the year of last reapproval.

1. Scope

1.1 This specification covers liquid petroleum asphalts of the rapid - curing type for use in the construction and treatment of pavements.

2. Applicable Documents

2.1 *ASTM Standards:*

D 5 Test for Penetration of Bituminous Materials[2]

D 95 Test for Water in Petroleum Products and Bituminous Materials by Distillation[2]

D 113 Test for Ductility of Bituminous Materials[2]

D 140 Sampling Bituminous Materials[2]

D 402 Test for Distillation of Cut-Back Asphaltic Products[2]

D 2042 Test for Solubility of Bituminous Materials in Organic Solvents[2]

D 2170 Test for Kinematic Viscosity of Asphalts[2]

3. Properties

3.1 The liquid asphalt shall not foam when heated to application temperature and shall conform to the requirements prescribed in Table 1.

4. Methods of Test

4.1 The material shall be sampled in accordance with Method D 140, and the properties enumerated in this specification shall be determined in accordance with the following ASTM methods:

4.1.1 *Flash Point (Tag Open-Cup)*—Method D 1310.

4.1.2 *Viscosity, Kinematic*—Method D 2170,

4.1.3 *Distillation*—Method D 402.

NOTE—If a 100-ml graduate does not permit sufficiently close readings to determine conformity to these specifications with the desired accuracy, receivers graduated in 0.1-ml divisions shall be used.

4.1.4 *Penetration*—Method D 5.

4.1.5 *Ductility*—Method D 113.

4.1.6 *Solubility in Trichloroethylene*—Method D 2042.

4.1.7 *Water*—Method D 95.

---

[1] This specification is under the jurisdiction of ASTM Committee D-4 on Road and Paving Materials.

Current edition approved Dec. 29, 1972. Published March 1973. Originally published as D 2028 - 63 T. Last previous edition D 2028 - 68.

[2] *Annual Book of ASTM Standards*, Part 11.

TABLE 1 Requirements for Liquid Asphalt (Rapid-Curing Type)

NOTE—If the ductility at 77 F (25 C) is less than 100, the material will be acceptable if its ductility at 60 F (15.5 C) is more than 100.

Designation	RC-70		RC-250		RC-800		RC-3000	
	Min	Max	Min	Max	Min	Max	Min	Max
Kinematic viscosity at 140 F (60 C), cSt	70	140	250	500	800	1600	3000	6000
Flash point (Tag open-cup), deg F	...	...	80+	...	80+	...	80+	...
(deg C)			(27+)		(27+)		(27+)	
Distillation test:								
Distillate, volume percent of total distillate to 680 F (360 C):								
to 374 F (190 C)	10	...	...	...	...	...	...	...
to 437 F (225 C)	50	...	35	...	15	...	...	...
to 500 F (260 C)	70	...	60	...	45	...	25	...
to 600 F (316 C)	85	...	80	...	75	...	70	...
Residue from distillation to 680 F (360 C), percent volume by difference	55	...	65	...	75	...	80	...
Tests on residue from distillation:								
Penetration at 77 F (25 C), 100 g, 5 s	80	120	80	120	80	120	80	120
Ductility at 77 F (25 C), cm	100	...	100	...	100	...	100	...
Solubility in trichloroethylene, percent	99.0	...	99.0	...	99.0	...	99.0	...
Water, percent	...	0.2	...	0.2	...	0.2	...	0.2

Standard Specification for
CATIONIC EMULSIFIED ASPHALT[1]

This Standard is issued under the fixed designation D 2397; the number immediately following the designation indicates the year of original adoption or, in the case of revision, the year of last revision. A number in parentheses indicates the year of last reapproval.

1. Scope

1.1 This specification covers six grades of cationic emulsified asphalt for use in pavement construction in the manner designated.

2. Applicable Documents

2.1 *ASTM Standards:*
D 140 Sampling Bituminous Materials[2]
D 244 Testing Emulsified Asphalts[2]

3. Requirements

3.1 The emulsified asphalt shall be homogeneous. Within 30 days after delivery and provided separation has not been caused by freezing, the emulsified asphalt shall be homogeneous after thorough mixing.

3.2 Emulsified asphalt shall conform to the requirements prescribed in Table 1.

4. Sampling

4.1 Samples of emulsified asphalt shall be taken in accordance with Methods D 140.

4.2 Samples shall be stored in clean, airtight sealed containers at a temperature of not less than 40°F (4.5°C) until tested.

5. Methods of Test

5.1 The properties of the emulsified asphalts given in Table 1 shall be determined in accordance with Methods D 244, with the following exception:

5.1.1 *Sieve Test*—Use distilled water in all wetting and washing operations in place of sodium oleate solution (2%).

---

[1] This specification is under the jurisdiction of ASTM Committee D-4 on Road and Paving Materials.
Current edition approved Oct. 29, 1973. Published December 1973. Originally published as D 2397 – 65 T. Last previous edition D 2397 – 71.
[2] *1974 Annual Book of ASTM Standards*, Part 15.

TABLE 2 Requirements and Typical Applications for Cationic Emulsified Asphalt

Type	Rapid-Setting				Medium-Setting				Slow-Setting			
Grade	CRS-1		CRS-2		CMS-2		CMS-2h		CSS-1		CSS-1h	
	min	max	min	max	min	max	min	max	min	max	min	max
Test on emulsions:												
Viscosity, Saybolt Furol at 77°F (25°C), s	20	100							20	100	20	100
Viscosity, Saybolt Furol at 122°F (50°C), s			100	400	50	450	50	450				
Settlement,[a] 5-day, %		5		5		5		5		5		5
Storage stability test,[b] 24-h, %		1		1		1		1		1		1
Classification test[c]	passes		passes									
or												
Demulsibility,[d] 35 ml 0.8 % sodium dioctylsulfosuccinate, %	40		40									
Coating, ability and water resistance:												
Coating, dry aggregate					good		good					
Coating, after spraying					fair		fair					
Coating, wet aggregate					fair		fair					
Coating, after spraying					fair		fair					
Particle charge test	positive		positive		positive		positive		positive		positive	
Sieve test, %		0.10		0.10		0.10		0.10		0.10		0.10
Cement mixing test, %										2.0		2.0
Distillation:												
Oil distillate, by volume of emulsion, %		3		3		12		12				
Residue, %	60		65		65		65		57		57	
Tests on residue from distillation test:												
Penetration, 77°F (25°C), 100 g, 5 s	100	250	100	250	100	250	40	90	100	250	40	90
Ductility, 77°F (25°C), 5 cm/min, cm	40		40		40		40		40		40	
Solubility in trichloroethylene, %	97.5		97.5		97.5		97.5		97.5		97.5	
Typical applications[e]	surface treatment, penetration macadam, sand seal coat, tack coat, mulch		surface treatment, penetration macadam, coarse aggregate seal coat (single and multiple)		cold plant mix, coarse aggregate seal coat (single and multiple), crack treatment, road mix, tack coat, sand seal coat		cold plant mix, hot plant mix, coarse aggregate seal coat (single and multiple), crack treatment, road mix, tack coat		cold plant mix, road mix, slurry seal coat, tack coat, fog seal, dust layer, mulch			

[a] The test requirement for settlement may be waived when the emulsified asphalt is used in less than 5 days time; or the purchaser may require that the settlement test be run from the time the sample is received until the emulsified asphalt is used, if the elapsed time is less than 5 days.

[b] The 24-h storage stability test may be used instead of the 5-day settlement test.

[c] Material failing the classification test will be considered acceptable if it passes the demulsibility test.

[d] The demulsibility test shall be made within 30 days from date of shipment.

[e] These typical applications are for use only as a guide for selecting and using the emulsion for pavement construction and maintenance.

Standard Specification for

ASPHALT FOR UNDERSEALING PORTLAND CEMENT CONCRETE PAVEMENTS[1]

This Standard is issued under the fixed designation D 3141; the number immediately following the designation indicates the year of original adoption or, in the case of revision, the year of last revision. A number in parentheses indicates the year of last reapproval.

1. Scope

1.1 This specification covers asphalt suitable for undersealing portland cement concrete and overlaid concrete pavements by pumping hot asphalt under the slabs.

2. Applicable Documents

2.1 *ASTM Standards:*

D 5 Test for Penetration of Bituminous Materials[2]

D 6 Test for Loss on Heating of Oil and Asphaltic Compounds[2]

D 36 Test for Softening Point of Asphalts and Tar Pitches (Ring-and-Ball Apparatus)[2]

D 92 Test for Flash and Fire Points by Cleveland Open Cup[3]

D 113 Test for Ductility of Bituminous Materials[2]

D 140 Sampling Bituminous Materials[2]

D 2042 Test for Solubility of Bituminous Materials in Organic Solvents[2]

3. Material

3.1 An asphalt of suitable consistency for pumping when heated to a temperature from 400 to 450 F (204 to 232 C) and for resistance to displacement in the pavement when cooled;

for sealing the underside of the slabs and joints, to fill cavities, and to correct vertical alignment by raising the slab.

4. Properties

4.1 The asphalt shall be homogeneous and free of water and shall conform to the requirements in Table 1.

5. Methods of Sampling and Testing

5.1 The asphalt shall be sampled and the properties enumerated in this specification shall be determined in accordance with the following ASTM methods:

5.1.1 *Sampling*—Method D 140.

5.1.2 *Softening Point*—Method D 36.

5.1.3 *Flash Point*—Method D 92.

5.1.4 *Penetration*—Method D 5.

5.1.5 *Ductility*—Method D 113.

5.1.6 *Loss on Heating*—Method D 6.

5.1.7 *Bitumen Soluble in Carbon Tetrachloride*—Method D 2042.

···· specification is under the jurisdiction of ASTM Committee D-4 on Road and Paving Materials.

Current edition approved Dec. 29, 1972. Published March 1973.

[2] *Annual Book of ASTM Standards*, Part 11.

[3] *Annual Book of ASTM Standards*, Parts 11, 17, 18, 29.

TABLE 1 Requirements for Asphalt for Undersealing
Portland Cement Concrete Pavements

	Min	Max
Softening point (ring-and-ball method), deg F (deg C)	180 (82)	200 (93)
Flash point (Cleveland open cup), deg F (deg C)	425 (218)	
Penetration:		
32 F (0 C), 200 g, 60 s	5	
77 F (25 C), 100 g, 5 s	15	30
115 F (46 C), 50 g, 5 s		60
Ductility at 77 F (25 C), (5 cm/min), cm	2	
Loss on heating at 325 F (163 C), 50 g, 5 h, percent		0.5
Penetration of residue, percent of original	70	
Proportion of bitumen soluble in carbon tetrachloride, percent[a]	99	

[a] Alternatively, trichloroethylene may be used as a solvent for determining solubility.

ASTM Standards Relating to Concrete and Cement*

 **Designation: C 31 – 69ᵉ**

American National Standard A37.17-1970
American National Standards Institute

Standard Method of
MAKING AND CURING CONCRETE TEST SPECIMENS IN THE FIELD[1]

This Standard is issued under the fixed designation C 31: the number immediately following the designation indicates the year of original adoption or, in the case of revision, the year of last revision. A number in parentheses indicates the year of last reapproval.

ᵉ NOTE—The title was editorially changed in October 1973.

1. Scope

1.1 This method covers procedures for making and curing test specimens from concrete being used in construction.

NOTE 1—For making and curing test specimens in the laboratory, see ASTM Method C 192, Making and Curing Concrete Test Specimens in the Laboratory.[2]

NOTE 2—The values stated in U.S. customary units are to be regarded as the standard.

2. Apparatus

2.1 Molds, General—Molds for specimens or fastenings thereto in contact with the concrete shall be made of steel, cast iron, or other nonabsorbent material, nonreactive with concrete containing portland or other hydraulic cements. Molds shall hold their dimensions and shape under conditions of severe use. Molds shall be watertight during use as judged by their ability to hold water poured into them. A suitable sealant, such as heavy grease, modeling clay, or microcrystalline wax shall be used where necessary to prevent leakage through the joints. Positive means shall be provided to hold base plates firmly to the molds. Molds shall be lightly coated with mineral oil or a suitable nonreactive release material before use.

2.2 Cylinder Molds:

2.2.1 Reusable Vertical Molds—Reusable vertical molds shall be made of heavy gage metal or other rigid nonabsorbent material (Note 3). The plane of the rim of the mold shall be at right angles of the axis. The molds shall not vary from the prescribed diameter by more than 1/16 in. (1.6 mm) nor from the prescribed height by more than 1/4 in. (6.4 mm). Molds shall be provided with a machined metal base plate in the instance of metal molds, a smooth flat metal or integrally molded flat bottom of the same material as the sides in the instance of molds other than metal, with means for securing it to the mold at a right angle to the axis of the cylinder.

NOTE 3—Satisfactory reusable molds may be made from cold-drawn, seamless steel tubing or from steel pipe. These tubular sections shall be cut to the proper length, slotted by machine on one side parallel to the axis, and fitted with a circumferential metal band and bolt or a set of two or three clamps for closing. Split tube molds should be machined inside, if necessary, to ensure compliance with dimensional tolerances after slotting and clamping. Satisfactory reusable molds may also be made from iron or steel castings. Molds made from less rigid materials than steel tubing or iron or steel castings may require special care to ensure that they are not deformed more than the stipulated tolerances during use.

2.2.2 Single-Use Molds—Single-use molds shall conform to ASTM Specification C 470, for Single-Use Molds for Forming 6 by 12-in. (152 by 305-mm) Concrete Test Cylinders.[2]

NOTE 4—Special attention and supervision may be required to ensure that the specified tolerances for absorption and elongation of cardboard molds are not exceeded. Molds made from formed, sheet metal or cardboard should be used with care to ensure that they are not deformed more than the

---

[1] This method is under the jurisdiction of ASTM Committee C-9 on Concrete and Concrete Aggregates and is the direct responsibility of Subcommittee C09.03.01 on Methods of Testing Concrete for Strength.
Current edition effective Oct. 3, 1969. Originally issued 1920. Replaces C 31 66.
[2] 1974 Annual Book of ASTM Standards, Part 14.

stipulated tolerances during use. The use of a tube of heavy metal around sheet metal molds when the specimen is being molded will preserve dimensional integrity.

2.3 *Beam Molds*—Beam molds shall be rectangular in shape and of the dimensions required to produce the specimens stipulated in 3.2. The inside surfaces of the molds shall be smooth and free from blemishes. The sides, bottom, and ends shall be at right angles to each other and shall be straight and true and free of warpage. Maximum variation from the nominal cross section shall not exceed ⅛ in. (3.2 mm) for molds with depth or breadth of 6 in. (152 mm) or more. Molds shall not be more than 1/16 in. (1.6 mm) shorter than the required length, but may exceed it by more than that amount.

2.4 *Tamping Rod*—The rod shall be a round, straight steel rod ⅝ in. (16 mm) in diameter and 24 in. (610 mm) long, with at least the tamping end rounded to a hemispherical tip of the same diameter. Both ends may be rounded, if preferred.

2.5 *Vibrators*—Internal vibrators may have rigid or flexible shafts, preferably powered by electric motors. The frequency or vibration shall be 7000 vibrations/min or greater while in use. The outside diameter or side dimension of the vibrating element shall be at least 0.75 in. (19 mm) and not greater than 1.50 in. (38 mm). The combined length of the shaft and vibrating element shall exceed the maximum depth of the section being vibrated by at least 3 in. (76 mm). External vibrators may be of two types: table or plank. The frequency for external vibrators shall be not less than 3600 vibrations/min, and preferably higher. For both table and plank vibrators, provision shall be made for clamping the mold securely to the apparatus. A vibrating-reed tachometer should be used to check the frequency of vibration.

NOTE 5—Vibratory impulses are frequently imparted to a table or plank vibrator through electromagnetic means, or by use of an eccentric weight on the shaft of an electric motor or on a separate shaft driven by a motor.

2.6 *Small Tools*—Tools and items which may be required such as shovels, pails, trowels, wood float, magnesium float, blunted trowels, straightedge, feeler gage, scoops, and rulers.

2.7 *Slump Apparatus*—The apparatus for measurement of slump shall conform to the requirements of ASTM Method C 143, Test for Slump of Portland Cement Concrete.[2]

2.8 *Sampling and Mixing Receptacle*—The receptacle shall be a suitable heavy gage metal pan, wheelbarrow, or flat, clean nonabsorbent mixing board of sufficient capacity to allow easy mixing by shovel or trowel of the entire sample.

2.9 *Air Content Apparatus*—The apparatus for measuring air content shall conform to the requirements of ASTM Method C 173, Test for Air Content of Freshly Mixed Concrete by the Volumetric Method,[2] or of ASTM Method C 231, Test for Air Content of Freshly Mixed Concrete by the Pressure Method.[2]

3. Test Specimens

3.1 *Compressive Strength Specimens*—Compressive strength specimens shall be cylinders of concrete cast and hardened in an upright position, with a length equal to twice the diameter. The standard specimen shall be the 6 by 12-in. (152 by 305 mm) cylinder when the nominal maximum size of the coarse aggregates does not exceed 2 in. (50 mm). When the nominal maximum size of the coarse aggregate exceeds 2 in. the diameter of the cylinder shall be at least three times the nominal maximum size of the coarse aggregate in the concrete (Note 6). Unless required by the project specifications, cylinders smaller than 6 by 12 in. shall not be made in the field.

NOTE 6—In general the nominal maximum size will be that size next larger than the sieve on which 15 percent of the coarse aggregate is retained. See ASTM Specification C 33, for Concrete Aggregates,[2] and ASTM Specification D 448, for Standard Sizes of Coarse Aggregates for Highway Construction.[2]

3.2 *Flexural Strength Specimens*—Flexural strength specimens shall be rectangular beams of concrete cast and hardened with long axes horizontal. The length shall be at least 2 in. (51 mm) greater than three times the depth as tested. The ratio of width to depth as molded shall not exceed 1.5. The standard beam shall be 6 by 6 in. (152 by 152 mm) in cross section, and shall be used for concrete with maximum size coarse aggregate up to 2 in. (50 mm). When the nominal maximum size of the coarse aggregate exceeds 2 in., the smaller cross-sectional dimension of the beam shall be at least three times the nominal maximum size of the coarse aggregate (Note 6). Unless required by project specifications, beams made in the field shall not have a width or depth of less than 6 in.

4. Sampling Concrete

4.1 Take samples of concrete for test specimens in accordance with ASTM Method C 172, Sampling Fresh Concrete.[2] Note the place of depositing in the structure of the sampled batch of concrete in the job records.

5. Slump and Air Content

5.1 *Slump*—Measure the slump of each batch of concrete, from which specimens are made, immediately after mixing, in accordance with the provisions of Method C 143. Discard concrete used for the slump test.

5.2 *Air Content*—Determine the air content, when required, in accordance with either Method C 173 or Method C 231. Discard concrete used for air content determination.

6. Molding Specimens

6.1 *Place of Molding*—Mold specimens promptly on a level, rigid, horizontal surface, free from vibration and other disturbances, at a place as near as practicable to the location where they are to be stored during the first 24 h. If it is not practicable to mold the specimens where they are to be stored, move them to the place of storage immediately after being struck off (Note 7). Avoid jarring, striking, tilting, or scarring of the surface of the specimens when moving the specimens to a safe place.

NOTE 7—A trowel slipped under the bottom of a cardboard mold will aid in preventing distortion of the bottom during moving.

6.2 *Placing the Concrete*—Place the concrete in the molds using a scoop, blunted trowel, or shovel. Select each scoopful, trowelful, or shovelful of concrete from the mixing pan to ensure that it is representative of the batch. It may be necessary to remix the concrete in the mixing pan with a shovel or trowel to prevent segregation during the molding of specimens. Move the scoop or trowel around the top edge of the mold as the concrete is discharged in order to ensure a

symmetrical distribution of the concrete and to minimize segregation of coarse aggregate within the mold. Further distribute the concrete by use of a tamping rod prior to the start of consolidation. In placing the final layer the operator shall attempt to add an amount of concrete that will exactly fill the mold after compaction. Do not add nonrepresentative concrete to an underfilled mold.

6.2.1 *Number of Layers*—Make specimens in layers as indicated in Table 1.

6.3 *Consolidation:*

6.3.1 *Methods of Consolidation*—Preparation of satisfactory specimens requies different methods of consolidation. The methods of consolidation are rodding, and internal or external vibration. Base the selection of the method of consolidation on the slump, unless the method is stated in the specifications under which the work is being performed. Rod concretes with a slump greater than 3 in. (75 mm). Rod or vibrate concretes with slump of 1 to 3 in. (25 to 75 mm). Vibrate concretes with slump of less than 1 in. (25 mm).

NOTE 8—Concretes of such low water content that they cannot be properly consolidated by the methods described herein, or requiring other sizes and shapes of specimens to represent the product or structure, are not covered by this method. Specimens for such concretes shall be made in accordance with the requirements of Method C 192 with regard to specimen size and shape and method of consolidation.

6.3.2 *Rodding*—Place the concrete in the mold, in the required number of layers of approximately equal volume. For cylinders, rod each layer with the rounded end of the rod using the number of strokes specified in Table 2. The number of roddings per layer required for beams is one for each 2 in.[2] (13 cm²) top surface area of the specimen. Rod the bottom layer throughout its depth. Distribute the strokes uniformly over the cross section of the mold and for each upper layer allow the rod to penetrate about ½ in. (12 mm) into the underlying layer when the depth of the layer is less than 4 in. (100 mm), and about 1 in. (25 mm) when the depth is 4 in. or more. If voids are left by the tamping rod, tap the sides of the mold lightly to close the voids. After each layer is rodded, spade the concrete along the sides and ends of beam molds with a trowel or other suitable tool.

6.3.3 *Vibration*—Maintain a standard duration of vibration for the particular kind of concrete, vibrator, and specimen mold involved. The duration of vibration required will depend upon the workability of the concrete and the effectiveness of the vibrator. Usually sufficient vibration has been applied as soon as the surface of the concrete has become relatively smooth. Continue vibration only long enough to achieve proper consolidation of the concrete. Overvibration may cause segregation. Fill the molds and vibrate in the required number of approximately equal layers. Place all the concrete for each layer in the mold before starting vibration of that layer. Add the final layer, so as to avoid overfilling by more than ¼ in. (6 mm). Finish the surface either during or after vibration where external vibration is used. Finish the surface after vibration when internal vibration is used. When the finish is applied after vibration, add only enough concrete with a trowel to overfill the mold about ⅛ in. (3 mm), work it into the surface and then strike it off.

6.3.3.1 *Internal Vibration*—The diameter of the vibrating element, or thickness of a square vibrating element, shall not exceed one third of the width of the mold in the case of beams. For cylinders, the ratio of the diameter of the cylinder to the diameter of the vibrating element shall be 4.0 or higher. In compacting the specimen the vibrator shall not be allowed to rest on or touch the bottom or sides of the mold. Carefully withdraw the vibrator in such a manner that no air pockets are left in the specimen. After vibration of each layer tap the sides of the molds to ensure removal of large entrapped air bubbles at the surface of the mold.

6.3.3.2 *Cylinders*—Use three insertions of the vibrator at different points for each layer. Allow the vibrator to penetrate through the layer being vibrated, and into the layer below, approximately 1 in. (25 mm).

6.3.3.3 *Beams*—Insert the vibrator at intervals not exceeding 6 in. (150 mm) along the center line of the long dimension of the specimen. For specimens wider than 6 in., use alternating insertions along two lines. Allow the shaft of the vibrator to penetrate into the bottom layer approximately 1 in. (25 mm).

6.3.4 *External Vibration*—When external vibration is used, take care to ensure that the mold is rigidly attached to or securely held against the vibrating element or vibrating surface (Note 8).

6.4 *Finishing*—After consolidation by any of the methods, unless the finishing has been performed during the vibration (6.3.3), strike off the surface of the concrete and float or trowel it as required. Perform all finishing with the minimum manipulation necessary to produce a flat even surface that is level with the rim or edge of the mold and that has no depressions or projections larger than ⅛ in. (3.2 mm).

6.4.1 *Cylinders*—After consolidation finish the top surfaces by striking them off with the tamping rod where the consistency of the concrete permits, or with a wood float or trowel. If desired, cap the top surface of freshly made cylinders with a thin layer of stiff portland cement paste which is permitted to harden and cure with the specimen. See Section 4 of ASTM Method C 617, Capping Cylindrical Concrete Specimens.[2]

6.4.2 *Beams*—Beams shall be finished with a wood or magnesium float.

7. Curing

7.1 *Covering After Finishing*—To prevent evaporation of water from the unhardened concrete cover the specimens immediately after finishing, preferably with a nonabsorptive, nonreactive plate or a sheet of tough, durable, impervious plastic. Wet burlap may be used for covering, but care must be exercised to keep the burlap wet until the specimens are removed from the molds. Placing a sheet of plastic over the burlap will facilitate keeping it wet. Protect the outside surfaces of cardboard molds from all contact with wet burlap or other sources of water for the first 24 h after cylinders have been molded in them. Water may cause the molds to expand and damage specimens at this early age.

7.2 *Initial Curing*—During the first 24 h after molding, store all test specimens under conditions that maintain the temperature immediately adjacent to the specimens in the range of 60 to 80 F (16 to 27 C) and prevent loss of moisture from the specimens. Storage temperatures may be regulated by means of ventilation or by evaporation of water from sand or burlap (Note 9), or by using heating devices such as stoves, electric light bulbs, or thermostatically controlled heating cables. A temperature record of the specimens may be established by means of maximum-minimum thermometers. Store specimens in tightly constructed, firmly braced wooden boxes, damp sand pits, temporary buildings at construction sites, under wet burlap in favorable weather, or in heavyweight closed plastic bags, or use other suitable methods, provided the foregoing requirements limiting specimen temperature and moisture loss are met. Specimens formed in cardboard molds (2.2.2) shall not be stored for the first 24 h in contact with wet sand or wet burlap or under any other condition that will allow the outside surfaces of the mold to absorb water.

NOTE 9—The temperature within damp sand and under wet burlap or similar materials will always be lower than the temperature in the surrounding atmosphere if evaporation takes place.

7.3 *Curing Cylinders for Checking the Adequacy of Laboratory Mixture Proportions for Strength or as the Basis for Acceptance or for Quality Control*—Remove test specimens made for checking the adequacy of the laboratory mixture proportions for strength, or as the basis for acceptance, from the molds at the end of 20 ± 4 h and stored in a moist condition at 73.4 ± 3 F (23 ± 1.7 C) until the moment of test (Note 9). As applied to the treatment of demolded specimens, moist curing means that the test specimens shall have free water maintained on the entire surface area at all times. This condition is met by immersion in saturated lime water and may be met by storage in a moist room or cabinet meeting the requirements of ASTM Specification C 511, for Moist Cabinets and Rooms Used in the Testing of Hydraulic Cements and Concretes.[2] Specimens shall not be exposed to dripping or running water.

7.4 *Curing Cylinders for Determining Form Removal Time or When a Structure May Be Put into Service*—Store test specimens made for determining when forms may be removed or when a structure may be put in service in or on the structure as near to the point of use as possible, and shall receive, insofar as practicable, the same protection from the elements on all surfaces as is given to the portions of the structure which they represent. Test specimens in the moisture condition resulting from the specified curing treatment. To meet these conditions, speci-

mens made for the purpose of determining when a structure may be put in service shall be removed from the molds at the time of removal of form work. Follow the provisions of 7.6, where applicable, for removal of specimens from molds.

7.5 *Curing Beams for Checking the Adequacy of Laboratory Mixture Proportions for Strength or as the Basis for Acceptance or for Quality Control*—Remove test specimens made for checking the adequacy of the laboratory mixture proportions for flexural strength, or as the basis for acceptance, or for quality control, from the mold between 20 and 48 h after molding and cure according to the provisions of 7.3 except that storage for a minimum period of 20 h immediately prior to testing shall be in saturated lime water at 73.4 ± 3 F (23 ± 1.7 C). At the end of the curing period, between the time the specimen is removed from curing until testing is completed, prevent drying of the surfaces of the specimen.

NOTE 10—Relatively small amounts of drying of the surface of flexural specimens induce tensile stresses in the extreme fibers that will markedly reduce the indicated flexural strength.

7.6 *Curing Beams for Determining when a Structure May Be Put into Service*—Cure test specimens for determining when a structure may be put into service, as nearly as practicable, in the same manner as the concrete in the structure. At the end of 48 ± 4 h after molding, take the specimens in the molds to a location preferably near a field laboratory and remove from the molds. Store specimens representing pavements or slabs on grade by placing them on the ground as molded, with their top surfaces up. Bank the sides and ends of the specimens with earth or sand that shall be kept damp, leaving the top surfaces exposed to the specified curing treatment. Store specimens representing structure concrete as near the point in the structure they represent as possible and afford them the same temperature protection and moisture environment as the structure. At the end of the curing period leave the specimens in place exposed to the weather in the same manner as the structure. Remove all beam specimens from field storage and store in lime water at 73.4 ± 3 F (23 ± 1.7 C) for 24 ± 4 h immediately before time of testing to ensure uniform moisture condition from specimen to specimen. Observe the precautions given in 7.5 to guard against drying between time of removal from curing to testing.

8. Shipment to Laboratory

8.1 Cylinders and beams shipped from the field to the laboratory for testing shall be packed in sturdy wooden boxes or other suitable containers surrounded by wet sand or wet sawdust, or other suitable packing material, and protected from freezing during shipment. Upon receipt by the laboratory they shall be placed immediately in the required curing at 73.4 ± 3 F (23 ± 1.7 C)

TABLE 1   Number of Layers Required for Specimens

Specimen Type and Size, as Depth, in. (mm)	Mode of Compaction	Number of Layers	Approximate Depth of Layer, in. (mm)
Cylinders:			
12 (305)	rodding	3 equal	4 (100)
Over 12 (305)	rodding	as required	4 (100)
12 (305) to 18 (460)	vibration	2 equal	half depth of specimen
Over 18 (460)	vibration	3 or more	8 (200) as near as practicable
Beams:			
6 (152) to 8 (200)	rodding	2 equal	half depth of specimen
Over 8 (200)	rodding	3 or more	4 (100)
6 (152) to 8 (200)	vibration	1	depth of specimen
Over 8 (200)	vibration	2 or more	8 (200) as near as practicable

TABLE 2   Number of Roddings to be Used in Molding Cylinder Specimens

Diameter of Cylinder. in. (mm)	Number of Strokes/Layer
6 (152)	25
8 (200)	50
10 (250)	75

American National Standard A37.18
American National Standards Institute
American Association State
Highway Officials Standard
AASHO No. T 22

Standard Method of Test for
COMPRESSIVE STRENGTH OF CYLINDRICAL CONCRETE SPECIMENS[1]

This Standard is issued under the fixed designation C 39; the number immediately following the designation indicates the year of original adoption or, in the case of revision, the year of last revision. A number in parentheses indicates the year of last reapproval.

1. Scope

1.1 This method covers determination of compressive strength of cylindrical concrete specimens such as molded cylinders and drilled cores.

NOTE 1—For methods of molding concrete specimens see ASTM Method C 192, Making and Curing Concrete Test Specimens in the Laboratory[2] and ASTM Method C 31, Making and Curing Concrete Compressive and Flexural Strength Test Specimens in the Field.[2] For methods of obtaining drilled cores see ASTM Method C 42, Obtaining and Testing Drilled Cores and Sawed Beams of Concrete.[2]

2. Apparatus

2.1 The testing machine may be of any type of sufficient capacity, and shall be capable of providing the rate of loading prescribed in 4.2. It must be power operated and must apply this load continuously rather than intermittently, and without shock.

2.2 It shall conform to the requirements of Sections 16, 17, and 18 of ASTM Methods E 4, Verification of Testing Machines.[2] If it has only one loading rate (meeting the requirements of 4.2), it must be provided with a supplemental means for loading at a rate suitable for calibration. This supplemental means of loading may be power or hand operated. The space provided for test specimens shall· be large enough to accommodate, in readable position, an elastic calibration device which is of sufficient capacity to cover the loading range of the testing machine and which complies with the requirements of ASTM Methods E 74, Verification of Calibration Devices for Verifying Testing Machines.[3]

NOTE 2—The type of elastic calibration device most generally available and most commonly used

for this purpose is the circular proving ring.

2.3 The testing machine shall be equipped with two steel bearing blocks with hardened faces (Note 3), one of which is a spherically seated block that will bear on the upper surface of the specimen, and the other a solid block on which the specimen shall rest. Bearing faces of the blocks shall have a minimum dimension at least 3 percent greater than the diameter of the specimen to be tested. Except for the concentric circles described below, the bearing faces shall not depart from a plane by more than 0.001 in. (0.025 mm) in any 6 in. (152 mm) of blocks 6 in. in diameter or larger, or by more than 0.001 in. in the diameter of any smaller block; and new blocks shall be manufactured within one half of this tolerance. When the diameter of the bearing face of the spherically seated block exceeds the diameter of the specimen by ½ in. (13 mm) or more, concentric circles not more than $\frac{1}{32}$ in. (0.8 mm) deep and not more than $\frac{3}{64}$ in. (1.2 mm) wide shall be inscribed to facilitate proper centering.

NOTE 3—It is desirable that the bearing faces of blocks used for compression testing of concrete have a Rockwell hardness of not less than HRC 55.

2.4 Bottom bearing blocks shall conform to the following requirements:

2.4.1 The bottom bearing block is specified

---

[1] This method is under the jurisdiction of ASTM Committee C-9 on Concrete and Concrete Aggregates and is the direct responsibility of Subcommittee C09.03.01 on Methods of Testing Concrete for Strength.
Current edition approved Sept. 29, 1972. Published October 1972. Originally published as C 39 – 21T. Last previous edition C 39 – 71.
[2] *1974 Annual Book of ASTM Standards*, Part 14.
[3] *1974 Annual Book of ASTM Standards*, Part 41.

for the purpose of providing a readily machinable surface for maintenance of the specified surface conditions (Note 4). The top and bottom surfaces shall be parallel to each other. The block may be fastened to the platen of the testing machine. Its least horizontal dimension shall be at least 3 percent greater than the diameter of the specimen to be tested. Concentric circles as described in 2.3 above are optional on the bottom block.

2.4.2 When the lower bearing block is used to assist in centering the specimen, the center of the concentric rings, when provided, or the center of the block itself must be directly below the center of the spherical head. Provision shall be made on the platen of the machine to assure such a position.

2.4.3 The bottom bearing block shall be at least 1 in. (25 mm) thick when new, and at least 0.9 in. (22.5 mm) thick after any resurfacing operations.

NOTE 4—If the testing machine is so designed that the platen itself can be readily maintained in the specified surface condition, a bottom block is not required.

2.5 The spherically seated bearing block shall conform to the following requirements:

2.5.1 The maximum diameter of the bearing face of the suspended spherically seated block shall not exceed the values given below:

Diameter of Test Specimens, in. (mm)	Maximum Diameter of Bearing Face, in. (mm)
2 (51)	4 (102)
3 (76)	5 (127)
4 (102)	6½ (165)
6 (152)	10 (254)
8 (203)	11 (279)

NOTE 5—Square bearing faces are permissible, provided the diameter of the largest possible inscribed circle does not exceed the above diameter.

2.5.2 The center of the sphere shall coincide with the surface of the bearing face within a tolerance of ±5 percent of the radius of the sphere. The diameter of the sphere shall be at least 75 percent of the diameter of the specimen to be tested.

NOTE 6—The preferred contact area is in the form of a ring (described as preferred "bearing" area) as shown on Fig. 1. The ball and the socket must be so designed by the manufacturer that the steel in the contact area does not permanently deform under repeated use, with loads up to 8000 psi (55.2 MPa) on the test specimen.

2.5.3 The curved surfaces of the socket and of the spherical portion shall be kept clean and shall be lubricated with a petroleum type oil such as conventional motor oil, not with a pressure type grease. After contacting the specimen and application of small initial load, further tilting of the spherically seated block is not intended and is undesirable.

2.5.4 If the radius of the sphere is smaller than the radius of the largest specimen to be tested, the portion of the bearing face extending beyond the sphere shall have a thickness not less than the difference between the radius of the sphere and radius of the specimen. The least dimension of the bearing face shall be at least as great as the diameter of the sphere (see Fig. 1).

2.5.5 The movable portion of the bearing block shall be held closely in the spherical seat, but the design shall be such that the bearing face can be rotated freely and tilted at least 4 deg in any direction.

2.6 If the load of a compression machine used in concrete tests is registered on a dial, the dial shall be provided with a graduated scale that can be read to at least the nearest 250 lbf (1110 N) of load (Note 7). The dial shall be readable within 1 percent of the indicated load at any given load level within the loading range. In no case shall the loading range of a dial be considered to include loads below the value which is 100 times the smallest change of load which can be read on the scale. The scale shall be provided with a graduation line equal to zero and so numbered. The dial pointer shall be of sufficient length to reach the graduation marks; the width of the end of the pointer shall not exceed the clear distance between the smallest graduations. Each dial shall be equipped with a zero adjustment which is easily accessible from the outside of the dial case, and with a maximum load indicator.

NOTE 7—As close as can reasonably be read is considered to be ¹⁄₃₂ in. (0.8 mm) along the arc described by the end of the pointer.

3. Test Specimens

3.1 Compression tests of moist-cured specimens shall be made as soon as practicable after removal from the curing room. Neither end of compressive test specimens when tested shall depart from perpendicularity to the axis by more than 0.5 deg (approximately equivalent to ⅛ in. in 12 in. (3 mm in 300 mm)). The ends of compression test specimens that are not plane within 0.002 in. (0.050 mm) shall be capped (Note 8). Test specimens shall be kept moist by any convenient method during the period between removal from moist storage and testing. They shall be tested in a moist condition. The diameter of the test specimen shall be determined to the nearest 0.01 in. (0.25 mm) by averaging two diameters measured at right angles to each other at about midheight of the specimen. This average diameter shall be used for calculating the cross-sectional area. When the length of the specimen is less than $1.8D$, or more than $2.2D$, the length shall be measured to the nearest $0.05D$.

NOTE 8—For methods of capping compression specimens see ASTM Method C 617, Capping Cylindrical Concrete Specimens.[2]

4. Procedure

4.1 *Placing the Specimen*—Place the plain (lower) bearing block, with its hardened face up, on the table or platen of the testing machine directly under the spherically seated (upper) bearing block. Wipe clean the bearing faces of the upper and lower bearing blocks and of the test specimen and place the test specimen on the lower bearing block. Carefully align the axis of the specimen with the center of thrust of the spherically seated block. As the spherically seated block is brought to bear on the specimen, rotate its movable portion gently by hand so that uniform seating is obtained.

4.2 *Rate of Loading*—Apply the load continuously and without shock. In testing machines of the screw type the moving head shall travel at a rate of approximately 0.05 in. (1.3

mm)/min when the machine is running idle. In hydraulically operated machines apply the load at a constant rate within the range 20 to 50 psi/s (0.14 to 0.34 MPa/s). During the application of the first half of the anticipated load a higher rate of loading shall be permitted. Make no adjustment in the controls of the testing machine while a specimen is yielding rapidly immediately before failure.

4.3 Apply the load until the specimen fails, and record the maximum load carried by the specimen during the test. Note the type of failure and the appearance of the concrete.

5. Calculation

5.1 Calculate the compressive strength of the specimen by dividing the maximum load carried by the specimen during the test by the average cross-sectional area determined as described in Section 3 and express the result to the nearest 10 psi (69 kPa).

6. Report

6.1 The report shall include the following:

6.1.1 Identification number,

6.1.2 Diameter (and length, if outside the range of $1.8D$ to $2.2D$), in inches (or millimeters),

6.1.3 Cross-sectional area, in square inches (or square centimeters),

6.1.4 Maximum load, in pounds-force (or newtons),

6.1.5 Compressive strength calculated to the nearest 10 psi (69 kPa),

6.1.6 Type of fracture, if other than the usual cone,

6.1.7 Defects in either specimen or caps, and,

6.1.8 Age of specimen.

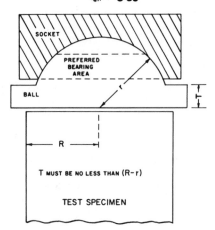

ⒶⓈⓉⓂ C 39

SOCKET

PREFERRED
BEARING
AREA

BALL

T

R

T MUST BE NO LESS THAN (R−r)

TEST SPECIMEN

NOTE—Provision shall be made for holding the ball in the socket and for holding the entire unit in the testing machine.

FIG. 1 Schematic Sketch of a Typical Spherical Bearing Block.

Standard Specification for
READY-MIXED CONCRETE[1]

This Standard is issued under the fixed designation C 94; the number immediately following the designation indicates the year of original adoption or, in the case of revision, the year of last revision. A number in parentheses indicates the year of last reapproval.

1. Scope

1.1 This specification covers ready-mixed concrete manufactured and delivered to a purchaser in a freshly mixed and unhardened state as hereinafter specified. Requirements for quality of concrete shall be either as hereinafter specified or as specified by the purchaser. In any case where the requirements of the purchaser differ from these in this specification, the purchaser's specification shall govern. This specification does not cover the placement, consolidation, curing, or protection of the concrete after delivery to the purchaser.

NOTE 1—As used throughout this specification the manufacturer shall be understood to be the contractor, subcontractor, supplier, or producer furnishing the ready-mixed concrete. The purchaser shall be understood to be the owner or representative thereof.

NOTE 2—The values stated in U.S. customary units are to be regarded as the standard.

2. Applicable Documents

2.1 The following documents of the issue in effect on date of material procurement form a part of this specification to the extent referenced herein:

2.1.1 *ASTM Standards:*
C 31 Making and Curing Concrete Compressive and Flexural Strength Test Specimens in the Field[2]
C 33 Specification for Concrete Aggregates[2]
C 39 Test for Compressive Strength of Cylindrical Concrete Specimens[2]
C 87 Test for Effect of Organic Impurities in Fine Aggregate on Strength of Mortar[2]
C 138 Test for Unit Weight, Yield, and Air Content (Gravimetric) of Concrete[2]
C 143 Test for Slump of Portland Cement Concrete[2]
C 150 Specification for Portland Cement[2]

C 172 Sampling Fresh Concrete[2]
C 173 Tests for Air Content of Freshly Mixed Concrete by the Volumetric Method[2]
C 231 Test for Air Content of Freshly Mixed Concrete by the Pressure Method[2]
C 260 Specification for Air Entraining Admixtures for Concrete[2]
C 330 Specification for Lightweight Aggregates for Structural Concrete[2]
C 494 Specification for Chemical Admixtures for Concrete[2]
C 567 Test for Unit Weight of Structural Lightweight Concrete[2]
C 595 Specification for Blended Hydraulic Cements[2]
C 618 Specification for Fly Ash and Raw or Calcined Natural Pozzolans for Use in Portland Cement Concrete[2]
E 329 Recommended Practice for Inspection and Testing Agencies for Concrete, Steel, and Bituminous Materials as Used in Construction[3]

2.2 *American Concrete Institute Standards:*
211.1-74 (Revised 1975) Recommended Practice for Selecting Proportions for Normal and Heavyweight Concrete
211.2-69 Recommended Practice for Selecting Proportions for Structural Lightweight Concrete
214-65 Recommended Practice for Evaluation of Compression Test Results of

---

[1] This specification is under the jurisdiction of ASTM Committee C-9 on Concrete and Concrete Aggregates and is the direct responsibility of Subcommittee C09.03.09 on Methods of Testing and Specifications for Ready-Mixed Concrete.
Current edition approved Oct. 25, 1974. Published December 1974. Originally published as C 94 – 33 T. Last previous edition C 94 – 74.
[2] *Annual Book of ASTM Standards*, Part 14.
[3] *Annual Book of ASTM Standards*, Parts 10, 14, and 15.

Field Concrete.

305-72 Recommended Practice for Hot Weather Concreting

306-66 (Reaffirmed 1972) Recommended Practice for Cold Weather Concreting

3. Basis of Purchase

3.1 The basis of purchase shall be the cubic yard or cubic metre of freshly mixed and unhardened concrete as discharged from the mixer.

3.2 The volume of freshly mixed and unhardened concrete in a given batch shall be determined from the total weight of the batch divided by the actual weight per cubic foot of the concrete. The total weight of the batch shall be calculated either as the sum of the weights of all materials, including water, entering the batch or as the net weight of the concrete in the batch as delivered. The weight per cubic foot shall be determined in accordance with Method C 138 from the average of at least three measurements, each on a different sample using a ½-ft³ (14 160-cm³) container. Each sample shall be taken from the midpoint of each of three different truck loads by the procedure outlined in Method C 172.

NOTE 3—It should be understood that the volume of hardened concrete may be, or appear to be, less than expected due to waste and spillage, over-excavation, spreading forms, some loss of entrained air, or settlement of wet mixtures, none of which are the responsibility of the producer.

4. Materials

4.1 In the absence of designated applicable specifications covering requirements for quality of materials, the following specifications shall govern:

4.1.1 *Cement*—Cement shall conform to Specification C 150 or Specification C 595. The purchaser should specify the type or types required, but if no type is specified, the requirements of Type I as prescribed in Specification C 150 shall apply.

NOTE 4—These different cements will produce concretes of different properties and should not be used interchangeably.

4.1.2 *Aggregates*—Aggregates shall conform to Specification C 33 or Specification C 330 if lightweight concrete is specified by the purchaser.

4.1.3 *Water*—The mixing water shall be clear and apparently clean. If it contains quantities of substances which discolor it or make it smell or taste unusual or objectionable or cause suspicion, it shall not be used unless service records of concrete made with it or other information indicates that it is not injurious to the quality of the concrete.

NOTE 5—Information on the effects of questionable mixing water may be secured by testing mortar made with the water in question in comparison with mortar mixed with potable water of known acceptable quality in accordance to Method C 87.

4.1.4 *Admixtures*—Admixtures shall conform to Specification C 260, Method C 618, or Specification C 494, whichever is applicable.

5. Quality of Concrete

5.1 In the absence of designated applicable general specifications, the purchaser shall specify the following:

5.1.1 Designated size, or sizes, of coarse aggregate,

5.1.2 Slump, or slumps, desired at the point of delivery (see Section 6 for acceptable tolerances),

5.1.3 When air-entraining concrete is specified, the average air content and tolerance for samples taken from the transportation unit at point of discharge (Note 6),

5.1.4 Which of Alternatives 1, 2, or 3 shall be used as a basis for determining the proportions of the concrete to produce the required quality, and

5.1.5 When structural lightweight concrete is specified, the unit weight as wet weight, air-dry weight, or oven-dry weight (Note 7).

NOTE 6—Tests for air content, both preliminary to construction and routine tests for control purposes during construction, are required. For the range of sizes of normal weight aggregate commonly used in ready-mixed concrete, the recommended average total air content for resistance to freezing and thawing is as follows:

Nominal Maximum Size, in. (mm)	Air Content, percent	Nominal Maximum Size, in. (mm)	Air Content, percent
⅜ (9.5)	8	1 (25.0)	5
½ (12.5)	7	1½ (37.5)	4.5
¾ (19.0)	6	2 (50)	4

Allowable tolerances are ±2 % for ⅜, ½, and ¾-in. (9.5, 12.5, and 19.0-mm) nominal maximum size aggregate concretes and ±1.5 % for 1, 1½, and 2-in. (25.0, 37.5, and 50-mm) nominal maximum size aggregate concretes. Air content less than shown above may not give the required resistance to freezing and thawing, which is the primary purpose of using air-entrained concrete. Air contents in excess of those recommended may reduce the strength without contributing additional protection.

NOTE 7—The unit weight of fresh concrete, which is the only unit weight determinable at the time of delivery, is always higher than the air-dry or oven-dry weight. Definitions of, and methods for determining or calculating air-dry and oven-dry weights, are covered by Method C 567.

5.2 Alternative No. 1:

5.2.1 When the purchaser assumes responsibility for the proportioning of the concrete mixture, he shall also specify the following:

5.2.1.1 Cement content in bags or pounds per cubic yard of concrete, or equivalent units,

5.2.1.2 Maximum allowable water content in gallons per cubic yard of concrete, or equivalent units, including surface moisture on the aggregates, but excluding water of absorption (Note 8), and

5.2.1.3 If admixtures are required, the type, name, and dosage to be used. The cement content shall not be reduced when admixtures are used under Alternative No. 1 without the written approval of the purchaser (Note 9).

NOTE 8—The purchaser, in selecting requirements for which he assumes responsibility should give consideration to requirements for workability, placeability, durability, surface texture, and density, in addition to those for structural design. The purchaser is referred to American Concrete Institute Standard 211.1-70 and American Concrete Institute Standard 211.2-69 for the selection of proportions that will result in concrete suitable for various types of structures and conditions of exposure. The water-cement ratio of most structural lightweight concretes cannot be determined with sufficient accuracy for use as a specification basis.

NOTE 9—In any given instance, the required dosage of air-entraining, accelerating, and retarding admixtures will vary. Therefore, a range of dosages shall be specified which will permit obtaining the desired effect.

5.2.2 At the request of the purchaser, the manufacturer shall, prior to the actual delivery of the concrete, furnish a statement to the purchaser giving the sources, specific gravities, and sieve analyses of the aggregates and the dry weights of cement and saturated-surface-dry weights of fine and coarse aggregate and quantities, type and name of admixture (if any) and of water per cubic yard or cubic metre of concrete that will be used in the manufacture of each class of concrete ordered by the purchaser.

5.3 Alternative No. 2:

5.3.1 When the purchaser requires the manufacturer to assume full responsibility for the selection of the proportions for the concrete mixture (Note 8), the purchaser shall also specify the following:

5.3.1.1 Requirements for compressive strength as determined on samples taken from the transportation unit at the point of discharge evaluated in accordance with Section 16. The purchaser shall specify the requirements in terms of the compressive strength of standard specimens cured under standard laboratory conditions for moist curing (see Section 18). Unless otherwise specified the age at test shall be 28 days.

5.3.2 At the request of the purchaser, the manufacturer shall, prior to the actual delivery of the concrete, furnish a statement to the purchaser, giving the dry weights of cement and saturated surface-dry weights of fine and coarse aggregate and quantities, type, and name of admixtures (if any) and of water per cubic yard or cubic metre of concrete that will be used in the manufacture of each class of concrete ordered by the purchaser. He shall also furnish evidence satisfactory to the purchaser that the materials to be used and proportions selected will produce concrete of the quality specified.

5.4 Alternative No. 3:

5.4.1 When the purchaser requires the manufacturer to assume responsibility for the selection of the proportions for the concrete mixture with the minimum allowable cement content specified (Note 8), the purchaser shall also specify the following:

5.4.1.1 Required compressive strength as determined on samples taken from the transportation unit at the point of discharge evaluated in accordance with Section 16. The purchaser shall specify the requirements for strength in terms of tests of standard specimens cured under standard laboratory conditions for moist curing (see Section 18). Unless otherwise specified the age at test shall be 28 days.

5.4.1.2 Minimum cement content in bags or pounds per cubic yard or kilograms per cubic metre of concrete.

5.4.1.3 If admixtures are required, the type, name, and dosage to be used. The cement content shall not be reduced when admixtures are used (Note 9).

NOTE 10—Alternative No. 3 can be distinctive and useful only if the designated minimum cement content is at about the same level that would ordinarily be required for the strength, aggregate size, and slump specified. At the same time, it must be an amount that will be sufficient to assure durability under expected service conditions, as well as satisfactory surface texture and density, in the event specified strength is attained with it. Attention is directed to the help to be secured in these matters from ACI Recommended Practices 211.1 and 211.2, referred to in Note. 8.

5.4.2 At the request of the purchaser, the manufacturer shall, prior to the actual delivery of the concrete, furnish a statement to the purchaser, giving the dry weights of cement and saturated surface-dry weights of fine and coarse aggregate and quantities, type, and name of admixture (if any) and of water per cubic yard or cubic metre of concrete that will be used in the manufacture of each class of concrete ordered by the purchaser. He shall also furnish evidence satisfactory to the purchaser that the materials to be used and proportions selected will produce concrete of the quality specified. Whatever strengths are attained the quantity of cement used shall not be less than the minimum specified.

5.5 The proportions arrived at by Alternatives 1, 2, or 3 for each class of concrete and approved for use in a project shall be assigned to a designation (such as 7CV, PK7, etc.) to facilitate identification of each concrete mixture delivered to the project. This is the designation required in 15.1.6 and supplies information on concrete proportions when they are not given separately on each delivery ticket as outlined in 15.2. A certified copy of all proportions as established in Alternatives 1, 2, and 3 shall be on file at the batch plant.

6. Tolerances in Slump

6.1 Unless other tolerances are included in the project specifications, the following shall apply.

6.1.1 When the project specifications for slump are written as a "maximum" or "not to exceed" requirement:

	Specified slump:	
	If 3 in. (76 mm) or less	If more than 3 in. (76 mm)
Plus tolerance:	0	0
Minus tolerance:	1½ in. (38 mm)	2½ in. (63 mm)

This option is to be used only if one addition of water is permitted on the job provided such addition does not increase the water-cement ratio above the maximum permitted by the specifications.

6.1.2 When the project specifications for slump are *not* written as a "maximum" or "not to exceed" requirement:

Tolerances for Nominal Slumps	
For Specified Slump of:	Tolerance
2 in. (51 mm) and less	± ½ in. (13 mm)
More than 2 through 4 in. (51 to 102 mm)	± 1 in. (25 mm)
More than 4 in. (102 mm)	± 1½ in. (38 mm)

6.2 Concrete, within the permissible ranges of slumps, shall be available in the batch from the time of beginning discharge for period of 15 min, excepting the first and last ¼ yd³ (¼ m³) as discharged. In the event the user is unprepared for discharge of the concrete from the vehicle upon its arrival at the prescribed destination, the producer shall not be held responsible for the limitation of minimum slump after a total waiting period of 30 min, at agitating speed or agitating and discharge, and the user shall assume full responsibility for the condition of the concrete thereafter.

7. Measuring Materials

7.1 Except as otherwise specifically permitted, cement shall be measured by weight. When fly ash or other pozzolans are specified in the mix design, they may be weighed cumulatively with cement. Cement and fly ash or pozzolans shall be weighed on a scale and in a weigh hopper which is separate and distinct from those used for other materials. Cement shall be weighed before fly ash or other pozzolan. When the quantity of cement exceeds 30 % of the full capacity of the scale, the quantity of cement, and the cumulative quantity of cement plus fly ash or cement plus pozzolan, shall be within ± 1 % of the required weight. For smaller batches to a minimum of 1 yd³ (1 m³), the quantity of cement, and the quantity of cement plus fly ash or cement plus pozzolan, used shall be not less than the required amount nor more than 4 % in excess. Under special circumstances, approved by the purchaser, cement may be measured in bags of standard weight (Note 11). No fraction of a bag of cement shall be used unless weighed.

NOTE 11—In the United States the standard weight of a bag of portland cement is 94 lb (42.6 kg) ± 3 percent.

7.2 Aggregate shall be measured by weight. Batch weights shall be based on dry materials and shall be the required weights of dry materials plus the total weight of moisture (both absorbed and surface) contained in the aggregate. The quantity of aggregate used in any batch of concrete as indicated by the scale shall be within ±2% of the required weight when weighed in individual aggregate weigh batchers. In a cumulative aggregate weigh batcher, the cumulative weight after each successive weighing shall be within ±1 % of the required cumulative amount when the scale is used in excess of 30 % of its capacity. For cumulative weights for less than 30 % of scale capacity, the tolerance shall be ±0.3 % of scale capacity or ±3 % of the required cumulative weight, whichever is less.

7.3 Mixing water shall consist of water added to the batch, ice added to the batch, water occurring as surface moisture on the aggregates, and water introduced in the form of admixtures. The added water shall be measured by weight or volume to an accuracy of 1 % of the required total mixing water. Added ice shall be measured by weight. In the case of truck mixers, any wash water retained in the drum for use in the next batch of concrete shall be accurately measured; if this proves impractical or impossible the wash water shall be discharged prior to loading the next batch of concrete. Total water (including any wash water) shall be measured or weighed to an accuracy of ±3 % of the specified total amount.

7.4 Powdered admixtures shall be measured by weight, and paste or liquid admixtures by weight or volume. Accuracy of weighing admixtures shall be within ±3 % of the required weight. Volumetric measurement shall be within an accuracy of ±3 % of the total amount required or plus and minus the volume of dose required for one sack of cement, whichever is greater.

NOTE 12—Admixture dispensers of the mechanical type capable of adjustment for variation of dosage, and of simple calibration, are recommended.

8. Batching Plant

8.1 Bins with adequate separate compartments shall be provided in the batching plant for fine and for each required size of coarse aggregate. Each bin compartment shall be designed and operated so as to discharge efficiently and freely, with minimum segregation, into the weighing hopper. Means of control shall be provided so that, as the quantity desired in the weighing hopper is approached, the material may be shut off with precision. Weighing hoppers shall be constructed so as to eliminate accumulations of tare materials and to discharge fully.

8.2 Indicating devices shall be in full view and near enough to be read accurately by the operator while charging the hopper. The operator shall have convenient access to all controls.

. 8.3 Scales in use shall be accurate when static load tested to ±0.4 % of the total capacity of the scale.

8.4 Scales for batching concrete ingredients may be either beam or springless dial scales and shall conform to the applicable sections of the current edition of the National Bureau of Standards *Handbook 44*, Specifications, Tolerances, and other Technical Requirements for Commercial Weighing and Measuring Devices,[4] except as may be otherwise specified. Methods for weighing (electric, hydraulic, load cells, etc.) other than beam or springless dial scales which meet the above weighing tolerances are also acceptable.

8.5 Adequate standard test weights shall be available for checking accuracy. All exposed fulcrums, clevises, and similar working parts of scales shall be kept clean. Beam scales shall be equipped with a balance indicator sensitive enough to show movement when a weight equal to 0.1 % of the nominal capacity of the scale is placed in the batch hopper. Pointer travel shall be a minimum of 5 % of the net-rated capacity of the largest weigh beam for underweight and 4 % for overweight.

8.6 The device for the measurement of the added water shall be capable of delivering to the batch the quantity required within the accuracy required in 7.3. The device shall be so arranged that the measurements will not be affected by variable pressures in the water supply line. Measuring tanks shall be equipped with outside taps and valves to provide for checking their calibration unless other means are provided for readily and accurately determining the amount of water in the tank.

NOTE 13—The scale accuracy limitations of the National Ready Mixed Concrete Association Plant Certification meet the requirements of Specification C 94.

[4] Available at Superintendent of Documents, U. S. Government Printing Office, Washington, D. C. 20402.

9. Mixers and Agitators

9.1 Mixers may be stationary mixers or truck mixers. Agitators may be truck mixers or truck agitators.

9.1.1 Stationary mixers shall be equipped with a metal plate or plates on which are plainly marked the mixing speed of the drum or paddles, and the maximum capacity in terms of the volume of mixed concrete. When used for the complete mixing of concrete, stationary mixers shall be equipped with an acceptable timing device that will not permit the batch to be discharged until the specified mixing time has elapsed.

9.1.2 Each truck mixer or agitator shall have attached thereto in a prominent place a metal plate or plates on which are plainly marked the gross volume of the drum, the capacity of the drum or container in terms of the volume of mixed concrete, and the minimum and maximum mixing speeds of rotation of the drum, blades, or paddles. When the concrete is truck mixed as described in 10.1.3, or shrink mixed as described in 10.1.2, the volume of mixed concrete shall not exceed 63 % of the total volume of the drum or container. When the concrete is central mixed as described in 10.1.1, the volume of concrete in the truck mixer or agitator shall not exceed 80 % of the total volume of the drum or container. Truck mixers and agitators shall be equipped with means by which the number of revolutions of the drum, blades, or paddles may be readily verified.

9.2 All stationary and truck mixers shall be capable of combining the ingredients of the concrete within the specified time or the number of revolutions specified in 9.5, into a thoroughly mixed and uniform mass and of discharging the concrete so that not less than 5 of the 6 requirements shown in Table X1 shall have been met.

NOTE 14—The sequence or method of charging the mixer will have an important effect on the uniformity of the concrete.

9.3 The agitator shall be capable of maintaining the mixed concrete in a thoroughly mixed and uniform mass and of discharging the concrete with a satisfactory degree of uniformity as defined by Appendix X1.

9.4 Slump tests of individual samples taken after discharge of approximately 15 % and 85

% of the load may be made for a quick check of the probable degree of uniformity (Note 15). These two samples shall be obtained within an elapsed time of not more than 15 min. If these slumps differ more than that specified in Appendix X1, the mixer or agitator shall not be used unless the condition is corrected, except as provided in 9.5.

NOTE 15—No samples should be taken before 10 % or after 90 % of the batch has been discharged. Due to the difficulty of determining the actual quantity of concrete discharged, the intent is to provide samples that are representative of widely separated portions, but not the beginning and end of the load.

9.5 Use of the equipment may be permitted when operation with a longer mixing time, a smaller load, or a more efficient charging sequence will permit the requirements of Appendix X1 to be met.

9.6 Mixers and agitators shall be examined or weighed routinely as frequently as necessary to detect changes in condition due to accumulations of hardened concrete or mortar and examined to detect wear of blades. When such changes are extensive enough to affect the mixer performance, the proof-tests described in Appendix X1 shall be performed to show whether the correction of deficiencies is required.

10. Mixing and Delivery

10.1 Ready-mixed concrete shall be mixed and delivered to the point designated by the purchaser by means of one of the following combinations of operations:

10.1.1 *Central-Mixed Concrete.*

10.1.2 *Shrink-Mixed Concrete.*

10.1.3 *Truck-Mixed Concrete.*

10.2 Mixers and agitators shall be operated within the limits of capacity and speed of rotation designated by the manufacturer of the equipment.

10.3 *Central-Mixed   Concrete*—Concrete that is mixed completely in a stationary mixer and transported to the point of delivery either in a truck agitator, or a truck mixer operating at agitating speed, or in nonagitating equipment approved by the purchaser and meeting the requirements of 10.1, shall conform to the following: The mixing time shall be counted from the time all the solid materials are in the drum. The batch shall be so charged into the mixer that some water will enter in advance of the cement and aggregate, and all water shall be in the drum by the end of the first one fourth of the specified mixing time.

10.3.1 Where no mixer performance tests are made, the acceptable mixing time for mixers having capacities of 1 yd³ (0.76 m³) or less shall be not less than 1 min. For mixers of greater capacity, this minimum shall be increased 15 s for each cubic yard or fraction thereof of additional capacity.

10.3.2 Where mixer performance tests have been made on given concrete mixtures in accordance with the testing program set forth in the following paragraphs, and the mixers have been charged to their rated capacity, the acceptable mixing time may be reduced for those particular circumstances to a point at which satisfactory mixing defined in 10.3.3 shall have been accomplished. When the mixing time is so reduced the maximum time of mixing shall not exceed this reduced time by more than 60 s for air-entrained concrete.

10.3.3 *Sampling for Uniformity Tests of Stationary Mixers*—Samples of concrete for comparative purposes shall be obtained immediately after arbitrarily designated mixing times, in accordance with one of the following procedures:

10.3.3.1 *Alternative Procedure 1*—The mixer shall be stopped, and the required samples removed by any suitable means from the concrete at approximately equal distances from the front and back of the drum, or

10.3.3.2 *Alternative Procedure 2*—As the mixer is being emptied, individual samples shall be taken after discharge of approximately 15 % and 85 % of the load. Any appropriate method of sampling may be used, provided the samples are representative of widely separated portions, but not the very ends of the batch (Note 15).

10.3.3.3 The samples of concrete shall be tested in accordance with Section 18, and differences in test results for the two samples shall not exceed those given in Appendix X1. Mixer performance tests shall be repeated whenever the appearance of the concrete or the coarse aggregate content of samples selected as outlined in this section indicates that adequate mixing has not been accomplished.

10.4 *Shrink-Mixed Concrete*—Concrete that

is first partially mixed in a stationary mixer, and then mixed completely in a truck mixer, shall conform to the following: The time of partial mixing shall be minimum required to intermingle the ingredients. After transfer to a truck mixer the amount of mixing at the designated mixing speed will be that necessary to meet the requirements for uniformity of concrete as indicated in Appendix X1. Tests to confirm such performance may be made in accordance with 10.3.3 and 10.3.3.3. Additional turning of the mixer, if any, shall be at a designated agitating speed.

10.5 *Truck-Mixed Concrete*—Concrete that is completely mixed in a truck mixer, 70 to 100 revolutions at the mixing speed designated by the manufacturer to produce the uniformity of concrete indicated in Appendix X1. Concrete uniformity tests may be made in accordance with 10.5.1 and if requirements for uniformity of concrete indicated in Appendix X1 are not met with 100 revolutions of mixing, after all ingredients including water, are in the drum, that mixer shall not be used until the condition is corrected, except as provided in 9.5. When satisfactory performance is found in one truck mixer, the performance of mixers of substantially the same design and condition of blades may be regarded as satisfactory. Additional revolutions of the mixer beyond the number found to produce the required uniformity of concrete shall be at a designated agitating speed.

10.5.1 *Sampling for Uniformity of Concrete Produced in Truck Mixers*—The concrete shall be discharged at the normal operating rate for the mixer being tested, with care being exercised not to obstruct or retard the discharge by an incompletely opened gate or seal. A minimum of two samples, each consisting of approximately 2 ft³ (0.1 m³ approximately) shall be taken after discharge of approximately 15 % and 85 % of the load (Notes 15 and 16). These samples shall be obtained within an elpased time of not more than 15 min. The samples shall be secured in accordance with Method C 172, but shall be kept separate to represent specific points in the batch rather than combined to form a composite sample. Between samples, where necessary to maintain slump, the mixer may be turned in mixing direction at agitating speed. During sampling the receptacle shall receive the full discharge of the chute. Additional samples may be taken at other points in the load, if desired. Regardless of the number of samples, sufficient personnel must be available to perform the required tests promptly. Segregation during sampling and handling must be avoided. Each sample shall be remixed the minimum amount to ensure uniformity before specimens are molded for a particular test.

NOTE 16—If more than two samples are tested, the uniformity requirements in Table X1 shall apply only to the two samples taken after discharge of approximately 15 % and 85 % of the load.

10.6 When a truck mixer or truck agitator is used for transporting concrete that has been completely mixed in a stationary mixer, any turning during transportation shall be at the speed designated by the manufacturer of the equipment as agitating speed.

10.7 When a truck mixer or agitator is approved for mixing or delivery of concrete, no water from the truck water system or elsewhere shall be added after the initial introduction of the mixing water for the batch except when on arrival at the job site the slump of the concrete is less than that specified. Such additional water to bring the slump within required limits shall be injected into the mixer under such pressure and direction of flow that the requirements for uniformity specified in Appendix X1 are met. The drum or blades shall be turned an additional 30 revolutions or more if necessary, at mixing speed, until the uniformity of the concrete is within these limits. Water shall not be added to the batch at any later time. Discharge of the concrete shall be completed within 1½ h, or before the drum has revolved 300 revolutions, whichever comes first, after the introduction of the mixing water to the cement and aggregates or the introduction of the cement to the aggregates. These limitations may be waived by the purchaser if the concrete is of such slump after the 1½-h time or 300-revolution limit has been reached that it can be placed, without the addition of water, to the batch. In hot weather, or under conditions contributing to quick stiffening of the concrete, a time less than 1½ h may be specified by the purchaser.

10.8 Concrete delivered in cold weather shall have the applicable minimum temperature indicated in the following table. (The purchaser shall inform the producer as to the type of construction for which the concrete is intended.)

	Minimum Concrete Temperature	
Air Temperature	Thin Sections and Unformed Slabs	Heavy Sections and Mass Concrete
	°F	
30 to 45	60	50
0 to 30	65	55
Below 0	70	60
	°C	
−1 to 7	16	10
−18 to −1	18	13
Below −18	21	16

The maximum temperature of concrete produced with heated aggregates, heated water, or both, shall at no time during its production or transportation exceed 90°F (32°C).

NOTE 17—When hot water is used rapid stiffening may occur if hot water is brought in direct contact with the cement. Additional information on cold weather concreting is contained in ACI 306-66.

10.9 Every effort should be made to maintain the temperature of the concrete produced during hot weather as low as practicable. In some situations difficulty may be encountered when concrete temperatures approach 90°F (32°C).

NOTE 18—Additional information is contained in ACI 305-72.

11. Use of Nonagitating Equipment

11.1 Central-mixed concrete may be transported in suitable nonagitating equipment approved by the purchaser. The proportions of the concrete shall be approved by the purchaser and the following limitations shall apply:

11.2 Bodies of nonagitating equipment shall be smooth, watertight, metal containers equipped with gates that will permit control of the discharge of the concrete. Covers shall be provided for protection against the weather when required by the purchaser.

11.3 The concrete shall be delivered to the site of the work in a thoroughly mixed and uniform mass and discharged with a satisfactory degree of uniformity as prescribed in

Appendix-X1.

11.4 Slump tests of individual samples taken after discharge of approximately 15 % and 85 % of the load may be made for a quick check of the probable degree of uniformity (Note 15). These two samples shall be obtained within an elapsed time of not more than 15 min. If these slumps differ more than that specified in Table X1, the nonagitating equipment shall not be used unless the conditions are corrected as provided in 11.5.

11.5 If the requirements of Appendix X1 are not met when the nonagitating equipment is operated for the maximum time of haul, and with the concrete mixed the minimum time, the equipment may still be used when operated using shorter hauls, or longer mixing times, or combinations thereof that will result in the requirements of Appendix X1 being met.

12. Inspection: Materials, Production, Delivery

12.1 The manufacturer shall afford the inspector all reasonable access, without charge, for making necessary checks of the production facilities and for securing necessary samples to determine if the concrete is being produced in accordance with this specification. All tests and inspection shall be so conducted as not to intefere unnecessarily with the manufacture and delivery of the concrete.

13. Inspection of Fresh Concrete and Sampling

13.1 The contractor shall afford the inspector all reasonable access, without charge, for the procurement of samples of fresh concrete at time of placement to determine conformance of it to this specification.

13.2 Samples of concrete shall be obtained in accordance with Method C 172, except when taken to determine uniformity of slump within any one batch or load of concrete (9.4, 10.3.3, 10.5.1, and 11.4).

14. Slump and Air Content

14.1 Slump and air-content tests shall be made at the time of placement at the option of the inspector as often as is necessary for control checks and acceptance purposes, and always when strength specimens are made (16.2).

14.2 If the measured slump or air content falls outside the specified limits, a check test shall be made immediately on another portion of the same sample. In the event of a second failure, the concrete shall be considered to have failed the requirements of the specification.

15. Certification

15.1 The manufacturer of the concrete shall furnish to the purchaser with each batch of concrete before unloading at the site, a delivery ticket on which is printed, stamped, or written, information concerning said concrete as follows:

15.1.1 Name of ready-mix batch plant,

15.1.2 Serial number of ticket,

15.1.3 Date and truck number,

15.1.4 Name of contractor,

15.1.5 Specific designation of job (name and location),

15.1.6 Specific class or designation of the concrete in conformance with that employed in the job specifications

15.1.7 Amount of concrete (cubic yards),

15.1.8 Time loaded or of first mixing of cement and aggregates,

15.1.9 Water added by receiver of concrete and his initials, and

15.1.10 Type and name of admixture and amount of same.

15.2 Additional information designated by the purchaser and required by the job specifications shall be furnished also upon request; such information may include:

15.2.1 Reading of revolution counter at the first addition of water,

15.2.2 Signature or initials of ready-mix representative,

15.2.3 Type and brand of cement,

15.2.4 Amount of cement,

15.2.5 Total water content by producer (or W/C ratio),

15.2.6 Maximum size of aggregate,

15.2.7 Weights of fine and coarse aggregate, and

15.2.8 Indication that all ingredients are as previously certified or approved.

16. Strength

16.1 When strength is used as a basis for acceptance of concrete, standard specimens shall be made in accordance to Method C 31. The specimens shall be cured under standard moisture and temperature conditions in accordance with Sections 7.2 and 7.3 of Method C 31 (see Section 17).

16.2 Strength tests as well as slump and air content tests shall generally be made with a frequency of not less than one test for each 150 yd³ (115 m³). Each test shall be made from a separate batch. On each day concrete is delivered, at least one strength test shall be made for each class of concrete.

16.3 For a strength test, two standard test specimens shall be made from a composite sample secured as required in Section 13. A test shall be the average of the strengths of the two specimens tested at the age specified in 5.3.1 or 5.4.1 (Note 19). If either of the specimens shows definite evidence other than low strength, of improper sampling, molding, handling, curing, or testing, it shall be discarded and the strength of the remaining cylinder shall then be considered the test result.

NOTE 19—Additional tests may be made at other ages to obtain information on the adequacy of the strength development or to check the adequacy of curing and protection of the concrete. Specimens made to chekc the adequacy of curing and protection should be cured in accordance with Section 7.4 of Method C 31.

16.4 The representative of the purchaser shall ascertain and record the delivery-ticket number for the concrete and the exact location in the work at which each load represented by a strength test is deposited.

16.5 To conform to the requirements of this specification, the average of all of the strength tests (see 16.3) representing each class of concrete shall be sufficient to ensure that the following requirements are met (Note 20 and Note 21).

16.5.1 For concrete in structures designed by the working stress method and all construction other than that covered in 16.5.2, not more than 20 percent of the strength tests shall have values less than the specified strength, f'_c, and the average of any six consecutive strength tests (Note 20) shall be equal to or greater than the specified strength.

16.5.2 For concrete, in structures designed by the ultimate strength method and in prestressed structures, not more than 10 percent of the strength tests shall have values less than the specified strength, f'_c, and the average of any three consecutive strength tests (Note 21) shall be equal to or greater than the specified strength.

NOTE 20—Due to variations in materials, operations, and testing the average strength necessary to meet these requirements will be substantially higher than the specified strength. The amount higher in-

creases as these variations increase and decreases as they are reduced. This is a function of the coefficient of variation and other factors of control explained in ACI 214-65. Pertinent data will be found in Table 1.

NOTE 21—When the number of tests made of any class of concrete totals six or less, the average of all the tests shall be equal to or greater than shown in the following table:

No. of Tests	Required Average Strength of Consecutive Tests, f'_c	
	Section 16.5.1	Section 16.5.2
1	0.79	0.86
2	0.90	0.97
3	0.94	1.02
4	0.97	1.05
5	0.99	1.07
6	1.00	1.08

17. Failure to Meet Strength Requirements

17.1 In the event that concrete tested in accordance with the requirements of Section 16 fails to meet the strength requirements of this specification, the manufacturer of the ready-mixed concrete and the purchaser shall confer to determine whether agreement can be reached as to what adjustment, if any, shall be made. If an agreement on a mutually satisfactory adjustment cannot be reached by the manufacturer and the purchaser, a decision shall be made by a panel of three qualified engineers, one of whom shall be designated by the purchaser, one by the manufacturer, and the third chosen by these two members of the panel. The question of responsibility for the cost of such arbitration shall be determined by the panel. Its decision shall be binding, except as modified by a court decision.

18. Methods of Sampling and Testing

18.1 Test ready-mixed concrete in accordance with the following methods:

18.1.1 *Compression Test Specimens—*Method C 31, using standard moist curing in accordance with Sections 7.2 and 7.3 of Method C 31.

18.1.2 *Compression Tests—*Method C 39.

18.1.3 *Yield, Weight per Cubic Foot—*Method C 138.

18.1.4 *Air Content—*Method C 138; Method C 173 or Method C 231.

18.1.5 *Slump—*Method C 143.

18.1.6 *Sampling Fresh Concrete—*Method C 172.

18.2 The testing laboratory performing acceptance tests of concrete shall meet the requirements of Recommended Practice E 329.

TABLE 1 Strength Requirements

AVERAGE STRENGTH REQUIREMENTS FOR LIMITING PROBABILITY OF TESTS FALLING BELOW THE SPECIFIED STRENGTH, $f'c$, TO ONE OUT OF EVERY TEN TESTS

Coefficient of Variation	5	10	15	20	25
Required Overdesign Factor	1.07	1.15	1:24	1.34	1.47
Design Strength	Required Average Strength[a]				
2000 psi	2140	2300	2480	2680	2940
2500 psi	2675	2875	3100	3350	3675
3000 psi	3210	3450	3720	4030	4420
3500 psi	3745	4025	4340	4690	5145
4000 psi	4270	4590	4960	5380	5890
4500 psi	4815	5175	5580	6030	6615
5000 psi	5340	5740	6200	6720	7360

AVERAGE STRENGTH REQUIREMENTS FOR LIMITING PROBABILITY OF TESTS FALLING BELOW THE SPECIFIED STRENGTH, $f'c$, TO ONE OUT OF EVERY FIVE TESTS

Coefficient of Variation	5	10	15	20	25
Required Overdesign Factor	1.04	1.09	1.14	1.20	1.27
Design Strength	Required Average Strength[a]				
2000 psi	2080	2180	2280	2400	2540
2500 psi	2600	2725	2850	3000	3180
3000 psi	3120	3270	3420	3600	3810
3500 psi	3640	3820	3990	4200	4450
4000 psi	4160	4360	4560	4800	5080
4500 psi	4680	4910	5130	5400	5720
5000 psi	5200	5450	5700	6000	6350

[a] Computed from Eq 7, and values of "t" for more than 30 samples from Table 4 (ACI 214-65). In the absence of statistical experience a coefficient of variation of 20 % shall be assumed.

APPENDIX

X1. CONCRETE UNIFORMITY REQUIREMENTS

X1.1 The variation within a batch as provided in Table X1 shall be determined for each property listed as the difference between the highest value and the lowest value obtained from the different portions of the same batch. For this specification the comparison will be between two samples, representing the first and last portions of the batch being tested. Test results conforming to the limits of five of the six tests listed in Table X1 shall indicate uniform concrete within the limits of this specification.

X1.2 *Coarse Aggregate Content*, using the washout test, shall be computed from the following relations:

$$P = (c/b) \times 100$$

where:
P = weight percent of coarse aggregate in concrete,
c = saturated surface dry weight in pounds (kg) of aggregate retained on the No. 4 (4.75-mm) sieve, resulting from washing all material finer than this sieve from the fresh concrete, and
b = weight of sample of fresh concrete in unit weight container, lb (kg).

X1.3 *Unit Weight of Air Free Mortar* shall be calculated as follows:

U.S. customary units:

$$M = \frac{b - c}{V - \left(\dfrac{V \times A}{100} + \dfrac{c}{G \times 62.4} \right)}$$

Metric units:

$$M = \frac{b - c}{V - \left(\dfrac{V \times A}{100} + \dfrac{c}{1000G} \right)}$$

where:
M = unit weight of air-free mortar, lb/ft³ (kg/m³),
b = weight of concrete sample in unit weight container, lb (kg),
c = saturated surface dry weight of aggregate retained on No. 4 (4.75-mm) sieve, lb (kg),
V = volume of unit weight container, ft³ (m³),
A = air content of concrete, percent, measured in accordance with 18.1.4 on the sample being tested, and
G = specific gravity of coarse aggregate (SSD).

TABLE X1 Requirements for Uniformity of Concrete

Test	Requirement, Expressed as Maximum Permissible Difference in Results of Tests of Samples Taken from Two Locations in the Concrete Batch
Weight per cubic foot (weight per cubic metre) calculated to an air-free basis, lb/ft³ (kg/m³)	1.0 (16)
Air content, volume percent of concrete	1.0
Slump:	
If average slump is 4 in. (102 mm) or less, in. (mm)	1.0 (25)
If average slump is 4 to 6 in. (102 to 152 mm), in. (mm)	1.5 (38)
Coarse aggregate content, portion by weight of each sample retained on No. 4 (4.75-mm) sieve, % . . . . /	6.0
Unit weight of air-free mortar[a] based on average for all comparative samples tested, %	1.6
Average compressive strength at 7 days for each sample,[b] based on average strength of all comparative test specimens, %	7.5[c]

[a] "Test for Variability of Constituents in Concrete," Designation 26, *Bureau of Reclamation Concrete Manual*. 7th Edition. Available from Superintendent of Documents, U. S. Government Printing Office, Washington, D. C. 20402.

[b] Not less than 3 cylinders will be molded and tested from each of the samples.

[c] Tentative approval of the mixer may be granted pending results of the 7-day compressive strength tests.

ASTM Designation: C 138 – 75

American National Standard A37.27
American National Standards Institute
American Association State
Highway Officials Standard
AASHO No.: T 121

Standard Method of Test for
UNIT WEIGHT, YIELD, AND AIR CONTENT (GRAVIMETRIC) OF CONCRETE[1]

This Standard is issued under the fixed designation C138; the number immediately following the designation indicates the year of original adoption or, in the case of revision, the year of last revision. A number in parentheses indicates the year of last reapproval.

1. Scope

1.1 This method covers determination of the weight per cubic foot (or cubic metre) of freshly mixed concrete and gives formulas for calculating the yield, cement content, and the air content of the concrete. Yield is defined as the volume of concrete produced from a mixture of known quantities of the component materials.

NOTE 1—The values stated in U.S. customary units are to be regarded as the standard.

2. Applicable Documents

2.1 *ASTM Standards:*
C 29 Test for Unit Weight of Aggregate[2]
C 150 Specification for Portland Cement[2]
C 172 Sampling Fresh Concrete[2]
C 188 Test for Specific Gravity of Hydraulic Cement[3]
C 231 Test for Air Content of Freshly Mixed Concrete by the Pressure Method.[2]

3. Apparatus

3.1 *Balance*—A balance or scale accurate to within 0.3 % of the test load at any point within the range of use. The range of use shall be considered to extend from the weight of the measure empty to the weight of the measure plus its contents at 160 lb/ft³ (2600 kg/m³).

3.2 *Tamping Rod*—A round, straight steel rod, ⅝ in. (16 mm) in diameter and approximately 24 in. (60 mm) in length, having the tamping end rounded to a hemispherical tip the diameter of which is ⅝ in.

3.3 *Internal Vibrator*—Internal vibrators may have rigid or flexible shafts, preferably powered by electric motors. The frequency of vibration shall be 7000 vibrations per minute or greater while in use. The outside diameter or the side dimension of the vibrating element shall be at least 0.75 in. (19 mm) and not greater than 1.50 in. (38 mm). The length of the shaft shall be at least 24 in. (600 mm).

3.4 *Measure*—A cylindrical container made from metal that is not readily attacked by cement paste. It shall be watertight and sufficiently rigid to retain its form and calibrated volume under rough usage. Measures that are machined to accurate dimensions on the inside and provided with handles are preferred. The minimum capacity of the measure shall conform to the requirements of Table 1. All measures, except for measuring bowls of air meters which are also used for Method C 138 tests, shall conform to the requirements of Method C 29. When measuring bowls of air meters are used, they shall conform to the requirements of Method C 231. The top rim of the air meter bowls shall be smooth and plane within 0.01 in. (0.25 mm).

NOTE 2—The top rim is satisfactorily plane if a 0.01-in. (0.25-mm) feeler gage cannot be inserted between the rim and a piece of ¼ in. (6 mm) or thicker plate glass laid over the top of the measure.

---

[1] This method is under the jurisdiction of ASTM Committee C-9 on Concrete and Concrete Aggregates and is the direct responsibility of Subcommittee C09.03.03 on Methods of Testing Fresh Concrete.
Current edition approved March 28, 1975. Published May 1975. Originally published as C 138 – 38 T. Last previous edition C 138 – 74.
[2] *Annual Book of ASTM Standards*, Part 14.
[3] *Annual Book of ASTM Standards*, Part 13.

3.5 *Strike-Off Plate*—A flat rectangular metal plate at least ¼ in. (6 mm) thick or a glass or acrylic plate at least ½ in. (12 mm) thick with a length and width at least 2 in. (50 mm) greater than the diameter of the measure with which it is to be used. The edges of the plate shall be straight and smooth within a tolerance of ¹⁄₁₆ in. (1.5 mm).

3.6 *Calibration Equipment*—A piece of plate glass, preferably at least ¼ in. (6 mm) thick and at least 1 in. (25 mm) larger than the diameter of the measure to be calibrated. A supply of water pump or chassis grease that can be placed on the rim of the container to prevent leakage.

3.7 *Mallet*—A mallet with a rubber or rawhide head weighing approximately ½ lb (0.23 kg) for use with measures 0.5 ft³ (14 dm³) or smaller or weighing approximately 1 lb (0.45 kg) for use with measures larger than 0.5 ft³.

4. Calibration of Measure

4.1 Calibrate the measure and determine the factor used to convert the weight in pounds (or kilograms) contained in the measure to weight in pounds per cubic foot (or kilograms per cubic metre. Follow the procedure outlined in Method C 29. Measures shall be recalibrated at least once a year or whenever there is reason to question the accuracy of the calibration.

5. Sample

5.1 Obtain the sample of freshly mixed concrete in accordance with Method C 172.

6. Procedure

6.1 Compact measures smaller than 0.4 ft³ (11 dm³) by rodding because of the danger of excessive loss of entrained air. For measures 0.4 ft³ or larger, base the selection of the method of consolidation on the slump, unless the method is stated in the specifications under which the work is being performed. The methods of consolidation are rodding and internal vibration. Rod concretes with a slump greater than 3 in. (75 mm). Rod or vibrate concrete with a slump of 1 to 3 in. (25 to 75 mm). Consolidate concretes with a slump less than 1 in. (25 mm) by vibration.

NOTE 3—The nonplastic concrete, such as is commonly used in the manufacture of pipe and unit masonry, is not covered by this method.

6.2 *Rodding*—Place the concrete in the measure in three layers of approximately equal volume. Rod each layer with 25 strokes of the tamping rod when the 0.5 ft³ (14 dm³) or smaller measures are used and 50 strokes when the 1 ft³ (28 dm³) measure is used. Rod the bottom layer throughout its depth but the rod shall not forcibly strike the bottom of the measure. Distribute the strokes uniformly over the cross section of the measure and for the top two layers, penetrate about 1 in. (25 mm) into the underlying layer. After each layer is rodded, tap the sides of the measure smartly ten or more times until no large bubbles of air appear on the surface and voids left by the 10 to 15 times with the appropriate mallet (see 3.7) to close any voids left by the tamping rod and to release any large bubbles of air that may have been trapped. Add the final layer so as to avoid overfilling.

6.3 *Internal Vibration*—Fill and vibrate the measure in two approximately equal layers. Place all of the concrete for each layer in the measure before starting vibration of that layer. Insert the vibrator at three different points for each layer. In compacting the bottom layer, do not allow the vibrator to rest on or touch the bottom or sides of the measure. In compacting the final layer, the vibrator shall penetrate into the underlying layer approximately 1 in. (25 mm). Take care that the vibrator is withdrawn in such a manner that no air pockets are left in the specimen. The duration of vibration required will depend upon the workability of the concrete and the effectiveness of the vibrator (Note 4). Continue vibration only long enough to achieve proper consolidation of the concrete (Note 5). Observe a constant duration of vibration for the particular kind of concrete, vibrator, and measure involved.

NOTE 4—Usually, sufficient vibration has been applied as soon as the surface of the concrete becomes relatively smooth.

NOTE 5—Overvibration may cause segregation and loss of appreciable quantities of intentionally entrained air.

6.4 On completion of consolidation the measure must not contain a substantial excess or deficiency of concrete. An excess of concrete protruding approximately ⅛ in. (3 mm) above the top of the mold is optimum. A small quantity of concrete may be added to correct a deficiency. If the measure contains a great excess of concrete at completion of consolidation, remove a representative portion of the excess concrete with a trowel or scoop immediately following completion of consolidation and before the measure is struck-off.

6.5 *Strike-Off*—After consolidation, strike-off the top surface of the concrete and finish it smoothly with the flat strike-off plate using great care to leave the measure just level full. The strike-off is best accomplished by pressing the strike-off plate on the top surface of the measure to cover about two thirds of the surface and withdrawing the plate with a sawing motion to finish only the area originally covered. Then place the plate on the top of the measure to cover the original two thirds of the surface and advance it with a vertical pressure and a sawing motion to cover the whole surface of the measure. Several final strokes with the inclined edge of the plate will produce a smooth finished surface.

6.6 *Cleaning and Weighing*—After strike-off, clean all excess concrete from the exterior of the measure and determine the net weight of the concrete in the measure to an accuracy consistent with the requirements of 3.1.

7. Calculations

7.1 *Unit Weight*—Calculate the net weight of the concrete in pounds (or kilograms) by subtracting the weight of the measure from the gross weight. Calculate the weight per cubic foot (or cubic metre) by multiplying the net weight by the calibration factor for the measure used, determined according to Method C 29.

7.2 *Yields*—Calculate the yield, Y, (volume of concrete produced per batch) by dividing the total weight of all materials batched, W_1, by the unit weight, W, determined in 6.1. The total weight of all materials batched is the sum of the weights of the cement, the fine aggregate in the condition used, the coarse aggregate in the condition used, the mixing water added to the batch and any other solid or liquid materials used.

7.3 *Relative Yield*—Relative yield is the ratio of the actual volume of concrete obtained to the volume as designed for the batch calculated as follows:

$$R_y = Y/Y_d$$

where:

R_y = relative yield, and
Y_d = volume of concrete which the batch was designed to produce, yd^3 (m^3).

NOTE 6—A value for R_y greater than 1.00 indicates an excess of concrete being produced whereas a value less than this indicates the batch to be "short" of its designed volume.

7.4 *Cement Content*—Calculate the actual cement content as follows:

$$N = N_t/Y$$

where:

N = actual cement content, lb/yd^3 (or kg/m^3) and
N_t = weight of cement in the batch, lb (or kg).

7.5 *Air Content*—Calculate the air content as follows:

$$A = [(T - W)/T] \times 100$$

or,

$$A = [(Y - V)/Y] \times 100$$

where:

A = air content (percentage of voids) in the concrete,
T = theoretical weight of the concrete computed on an airfree basis, lb/ft^3 (or kg/m^3) (Note 7),
W = unit weight of concrete, lb/ft^3 (or kg/m^3), and
V = total absolute volume of the component ingredients in the batch, ft^3 (or m^3).

NOTE 7—The theoretical weight per cubic foot (or cubic metre) is, customarily, a laboratory determination, the value for which is assumed to remain constant for all batches made using identical component ingredients and proportions. It is calculated from the equation:

$$T = W_1/V$$

The absolute volume of each ingredient in cubic feet is equal to the quotient of the weight of that ingredient divided by the product of its specific gravity times 62.4. The absolute volume of each ingredient in cubic metres is equal to the weight of the ingredient in kilograms divided by 1000 times its specific gravity. For the aggregate components, the bulk specific gravity and weight should be based on the saturated, surface-dry condition. For cement, the actual specific gravity should be determined by Method C 188. A value of 3.15 may be used for cements manufactured to meet the requirements of Specification C 150.

TABLE 1 Minimum Capacity of Measures

Maximum Nominal Size of Coarse Aggregate[a]		Capacity of Measure, min[b]	
in.	mm	ft³	dm³
1	25.0	0.2	6
1½	37.5	0.4	11
2	50	0.5	14
3	75	1.0	28
4½	114	2.5	71
6	152	3.5	99

[a] Aggregate of a given maximum nominal size may contain up to 10 % of particles retained on the sieve referred to.
[b] To provide for wear, measures may be up to 5 % smaller than indicated in this table.

The American Society for Testing and Materials takes no position respecting the validity of any patent rights asserted in connection with any item mentioned in this standard. Users of this standard are expressly advised that determination of the validity of any such patent rights, and the risk of infringement of such rights, is entirely their own responsibility.

American National Standard A37.29
American National Standards Institute

Standard Method of Test for
SLUMP OF PORTLAND CEMENT CONCRETE[1]

This Standard is issued under the fixed designation C 143: the number immediately following the designation indicates the year of original adoption or, in the case of revision, the year of last revision. A number in parentheses indicates the year of last reapproval.

1. Scope

1.1 This method covers determination of slump of concrete, both in the laboratory and in the field.

NOTE 1—This method is considered applicable to plastic concrete having coarse aggregate up to $1\frac{1}{2}$ in. (38 mm) in size. If the coarse aggregate is larger than $1\frac{1}{2}$ in. in size, the method is applicable when it is made on the fraction of concrete passing a $1\frac{1}{2}$-in. sieve with the larger aggregate being removed in accordance with Section 4 of ASTM Method C 172, Sampling Fresh Concrete.[2] This method is not considered applicable to nonplastic and noncohesive concrete.

NOTE 2—The values stated in U.S. customary units are to be regarded as the standard. The metric equivalents of U.S. customary units may be approximate.

2. Apparatus

2.1 *Mold*—The test specimen shall be formed in a mold made of metal not readily attacked by the cement paste. The metal shall not be thinner than No. 16 gage (Bwg) and if formed by the spinning process, there shall be no point on the mold at which the thickness is less than 0.045 in. (1.14 mm). The mold shall be in the form of the lateral surface of the frustum of a cone with the base 8 in. (203 mm) in diameter, the top 4 in. (102 mm) in diameter, and the height 12 in. (305 mm). Individual diameters and heights shall be within $\pm\frac{1}{8}$ in. (3.2 mm) of the prescribed dimensions. The base and the top shall be open and parallel to each other and at right angles to the axis of the cone. The mold shall be provided with foot pieces and handles similar to those shown in Fig. 1. The mold may be constructed either with or without a seam. When a seam is required, it should be essentially as shown in Fig. 1. The interior of the mold shall be relatively smooth and free from projections such as protruding rivets. The mold shall be free

from dents. A mold which clamps to a nonabsorbent base plate is acceptable instead of the one illustrated provided the clamping arrangement is such that it can be fully released without movement of the mold.

2.2 *Tamping Rod*—The tamping rod shall be a round, straight steel rod $\frac{5}{8}$ in. (16 mm) in diameter and approximately 24 in. (600 mm) in length, having the tamping end rounded to a hemispherical tip the diameter of which is $\frac{5}{8}$ in.

3. Sample

3.1 The sample of concrete from which test specimens are made shall be representative of the entire batch. It shall be obtained in accordance with Method C 172.

4. Procedure

4.1 Dampen the mold and place it on a flat, moist, nonabsorbent (rigid) surface. It shall be held firmly in place during filling by the operator standing on the two foot pieces. From the sample of concrete obtained in accordance with Section 3, immediately fill the mold in three layers, each approximately one third the volume of the mold.

NOTE 3—One third of the volume of the slump mold fills it to a depth of $2\frac{5}{8}$ in. (67 mm); two thirds of the volume fills it to a depth of $6\frac{1}{8}$ in. (155 mm).

4.2 Rod each layer with 25 strokes of the tamping rod. Uniformly distribute the strokes

---

[1] This method is under the jurisdiction of ASTM Committee C-9 on Concrete and Concrete Aggregates and is the direct responsibility of Subcommittee C09.03.03 on Methods of Testing Fresh Concrete.

Current edition approved July 29, 1974. Published October 1974. Originally published as D 138 – 22 T. Last previous edition C 143 – 71.

[2] *Annual Book of ASTM Standards*, Part 14.

The American Society for Testing and Materials takes no position respecting the validity of any patent rights asserted in connection with any item mentioned in this standard. Users of this standard are expressly advised that determination of the validity of any such patent rights, and the risk of infringement of such rights, is entirely their own responsibility.

over the cross section of each layer. For the bottom layer this will necessitate inclining the rod slightly and making approximately half of the strokes near the perimeter, and then progressing with vertical strokes spirally toward the center. Rod the bottom layer throughout its depth. Rod the second layer and the top layer each throughout its depth, so that the strokes just penetrate into the underlying layer.

4.3 In filling and rodding the top layer, heap the concrete above the mold before rodding is started. If the rodding operation results in subsidence of the concrete below the top edge of the mold, add additional concrete to keep an excess of concrete above the top of the mold at all times. After the top layer has been rodded, strike off the surface of the concrete by means of a screeding and rolling motion of the tamping rod. Remove the mold immediately from the concrete by raising it carefully in a vertical direction. Raise the mold a distance of 12 in. (300 mm) in 5 ± 2 s by a steady upward lift with no lateral or torsional motion. Complete the entire test from the

start of the filling through removal of the mold without interruption and complete it within an elapsed time of 2½ min.

4.4 Immediately measure the slump by determining the difference between the height of the mold and the height over the original center of the base of the specimen. If a decided falling away or shearing off of concrete from one side or portion of the mass occurs (Note 4), disregard the test and make a new test on another portion of the sample.

NOTE 4—If two consecutive tests on a sample of concrete show a falling away or shearing off of a portion of the concrete from the mass of the specimen, the concrete probably lacks necessary plasticity and cohesiveness for the slump test to be applicable.

5. Report

5.1 Record the slump in terms of inches (millimetres) to the nearest ¼ in. (6 mm) of subsidence of the specimen during the test as follows:

Slump = 12 − inches of height after subsidence.

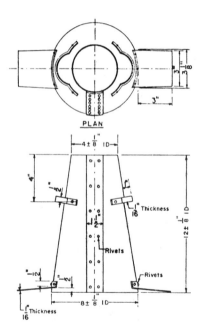

PLAN

Metric Equivalents									
in.	¹⁄₁₆	¹⁄₈	¹⁄₂	1	1½	3	3⅛	4	8	12
mm	1.6	3.2	12.7	25.4	38.1	76.2	79.4	102	203	305

FIG. 1 Mold for Slump Test.

Standard Method of
SAMPLING FRESH CONCRETE[1]

This Standard is issued under the fixed designation C 172; the number immediately following the designation indicates the year of original adoption or, in the case of revision, the year of last revision. A number in parentheses indicates the year of last reapproval.

1. Scope

1.1 This method covers procedures for obtaining representative samples of fresh concrete as delivered to the project site on which tests are to be performed to determine compliance with quality requirements of the specifications under which the concrete is furnished (Note 2). The method includes sampling from stationary, paving and truck mixers, and from agitating and nonagitating equipment used to transport central-mixed concrete.

NOTE 1—The values stated in U.S. customary units are to be regarded as the standard. The metric equivalents of U.S. customary units may be approximate.

NOTE 2—Composite samples are required by this method, unless specifically excepted by procedures governing the tests to be performed such as tests to determine uniformity of consistency and mixer efficiency. Procedures used to select the specific test batches are not described in this method, but it is recommended that random sampling be used to determine over-all specification compliance.

1.2 This method also covers the procedures to be used for preparing a sample of concrete for further testing where it is desirable or necessary to remove the aggregate larger than a designated size. This removal of larger aggregate particles is preferably accomplished by wet-sieving.

2. Sampling

2.1 The elapsed time between obtaining the first and final portions of the composite samples shall be as short as possible, but in no instance shall it exceed 15 min.

2.1.1 Transport the individual samples to the place where fresh concrete tests are to be performed or where test specimens are to be molded. They shall then be combined and remixed with a shovel the minimum amount necessary to ensure uniformity.

2.1.2 Start tests for slump or air content, or both, within 5 min after the sampling is completed. Complete these tests as expeditiously as possible. Start molding specimens for strength tests within 15 min after fabricating the composite sample. Keep the elapsed time between obtaining and using the sample as short as possible and protect the sample from the sun, wind, and other sources of rapid evaporation, and from contamination.

3. Procedure

3.1 *Size of Sample*—Make the samples to be used for strength tests a minimum of 1 ft³ (28 liters). Smaller samples may be permitted for routine air content and slump tests and the size shall be dictated by the maximum aggregate size.

3.2 The procedures used in sampling shall include the use of every precaution that will assist in obtaining samples that are truly representative of the nature and condition of concrete sampled as follows:

NOTE 3—Sampling should normally be performed as the concrete is delivered from the mixer to the conveying vehicle used to transport the concrete to the forms; however, specifications may require other points of sampling, such as at the discharge of a concrete pump.

3.2.1 *Sampling from Stationary Mixers, Except Paving Mixers*—Sample the concrete at two or more regularly spaced intervals during discharge of the middle portion of the batch. Take the samples, so obtained, within the time limit specified in Section 2, and com-

[1] This method is under the jurisdiction of ASTM Committee C-9 on Concrete and Concrete Aggregates and is the direct responsibility of Subcommittee C09.03.03 on Methods of Testing Fresh Concrete.
Current edition effective Jan 8, 1971. Originally issued 1942. Replaces C 172-68.

posite them into one sample for test purposes. Do not obtain samples from the very first or last portions of the batch discharge. Perform sampling by passing a receptacle completely through the discharge stream, or by completely diverting the discharge into a sample container. If discharge of the concrete is too rapid to divert the complete discharge stream, discharge the concrete into a container or transportation unit sufficiently large to accommodate the entire batch and then accomplish the sampling in the same manner as given above. Take care not to restrict the flow of concrete from the mixer, container, or transportation unit so as to cause segregation. These requirements apply to both tilting and nontilting mixers.

3.2.2 *Sampling from Paving Mixers*— Sample the concrete after the contents of the paving mixer have been discharged. Obtain samples from at least five different portions of the pile and then composite into one sample for test purposes. Avoid contamination with subgrade material or prolonged contact with an absorptive subgrade. To preclude contamination or absorption by the subgrade, sample the concrete by placing three shallow containers on the subgrade and discharging the concrete across the containers. Composite the samples so obtained into one sample for tests purposes. The containers shall be of a size sufficient to provide a composite sample size that is in agreement with the maximum aggregate size.

NOTE 4—In some instances, the containers may have to be supported above the subgrade to prevent displacement during discharge.

3.2.3 *Sampling from Revolving Drum Truck Mixers or Agitators*—Sample the concrete at two or more regularly spaced intervals during discharge of the middle portion of the batch. Take the samples so obtained within the time limit specified in Section 2 and composite them into one sample for test purposes. In any case do not obtain samples until after all of the water has been added to the mixer; also do not obtain samples from the very first or last portions of the batch discharge. Sample by repeatedly passing a receptacle through the entire discharge stream or by completely diverting the discharge into a sample container. Regulate the rate of discharge of the batch by the rate of revolution of the drum and not by the size of the gate opening.

3.2.4 *Sampling from Open-Top Truck Mixers, Agitators, Nonagitating Equipment, or Other Types of Open-Top Containers*— Take samples by whichever of the procedures described in 3.2.1, 3.2.2, or 3.2.3 is most applicable under the given conditions.

4. Additional Procedure for Large Maximum Size Aggregate Concrete

4.1 When the concrete contains aggregate larger than that appropriate for the size of the molds or equipment to be used, wet-sieve the sample as described below except make unit-weight tests for use in yield computations on the full mix.

NOTE 5—The effect of wet-sieving on the test results should be considered. For example, wet-sieving concrete causes the loss of a small amount of air due to additional handling. The air content of the wet-sieved fraction of concrete is greater than that of the total concrete because the larger size aggregate which is removed does not contain air. The apparent strength of wet-sieved concrete in smaller specimens is usually greater than that of the total concrete in larger appropriate size specimens. The effect of these differences may need to be considered or determined by supplementary testing for quality control or test result evaluation purposes.

4.2 *Definition:*

4.2.1 *wet-sieving concrete*—the process of removing aggregate larger than a designated size from the fresh concrete by sieving it on a sieve of the designated size.

4.3 *Apparatus:*

4.3.1 *Sieves*, as designated, conforming to ASTM Specification E 11, for Wire-Cloth Sieves for Testing Purposes.[2]

4.3.2 *Wet-Sieving Equipment*—Equipment for wet-sieving concrete shall be a sieve as noted in 4.3.1 of suitable size and conveniently arranged and supported so that one can shake it rapidly by either hand or mechanical means. Generally, a horizontal back and forth motion is preferred. The equipment shall be capable of rapidly and effectively removing the designated size of aggregate (Note 6).

4.3.3 *Hand Tools*—Shovels, hand scoops, plastering trowels, and rubber gloves as required.

NOTE 6—The Manual of Concrete Testing[2] gives descriptions and pictures of several pieces of equipment which have proven satisfactory for this purpose.

---

[2] *1974 Annual Book of ASTM Standards.* Part 14.

4.4 *Procedure:*

4.4.1 *Wet-Sieving*—After sampling the concrete, pass the concrete over the designated sieve and remove and discard the aggregate retained. This shall be done before remixing. Shake or vibrate the sieve by hand or mechanical means until no undersize material remains on the sieve. Mortar adhering to the aggregate retained on the sieve shall not be wiped from it before it is discarded. Place only enough concrete on the sieve at any one time so that after sieving, the thickness of the layer of retained aggregate is not more than one particle thick. The concrete which passes the sieve shall fall into a batch pan of suitable size which has been dampened before use or onto a clean, moist, nonabsorbent surface. Scrape any mortar adhering to the sides of the wet-sieving equipment into the batch. After removing the larger aggregate particles by wet-sieving remix the batch with a shovel the minimum amount necessary to ensure uniformity and proceed testing immediately.

Standard Method of Test for
AIR CONTENT OF FRESHLY MIXED CONCRETE BY THE VOLUMETRIC METHOD[1]

This Standard is issued under the fixed designation C 173; the number immediately following the designation indicates the year of original adoption or, in the case of revision, the year of last revision. A number in parentheses indicates the year of last reapproval.

1. Scope

1.1 This method covers determination of the air content of freshly mixed concrete containing any type of aggregate, whether it be dense, cellular, or lightweight.

2. Applicable Documents

2.1 *ASTM Standards:*
C 29 Test for Unit Weight of Aggregate[2]
C 138 Test for Unit Weight, Yield, and Air Content (Gravimetric) of Concrete[2]
C 172 Sampling Fresh Concrete[2]
C 231 Test for Air Content of Freshly Mixed Concrete by the Pressure Method[2]

3. Apparatus

3.1 *Airmeter*—An airmeter consisting of a bowl and a top section (Fig. 1) conforming to the following requirements:

3.1.1 *Bowl*—The bowl shall be constructed of machined metal of such thickness as to be sufficiently rigid to withstand normal field use and of such composition as not to be readily attacked by cement paste. The bowl shall have a diameter equal to 1 to 1.25 times the height and be constructed with a flange at or near the top surface. Bowls shall not have a capacity of less than 0.075 ft³ (0.002 m³).

3.1.2 *Top Section*—The top section shall be constructed or machined metal of thickness sufficiently rigid to withstand normal field use and of composition not readily attacked by cement paste. The top section shall have a capacity at least 20 % larger than the bowl and shall be equipped with a flexible gasket and with hooks or lugs to attach to the flange on the bowl to make a watertight connection. The top section shall be equipped with a glass-lined or transparent plastic neck, graduated in increments not greater than 0.5 % from 0 at the top to 9 %, or more, of the volume of the bowl. Graduations shall be accurate to ±0.1 % by volume of the bowl. The upper end of the neck shall be threaded and equipped with a screw cap having a gasket to make a watertight fit.

3.2 *Funnel*—A metal funnel with a spout of a size permitting it to be inserted through the neck of the top section and long enough to extend to a point just above the bottom of the top section. The discharge end of the spout shall be so constructed that when water is added to the container there will be a minimum disturbance of the concrete.

3.3 *Tamping Rod*—A round, straight steel rod, ⅝ in. or 16 mm in diameter at least 12 in. or 300 mm long with both ends rounded to a hemispherical tip of the same diameter.

3.4 *Strike-off Bar*—A flat, straight steel bar at least ⅛ by ¾ by 12 in. or 3 by 20 by 300 mm long.

3.5 *Measuring Cup*—A metal cup having a capacity equal to 1.03 ± 0.04 % of the volume of the bowl of the air meter.

NOTE 1—The volume of the measuring cup is slightly larger than 1.0 % of the volume of the bowl to compensate for the volume contraction that takes place when 70 % isopropyl alcohol is mixed with water. Other alcohols or defoaming agents may be used if calculations show that their use will result in an error in indicated air content less than 0.1 %.

[1] This method is under the jurisdiction of ASTM Committee C-9 on Concrete and Concrete Aggregates and is the direct responsibility of Subcommittee C09.03.03 on Methods of Testing Fresh Concrete.
Current edition approved March 28, 1975. Published May 1975. Originally published as C 173 – 42. Last previous edition C 173 – 74.
[2] *Annual Book of ASTM Standards.* Part 14.

3.6 *Syringe*—A small rubber bulb syringe having a capacity at least that of the measuring cup.

3.7 *Pouring Vessel*—A metal or glass container of approximately 1-qt or 1-litre capacity.

3.8 *Trowel*—A blunt-nosed brick mason's trowel.

3.9 *Scoop*—A small metal scoop.

3.10 *Isopropyl Alcohol*—Use 70 % by volume isopropyl alcohol (approximately 65 % by weight). (Notes 1 and 2).

3.11 *Mallet*—A mallet with a rubber or rawhide head weighing approximately ½ lb (0.23 kg).

NOTE 2—Seventy percent isopropyl alcohol is commonly available as rubbing alcohol. More concentrated grades can be diluted with water to the required concentration.

4. Calibration of Apparatus

4.1 The volume of the bowl of the airmeter, in cubic feet or cubic metres shall be determined by accurately weighing the amount of water required to fill it at room temperature, and dividing this weight by the unit weight of water at the same temperature. Follow the calibration procedure outlined in Section 4 of Method C 29.

4.2 Determine the accuracy of the graduations on the neck of the top section of the airmeter by filling the assembled measuring bowl and top section with water to the level of the mark for any air content. Add a quantity of water at room temperature, equal to 1.0 % of the volume of the bowl, to the water already in the neck. The height of the water column shall increase by an amount equivalent to 1.0 % of air.

4.3 Determine the volume of the measuring cup using water at 70°F (21.1°C) by the method outlined in 4.1. A quick check can be made by adding 1 or more cups of water to the assembled apparatus and observing the increase in the height of the water column after filling to a given level as described in 4.2.

5. Sample

5.1 Obtain the sample of freshly mixed concrete in accordance with applicable provisions of Method C 172. If the concrete contains coarse aggregate particles that would be retained on a 1½-in. (37.5-mm) sieve, wet sieve a representative sample over a 1-in. (25-mm) sieve to yield somewhat more than enough material to fill the measuring bowl. The wet sieving procedure is described in Method C 172. Carry out the wet sieving operation with the minimum practicable disturbance of the mortar. Make no attempt to wipe adhering mortar from coarse aggregate particles retained on the sieve.

6. Procedure

6.1 *Rodding and Tapping*—Using the scoop, aided by the trowel if necessary, fill the bowl with freshly mixed concrete in three layers of equal depth. Rod each layer 25 times with the tamping rod. After each layer is rodded, tap the sides of the measure 10 to 15 times smartly with the mallet to close any voids left by the tamping rod and to release any large bubbles of air that may have been trapped.

6.2 *Striking Off*—After placement of the third layer of concrete in accordance with 6.1, strike off the excess concrete with the strike-off bar until the surface is flush with the top of the bowl. Wipe the flange of the bowl clean.

6.3 *Adding Water*—Clamp the top section into position on the bowl, insert the funnel, and add water until it appears in the neck. Remove the funnel and adjust the water level, using the rubber syringe, until the bottom of the meniscus is level with the zero mark. Attach and tighten the screw cap.

6.4 *Agitating and Rolling*—Invert and agitate the unit until the concrete settles free from the base; and then, with the neck elevated, roll and rock the unit until the air appears to have been removed from the concrete. Set the apparatus upright, jar it lightly, and allow it to stand until the air rises to the top. Repeat the operation until no further drop in the water column is observed.

6.5 *Dispelling Bubbles*—When all the air has been removed from the concrete and allowed to rise to the top of the apparatus, remove the screw cap. Add, in 1-cup increments using the syringe, sufficient isopropyl alcohol to dispel the foamy mass on the surface of the water.

6.6 *Reading*—Make a direct reading of the liquid in the neck, reading to the bottom of the meniscus, and estimating to the nearest 0.1 %.

C 173

7. Calculation

7.1 Calculate the air content percent of the concrete in the measuring bowl in percent by adding to the reading from 6.6 the amount of alcohol used in accordance with 6.5.

7.2 When the sample tested represents that portion of the mixture obtained by wet sieving over a 1-in. (25-mm) sieve, calculate the air content of the mortar or of the full mixture using the formulas given in Method C 231. Use appropriate quantities coarser or finer than the 1-in. sieve instead of the 1½-in. (37.5-mm) sieve specified in Method C 231.

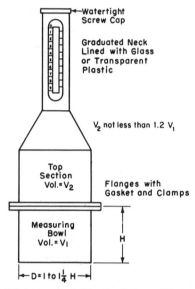

FIG. 1 Apparatus for Measuring Air Content of Fresh Concrete by Volumetric Method.

Standard Method of Test for

AIR CONTENT OF FRESHLY MIXED CONCRETE BY THE PRESSURE METHOD [1]

This Standard is issued under the fixed designation C 231; the number immediately following the designation indicates the year of original adoption or. in the case of revision. the year of last revision. A number in parentheses indicates the year of last reapproval.

1. Scope

1.1 This method covers determination of the air content of freshly mixed concrete from observation of the change in volume of concrete with a change in pressure.

1.2 This method is intended for use with concretes and mortars made with relatively dense aggregates for which the aggregate correction factor can be satisfactorily determined by the technique described in Section 4. It is not applicable to concretes made with lightweight aggregates, air-cooled blast-furnace slag, or aggregates of high porosity. In these cases, ASTM Method C 173, Test for Air Content of Freshly Mixed Concrete by the Volumetric Method,[2] should be used.

Note 1—The values stated in U.S. customary units are to be regarded as the standard.

2. Apparatus

2.1 *Air Meters*—There are available satisfactory apparatus of two basic operational designs employing the principle of Boyle's law. For purposes of reference herein these are designated Meter Type A and Meter Type B.

2.1.1 *Meter Type A*—An air meter consisting of a measuring bowl and cover assembly (see Fig. 1) conforming to the requirements of 2.2 and 2.3. The operational principle of this meter consists of introducing water to a predetermined height above a sample of concrete of known volume, and the application of a predetermined air pressure over the water. The determination consists of the reduction in volume of the air in the concrete sample by observing the amount the water level is lowered under the applied pressure, the latter amount being calibrated in terms of percent of air in the concrete sample.

2.1.2 *Meter Type B*—An air meter consisting of a measuring bowl and cover assembly (see Fig. 2) conforming to the requirements of 2.2 and 2.3. The operational principle of this meter consists of equalizing a known volume of air at a known pressure in a sealed air chamber with the unknown volume of air in the concrete sample, the dial on the pressure gage being calibrated in terms of percent air for the observed pressure at which equalization takes place. Working pressures of 7.5 to 30.0 psi (51 to 207 kPa) have been used satisfactorily.

2.2 *Measuring Bowl*—The measuring bowl shall be essentially cylindrical in shape, made of steel or other hard metal not readily attacked by the cement paste, having a minimum diameter equal to 0.75 to 1.25 times the height, and a capacity of at least 0.20 ft³ (0.006 m³). It shall be flanged or otherwise constructed to provide for a pressure tight fit between bowl and cover assembly. The interior surfaces of the bowl and surfaces of rims, flanges and other component fitted parts shall be machined smooth. The measuring bowl and cover assembly shall be sufficiently rigid to limit the expansion factor, D, of the apparatus assembly (Appendix A5) to not more than 0.1 percent of air content on the indicator scale when under normal operating

---

[1] This method is under the jurisdiction of ASTM Committee C-9 on Concrete and Concrete Aggregates, and is the direct responsibility of Subcommittee C09 03.03 on Methods of Testing Fresh Concrete.
Current edition approved March 28, 1975. Published May 1975. Originally published as C 231 – 49 T. Last previous edition C 231 – 74.
[2] *Annual Book of ASTM Standards*, Part 14.

pressure.

2.3 *Cover Assembly:*

2.3.1 The cover assembly shall be made of steel or other hard metal not readily attacked by the cement paste. It shall be flanged or otherwise constructed to provide for a pressure-tight fit between bowl and cover assembly and shall have machined smooth interior surfaces contoured to provide an air space above the level of the top of the measuring bowl. The cover shall be sufficiently rigid to limit the expansion factor of the apparatus assembly as prescribed in 2.2.

2.3.2 The cover assembly shall be fitted with a means of direct reading of the air content. The cover for the Type A meter shall be fitted with a standpipe, which may be a graduated precision-bore glass tube or may be metal of uniform bore with a glass water gage attached. In the Type B meter, the dial of the pressure gage shall be calibrated to indicate the percent of air. Graduations shall be provided for a range in air content of at least 8 percent easily readible to 0.1 percent as determined by the proper air pressure calibration test.

2.3.3 The cover assembly shall be fitted with air valves, air bleeder valves, and petcocks for bleeding off or through which water may be introduced as necessary for the particular meter design. Suitable means for clamping the cover to the bowl shall be provided to make a pressure-tight seal without entrapping air at the joint between the flanges of the cover and bowl. A suitable hand pump shall be provided with the cover either as an attachment or as an accessory.

2.4 *Calibration Vessel*—A measure having an internal volume equal to a percent of the volume of the measuring bowl corresponding to the approximate percent of air in the concrete to be tested; or, if smaller, it shall be possible to check calibration of the meter indicator at the approximate percent of air in the concrete to be tested by repeated filling of the measure. When the design of the meter requires placing the calibration vessel within the measuring bowl to check calibration, the measure shall be cylindrical in shape and of an inside depth ½ in. (13 mm) less than that of the bowl. A satisfactory measure of this type may be machined from No. 16 gage

brass tubing, of a diameter to provide the volume desired, to which a brass disk ½ in. in thickness is soldered to form an end. When design of the meter requires withdrawing of water from the water-filled bowl and cover assembly to check calibration, the measure may be an integral part of the cover assembly or may be a separate cylindrical measure similar to the above described cylinder.

2.5 *Coil Spring or Other Device for Holding Calibration Cylinder in Place* (Note 2):

2.6 *Spray Tube*—A brass tube of appropriate diameter, which may be an integral part of the cover assembly or which may be provided separately. It shall be so constructed that when water is added to the container, it is sprayed to the walls of the cover in such a manner as to flow down the sides causing a minimum of disturbance to the concrete.

2.7 *Trowel*—A standard brick mason's trowel.

2.8 *Tamping Rod*, as described in ASTM Method C 143, Test for Slump of Portland Cement Concrete.[2]

2.9 *Mallet*, with a rubber or rawhide head weighing approximately ½ lb (0.23 kg).

2.10 *Strike-Off Bar*—A flat straight bar of steel or other suitable metal.

2.11 *Funnel*, with the spout fitting into spray tube.

2.12 *Measure for Water*, having the necessary capacity to fill the indicator with water from the top of the concrete to the zero mark.

2.13 *Vibrator*, as described in ASTM Method C 192, Making and Curing Concrete Test Specimens in the Laboratory.[2]

2.14 *Sieves*, 1½-in. (37.5-mm) with not less than 2 ft[2] (0.19 m[2]) of sieving area.

NOTE 2—The designs of various available types of airmeters are such that they differ in operating techniques and therefore, all of the items described in 2.5 through 2.13 may not be required. The items required shall be those necessary for use with the particular design of apparatus used to satisfactorily determine air content in accordance with the procedures prescribed herein.

3. Calibration of Apparatus

3.1 Make calibration tests in accordance with procedures prescribed in the appendix. Rough handling will affect the calibration of both Types A and B meters. Changes in barometric pressure will affect the calibration of Type A meter but not Type B meter. The steps described in A1.2 to A1.6, as applicable to the meter type under consideration, are prerequisites for the final calibration test to determine the operating pressure, P, on the pressure gage of the Type A meter as described in A1.7, or to determine the accuracy of the graduations indicating air content on the dial face of the pressure gage of the Type B meter. Normally the steps in A1.2 to A1.6 need be made only once (at the time of initial calibration), or only occasionally to check volume constancy of the calibration cylinder and measuring bowl. On the other hand, the calibration test described in A1.7 and A1.9, as applicable to the meter type being checked, must be made as frequently as necessary to ensure that the proper gage pressure, P, is being used for the Type A meter or that the correct air contents are being indicated on the pressure gage air content scale for the Type B meter. A change in elevation of more than 600 ft (183 m) from the location at which a Type-A meter was last calibrated will require recalibration in accordance with A1.7.

4. Determination of Aggregate Correction Factor

4.1 *Procedure*—Determine the aggregate correction factor on a combined sample of fine and coarse aggregate as directed in 4.2 to 4.4. It is determined independently by applying the calibrated pressure to a sample of inundated fine and coarse aggregate in approximately the same moisture condition, amount, and proportions occurring in the concrete sample under test.

4.2 *Aggregate Sample Size*—Calculate the weights of fine and coarse aggregate present in the sample of fresh concrete whose air content is to be determined, as follows:

$$F_a = (S/B) \times F_b \qquad (1)$$
$$C_a = (S/B) \times C_b \qquad \cdot (2)$$

where:

F_a = weight of fine aggregate in concrete sample under test, lb (kg),

S = volume of concrete sample (same as volume of measuring bowl), ft^3 (m^3),

B = volume of concrete produced per batch (Note 3), ft^3 (m^3),

F_b = total weight of fine aggregate in the moisture condition used in batch, lb (kg),

C_a = weight of coarse aggregate in concrete sample under test, lb (kg), and

C_b = total weight of coarse aggregate in the moisture condition used in batch, lb (kg).

NOTE 3—The volume of concrete produced per batch can be determined in accordance with applicable provisions of ASTM Method C 138, Test for Unit Weight, Yield, and Air Content (Gravimetric) of Concrete.[2]

NOTE 4—The term "weight" is temporarily used in this standard because of established trade usage. The word is used to mean both "force" and "mass," and care must be taken to determine which is meant in each case (SI unit for force = newton and for mass = kilogram).

4.3 *Placement of Aggregate in Measuring Bowl*—Mix representative samples of fine aggregate F_a, and coarse aggregate C_a, and place in the measuring bowl filled one-third full with water. Place the mixed aggregate, a small amount at a time, into the measuring bowl; if necessary, add additional water so as to inundate all of the aggregate. Add each scoopful in a manner that will entrap as little air as possible and remove accumulations of foam promptly. Tap the sides of the bowl and lightly rod the upper 1 in. (25 mm) of the aggregate about ten times. Stir after each addition of aggregate to eliminate entrapped air.

4.4 *Aggregate Correction Factor Determination:*

4.4.1 *Initial Procedure for Types A and B Meters*—When all of the aggregate has been placed in the measuring bowl, remove excess foam and keep the aggregate inundated for a period of time approximately equal to the time between introduction of the water into the mixer and the time of performing the test for air content before proceeding with the determination as directed in 4.4.2 or 4.4.3.

4.4.2 *Type A Meter*—Complete the test as described in 6.2.1 and 6.2.2. The aggregate correction factor, G, is equal to $h_1 - h_2$ (see Fig. 1) (Note 5).

4.4.3 *Type B Meter*—Perform the procedures as described in 6.3.1. Remove a volume of water from the assembled and filled apparatus approximately equivalent to the volume of air that would be contained in a typical concrete sample of a size equal to the volume of the bowl. Remove the water in the manner described in A1.9 of the appendix for the calibration tests. Complete the test as described in 6.3.2. The aggregate correction factor, G, is equal to the reading on the air-content scale minus the volume of water removed from the bowl expressed as a percent of the volume of the bowl (see Fig. 1).

NOTE 5—The aggregate correction factor will vary with different aggregates. It can be determined only by test, since apparently it is not directly related to absorption of the particles. The test can be easily made and must not be ignored. Ordinarily the factor will remain reasonably constant for given aggregates, but an occasional check test is recommended.

5. Preparation of Concrete Test Sample

5.1 Obtain the sample of freshly mixed concrete in accordance with applicable procedures of ASTM Method C 172, Sampling Fresh Concrete.[2] If the concrete contains coarse aggregate particles that would be retained on a 2-in. (50-mm) sieve, wet-sieve a sufficient amount of the representative sample over a 1½-in. (37.5-mm) sieve, as described in Method C 172, to yield somewhat more than enough material to fill the measuring bowl of the size selected for use. Carry out the wet-sieving operation with the minimum practicable disturbance of the mortar. Make no attempt to wipe adhering mortar from coarse aggregate particles retained on the sieve.

6. Procedure for Determining Air Content of Concrete

6.1 *Placement and Consolidation of Sample:*

6.1.1 Place a representative sample of the concrete, prepared as described in Section 5, in the measuring bowl in equal layers. Consolidate each layer by the rodding procedure (6.1.2) or by vibration (6.1.3). Strike-off the finally consolidated layer (6.1.4). Vibration shall not be employed to consolidate concrete having a slump greater than 3 in. (76 mm).

6.1.2 *Rodding*—Place the concrete in the measuring bowl in three layers of approximately equal volume. Consolidate each layer of concrete by 25 strokes of the tamping rod evenly distributed over the cross section. After each layer is rodded, tap the sides of the measure smartly 10 to 15 times with the mallet to close any voids left by the tamping rod and to release any large bubbles of air that may have been trapped. Rod the bottom layer throughout its depth but the rod shall not forcibly strike the bottom of the measure. In rodding the second and final layers, use only enough force to cause the rod to penetrate the surface of the previous layer about 1 in. (25 mm). Add the final layer of concrete in a manner to avoid excessive overfilling (6.1.4).

6.1.3 *Vibration*—Place the concrete in the measuring bowl in two layers of approximately equal volume. Place all of the concrete for each layer before starting vibration of that layer. Consolidate each layer by three insertions of the vibrator evenly distributed over the cross section. Add the final layer in a manner to avoid excessive overfilling (6.1.4). In consolidating the bottom layer, do not allow the vibrator to rest on or touch the bottom or sides of the measuring bowl. Take care in withdrawing the vibrator to ensure that no air pockets are left in the specimen. Observe a standard duration of vibration for the particular kind of concrete, vibrator, and measuring bowl involved. The duration of vibration required will depend upon the workability of the concrete and the effectiveness of the vibrator. Continue vibration only long enough to achieve proper consolidation of the concrete. Overvibration may cause segregation and loss of intentionally entrained air. Usually, sufficient vibration has been applied as soon as the surface of the concrete becomes relatively smooth and has a glazed appearance. Never continue vibration long enough to cause escape of froth from the sample.

6.1.4 *Strike Off*—After consolidation of the concrete, strike off the top surface by sliding the strike-off bar across the top flange or rim of the measuring bowl with a sawing motion until the bowl is just level full. On completion of consolidation, the bowl must not contain a great excess or deficiency of concrete. Removal of approximately ⅛ in. (3 mm) during strike off is optimum. A small quantity of representative concrete may be added to correct a deficiency. If the measure contains a great excess, remove a representative portion of concrete with a trowel or scoop before the measure is struck off.

NOTE 6—Any portion of the test method not specifically designated as pertaining to Type A or Type B meter shall apply to both types.

6.2 Procedure—Type A Meter:

6.2.1 *Preparation for Test*—Thoroughly clean the flanges or rims of the bowl and of the cover assembly so that when the cover is clamped in place a pressure-tight seal will be obtained. Assemble the apparatus and add water over the concrete by means of the tube until it rises to about the halfway mark in the standpipe. Incline the apparatus assembly about 30 deg from vertical and, using the bottom of the bowl as a pivot, describe several complete circles with the upper end of the column, simultaneously tapping the cover lightly to remove any entrapped air bubbles above the concrete sample. Return the apparatus assembly to a vertical position and fill the water column slightly above the zero mark, while lightly tapping the sides of the bowl. Remove foam on the surface of the water column with a syringe or with a spray of alcohol to provide a clear meniscus. Bring the water level to the zero mark of the graduated tube before closing the vent at the top of the water column (see Fig. 1 A).

NOTE 7—The internal surface of the cover assembly should be kept clean and free from oil or grease; the surface should be wet to prevent adherence of air bubbles that might be difficult to dislodge after assembly of the apparatus.

6.2.2 *Test Procedure*—Apply slightly more than the desired test pressure, P, (about 0.2 psi (1380 Pa) more) to the concrete by means of the small hand pump. To relieve local restraints, tap the sides of the measure sharply and, when the pressure gage indicates the exact test pressure, P, (as determined in accordance with A1.7, read the water level, H_1, and record to the nearest division or half-division on the graduated precision-bore tube or gage glass of the standpipe (see Fig. 1 B). For extremely harsh mixes it may be necessary to tap the bowl vigorously until further tapping produces no change in the indicated air content. Gradually release the air pressure through the vent at the top of the water column and tap the sides of the bowl lightly for about 1 min. Record the water level, H_2, to the nearest division or half-division (see

Fig. 1 C). The apparent air content, A_1, is equal to $h_1 - h_2$.

6.2.3 *Check Test*—Repeat the steps described in 6.2.2 without adding water to reestablish the water level at the zero mark. The two consecutive determinations of apparent air content should check within 0.2 percent of air and shall be averaged to give the value A_1 to be used in calculating the air content, A, in accordance with Section 7.

6.2.4 In the event the air content exceeds the range of the meter when it is operated at the normal test pressure P, reduce the test pressure to the alternative test pressure P_1 and repeat the steps outlined in 6.2.2 and 6.2.3.

NOTE 8—See A1.7 for exact calibration procedures. An approximate value of the alternative pressure, P_1, such that the apparent air content will equal twice the meter reading can be computed from the following relationship:

$$P_1 = P_a P/(2P_a + P)$$

where:
P_1 = alternative test pressure. psi (or kPa),
P_a = atmospheric pressure, psi (approximately 14.7 psi (101 kPa) but will vary with altitude and weather conditions) (or kPa), and
P = normal test or operating gage pressure, psi (or kPa).

6.3 Procedure—Type B Meter.

6.3.1 *Preparation for Test:* Thoroughly clean the flanges or rims, of the bowl and the cover assembly so that when the cover is clamped in place a pressure-tight seal will be obtained. Assemble the apparatus. Close the air valve between the air chamber and the measuring bowl and open both petcocks on the holes through the cover. Using a rubber syringe, inject water through one petcock until water emerges from the opposite petcock. Jar the meter gently until all air is expelled from this same petcock.

6.3.2 *Test Procedure*—Close the airbleeder valve on the air chamber and pump air into the air chamber until the gage hand is on the initial pressure line. Allow a few seconds for the compressed air to cool to normal temperature. Stabilize the gage hand at the initial pressure line by pumping or bleeding-off air as necessary, tapping the gage lightly. Close both petcocks on the holes through the cover. Open the air valve between the air chamber and the measuring bowl. Tap the sides of the measuring bowl sharply to relieve local restraints.

Lightly tap the pressure gage to stabilize the gage hand and read the percentage of air on the dial of the pressure gage. Release the pressure by opening both petcocks (Fig. 1, A and B) before removing the cover.

NOTE 9—The main air valve should be closed before releasing pressure from either the container or the air chamber. Failure to do so will result in water being drawn into the air chamber thus introducing an error in subsequent measurements. In the event water enters the air chamber it must be bled from the air chamber through the bleeder valve followed by several strokes of the pump to blow out the last traces of water.

7. Calculation

7.1 *Air Content of Sample Tested*—Calculate the air content of the concrete in the measuring bowl as follows:

$$A_s = A_1 - G \qquad (3)$$

where:

A_s = air content of the sample tested, percent,

A_1 = apparent air content of the sample tested, percent (see 6.2.2 and 6.3.2), and

G = aggregate correction factor, percent (Section 4).

7.2 *Air Content of Full Mixture*—When the sample tested represents that portion of the mixture that is obtained by wet sieving to remove aggregate particles larger than a 1½-in. (37.5-mm) sieve, the air content of the full mixture may be calculated as follows:

$$A_t = 100 \, A_s V_c/(100 \, V_t - A_s V_a) \qquad (4)$$

where: (Note 10)

A_t = air content of the full mixture, percent.

V_c = absolute volume of the ingredients of the mixture passing a 1½-in. sieve, air-free, as determined from the original batch weights, ft^3 (m^3),

V_t = absolute volume of all ingredients of the mixture, airfree, ft^3 (m^3), and

V_a = absolute volume of the aggregate in the mixture coarser than a 1½-in. sieve, as determined from original batch weights, ft^3 (m^3).

7.3 *Air Content of the Mortar Fraction*—When it is desired to know the air content of the mortar fraction of the mixture, calculate it as follows:

$$A_m = 100 \, A_s V_c/[100 \, V_m + A_a(V_c - V_m)] \qquad (5)$$

where: (Note 10)

A_m = air content of the mortar fraction, percent, and

V_m = absolute volume of the ingredients of the mortar fraction of the mixture, airfree, ft^3 (m^3).

NOTE 10—The values for use in Eqs 4 and 5 are most conveniently obtained from data on the concrete mixture tabulated as follows for a batch of any size:

	Absolute Volume, ft^3 (m^3)
Cement	
Water	
Fine aggregate	
Coarse aggregate (No. 4 (4.75-mm) to 1½-in. (37.5-mm))	
Coarse aggregate (1½ -in.)	V_a
Total	V_t

The Cement, Water, Fine aggregate braced as V_m; Cement through Coarse aggregate (No. 4 to 1½-in.) braced as V_c.

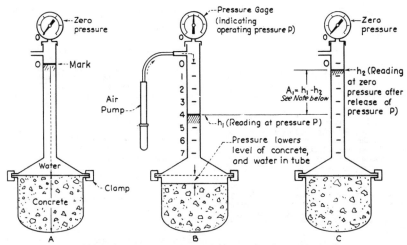

Note: $A_1 = h_1 - h_2$ when bowl contains concrete as shown in this figure; when bowl contains only aggregate and water, $h_1 - h_2 = G$ (aggregate correction factor). $A_1 - G = A$ (entrained air content of concrete)

FIG. 1 Illustration of the Pressure Method for Air Content—Type-A Meter.

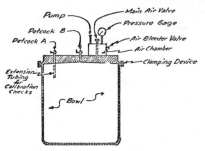

FIG. 2 Schematic Diagram—Type-B Meter.

APPENDIX

A1. CALIBRATION OF APPARATUS

A1.1 Calibration tests shall be performed in accordance with the following procedures as applicable to the meter type being employed.

A1.2 *Calibration of the Calibration Vessel*—Determine accurately the weight of water, w, required to fill the calibration vessel, using a scale accurate to 0.1 percent of the weight of the vessel filled with water. This step shall be performed for Type A and B meters.

A1.3 *Calibration of the Measuring Bowl*—Determine the weight of water, W, required to fill the measuring bowl, using a scale accurate to 0.1 percent of the weight of the bowl filled with water. Slide a glass plate carefully over the flange of the bowl in a manner to ensure that the bowl is completely filled with water. A thin film of cup grease smeared on the flange of the bowl will make a watertight joint between the glass plate and the top of the bowl. This step shall be performed for Type A and B meters.

A1.4 *Effective Volume of the Calibration Vessel, R*—The constant R represents the effective volume of the calibration vessel expressed as a percentage of the volume of the measuring bowl.

A1.4.1 For meter Types A, calculate R as follows (Note A1):

$$R = 0.98 \, w/W \qquad (A1)$$

where:
w = weight of water required to fill the calibration vessel, and
W = weight of water required to fill the measuring bowl.

NOTE A1—The factor 0.98 is used to correct for the reduction in the volume of air in the calibration vessel when it is compressed by a depth of water equal to the depth of the measuring bowl. This factor is approximately 0.98 for an 8-in. (203-mm) deep measuring bowl at sea level. Its value decreases to approximately 0.975 at 5000 ft (1524 m) above sea level and 0.970 at 13 000 ft (3962 m) above sea level. The value of this constant will decrease by about 0.01 for each 4-in. (102-mm) increase in bowl depth. The depth of the measuring bowl and atmospheric pressure do not affect the effective volume of the calibration vessel for meter Types B.

A1.4.2 For meter Types B calculate R as follows (Note A1):

$$R = w/W \qquad (A2)$$

A1.5 *Determination of, or Check of, Allowance for Expansion Factor, D:*

A1.5.1 For meter assemblies of Type A determine the expansion factor, D (Note A2) by filling the apparatus with water only (making certain that all entrapped air has been removed and the water level is exactly on the zero mark (Note A3)) and applying an air pressure approximately equal to the operating pressure, P, determined by the calibration test described in A1.7. The amount the water column lowers will be the equivalent expansion factor, D, for that particular apparatus and pressure (Note A4).

NOTE A2—Although the bowl, cover, and clamping mechanism of the apparatus must of necessity be sturdily constructed so that it will be pressure-tight, the application of internal pressure will result in a small increase in volume. This expansion will not affect the test results because, with the procedure described in Sections 4 and 6, the amount of expansion is the same for the test for air in concrete as for the test for aggregate correction factor on combined fine and coarse aggregates, and is thereby automatically cancelled. However, it does enter into the calibration test to determine the air pressure to be used in testing fresh concrete.

NOTE A3—The water columns on some meters of Type-A design are marked with an initial water level and a zero mark, the difference between the two marks being the allowance for the expansion factor. This allowance should be checked in the same manner as for meters not so marked and in such a case, the expansion factor should be omitted in computing the calibration readings in A1.7.

NOTE A4—It will be sufficiently accurate for this purpose to use an approximate value for P determined by making a preliminary calibration test as described in A1.7 except that an approximate value

for the calibration factor, K, shall be used. For this test $K = 0.98R$ which is the same as Eq A2 except that the expansion reading, D, as yet unknown, is assumed to be zero.

A1.5.2 For meters of Type B design, the allowance for the expansion factor, D, is included in the difference between the initial pressure indicated on the pressure gage and the zero percent mark on the air-content scale on the pressure gage. This allowance shall be checked by filling the apparatus with water (making certain that all entrapped air has been removed), pumping air into the air chamber until the gage hand is stabilized at the indicated initial pressure line, and then releasing the air to the measuring bowl (Note A5). If the initial pressure line is correctly positioned, the gage should read zero percent. The initial pressure line shall be adjusted if two or more determinations show the same variation from zero percent and the test repeated to check the adjusted initial pressure line.

NOTE A5–This procedure may be accomplished in conjunction with the calibration test described in A1.9.

A1.6 *Calibration Reading, K*—The calibration reading, K, is the final meter reading to be obtained when the meter is operated at the correct calibration pressure.

A1.6.1 For meter Types A, the calibration reading, K, is as follows:

$$K = R + D \qquad (A3)$$

where:
R = effective volume of the calibration vessel (A4.1), and
D = expansion factor (A5.1, Note A6).

A1.6.2 For meter Types B the calibration reading, K, equals the effective volume of the calibration vessel (A4.2) as follows:

$$K = R \qquad (A4)$$

NOTE A6—If the water column indicator is graduated to include an initial water level and a zero mark, the difference between the two marks being equivalent to the expansion factor, the term D shall be omitted from Eq A3.

A1.7 *Calibration Test to Determine Operating Pressure, P, on Pressure Gage, Type A Meter*—If the rim of the calibration cylinder contains no recesses or projections, fit it with three or more spacers equally spaced around the circumference. Invert the cylinder and place it at the center of the dry bottom of the measuring bowl. The spacers will provide an opening for flow of water into the calibration cylinder when pressure is applied. Secure the inverted cylinder against displacement and carefully lower the cover assembly. After the cover is clamped in place, carefully adjust the apparatus assembly to a vertical position and add water at air temperature, by means of the tube and funnel, until it rises above the zero mark on the standpipe. Close the vent and pump air into the apparatus to the approximate operating pressure. Incline the assembly about 30 deg from vertical (Note A7) and, using the bottom of the bowl as a pivot, describe several complete circles with the upper end of the standpipe, simultaneously tapping the cover and sides of the bowl lightly to remove any entrapped air adhering to the inner surfaces of the apparatus. Return the apparatus to a vertical position, gradually release the pressure (to avoid loss of air from the calibration vessel), and open the vent. Bring the water level exactly to the zero mark by bleeding water through the petcock in the top of the conical cover. After closing the vent, apply pressure until the water level has dropped an amount equivalent to about 0.1 to 0.2 percent of air more than the value of the calibration reading, K, determined as described in A1.6. To relieve local restraints, lightly tap the sides of the bowl, and when the water level is exactly at the value of the calibration reading, K, read the pressure, P, indicated by the gage and record to the nearest 0.i psi (690 Pa). Gradually release the pressure and open the vent to determine whether the water level returns to the zero mark when the sides of the bowl are tapped lightly (failure to do so indicates loss of air from the calibration vessel or loss of water due to a leak in the assembly). If the water level fails to return to within 0.05 percent air of the zero mark and no leakage beyond a few drops of water is found, some air probably was lost from the calibration cylinder. In this case, repeat the calibration procedure step by step from the beginning of this paragraph. If the leakage is more than a few drops of water, tighten the leaking joint before repeating the calibration procedure. Check the indicated pressure reading promptly by bringing the water level exactly to the zero mark, closing the vent, and applying the pressure, P, just determined. Tap the gage lightly with a finger. When the gage indicates the exact pressure, P, the water column should read the value of the calibration factor, K, used in the first pressure application within about 0.05 percent of air.

NOTE A7: **Caution**—The apparatus assembly must not be moved from the vertical position until pressure has been applied which will force water about one third of the way up into the calibration cylinder. Any loss of air from this cylinder will nullify the calibration.

A1.8 *Calibration Test to Determine Alternative Operating Pressure P_1—Meter Type A*—The range of air contents which can be measured with a given meter can be doubled by determining an alternative operating pressure P_1 such that the meter reads half of the calibration reading, K, (Eq. A3). Exact calibration will require determination of the expansion factor at the reduced pressure in A1.5. For most purposes the change in expansion factor can be disregarded and the alternative operating pressure determined during the determination of the regular operating pressure in A1.7.

A1.9 *Calibration Test to Check the Air Content Graduations on the Pressure Gage, Type B Meter*—Fill the measuring bowl with water as described in A1.3. Screw the short piece of tubing or pipe furnished with the apparatus into the threaded petcock hole on the underside of the cover assembly. Assemble the apparatus. Close the air valve between the air chamber and the measuring bowl and open the two petcocks on holes through the cover assembly. Add water through the petcock on the cover assembly having the extension below until all air is expelled from the second petcock. Pump air into the air chamber until the pressure reaches the indicated initial pressure line. Allow a few seconds for the compressed air to cool to normal temperature. Stabilize the gage hand at the initial pressure line by pumping or bleeding off air as necessary, tapping the gage lightly. Close the petcock not provided with the tube or pipe extension on the under side of the cover. Remove water from the assembly to the calibrating vessel controlling the flow, depending on the particular meter design, by opening the petcock provided with the tube or pipe extension and cracking the air valve between the air chamber and the measuring bowl, or by opening the air valve and using the petcock to control flow. Perform the calibration at an air content which is within the normal range of use. If the calibration vessel (A1.2) has a capacity within the normal range of use, remove exactly that amount of water. With some meters the calibrating vessel is quite small and it will be necessary to remove several times that volume to obtain an air content within the normal range of use. In this instance, carefully collect the water in an auxiliary container and determine the amount removed by weighing to the nearest 0.1 percent. Calculate the correct air content, R, by using Eq A2. Release the air from the apparatus at the petcock not used for filling the calibration vessel and if the apparatus employs an auxiliary tube for filling the calibration container, open the petcock to which the tube is connected to drain the tube back into the measuring bowl (Note A8). At this point of procedure the measuring bowl contains the percentage of air determined by the calibration test of the calibrating vessel. Pump air into the air chamber until the pressure reaches the initial pressure line marked on the pressure gage, close both petcocks in the cover assembly, and then open the valve between the air chamber and the measuring bowl. The indicated air content on the pressure gage dial should correspond to the percentage of air determined to be in the measuring bowl. If two or more determinations show the same variation from the correct air content, the dial hand shall be reset to the correct air content and the test repeated until the gage reading corresponds to the calibrated air content within 0.1 percent. If the dial hand was reset to obtain the correct air content, recheck the initial pressure mark as in A1.5.2. If a new initial pressure reading is required, repeat the calibration to check the accuracy of the graduation on the pressure gage described earlier in this section. If difficulty is encountered in obtaining consistent readings, check for leaks, for the presence of water inside the air chamber (see Fig. 2), or the presence of air bubbles clinging to the inside surfaces of the meter from the use of cool aerated water. In this latter instance use deaerated water which can be obtained by cooling hot water to room temperature.

NOTE A8—If the calibrating vessel is an integral part of the cover assembly, the petcock used in filling the vessel should be closed immediately after filling the calibration vessel and not opened until the test is complete.

Designation: C 260 – 74

American National Standard A37 132
American National Standards Institute

Standard Specification for

AIR-ENTRAINING ADMIXTURES FOR CONCRETE[1]

This Standard is issued under the fixed designation C 260; the number immediately following the designation indicates the year of original adoption or, in the case of revision, the year of last revision. A number in parentheses indicates the year of last reapproval.

1. Scope

1.1 This specification covers materials proposed for use as air-entraining admixtures to be added to concrete mixtures in the field.

NOTE 1—The values stated in U.S. customary units are to be regarded as the standard.

2. Applicable Documents

2.1 The following documents of the issue in effect on date of material procurement form a part of this specification to the extent referenced herein:

2.1.1 *ASTM Standards:*
C 183 Sampling Hydraulic Cement[2]
C 233 Testing Air-Entraining Admixtures for Concrete[3]

3. Definition

3.1 For the purpose of this specification an air-entraining admixture is defined as a material that is used as an ingredient of concrete, added to the batch immediately before or during its mixing, for the purpose of entraining air.

4. General Requirements

4.1 At the request of the purchaser, the manufacturer shall state in writing that the air-entraining admixture supplied for use in the work is essentially identical in concentration, composition, and performance, to the air-entraining admixture tested under this specification.

NOTE 2—It is recommended that, whenever practicable, tests with the air-entraining admixture be made using all of the ingredients of the concrete proposed for the specific work, because the effect produced by the air-entraining admixture may vary with the properties of the other ingredients of the concrete.

4.2 Requirements for establishing compositional or chemical equivalence of a subsequent lot relative to a previous lot that was subjected to quality tests and found to comply with the requirements of 5.1 may be determined by agreement between the purchaser and the manufacturer.

NOTE 3—Ultraviolet light absorption of solutions and infrared spectroscopy of dried residues have been found to be valuable for these purposes. The specific procedures to be employed and the criteria to establish equivalence should be stipulated with due regard to the composition and properties of the sample.

4.3 At the request of the purchaser, the manufacturer shall state in writing the chloride content of the air-entraining admixture and whether or not chloride was added during its manufacture.

NOTE 4—Admixtures that contain chlorides may accelerate corrosion of embedded metals.

4.4 At the request of the purchaser, the manufacturer shall recommend appropriate test procedures, such as infrared spectrophotometry, pH value and solids content, for establishing the equivalence of materials from

[1] This specification is under the jurisdiction of ASTM Committee C-9 on Concrete and Concrete Aggregates and is the direct responsibility of Subcommittee C09.03.08 on Methods of Testing and Specifications for Admixtures.
Current edition approved July 29, 1974. Published October 1974. Originally published as C 260 – 50 T. Last previous edition C 260 – 73.
[2] *Annual Book of ASTM Standards*, Part 13.
[3] *Annual Book of ASTM Standards*, Part 14.

different lots or different portions of the same lot.

5. Optional Uniformity Requirements

5.1 A series of two or more samples from a manufacturing lot will be considered sufficiently uniform to be properly composited into a single sample for quality testing provided they do not differ more than the amounts indicated in 5.4.

5.2 A single sample from a subsequent lot or a composite sample prepared by combining two or more samples from a subsequent lot that do not differ by more than the amounts indicated in 5.4, may be considered sufficiently similar to a sample from a previous lot that was subjected to quality tests and found to comply with the requirements of 6.1, so that it may be regarded as also in compliance with these requirements, provided it does not differ from the sample so tested by more than the amounts indicated in 5.4.

5.3 Determinations of uniformity shall be made in accordance with the procedures given in 10.1 of C 233.

5.4 Allowable differences in results of uniformity determinations shall not exceed the following amounts:

5.4.1 The pH of samples tested shall not deviate from the pH of any previous sample by more than 1.0.

5.4.2 The specific gravity of the check test sample shall not differ from the specific gravity of the acceptance sample by more than 10 percent of the difference between the specific gravity of the acceptance sample and that of reagent water at the same temperature.

5.4.3 The air content in percent of C 185 mortars prepared from successive lots shall not differ by more than 2.0 from that for the acceptance sample.

6. Performance Requirements

6.1 The air-entraining admixture shall conform to the following requirements:

6.1.1 *Bleeding*—The bleeding of concrete made with the admixture under test shall not exceed that of concrete made with the reference admixture by more than 2 percentage points, the bleeding being computed as a percentage of the net amount of mixing water in each concrete. The net mixing water is the water in excess of that present as absorbed water in the aggregates.

6.1.2 *Time of Setting*—Both the initial and final times of setting of concrete containing the admixture under test shall not deviate from that of the concrete made with the reference admixture by more than ± 1 h and 15 min.

6.1.3 *Compressive Strength*—The compressive strength at any test age of concrete containing the admixture under test shall be not less than 90 percent of that of similar concrete containing the reference admixture at the same test age.

6.1.4 *Flexural Strength*—The flexural strength at any test age of concrete containing the admixture under test shall be not less than 90 percent of that of similar concrete containing the reference admixture at the same test age (Note 3).

6.1.5 *Resistance to Freezing and Thawing* —The relative durability factor of concrete containing the admixture under test shall be not less than 80. The relative durability factor shall be calculated as follows:

$$DF \text{ (or } DF_1) = PN/300$$
$$RDF = (DF/DF_1) \times 100$$

where:

DF = durability factor of the concrete containing the admixture under test,

DF_1 = durability factor of the concrete containing the reference admixture,

P = relative dynamic modulus of elasticity in percentage of the dynamic modulus of elasticity at zero cycles (values of P will be 60 or greater),

N = number of cycles at which P reaches 60 percent, or 300 if P does not reach 60 percent prior to the end of the test (300 cycles), and

RDF = relative durability factor.

6.1.6 *Length Change*—The length change on drying of concrete containing the admixture under test shall not be greater than 120 percent of that of similar concrete containing the reference admixture when compared after 14 days of drying. If the length change of the reference concrete at the end of 14 days of drying is less than 0.030 percent, the increase in length change on drying of the concrete containing the admixture under test shall be not more than 0.006, expressed as a percentage change in length, greater than that of the reference concrete.

NOTE 4—Applicable only when specifically required by the purchaser for use in structures where flexural strength or volume change may be of critical importance.

7. Sampling

7.1 Opportunity shall be provided the purchaser for careful sampling and inspection, either at the point of manufacture or at the site of the work, as may be specified by the purchaser.

7.2 Samples shall be either 'grab' or 'composite' samples, as specified or required by this specification. A grab sample is one obtained in a single operation. A composite sample is one obtained by combining three or more grab samples.

7.3 For the purpose of this specification, it is recognized that samples will be taken for the two following reasons:

7.3.1 *Quality Tests*—A sample taken for the purpose of evaluating the quality of a source or lot of admixture will be required to meet all the applicable requirements of this specification. Samples used to determine conformance with the requirements of this specification shall be composites of grab samples taken from sufficient locations to ensure that the composite sample will be representative of the lot.

7.3.2 *Uniformity Tests*—A sample taken for the purpose of evaluating the uniformity of a single lot or of different lots from the same source will generally be subjected to a limited number of tests as the result of agreement between the purchaser and manufacturer (see Section 4). Such samples shall be composite samples from individual lots when different lots from the same source are being compared. When the uniformity of a single lot is being determined, grab samples shall be used.

7.4 *Liquid Air-Entraining Admixtures*—Liquid admixtures shall be agitated thoroughly immediately prior to sampling. Grab samples taken for quality or uniformity tests shall represent not more than 2500 gal (9500 liters) of admixture and shall have a volume of at least 1 qt (0.9 liter). A minimum of three grab samples shall be taken. Composite

samples shall be prepared by thoroughly mixing the grab samples selected and the resultant mixture sampled to provide at least 1 gal (4 liters) for quality tests. Grab samples shall be taken from different locations well distributed throughout the quantity to be represented.

7.4.1 Admixtures in bulk storage tanks shall be sampled equally from the upper, intermediate, and lower levels by means of drain cocks in the sides of the tanks or a weighted sampling bottle fitted with a stopper that can be removed after the bottle is lowered to the desired depth.

7.4.2 Samples shall be packaged in impermeable, airtight containers that are resistant to attack by the admixture.

7.5 *Nonliquid Air-Entraining Admixtures* —Grab samples taken for quality or uniformity tests shall represent not more than 2 tons (2 metric tons) of admixture and shall weigh at least 2 lb (1 kg). A minimum of four grab samples shall be taken. Composite samples shall be prepared by thoroughly mixing the grab samples selected and the resultant mixture sampled to provide at least 5 lb (2.3 kg) for the composite sample. Grab samples shall be taken from different locations well distributed throughout the quantity to be represented.

7.5.1 Samples of packaged admixtures shall be obtained by means of a tube sampler as described in Method C 183.

7.5.2 Samples shall be packaged in moisture-proof, airtight containers.

7.6 Samples shall be thoroughly mixed before testing to assure uniformity. When recommended by the manufacturer, the entire sample of a nonliquid admixture shall be dissolved in water prior to testing.

8. Methods of Test

8.1 Determine the properties enumerated in Section 5 in accordance with Method C 233. It is recommended that, whenever practicable, tests be made in accordance with Section 2.4 of Methods C 233, using the cement proposed for the specific work.

9. Rejection

9.1 The air-entraining admixture may be rejected if it fails to meet any of the applicable requirements of this specification.

9.2 After completion of tests, an admixture stored at the point of manufacture for more than 6 months prior to shipment, or an admixture in local storage in the hands of a seller for more than 6 months, may be retested before use and may be rejected if it fails to conform to any of the applicable requirements of this specification.

9.3 Packages or containers varying more than 5 percent from the specified weight or volume may be rejected. If the average weight or volume of 50 packages or containers taken at random is less than that specified, the entire shipment may be rejected.

10. Packaging and Marking

10.1 The proprietary name of the air-entraining admixture and the net quantity in pounds or gallons (kilograms or liters) shall be plainly indicated on the packages or containers in which the admixture is delivered. Similar information shall be provided in the shipping advices accompanying packaged or bulk shipments of admixtures.

Standard Specification for
CHEMICAL ADMIXTURES FOR CONCRETE[1]

This Standard is issued under the fixed designation C 494; the number immediately following the designation indicates the year of original adoption or, in the case of revision, the year of last revision. A number in parentheses indicates the year of last reapproval.

ᵉ NOTE—Editorial correction was made in Section 16.1.3 in January 1972.

1. Scope

1.1 This specification covers materials for use as chemical admixtures to be added to portland cement concrete mixtures in the field for the purpose or purposes indicated for the five types as follows:

1.1.1 *Type A*—Water-reducing admixutres,

1.1.2 *Type B*—Retarding admixtures,

1.1.3 *Type C*—Accelerating admixtures,

1.1.4 *Type D*—Water-reducing and retarding admixtures, and

1.1.5 *Type E*—Water-reducing and accelerating admixtures.

NOTE 1—The purchaser should ensure that the admixture supplied for use in the work is equivalent in composition to the admixture subjected to test under this specification. It is recommended that, whenever practicable, tests be made using the cement, aggregates, and air-entraining admixture proposed for the specific work (see 10.4) because the specific effects produced by chemical admixtures may vary with the properties of the other ingredients of the concrete.

NOTE 2—Admixtures that contain relatively large amounts of chloride may accelerate corrosion of prestressing steel. Where corrosion of such steel is of major concern, compliance with the requirements of this specification does not constitute assurance of acceptability of the admixture for use in prestressed concrete.

NOTE 3—The values stated in U.S. customary units are to be regarded as the standard. The metric equivalents of U.S. customary units may be approximate.

2. Definitions

2.1 *water-reducing admixture*—an admixture that reduces the quantity of mixing water required to produce concrete of a given consistency.

2.2 *retarding admixture*—an admixture that retards the setting of concrete.

2.3 *accelerating admixture*—an admixture that accelerates the setting and early strength development of concrete.

2.4 *water-reducing and retarding admixture*—an admixture that reduces the quantity of mixing water required to produce concrete of a given consistency and retards the setting of concrete.

2.5 *water-reducing and accelerating admixture*—an admixture that reduces the quantity of mixing water required to produce concrete of a given consistency and accelerates the setting and early strength development of concrete.

3. Basis of Purchase

3.1 The purchaser shall specify the type of chemical admixture desired.

4. General Requirements

4.1 Concrete in which each of the five types of admixtures shown in 1.1.1 through 1.1.5 are used shall conform to the respective requirements prescribed in Table 1.

4.2 At the request of the purchaser, the manufacturer shall state in writing that the admixture supplied for use in the work is identical in all essential respects, including concentration, to the admixture tested under this specification.

4.3 At the request of the purchaser, when the admixture is to be used in prestressed concrete, the manufacturer shall state in writing the chloride content of the admixture and whether or not chloride has been added during its manufacture.

---

[1] This specification is under the jurisdiction of ASTM Committee C-9 on Concrete and Concrete Aggregates and is the direct responsibility of Subcommittee C09.03.08 on Methods of Testing and Specifications for Admixtures.
Current edition effective Jan. 8, 1971. Originally issued 1962. Replaces C 494 – 68.

4.4 At the request of the purchaser, the manufacturer shall recommend appropriate test procedures, such as infrared spectrophotometry, pH value and solids content, for establishing the equivalence of materials from different lots or different portions of the same lot.

5. Optional Uniformity Requirements

5.1 Requirements for uniformity of a lot, or of different lots from the same source, may be established by agreement between the purchaser and the manufacturer. It is expected that such requirements will in most cases be based on test procedures recommended by the manufacturer as being appropriate for a specific admixture.

6. Packaging and Marking

6.1 When the admixture is delivered in packages or containers, the proprietary name of the admixture, the type under this specification, and the net weight or volume shall be plainly marked thereon. Similar information shall be provided in the shipping advices accompanying packaged or bulk shipments of admixtures.

7. Storage

7.1 The admixture shall be stored in such a manner as to permit easy access for proper inspection and identification of each shipment, and in a suitable weathertight building that will protect the admixture from dampness and freezing.

8. Sampling and Inspection

8.1 Every facility shall be provided the purchaser for careful sampling and inspection, either at the point of manufacture or at the site of the work, as may be specified by the purchaser.

8.2 Samples shall be either 'grab' or 'composite' samples, as specified or required by this specification. A grab sample is one obtained in a single operation. A composite sample is one obtained by combining three or more grab samples.

8.3 For the purposes of this specification, it is recognized that samples will be taken for two reasons:

8.3.1 *Quality Tests*—A sample taken for the purpose of evaluating the quality of a

source or lot of admixture will be required to meet all the applicable requirements of this specification. Samples used to determine conformance with the requirements of this specification shall be composites of grab samples taken from sufficient locations to ensure that the composite sample will be representative of the lot.

8.3.2 *Uniformity Tests*—A sample taken for the purpose of evaluating the uniformity of a single lot, or of different lots from the same source, will generally be subjected to a limited number of tests as the result of agreement between the purchaser and manufacturer (see 5.1). Such samples shall be composite samples from individual lots when different lots from the same source are being compared. When the uniformity of a single lot is being determined, grab samples shall be used.

8.4 *Liquid Admixtures*—Liquid admixtures shall be agitated thoroughly immediately prior to sampling. Grab samples taken for quality or uniformity tests shall represent not more than 2500 gal (9500 liters) of admixture and shall have a volume of at least 1 qt (1 liter). A minimum of three grab samples shall be taken. Composite samples shall be prepared by thoroughly mixing the grab samples selected and the resultant mixture sampled to provide at least 1 gal (4 liters) for quality tests. Grab samples shall be taken from different locations well distributed throughout the quantity to be represented.

8.4.1 Admixtures in bulk storage tanks shall be sampled equally from the upper, intermediate, and lower levels by means of drain cocks in the sides of the tanks or a weighted sampling bottle fitted with a stopper that can be removed after the bottle is lowered to the desired depth.

8.4.2 Samples shall be packaged in impermeable, airtight containers which are resistant to attack by the admixture.

8.5 *Nonliquid Admixtures*—Grab samples taken for quality or uniformity tests shall represent not more than 2 tons (2 metric tons) of admixture and shall weigh at least 2 lb (1 kg). A minimum of four grab samples shall be taken. Composite samples shall be prepared by thoroughly mixing the grab samples selected and the resultant mixture sampled to provide at least 5 lb (2.3 kg) for the composite sample. Grab samples shall be taken from different locations well distributed throughout the quantity to be represented.

8.5.1 Samples of packaged admixtures shall be obtained by means of a tube sampler as described in ASTM Method C 183, Sampling Hydraulic Cement.[2]

8.5.2 Samples shall be packaged in moisture-proof, airtight containers.

8.6 Samples shall be throughly mixed before testing to assure uniformity. When recommended by the manufacturer, the entire sample of a nonliquid admixture shall be dissolved in water prior to testing.

9. Rejection

9.1 The admixture may be rejected if it fails to meet any of the applicable requirements of this specification.

9.2 An admixture stored at the point of manufacture, for more than 6 months prior to shipment, or an admixture in local storage in the hands of a vendor for more than 6 months, after completion of tests, may be retested before use and may be rejected if it fails to conform to any of the applicable requirements of this specification.

9.3 Packages or containers varying more than 5 percent from the specified weight or volume may be rejected. If the average weight or volume of 50 packages taken at random is less than that specified, the entire shipment may be rejected.

9.4 When the admixture is to be used in non-air-entrained concrete, it may be rejected if the test concrete containing it has an air content greater than 3.0 percent; when the admixture is to be used in air-entrained concrete, it may be rejected if the test concrete containing it has an air content greater than 7.0 percent.

METHODS OF TEST

NOTE 4—These tests are based on arbitrary stipulations which make possible highly standardized testing in the laboratory and are not intended to simulate actual job conditions.

10. Materials

10.1 *Cement*—The cement used in any series of tests shall be either the cement proposed for specific work in accordance with 10.4 or a thorough blend of equal parts of three cements from three mills (Note 5). Each cement of the blend shall be either Type I or Type II portland cement conforming to ASTM Specification C 150, for Portland Cement.[3] If, when tested as prescribed in 13.3, the air content of the concrete made without admixture is more than 2.0 percent, prepare a different blend of equal parts of three cements so that the air content of the concrete will be 2.0 percent or less.

NOTE 5—It is recommended that equal quantities of each of the cements be weighed out in the amount required for each batch of concrete.

10.2 *Aggregates*—Except when tests are made in accordance with 10.4 using the aggregates proposed for specific work, the fine and coarse aggregates used in any series of tests shall come from single lots of well-graded, sound materials that conform to the requirements of ASTM Specification C 33, for Concrete Aggregates,[3] except that the grading of the aggregates shall conform to the following requirements:

10.2.1 *Fine Aggregate Grading:*

Sieve	Weight Percent Passing
No. 4 (4.75-mm)	100
No. 16 (1.18-mm)	65 to 75
No. 50 (300 μm)	12 to 20
No. 100 (150 μm)	2 to 5

10.2.2 *Coarse Aggregate Grading*—Separate the coarse aggregate on the 1 in. (25.0 mm), $^3/_4$ in. (19.0 mm), $^1/_2$ in. (12.5 mm), and $^3/_8$ in. (9.5 mm) and No. 4 (4.75 mm) sieves and recombine for use by taking equal portions by weight of the four sizes of material produced by the separation, discarding the oversize and under size.

10.3 *Air-Entraining Admixture*—Except when tests are made in accordance with 10.4 using the air-entraining admixture proposed for specific work, the air-entraining admixture used in the concrete mixtures specified in Section 11 shall be a material such that when used to entrain the specified amount of air in the concrete mixture will give concrete of satisfactory resistance to freezing and thawing. The material to be so used will be designated by the person or agency for whom the testing is to be performed. If no material is designated, "neutralized Vinsol resin"[4] shall be used.

---

[2] *1974 Annual Book of ASTM Standards*, Part 13.
[3] *1974 Annual Book of ASTM Standards*, Part 14.
[4] Vinsol resin is manufactured by Hercules Inc., Wilmington, Del.

NOTE 6—Neutralization may be accomplished by treating 100 parts of the Vinsol resin with 9 to 15 parts of NaOH by weight. In an aqueous solution, the ratio of water to the resinate shall not exceed 12 plus 1 by weight.

10.4 *Materials for Tests for Specific Uses* —To test a chemical admixture for use in specific work, the cement, aggregates, and air-entraining admixture used shall be representative of those proposed for use in the work. Add the chemical admixture in the same manner and at the same time during the batching and mixing sequence as it will be added on the job. Proportion the concrete mixtures to have the cement content specified for use in the work. If the maximum size of coarse aggregate is greater than 1 in. (25.4 mm), screen the concrete over a 1-in. (25.0-mm) sieve prior to fabricating the test specimens.

10.5 *Preparation and Weighing*—Prepare all material and make all weighings as prescribed in ASTM Method C 192, Making and Curing Concrete Test Specimens in the Laboratory.[3]

11. Proportioning of Concrete Mixtures

11.1 *Proportions*—Except when tests are being made for specific uses (see 10.4), all concrete shall be proportioned using the ACI Recommended Practice for Selecting Proportions for Concrete (ACI 613-54)[5] to conform to the requirements described in 11.1.1 through 11.1.4. Unless otherwise specified, the admixture shall be added with the first increment of mixing water that is added to the mixer.

NOTE 7—The effects of a chemical admixture on the time of setting and water requirement of concrete may vary with the time of its addition during the batching and mixing sequence. Consequently, specifications for particular work should require that the admixture be added in the same manner and at the same time during the batching and mixing sequence as it will be added on the job.

11.1.1 The cement content shall be 5.5 ± 0.05 bags/yd³ (307 ± 3 kg/m³).

11.1.2 The first trial mixture shall contain the amount of coarse aggregate shown in Table 6 of ACI 613-54 for the maximum size of aggregate and for the fineness modulus of the sand being used.

NOTE 8—Values in Table 6 of ACI 613-54 are intended to assure workable mixtures with the least favorable combinations of aggregate likely to be used. It is suggested, therefore, that for a closer approximation of the proportions required for this test, the values selected from Table 6 be increased by about 7 percent for the first trial mixture.

11.1.3 For the non-air-entrained mixtures, the air content used in calculating the proportions shall be 1.5 percent, as shown in Table 3 of ACI 613-54. For the air-entrained mixtures, the air content used for this purpose shall be 5.5 percent.

11.1.4 Adjust the water content to obtain a slump of $2\frac{1}{2} \pm \frac{1}{2}$ in. (63 ± 12 mm). The workability of the concrete mixture shall be suitable for consolidation by hand rodding and the concrete mixture shall have the minimum water content possible. Achieve these conditions by final adjustments in the proportion of fine aggregate to total aggregate or in the amount of total aggregate, or both, while maintaining the yield and slump in the required ranges.

11.2 *Conditions*—Prepare concrete mixtures both with and without the admixture under test. Refer herein to the concrete mixture without the chemical admixture as the reference or control concrete mixture. Add the admixture in the manner recommended by the manufacturer and in the amount necessary to comply with the applicable requirements of the specifications for water reduction or time of setting, or both. When desired by the person or agency for whom the tests are being performed, the admixture may be added in an amount such as to produce a specific time of setting of the concrete mixture within the limits of the applicable provisions of this specification.

11.2.1 *Non-Air-Entrained Concrete*—When the admixture is to be tested for use only in non-air-entrained concrete, the air content of both the mixture containing the admixture under test and the reference concrete mixture shall be 3.0 percent or less, and the difference between the air contents of the two mixtures shall not exceed 0.5. If necessary, the air-entraining admixture specified in 10.3 shall be added to the reference concrete mixture. Tests for resistance to freezing and thawing shall not be made.

11.2.2 *Air-Entrained Concrete*—When the

---

[5] Available from the American Concrete Institute, P.O. Box 4754, Redford Station, Detroit, Mich. 48219.

admixture is to be tested for use only in air-entrained concrete, the air-entraining admixture specified in 10.3 shall be added to the reference concrete mixture and, if necessary, to the concrete mixture containing the admixture under test in sufficient amounts to produce air contents in the range 3.5 to 7.0 percent, except that for tests for resistance to freezing and thawing, the range shall be 5.0 to 7.0 percent. In both cases the difference between the air content of the reference concrete and that of the concrete containing the admixture under test shall not exceed 0.5.

12. Mixing

12.1 Machine mix the concrete as prescribed in Method C 192. The concrete shall be mixed for 2 min after all materials have been introduced into the mixer, allowed to rest in the mixer for 3 min, remixed for 1 min, and then discharged.

13. Tests and Properties of Freshly Mixed Concrete

13.1 Samples of freshly mixed concrete from at least three separate batches for each condition of concrete shall be tested in accordance with the methods described in 13.2 through 13.6, and the minimum number of tests shall be as prescribed in Table 2.

13.2 *Slump*—ASTM Method C 143, Test for Slump of Portland Cement Concrete.[3]

13.3 *Air Content*—ASTM Method C 231, Test for Air Content of Freshly Mixed Concrete by the Pressure Method.[3]

13.4 *Time of Setting*—ASTM Method C 403, Test for Time of Setting of Concrete Mixtures by Penetration Resistance,[3] except that the temperature of each of the ingredients of the concrete mixtures, just prior to mixing, and the temperature at which the time of setting specimens are stored during the test period shall be 73 ± 3 F $(23.0 \pm 1.7$ C).

13.5 *Water Content:*

13.5.1 Report the water-cement ratio of the concrete, computed to the nearest 0.001, as follows: Determine the net water content of the batch as the weight of water in the batch in excess of that present as absorbed water in the aggregates. Determine the weight per unit volume of concrete in the batch as prescribed in ASTM Method C 138, Test for Unit Weight, Yield, and Air Content (Gravimetric) of Concrete.[3] Determine the water-cement ratio by dividing the net weight of water by the weight of cement in the batch.

13.5.2 Calculate the relative water content of the concrete containing the admixture under test as a percentage of the water content of the reference concrete as follows: Divide the average water content of all batches of concrete containing the admixture under test by the average water content of all batches of the reference concrete and multiply the quotient by 100.

14. Preparation of Test Specimens

14.1 Make specimens for tests of hardened concrete, representing each test and age of test and each condition of concrete being compared, from at least three separate batches, and the minimum number of specimens shall be as prescribed in Table 2. On a given day make at least one specimen for each test and age of test from each condition of concrete except make at least two specimens for the freezing and thawing test from each condition of concrete. Complete the preparation of all specimens in three days of mixing.

14.2 *Manifestly Faulty Specimens*—Visually examine each group of specimens representing a given test or a given age of test, including test of freshly mixed concrete, before or during the test, or both, whichever is appropriate. Discard any specimen found to be manifestly faulty by such examination without testing. Visually examine all specimens representing a given test at a given age after testing, and should any specimen be found to be manifestly faulty the test results thereof shall be disregarded. Should more than one specimen representing a given test at a given age be found manifestly faulty either before or after testing, the entire test shall be disregarded and repeated. The test result reported shall be the average of the individual test results of the specimens tested or, in the event that one specimen or one result has been discarded, it shall be the average of the test results of the remaining specimens.

15. Test Specimens of Hardened Concrete

15.1 *Number of Specimens*—Six or more test specimens for the freezing and thawing test and three or more test specimens for each other type of test and age of test specified in Table 2 shall be made for each condition of concrete to be compared.

15.2 *Types of Specimens*—Specimens made from concrete with and without the chemical admixture under test shall be prepared in accordance with the following:

15.2.1 *Compressive Strength*—Make and cure test specimens in accordance with Method C 192.

15.2.2 *Flexural Strength*—Make and cure test specimens in accordance with Method C 192.

15.2.3 *Resistance to Freezing and Thawing* —Test specimens shall consist of prisms made and cured in accordance with the applicable requirements of Method C 192. The prisms shall be not less than 3 in. (76 mm) nor more than 5 in. (127 mm) in width and depth and not less than 16 in. (406 mm) in length. Make one set of specimens from the concrete mixture containing the chemical admixture under test and from the reference concrete mixture, the air content of each mixture being as specified in 11.2.2.

15.2.4 *Length Change*—Make and cure test specimens in accordance with ASTM Method C 157, Test for Length Change of Cement Mortar and Concrete.[3] The moist-curing period, including the period in the molds, shall be 14 days.

16. Tests on Hardened Concrete

16.1 Test specimens of hardened concrete in accordance with the following methods (see Table 1):

16.1.1 *Compressive Strength*—ASTM Method C 39, Test for Compressive Strength of Molded Concrete Cylinders.[3] Test specimens at ages of 3, 7, and 28 days, 6 months, and 1 year. Calculate the compressive strength of the concrete containing the admixture under test as a percentage of the compressive strength of the reference concrete as follows:

16.1.1.1 Divide the average compressive strength of the specimens made from the concrete containing the admixture under test at a given age of test by the average compressive strength of the specimens made from the reference concrete at the same age of test and multiply the quotient by 100.

NOTE 9—When tests are conducted with materials representative of those proposed for use in specific work in accordance with 10.4, and if the results of the tests are required in a period of time that will not permit curing of specimens to ages of 6 months and 1 year, the tests at those ages as required in accordance with 16.1.1 may be waived.

16.1.2 *Flexural Strength*—ASTM Method C 78, Test for Flexural Strength of Concrete (Using Simple Beam with Third-Point Loading).[3] Test specimens at ages 3, 7, and 28 days. Calculate the flexural strength of the concrete containing the admixture under test as a percentage of the flexural strength of the reference concrete as follows:

16.1.2.1 Divide the average flexural strength of the specimens made from the concrete containing the admixture under test at a given age of test by the average flexural strength of the specimens made from the reference concrete at the same age of test, and multiply the quotient by 100.

16.1.3 *Resistance to Freezing and Thawing* —Procedure A of ASTM Method C 666, Test for Resistance of Concrete to Rapid Freezing and Thawing.[3] Place specimens under test at the age of 14 days. Calculate the relative durability factors as shown in ASTM Specification C 260, for Air-Entraining Admixtures for Concrete.[3]

16.1.4 *Length Change*—Test specimens shall consist of molded prisms made and tested in accordance with Method C 157 except that moist curing period, including the period in the molds, shall be 14 days. Then store the specimens in air under conditions specified in Section 7.1.2 of Method C 157 for a period of 14 days, at which time determine the length change of the specimen. Consider the drying shrinkage to be the length change during the drying period, based on an initial measurement at the time of removal of the specimen from the mold, and express it as percent to the nearest 0.001 percent based on the specimen gage length. If the length change of the reference concrete after 14 days of drying is 0.030 percent or greater, the length change on drying of concrete containing the admixture under test, expressed as percent of the length change of the reference concrete, shall not exceed the maximum specified in Table 1. If the length change of the reference concrete after 14 days of drying is less than 0.030 percent, the length change on drying of concrete

C 494

containing the admixture under test shall be not more than 0.010, expressed as a percentage change in length, greater than that of the reference concrete.

NOTE 10—Since the specific effects produced by chemical admixtures may vary with the properties of the other ingredients of the concrete, results of length change tests using aggregates of such a nature that the length change on drying is low may not accurately indicate relative performance to be expected with other aggregates having properties such as to produce concrete of high length change on drying.

17. Report

17.1 The report shall include the following:

17.1.1 Results of the tests specified in Sections 13 and 16, and the relevant specification requirements with which they are compared,

17.1.2 Brand name, manufacturer's name, and lot number, character of the material, and quantity represented by the sample of the admixture under test,

17.1.3 Brand name, manufacturer's name, and other pertinent data on the material used as the air-entraining admixture,

17.1.4 Brand name, manufacturer's name, type, and test data on the portland cement or cements used,

17.1.5 Description of, and test data on the fine and coarse aggregates used,

17.1.6 Detailed data on the concrete mixtures used, including amounts and proportions of admixtures used, actual cement factors, water-cement ratios, unit water contents, ratios of fine to total aggregate, slump, and air content, and

17.1.7 In the event that, in accordance with the provisions of Note 9, some of the tests have been waived, the circumstances under which such action was taken shall be stated.

TABLE 1 Physical Requirements[a]

	Type A, Water-Reducing	Type B, Retarding	Type C, Accelerating	Type D, Water Reducing and Retarding	Type E, Water Reducing and Accelerating
Water content, max, percent of control	95	...	...	95	95
Time of setting, allowable deviation from control, h:min:					
Initial: at least	...	1:00 later	1:00 earlier	1:00 later	1:00 earlier
not more than	1:00 earlier nor 1:30 later	3:30 later	3:30 earlier	3:30 later	3:30 earlier
Final: at least	...	...	1:00 earlier	...	1:00 earlier
not more than	1:00 earlier nor 1:30 later	3:30 later	...	3:30 later	...
Compressive strength, min, percent of control[b]:					
3 days	110	90	125	110	125
7 days	110	90	100	110	110
28 days	110	90	100	110	110
6 months	100	90	90	100	100
1 year	100	90	90	100	100
Flexural strength, min, percent of control[b]:					
3 days	100	90	110	100	110
7 days	100	90	100	100	100
28 days	100	90	90	100	100
Length change, max. shrinkage (alternative requirements)[c]:					
Percent of control	135	135	135	135	135
Increase over control	0.010	0.010	0.010	0.010	0.010
Relative durability factor, min,[d]	80	80	80	80	80

[a] The values in the table include allowance for normal variation in test results. The object of the 90 percent compressive strength requirement for a Type-B admixture is to require a level of performance comparable to that of the reference concrete.

[b] The compressive and flexural strength of the concrete containing the admixture under test at any test age shall be not less than 90 percent of that attained at any previous test age. The objective of this limit is to require that the compressive or flexural strength of the concrete containing the admixture under test shall not decrease with age.

[c] Alternative requirements, see 16.1.5, percent of control limit applies when length change of control is 0.030 percent or greater; increase over control limit applies when length change of control is less than 0.030 percent.

[d] This requirement is applicable only when the admixture is to be used in air-entrained concrete which may be exposed to freezing and thawing while wet.

TABLE 2 Types and Minimum Number of Specimens and Tests

	Number of Types of Specimens[a]	Number of Test Ages	Number of Conditions of Concrete[b]	Number of Specimens, min
Water content	...	1	2	[c]
Slump	1	1	2	[c]
Air content	1	1	2	[c]
Time of setting	1	[d]	2	6
Compressive strength	1	5	2	30
Flexural strength	1	3	2	18
Freezing and thawing	1	1	2	12
Length change	1	1	2	6

[a] See Section 13 and 15.2.
[b] See 11.2.
[c] Determined on each batch of concrete mixed.
[d] See 13.4.

Standard Method of
CAPPING CYLINDRICAL CONCRETE SPECIMENS[1]

This Standard is issued under the fixed designation C 617; the number immediately following the designation indicates the year of original adoption or, in the case of revision, the year of last revision. A number in parentheses indicates the year of last reapproval.

1. Scope

1.1 This method covers apparatus, materials, and procedures for capping freshly molded concrete cylinders with neat cement and hardened cylinders and drilled concrete cores with high-strength gypsum plaster or sulfur mortar.

1.2 A cap shall be at least as strong as the concrete. The surfaces of capped compression specimens shall be plane within a tolerance of 0.002 in. (0.05 mm) across any diameter. During capping operations, the planeness of the caps of every tenth specimen should be checked by means of a straightedge and feeler gage, making a minimum of three measurements on different diameters, to ensure that the surfaces of the caps do not depart from a plane by more than 0.002 in.

NOTE 1—The values stated in U.S. customary units are to be regarded as the standard. The metric equivalents of U.S. customary units may be approximate.

2. Applicable Documents

2.1 *ASTM Standards:*
C 109 Test for Compressive Strength of Hydraulic Cement Mortars (Using 2-in. (50-mm) Cube Specimens)[2]
C 150 Specification for Portland Cement[3]
C 287 Specification for Chemical-Resistant Sulfur Mortar[4]
C 472 Physical Testing of Gypsum Plasters and Gypsum Concrete[2]
2.2 *ANSI Standards:*
B46.1 Standard for Surface Texture

3. Capping Equipment

3.1 *Capping Plates*—Neat cement caps and high-strength gypsum-plaster caps shall be formed against a glass plate at least ¼ in. (6 mm) thick, a machined metal plate at least ½

in. (13 mm) thick, or a polished plate of granite or diabase at least 3 in. (76 mm) thick. Sulfur mortar caps shall be formed against similar metal or stone plates. In all cases, plates shall be at least 1 in. (25 mm) greater in diameter than the test specimen and the working surfaces shall not depart from a plane by more than 0.002 in. (0.05 mm) in 6 in. (152 mm). The surface roughness of newly finished metal plates shall not exceed that set forth in Table 4 of American National Standard B46.1, of 125 µin. for any type of surface and direction of lay. The surface when new shall be free of gouges, grooves, or indentations beyond those caused by the finishing operation. Metal plates that have been in use shall be free of gouges, grooves, and indentations greater than 0.010 in. (0.25 mm) deep or greater than 0.05 in.[2] (32 mm[2]) in surface area. If a recess is machined into the metal plate, the thickness of the plate beneath the recessed area shall be at least ½ in. In no case shall the recess in the plate be deeper than ½ in.

NOTE 2—In vertical capping devices, use of two-piece metal capping plates is advantageous as this facilitates refinishing of the capping surface should it become necessary to do so. In such devices, the lower section is a solid plate and the upper section has a circular hole which forms the recess. The two sections are customarily fastened together with machine screws. It is advantageous to have the upper surface of the lower plate case hardened. A Rockwell hardness of HRC 48 is suggested.

---

[1] This method is under the jurisdiction of ASTM Committee C-9 on Concrete and Concrete Aggregates and is the direct responsibility of Subcommittee C09.03.01 on Methods of Testing Concrete for Strength.
Current edition approved March 29, 1973. Published May 1973. Originally published as C 617 - 68. Last previous edition C 617 - 71a.
[2] *1974 Annual Book of ASTM Standards*, Part 13.
[3] *1974 Annual Book of ASTM Standards*, Part 14.
[4] *1974 Annual Book of ASTM Standards*, Part 16.

3.2 *Alignment Devices*—Suitable alignment devices such as guide bars or bull's-eye levels shall be used in conjunction with capping plates to ensure that no single cap will depart from perpendicularity to the axis of a cylindrical specimen by more than 0.5 deg (approximately equivalent to ⅛ in. in 12 in. (3.2 mm in 305 mm)). The same requirement is applicable to the relationship between the axis of the alignment device and the surface of a capping plate when guide bars are used. In addition, the location of each bar with respect to its plate must be such that no cap will be off-centered on a test specimen by more than ¹⁄₁₆ in. (2 mm).

3.3 *Melting Pots for Sulfur Mortars*—Pots used for melting sulfur mortars shall be equipped with automatic temperature controls and shall be made of metal or lined with a material that is nonreactive with molten sulfur.

NOTE 3: **Caution**—Melting pots equipped with peripheral heating will ensure against accidents during reheating of cooled sulfur mixtures which have a crusted-over surface. When using melting pots not so equipped, a build-up of pressure under the hardened surface crust on subsequent reheating may be avoided by use of a metal rod which contacts the bottom of the pot and projects above the surface of the fluid sulfur mix as it cools. The rod should be of sufficient size to conduct enough heat to the top on reheating to melt a ring around the rod first and thus avoid the development of pressure. A large metal ladle can be substituted for the rod.

NOTE 4—Sulfur melting pots should be used under a hood to exhaust the fumes to outdoors. Heating over an open flame is dangerous because the flash point of sulfur is approximately 440 F (227 C) and the mixture can ignite due to overheating. Should the mixture start to burn, covering will snuff out the flame. The pot should be recharged with fresh material after the flame has been extinguished.

4. Capping Materials

4.1 *Fresh Specimens*—The top surface of freshly molded specimens may be capped with a thin layer of stiff portland cement paste. The portland cement shall conform to the requirements of Specification C 150.

4.2 *Hardened Specimens (Moist-Cured)*—Hardened specimens which have been moist cured may be capped with high-strength gypsum plaster or sulfur mortar meeting the requirements set forth below:

4.2.1 *High-Strength Gypsum Plaster*—Unadulterated neat high-strength gypsum

plaster may be used if 2-in. (50-mm) cubes are found to develop a strength of at least 5000 psi (34 MN/m²) when subjected to the same environment for the same length of time as capped specimens. The cubes shall be made in accordance with the procedure for molding specimens in Section 14.2 of Methods C 472 using the same percent of mixing water as will be used in preparing the capping material.

NOTE 5—Low-strength molding plasters, commonly called plaster of paris, or mixtures of plaster and portland cement, are unsuitable for capping specimens.

NOTE 6—The percent of mixing water based on the weight of the dry plaster should be between 26 and 30. Use of minimum percentages of mixing water and vigorous mixing will usually permit development of acceptable strength at ages of 1 or 2 h.

4.2.2 *Sulfur Mortar*—Proprietary or laboratory prepared sulfur mortars may be used if allowed 2 h in which to harden. When tested in accordance with 4.2.2.1 and 4.2.2.2, each sulfur mortar shall conform to the following requirements:

Compressive strength (aged 2 h): min, psi	5,000
MN/m²	34.5
Composition:	
Combustible materials, percent	55.0 to 70.0
Incombustible filler, percent	30.0 to 45.0

4.2.2.1 *Determination of Compressive Strength*—Prepare test specimens using a cube mold and base plate conforming to the requirements of Method C 109 and a metal cover plate conforming in principle to the design shown in Fig. 1 (Note 7). Bring the various parts of the apparatus to a temperature of 68 to 86 F (20 to 30 C), lightly coat the surfaces that will be in contact with the sulfur mortar with mineral oil, and assemble near the melting pot. Bring the temperature of the molten-sulfur mortar in the pot within a range of 265 to 290 F (129 to 143 C), stir thoroughly, and begin casting cubes. Using a ladle, or other suitable pouring device, quickly fill each of the three compartments until the molten material reaches the top of the filling hole. Allow sufficient time for maximum shrinkage, due to cooling, and solidification to occur (approximately 15 min) and refill each hole with molten material (Note 8). After solidification is complete, remove the cubes from the mold without breaking off the knob formed by the filling hole in the cover plate. Remove oil, sharp edges, and fins from the cubes and check the planeness of the bearing surfaces in the manner described in Note 7 of Method C 109. After storage at room temperature for 2 h, test cubes in compression following the procedure described in Section 7.6.3 of Method C 109 and calculate the compressive strength in pounds per square inch (meganewtons per square meter).

NOTE 7—If desired, a plane phenol formaldehyde (bakelite) plate of ⅛-in. (3-mm) thickness, provided with three appropriately spaced filling holes, may be inserted between the cover plate and the mold to slow the rate of cooling of test specimens.

NOTE 8—The second filling helps to prevent the formation of a large void or shrinkage pipe in the body of a cube. However, such defects may occur no matter how much care is exercised, and it therefore is advisable to inspect the interior of tested sulfur mortar cubes for homogeneity whenever the strength values obtained are significantly lower than anticipated.

4.2.2.2 *Determination of Composition*— Obtain samples from caps on concrete cylinders or from cast specimens similar to caps in size and thickness. Divide each cap-size specimen into eight approximately equal triangular sections, and secure test samples by breaking either two or four of the triangular sections into small pieces with the fingers. Weigh 20 to 25 g of fragmented material in a previously ignited, cooled, and tared Coors No. 3, high-form porcelain crucible. Place the crucible on a ring approximately 2 in. (50 mm) above a Terrel-type bunsen burner and adjust the flame so that the sulfur burns slowly without spattering (Note 9). When the sulfur has been completely consumed, adjust the burner for high heat and ignite the residue for 30 min. Cool the crucible and residue in a desiccator and weigh. Continue to ignite, cool, and weigh the crucible until a constant weight is obtained. Calculate the percentage of combustible materials, C, as follows:

$$C = \frac{A}{B} \times 100$$

where:
A = original weight of sample less weight of the residue after ignition, and
B = original weight of sample.

NOTE 9—Where the filler is known or found to be composed of carbonate minerals the ignition test shall be made at a carefully controlled temperature, in the range of 600 to 650 C, to prevent calcination of the mineral. Small amounts of plasticizer and carbon filler will be included in the reported value

for combustibles using the simple test herein described.

NOTE 10—A refereee procedure for the determination of the percent of sulfur contained in sulfur mortar may be found in Section 7.1.3 of Specification C 287.

4.3 *Hardened Specimens (Air-Dried)*— Hardened specimens which must be tested in an air-dry condition, or must be soaked for 20 to 28 h before testing may be capped with sulfur mortar conforming to the requirements of 4.2.2.

5. Capping Procedures

5.1 *Freshly Molded Cylinders*—Use only neat portland cement pastes (Note 11) to cap freshly molded cylinders. Make caps as thin as practicable. Do not apply the neat paste to the exposed end until the concrete has ceased settling in the molds, generally from 2 to 4 h after molding. During the molding of the cylinder, strike off the upper end even with or slightly below the plane of the rim of the mold. Mix the neat paste to a stiff consistency 2 or 4 h before it is to be used, in order to allow the paste to go through its period of initial shrinkage. The strength of the paste will depend on the consistency, water-cement ratio, curing, brand, and type of cement. For Type I and Type II cement pastes, the optimum consistency is generally produced at a water-cement ratio of 0.32 to 0.36 by weight. For Type III cement, the water ratio should generally be between 0.35 to 0.39 by weight. The paste will stiffen during the 2 to 4-h waiting period and the use of retempering water is not recommended. However, if retempering water is used, the amount should not increase the water-cement ratio by more than 0.05 by weight. Remove free water and laitance from the top of the specimen immediately before capping. Form the cap by placing a conical mound of paste on the specimen and then gently pressing a freshly oiled capping plate on the conical mound until the plate contacts the rim of the mold. A very slight twisting motion may be required to extrude excess paste and minimize air voids. in the paste. The capping plate must not rock during this operation. Carefully cover the capping plate and mold with a double layer of damp burlap and a polyethylene sheet to prevent drying. Removal of the capping plate after hardening may be accomplished by tapping the edge with a rawhide hammer in a direction parallel to the plane of the cap.

Note 11—Type I neat cement caps generally require at least 6 days to develop acceptable strength and Type III neat cement caps at least 2 days. Dry concrete specimens will absorb water from freshly mixed neat cement paste and produce unsatisfactory caps. Neat cement paste caps will shrink and crack on drying and, therefore, should be used only for specimens which are to be moist cured continuously until time of testing.

5.2 Hardened Concrete Specimens:

5.2.1 *General*—Cap, saw, or grind the ends of hardened cylinders that are not plane within 0.002 in. (0.05 mm) to meet that tolerance. Caps should be about ⅛ in. (3-mm) thick, and in no instance shall any part of a cap be more than ⁵⁄₁₆ in. (8 mm) thick. If either or both ends of a specimen have coatings or deposits of oily or waxy materials that would interfere with the bond of the cap, remove such coatings or deposits. If necessary, the ends of a specimen may be slightly roughened with a steel file or wire brush to produce proper adhesion of the cap. If desired, capping plates may be coated with a thin layer of mineral oil or grease to prevent the capping material from adhering to the surface of the plate.

5.2.2 *Capping with High-Strength Gypsum Plaster*—Mix high-strength plaster for capping, using the same percent of mixing water as was used in making the qualification test described in 3.2.1.

5.2.3 *Capping with Sulfur Mortar*—Prepare sulfur mortar for use by heating to about 265 F (130 C), as periodically determined by an all-metal thermometer inserted near the center of the mass. Empty the pot and recharge with fresh material at frequent enough intervals to ensure that the oldest material in the pot has not been used more than five times (Note 12). Fresh sulfur mortar must be dry at the time it is placed in the pot as dampness may cause foaming. Keep water away from molten sulfur mortar for the same reason. The capping plate or device should be warmed slightly before use to slow the rate of hardening and permit the production of thin caps. Oil the capping plate lightly and stir the molten sulfur mortar immediately prior to pouring each cap. The ends of moist cured specimens shall be dry enough at the time of capping to preclude the formation of steam or foam pockets under or in the cap larger than ¼ in. (6 mm) in diameter. To ensure that the cap shall be bonded to the surface of the specimen, the end of the specimen shall not be oiled prior to application of the cap.

Note 12—Reuse of material must be restricted in order to minimize loss of strength and pourability occasioned by contamination of the mortar with oil and miscellaneous debris, and loss of sulfur through volatilization.

6. Protection of Specimens After Capping

6.1 Moist cured specimens shall be maintained in a moist condition between the completion of capping and the time of testing by returning them to moist storage or wrapping them with a double layer of wet burlap. Specimens with gypsum plaster caps shall not be immersed in water and shall not be stored in a moist room for more than 4 h. If stored in a moist room, the plaster caps shall be protected against water dripping on their surfaces.

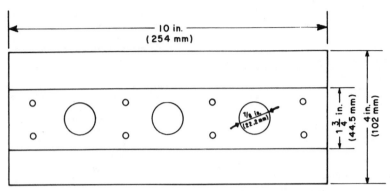

COVER PLATE – Plan View

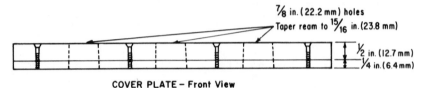

⁷⁄₈ in. (22.2 mm) holes
Taper ream to ¹⁵⁄₁₆ in. (23.8 mm)

½ in. (12.7 mm)
¼ in. (6.4 mm)

COVER PLATE – Front View

FIG. 1 Sketch of Cover Plate for 2-in. (50-mm) Cube Mold.

Standard Specification for
PORTLAND CEMENT[1]

This Standard is issued under the fixed designation C 150; the number immediately following the designation indicates the year of original adoption or, in the case of revision, the year of last revision. A number in parentheses indicates the year of last reapproval.

1. Scope

1.1 This specification[2] covers eight types of portland cement, as follows (see Note 1):

1.1.1 *Type I*—For use when the special properties specified for any other type are not required.

1.1.2 *Type IA*—Air-entraining cement for the same uses as Type I, where air-entrainment is desired.

1.1.3 *Type II*—For general use, more especially when moderate sulfate resistance or moderate heat of hydration is desired.

1.1.4 *Type IIA*—Air-entraining cement for the same uses as Type II, where air-entrainment is desired.

1.1.5 *Type III*—For use when high early strength is desired.

1.1.6 *Type IIIA*—Air-entraining cement for the same use as Type III, where air-entrainment is desired.

1.1.7 *Type IV*—For use when a low heat of hydration is desired.

1.1.8 *Type V*—For use when high sulfate resistance is desired.

NOTE 1—Attention is called to the fact that cements conforming to the requirements for all of these types may not be carried in stock in some areas. In advance of specifying the use of other than Type-I cement, it should be determined whether the proposed type of cement is or can be made available.

NOTE 2—The values stated in U.S. customary units are to be regarded as the standard. The metric equivalents of U.S. customary units may be approximate.

2. Definitions

2.1 *portland cement*—a hydraulic cement produced by pulverizing clinker consisting essentially of hydraulic calcium silicates, usually containing one or more of the forms of calcium sulfate as an interground addition.

2.2 *air-entraining portland cement*—a hydraulic cement produced by pulverizing clinker consisting essentially of hydraulic calcium silicates, usually containing one or more of the forms of calcium sulfate as an interground addition, and with which there has been interground an air-entraining addition.

3. Basis of Purchase

3.1 The purchaser should specify the type desired, and indicate which, if any, of the optimal requirements apply. When the type is not specified, the requirements of Type I shall apply.

4. Additions

4.1 The cement covered by this specification shall contain no addition except as provided for below.

4.1.1 Water or calcium sulfate, or both, may be added in amounts such that the limits shown in **Table 1** for sulfur trioxide and loss-on-ignition shall not be exceeded.

4.1.2 At the option of the manufacturer, processing additions may be used in the manufacture of the cement, provided such materials in the amounts used have been shown to meet the requirements of ASTM Specifications C 465, for Processing Additions for Use

[1] This specification is under the jurisdiction of ASTM Committee C-1 on Cement and is the direct responsibility of Subcommittee on Portland Cement.

Current edition approved June 27, 1974. Published August 1974. Originally published as C 150 – 40 T. Last previous edition C 150 – 73a.

[2] The 1973 and 1973a revisions of this specification change the strength requirements in Table 2, correct errors in the strength requirements in Table 2A, and eliminate the bag and barrel size from Section 12.1.

in the Manufacture of Portland Cement.[3]

4.1.3 Air-entraining portland cement shall contain an interground addition conforming to the requirements of ASTM Specification C 226, for Air-Entraining Additions for Use in the Manufacture of Air-Entraining Portland Cement.[3]

5. Chemical Requirements

5.1 Portland cement of each of the eight types shown in Section 1 shall conform to the respective standard chemical requirements prescribed in Table 1. Optional chemical requirements are shown in Table 1A.

6. Physical Requirements

6.1 Portland cement of each of the eight types shown in Section 1 shall conform to the respective standard physical requirements prescribed in Table 2. Optional physical requirements are shown in Table 2A.

7. Methods of Test

7.1 Sample the cement and determine the properties enumerated in this specification in accordance with the following ASTM methods:

7.1.1 *Sampling*—Methods C 183, Sampling Hydraulic Cement.[3]

7.1.2 *Air Content of Mortar*—Method C 185, Test for Air Content of Hydraulic Cement Mortar.[3]

7.1.3 *Chemical Analysis*—Methods C 114, for Chemical Analysis of Hydraulic Cement.[3]

7.1.4 *Strength*—Method C 109, Test for Compressive Strength of Hydraulic Cement Mortars (Using 2-In. Cube Specimens).[3]

7.1.5 *False Set*—Method C 451, Test for False Set of Portland Cement (Paste Method).[3]

7.1.6 *Fineness by Air Permeability*—Method C 204, Test for Fineness of Portland Cement by Air Permeability Apparatus.[3]

7.1.7 *Fineness by Turbidimeter*—Method C 115, Test for Fineness of Portland Cement by the Turbidimeter.[3]

7.1.8 *Heat of Hydration*—Method C 186, Test for Heat of Hydration of Portland Cement.[3]

7.1.9 *Autoclave Expansion*—Method C 151, Test for Autoclave Expansion of Portland Cement.[3]

7.1.10 *Time of Setting by Gillmore Needles*—Method C 266, Test for Time of Setting of Hydraulic Cement by Gillmore Needles.[3]

7.1.11 *Time of Setting by Vicat Needle*—Method C 191, Test for Time of Setting of Hydraulic Cement by Vicat Needle.[3]

7.1.12 *Sulfate Expansion*—Method C 452, Test for Potential Expansion of Portland Cement Mortars Exposed to Sulfate.[3]

8. Inspection

8.1 Inspection of the material shall be made as agreed upon by the purchaser and the seller as part of the purchase contract.

9. Testing Time Requirements

9.1 The following periods from time of sampling shall be allowed for completion of testing:

1-day test	6 days
3-day test	8 days
7-day test	12 days
28-day test	33 days

10. Rejection

10.1 The cement may be rejected if it fails to meet any of the requirements of this specification.

10.2 Cement remaining in bulk storage at the mill, prior to shipment, for more than 6 months, or cement in bags in local storage in the hands of a vendor for more than 3 months, after completion of tests, may be retested before use and may be rejected if it fails to conform to any of the requirements of this specification.

10.3 Packages varying more than 3 percent from the weight marked thereon may be rejected; and if the average weight of packages in any shipment, as shown by weighing 50 packages taken at random, is less than that marked on the packages, the entire shipment may be rejected.

11. Manufacturer's Statement

11.1 At the request of the purchaser, the manufacturer shall state in writing the nature, amount, and identity of the air-entraining agent used, and of any processing addition that may have been used, and also, if requested, shall supply test data showing com-

---

[3] *1974 Annual Book of ASTM Standards*, Part 13.

C 150

pliance of such air-entraining addition with the provisions of Specification C 226, and of any such processing addition with Specification C 465.

12. Packaging and Marking

12.1 When the cement is delivered in packages, the words "Portland Cement," the type of cement, the name and brand of the manufacturer, and the weight of the cement contained therein shall be plainly marked on each package. When the cement is an air-entraining type, the words "air-entraining" shall be plainly marked on each package. Similar information shall be provided in the shipping advices accompanying the shipment of packaged or bulk cement. All packages shall be in good condition at the time of inspection.

13. Storage

13.1 The cement shall be stored in such a manner as to permit easy accesss for proper inspection and identification of each shipment, and in a suitable weather-tight building that will protect the cement from dampness and minimize warehouse set.

14. Manufacturer's Certification

14.1 Upon request of the purchaser in the contract or order, a manufacturer's certification that the material was tested in accordance with this specification together with a report of the test results shall be furnished at the time of shipment.

TABLE 1 Standard Chemical Requirements

Cement Type[a]	I and IA	II and IIA	III and IIIA	IV	V
Silicon dioxide (SiO_2), min, percent	...	21.0	...	...	...
Aluminum oxide (Al_2O_3), max, percent	...	6.0	...	...	...
Ferric oxide (Fe_2O_3), max, percent	...	6.0	...	6.5	...
Magnesium oxide (MgO), max, percent	5.0	5.0	5.0	5.0	5.0
Sulfur trioxide (SO_3), max, percent					
When ($3 CaO \cdot Al_2O_3$)[b] is 8 percent or less	3.0	3.0	3.5	2.3	2.3
When ($3 CaO \cdot Al_2O_3$)[b] is more than 8 percent	3.5	[c]	4.5	[c]	[c]
Loss on ignition, max, percent	3.0	3.0	3.0	2.5	3.0
Insoluble residue, max, percent	0.75	0.75	0.75	0.75	0.75
Tricalcium silicate ($3CaO \cdot SiO_2$)[b] max, percent	...	...	...	35	...
Dicalcium silicate ($2CaO \cdot SiO_2$)[b] min, percent	...	...	...	40	...
Tricalcium aluminate ($3CaO \cdot Al_2O_3$)[b] max, percent	...	8	15	7	5
Tetracalcium aluminoferrite plus twice the tricalcium aluminate[b] ($4CaO \cdot Al_2O_3 \cdot Fe_2O_3 + 2(3CaO \cdot Al_2O_3)$), or solid solution ($4CaO \cdot Al_2O_3 \cdot Fe_2O_3 + 2CaO \cdot Fe_2O_3$), as applicable, max, percent	...	...	...	...	20.0

[a] See Note 1.

[b] The expressing of chemical limitations by means of calculated assumed compounds does not necessarily mean that the oxides are actually or entirely present as such compounds.

When the ratio of percentages of aluminum oxide to ferric oxide is 0.64 or more, the percentages of tricalcium silicate, dicalcium silicate, tricalcium aluminate, and tetracalcium aluminoferrite shall be calculated from the chemical analysis as follows:

Tricalcium silicate = (4.071 × percent CaO) − (7.600 × percent SiO_2) − (6.718 × percent Al_2O_3) − (1.430 × percent Fe_2O_3) − (2.852 × percent SO_3)

Dicalcium silicate = (2.867 × percent SiO_2) − (0.7544 × percent C_3S)

Tricalcium aluminate = (2.650 × percent Al_2O_3) − (1.692 × percent Fe_2O_3)

Tetracalcium aluminoferrite = 3.043 × percent Fe_2O_3

When the alumina-ferric oxide ratio is less than 0.64, a calcium aluminoferrite solid solution (expressed as ss($C_4AF + C_2F$)) is formed. Contents of this solid solution and of tricalcium silicate shall be calculated by the following formulas:

ss($C_4AF + C_2F$)) = (2.100 × percent Al_2O_3) + (1.702 × percent Fe_2O_3)

Tricalcium silicate = (4.071 × percent CaO) − (7.600 × percent SiO_2) − (4.479 × percent Al_2O_3) − (2.859 × percent Fe_2O_3) − (2.852 × percent SO_3).

No tricalcium aluminate will be present in cements of this composition. Dicalcium silicate shall be calculated as previously shown.

In the calculation of C_3A, the values of Al_2O_3 and Fe_2O_3 determined to the nearest 0.01 percent shall be used. In the calculation of other compounds the oxides determined to the nearest 0.1 percent shall be used.

Values for C_3A and for the sum of $C_4AF + 2C_3A$ shall be reported to the nearest 0.1 percent. Values for other compounds shall be reported to the nearest 1 percent.

[c] Not applicable.

TABLE 1A Optional Chemical Requirements

NOTE—These optional requirements apply only when specifically requested

Cement Type[a]	I and IA	II and IIA	III and IIIA	IV	V	Remarks
Tricalcium aluminate ($3CaO \cdot Al_2O_3$),[b] max, percent	...	...	8	...	...	for moderate sulfate resistance
Tricalcium aluminate ($3CaO \cdot Al_2O_3$),[b] max, percent	...	...	5	...	...	for high sulfate resistance
Sum of tricalcium silicate and tricalcium aluminate,[b] max, percent	...	58[c]	...	...	...	for moderate heat of hydration
Alkalies ($Na_2O + O \cdot 658K_2O$), max, percent	0.60[d]	0.60[d]	0.60[d]	0.60[d]	0.60[d]	low-alkali cement

[a] See Note 1.

[b] The expressing of chemical limitations by means of calculated assumed compounds does not necessarily mean that the oxides are actually or entirely present as such compounds.

When the ratio of percentages of aluminum oxide to ferric oxide is 0.64 or more, the percentages of tricalcium silicate, dicalcium silicate, tricalcium aluminate and tetracalcium aluminoferrite shall be calculated from the chemical analysis as follows:

Tricalcium silicate = (4.071 × percent CaO) − (7.600 × percent SiO_2) − (6.718 × percent Al_2O_3) − (1.430 × percent Fe_2O_3) − (2.852 × percent SO_3)

Dicalcium silicate = (2.867 × percent SiO_2) − (0.7544 × percent C_3S)

Tricalcium aluminate = (2.650 × percent Al_2O_3) − (1.692 × percent Fe_2O_3)

Tetracalcium aluminoferrite = 3.043 × percent Fe_2O_3

When the alumina-ferric oxide ratio is less than 0.64, a calcium aluminoferrite solid solution (expressed as ss ($C_4AF + C_2F$)) is formed. Contents of this solid solution and of tricalcium silicate shall be calculated by the following formulas:

ss($C_4AF + C_2F$)) = (2.100 × percent Al_2O_3) + (1.702 × percent Fe_2O_3)

Tricalcium silicate = (4.071 × percent CaO) − (7.600 × percent SiO_2) − (4.479 × percent Al_2O_3) − (2.859 × percent Fe_2O_3) − (2.852 × percent SO_3).

No tricalcium aluminate will be present in cements of this composition. Dicalcium silicate shall be calculated as previously shown.

In the calculation of C_3A, the values of Al_2O_3 and Fe_2O_3 determined to the nearest 0.01 percent shall be used. In the calculation of other compounds the oxides determined to the nearest 0.1 percent shall be used.

Values for C_3A and for the sum of $C_4AF + 2C_3A$ shall be reported to the nearest 0.1 percent. Values for other compounds shall be reported to the nearest 1 percent.

[c] This limit applies when moderate heat of hydration is required and tests for heat of hydration are not requested.

[d] This limit may be specified when the cement is to be used in concrete with aggregates that may be deleteriously reactive. Reference should be made to ASTM Specifications C 33, for Concrete Aggregates, *1974 Annual Book of ASTM Standards*, Part 14, for suitable criteria of deleterious reactivity.

TABLE 2 Standard Physical Requirements

Cement Type[a]	I	IA	II	IIA	III	IIIA	IV	V
Air content of mortar,[b] volume percent:								
max	12	22	12	22	12	22	12	12
min	...	16	...	16	...	16	...	...
Fineness, specific surface, cm²/g (alternative methods):								
Turbidimeter test, min	1600	1600	1600	1600	...	...	1600	1600
Air permeability test, min	2800	2800	2800	2800	...	...	2800	2800
Autoclave expansion, max, percent	0.80	0.80	0.80	0.80	0.80	0.80	0.80	0.80
Strength, not less than the values shown for the ages indicated below:[d]								
Compressive strength, psi (MPa)								
1 day	...	...	...	...	1800 (12.4)	1450 (10.0)	...	...
3 days	1800 (12.4)	1450 (10.0)	1500 (10.3) 1000[f] (6.9)[f]	1200 (8.3) 800[f] (5.5)[f]	3500 (24.1)	2800 (19.3)	...	1200 (8.3)
7 days	2800 (19.3)	2250 (15.5)	2500 (17.2) 1700 [f] (11.7)[f]	2000 (13.8) 1350[f] (9.3)[f]	...	...	1000 (6.9)	2200 (15.2)
28 days	...	...	...	...	...	...	2500 (17.2)	3000 (20.7)
Time of setting (alternative methods):[e]								
Gillmore test:								
Initial set, min, not less than	60	60	60	60	60	60	60	60
Final set, h, not more than	10	10	10	10	10	10	10	10
Vicat test:								
Initial set, min, not less than	45	45	45	45	45	45	45	45
Final set, h, not more than	8	8	8	8	8	8	8	8

[a] See Note 1.

[b] Compliance with the requirements of this specification does not necessarily ensure that the desired air content will be obtained in concrete.

[c] Either of the two alternative fineness methods may be used at the option of the testing laboratory. However, in case of dispute, or when the sample fails to meet the requirements of the air-permeability test, the turbidimeter test shall be used, and the requirements in this table for the turbidimetric method shall govern.

[d] The strength at any age shall be higher than the strength at any preceding age.

[e] The purchaser should specify the type of setting-time test required. In case he does not so specify, or in case of dispute, the requirements of the Vicat test only shall govern.

[f] When the optional heat of hydration or the chemical limit on the sum of the tricalcium silicate and tricalcium aluminate is specified.

TABLE 2a Optional Physical Requirements

NOTE—These optional requirements apply only when specifically requested.

Cement Type[a]	I	IA	II	IIA	III	IIIA	IV	V
False set, final penetration, min, percent	50	50	50	50	50	50	50	50
Heat of hydration:								
7 days, max, cal/g	...	...	70[b]	70[b]	...	...	60	...
28 days, max, cal/g	...	...	80[b]	80[b]	...	...	70	...
Strength, not less than the values shown:								
Comprehensive strength, psi (MPa)								
7 days	...	...	...	...	[c]	[c]	...	...
28 days	3500	2800	3500	2800	...	...	...	...
	(24.1)	(19.3)	(24.1)	(19.3)				
			2800[b]	2250[b]				
			(19.3)[b]	(15.5)[b]				
Sulfate expansion,[d] 14 days, max, percent	...	...	...	...	...	...	...	0.045

[a] See Note 1.

[b] When the heat of hydration requirements are specified, the sum of the tricalcium silicate and tricalcium aluminate shall not be specified. These strength requirements apply when either heat of hydration requirements or the sum of tricalcium silicate and tricalcium aluminate are specified.

[c] The strength at any age shall be higher than the strength at any preceding age.

[d] When the sulfate expansion is specified, it shall be instead of the limits of C_3A and $C_4AF + 2 C_3A$ listed in Table 1.

The American Society for Testing and Materials takes no position respecting the validity of any patent rights asserted in connection with any item mentioned in this standard. Users of this standard are expressly advised that determination of the validity of any such patent rights, and the risk of infringement of such rights, is entirely their own responsibility.

 Designation: C 618 – 73

American National Standard A37.122
American National Standards Institute

Standard Specification for

FLY ASH AND RAW OR CALCINED NATURAL POZZOLANS FOR USE IN PORTLAND CEMENT CONCRETE[1]

This Standard is issued under the fixed designation C 618; the number immediately following the designation indicates the year of original adoption or, in the case of revision, the year of last revision. A number in parentheses indicates the year of last reapproval.

1. Scope

1.1 This specification covers the use of pozzolan as an admixture in concrete where pozzolanic action is desired, where a suitable fine material may be desired to promote workability and plasticity, or where both effects are to be achieved.

NOTE 1—This specification covers the use of pozzolan as an ingredient of concrete to be added to the batch immediately before or during its mixing in combination with the following:
Portland Cement and Air-Entraining Portland Cement—ASTM Specification C 150, for Portland Cement.[2]
Portland Blast-Furnace Slag Cement and Portland-Pozzolan Cement—ASTM Specification C 595, for Blended Hydraulic Cements.[2]
The user should recognize that replacement of a portion of any of these cements by pozzolan may reduce early strength, and partial replacement of blended cements by these materials will in most cases reduce early strength and may reduce resistance of concrete to the effects of freezing and thawing. Care should be exercised to ensure strength and freezing and thawing resistance adequate for the contemplated use of the concrete.

NOTE 2—A pozzolan may tend to reduce the entrained air content of concrete. Hence, if pozzolan is added to any concrete for which entrainment of air is specified, provision should be made to assure that the specified air content is maintained, such as by use of additional air-entraining admixture or use of an air-entraining admixture in combination with air-entraining hydraulic cement.

NOTE 3—The values stated in U.S. customary units are to be regarded as the standard. The metric equivalents of U.S. customary units may be approximate.

2. Definitions

2.1 *pozzolan*—a siliceous or siliceous and aluminous material which in itself possesses little or no cementitious value but will, in finely divided form and in the presence of moisture, chemically react with calcium hydroxide at ordinary temperatures to form compounds possessing cementitious properties. For purposes of this specification pozzolans are segregated into three classes:

2.1.1 *pozzolan Class N*—raw or calcined natural pozzolans that comply with the applicable requirements for the class as given herein, such as some diatomaceous earths; opaline cherts and shales; tuffs and volcanic ashes or pumicites, any of which may or may not be processed by calcination; and various materials requiring calcination to induce satisfactory properties, such as some clays and shales.

2.1.2 *pozzolan Class F*—fly ashes that meet the applicable requirements for this class as given herein. Fly ash is the finely divided residue that results from the combustion of ground or powdered coal and is transported from the combustion chamber by exhaust gases.

2.1.3 *pozzolan Class S*—any material that meets the applicable requirements for this

[1] This specification is under the jurisdiction of ASTM Committee C-9 on Concrete and Concrete Aggregates. This tentative is the direct responsibility of Subcommittee C09.03.08 on Methods of Testing and Specifications for Admixtures.
Current edition approved Oct. 29, 1973. Published December 1973. Originally published as C 618 – 68 T to replace C 350 and C 402. Last previous edition C 618 – 72.
[2] *1974 Annual Book of ASTM Standards*, Part 14.

class as given herein. Examples of materials in this class include certain processed pumicites, and certain calcined and ground shales, clays, and diatomites.

3. Chemical Requirements

3.1 Pozzolan shall conform to the chemical requirements prescribed in Table 1.

4. Physical Requirements

4.1 Pozzolan shall conform to the physical requirements prescribed in Table 2.

4.2 Use of a pozzolan will in most instances increase the proportion of an air-entraining admixture that is required to produce a given air content in concrete. Some air-entraining agents contain substances that will accelerate or retard the setting of the cement and rate of hardening of the concrete. If use of the pozzolan substantially increases the proportion of air-entraining admixture that is required, any such effects should be evaluated and their significance established with respect to the requirements of the work.

5. Methods of Sampling and Testing

5.1 Sample the pozzolan in accordance with the requirements of ASTM Methods C 311, Sampling and Testing Fly Ash For Use as an Admixture in Portland Cement Concrete.[2] Determine the porperties enumerated in this specification in accordance with procedures stipulated below. Use pozzolans other than fly ash instead of fly ash in applicable tests under Methods C 311. Use cement of the type proposed for use in the work and, if available, from the mill proposed as the source of the cement, in all tests requiring the use of hydraulic cement.

5.1.1 *Chemical Analysis for Combined Amounts of Silicon Dioxide (SiO_2), Aluminum Oxide (Al_2O_3), and Iron Oxide (Fe_2O_3)* —Determine the silicon dioxide (SiO_2) in accordance with Section 12 of Methods C 311. Treat the filtrate reserved from the silicon dioxide determination in accordance with Section 13 of ASTM Methods C 114, Chemical Analysis of Hydraulic Cement.[3] Reserve the combined filtrate for the determination of magnesium oxide (MgO), if this determination is required. Calculate the combined per-

centage of silicon dioxide (SiO_2), aluminum oxide (Al_2O_3), and iron oxide (Fe_2O_3) by adding the percentage of SiO_2 determined in accordance with Section 12 of Methods C 311 to the percentage of ammonium hydroxide group calculated in accordance with Section 14 of Methods C 114. Report the result to the nearest 0.1.

5.1.1.1 Determine the combined percentage of SiO_2, Al_2O_3, and Fe_2O_3 on composite samples representing each 1000 tons (910 Mg) of pozzolan to be used in the work. When the total number of tons sampled is less than 1000, make the determination on the quantity sampled.

5.1.2 *Fineness, Surface Area*—Determine the specific surface of the pozzolan in accordance with ASTM Method C 204, Test for Fineness of Portland Cement by Air Permeability Apparatus,[3] using Eq 7 or 8 of Section 5 of Method C 204, except use the determined value for specific gravity in calculating the weight of the sample. Calculate the surface area of the pozzolan as follows:

$$Sv = \rho S$$

where:

Sv = surface area of test sample, cm^2/cm^3,
S = specific surface of test sample, cm^2/g, and
ρ = specific gravity of test sample.

5.1.3 *Fineness, Amount Retained When Wet-Sieved on No. 325 (45-μm) Sieve*—Determine the amount of the pozzolan retained when wet-sieved on No. 325 (45-μm) sieve in accordance with ASTM Method C 430, Test for Fineness of Hydraulic Cement by the No. 325 (45-μm) Sieve,[3] except use a representative sample of the pozzolan instead of hydraulic cement in the determination.

5.1.4 *Pozzolanic Activity Index with Portland Cement:*

5.1.4.1 *Specimens*—Mold the specimens from a control mix and from a test mix in accordance with ASTM Method C 109, Test for Compressive Strength of Hydraulic Cement Mortars (Using 2-in. (51-mm) Cube Specimens).[3] The portland cement used in the control mix shall meet the requirements of

---

[3] *1974 Annual Book of ASTM Standards*, Part 13.

Specification C 150, and shall be the type, and if available, the brand of cement to be used in the work. In the test mix replace 35 percent of the absolute volume of the amount of cement used in the control mix by an equal absolute volume of the test sample. Make three-cube batches as follows:

Control Mix:
250 g portland cement
687.5 g graded Ottawa sand
X ml water required for flow of 100 to 115.
Test Mix:
162.5 g, portland cement
87.5 × sp gr of the sample/sp gr of the portland cement g of sample
687.5 g, graded Ottawa sand
Y ml water required for flow of 100 to 115.

5.1.4.2 *Storage of Specimens*—After molding, keep all of the specimens in the molds on the base plates and place immediately in a moist closet or moist room at 73.4 ± 3 F (22.9 ± 1.7 C) for from 20 to 24 h with their upper surfaces exposed to moist air but protected from dripping water. Remove all specimens from the molds 20 to 24 h after molding and place in close-fitting metal or glass containers (Note 4), seal the containers airtight, and store at 100 ± 3 F (37.8 ± 1.7 C) for 27 days. Allow the specimens to cool to 73.4 ± 3 F before testing.

Note 4—Use any metal container having a capacity of three cubes if it can be sealed airtight by soldering. Containers of light-tinned sheet metal with inside dimensions 2½ by 2½ by 6¼ in. (51.6 by 51.6 by 209.6 mm) have been found to be satisfactory. Widemouth Mason jars of 1-qt (1-liter) capacity have been found to be satisfactory, provided care is taken to prevent breakage.

5.1.4.3 *Test Age*—Test the three specimens of the control mix and the three specimens of the test mix at an age of 28 days.

5.1.4.4 *Calculation*—Calculate the pozzolanic activity index with portland cement as follows:

Pozzolanic activity index with
portland cement = $(A/B) \times 100$

where:
A = average compressive strength of test mix cubes, psi (N/m²), and
B = average compressive strength of control mix cubes, psi (N/m²).

5.1.4.5 *Number of Tests*—Determine the pozzolanic activity index with portland cement on composite samples representing each 100 tons (91 Mg) of pozzolan to be used in the

work. When the total number of tons sampled is less than 100, make the determination on the quantity sampled.

5.1.5 *Pozzolanic Activity Index with Lime* —Determine the pozzolanic activity index with lime in accordance with Section 7.16.5 of ASTM Specification C 595. Designate the average compressive strength of the specimens calculated in accordance with Section 7.16.5 of Specification C 595, as the pozzolanic activity index with lime.

5.1.5.1 Determine the pozzolanic activity index with lime on composite samples representing each 1000 tons (910 Mg) of pozzolan to be used in the work. When the total number of tons sampled is less than 1000, make the determination on the quantity sampled.

5.1.6 *Water Requirement*—Calculate the water requirement for the values for *X* and *Y* determined in accordance with 5.1.4.1 as follows:

Water requirement, percentage of control
= $(Y/X) \times 100$

where:
Y = milliliters of water required for flow of 100 to 115 in the test mix, and
X = milliliters of water required for flow of 100 to 115 in the control mix.

5.1.7 *Increase of Drying Shrinkage of Mortar Bars*—Determine the drying shrinkage of mortar bars in accordance with Sections 23, 24, and 25 of Methods C 311, except mold three mortar bars from both the control mix and the test mix specified in Section 19 of Methods C 311.

5.1.7.1 For purposes of this specification, calculate the increase of drying shrinkage of mortar bars as follows:

Increase of drying shrinkage of mortar bars,
percent = $S_t - S_c$

where:
S_t = average drying shrinkage of the test specimens calculated, and
S_c = average drying shrinkage of the control specimens calculated in accordance with Section 25 of Methods C 311.

Report the result to the nearest 0.01. If the average drying shrinkage of the control specimens is larger than the average drying shrinkage of the test specimens, prefix a minus sign to the increase of drying shrinkage of mortar bars reported.

5.1.8 *Soundness*—Determine soundness in accordance with Section 26 of Methods C 311.

5.1.9 *Amount of Air-Entraining Admixture in Concrete*—Determine the amount of air-entraining admixture in concrete in accordance with Section 27 of Methods C 311 on composite samples representing each 1000 tons (910 Mg) of pozzolan to be used in the work. When the total number of tons sampled is less than 1000, make the determination on the quantity sampled.

5.1.10 *Uniformity of Specific Gravity*—Determine uniformity of specific gravity in accordance with Section 17 of Methods C 311.

5.1.11 *Uniformity Requirements (Quantity of Air-Entraining Admixture)*—To establish conformance with the uniformity requirements if air entrainment is specified, determine the quantity of air-entraining admixture required to produce an air content of 18.0 volume percent in mortar in accordance with the requirements of ASTM Method C 185, Test for Air Content of Hydraulic Cement Mortar,[3] except that the mortar shall contain a quantity of the pozzolan under test equivalent to 25 weight percent of the cement instead of an equal weight of the standard sand.

5.1.12 *Reactivity with Cement Alkalies (Reduction of Mortar Expansion)*—Determine the reduction of mortar expansion in accordance with ASTM Method C 441, Test for Effectiveness of Mineral Admixtures in Preventing Excessive Expansion of Concrete Due to the Alkali-Aggregate Reaction.[2]

5.1.13 *Reactivity with Cement Alkalies (Mortar Expansion)*—Determine the mortar expansion in accordance with the requirements of Method C 441 for the job mixture (see especially Sections 4.3, 9.1.1, 9.1.2, and 9.1.4 of Method C 441).

6. Storage and Inspection

6.1 The pozzolan shall be stored in such a manner as to permit easy access for proper inspection and identification of each shipment. Every facility shall be provided the purchaser for careful sampling and inspection, either at the source or at the site of the work as may be specified by the purchaser.

7. Rejection

7.1 The pozzolan may be rejected if it fails to meet any of the requirements of this specification.

7.2 Packages varying more than 5 percent from the stated weight may be rejected. If the average weight of the packages in any shipment, as shown by weighing 50 packages taken at random, is less than that specified, the entire shipment may be rejected.

8. Packaging and Marking

8.1 When the pozzolan is delivered in packages, the words "Pozzolan Class N (F or S, as appropriate) for Use in Portland Cement Concrete, ASTM Designation: C 618; Not to Be Used in Concrete Without Cement," the name and brand of the producer, and the weight of the material contained therein shall be plainly marked on each package. Similar information shall be provided in the shipping invoices accompanying the shipment of packaged or bulk pozzolan.

TABLE 1 Chemical Requirements

	Pozzolan Class		
	N	F	S
Silicon dioxide (SiO_2) plus aluminum oxide (Al_2O_3) plus iron oxide (Fe_2O_3), min, percent	70.0	70.0	70.0
Magnesium oxide (MgO), max, percent	5.0	...	5.0
Sulfur trioxide (SO_3), max, percent	4.0	5.0	4.0
Moisture content, max, percent	3.0	3.0	3.0
Loss on ignition, max, percent	10.0	12.0	10.0
Available alkalies as Na_2O, max, percent[a]	...	1.5[a]	1.5[a]

[a] Applicable only when specifically required by the purchaser for pozzolan to be used in concrete containing reactive aggregate and cement required to meet a limitation on content of alkalies.

TABLE 2 Physical Requirements

	Pozzolan Class		
	N	F	S
Fineness:			
Surface area, min, cm²/cm³	12 000	6 500	6 500
Amount retained when wet-sieved on No. 325 (45-μm) sieve, max, percent[a]	20	34	...
Multiple factor, calculated as the product of loss on ignition and fineness, amount retained when wet-sieved on No. 325 (425-μm) sieve, max, percent	...	255	...
Pozzolanic activity index:[b]			
With portland cement, at 28 days, min, percent of control	75	85	85
With lime, at 7 days, min, psi (kPa)	800 (5500)	800 (5500)	800 (5500)
Water requirement, max, percent of control	115	105	105
Increase of drying shrinkage of mortar bars at 28 days, max, percent	0.03	0.03	0.03
Soundness:[c]			
Autoclave expansion or contraction, max, percent	0.5	0.5	0.5
Amount of air-entraining admixture in concrete,[d] ratio to control, max	2.0[e]	...	...
Uniformity requirements:			
The specific surface and specific gravity of individual samples shall not vary from the average established by the ten preceding samples, or by all preceding samples if the number is less than ten, by more than:			
Specific surface, max variation from average, percent	15	15	15
Specific gravity, max variation from average, percent	5	5	5
In addition, when air-entraining concrete is specified, the quantity of air-entraining agent required to produce an air content of 18.0 volume percent of mortar shall not vary from the average established by the ten preceding tests, or by all preceding tests if less than ten, by more than, percent	20	20	20
Reactivity with cement alkalies:[f]			
Reduction of mortar expansion at 14 days, min, percent	75	...	...
Mortar expansion at 14 days, max, percent	0.020	0.020	0.020

[a] Care should be taken to avoid the retaining of agglomerations of extremely fine material.

[b] Neither the pozzolanic activity index with portland cement nor the pozzolanic activity index with lime is to be considered a measure of the compressive strength of concrete containing the pozzolan. The pozzolanic activity index with portland cement is determined by an accelerated test, and is intended to evaluate the contribution to be expected from the pozzolan to the longer strength development of concrete. The weight of pozzolan specified for the test to determine the pozzolanic activity index with portland cement is not considered to be the proportion recommended for the concrete to be used in the work. The optimum amount of pozzolan for any specific project is determined by the required properties of the concrete and other constituents of the concrete and should be established by testing.

[c] The specimen shall remain firm and hard and show no distortion, cracking, checking, pitting, or disintegration visible to the unaided eye when subjected to the autoclave-expansion test.

[d] Applicable only if air-entrained concrete is specified. Proper air entrainment is recommended for concrete that may be exposed to freezing and thawing.

[e] If the specified limit is exceeded, the test mixture shall meet the requirements of ASTM Specification C 260, for Air-Entraining Admixture for Concrete, which appears in the *1974 Annual Book of ASTM Standards*, Part 14.

[f] The indicated tests for reactivity with cement alkalies are optional and alternative requirements to be applied only at the purchaser's request. They need not be requested unless the pozzolan is to be used with aggregate that is regarded as deleteriously reactive with alkalies in cement. The test for reduction of mortar expansion may be made using any high-alkali cement in accordance with 5.1.12 if the portland cement to be used in the work is not known, or is not available at the time the pozzolan is tested. The test for mortar expansion is preferred over the test for reduction of mortar expansion if the portland cement to be used in the work is known and available. The test for mortar expansion should be performed with each of the cements to be used in the work.

Designation: D 143 – 52
(Reapproved 1972)

American National Standard 04.1-1973(R-1969)
Approved April 16, 1973
By American National Standards Institute

AMERICAN SOCIETY FOR TESTING AND MATERIALS
1916 Race St., Philadelphia, Pa. 19103
Reprinted from the Annual Book of ASTM Standards, Copyright ASTM
If not listed in the current combined index, will appear in the next edition.

Standard Methods of Testing
SMALL CLEAR SPECIMENS
OF TIMBER[1]

This Standard is issued under the fixed designation D 143; the number immediately following the designation indicates the year of original adoption or, in the case of revision, the year of last revision. A number in parentheses indicates the year of last reapproval.

PART I. PRIMARY METHODS

Part I, Primary Methods, is the basic procedure intended for the broadest possible use in evaluating the strength and related properties of wood in the form of small clear specimens. These methods afford satisfactory results, have been widely used, and extensive data based on their use have been obtained and published. Any departure in cross-section of specimens from the 2 by 2-in. (5 by 5-cm) size employed in the Primary Methods introduces a variable that appreciably affects the results for certain properties, and thereby limits the full comparability desired for obtaining uniform results among different species. Only when relatively small trees, generally less than 12 in. (30 cm) in diameter, are available to produce the test specimens, and only when such trees because of crook, cross grain, knots, or other defects are of such quality that the longer specimens required in Part I, Primary Methods, cannot be obtained, should Part II, Secondary Methods, be employed.

INTRODUCTION

The everyday use of timber for multitudinous purposes makes manifest a continual need for data on its mechanical properties. The great variety of species, the variability of the material, the continually changing conditions of supply, the many factors affecting test results, all combine to make the technique of testing wood unique in its complexity.

In the preparation of these methods for testing small clear specimens, consideration was given both to the desirability of adopting methods that would yield results comparable to those already available and to the possibility of embodying such improvements as experience has shown desirable. In view of the many thousands of tests made under a single comprehensive plan by the U.S. Forest Service, the Forest Products Laboratories of Canada, and other similar organizations, the methods naturally conform closely to the methods used by these institutions. These methods are the outgrowth of a study of both American and European experience and methods. Their general adoption will tend toward a world-wide unification of results, permitting an interchange and correlation of data, and will establish the basis for a cumulative body of fundamental information on the timber species of the world.

---

[1] These methods are under the jurisdiction of ASTM Committee D-7 on Wood.
Current edition effective Sept. 30, 1952. Originally issued 1922. Replaces D 143 – 50 T.

These methods represent the entire procedure from selection of the trees to the carrying out of the tests, thus controlling factors, such as the size and proportion of test specimens and rate of loading, that may influence results. No attempt has been made to cover methods of computation and analysis, as these questions may be considered independently at any time. Such sample data and computation sheets and cards have been incorporated, however, as were thought to be of assistance to the investigator in systematizing records.

1. Scope

1.1 These methods cover tests on small clear specimens of wood that are made to afford:

1.1.1 Data for comparing the mechanical properties of various species,

1.1.2 Data for the establishment of correct strength functions which, in conjunction with results of tests of timbers in structural sizes,[2] afford the basis for fixing allowable stresses, and

1.1.3 Data upon which to determine the influence on the mechanical properties of such factors as density, locality of growth, position in cross section, height of timber in the tree, change of properties with seasoning, and change from sapwood to heartwood.

NOTE 1—The values stated in U.S. customary units are to be regarded as the standard. The metric equivalents of U.S. customary units may be approximate.

2. Summary of Method

2.1 The principal mechanical tests are static bending, compression parallel to grain, impact bending, toughness, compression perpendicular to grain, hardness, shear parallel to grain,[3] cleavage, and tension parallel to grain. The tension-perpendicular-to-grain and nail-withdrawal tests also included are optional. These tests are made on both green and air-dry material as specified in these methods. In addition, methods for evaluating such physical properties as specific gravity, shrinkage in volume, radial shrinkage, and tangential shrinkage are presented.

2.2 The procedures for collection and preparation of the material for testing and for the various tests appear in the following order:

COLLECTION OF MATERIAL

Selection

3. Authentic Identification

3.1 The material shall be from trees selected in the forest by one qualified to identify the species and to select the trees. Whenever practicable this should be a member of the timber mechanics staff of the laboratory concerned, and where necessary, herbarium samples including leaves, fruit, twigs, and bark

---

[2] See ASTM Methods D 198, Static Tests of Timbers in Structural Sizes, *1974 Annual Book of ASTM Standards*, Part 22.

[3] The test for shearing strength perpendicular to the grain (sometimes termed "vertical shear") is not included as one of the principal mechanical tests since in such a test the strength is limited by the shearing resistance parallel to the grain.

shall be obtained to ensure positive identification.

4. Selection and Number of Trees

4.1 For each species to be tested, at least five trees representative of the species shall be selected.

5. Selection and Number of Bolts

5.1 The material of each species selected for test shall be representative of the merchantable bole of the tree. One method of selection that has been found satisfactory is as follows:

5.2 From one tree of each group of five, select 8-ft (2.4-m) sections (each section representing two 4-ft (1.2-m) bolts) from various heights to afford information on the variation of properties with height in tree, as indicated in Fig. 1 and as follows:

Length of Merchantable Bolt, ft (m)	Bolts to be Selected (for explanation of letter designation of bolts, see Section 9)
16 (4.9 m)	a, b; c, d
20 (6.0 m)	a, b; c, d
24 (7.2 m)	a, b; c, d; e
28 (8.4 m)	a, b; c, d; f, g
32 (9.6 m)	a, b; c, d; g, h
36 (10.8 m)	a, b; c, d; h, i
40 (12.0 m)	a, b; c, d; g, h; i, j
44 (13.2 m)	a, b; c, d; g, h; j, k
48 (14.4 m)	a, b; c, d; g, h; k, l
52 (15.6 m)	a, b; c, d; g, h; l, m
56 (16.8 m)	a, b; c, d; g, h; m, n
60 (18.0 m)	a, b; c, d; i, j; n, o
64 (19.2 m)	a, b; c, d; i, j; o, p
72 (21.6 m)	a, b; c, d; i, j; q, r
80 (24.0 m)	a, b; c, d; i, j; o, p; s, t
96 (28.8 m)	a, b; c, d; i, j; o, p; w, x
Over 96	a, b; c, d; k, l; s, t; and last two bolts (each 4 ft (1.2-m) in length) at top of merchantable length

5.3 From the other trees called for in Section 4, take the 8-ft section[4] (c-d bolts) next above the 8-ft butt log.

6. Substitution of Flitches for Bolts

6.1 In cases where the logs or bolts are over 60 in. (1.5 m) in diameter, a single flitch 6 in. (15 cm) in thickness, taken through the pith in a north and south direction and representing the full diameter of the log, may be substituted, in the same length, for the full log or bolt specified in Section 5.

7. Selection for Important Species

7.1 For important species of wide geographical distribution, test material shall be selected from two or more localities or sites. The number of trees of a species selected from each site or locality shall conform to the requirements of Sections 4 and 5.

Field Marking

8. Tree Designation

8.1 Each tree shall be given an arabic number, the numbering in any given shipment to be consecutive for trees of a given species.

9. Bolt Designation

9.1 Each 4 ft (1.2 m) of length of a tree or log shall be considered a "bolt." Bolts shall be designated by small letters, beginning with *a* for the 4-ft section next above the stump. Bolt letters, therefore, indicate position with respect to height in tree.

10. Marking

10.1 The tree number and bolt designation shall be plainly marked upon each log selected by the collector. Thus the 16-ft (4.8-m) butt log of Tree No. 2 would be designated 2*abcd*. Steel dies are recommended for marking the butt end of the logs.

11. Indication of Cardinal Point

11.1 The north side of each log shall be indicated in some convenient manner.

12. Shipment Number

12.1 All material collected from a given locality and shipped at one time shall be given a shipment number or other designation.

Field Descriptions

13. Field Descriptions

13.1 Complete field notes describing the material shall be fully and carefully made by the collector. These notes shall, in general, supply data as outlined in Table A1.

---

[4] The 8-ft lengths specified are intended to provide test material in sticks of this net length. It is recommended that the bolts or sections be cut in the woods to 9-ft lengths to allow for trimming, etc.

13.2 Photographs of the standing trees selected should be taken, when practicable.

Preparation for Shipment

14. Preparation for Shipment

14.1 The bark will be left on each log, and care shall be taken to keep the bark intact. The ends of the logs shall be carefully painted to retard or prevent end drying and end checking.

14.2 Record shall be made of the shipment routing, bill of lading, kind of shipment, date of shipment, and condition of material when shipped.

14.3 Record shall also be made of date of receipt of shipment at destination, its condition, and method of storage.

DISPOSITION AT DESTINATION

Storage of Logs at Destination

15. Storage of Logs

15.1 Material shall not be kept in the bolt or log form long enough to permit damage by checks, decay, stains, or insect attack. The logs shall be piled on skids, free from contact with the soil, and shall not be stored where subjected to artificial heat. In addition they should preferably be protected from the sun and, when necessary, sprinkled regularly with water to prevent drying. As an alternative to piling on skids, the logs may be stored in water prior to testing.

*Photographing, Sawing, and
Final Marking*

NOTE 2—In sawing, marking, and selecting test sticks, the aim should be to obtain specimens representative of the material collected. The procedure described herein is one that has been found satisfactory for most species.

16. Photographing Ends of Bolts

16.1 The top end of each *d* or *c-d* bolt shall be photographed. It is suggested that a rule be placed on the log so as to indicate the scale of the photograph and that the cardinal points be indicated on the cross-section. Figure 2 shows a photograph of this kind.

17. Sawing of Bolts

17.1 All bolts shall be marked on the top end into $2\frac{1}{2}$ by $2\frac{1}{2}$-in. (6 by 6-cm) squares as shown in Fig. 3, and sawed into nominal $2\frac{1}{2}$ by $2\frac{1}{2}$-in. sticks. The letters *N, E, S,* and *W* indicate the cardinal points.

17.2 When flitches are substituted for bolts (Section 6), the same general marking and numbering scheme of 17.1 shall be followed insofar as it is applicable.

18. Marking of Test Sticks

18.1 All test sticks shall bear the shipment number, the tree number, stick number, and bolt designation, to be known respectively as Shipment No., Piece No., Stick No., and mark. Thus, 400-1-*N4d* represents Stick *N4* of Bolt *d*, Tree 1, Shipment 400.

Matching for Tests of Air-Dry Material

19. Composite Bolts

19.1 The collection of the material (Section 5) has been arranged to provide for tests of both green and air-dry specimens that are closely matched by selection from adjacent parts of the same tree. The 8-ft (2.4-m) long bolts, after being marked in accordance with 17.1, shall be sawed into $2\frac{1}{2}$ by $2\frac{1}{2}$-in. (6 by 6-cm) by 8-ft sticks, and numbered and lettered in accordance with Section 18. Each $2\frac{1}{2}$ by $2\frac{1}{2}$-in. by 8-ft stick shall then be cut into two 4-ft (1.2-m) pieces, making sure that each part carries the proper designation and bolt letter.

19.2 Part of the $2\frac{1}{2}$ by $2\frac{1}{2}$-in. by 4-ft (1.2-m) sticks from each 8-ft bolt are to provide specimens to be tested green (unseasoned) and the other part are to provide specimens to be air-dried and tested. To afford matching, the 4-ft sticks of one bolt shall be interchanged with the 4-ft sticks of the next adjacent bolt from the same tree to form two composite bolts, each being complete and being made of equal portions of the adjacent 4-ft bolts. The sticks from one of these composite bolts shall be tested green and those from the other shall be tested after air-drying. Thus, the sticks of each composite bolt shall be regarded as if they were from the same bolt.

19.3 The above procedure provides for end-to-end matching (end matching) of sticks to be tested air-dry with those to be tested green, which is to be preferred when practicable. If, because of the nature of the material, end matching is not practicable, side matching may be used.

20. Schedule for Forming Composite Bolts

20.1 The division of sticks into composite bolts, part to be tested green and part to be air-dried and tested, shall be made according to the following schedule, in which the numbers refer to stick numbers:

Selection of Sticks from *a* and *b* Bolts

Composite Bolt to Be Tested Green:

| Bolt *a* | 1 | 4, 5 | 8, 9 | |
| Bolt *b* | 2, 3 | 6, 7 | 10, etc. | |

Composite Bolt to Be Air-Dried and Tested:

| Bolt *a* | 2, 3 | 6, 7 | 10, etc. | |
| Bolt *b* | 1 | 4, 5 | 8, 9 | |

Selection of Sticks from *c* and *d* Bolts

Composite Bolt to Be Tested Green:

| Bolt *c* | 1 | 4, 5 | 8, 9 | |
| Bolt *d* | 2, 3 | 6, 7 | 10, etc. | |

Composite Bolt to Be Air-Dried and Tested:

| Bolt *c* | 2, 3 | 6, 7 | 10, etc. | |
| Bolt *d* | 1 | 4, 5 | 8, 9 | |

Selection of Sticks from *e* and *f* Bolts

Composite Bolt to Be Tested Green:

| Bolt *e* | 1 | 4, 5 | 8, 9 | |
| Bolt *f* | 2, 3 | 6, 7 | 10, etc. | |

Composite Bolt to Be Air-Dried and Tested:

| Bolt *e* | 2, 3 | 6, 7 | 10, etc. | |
| Bolt *f* | 1 | 4, 5 | 8, 9 | |

20.2 The selection of sticks from other 8-ft (2.4-m) bolts of the tree to form the composite bolts to be tested green and to be air-dried and tested shall be made in accordance with the system as indicated in 20.1.

20.3 As an example of composite bolts, assume that the cross-section, Fig. 3, represents the end of an 8-ft (2.4-m) section comprising the *c* and *d* bolts.

20.3.1 The following sticks are selected for the composite bolt to be tested green: *N*1*c*, *N*2*d*, *N*3*d*, *N*4*c*, *N*5*c*, *N*6*d*, *N*7*d*, *N*8*c*, *N*9*c*, *N*10*d*, *N*11*d*, *N*12*c*; *E*3*d*, *E*4*c*, *E*5*c*, *E*6*d*, *E*7*d*, *E*8*c*, *E*9*c*, *E*10*d*, *E*11*d*, *E*12*c*; *S*1*c*, *S*2*d*, *S*3*d*, *S*4*c*, *S*5*c*, *S*6*d*, *S*7*d*, *S*8*c*, *S*9*c*, *S*10*d*, *S*11*d*, *S*12*c*; *W*3*d*, *W*4*c*, *W*5*c*, *W*6*d*, *W*7*d*, *W*8*c*, *W*9*c*, *W*10*d*, *W*11*d*, *W*12*c*.

20.3.2 The following sticks are selected for the composite bolt to be air-dried and tested: *N*1*d*, *N*2*c*, *N*3*c*, *N*4*d*, *N*5*d*, *N*6*c*, *N*7*c*, *N*8*d*, *N*9*d*, *N*10*c*, *N*11*c*, *N*12*d*; *E*3*c*, *E*4*d*, *E*5*d*, *E*6*c*, *E*7*c*, *E*8*d*, *E*9*d*, *E*10*c*, *E*11*c*, *E*12*d*; *S*1*d*, *S*2*c*, *S*3*c*, *S*4*d*, *S*5*d*, *S*6*c*, *S*7*c*, *S*8*d*, *S*9*d*, *S*10*c*, *S*11*c*, *S*12*d*; *W*3*c*, *W*4*d*, *W*5*d*, *W*6*c*, *W*7*c*, *W*8*d*, *W*9*d*, *W*10*c*, *W*11*c*, *W*12*d*.

Disposition of Sticks

21. Green Material

21.1 The sticks (2½ by 2½ in. by 4 ft) (6 by 6 cm by 1.2 m) to be tested green shall be kept in an unseasoned condition, while awaiting preparation for test, by being stored in a framed pit or other suitable container, where they shall be close piled and covered with damp sawdust, or in some other suitable manner. As material is required for test, it shall be removed from this pit or container, surfaced on all four sides to 2 by 2 in. (5 by 5 cm) in cross section, sawed to test size, and kept covered with a damp cloth in a tightly closed container at a temperature of 68 ± 6 F (20 ± 3 C) (see Note 3, 22.5) until the time of test. Care shall be taken to avoid as much as possible the storage of green material in any form. Sticks to be tested in a green condition usually should not be sawed from the log form in quantities greater than is required to meet the testing demands for from a few days to not more than 2 weeks, depending on the prevailing conditions.

22. Air-Dry Material

22.1 The ends of the sticks to be air-dried (2½ by 2½ in. by 4 ft) (6 by 6 cm by 1.2 m) shall be dipped in melted paraffin or other substance suitable to retard checking. The material shall be piled so as to have a space of at least ½ in. (1.3 cm) on each side of each stick to permit circulation of air. The material shall be stored in a place allowing free access of air, but protected from sunshine, rain, snow, and moisture from the ground. The sticks in drying shall not be subjected to artificial heat.

22.2 All of the sticks from each composite bolt to be air-dried shall be weighed when stored and at sufficiently frequent intervals thereafter to get accurate data on the progress of seasoning. No material shall be considered thoroughly air-dried and properly conditioned for testing until practically constant weight has been reached. (Wood absorbs and gives off moisture with changing atmospheric conditions; consequently it never comes to absolutely constant weight.)

22.3 When the material has reached equilibrium, moisture sections approximately 1 in. (2.5 cm) in length shall be taken from about 10 percent of the sticks to determine the actual moisture content. These moisture specimens shall be cut not less than 1 ft (0.3 m) from the ends of the sticks, and in such a way as to prevent any appreciable loss of material for testing. When conditioned to approximately 12 percent moisture content, the material shall be surfaced on four sides to 2 by 2 in. (5 by 5 cm) in cross-section and tested.

22.4 When adequate facilities are available, the stocks may be kiln-dried instead of air-dried in order to reduce the drying time. The preparation of the sticks and procedures followed shall be similar to those used in air-drying, and the drying shall be continued until the sticks have a moisture content of approximately 12 percent. The kilns shall be operated in a manner and at such temperatures as are in accordance with best practices for drying the species in question without injury to the strength, and the drying shall be done to avoid kiln-drying defects such as "casehardening," "honeycombing," or "collapse." A record of operating conditions of the kiln shall be kept for the entire run and shall include humidity conditions and temperatures at the hottest part of the kiln. In general, the maximum kiln temperature shall not exceed 130 F (54 C), but the exact permissible limits such as are suitable for kiln-drying airplane stock without injury depend on the species.

22.5 The seasoned sticks, whether kiln-dried or air-dried, preferably should be stored in a room having controlled temperature and humidity (at 68 ± 6 F (20 ± 3 C) and 65 ± 1 percent relative humidity) before test to reduce the moisture gradient within the material, and to bring the material into equilibrium, which will be approximately 12 percent moisture content for most species.

NOTE 3—In following the recommendation that the temperature be controlled at 68 ± 6 F (20 ± 3 C), it should be understood that it is desirable to maintain the temperature as nearly constant as possible at some temperature within this range.

ORDER, SELECTION, AND NUMBER OF TESTS

Order of Tests

23. Order of Tests

23.1 The order of tests in all cases shall be such as to eliminate as far as possible from the comparisons the effect of changes in the specimen due to such factors as storage and weather conditions.

Selection of Specimens

24. Preference in Selecting Specimens

24.1 In case the material from a given bolt should be insufficient to furnish all the test specimens hereinafter required (logs or bolts less than 24 in. (0.6 m) in diameter), additional bolts may be selected. If additional material is not available, the preferential order of mechanical tests to be used in selecting specimens shall be as follows: static bending, compression parallel to grain, impact bending, toughness, compression perpendicular to grain, hardness, shear parallel to grain, cleavage, tension parallel to grain, tension perpendicular to grain, and nail withdrawal.

25. Test Specimens from Bending Specimens After Failure

25.1 In some instances where the sticks do not provide sufficient material for all the tests, certain test specimens may be taken from the uninjured portion of the static and impact bending specimens remaining after test, provided proper care is used in the selection.

26. Quality of Test Material

26.1 Only clear straight-grained material, free of decay and other defects, shall be used for the tests. However, small knots and other similar defects may be permitted in such specimens as static bending when their location is such that it is certain they will not in any way influence the failure or otherwise affect the strength of the specimen.

Number of Tests for Each Bolt

27. Static Bending

27.1 One static bending specimen shall be taken from each pair of sticks. A pair consists of two adjacent sticks equi-distant from the pith, as *W*3 and *W*4, Fig. 3. In the composite bolts tested to afford a comparison of the strength of green and air-dry material, the pair of sticks shall be constituted as above, except that the sticks in this case will be from different bolts. Thus, *W*3*d* and *W*4*c* constitute one pair of sticks to be tested green, and *W*3*c* and *W*4*d* the corresponding pair to be tested air-dry (Section 20).

28. Compression Parallel to Grain

28.1 One compression-parallel-to-grain specimen shall be taken from each stick. Load-compression curves shall preferably be taken on all of the specimens.

29. Impact Bending

29.1 Eight impact-bending specimens shall be taken from each bolt, selection being made from the sticks remaining after obtaining the static bending tests. Two of the specimens shall be selected from near the pith, two from near the periphery, and four that are representative of the cross-section.

30. Toughness

30.1 Two toughness specimens shall be selected from the uninjured portion or end of each impact bending specimen or companion static bending specimen, making a total of 32 toughness specimens for each bolt. One from each group of two specimens from the same stick shall be tested with the load applied radially and the other tested with the load applied tangentially.

31. Compression Perpendicular to Grain

31.1 One compression-perpendicular-to-grain specimen shall be taken from each of 50 percent of the sticks selected for static bending.

32. Hardness

32.1 One hardness specimen shall be taken from each of the other 50 percent of the static-bending sticks.

33. Shear Parallel to Grain

33.1 Twelve shear-parallel-to-grain specimens shall be selected from the unused portion or ends of six sticks from which bending specimens have been selected. Two specimens shall be taken from near the pith, two from near the periphery, and eight that are representative of the average growth of the cross section of the bolt. These twelve specimens shall be selected in pairs from the six sticks. One of each pair of specimens from the same stick shall be tested in radial shear (surface of failure radial) and the other in tangential shear (surface of failure tangential).

34. Cleavage Perpendicular to Grain

34.1 Twelve cleavage specimens shall be selected from six sticks in a manner similar to that for shear (Section 33). One of each pair of specimens from the same stick shall be tested in radial cleavage (surface of failure radial) and the other in tangential cleavage (surface of failure tangential).

35. Tension Parallel to Grain

35.1 Six tension-parallel-to-grain specimens shall be chosen of which one shall be selected from near the pith, one from near the periphery, and four that are representative of the cross-section.

36. Tension Perpendicular to Grain

36.1 Twelve tension-perpendicular-to-grain specimens shall be selected from six sticks in a manner similar to that for shear (Section 33). One of each pair of specimens from the same stick shall be tested in radial tension (surface of failure radial) and the other in tangential tension (surface of failure tangential).

37. Nail Withdrawal

37.1 Twelve nail withdrawal specimens shall be selected from the unused portion or ends of twelve of the sticks from which bending or tension-parallel-to-grain specimens have been selected or, if necessary, from the uninjured portion of specimens from other tests. Six nail withdrawal specimens shall be tested in the green and six in the air-dry condition. The specimens for testing in both the green and the air-dry conditions shall be selected so as to give one from near the pith, one from near the periphery, and four that are representative of the average growth of the cross-section of the bolt.

38. Specific Gravity and Shrinkage in Volume

38.1 Six specific gravity and shrinkage-in-volume specimens shall be selected from the unused portion of bending or tension-parallel-to-grain sticks, selected so as to give one from near the pith, one from near the periphery, and four that are representative of the average growth of the cross-section of the bolt. These specimens shall be selected only from the sticks to be tested in a green condition.

39. Radial Shrinkage

39.1 Four radial shrinkage specimens shall be obtained from each *d* bolt, and where possible from the upper bolt of each pair of bolts selected at other heights in the tree. They shall be cut from the "sectors" or "quadrants" remaining after sawing (Fig. 3) or from disks cut from near the end of the bolt. When a disk is used, care must be taken to see that it is green and has not been affected by shrinking and checking, which is common near the end of the bolt. The specimens shall not be surfaced. Radial shrinkage specimens shall be cut with their greatest dimension in the radial direction. Two shall be taken from the heartwood and the other two from near the periphery. When possible, two specimens shall consist entirely of sapwood.

40. Tangential Shrinkage

40.1 Four tangential shrinkage specimens shall be obtained from each *d* bolt, and where possible from the upper bolt of each pair of bolts selected at other heights in the tree. They shall be selected at the same time and in a manner similar to radial-shrinkage specimens (Section 39), except that the greatest dimension shall be in a tangential direction. The specimens shall not be surfaced. Two shall be taken from the heartwood; the other two shall be taken from near the periphery and when possible shall consist entirely of sapwood. The heartwood and the sapwood specimens shall be taken adjacent to the respective specimens selected for radial shrinkage.

PHOTOGRAPHS OF STICKS

41. Sticks to be Photographed

41.1 Four of the static bending sticks from each species shall be selected for photographing, as follows: two average growth, one fast growth, and one slow growth. These sticks shall be photographed in cross-section and on the radial and tangential surfaces. Figure 4 is a typical photograph of a cross-section of 2 by 2-in. (5 by 5-cm) test specimens and Fig. 5 of the tangential surface of such specimens.

CONTROL OF MOISTURE CONTENT AND TEMPERATURE

NOTE 4—In recognition of the significant influence of temperature and humidity on the strength of wood, it is highly desirable that these factors be controlled to ensure comparable test results.

42. Control of Moisture Content

42.1 As prescribed in Section 22, sticks for test in the air-dry condition shall be brought practically to constant weight before test. Should any changes in moisture content occur during final preparation of specimens, the specimens shall be reconditioned before test to constant weight under conditions as prescribed in 22.5. Tests shall then be carried out in such manner that large changes in moisture content will not occur. To prevent such changes, it is desirable that the testing room and rooms for preparation of test specimens have some means of humidity control.

43. Control of Temperature

43.1 Independent of the effect on strength of the moisture content of the test specimens as influenced by temperature, is the significant effect of temperature itself on the mechanical properties. The specimens when tested shall be at a temperature of 68 ± 6 F $(20 \pm 3$ C$)$ (see Note 3, 22.5). The temperature at time of test shall in all instances be recorded as a specific part of the test record.

RECORD OF HEARTWOOD AND SAPWOOD

44. Proportion of Sapwood

44.1 The estimated proportion of sapwood present shall be recorded for each test specimen.

STATIC BENDING

45. Size of Specimens

45.1 The static bending tests shall be made on 2 by 2 by 30-in. (5 by 5 by 76-cm) specimens. The actual height and width at the center and the length shall be measured (Section 127).

46. Loading Span and Supports

46.1 Center loading and a span length of 28 in. (70 cm) shall be used. Both supporting knife edges shall be provided with bearing plates and rollers of such thickness that the distance from the point of support to the central plane is not greater than the depth of the specimen (Fig. 6). The knife edges shall be adjustable laterally to permit adjustment for slight twist or warp in the specimen.[5] Alternatively, the method of supporting the specimen in trunnion-type supports that are free to move in a horizontal direction may be employed.

47. Bearing Block

47.1 A bearing block of the form and size of that shown in Fig. 7 shall be used for applying the load.

48. Placement of Growth Rings

48.1 The specimen shall be placed so that the load will be applied through the bearing block to the tangential (flat-sawed) surface nearest the pith.

49. Speed of Testing

49.1 The load shall be applied continuously throughout the test at a rate of motion of the movable crosshead of 0.10 in. (2.5 mm)/min (Section 128).

50. Load-Deflection Curves

50.1 Load-deflection curves shall be taken to or beyond the maximum load for all static bending tests. In at least one third of the tests, the curves shall be continued to a 6-in. (15-cm) deflection, or until the specimen fails to support a load of 200 lb (90 kg).

50.2 Deflections of the neutral plane at the center of the length shall be taken with respect to points in the neutral plane above the supports.

50.3 Within the proportional limit, deflection readings shall be taken to 0.001 in. (0.02 mm). After the proportional limit is reached, less refinement is necessary in observing deflections, but it is convenient to read them by means of the dial gage (Fig. 6) until it reaches the limit of its capacity, normally approximately 1 in. (2.5 cm). Where deflections beyond 1 in. are encountered, the deflections may be measured by means of the scale mounted on the loading head (Fig. 6) and a wire mounted at the neutral axis of the specimen on the side opposite the yoke. Deflections are read to the nearest 0.01 in. (0.2 mm) at 0.10-in. (2.5-mm) intervals and also after abrupt changes in load.

50.4 The load and deflection of first failure, the maximum load, and points of sudden change shall be read and shown on the curve sheet[6] although they may not occur at one of the regular load or deflection increments.

51. Description of Static Bending Failures

51.1 Static bending (flexural) failures shall be classified according to the appearance of the fractured surface and the manner in which the failure develops (Fig. 8). The fractured surfaces may be roughly divided into "brash" and "fibrous," the term "brash" indicating abrupt failure and the term "fibrous" indicating a fracture showing splinters.

52. Weight and Moisture Content

52.1 The specimen shall be weighed immediately before test, and after test a moisture section approximately 1 in. (2.5 cm) in length shall be cut near the failure (Section 126).

COMPRESSION PARALLEL TO GRAIN

53. Size of Specimens

53.1 The compression-parallel-to-grain tests shall be made on 2 by 2 by 8-in. (5 by 5 by 20-cm) specimens. The actual cross-section dimensions and the length shall be measured (Section 127).

54. End Surfaces Parallel

54.1 Special care shall be used in preparing the compression-parallel-to-grain test specimens to ensure that the end grain surfaces will be parallel to each other and at right angles to the longitudinal axis. If deemed necessary, at least one platen of the testing machine shall

---

[5] Details of laterally adjustable supports may be found in Fig. 4 of ASTM Methods D 805, Testing Veneer, Plywood, and Other Glued Veneer Constructions, *1974 Annual Book of ASTM Standards*, Part 22.
[6] See Fig. A1 for a sample static bending data sheet form.

be equipped with a spherical bearing to obtain uniform distribution of load over the ends of the specimen.

55. Speed of Testing

55.1 The load shall be applied continuously throughout the test at a rate of motion of the movable crosshead of 0.003 in./in. (cm/cm) of specimen length/min (Section 128).

56. Load-Compression Curves

56.1 Load-compression curves shall be taken over a central gage length not exceeding 6 in. (15 cm) and preferably on all of the specimens. Load-compression readings shall be continued until the proportional limit is well passed, as indicated by the curve.[7]

56.2 Deformations shall be read to 0.0001 in. (0.002 mm).

56.3 Figures 9 and 10 illustrate two types of compressometers that have been found satisfactory for wood testing.

57. Position of Test Failures

57.1 In order to obtain satisfactory and uniform results, it is necessary that the failures be made to develop in the body of the specimen. With specimens of uniform cross-section, this result can best be obtained when the ends are at a very slightly lower moisture content than the body. With green material it will usually suffice to close-pile the specimens, cover the body with a damp or wet cloth, and expose the ends for a short time. For air-dry material, it may sometimes be advisable to pile the specimens in a similar manner and place them in a desiccator should the failures in test indicate that a slight end-drying is necessary.

58. Description of Compression Failures

58.1 Compression failures shall be classified according to the appearance of the fractured surface (Fig. 11). In case two or more kinds of failures develop, all shall be described in the order of their occurrence; thus, shearing followed by brooming. The failure shall also be sketched in its proper position on the data sheet.

59. Weight and Moisture Content

59.1 The specimen shall be weighed immediately before test, and after test a moisture section approximately 1 in. (2.5 cm) in length shall be cut from the body near the failure (Section 126).

60. Ring and Summer Wood Measurement

60.1 When practicable, the number of rings per inch (centimeter) and the proportion of summer wood shall be measured over a representative inch (centimeter) of cross section of the test specimen. In determining the proportion of summer wood, it is essential that the end surface be prepared so as to permit accurate summer wood measurement. When the fibers are broomed over at the ends from sawing, a light sanding, planing, or similar treatment of the ends is recommended.

IMPACT BENDING

61. Size of Specimens

61.1 The impact bending tests shall be made on 2 by 2 by 30-in. (5 by 5 by 76-cm) specimens. The actual height and width at the center and the length shall be measured (Section 127).

62. Loading and Span

62.1 Center loading and a span length of 28 in. (70 cm) shall be used.

63. Bearing Block

63.1 A metal tup of curvature corresponding to the bearing block shown in Fig. 7 shall be used in applying the load.

64. Placement of Growth Rings

64.1 The specimen shall be placed so that the load will be applied through the bearing block to the tangential or flat-sawed surface nearest the pith.

65. Procedure

65.1 Make the tests by increment drops in a Hatt-Turner or similar impact machine (see Fig. 12). The first drop shall be 1 in. (2.5 cm), after which increase the drops by 1-in. (2.5-cm) increments until a height of 10 in. (25 cm) is reached. Then use a 2-in. (5-cm) increment until complete failure occurs or until a 6-in.

---

[7] See Fig. A2 for a sample compression-parallel-to-grain data sheet form.

(15-cm) deflection is reached.

66. Weight of Hammer

66.1 A 50-lb (22.5-kg) hammer shall be used when, with drops up to the capacity of the machine (about 68 in. (1.7 m) for the small Hatt-Turner impact machine), it is practically certain that complete failure or a 6-in. (15-cm) deflection will result for all specimens of a species. For all other cases a 100-lb (45-kg) hammer shall be used.

67. Deflection Records

67.1 When desired, graphical drum records[8] giving the deflection for each drop and the set, if any, shall be made until the first failure occurs. This record will also afford data from which the exact height of drop can be scaled for at least the first four falls.

68. Drop Causing Failure

68.1 The height of drop causing complete failure or a 6-in. (15-cm) deflection shall be observed for each specimen.

69. Description of Failure

69.1 The failure shall be sketched on the data sheet[9] and described in accordance with the directions for static bending under Section 51.

70. Weight and Moisture Content

70.1 The specimen shall be weighed immediately before test, and after test a moisture section approximately 1 in. (2.5 cm) in length shall be cut near the failure (Section 126).

TOUGHNESS

NOTE 5—A single-blow impact test on a small specimen is recognized as a valuable and desirable test. Several types of machines such as the Toughness, Izod, and Amsler have been used, but insufficient information is available to decide whether one procedure is superior to another, or whether the results by the different methods can be directly correlated. If the Toughness machine is used, the following procedure has been found satisfactory. To aid in standardization and to facilitate comparisons, the size of the toughness specimen has been made equal to that accepted internationally.

71. Size of Specimen

71.1 The toughness tests shall be made on 0.79 by 0.79 by 11-in. (2 by 2 by 28-cm) specimens. The actual height and width at the cen-

ter and the length shall be measured (Section 127).

72. Loading and Span

72.1 Center loading and a span length of 9.47 in. (24 cm) shall be used. The load shall be applied to a radial or tangential surface on alternate specimens.

73. Bearing Block

73.1 An aluminum tup (Fig. 13) having a radius of $^3/_4$ in. (18 mm) shall be used in applying the load.

74. Apparatus and Procedure

74.1 Make the tests in a Forest Products Laboratory type toughness machine (Fig. 13). Adjust the machine before test so that the pendulum hangs truly vertical and adjust it to compensate for friction. Adjust the cable so that the load is applied to the specimen when the pendulum swings to 15 deg from the vertical so as to produce complete failure by the time the downward swing is completed. Choose the weight position and initial angle (30, 45, or 60 deg) of the pendulum so that complete failure of the specimen is obtained on one drop. Most satisfactory results are obtained when the difference between the initial and final angle is at least 10 deg.

75. Calculation

75.1 The initial and final angle shall be read to the nearest 0.1 deg by means of the vernier (Fig. 13) attached to the machine.[10] The toughness shall then be calculated as follows:

$$T = wL (\cos A_2 - \cos A_1)$$

where:

T = toughness (work per specimen), in. · lb (cm · kg),

w = weight of pendulum, lb (kg),

L = distance from center of the supporting axis to center of gravity of the pendulum, in. (cm),

A_1 = initial angle (Note 5), deg, and

---

[8] See Fig. A3 for a sample drum record.
[9] See Fig. A5 for a sample impact bending data sheet form. Figure A4 shows a sample data and computation card.
[10] See Fig. A6 for a sample data and computation sheet for the toughness test.

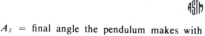

A_2 = final angle the pendulum makes with the vertical after failure of the test specimen, deg.

NOTE 6—Since friction is compensated for in the machine adjustment, the initial angle may be regarded as exactly 30, 45, or 60 deg, as the case may be.

76. Weight and Moisture Content

76.1 The specimen shall be weighed immediately before test, and after test a moisture section approximately 2 in. (5 cm) in length shall be cut from the body near the failure (Section 126).

COMPRESSION PERPENDICULAR TO GRAIN

77. Size of Specimens

77.1 The compression-perpendicular-to-grain tests shall be made on 2 by 2 by 6-in. (5 by 5 by 15-cm) specimens. The actual height, width, and length shall be measured (Section 127).

78. Loading

78.1 The load shall be applied through a metal bearing plate 2 in. (5 cm) in width, placed across the upper surface of the specimen at equal distances from the ends and at right angles to the length (Fig. 14).

79. Placement of Growth Rings

79.1 The specimens shall be placed so that the load will be applied through the bearing plate to a radial (quarter-sawed) surface.

80. Speed of Testing

80.1 The load shall be applied continuously throughout the test at a rate of motion of the movable crosshead of 0.012 in. (0.3 mm)/min (Section 128).

81. Load-Compression Curves

81.1 Load-compression curves[11] shall be taken for all specimens up to 0.1-in. (2.5-mm) compression, after which the test shall be discontinued. Compression shall be measured between the loading surfaces.

81.2 Deflection readings shall be taken to 0.0001 in. (0.002 mm).

82. Weight and Moisture Content

82.1 The specimen shall be weighed imme-

diately before test, and after test a moisture section approximately 1 in. (2.5 cm) in length shall be cut adjacent to the part under load (Section 126).

HARDNESS

83. Size of Specimens

83.1 The hardness tests shall be made on 2 by 2 by 6-in. (5 by 5 by 15-cm) specimens. The acutal cross-section dimensions and length shall be measured (Section 127).

84. Procedure

84.1 Use the modified ball test with a "ball" 0.444 in. (1.13 cm) in diameter for determining hardness (Fig. 15). Record the load at which the "ball" has penetrated to one half its diameter, as determined by an electric circuit indicator or by the tightening of the collar against the specimen.

85. Number of Penetrations

85.1 Two penetrations shall be made on a tangential surface, two on a radial surface, and one on each end. The choice between the two radial and between the two tangential surfaces shall be such as to give a fair average of the piece. The penetrations shall be far enough from the edge to prevent splitting or chipping.[12]

86. Speed of Testing

86.1 The load shall be applied continuously throughout the test at a rate of motion of the movable crosshead of 0.25 in. (6 mm)/min (Section 128).

87. Weight and Moisture Content

87.1 The specimen shall be weighed immediately before test, and after test a moisture section approximately 1 in. (2.5 cm) in length shall be cut (Section 126).

SHEAR PARALLEL TO GRAIN

NOTE 7—The following describes one method of making the shear-parallel-to-grain test that has been extensively used and found satisfactory.

---

[11] See Fig. A7 for a sample compression-perpendicular-to-grain data sheet form.

[12] See Fig. A8 for a sample data and computation sheet for the hardness test.

88. Size of Specimens

88.1 The shear-parallel-to-grain tests shall be made on 2 by 2 by 2$\frac{1}{2}$-in. (5 by 5 by 6.3-cm) specimens notched as illustrated in Fig. 16 to produce failure on a 2 by 2-in. (5 by 5-cm) surface. The actual dimensions of the shearing surface shall be measured (Section 127).

89. Procedure

89.1 Use a shear tool similar to that illustrated in Fig. 17, providing a $\frac{1}{8}$-in. (3-mm) offset between the inner edge of the supporting surface and the plane along which the failure occurs. Apply the load to, and support the specimen on, end-grain surfaces. Take care in placing the specimen in the shear tool to see that the crossbar is adjusted so that the edges of the specimen are vertical and the end rests evenly on the support over the contact area. Observe the maximum load only.

90. Speed of Testing

90.1 The load shall be applied continuously throughout the test at a rate of motion of the movable crosshead of 0.024 in. (0.6 mm)/min (Section 128).

91. Test Failures

91.1 The failure shall be sketched on the data sheet.[13] In all cases where the failure at the base of the specimen extends back onto the supporting surface, the test shall be culled.

92. Moisture Content

92.1 The portion of the test piece that is sheared off shall be used as a moisture specimen (Section 126).

CLEAVAGE

93. Size of Specimens

93.1 The cleavage tests shall be made on specimens of the form and size shown in Fig. 18. The actual width and length at minimum section shall be measured (Section 127).

94. Procedure

94.1 The specimens shall be held during test in grips as shown in Figs. 19 and 20. Observe the maximum load only.

95. Speed of Testing

95.1 The load shall be applied continuously throughout the test at a rate of motion of the movable crosshead of 0.10 in. (2.5 mm)/min (Section 128).

96. Sketch of Failure

96.1 The failure shall be sketched on the data sheet.[14]

97. Moisture Content

97.1 One of the pieces remaining after failure, or a section split along the surface of failure, shall be used as a moisture specimen (Section 126).

TENSION PARALLEL TO GRAIN

NOTE 8—One method of determining the tension-parallel-to-grain strength of wood is given in the following procedure.

98. Size of Specimens

98.1 The tension-parallel-to-grain tests shall be made on specimens of the size and shape shown in Fig. 21. The specimen shall be so oriented that the direction of the annual rings at the critical section, as shown on the ends of the specimens, shall be perpendicular to the greater cross-sectional dimension. The actual cross-sectional dimensions at minimum section shall be measured (Section 127).

99. Procedure

99.1 Fasten the specimen in special grips (Fig. 22). Take load-extension curves for a 2-in. (5-cm) central gage length on all specimens. Continue the load-extension readings until the proportional limit is passed.

99.2 Read deformations to 0.0001 in. (0.002 mm).

99.3 Figure 22 illustrates gripping devices and a type of extensometer that have been found satisfactory.

100. Speed of Testing

100.1 The load shall be applied continuously throughout the test at a rate of motion

---

[13] See Fig. A9 for a sample data and computation sheet for the tangential-shear-parallel-to-grain test.

[14] See Fig. A10 for a sample data and computation sheet for the cleavage test.

of the movable crosshead of 0.05 in. (1 mm)/min (Section 128).

101. Sketch of Failure

101.1 The failure shall be sketched on the data sheet.[15]

102. Moisture Content

102.1 A moisture section about 3 in. (7.5 cm) in length shall be cut from the reduced section near the failure (Section 126).

TENSION PERPENDICULAR TO GRAIN
(Optional Test)

103. Size of Specimens

103.1 The tension-perpendicular-to-grain tests shall be made on specimens of the size and shape shown in Fig. 23. The actual width and length at minimum sections shall be measured (Section 127).

104. Procedure

104.1 Fasten the specimens during test in grips as shown in Figs. 24 and 25. Observe the maximum load only.

105. Speed of Testing

105.1 The load shall be applied continuously throughout the test at a rate of motion of the movable crosshead of 0.10 in. (2.5 mm)/min (Section 128).

106. Sketch of Failure

106.1 The failure shall be sketched on the data sheet.[16]

107 Moisture Content

107.1 One of the pieces remaining after failure, or a section split along the surface of failure, shall be used as a moisture specimen (Section 126).

NAIL WITHDRAWAL
(Optional Test)

NOTE 9—Presented herewith is a recommended procedure for making nail withdrawal tests. When necessary, alternative procedures that give comparable results may be used.

108. Size of Specimens

108.1 The nail withdrawal tests shall be made on 2 by 2 by 6-in. (5 by 5 by 15-cm)

specimens. The actual cross-sectional dimensions and length shall be measured (Section 127).

109. Nails

109.1 Nails used for withdrawal tests shall be nominally 0.0985 in. (2.5 mm) in diameter.[17] Bright diamond-point nails shall be used, and all nails shall be cleaned before use to remove any coating or surface film that may be present as a result of manufacturing operations. Each nail shall be used but once.

110. Preparation of Specimens

110.1 Nails shall be driven at right angles to the face of the specimen to a total penetration of $1\frac{1}{4}$ in. (3.2 cm). Two nails shall be driven on a tangential surface, two on a radial surface, and one on each end. The choice between the two radial and between the two tangential surfaces shall be such as to give a fair average of the piece. On radial and tangential faces, the nails shall be driven a sufficient distance from the edges and ends of the specimen to avoid splitting. In general, nails should not be driven closer than $\frac{3}{4}$ in. (18 mm) from the edge or $1\frac{1}{2}$ in. (37 mm) from the end of a piece, and the two nails on a radial or tangential face should not be driven in line with each other or less than 2 in. (5 cm) apart.

111. Procedure

111.1 Withdraw all six nails in a single specimen immediately after driving. Fasten the specimens during the test in grips as shown in Figs. 26 and 27. Observe the maximum load only.[18]

112. Speed of Testing

112.1 The load shall be applied continuously throughout the test at a rate of motion of the movable crosshead of 0.075 in. (2 mm)/min (Section 128).

[15] See Fig. A11 for a sample tension-parallel-to-grain data and computation sheet.
[16] See Fig. A12 for a sample data and computation sheet for the tension-perpendicular-to-grain test.
[17] A fivepenny common nail meets this requirement. If difficulty is experienced in woods of higher density in pulling the nails without breaking the heads, a sevenpanny, cement-coated sinker nail, with coating removed by use of a suitable solvent, may be used.
[18] See Fig. A13 for a sample nail-withdrawal test data sheet form.

113. Weight and Moisture Content

113.1 The specimen shall be weighed immediately before driving the nails and after test a moisture section approximately 1 in. (2.5 cm) in length shall be cut from the body of the specimen (Section 126).

SPECIFIC GRAVITY AND SHRINKAGE IN VOLUME

114. Size of Specimens

114.1 The specific gravity and shrinkage in volume tests shall be made on 2 by 2 by 6-in. (5 by 5 by 15-cm) specimens. The actual cross-sectional dimensions and length shall be measured (Section 127).

115. Procedure

115.1 Obtain both specific gravity and shrinkage-in-volume determinations on the same specimen. These determinations should be made at approximately 12 percent moisture content and in the oven-dry condition.

115.2 A carbon impression of the end of the green specimen may be made on the back of the data sheet.[19] In like manner, a carbon impression of the same end may be made after the specimen has been conditioned (115.4 and 115.5).

115.3 Weigh the specimen when green (Section 126) and determine the volume by the immersion method.

115.4 Open-pile the green specimens after immersion and allow them to air-season under room conditions to a uniform moisture content of approximately 12 percent. The specimens should then be weighed and the volume determined by the immersion method.

115.5 Then, open-pile the specimens used for specific gravity and shrinkage determinations at 12 percent moisture content, or duplicate specimens on which green weight and volume measurements have been made prior to conditioning to approximately 12 percent moisture content, in an oven and dry at 103 ± 2 C until approximately constant weight is reached.

115.6 After over-drying, weigh the specimens (Section 126) and while still warm immerse them in a hot paraffin bath, taking care to remove them quickly to ensure a thin coating.

115.7 Determine the volume of the paraffin-coated specimen by immersion as before.

115.8 Figure 28 illustrates the apparatus used in determining the specific gravity and shrinkage in volume. The use of an automatic balance will facilitate increased rapidity and accuracy of measurements.

RADIAL AND TANGENTIAL SHRINKAGE

116. Size of Specimen

116.1 The radial- and tangential-shrinkage determinations shall be made on 1 by 4 by 1-in. (2.5 by 10 by 2.5-cm) specimens.

117. Initial Measurement

117.1 The specimen shall be measured across the 4-in. (10-cm) dimension in which the shrinkage is to be determined (Section 127).

118. Weight

118.1 The specimen shall be weighed when green and after subsequent oven-drying (Section 126).

119. Drying

119.1 The green specimens shall be open-piled and allowed to air-season under room conditions to a uniform moisture content of approximately 12 percent.

119.2 The specimens shall then be open-piled in an oven and dried at 103 ± 2 C until approximately constant weight in attained.

120. Final Measurement

120.1 Measurements shall be made on the air-dry and on the oven-dry specimens.[20]

121. Method of Measurement

121.1 Figure 29 illustrates the method of making the radial- and tangential-shrinkage measurements. An ordinary micrometer of required accuracy is suitable for this work (Section 127).

---

[19] See Fig. A14 for a sample data and computation sheet for the specific gravity and shrinkage-in-volume test.

[20] See Fig. A15 for a sample data and computation sheet for the radial- and tangential-shrinkage test.

MOISTURE DETERMINATION

122. Selection

122.1 The sample for moisture determinations of each test specimen shall be selected as hereinbefore described for each test.

123. Weighing

123.1 Immediately after obtaining the moisture sample, all loose splinters shall be removed and the sample shall be weighed (Section 126).

124. Drying

124.1 The moisture samples shall be open-piled in an oven and dried at a temperature of 103 ± 2 C until approximately constant weight is attained, after which the oven-dry weight shall be determined (Section 125).

125. Moisture Content

125.1 The loss in weight, expressed in percentage of the over-dry weight as above determined, shall be considered the moisture content of the specimen.

PERMISSIBLE VARIATIONS

126. Weights

126.1 The weight of test specimens and of moisture samples shall be determined to an accuracy of not less than ± 0.2 percent.

127. Measurements

127.1 Measurements of test specimens shall be made to an accuracy of not less than ± 0.3 percent, except that in no case shall the measurements be made to less than 0.01 in. (0.2 mm), except measurements of the radial and tangential shrinkage specimens that shall be made to the nearest 0.001 in. (0.02 mm).

128. Testing Machine Speeds

128.1 The testing machine speed used should not vary by more than ± 25 percent from that specified for a given test. If the specified speed cannot be obtained, the speed used shall be recorded on the data sheet. The crosshead speed shall mean the free-running or no-load speed of crosshead for testing machines of the mechanical drive type and the loaded crosshead speed for testing machines of the hydraulic loading type.

CALIBRATION

129. Calibration

129.1 All apparatus used in obtaining data shall be calibrated at sufficiently frequent intervals to ensure accuracy.[21]

---

[21] ASTM Methods E 4, Verification of Testing Machines, *1974 Annual Book of ASTM Standards*, Part 10.

PART II. SECONDARY METHODS

Part II, Secondary Methods, is intended for use in evaluating the properties of wood only when relatively small trees, generally less than 12 in. (30 cm) in diameter, are available to provide the test specimens and only when such trees because of crook, cross grain, knots or other defects are of such quality that the longer clear, straight-grained specimens required by Part I, Primary Methods, cannot reasonably be obtained. Whenever possible, the procedure for Part I, Primary Methods, shall be used regardless of size of trees.

INTRODUCTION

The standard methods of testing small clear specimens of timber, Part I, Primary Methods, provide for cutting the bolts (log sections) systematically into sticks of nominal $2\frac{1}{2}$ by $2\frac{1}{2}$ in. (6 by 6 cm) in cross section, that are later surfaced to provide the test specimens 2 by 2 in. (5 by 5 cm) in cross section, on which the system is based. These methods have served as an excellent basis for the evaluation of the various mechanical and related physical properties of different species of wood. They have been extensively used, and a large amount of data based on these methods have been obtained and published.

The 2 by 2-in. test specimen has the advantage that it embraces a number of growth rings, is less influenced by springwood and summerwood differences than smaller specimens, and is large enough to represent a considerable proportion of the material. Because of the cross-sectional size and the length of specimen required for some of the tests (30 in. (76 cm) for static and impact bending) it is, however, sometimes difficult to obtain test specimens in adequate number and entirely free of defects from bolts representing smaller trees, particularly trees under 12 to 15 in. (30 to 38 cm) in diameter. With increasing need for evaluating the properties of species involving smaller trees, and the increasing importance of second-growth timber that is expected to be harvested much before it reaches the sizes attained in virgin stands, there has developed a need for secondary methods of test in which at least the longer test specimens are smaller than 2 by 2 in. in cross section. It is axiomatic that test results are intimately related to and dependent upon the test methods employed. The problem has hence been to develop secondary methods that give test results directly comparable to those obtained by the present primary methods employing 2 by 2-in. cross section for all test specimens, and thus ensure a continuing accumulation of data directly comparable to the extensive data already available. Such methods are provided by Part II, Secondary Methods, for testing small clear specimens of timber.

The exceedingly rapid rate of growth and corresponding wide annual rings in much second-growth material, together with the desirability of incorporating more than a single year's growth increment in a test specimen, has necessitated limiting the minimum cross section of test piece in these secondary methods to 1 by 1 in. (2.5 by 2.5 cm). This cross section is established for the compression-parallel-to-grain and static-bending tests. The 2 by 2-in. cross section is retained for impact bending, and for the other tests not requiring specimens longer than 6 in. (15 cm) namely, compression perpendicular to grain, hardness, shear parallel to grain, cleavage, and tension perpendicular to grain. Toughness and tension parallel to grain are special tests based on specimens of smaller cross section.

Investigations have shown that for the more important properties obtained from static bending and compression-parallel-to-grain tests (modulus of rupture and modulus of elasticity in static bending, and maximum crushing strength and modulus of elasticity in compression parallel to grain) results from specimens of 1 by 1 in. in cross section can be substituted directly for those obtained from specimens of 2 by 2 in. in cross section with but little error. Present data indicate that values of fiber stress at proportional limit in static bending and in compression parallel to grain may be slightly higher for the 1 by 1-in. than for the 2 by 2-in. specimens, based on standardized testing procedures appropriate to the two sizes, but no special reason why this should be expected is apparent. The work values in static bending, however, are related somewhat to size of specimen, and total work also to the arbitrary load and deflection limit established for terminating the test. The relationship of work values for the two sizes also varies among different species, hence work values in static bending should not be regarded as directly comparable as between the Primary Methods and the Secondary Methods. In reporting results of tests it is recommended that the size of specimen be given, or that the data be referenced to the Primary or Secondary Methods.

Since exactly the same size and form of test specimens for compression perpendicular to grain, hardness, impact bending, shear parallel to grain, cleavage, tension parallel to grain, tension perpendicular to grain, and toughness are used for the Primary and the Secondary Methods, identical test results are obviously obtained.

Since the procedure for the Secondary Methods for many features, such as in selection and care of material, and in conducting certain tests, is identical with the Primary Methods, the Secondary Methods presented herewith are referenced to the Primary Methods, and procedure is given only where it differs therefrom. For convenience the section numbers in the Secondary Methods correspond in the last two digits with the numbering of the Primary Methods but the numbering begins with 201 in the former. Thus Section 201 in the Secondary Methods corresponds in subject matter to Section 1 of the Primary Methods, etc.

201. Scope

201.1 See Section 1.

202. Summary of Method

202.1 See 2.1.

202.2 The procedures for collection and preparation of the material for testing and for the various tests appear in the following order:

COLLECTION OF MATERIAL

Selection

203. Authentic Identification

203.1 See Section 3.

204. Selection and Number of Trees

204.1 For each species to be tested, at least ten trees representative of the species shall be selected.

205. Selection and Number of Bolts

205.1 See 5.2.

205.2 From the other trees called for in Section 204, take the 8-ft (2.4-m) section[4] (*c-d* bolts) next above the 8-ft butt log if this section falls within the merchantable length of the tree, otherwise taken the 8-ft section comprising the two highest standard bolts (multiples of 4-ft (1.2-m)) within the merchantable length.

206. Substitution of Flitches for Bolts

206.1 For the small trees to which this secondary method is applicable, bolts representing the full diameter of the log are required, and flitches should not be substituted for bolts.

207. Selection for Important Species

207.1 For important species of wide geographical distribution, test material shall be selected from two or more localities or sites. The number of trees of a species selected from each site or locality shall conform to the requirements of Sections 204 and 205.

Field Marking

208. Tree Designation

208.1 See Section 8.

209. Bolt Designation

209.1 See Section 9.

210. Marking

210.1 See Section 10.

211. Indication of Cardinal Point

211.1 See Section 11.

212. Shipment Number

212.1 See Section 12.

Field Descriptions

213. Field Descriptions

213.1 See Section 13.

Preparation for Shipment

214. Preparation for Shipment

214.1 See Section 14.

DISPOSITION AT DESTINATION

Storage of Logs at Destination

215. Storage of Logs

215.1 See Section 15.

Photographing, Sawing, and Final Marking

NOTE 10—In sawing, marking, and selecting test sticks, the aim should be to obtain specimens representative of the material collected. The procedure described herein is one that has been found satisfactory for most species.

216. Photographing Ends of Bolts

216.1 See Section 16.

217. Sawing of Bolts

217.1 All bolts shall be marked on the top end into $2\frac{1}{2}$-in. (6 by 6-cm) or $1\frac{1}{4}$ by $1\frac{1}{4}$-in. (3 by 3-cm) squares as shown in Fig. 30, and sawed into nominal $2\frac{1}{2}$ or $1\frac{1}{4}$-in. sticks. The letters N, E, S, and W indicate the cardinal points. For trees that are not circular or for intermediate sizes where more than the required distance is available, sticks may be moved outward toward the periphery to whatever position between the pith and bark would products sticks with a minimum of defects. For example, in trees 9 to 12 in. (23 to 30 cm) in diameter, sticks N1-4 and S1-4 could be moved outward as much as $1\frac{1}{2}$ in. (3.8 cm) if desired.

218. Marking of Test Sticks

218.1 All test sticks shall bear the shipment number, the tree number, stick number, and bolt designation, to be known respectively as Shipment No., Piece No., Stick No., and mark. Thus, 800-1-N1-4d represents the $2\frac{1}{2}$ by $2\frac{1}{2}$-in. (6 by 6 cm) Stick N1-4 of Bolt d,

Tree 1, Shipment 800, and 800-1-W4c represents the $1\frac{1}{4}$ by $1\frac{1}{4}$-in. (3 by 3-cm) Stick W4 of Bolt c, Tree 1, Shipment 800.

Matching for Tests of Air-Dry Material

219. Composite Bolts

219.1 The collection of material (Section 205) has been arranged to provide for tests of both green and air-dry specimens that are closely matched by selection from adjacent parts of the same tree. The 8-ft (2.4-m) long bolts, after being marked in accordance with Section 217, shall be sawed into $2\frac{1}{2}$ by $2\frac{1}{2}$-in. (6 by 6-cm) or $1\frac{1}{4}$ by $1\frac{1}{4}$-in. (3 by 3-cm) by 8-ft (2.4-m) sticks, and numbered and lettered in accordance with Section 218. Each 8-ft stick shall then be cut into two 4-ft (1.2-m) pieces, making sure that each part carries the proper designation and bolt letter. If the 8-ft bolt is not straight it may be found more desirable to cut it into 4-ft lengths before cutting the $2\frac{1}{2}$- or $1\frac{1}{4}$-in. square pieces. If this is done care must be taken to secure end-matched sticks in the two 4-ft bolts, and to ensure that each part carries the proper designation and bolt letter.

219.2 Part of the $2\frac{1}{2}$ by $2\frac{1}{2}$-in. and $1\frac{1}{4}$ by $1\frac{1}{4}$-in. by 4-ft sticks from each 8-ft bolt is to provide specimens to be tested green (unseasoned) and the other part is to provide specimens to be air-dried and tested. To afford matching, the 4-ft sticks of one bolt shall be interchanged with the 4-ft sticks of the next adjacent bolt from the same tree to form two composite bolts, each being complete and being made of equal portions of the adjacent 4-ft bolts. The sticks from one of these composite bolts shall be tested green and those from the other shall be tested after air-drying. Thus, the sticks of each composite bolt shall be regarded as if they were from the same bolt.

219.3 The above procedure provides for end-to-end matching (end matching) of sticks to be tested air-dry with those to be tested green, which is to be preferred when practicable. If, because of the nature of the material, end matching is not practicable, side matching of $1\frac{1}{4}$ by $1\frac{1}{4}$-in. sticks may be used.

220. Schedule for Forming Composite Bolts

220.1 The division of sticks into composite

bolts, part to be tested green and part to be air-dried and tested, shall be made according to the following schedule, in which the numbers refer to stick numbers:

Selection of Sticks from Bolts

Composite Bolt (ab, cd, etc.) to Be Tested Green:
Lower bolt   N1–4, S5–8, E4, E5, E8, W4, W5, W8
Upper bolt   S1–4, N5–8, E3, E6, E7, W3, W6, W7

Composite Bolt (ab, cd, etc.) to Be Air-Dried and Tested:
Lower bolt   S1–4, N5–8, E3, E6, E7, W3, W6, W7
Upper bolt   N1–4, S5–8, E4, E5, E8, W4, W5, W8

220.2 As an example of composite bolts, assume that the full cross-section, Fig. 30, represents the end of an 8-ft (2.4-m) section comprising the *c* and *d* bolts.

220.2 The following sticks are selected for the composite bolt to be tested green:
$2\frac{1}{2}$ by $2\frac{1}{2}$-in. (6 by 6-cm) sticks:
N1–4c, N5–8d, S1–4d, S5–8c
$1\frac{1}{4}$ by $1\frac{1}{4}$-in. (3 by 3-cm) sticks:
E3d, E4c, E5c, E6d, E7d, E8c, W3d, W4c, W5c, W6d, W7d, W8c

220.2.2 The following sticks are selected for the composite bolt to be air-dried and tested:
$2\frac{1}{2}$ by $2\frac{1}{2}$-in. (6 by 6-cm) sticks:
N1–4d, N5–8c, S1–4c, S5–8d
$1\frac{1}{4}$ by $1\frac{1}{4}$-in. (3 by 3-cm) sticks:
E3c, E4d, E5d, E6c, E7c, E8d, W3c, W4d, W5d, W6c, W7c, W8d

Disposition of Sticks

221. Green Material

221.1 The sticks ($2\frac{1}{2}$ by $2\frac{1}{2}$ in. by 4 ft (6 by 6 cm by 1.2 m), or $1\frac{1}{4}$ by $1\frac{1}{4}$ in. by 4 ft (3 by 3 cm by 1.2 m)) to be tested green, shall be kept in an unseasoned condition, while awaiting preparation for test, by being stored in a framed pit or other suitable container where they shall be close piled and covered with damp sawdust, or in some other suitable manner. As material is required for test, it shall be removed from this pit or container, surfaced on all four sides to 2 by 2 in. (5 by 5 cm) or 1 by 1 in. (2.5 by 2.5 cm) cross section, sawed to test size, and kept covered with a damp cloth in a tightly closed container at a temperature of about 68 ± 6 F (20 ± 3 C) (see Note 3, 22.5) until the time of test. Care shall be taken to avoid as much as possible the storage of green material in any form. Sticks

to be tested in a green condition usually should not be sawed from the log form in quantities greater than is required to meet the testing demands for from a few days to not more than 2 weeks, depending on the prevailing conditions.

222. Air-Dry Material

222.1 The ends of the sticks to be air-dried ($2\frac{1}{2}$ by $2\frac{1}{2}$ in. by 4 ft (6 by 6 cm by 1.2 m), or $1\frac{1}{4}$ by $1\frac{1}{4}$ in. by 4 ft (3 by 3 cm by 1.2 m)) shall be dipped in melted paraffin or other substance suitable to retard checking. The material shall be piled so as to have a space of at least $\frac{1}{2}$ in. (1.3 cm) on each side of each stick to permit circulation of air. The material shall be stored in a place allowing free access of air, but protected from sunshine, rain, snow, and moisture from the ground. The sticks in drying shall not be subjected to artificial heat.

222.2 See 22.2.

222.3 When the material has reached equilibrium, moisture sections approximately 1 in. (2.5 cm) in length shall be taken from about 10 percent of the sticks to determine the actual moisture content. These moisture specimens shall be cut not less than 1 ft (0.3 m) from the ends of the sticks, and in such a way as to prevent any appreciable loss of material for testing. When conditioned to approximately 12 percent moisture content the sticks shall be surfaced on four sides to 2 by 2 in. (5 by 5 cm) or 1 by 1 in. (2.5 by 2.5 cm) in cross-section, sawed to test size, and tested.

222.4 See 22.4.
222.5 See 22.5.

ORDER, SELECTION, AND NUMBER OF TESTS

Order of Tests

223. Order of Tests

223.1 See Section 23.

Selection of Specimens

224. Preference in Selecting Specimens

224.1 In case the material from a given bolt should be insufficient to furnish all the test specimens hereinafter required, additional bolts may be selected. If additional material is not available, the preferential order of mechanical tests to be used in selecting specimens shall be as follows: static bending, compression parallel to grain, impact bending, toughness, compression perpendicular to grain, hardness, shear parallel to grain, cleavage, tension parallel to grain, tension perpendicular to grain, and nail withdrawal.

225. Test Specimens from Bending Specimens After Failure

225.1 See Section 25.

226. Quality of Test Material

226.1 See Section 26.

Number of Test for Each Bolt

227. Static Bending

227.1 One static bending specimen shall be taken from each pair of $1\frac{1}{4}$ by $1\frac{1}{4}$-in. (3 by 3-cm) sticks. A pair consists of two adjacent sticks equidistant from the pith, as $W7$ and $W8$, Fig. 30. In the composite bolts tested to afford a comparison of the strength of green and air-dry material, the pair of sticks shall be constituted as above, except that the sticks in this case will be from different bolts. Thus, $W3d$ and $W4c$ constitute one pair of sticks to be tested green, and $W3c$ and $W4d$ the corresponding pair to be tested air-dry (Section 220). Effort shall be made to select sticks so that both bolts of the composite bolt are represented in the green and the dry tests.

228. Compression Parallel to Grain

228.1 One compression-parallel-to-grain specimen shall be taken from each pair of $1\frac{1}{4}$ by $1\frac{1}{4}$-in. (3 by 3-cm) sticks, as for static bending. Effort shall be made to select sticks so that both bolts of a composite bolt are represented in the green and the dry tests. Load-compression curves shall preferably be taken on all of the specimens.

229. Impact Bending

229.1 One impact bending specimen shall be taken from each of 50 percent of the $2\frac{1}{2}$ by $2\frac{1}{2}$-in. (6 by 6-cm) sticks from each bolt. Effort shall be made to secure the best possible representation of the cross section.

230. Toughness

230.1 Two toughness specimens shall be selected from each stick used for static bending.

231. Compression Perpendicular to Grain

231.1 One compression-perpendicular-to-grain specimen shall be taken from each $2\frac{1}{2}$ by $2\frac{1}{2}$-in. (6 by 6-cm) stick selected for impact-bending specimens.

232. Hardness

232.1 One hardness specimen shall be taken from each $2\frac{1}{2}$ by $2\frac{1}{2}$-in. (6 by 6-cm) stick used for impact bending and compression-perpendicular-to-grain tests.

233. Shear Parallel to Grain

233.1 Two shear-parallel-to-grain specimens shall be selected from each of the $2\frac{1}{2}$ by $2\frac{1}{2}$-in. (6 by 6-cm) sticks from each bolt remaining after selection of sticks for impact bending tests. One of each pair of specimens from the same stick shall be tested in radial shear (surface of failure radial) and the other in tangential shear (surface of failure tangential).

234. Cleavage Perpendicular to Grain

234.1 Two cleavage specimens shall be taken from each of the $2\frac{1}{2}$ by $2\frac{1}{2}$-in. (6 by 6-cm) sticks selected for shear-parallel-to-grain specimens. One of each pair of specimens from the same stick shall be tested in radial cleavage (surface of failure radial) and the other in tangential cleavage (surface of failure tangential).

235. Tension Parallel to Grain

235.1 One tension-parallel-to-grain specimen shall be taken from each pair of $1\frac{1}{4}$ by $1\frac{1}{4}$-in. (3 by 3-cm) sticks.

236. Tension Perpendicular to Grain

236.1 Two tension-perpendicular-to-grain specimens shall be taken from each of the $2\frac{1}{2}$ by $2\frac{1}{2}$-in. (6 by 6-cm) sticks selected for shear-parallel-to-grain specimens. One of each pair of specimens from the same stick shall be tested in radial tension (surface of failure radial) and the other in tangential tension (surface of failure tangential).

237. Nail Withdrawal

237.1 Four nail-withdrawal specimens shall

be selected from the uninjured portion of 2 by 2-in. (5 by 5-cm) specimens from other tests, selected to give satisfactory representation of the cross-section of the bolt. Two specimens shall be tested in the green condition and two in the air-dry condition.

238. Specific Gravity and Shrinkage in Volume

238.1 Two to four specific gravity and shrinkage-in-volume specimens shall be selected from the unused portions of $2\frac{1}{2}$ by $2\frac{1}{2}$-in. (6 by 6-cm) sticks, selected to give the best possible representation of the cross section and tree heights included in composite bolts. These specimens shall be selected only from the sticks to be tested in a green condition.

239. Radial Shrinkage

239.1 Two radial-shrinkage specimens shall be obtained from each d bolt, and where possible from the upper bolt of each pair of bolts selected at other heights in the tree. They shall be cut from disks cut from near the end of the bolt. Care shall be taken to see that the disks are green and have not been affected by shrinking and checking, which is common near the end of the bolt. The specimens shall not be surfaced. Radial shrinkage specimens shall be cut with their greatest dimension in the radial direction. One specimen shall be taken outward from near the pith and the other inward from near the bark.

240. Tangential Shrinkage

240.1 Two tangential-shrinkage specimens shall be obtained from each d bolt, and where possible from the upper bolt of each pair of bolts selected at other heights in the tree. They shall be selected at the same time and in a manner similar to radial-shrinkage specimens (Section 239), except that the greatest dimension shall be in a tangential direction. The specimens shall not be surfaced. One shall be taken from the near periphery and the other nearer the pith to represent an earlier period of growth. The tangential-shrinkage specimens shall be adjacent to the specimens selected for radial shrinkage.

241. Sticks to be Photographed

241.1 See Section 41.

NOTE 11—In recognition of the significant influence of temperature and humidity on the strength of wood, it is highly desirable that these factors be controlled to ensure comparable test results.

242. Control of Moisture Content

242.1 See Section 42.

243. Control of Temperature

243.1 See Section 43.

244. Proportion of Sapwood

244.1 See Section 44.

245. Size of Specimens

245.1 The static bending tests shall be made on nominal 1 by 1 by 16-in. (2.5 by 2.5 by 41-cm) specimens. The actual height and width at the center, and the length shall be measured (Section 127).

246. Loading Span and Supports

246.1 Center loading and span length of 14 in. (35 cm) shall be used. Both supporting knife edges shall be provided with bearing plates and rollers of such thickness that the distance from the point of support to the central plane is not greater than the depth of the specimen (Fig. 6). The knife edges shall be adjustable laterally to permit adjustment for slight twist or warp in the specimen.[5] Alternatively, the method of supporting the specimen in trunnion-type supports that are free to move in a horizontal direction may be employed.

247. Bearing Block

247.1 A bearing block having a radius of curvature of $1\frac{1}{2}$ in. (3.7 cm) for a chord length of not less than 2 in. (5 cm) shall be used.

248. Placement of Growth Rings

248.1 See Section 48.

249. Speed of Testing

249.1 The load shall be applied continuously throughout the test at a rate of the movable crosshead of 0.05 in. (1.3 mm)/min (Section 128).

250. Load-Deflection Curves

250.1 Load-deflection curves shall be taken to or beyond the maximum load for all static bending tests. In at least one-third of the tests, the curves shall be continued to a 3-in. (7.5-cm) deflection, or until the specimen fails to support a load of 50 lb (22.5 kg).

250.2 See 50.2.

250.3 See 50.3.

250.4 See 50.4.

251. Description of Static Bending Failures

251.1 See Section 51.

252. Weight and Moisture Content

252.1 See Section 52.

COMPRESSION PARALLEL TO GRAIN

253. Size of Specimens

253.1 The compression-parallel-to-grain tests shall be made on nominal 1 by 1 by 4-in. (2.5 by 2.5 by 10-cm) specimens. The actual cross-section dimensions and the length shall be measured (Section 127).

254. End Surfaces Parallel

254.1 See Section 54.

255. Speed of Testing

255.1 See Section 55.

256. Load-Compression Curves

256.1 Load-compression curves shall be taken over a central gage length of 2 in. (5 cm), and preferably on all of the specimens. Load-compression readings shall be continued until the proportional limit is well passed, as indicated by the curve.[7]

256.2 Deformations shall be read to 0.0001 in. (0.002 mm).

256.3 Figures 9 and 10 illustrate two types

of compressometers of 6-in. (15-cm) gage length that have been found satisfactory for wood testing. Similar apparatus is available for measurements of compression over a 2-in. (5-cm) gage length.

257. Position of Test Failures

257.1 See Section 57.

258. Description of Compression Failures

258.1 See Section 58.

259. Weight and Moisture Content

259.1 See Section 59.

260. Ring and Summer Wood Measurement

260.1 See Section 60.

IMPACT BENDING

261 to 270. See Sections 61 to 70, inclusive.

TOUGHNESS

271 to 276. See Sections 71 to 76, inclusive.

NOTE 12—A single-blow impact test on a small specimen is recognized as a valuable and desirable test. Several types of machines such as the Toughness, Izod, and Amsler have been used, but insufficient information is available to decide whether one procedure is superior to another, or whether the results by the different methods can be directly correlated. If the Toughness machine is used, the procedure described in Sections 71 to 76, inclusive, has been found satisfactory. To aid in standardization and to facilitate comparisons, the size of the toughness specimen has been made equal to that accepted internationally.

COMPRESSION PERPENDICULAR TO GRAIN

277 to 282. See Sections 77 to 82, inclusive.

HARDNESS

283 to 287. See Sections 83 to 87, inclusive.

SHEAR PARALLEL TO GRAIN

288 to 292. See Sections 88 to 92, inclusive.

NOTE 13—Sections 88 to 92, inclusive, describe one method of making the shear-prallel-to-grain test that has been extensively used and found satisfactory.

CLEAVAGE

293 to 298. See Sections 93 to 97, inclusive.

TENSION PARALLEL TO GRAIN

298 to 302. See Sections 98 to 102, inclu-

sive.

Note 14—One method of determining the tension-parallel-to-grain strength of wood is given in Sections 98 to 102, inclusive.

TENSION PERPENDICULAR TO GRAIN

(Optional Test)

303 to 307. See Sections 103 to 107, inclusive.

NAIL WITHDRAWAL

(Optional Test)

308 to 313. See Sections 108 to 113, inclusive.

Note 15—A recommended procedure for nail-withdrawal test is given in Sections 108 to 113, inclusive. When necessary, alternate procedures that give comparable results may be used.

SPECIFIC GRAVITY AND SHRINKAGE IN VOLUME

314 and 315. See Sections 114 and 115.

RADIAL AND TANGENTIAL SHRINKAGE

316 to 321. See Sections 116 to 121, inclusive.

MOISTURE DETERMINATION

322 to 325. See Sections 122 to 125, inclusive.

PERMISSIBLE VARIATIONS

326 to 328. See Sections 126 to 128, inclusive.

CALIBRATION

329. See Section 129.

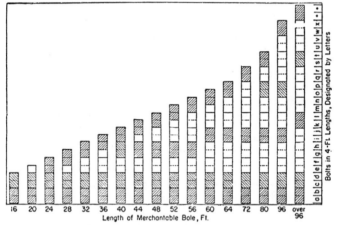

Letters *a, b, c,* etc. indicate 4-ft (1.2-m) units of the merchantable length, called bolts, and designate height in the tree.
* Indicates bolts to be taken from the top of the merchantable length, to be lettered appropriately according to their actual height in the tree.

FIG. 1   Diagram Indicating Number and Position of Bolts to be Collected from Trees Having Boles of Various Merchantable Lengths, to Evaluate Effect of Height in Tree on Properties of the Wood.

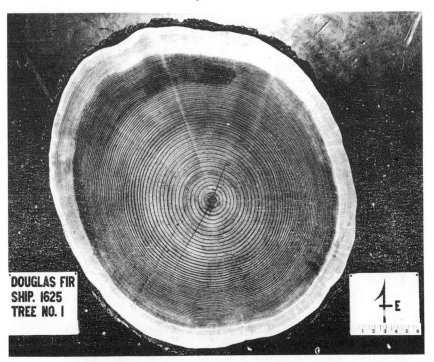

FIG. 2 Section of Log Selected for Test Material.

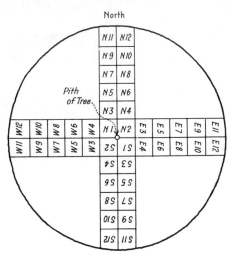

FIG. 3 Sketch Showing Method of Cutting
Up the Bolt and Marking the Sticks.

FIG. 4 Cross-Sections of Bending Specimens Showing Different Rates of Growth of Longleaf Pine (2 by 2-in. (5 by 5-cm) Specimens).

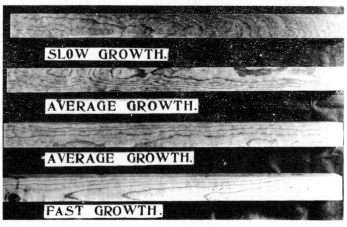

FIG. 5 Tangential Surfaces of Bending Specimens of Different Rates of Growth of Jeffrey Pine (2 by 2 by 30-in. (5 by 5 by 76-cm) Specimens).

FIG. 6   Static Bending Test Assembly Showing Method of Load Application, Specimen Supported on Rollers and Laterally Adjustable Knife Edges, and Method of Measuring Deflection at Neutral Axis by Means of Yoke and Dial Attachment. (Adjustable scale mounted on loading head is used to measure increments of deformation beyond the dial capacity.)

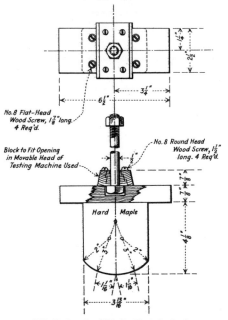

FIG. 7   Details of Bearing Block for Static
Bending Tests.

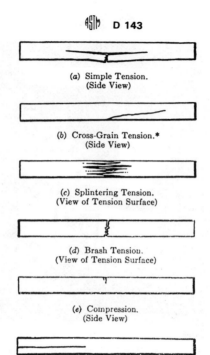

(a) Simple Tension.
(Side View)

(b) Cross-Grain Tension.*
(Side View)

(c) Splintering Tension.
(View of Tension Surface)

(d) Brash Tension.
(View of Tension Surface)

(e) Compression.
(Side View)

(f) Horizontal Shear.
(Side View)

* The term "cross grain" shall be considered to include all deviations of grain from the direction of the longitudinal axis or longitudinal edges of the specimen. It should be noted that spiral grain may be present even to a serious extent without being evident from a casual observation.

The presence of cross grain having a slope that deviates more than 1 in 20 from the longitudinal edges of the specimen shall be cause for culling the test.

FIG. 8   Types of Failures in Static Bending.

FIG. 9   Compression-Parallel-to-Grain Test Assembly Showing Method of Measuring Deformations by Means of Roller-Type Compressometer.

FIG. 10   Compression-Parallel-to-Grain Test Assembly Using an Automatic Autographic Type of Compressometer to Measure Deformations. (The wire in the lower right-hand corner connects the compressometer with the recording unit.)

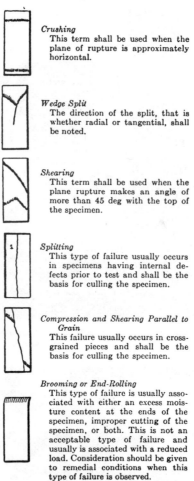

Crushing
This term shall be used when the plane of rupture is approximately horizontal.

Wedge Split
The direction of the split, that is whether radial or tangential, shall be noted.

Shearing
This term shall be used when the plane rupture makes an angle of more than 45 deg with the top of the specimen.

Splitting
This type of failure usually occurs in specimens having internal defects prior to test and shall be the basis for culling the specimen.

Compression and Shearing Parallel to Grain
This failure usually occurs in cross-grained pieces and shall be the basis for culling the specimen.

Brooming or End-Rolling
This type of failure is usually associated with either an excess moisture content at the ends of the specimen, improper cutting of the specimen, or both. This is not an acceptable type of failure and usually is associated with a reduced load. Consideration should be given to remedial conditions when this type of failure is observed.

FIG. 11 Types of Failures in Compression.

FIG. 12 Hatt-Turner Impact Machine, Illustrating
Method of Conducting Impact Bending Test.

FIG. 13 Toughness Test Assembly.

FIG. 14 Compression-Perpendicular-to-Grain Test Assembly Showing Method of Load Application and Measurement of Deformation by Means of Averaging-Type Compressometer.

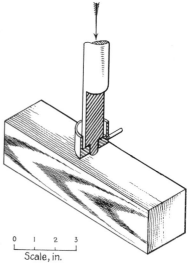

0   1   2   3
Scale, in.

FIG. 15 Diagrammatic Sketch of Method of Conducting Hardness Test.

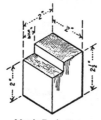

Metric Equivalents

in.	$^3/_4$	2	$2^1/_2$
cm	2	5	6

FIG. 16 Shear-Parallel-to-Grain Test Specimen.

FIG. 17 Shear-Parallel-to-Grain Test Assembly Showing Method of Load Application Through
Adjustable Seat to Provide Uniform Lateral Distribution of Load.

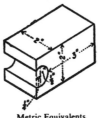

Metric Equivalents

in.	$\frac{1}{4}$	$\frac{1}{2}$	2	3
cm	0.6	1.3	5	7.6

FIG. 18 Cleavage Test Specimen.

FIG. 19   Cleavage Test Assembly.

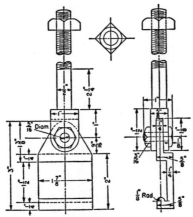

Note—Two peices included in one set:
One piece with shank 8" long.
One piece with shank 5 1/2" long.

Metric Equivalents

in.	mm	in.	mm
1/8	3	1 3/8	34
3/16	4.5	1 1/2	38
1/4	6	1 7/8	46
5/16	7.5	2	51
1/2	12.7	2 1/4	57
9/16	13.5	3	76
5/8	15	5 1/2	140
1	25.4	8	203
1 1/8	28		

Note—Two pieces included in one set:
One piece with shank 8" long.
One piece with shank 5 1/2" long.

FIG. 20 Design Details of Grips for Cleavage Test.

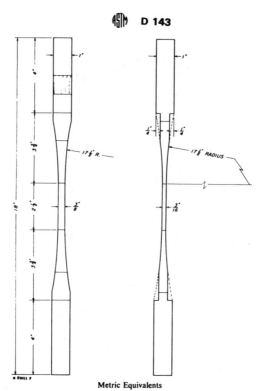

Metric Equivalents

in.	³/₁₆	¹/₄	³/₈	1	2¹/₂	3³/₄	4	17¹/₂	18
cm	0.45	0.6	0.9	2.5	6	9.5	10	44	45.7

FIG. 21 Tension-Parallel-to-Grain Test Specimen.

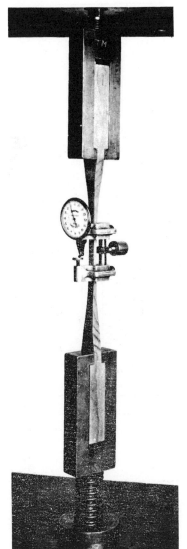

Metric Equivalents

in	$^1/_4$	$^1/_2$	1	2
cm	0.6	1.3	2.5	5

FIG. 23   Tension-Perpendicular-to-Grain Test Specimen.

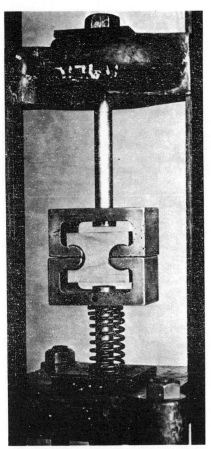

FIG. 22   Tension-Parallel-to-Grain Test Assembly Showing Grips and Use of 2-in. (5-cm) Gage Length Extensometer for Measuring Deformation.

FIG. 24   Tension-Perpendicular-to-Grain Test Assembly.

455

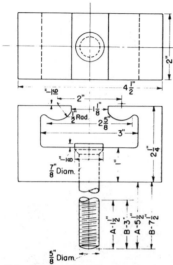

Note— Two pieces included in one set:
One marked A.
One marked B.
Scale-Full Size

Metric Equivalents

in.	cm	in.	cm
$1/16$	0.15	2	5
$1/8$	0.3	$2\,1/4$	5.7
$1/2$	1.3	$2\,5/8$	6.6
$5/8$	1.5	3	7.6
$7/8$	2	$4\,1/2$	11
1	2.5	$5\,1/2$	14
$1\,1/8$	3	$7\,1/2$	19
$1\,1/2$	3.8		

**FIG. 25   Design Details of Grips for Tension-
Perpendicular-to-Grain Test.**

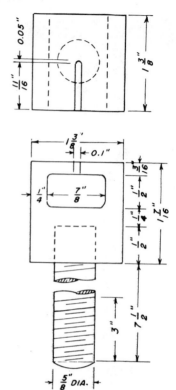

Metric Equivalents

in.	cm	in.	cm
0.05	0.12	$11/16$	1.7
0.1	0.25	$7/8$	2.
$1/16$	0.45	$1\,3/8$	3.4
$1/4$	0.6	$1\,7/16$	3.6
$1/2$	1.3	3	7.6
$5/8$	1.5	$7\,1/2$	19

**FIG. 26   Design Details of Grip for Nail
Withdrawal Test.**

FIG. 27 Nail Withdrawal Test Assembly Showing Specimen in Position for Withdrawal of Nail Driven in One End of the Specimen.

FIG. 28 Specific Gravity and Shrinkage-in-Volume Test Set-Up

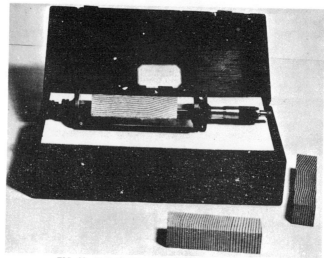

FIG. 29 Radial- and Tangential-Shrinkage Test Assembly.

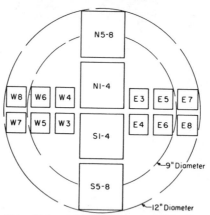

Note—Sticks cut from the *N-S* axis shall be 2½ by 2½ in. (6 by 6 cm) when green. Sticks cut from the *E-W* axis shall be 1¼ by 1¼ in. (3 by 3 cm) when green.

FIG. 30 Sketch Showing Method of Cutting Up the Bolt and Marking the Sticks for the Secondary Methods.

Ship Descr. 1

TABLE A1 Shipment Description—Field Notes

Date___*Sept. 1946*___

Shipment No.___*1625*___ Species___*Douglas-fir*___ Project No.___*259*___
State___*Oregon*___ County___*Lane*___
Local contact: National Forest___*Willamette*___ Private owner___———___
Name___————————___ Address___*Eugene, Oregon*___

A. General ecological description of locality.*
  1. Climatic factors:
    a. Precipitation in inches: average annual amount___*38.4*___; seasonal distribution—
      spring___*9.4*___, summer___*2.5*___, autumn___*10.5*___, winter___*16.0*___
    b. Temperature, degrees Fahrenheit: mean annual___*52*___, mean summer___*64*___
      mean winter___*41*___, maximum summer___*99*___, minimum winter___*−3*___
      Season between killing frosts: (dates)___*Oct. 31*___ to___*April 17*___
    c. Relative humidity: high, medium, or low in spring___*high*___ summer,___*low*___
      autumn___*high*___, winter___*high*___
    d. Prevailing wind direction:___*Westerly;*___ summer_____ winter_____
  2. Topographic factors:
    a. Character of topography: level, rolling, *mountainous*, to *precipitous*

    b. Elevations: absolute___*3,000 ft.*___, relative___*2,000 to 4,000 ft.*___
    c. Presence of streams, lakes, swamps: numerous, *few*, *permanent*, intermittent___*(Salt Creek*
      Valley)
    d. Geological history—original rock formations: (1) *igneous*, (2) sedimentary—shales, sand stones,
      limestones———————————————————————————————

    Secondary formations: *local*, glacial, alluvial, loessal___*from basalt or tuffaceous conglomerate. The*
    soils are mainly derived from weathered consolidated rocks. Stones and boulders are abundant over the
    surface and embedded in soil material.
  * Prepare page 1 of this form for each shipment. Underline descriptive words and fill in all blank spaces that
apply. Use reverse of this form for additional notes.

Ship. Descr. 2

TABLE A1 (*Continued*)

Date __*Sept. 23–25, 1946*__

Shipment No. __*1625*__ Species __*Douglas-fir*__ Project No. __*259*__
State __*Oregon*__ Co. __*Lane*__ Twp. __*22S*__ Range __*5E*__ Sec. __*22*__
Locate on *map* or sketch; __*4*__ miles to __*McCredie Springs, Oregon*__

B. Site description*
   1. Site quality class: I, *II*, III, IV, V; or age __*100 years*__, height __*170 ft.*__ of dominant trees
   2. Physiography
      a. Elevation: absolute __*3,000 ft.*__, range over area __*±50 ft.*__
      b. Surface: level, undulating; *slope* _____, upper _____, *lower* __*cove*__, degree __*15°*__; ridge, valley bottom
      c. Aspect: N, NE, E, SE, S, *SW*, W, NW
      d. Distance to streams, lakes, swamps __*Salt Creek—1⅛ mile*__
      e. Soil type: sand, sandy loam, *loam*, clay loam, clay
         U. S. Soil Survey name __*Olympic Series*__
         (1) Color __*brown*__, (2) *acid* or alkaline, (3) depth __*3 to 6 ft.*__
         (4) *boulders, stones,* or gravel __*numerous*__
      f. Soil moisture: dry, *moist*, wet, flooded.
         (1) Natural drainage: *good*, medium, poor
         (2) Depth of water table, _____ feet
C. Forest description:
   1. Origin: *natural*, artificial; *seed*, sprout, planted_____
   2. History: fires, *lumbering;* wind, snow, sleet, tapping for exudates
      a. Year: *1941 to 1945* ___, ___, __*Some pilling removed*__
   3. Pathological condition: *good*, medium, poor.
      a. Species attacked __————————__.   Injury to trunk, branch, leaf, root

   4. Type name __*Douglas-fir*__; all aged, *even aged*--------------------------------
      a.

Species *Douglas-fir*	Percent *100*	age *Av.* or range *100 years*	D.B.H. *Av.* or *range* *12 to 48 in.*

   b. No. of trees over __*10*__ in. d.b.h. per acre __*100*__ (¼ acre, 57 ft. radius; ⅛ acre, 41.7 ft. radius; ¹⁄₁₀ acre, 37.3 ft. radius).
   c. Density of crown cover: 0.1, 0.2, 0.3, 0.4, 0.5, 0.6, 0.7, *0.8*, 0.9, 1.0.
   d. Underbrush: species __*Vine maple*__

      amount --
   5. Forest floor
      a. Ground cover: weeds, grass, *bracken*, briars, vines. __*Sword fern, Salal brush.*__
      b. Litter: kind __*Dead needles and branches*__ amount __*moderate*__
      c. Raw humus or duff: depth __*1 in.*__
      d. Humus: depth __*½ in.*__
   6. Photographs: *yes*, no. Taken by __*A. K.*__
   7. Trees collected: *Nos. 1 to 10.*
* Prepare page 2 of this form for each site or forest. Underline descriptive words and fill in all blank spaces that apply. Use reverse of this form for additional notes.

Ship. Descr. 3

TABLE A1 (*Continued*)

Shipment No. _____1625_____ Species ___Douglas-fir___ Project No. ___259___

State ___Oregon___ Co. ___Lane___ Twp. ___22S___ Range ___5E___ Sec. ___22___

D. Tree description:* Tree No. ___6___

   1. Date sawed ___Sept. 24, 1946___ How removed from woods ___Truck___ Date ___Oct. 9, 1946___

   2. Tree class: Open, *dominant*, codominant, intermediate, suppressed.

   3. Origin: *seedling*, sprout. 4. Age at stump ___99___ years.

   5. D.B.H.o.b. ___25___ in. Total ht. ___165___ ft. Merch. l. ___132___ ft. Top d.i.b. ___8 in.___

   6. Stu ht. ___24___ in. Root swelling ht. ___12___ in. Av. dia. stump. i.b. ___23___ in.

   7. Crown length ___60___ ft, width ___30___ ft, projection, ft E. ___20___ W ___10___ N ___15___

      S ___15___

   8. Foliage density: thick, *medium*, thin.

   9. Lean: direction ___———___ ; 2, 4, 6 ___———___ deg. Crook: form,), (_____

 10. Locate position and size of adjacent trees and stumps on diagram of concentric circles assuming the tree to stand at the center and the intervals to be 5 (or 10) ft. Indicate d.b.h. and species by appropriate abbreviations.

Legend:
   All trees Douglas-fir except as indicated.

 11. Give approximate time of cutting any adjacent trees ___1941___

 12. Photographs of standing tree ___one___

E. Specimens shipped:

   1. Herbarium material: leaves ___———___ , fruit ___———___ , flowers ___———___

   2. Size of pieces and location in tree:

	Mark	Height above ground of lower end, ft	Length, ft	Diameters i. b., in. Bottom	Top
First section	128	2	20	23	20
Second section	129	22	20	20	19
Third section	130	58	24	18	15
Fourth section	131	106	12	12	10
	—	—	—	—	—
	—	—	—	—	—
	—	—	—	—	—

   3. Defects: Kind ___———___ Extent ___———___

   4. Photographs of sections ___———___

 * Prepare page 3 of this form for each tree. Underline descriptive words and fill in all blank spaces that apply. Use reverse of this form for additional notes.

Ship, Descr. FG

TABLE A1 (*Concluded*)
UNITED STATES DEPARTMENT OF AGRICULTURE
FOREST SERVICE
FG. Shipping, Routing, and Storing

Shipment No. _1625_

Project No. _259_

Consisting of:

Species	No. of pieces	Species	No. of species
Douglas-fir (samples from 10 trees)	*40 logs*		

Date cut _Sept. 24–25, 1946_
In state of _Oregon_ County _Lane_ Township
Manufactured at _____ Date
Shipped from _Oakridge, Oregon_ Date _Oct. 17, 1947_
Via _Southern Pacific Railroad_
In car _CNJ_ No. _89026_
      Initial
Condition when shipped _Green; ends of logs painted_

Received at _Madison, Wisconsin_ Date _Nov. 1, 1946_
Condition when received _Good_
How stored _On skids in yard._
Records: Correspondence _Pacific Northwest Forest Experiment Station (Portland, Oregon)_
      Photographs
      Remarks

ASTM **D 143**

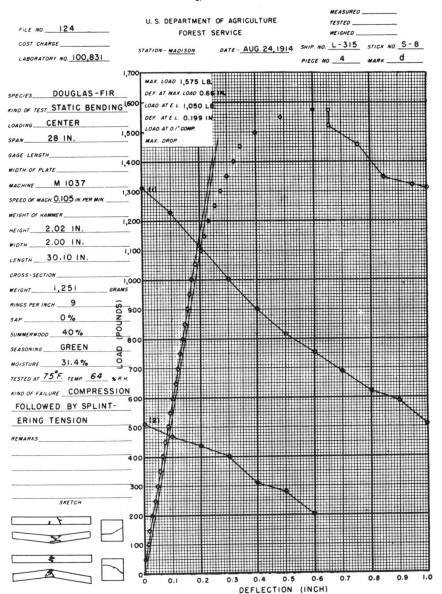

U. S. DEPARTMENT OF AGRICULTURE
FOREST SERVICE

MEASURED _____
TESTED _____
WEIGHED _____

FILE NO. __124__

COST CHARGE _____

LABORATORY NO. __100,831__

STATION - __MADISON__   DATE - __AUG. 24, 1914__   SHIP. NO. __L-315__   STICK NO. __S-8__

PIECE NO. __4__   MARK __d__

SPECIES __DOUGLAS-FIR__

KIND OF TEST __STATIC BENDING__

LOADING __CENTER__

SPAN __28 IN.__

GAGE LENGTH _____

WIDTH OF PLATE _____

MACHINE __M 1037__

SPEED OF MACH. __0.105 IN. PER MIN.__

WEIGHT OF HAMMER _____

HEIGHT __2.02 IN.__

WIDTH __2.00 IN.__

LENGTH __30.10 IN.__

CROSS-SECTION _____

WEIGHT __1,251__ GRAMS

RINGS PER INCH __9__

SAP __0 %__

SUMMERWOOD __40 %__

SEASONING __GREEN__

MOISTURE __31.4 %__

TESTED AT __75°F.__ TEMP. __64__ % R.H.

KIND OF FAILURE __COMPRESSION__
__FOLLOWED BY SPLINT-__
__ERING TENSION__

REMARKS _____

SKETCH

MAX. LOAD 1,575 LB.
DEF. AT MAX. LOAD 0.66 IN.
LOAD AT E.L. 1,050 LB.
DEF. AT E.L. 0.199 IN.
LOAD AT 0.1" COMP.
MAX. DROP

LOAD (POUNDS)

DEFLECTION (INCH)

FIG. A1 Sample Data Sheet for Static Bending Test.

463

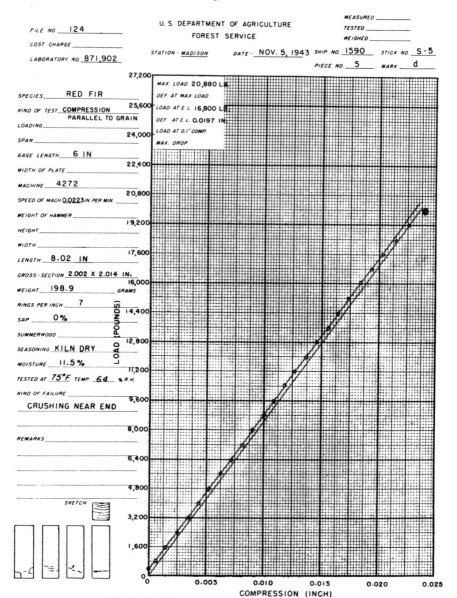

U. S. DEPARTMENT OF AGRICULTURE
FOREST SERVICE

STATION - _MADISON_   DATE - _NOV. 5, 1943_   SHIP. NO. _1590_   STICK NO. _S-5_

PIECE NO. _5_   MARK _d_

MEASURED _____
TESTED _____
WEIGHED _____

FILE NO. _124_

COST CHARGE _____

LABORATORY NO. _871,902_

SPECIES _RED FIR_

KIND OF TEST _COMPRESSION_
           PARALLEL TO GRAIN

LOADING _____

SPAN _____

GAGE LENGTH _6 IN_

WIDTH OF PLATE _____

MACHINE _4272_

SPEED OF MACH. _0.0223 IN. PER MIN._

WEIGHT OF HAMMER _____

HEIGHT _____

WIDTH _____

LENGTH _8.02 IN_

CROSS-SECTION _2.002 X 2.014 IN._

WEIGHT _198.9_ GRAMS

RINGS PER INCH _7_

SAP _0%_

SUMMERWOOD _____

SEASONING _KILN DRY_

MOISTURE _11.5%_

TESTED AT _75°F._ TEMP. _64_ % R.H.

KIND OF FAILURE _____

CRUSHING NEAR END

REMARKS _____

SKETCH

MAX. LOAD _20,880 LB._
DEF. AT MAX. LOAD
LOAD AT E.L. _16,800 LB._
DEF. AT E.L. _0.0197 IN._
LOAD AT 0.1" COMP.
MAX. DROP

FIG. A2 Sample Data Sheet for Compression-Parallel-to-Grain Test.

FIG. A3 Sample Drum Record of Impact Bending Test.

L-315   E-12   **IMPACT BENDING**   101151
(Ship. No.)   (Stick No.)   (Lab. No.)
1   C   Station MADISON   Date Aug, 20, 1914   124
(Piece No.)   (Mark)   (Project No)

Species __Douglas Fir__ Grade __Clear__ Seasoning __Green__
Rings __8__ Sap __100__ % Summerwood __30__ % Moisture __61.4__ %
Hammer __50__ lbs. Span __28 in.__ Length __29.94 in.__ Height __2.00 in.__ Width __2.00 in.__ Weight __1370 g.__

Drop No.	Head.	Def.	Def²	Set.	Drop No.	Head.	Def.	Def²	Set.		
1	1.0	0.13	0.017		11	12.0	0.50	0.250		Sp. Gr. (at test),	0.698
2	2.0	0.18	0.032		12	14.0	0.55	0.302		Sp. Gr. (oven dry),	0.432
3	3.0	0.22	0.048		13	16.0	0.62	0.384		F. S. at E. L.,	10 610
4	4.0	0.26	0.068		14	18.0	0.67	0.593		M. of E.,	1776
5	5.0	0.30	0.090		15					E. Resil.,	3.51
6	6.0	0.34	0.116		16					Max. Drop,	22 in.
7	7.0	0.36	0.130		17					d,	0.010
8	8.0	0.38	0.144		18					H	7.88
9	9.0	0.43	0.185		19					Δ	0.39
10	10.0	0.46	0.212		20						

Failure: __Compression Followed by Splintering Tension.__

FIG. A4 Sample Data and Computation Card for Impact Bending Test.

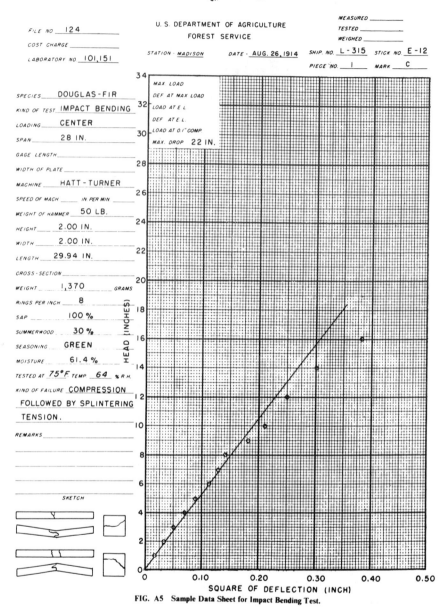

FIG. A5 **Sample Data Sheet for Impact Bending Test.**

ASTM D 143

TOUGHNESS

STATION - *Madison*

SPECIES *PACIFIC SILVER FIR*　　SHIPMENT NO. *1,651*

PROJECT *Str. IL*　　SEASONING *GREEN*　　MEASURED BY _____

COST CHARGE *01-3-005*　　SPAN *9.47 IN.*　　WEIGHED BY _____

LABORATORY NOS. *268,779A-806A* MACHINE NO. *4,715*　　TESTED BY _____

DATE *FEB. 1, 1950*　　TEMP. *75* °F.　REL. HUMIDITY *64* %

STICK NO.	LAB. NO.	DIMENSIONS L" x H" x W"	WEIGHT GM.	MOIST. %	SP. GR	POSITION OF RINGS * RAD.	POSITION OF RINGS * TANG.	WEIGHT	INITIAL ANGLE °	FINAL ANGLE °	FINAL ANGLE '	TOUGHNESS INCH - POUNDS	REMARKS
								3	45				
22E-3-d-1	785A	11.02 X .794 X .797	53.80	32.0	.357	v				32	30	143.8	
2	786A	11.02 X .789 X .790	52.54	31.8	.354		v			31	56	149.7	
22E-5-c-1	787A	11.02 X .792 X .795	53.56	35.7	.347	v				33	10	136.8	
2	788A	11.02 X .794 X .795	53.00	39.6	.333		v			34	4	127.6	

* "RAD" LOAD APPLIED TO RADIAL FACE; "TANG." LOAD APPLIED TO TANGENTIAL FACE.

FIG. A6　Sample Data and Computation Sheet for Toughness Test.

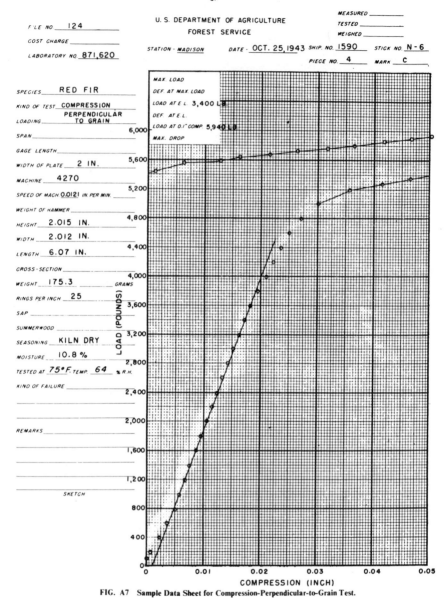

FIG. A7 Sample Data Sheet for Compression-Perpendicular-to-Grain Test.

468

HARDNESS

SPECIES _PACIFIC SILVER FIR_   SHIPMENT NO. _1,651_

PROJECT _Str. IL_   SEASONING _GREEN_   MEASURED BY _____

COST CHARGE _01-3-005_   MACHINE SPEED _0.244_   WEIGHED BY _____

LABORATORY NOS. _268,281A-290A_   MACHINE NO. _4,271_   TESTED BY _____

DATE _JAN. 31, 1951_   TEMP. _75_ °F. REL. HUMIDITY _64_ %

STICK NO.	DIMENSIONS L" x H" x W"	WEIGHT GM.	MOIST. %	SP. GR.	HARDNESS RADIAL SURFACE LB.	TANGENTIAL SURFACE LB.	END SURFACE LB.	REMARKS	SKETCH
23-N-7-d	6.02 X 1.996 X 1.994	241.3	47.5	.416	530	470	465		
					500	515	530		
			AVERAGE		515	492	498		
	AVERAGE RADIAL AND TANGENTIAL				504				
			AVERAGE						
	AVERAGE RADIAL AND TANGENTIAL								
23-E-8-C	6.04 X 1.992 X 1.992	273.3	71.1	.406	370	455	510		
					415	435	555		
			AVERAGE		392	.445	532		
	AVERAGE RADIAL AND TANGENTIAL				418				
			AVERAGE						
	AVERAGE RADIAL AND TANGENTIAL								
			AVERAGE						
	AVERAGE RADIAL AND TANGENTIAL								
			AVERAGE						
	AVERAGE RADIAL AND TANGENTIAL								
			AVERAGE						
	AVERAGE RADIAL AND TANGENTIAL								
			AVERAGE						
	AVERAGE RADIAL AND TANGENTIAL								
			AVERAGE						
	AVERAGE RADIAL AND TANGENTIAL								
			AVERAGE						
	AVERAGE RADIAL AND TANGENTIAL								

FIG. A8   Sample Data and Computation Sheet for Hardness Test.

SHEAR

STATION - *Madison*

SPECIES _PACIFIC SILVER FIR_   SHIPMENT NO. _1,651_

PROJECT _Str. IL_   SEASONING _GREEN_   MEASURED BY____

COST CHARGE _01-3-005_   MACHINE SPEED _0.0215_   WEIGHED BY____

LABORATORY NOS. _267,024A-029A_   MACHINE NO. _4,271_   TESTED BY____

DATE _JAN. 16, 1951_   TEMP. _75_ °F. REL. HUMIDITY _64_ %

STICK NO.	SHEARING SURFACE	SHEARING AREA L" x W"	MAXIMUM LOAD LB.	SHEARING STRENGTH P.S.I.	MOISTURE CONTENT %	REMARKS	SKETCH
22-N-2-d	R.	2.016 x 2.000	2770	687	40.1		
22-N-6-d	T.	2.020 x 1.998	2775	688	41.1		

FIG. A9   Sample Data and Computation Sheet for Shear-Parallel-to-Grain Test.

D 143

CLEAVAGE

STATION - *Madison*

SPECIES *PACIFIC SILVER FIR*　　SHIPMENT NO. *1,651*

PROJECT *Str. IL*　　SEASONING *GREEN*　　MEASURED BY _____

COST CHARGE *01-3-005*　　MACHINE SPEED *0.1110*　　WEIGHED BY _____

LABORATORY NOS. *267,036A-041A*　　MACHINE NO. *4269*　　TESTED BY _____

DATE *JAN. 17, 1951*　　TEMP. *75* °F.　REL. HUMIDITY *64* %

STICK NO.	CLEAVAGE SURFACE	CLEAVAGE AREA L" x w"	MAXIMUM LOAD LB.	LOAD PER INCH OF WIDTH LB.	MOISTURE CONTENT %	REMARKS	SKETCH
22-N-6-d	R.	3.03 x 2.005	315	157	36.9		
22-N-6-d	T.	3.03 x 2.007	330	165	38.5		

FIG. A10　Sample Data and Computation Sheet for Cleavage Test.

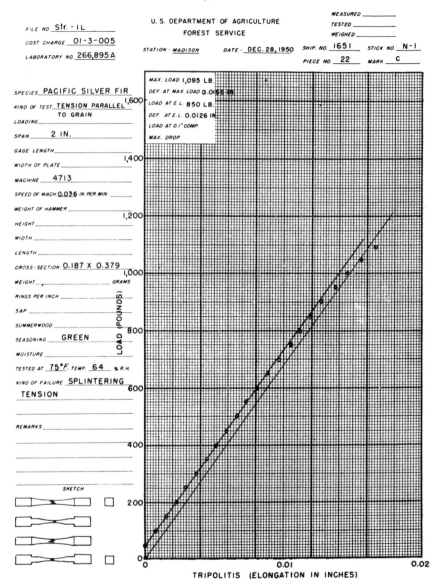

FIG. A11 Sample Data Sheet for Tension-Parallel-to-Grain Test.

472

TENSION PERPENDICULAR TO GRAIN

STATION - _Madison_

SPECIES _PACIFIC SILVER FIR_   SHIPMENT NO. _1,651_

PROJECT _Str. IL_   SEASONING _GREEN_   MEASURED BY _____

COST CHARGE _01-3-005_   MACHINE SPEED _0.1080_   WEIGHED BY _____

LABORATORY NOS. _267,048A-053A_   MACHINE NO. _4,713_   TESTED BY _____

DATE _JAN. 16, 1951_   TEMP. _75_ °F. REL. HUMIDITY _64_ %

STICK NO.	TENSION SURFACE	TENSION AREA L" x w"	MAXIMUM LOAD LB.	TENSILE STRENGTH P.S.I.	MOISTURE CONTENT %	REMARKS	SKETCH
22-N-6-d	R.	0.98 x 2.011	575	292	33.0		
22-N-6-d	T.	1.00 x 2.001	635	317	32.4		

FIG. A12 Sample Data and Computation Sheet for Tension-Perpendicular-to-Grain Test.

D 143

NAIL WITHDRAWAL

STATION - _Madison_

SPECIES _PACIFIC SILVER FIR_   SHIPMENT NO. _1,651_

PROJECT _Str. I L_   SEASONING _GREEN_   MEASURED BY _____

COST CHARGE _01-3-005_   MACHINE SPEED _0.071_   WEIGHED BY _____

LABORATORY NOS. _270,270A-278A_   MACHINE NO. _4269_   TESTED BY _____

DATE _FEB. 2, 1951_   NAILS, TYPE _7d PLAIN (SINKER) DRIVEN 1¼"_   TEMP. _75_ °F. REL. HUMIDITY _64_ %

STICK NO.	DIMENSIONS L" x H" x W"	WEIGHT GM.	MOIST. %	SP. GR.	WITHDRAWAL LOADS			REMARKS	SKETCH
					RADIAL SURFACE LB.	TANGENTIAL SURFACE LB.	END SURFACE LB.		
23-N-5-C	6.05 X 1.990 X 1.989	326.4	77.7	.468	180	205	105		
					175	200	110		
				AVERAGE	178	202	108		
23-N-7-d	602 X 1.996 X 1.994	241.3	47.5	.416	180	175	110		
					185	155	75		
				AVERAGE	182	165	92		
				AVERAGE					
				AVERAGE					
				AVERAGE					
				AVERAGE					
				AVERAGE					
				AVERAGE					
				AVERAGE					
				AVERAGE					
				AVERAGE					

FIG. A13   Sample Data and Computation Sheet for Nail Withdrawal Test.

SPECIFIC GRAVITY AND VOLUMETRIC SHRINKAGE

STATION - _Madison_
SPECIES _PACIFIC SILVER FIR_   SHIPMENT NO. _1,651_

PROJECT _Str. IL_   MEASURED BY _____

COST CHARGE _01-3-005_   WEIGHED BY _____

LABORATORY NOS. _267,060A-065A_   VOLUME BY _____

DATE _____

STICK NO.	DIMENSIONS L" x H" x W"	SEASONING	DATE	RINGS PER INCH %	SAP %	SUMMER-WOOD %	WEIGHT GM.	MOISTURE %	VOLUME C.C.	I. SPECIFIC GRAVITY	WEIGHT POUNDS PER CUBIC FOOT	VOLUMETRIC * SHRINKAGE %
22-N-4-C	6.05 X 2.001 X 2.002	GREEN	1-9-'51	18	0		201.3	34.3	393.8	.381		
		OVEN-DRY	6-19-'51				149.9	0	332.1	.451	28.1	15.7
REMARKS		AIR-DRY	6-13-'51				168.0	12.07	360.3	.416		
REMARKS												
22-S-5-C	6.03 X 2.004 X 2.001	GREEN	1-9-'51	17	0		223.1	55.5	392.0	.366		
		OVEN-DRY	6-19-'51				143.5	0	334.2	.429	26.8	14.7
REMARKS		AIR-DRY	6-13-'51				160.9	12.13	360.9	.398		
REMARKS												
REMARKS												
REMARKS												
REMARKS												
REMARKS												
REMARKS												

* BASED ON ORIGINAL VOLUME (GREEN, AIR-DRY OR KILN-DRY).   NOTE: USE BACK OF SHEET FOR CARBON IMPRESSIONS.
I. **BASED ON WEIGHT WHEN OVEN-DRY**

FIG. A14   Sample Data and Computation Sheet for Specific Gravity and Shrinkage-in-Volume Test.

SHRINKAGE - RADIAL AND TANGENTIAL

SPECIES _PACIFIC SILVER FIR_   STATION - _Madison_   SHIPMENT NO. ___1,651___

PROJECT _Str. IL_

COST CHARGE _01-3-005_   MEASURED BY _____

LABORATORY NOS. _266,857A - 864A_   WEIGHED BY _____

DATE _____

STICK NO.	NOMINAL SIZE L" X H" X W"	SHRINKAGE DIRECTION	SEASONING	DATE	RINGS PER INCH	SAP %	SUMMERWOOD %	WIDTH IN.	WEIGHT GM.	MOISTURE %	SHRINKAGE ⁴ %
22-2-cd	1 X 1 X 4	R.	GREEN	12/26/50	17	15		3.997	35.50	52.5	
			AIR-DRY								
			OVEN-DRY	4/6/51				3.784	23.28		5.3
REMARKS											
22-2-cd	1 X 1 X 4	T.	GREEN	12/26/50	12	10		3.995	40.00	77.8	
			AIR-DRY								
			OVEN-DRY	4/6/51				3.602	22.50		9.8
REMARKS											
			GREEN								
			AIR-DRY								
			OVEN-DRY								
REMARKS											
			GREEN								
			AIR-DRY								
			OVEN-DRY								
REMARKS											
			GREEN								
			AIR-DRY								
			OVEN-DRY								
REMARKS											
			GREEN								
			AIR-DRY								
			OVEN-DRY								
REMARKS											
			GREEN								
			AIR-DRY								
			OVEN-DRY								
REMARKS											
			GREEN								
			AIR-DRY								
			OVEN-DRY								
REMARKS											
			GREEN								
			AIR-DRY								
			OVEN-DRY								
REMARKS											
			GREEN								
			AIR-DRY								
			OVEN-DRY								
REMARKS											

** BASED ON GREEN WIDTH.

FIG. A15 Sample Data and Computation Sheet for Radial- and Tangential-Shrinkage Tests.

By publication of this standard no position is taken with respect to the validity of any patent rights in connection therewith, and the American Society for Testing and Materials does not undertake to insure anyone utilizing the standard against liability for infringement of any Letters Patent nor assume any such liability.

AMERICAN SOCIETY FOR TESTING AND MATERIALS
1916 Race St., Philadelphia, Pa. 19103
Reprinted from the Annual Book of ASTM Standards, Copyright ASTM
If not listed in the current combined index, will appear in the next edition.

Standard Specification for

GENERAL REQUIREMENTS FOR ROLLED STEEL PLATES, SHAPES, SHEET PILING, AND BARS FOR STRUCTURAL USE[1]

This standard is issued under the fixed designation A 6; the number immediately following the designation indicates the year of original adoption or, in the case of revision, the year of last revision. A number in parentheses indicates the year of last reapproval.

This specification has been approved for use by agencies of the Department of Defense and for listing in the DoD Index of Specifications and Standards.

1. Scope

1.1 This specification[2] covers a group of common requirements which, unless otherwise specified in the material specification, apply to rolled steel plates, shapes, sheet piling, and bars under each of the following specifications issued by the American Society for Testing and Materials:

ASTM Designation[3]	Title of Specification
A 36	Structural Steel
A 131	Structural Steel for Ships
A 242	High-Strength Low-Alloy Structural Steel
A 283	Low and Intermediate Tensile Strength Carbon Steel Plates of Structural Quality
A 284	Low and Intermediate Tensile Strength Carbon-Silicon Steel Plates for Machine Parts and General Construction
A 328	Steel Sheet Piling
A 441	High-Strength Low-Alloy Structural Manganese Vanadium Steel
A 514	High-Yield Strength, Quenched and Tempered Alloy Steel Plate Suitable for Welding
A 529	Structural Steel with 42 000 psi (290 MPa) Minimum Yield Point (½ in. (12.7 mm) Maximum Thickness)
A 572	High-Strength Low-Alloy Columbium-Vanadium Steels of Structural Quality
A 573	Structural Carbon Steel Plates of Improved Toughness
A 588	High-Strength Low-Alloy Structural Steel with 50 000 psi Minimum Yield Point to 4 in. Thick
A 633	Normalized High-Strength Low-Alloy Structural Steel
A 656	High-Strength Low-Alloy, Hot-Rolled, Structural Vanadium-Aluminum-Nitrogen Steel
A 678	Quenched and Tempered Carbon Steel Plates for Structural Applications
A 690	High-Strength Low-Alloy Steel H-Piles and Sheet Piling for Use in Marine Environments
A 699	Low-Carbon Manganese-Molybdenum-Columbium Alloy Steel Plates. Shapes. and Bars
A 709	Structural Steel for Bridges
A 710	Low-Carbon Age-Hardening Nickel-Copper-Chromium-Molybdenum-Columbium and Nickel-Copper-Columbium Alloy Steels
A 769	Electric Resistance Welded Steel Shapes

1.2 Appendix X1 lists permissible variations in dimensions and weight in SI (metric) units. The values listed are not exact conversions of the values in Tables 1 through 31 but are, instead, rounded or rationalized values which are more nearly consistent with the values in specifications utilizing metric units. Conformance to Appendix X1 is mandatory only when so agreed between the purchaser and the manufacturer. Furthermore, publication herein of such tolerances does not infer that individual manufacturers will accept such requirements.

1.3 Appendix X2 describes the production and some of the characteristics of coiled product from which structural plate may be produced.

1.4 Annex A1 lists the dimensions of some shape profiles. Conformance to the SI units for dimensions and mass (Note 1) is not mandatory unless otherwise agreed prior to acceptance of the order by the manufacturer.

NOTE 1—The term "weight" is used when U.S. customary units are the standard; however, under SI, the preferred term is "mass."

---

[1] This specification is under the jurisdiction of ASTM Committee A-1 on Steel, Stainless Steel and Related Alloys, and is the direct responsibility of Subcommittee A01.02 on Structural Steel.

Current edition approved April 25 and Sept. 2, 1980. Published November 1980. Originally published as A 6 – 49 T. Last previous edition A 6 – 79b.

[2] For ASME Boiler and Pressure Vessel Code applications see related Specification SA-6 in Section II of that Code.

[3] *Annual Book of ASTM Standards*, Part 4.

1.5 This specification also covers a group of supplementary requirements that are applicable to several of the above specifications as indicated therein. These are provided for use when additional testing or inspection is desired and apply only when specified individually by the purchaser in the order.

1.6 In case of any conflict in requirements, the requirements of the individual material specification shall prevail over those of this general specification.

1.7 The purchaser may specify additional requirements which do not negate any of the provisions of this general specification or of the individual material specifications. Such additional requirements, the acceptance of which are subject to negotiation with the supplier, must be included in the order information (see Section 4).

NOTE 2—The values stated in inch-pound units are to be regarded as the standard.

2. Applicable Documents

2.1 *ASTM Standards:*

A 370 Methods and Definitions for Mechanical Testing of Steel Products[4]

A 673 Specification for Sampling Procedure for Impact Testing of Structural Steel[3]

A 700 Recommended Practices for Packaging, Marking, and Loading Methods for Steel Products for Domestic Shipment[5]

E 30 Chemical Analysis of Steel, Cast Iron, Open-Hearth Iron, and Wrought Iron[6]

E 59 Sampling Steel and Iron for Determination of Chemical Composition[6]

E 112 Estimating the Average Grain Size of Metals[7]

E 350 Chemical Analysis of Carbon Steel, Low-Alloy Steel, Silicon Electrical Steel, Ingot Iron, and Wrought Iron[6]

2.2 *American Welding Society Standards:*[8]

A5.1 Mild Steel Covered Arc-Welding Electrodes

A5.5 Low-Alloy Steel Covered Arc-Welding Electrodes

2.3 *Military Standard:*

MIL-STD-129 Marking for Shipment and Storage[9]

MIL-STD-163 Steel Mill Products Preparation for Shipment and Storage[9]

2.4 *Federal Standard:*

Fed. Std. No. 123 Marking for Shipments (Civil Agencies)[9]

3. Description of Terms

3.1 *Plates* (other than floor plates or coiled product)—Flat hot-rolled steel classified as follows:

3.1.1 *When Ordered to Thickness:*

3.1.1.1 Over 8 in. (200 mm) in width and 0.230 in. (6 mm) or over in thickness.

3.1.1.2 Over 48 in. (1220 mm) in width and 0.180 in. (5 mm) or over in thickness.

3.1.2 *When Ordered to Weight:*

3.1.2.1 Over 8 in. (200 mm) in width and 9.62 lb/ft^2 (47.1 kg/m^2) or heavier.

3.1.2.2 Over 48 in. (1220 mm) in width and 7.53 lb/ft^2 (39.2 kg/m^2) or heavier.

3.1.3 Slabs, sheet bars, and skelp, though frequently falling in the foregoing size ranges, are not classed as plates.

3.1.4 Coiled product is excluded from qualification to this specification until cut to length (see 5.3.2).

3.2 *Shapes (Flanged Sections):*

3.2.1 *Structural-Size Shapes*—Rolled flanged sections having at least one dimension of the cross section 3 in. (75 mm) or greater. Structural shape size groupings used for tensile property classification are listed in Table A.

3.2.2 *Bar Size Shapes*—Rolled flanged sections having a maximum dimension of the cross section less than 3 in. (75 mm).

3.2.3 *"W" Shapes* are doubly-symmetric wide-flange shapes used as beams or columns whose inside flange surfaces are substantially parallel. A shape having essentially the same nominal weight and dimensions as a "W" shape listed in the tabulation but whose inside flange surfaces are not parallel may also be considered a "W" shape having the same nomenclature as the tabulated shape, provided its average flange thickness is essentially the same as the flange thickness of the "W" shape.

3.2.4 *"HP" Shapes* are wide-flange shapes generally used as bearing piles whose flanges and webs are of the same nominal thickness and whose depth and width are essentially the same.

[4] *Annual Book of ASTM Standards*, Parts 1, 2, 3, 4, 5, and 10.

[5] *Annual Book of ASTM Standards*, Parts 1, 3, 4, and 5.

[6] *Annual Book of ASTM Standards*, Part 12.

[7] *Annual Book of ASTM Standards*, Part 11.

[8] Available from American Welding Society, 2501 North West 7th St., Miami, Fla. 33125.

[9] Available from the procuring activity or as directed by the contracting office or from the Naval Publications and Forms Center, 5801 Tabor Ave., Philadelphia, Pa. 19120.

3.2.5 *"S" Shapes* are doubly-symmetric shapes produced in accordance with dimensional standards adopted in 1896 by the Association of American Steel Manufacturers for American Standard beam shapes. The essential part of these standards is that the inside flange surfaces of American Standard beam shapes have approximately 16⅔ % slope.

3.2.6 *"M" Shapes* are doubly-symmetric shapes that cannot be classified as "W," "S," or "HP" shapes.

3.2.7 *"C" Shapes* are channels produced in accordance with dimensional standards adopted in 1896 by the Association of American Steel Manufacturers for American Standard channels. The essential part of these standards is that the inside flange surfaces of American Standard channels have approximately a 16⅔ % slope.

3.2.8 *"MC" Shapes* are channels that cannot be classified as "C" shapes.

3.2.9 *"L" Shapes* are equal-leg and unequal-leg angles.

3.3 *Sheet Piling*—Steel sheet piling consists of rolled sections that can be interlocked, forming a continuous wall when individual pieces are driven side by side.

3.4 *Bars*—Rounds, squares, and hexagons, of all sizes; flats ¹³⁄₆₄ in. (0.2031 in.) (5.16 mm) and over in specified thickness, not over 6 in. (150 mm) in specified width; and flats 0.230 in. (5.84 mm) and over in specified thickness, over 6 to 8 in. (200 mm) incl, in specified width.

3.5 *Exclusive*—When used in relation to ranges, as for ranges of thickness in the tables of permissible variations in dimensions, the term is intended to exclude only the greater value of the range. Thus, a range from 60 to 72 in. (1524 to 1829 mm) exclusive includes 60, but does not include 72.

3.6 *Rimmed Steel*—Steel containing sufficient oxygen to give a continuous evolution of carbon monoxide while the ingot is solidifying, resulting in a case or rim of metal virtually free of voids.

3.7 *Semi-killed Steel*—Incompletely deoxidized steel containing sufficient oxygen to form enough carbon monoxide during solidification to offset solidification shrinkage.

3.8 *Capped Steel*—Rimmed steel in which the rimming action is limited by an early capping operation. Capping may be carried out mechanically by using a heavy metal cap on a bottle-top mold or it may be carried out chemically by an addition of aluminum or ferrosilicon to the top of the molten steel in an open-top mold.

3.9 *Killed Steel*—Steel deoxidized, either by addition of strong deoxidizing agents or by vacuum treatment, to reduce the oxygen content to such a level that no reaction occurs between carbon and oxygen during solidification.

3.10 *Groupings for Tensile Property Classification*—In some of the material specifications, the tensile property requirements vary for different sizes of shapes due to mass effect, etc. For the convenience of those using the specifications, the various sizes of shapes have been divided into groups based on section thickness at the standard tension test location (webs of beams, channels, and zees; legs of angles; and stems of tees). The material specifications designate shape sizes by reference to the group designations. The groupings are shown in Table A.

4. Ordering Information

4.1 Orders shall include the following information, as necessary, to adequately describe the desired material:

4.1.1 ASTM designation and grade, etc. (if applicable),

4.1.2 Name of material (shapes, plates, bars),

4.1.3 Shape designation, or size and thickness or diameter, and length,

4.1.4 Condition, if other than as-rolled (normalized, etc.),

4.1.5 Either plates from coil or discrete cut lengths of flat product may be supplied, unless one is specifically excluded on the order (see Appendix X2).

4.1.6 Should the processor (5.3.2) intend to qualify plates cut from a coiled product as structural plates, the order to the manufacturer (5.3.1) should state the intended ASTM specification number, grade, and type.

4.1.7 Supplementary requirements, if any, including any additional information called for in the supplementary requirements.

5. Manufacture

5.1 Unless otherwise specified in the material specification, the steel shall be made by the open-hearth, basic-oxygen, or electric-furnace process. Additional refining by vacuum-arc-remelt (VAR) or electroslag-remelt (ESR) is permitted.

5.2 Plates are produced in either discrete cut lengths of flat product or from coils.

5.2.1 Plates produced from coil means plates that have been cut to individual lengths from a coiled product and are furnished without heat treatment. For the purposes of this paragraph, stress relieving is not considered to be a heat treatment.

5.2.2 Plates that are heat treated (except stress relieving) after decoiling shall be considered to be discrete cut lengths of flat product.

5.3 When plates are produced from coils:

5.3.1 The manufacturer directly controls one or more of the operations (that is, melting, rolling, coiling, etc.), that affect the chemical composition or the mechanical properties, or both, of the material.

5.3.2 The processor decoils, cuts to length, and marks; performs and certifies tests, examinations, repairs, inspection, or operations not intended to affect the properties of the material. The processor may subsequently heat treat the plate (see Section 6). Specific sections of this specification for which the processor is responsible are 9, 10, 11, 12, 13, 14, 15, 18, and 19.

5.3.3 When part of a heat is rolled into discrete plates of flat product and the balance of the heat into coiled product, each part must be tested separately.

6. Heat Treatment

6.1 When material is required to be heat treated, the heat treatment may be performed either by the manufacturer, processor, or fabricator unless otherwise specified in the material specification.

6.2 When heat treatment is required and is to be performed by the fabricator, the order shall so state.

6.3 When heat treatment is to be performed by the manufacturer or processor, the material shall be heat treated as specified in the material specification. The purchaser may specify the heat treatment to be used provided it is not in conflict with the requirements of the material specification.

6.4 When normalizing is to be performed by the fabricator, it may be accomplished by heating uniformly for hot forming. The temperature to which the plates are heated for hot forming

shall not significantly exceed the normalizing temperature.

6.5 When no heat treatment is required, the manufacturer or processor may, at his option, heat treat the plates by normalizing, stress relieving, or normalizing and then stress relieving to meet the material specification.

7. Chemical Analysis

7.1 *Heat Analysis*—An analysis of each heat shall be made by the manufacturer to determine the percentage of carbon, manganese, phosphorus, sulfur, and any other elements specified or restricted by the applicable specification. This analysis shall be made from a test sample preferably taken during the pouring of the heat. The heat analysis shall be reported to the purchaser or his representative and shall conform to the heat analysis requirements of the applicable specification.

7.1.1 When vacuum-arc-remelting or electroslag remelting is used, a heat is defined as all the ingots remelted from a single primary melt. The heat analysis shall be obtained from one remelted ingot, or the product of one remelted ingot, of each primary melt providing the heat analysis of the primary melt meets the heat analysis requirements of the material specification. If the heat analysis of the primary melt does not meet the heat analysis requirements of the material specification, one test sample shall be taken from the product of each remelted ingot. In either case, the analyses so obtained from the remelted material shall conform to the heat analysis requirements of the applicable specification.

7.2 *Product Analysis*—The purchaser may analyze finished material representing each heat. Sampling shall be in accordance with Method E 59. The chemical composition thus determined shall conform to the requirements of the product specification subject to the product analysis tolerances in Table B. If a range is specified, the determinations of any element in a heat may not vary both above and below the specified range. Rimmed or capped steel is characterized by a lack of homogeneity in its composition, especially for the elements carbon, phosphorus, and sulfur; therefore, the limitations for these elements shall not be applicable unless misapplication is clearly indicated.

7.3 *Referee Analysis*—For referee purposes, Methods E 30 or E 350 shall be used.

8. Metallurgical Structure

8.1 When a fine austenitic grain size is specified, the steel shall have a grain size number of 5 or finer as determined by the McQuaid-Ehn test. Determination shall be in accordance with Plate IV of Methods E 112, by carburizing for 8 h at 1700°F (925°C). Conformance to this grain size of 70 % of the grains in the area examined shall constitute the basis of acceptance. One test per heat shall be made.

9. Quality

9.1 *General*—The material shall be free of injurious defects and shall have a workmanlike finish.

9.2 *Plate Conditioning:*

9.2.1 Plates may be conditioned by the manufacturer or processor for the removal of imperfections or depressions on the top and bottom surfaces by grinding, provided the area ground is well faired without abrupt changes in contour and the grinding does not reduce the thickness of the plate by (*1*) more than 7 % under the nominal thickness for plates ordered to weight per square foot or per square metre, but in no case more than ⅛ in. (3 mm); or (*2*) below the permissible minimum thickness for plates ordered to thickness in inches or millimetres.

9.2.2 Imperfections on the top and bottom surfaces of plates may be removed by chipping, grinding, or arc-air gouging and then by depositing weld metal (see 9.5), subject to the following limiting conditions:

9.2.2.1 The chipped, ground, or gouged area shall not exceed 2 % of the area of the surface being conditioned.

9.2.2.2 After removal of any imperfections preparatory to welding, the thickness of the plate at any location must not be reduced by more than 30 % of the nominal thickness of the plate. (Specification A 131 restricts the reduction in thickness to 20 % maximum.)

9.2.3 The edges of plates may be conditioned by the manufacturer or processor to remove injurious imperfections by grinding, chipping, or arc-air gouging and welding (see 9.5). Prior to welding, the depth of depression, measured from the plate edge inward, shall be limited to the thickness of the plate, with a maximum

depth of 1 in. (25 mm).

9.3 *Structural Size Shapes, Bar Size Shapes, and Steel Sheet Piling Conditioning:*

9.3.1 These products may be conditioned by the manufacturer for the removal of injurious imperfections or surface depressions by grinding, or chipping and grinding, provided the area ground is well faired without abrupt changes in contour and the depression does not extend below the rolled surface by more than (*1*) ¹⁄₃₂ in. (1 mm), for material less than ⅜ in. (10 mm) in thickness; (*2*) ¹⁄₁₆ in. (2 mm), for material ⅜ to 2 in. (50 mm) inclusive in thickness; or (*3*) ⅛ in. (3 mm), for material over 2 in. in thickness.

9.3.2 Imperfections that are greater in depth than the limits previously listed may be removed and then weld metal deposited (see 9.5), subject to the following limiting conditions:

9.3.2.1 The total area of the chipped or ground surface of any piece prior to welding shall not exceed 2 % of the total surface area of that piece.

9.3.2.2 The reduction of thickness of the material resulting from removal of imperfections prior to welding shall not exceed 30 % of the nominal thickness at the location of the imperfection, nor shall the depth of depression prior to welding exceed 1¼ in. (32 mm) in any case except as noted in 9.3.2.3.

9.3.2.3 The toes of angles, beams, channels, and zees and the stems and toes of tees may be conditioned by grinding, chipping, or arc-air gouging and welding (see 9.5). Prior to welding, the depth of depression, measured from the toe inward, shall be limited to the thickness of the material at the base of the depression, with a maximum depth limit of ½ in. (13 mm).

9.3.2.4 The interlock of any sheet piling section may be conditioned by welding (see 9.5) and grinding to correct or build up the interlock at any location not to exceed 2 % of the total surface area.

9.4 *Bar Conditioning:*

9.4.1 Bars may be conditioned by the manufacturer for the removal of imperfections by grinding, chipping, or some other means, provided the conditioned area is well faired and the affected sectional area is not reduced by more than the permissible variations prescribed in the applicable tables designated in Section 13.

9.4.2 Imperfections that are greater in depth than the limitations of 9.4.1 may be removed by chipping or grinding and then by depositing weld metal (see 9.5) subject to the following limiting conditions:

9.4.2.1 The total area of the chipped or ground surface of any piece, prior to welding, shall not exceed 2 % of the total surface area of the piece.

9.4.2.2 The reduction of sectional dimension of a round, square, or hexagon bar, or the reduction in thickness of a flat bar, resulting from removal of an imperfection, prior to welding, shall not exceed 5 % of the nominal dimension or thickness at the location of the imperfection.

9.4.2.3 For the edges of flat bars, the depth of the conditioning depression prior to welding shall be measured from the edge inward and shall be limited to a maximum depth equal to the thickness of the flat bar or ½ in. (13 mm), whichever is less.

9.5 *Repair by Welding:*

9.5.1 *Steels Other Than Quenched and Tempered:*

9.5.1.1 All welding shall be performed by competent welders using low hydrogen welding electrodes conforming to both the proper series and latest issue of AWS Specification A5.1, or AWS Specification A5.5. The electrodes shall be protected from moisture during storage and use.

9.5.1.2 The manufacturer or processor shall establish and follow documented welding procedures that are appropriate for the material being welded.

9.5.2 *Quenched and Tempered Steels:*

9.5.2.1 When so specified in the purchase order, prior approval for repair by welding shall be obtained from the purchaser.

9.5.2.2 The manufacturer or processor shall establish and follow the documented welding procedures that are appropriate for the material being welded. When specified on the purchase order, such procedures shall be subject to approval by the purchaser. The welding operator shall be competent to follow such procedures.

9.5.2.3 After removal of any imperfections and prior to welding, the cavity shall be examined by a magnetic particle method or a liquid penetrant method to ensure that the imperfection has been completely removed. When magnetic particle examination is employed, the cavity shall be examined parallel and normal to the length of the cavity.

9.5.2.4 Electrodes shall be protected from moisture during storage and use.

9.5.2.5 Electrodes and base metal shall be free of hydrogen-producing contaminants such as oil, grease, or other organic materials. The base metal shall be maintained in a dry condition during welding.

9.5.2.6 For material in its heat-treated condition, all welding shall be performed using either the shielded metal-arc (SMA) or gas metal-arc (GMA) process. For SMA welding, low hydrogen electrodes conforming to the latest edition of AWS Specification A5.5 shall be employed. The electrodes shall be selected to provide weld-metal deposits compatible with the minimum specified base metal properties. Moisture content shall not exceed the tolerable level for the steel being welded. For GMA welding, any composition that provides weld-metal deposits compatible with the minimum specified base metal properties may be employed. Gases used for shielding shall be of welding quality. When weld repairs by either process are to be post-weld heat treated, special care must be exercised in selection of electrodes to avoid those compositions which embrittle as a result of such heat treatment.

9.5.2.7 The heat-affected zone of quenched and tempered alloy steels may be affected adversely by excessive heat input or excessive preheating, or both. Similarly, insufficient preheat and heat input in the welding of quenched and tempered alloy steels may result in undesirable defects. Therefore, suitable combinations of heat input and preheat (including interpass temperature) shall be employed.

9.5.2.8 For material that is to be quenched and tempered after repair-welding, electrodes for SMA or GMA welding shall be selected to provide weld deposits whose mechanical properties after heat treatment meet the requirements of the base metal.

9.5.2.9 Repairs on material that is subsequently thermally treated at the mill shall be examined after heat treatment; repairs on material that is not subsequently thermally treated at the mill shall be examined no sooner than 48 h after welding. In either case the repaired area shall be examined by one of the methods and in the same manner prescribed in 9.5.2.3.

9.5.2.10 The location of weld repairs shall be marked on the finished piece.

9.5.3 *Repair Quality*—The welds and adjacent heat-affected zone shall be sound and free of cracks, the weld metal being thoroughly fused to all surfaces and edges without undercutting or overlap. Any visible cracks, porosity, lack of fusion, or undercut in any layer shall be removed prior to deposition of the succeeding layer. Weld metal shall project at least ¹⁄₁₆ in. (2 mm) above the rolled surface after welding, and the projecting metal shall be removed by chipping or grinding, or both, to make it flush with the rolled surface, and to produce a workmanlike finish.

9.5.4 *Inspection of Repair*—The manufacturer or processor shall maintain an inspection program to inspect the work to see that:

9.5.4.1 Imperfections have been completely removed.

9.5.4.2 The limitations specified above have not been exceeded.

9.5.4.3 Established welding procedures have been followed, and

9.5.4.4 Any weld deposit is of acceptable quality as defined above.

10. Test Methods

10.1 All tests shall be conducted in accordance with Methods and Definitions A 370.

11. Tension Tests

11.1 *Condition*—Test specimens shall be prepared for testing from the material in its delivered condition except that test specimens for heat-treated material may be from a separate piece of full thickness or full section from the same heat similarly treated.

11.2 *Orientation*—For plates wider than 24 in. (610 mm), test specimens shall be taken such that the longitudinal axis of the specimen is transverse to the final direction of rolling of the plate. Test specimens for all other products shall be taken such that the longitudinal axis of the specimen is parallel to the final direction of rolling.

11.3 *Location:*

11.3.1 *Plates*—Test specimens shall be taken from a corner of the plate.

11.3.2 *Shapes*—Test specimens shall be selected from the webs of beams, channels, and zees, from the legs of angles and bulb angles, and from the stems of rolled tees.

11.3.3 *Bars:*

11.3.3.1 Test specimens for bars to be used for pins and rollers less than 3 in. (75 mm) in diameter shall be taken so that the axis is midway, if practicable, between the center and the surface. Test specimens for pins and rollers 3 in. and over in diameter should be taken so that the axis is 1 in. (25 mm) from the surface.

11.3.3.2 Test specimens for bars other than those covered by 11.3.3.1 shall be taken as

specified in Supplement I of Methods and Definitions A 370.

11.4 *Number of Tests*—Except as specified in 11.4.1, two tests shall be made from each heat and each strength gradation, where applicable, with the test coupons being taken from different as-produced pieces. However, for material 2 in. (50 mm) and under in thickness, when the material from one heat and one strength gradation differs ³⁄₈ in. (10 mm) or more in thickness, one test shall be made from at least the thickest and the thinnest material rolled in that strength gradation regardless of weight represented. For material over 2 in. thick, when the material from heat and strength differs 1 in. (25 mm) or more in thickness, one test shall be made from at least the thickest and the thinnest material rolled in that strength gradation that is more than 2 in. thick regardless of the weight represented.

11.4.1 *Plates Provided from Coils:*

11.4.1.1 When plates are provided from coils, tension tests shall be taken from not less than two coils from each heat and each strength gradation where applicable, if more than one coil from the heat is to be qualified by the tension tests. If only one coil from a heat is to be qualified, tests need only be taken from the coil to be qualified.

11.4.1.2 When the material from one heat and one strength gradation differs ¹⁄₁₆ in. (1.6 mm) or more in thickness, tests shall be made from both the thickest and the thinnest material rolled in that strength gradation regardless of the number of coils represented.

11.4.1.3 Two tension tests shall be taken from each coil tested. One tension-test specimen shall be taken immediately prior to the first plate produced to the qualifying specification and a second test shall be taken from the approximate center lap. If, during decoiling, the amount of material decoiled is less than that required to reach the approximate center lap, the second test for the qualification of a particular shipment may be taken from a location adjacent to the end of the innermost portion shipped. For successive shipments from the same coil, an additional test shall be taken adjacent to the innermost portion shipped until a test is obtained from the approximate center lap.

11.5 *Preparation:*

11.5.1 *Plates:*

11.5.1.1 Test specimens for plates under ³⁄₄ in. (19 mm) in thickness shall conform to the requirements of Fig. 4 of Methods and Definitions A 370, *except that the ¼-in. (6.35-mm) wide subsize specimen is not permitted.*

11.5.1.2 Except as required in 11.5.1.3, test specimens for plates ¾ in. (19 mm) and over in thickness shall conform to the requirements for either the 1½-in. (40-mm) or ½-in. (12.5-mm) wide specimen of Fig. 4 of Methods and Definitions A 370, or to the requirements for the ½-in. diameter specimen of Fig. 5 of A 370.

11.5.1.3 Test specimens for quenched and tempered plates over 1½ in. (38 mm) in thickness shall conform to the requirements for the ½-in. (12.5-mm) diameter specimen of Fig. 5 of Methods and Definitions A 370.

11.5.1.4 When the 0.500-in. (13-mm) diameter specimen (Fig. 5 of A 370) is used, the axis of the specimen shall be located as near as practical midway between the center of thickness and the top or bottom surface of the plate.

11.5.2 *Shapes:*

11.5.2.1 Test specimens for materials under ¾ in. (19 mm) in thickness shall conform to the requirements of Fig. 4 of Methods and Definitions A 370, *except that the ¼-in. (6.35-mm) wide subsize specimen is not permitted.*

11.5.2.2 Test specimens for material ¾ in. (19 mm) and over in thickness shall conform to the requirements of either the 1½-in. (40-mm) wide or the ½-in. (12.5-mm) wide specimen of Fig. 4 of Methods and Definitions A 370, or to the requirements for the ½-in. diameter specimen of Fig. 5 of A 370.

(*a*) When the ½-in. (12.5-mm) diameter specimen of Fig. 5 of Methods and Definitions A 370 is used, the axis of the specimen shall be located as near as practical midway between the center of thickness and an adjacent surface of the shape.

(*b*) Test specimens for material over 1½ in. (38 mm) in thickness may be machined to a thickness of at least ¾ in. (19 mm) for a length of at least 9 in. (230 mm).

11.5.3 *Bars:*

11.5.3.1 Except as otherwise provided below, test specimens for bars shall be in accordance with Supplement I of Methods and Definitions A 370.

11.5.3.2 Except as provided in 11.5.3.5, test specimens for bars under ¾ in. (19 mm) in thickness may conform to the requirements of Fig. 4 of Methods and Definitions A 370, *except that the ¼-in. (6.35-mm) wide subsize specimen is not permitted.*

11.5.3.3 Except as provided in 11.5.3.5, test specimens for bars ¾ in. (19 mm) and over in thickness or diameter may conform to the requirements for either the 1½-in. (40-mm) or ½-in. (12.5-mm) wide specimen of Fig. 4 of Methods and Definitions A 370, or to the requirements for the ½-in. diameter specimen of Fig. 5 of A 370.

11.5.3.4 Test specimens for bars other than those to be used for pins and rollers may be machined to a thickness or diameter of at least ¾ in. (19 mm) for a length of at least 9 in. (230 mm).

11.5.3.5 Test specimens for bars to be used for pins and rollers shall conform to the requirements of Fig. 5 of Methods and Definitions A 370 for the ½-in. (12.5-mm) diameter specimen.

11.6 *Elongation Requirement Adjustments:*

11.6.1 Due to the specimen geometry effect encountered when using the rectangular tension test specimen for testing thin plates, adjustments in elongation requirements must be provided. For plates under 0.312 in. (7.92 mm) in thickness, a deduction of 1.25 % from the specified percentage of elongation shall be made for each decrease of 0.031 in. (0.79 mm) of the specified thickness under 0.312 in.

11.6.2 Due to the inherently lower elongation that is obtainable in material of thicker plates, adjustments in elongation requirements must be provided. For plates over 3.5 in. (88.9 mm) in thickness, a deduction of 0.5 % from the specified percentage of elongation in 2 in. (50 mm) shall be made for each increase of 0.5 in. (13 mm) of the specified thickness over 3.5 in. This deduction shall not exceed 3 %.

11.6.3 A characteristic of certain types of alloy steels is a local disproportionate increase in the degree of necking down or contraction of the specimens under tension test, resulting in a decrease in the percentage of elongation as the gage length is increased. The effect is not so pronounced in the thicker plates. On such material, when so stated in the material specification for plates up to ¾ in. (19 mm), inclusive, in thickness, if the percentage of elongation of an 8-in. or 200-mm gage length test specimen falls not more than 3 % below the amount prescribed, the elongation shall be considered satisfactory provided the percentage of elongation in 2 in. (50 mm) across the break is not less than 25 %.

12. Identification of Material

12.1 *Plates*—Each plate shall be steel die-stamped, marked, or stenciled in one place with heat number, manufacturer's name, brand, or trademark, size and thickness. For plates provided from coils, the processor identity rather than that of the manufacturer shall be used. However, in the case of secured lifts of plates ⅜ in. (10 mm) (or of material specified for bridge construction ⁵⁄₁₆ in. (8 mm)) and under in thickness of all sizes, and of plates 36 in. (915 mm) and under in width in all thicknesses, such markings may be placed on only the top piece of each lift, or may be shown on a substantial tag attached to each lift, unless otherwise specified. See also 12.5.

12.2 *Shapes*—Shapes shall be marked with the heat number, size of section, length, and mill identification marks on each piece. Either the manufacturer's name, brand, or trademark shall be shown in raised letters at intervals along the length. Small shapes with the greatest cross-sectional dimension not greater than 6 in. (150 mm) may be bundled for shipment with each lift marked or tagged showing the previously listed identification. See also 12.5.

12.3 *Steel Sheet Piling*—Steel sheet piling shall be marked with the heat number, size of section, length, and mill identification marks on each piece. Either the manufacturer's name, brand, or trademark shall be shown in raised letters at intervals along the length.

12.4 *Bars*—Bars in secured lifts shall be identified with a tag showing purchaser's order number, grade or specification, size, length, weight of lift, and heat number. Bars are not required to be die-stamped.

12.5 *Specification Identification*—In addition to the requirements of 12.1 or 12.2 material ordered to one of the specifications and grades for which a color code is given in 12.5.3 shall be marked with the applicable specification number and grade. Color identification shall be applied as stated in 12.5.1, 12.5.2, and 12.5.3.

12.5.1 *Plates*—When specified by the purchaser, each plate (except for plates in secured lifts) shall be marked with the color designated in 12.5.3 along one edge or on the rolled surface within 12 in. (300 mm) of the heat number identification. Plates in secured lifts may have the color identification marked with a vertical stripe for the full height of the lift. Each plate in the lift shall be marked by this stripe. Color markings shall be distinct and of sufficient size to be clearly visible.

12.5.2 *Shapes*—Each structural shape or lift shall be marked with the color designated in 12.5.3 on one cut end or across the rolled face

of one flange or leg, adjacent to one cut end. Color markings shall be distinct and of sufficient size to be clearly visible.

12.5.3 *Colors*—The following color system shall be used to identify the individual specifications:

A 242	blue
A 283 (Grade D)	orange
A 441	yellow
A 514	red
A 529	black
A 572 Grade 42	green and white
A 572 Grade 50	green and yellow
A 572 Grade 60	green and gray
A 572 Grade 65	green and blue
A 588	blue and yellow
A 709 Grade 50	green and yellow
A 709 Grade 50W	blue and yellow
A 709 Grade 100	red
A 709 Grade 100W	red and orange

12.6 *Heat Treatment Identification:*

12.6.1 Material that is eventually required to be heat treated by the material specification, but that is released on the basis of heat-treated test specimens, shall be identified with the letter "G" following the specification designation.

12.6.2 Material that has been given the required full heat treatment by the manufacturer or processor shall be identified with the letters "MT" following the specification designation.

13. Permissible Variations in Dimensions or Weight

13.1 One cubic foot of rolled steel is assumed to weigh 490 lb. One cubic metre of rolled steel is assumed to have a mass of 7850 kg.

13.2 *Plates*—The permissible variations for dimensions shall not exceed the applicable limits in Tables 1 to 16 inclusive, except as specified in Supplementary Requirement S17.

13.3 *Shapes:*

13.3.1 Annex A1 lists the designations and dimensions, in both U.S. customary and SI (metric) units, of shapes that are most commonly available. Radii of fillets and toes of shape profiles vary with individual manufacturers and therefore are not specified.

13.3.2 The permissible variations from nominal U.S. customary dimensions shall not exceed the applicable limits in Tables 17 to 26 inclusive. Permissible variations for special shapes not listed in those tables are subject to negotiation between the manufacturer and the purchaser.

NOTE 3—Tolerances are shown in Tables 17 to

485

26, incl, for some shapes that are not listed in Annex A1 (that is, bulb angles, tees, zees). Addition of such sections to Annex A1 will be considered by Subcommittee A01.02 when and if a need for such listing is shown.

13.3.3 *Shapes Having One Dimension of the Cross Section 3 in. (75 mm) or Greater (Structural-Size Shapes)*—The cross-sectional area or weight of each shape shall not vary more than 2.5 % from the theoretical or specified amounts.

13.4 *Sheet Piling*—The weight of each steel sheet pile shall not vary more than 2.5 % from the theoretical or specified weight. The length of each steel sheet pile shall not vary more than 5 in. (125 mm) over, and shall not be less than the length specified.

13.5 *Bars*—The variations from nominal dimensions of hot-rolled bars shall not exceed the applicable limits in Tables 27 to 32 inclusive.

14. Inspection and Testing

14.1 The inspector representing the purchaser shall have free entry, at all times, while work on the contract of the purchaser is being performed, to all parts of the manufacturer's works that concern the manufacture of the material ordered. The manufacturer shall afford the inspector all reasonable facilities to satisfy him that the material is being furnished in accordance with this specification. All tests (except product analysis) and inspection shall be made at the place of manufacturer prior to shipment, unless otherwise specified, and shall be conducted so as not to interfere with the operation of the works.

14.2 When plates are produced from coils, 14.1 shall apply to the processor instead of the manufacturer, and the place of process shall apply instead of the place of manufacture. When plates are produced from coils and the processor is different from the manufacturer, the inspector representing the purchaser shall have free entry at all times while work on the contract of the purchaser is being performed to all parts of the manufacturer's works that concerns the manufacturer of the material ordered.

15. Retests

15.1 If any test specimen shows defective machining or develops flaws, it may be discarded and another specimen substituted.

15.2 If the percentage of elongation of any tension test specimen is less than that specified

and any part of the fracture is more than ¾ in. (19 mm) from the center of the gage length of a 2-in. (50-mm) specimen or is outside the middle half of the gage length of an 8-in. (200-mm) specimen, as indicated by scribe scratches marked on the specimen before testing, a retest shall be allowed.

15.3 Except as provided in 15.3.1, if the results from an original tension specimen fails to meet the specified requirements, but are within 2000 psi (14 MPa) of the required tensile strength, within 1000 psi (7 MPa) of the required yield strength or yield point, or within 2 percentage units of the required elongation, a retest shall be permitted to replace the failing test. A retest shall be performed for the failing original test, with the specimen being randomly selected from the heat. If the results of the retest meet the specified requirements, the heat or lot shall be approved.

15.3.1 For plates produced from coils, both tests from each coil tested to qualify a heat must meet all mechanical property requirements. Should either test fail to do so, then that coil cannot be used to qualify the parent heat. However, that portion of that individual coil which is bracketed by acceptable tests (see 11.4.1.3) may be qualified.

15.4 Quenched and tempered steel plates are subject to the additional retest requirements contained in the material specification.

16. Rejection

16.1 Unless otherwise specified, any rejection based on product analysis made in accordance with the material specification shall be reported to the manufacturer or processor within 5 working days from receipt of samples by the purchaser.

16.2 Samples that represent rejected material shall be preserved for 2 weeks from the date of the test report. In case of dissatisfaction with the results of the tests, the manufacturer or processor may make claim for a rehearing within that time.

16.3 Material that shows injurious defects subsequent to its acceptance at the manufacturer's or processor's works will be rejected, and the manufacturer or processor shall be notified.

17. Retreatment

17.1 If any heat-treated material fails to

meet the mechanical requirements of the applicable specification, the material may be reheat treated. All mechanical property tests shall be repeated and the material surface shall be reexamined for defects when the material is resubmitted for inspection.

18. Test Reports

18.1 When test reports are required by the purchase order, the test reports shall show the heat analysis and the results of two tension tests from material of thicknesses sufficient to qualify the material shipped. However, only one test need be reported when the amount of material from a shipment is less than 10 tons (9 Mg) and the thickness variations described in 11.4 were not exceeded. Furthermore, only one test need be reported when the shipment consists of a single piece weighing 10 tons or more.

18.2 The thickness of the product tested may not necessarily be the same as an individual ordered thickness since it is the heat that is tested rather than each ordered item. Tests from material thicknesses in accordance with 11.4 and encompassing the thicknesses in a shipment shall be sufficient for qualifying the material in the shipment. These test thicknesses may or may not be within previously tested and shipped thicknesses from the same heat.

18.3 For plates produced from coils, both tests results shall be reported for each qualifying coil.

18.4 For plates produced from coils, the test report must carry the processor's name.

19. Packaging, Marking, and Loading for Shipment

19.1 Packaging, marking, and loading for shipment shall be in accordance with those procedures recommended by Recommended Practices A 700.

19.2 When Level A is specified, and when specified in the contract or order, and for direct procurement by or direct shipment to the U. S. government, preservation, packaging, and packing shall be in accordance with the Level A requirements of MIL-STD-163.

19.3 When specified in the contract or order, and for direct procurement by or direct shipment to the U. S. government, marking for shipment, in addition to requirements specified in the contract or order, shall be in accordance with MIL-STD-129 for military agencies and with Fed. Std. No. 123 for civil agencies.

SUPPLEMENTARY REQUIREMENTS

The following standardized supplementary requirements are for use when desired by the purchaser. Those which are considered suitable for use with each material specification are listed in the specification. Other tests may be performed by agreement between the supplier and the purchaser. These additional requirements shall apply only when specified in the order, in which event the specified tests shall be made by the manufacturer or processor before shipment of the material.

S1. Vacuum Treatment

S1.1 The steel shall be made by a process which includes vacuum degassing while molten. Unless otherwise agreed upon with the purchaser, it is the responsibility of the manufacturer to select suitable process procedures.

S2. Product Analysis

S2.1 Product analyses shall be made for those elements listed in the material specification. Test frequency shall be as specified on the order. Specimens for analysis shall be taken adjacent to or from the tension test specimen, or from a sample taken from the same relative location as that from which the tension test specimen was taken.

S3. Simulated Post-Weld Heat Treatment of Mechanical Test Coupons

S3.1 The test specimens representing the material shall be thermally treated to simulate heat treatments below the critical temperature which the material may receive during fabrication after heat treatment for mechanical properties. The temperature range, time, and cooling rates shall be as specified in the order.

S4. Additional Tension Test

S4.1 One tension test shall be made from each unit plate rolled from a slab or directly from an ingot, except that for quenched and tempered plates, a test shall be taken from each unit plate heat treated. The results obtained shall be reported on the mill test reports when such tests are required by the order.

S5. Charpy V-Notch Impact Test

S5.1 Charpy V-notch impact tests shall be conducted in accordance with Specification A 673.

S5.2 The frequency of testing, the test temperature to be used, and the absorbed energy requirements shall be as specified on the order.

S6. Drop-Weight Test (for Material 0.625 in. (15.8 mm) and over in Thickness)

S6.1 Drop-weight tests shall be made in accordance with Method E 208. The specimens shall represent the material in the final condition of heat treatment. Agreement shall be reached between the purchaser and the manufacturer or processor as to the number of pieces to be tested and whether a maximum nil-ductility transition (NDT) temperature is mandatory or if the test results are for information only.

S8. Ultrasonic Examination

S8.1 The material shall be ultrasonically examined in accordance with the requirements specified on the order.

S14. Bend Test

S14.1 Bend tests shall be performed with material in the condition prescribed by the material specification. The frequency of testing shall be the same as that specified for tension testing. The bend test specimens shall be taken from the same relative location as the tension test specimen. The longitudinal axis of the specimen shall be parallel to the final direction of rolling.

S14.1.1 Except as provided below, bend test specimens for flats, plates, and shapes shall be at least 1¼ in. (32 mm) in width, with both edges parallel throughout the section in which bending occurs, and may be machined, sheared, or gas-cut.

S14.1.2 Bend test specimens for plates over ¾ in. (19 mm) in thickness and with a specified minimum tensile strength exceeding 90 ksi (620

MPa), and for other material over 1½ in. (38 mm) in thickness or diameter, except bars to be used for pins and rollers, may be machined to a thickness or diameter of at least ¾ in. or to a 1 by ½-in. (25 by 13-mm) section. When the test is made on a specimen of reduced thickness, the rolled surface shall be on the outer curve of the bend.

S14.1.3 Bend test specimens for bars to be used for pins and rollers shall be 1 by ½ in. (25 by 13 mm) in cross section.

S14.1.4 The sides of the bend test specimens may have the corners rounded to a radius not over 1/16 in. (2 mm) for specimens 2 in. (50 mm) and under in thickness, and not over ⅛ in. (3 mm) for specimens over 2 in. in thickness.

S14.2 The bend test specimens shall withstand being bent cold, without cracking on the outside of the bent portion, to an inside diameter that shall have a relation to the thickness of the specimen as prescribed in Table C for the material specification.

S14.3 If a bend specimen fails due to conditions of bending more severe than required by the specification, a retest shall be permitted, either on a duplicate specimen or on a remaining portion of the failed specimen.

S14.4 If a sheared or gas-cut bend test specimen fails due to conditions associated with the sheared or gas-cut edges, a retest shall be permitted on a duplicate machined specimen.

S15. Reduction of Area Measurement

S15.1 The reduction of area, as determined on the 0.500-in. (12.7-mm) diameter round tension test specimen in accordance with Methods and Definitions A 370, shall not be less than 40 %.

S17. Metric Thickness Tolerances

S17.1 When plates are ordered to thickness in metric units, the thickness tolerances of Table X1.1 shall apply instead of those in Table 1.

S18. Maximum Tensile Strength

S18.1 Steel having a specified minimum tensile strength of less than 70 ksi (485 MPa) shall not exceed the minimum specified tensile strength by more than 30 ksi (210 MPa).

S18.2 Steel having a minimum specified tensile strength of 70 ksi (485 MPa) or higher shall not exceed the minimum specified tensile strength by more than 25 ksi (180 MPa).

TABLE A   Shape Size Groupings for Tensile Property Classification

NOTE 1—Metric equivalents, from Annex A1, are shown in parentheses.
NOTE 2—Tees cut from W, M and S. shapes fall in the same group as the shape from which they are cut.

Shape Type	Group 1	Group 2	Group 3	Group 4	Group 5
W Shapes	W24 × 55 & 62 (W610 × 82 & 92)	W36 × 135 to 210 incl (W920 × 201 to 313 incl)	W36 × 230 to 300 incl (W920 × 342 to 446 incl)	W14 × 233 to 550 incl (W360 × 347 to 818 incl)	W14 × 605 to 730 incl (W360 × 900 to 1086 incl)
	W21 × 44 to 57 incl (W530 × 66 to 85 incl)	W33 × 118 to 152 incl (W840 × 176 to 226 incl)	W33 × 201 to 241 incl (W840 × 299 to 359 incl)	W12 × 210 to 336 incl (W310 × 313 to 500 incl)	
	W18 × 35 to 71 incl (W460 × 52 to 106 incl)	W300 × 99 to 211 incl (W760 × 147 to 314 incl)	W14 × 145 to 211 incl (W360 × 216 to 314 incl)		
	W16 × 26 to 57 incl (W410 × 38.8 to 85 incl)	W27 × 84 to 178 incl (W690 × 125 to 265 incl)	W12 × 120 to 190 incl (W310 × 179 to 283 incl)		
	W14 × 22 to 53 incl (W360 × 32.9 to 79 incl)	W24 × 68 to 162 incl (W610 × 101 to 241 incl)			
	W12 × 14 to 58 incl (W310 × 21.0 to 86 incl)	W21 × 62 to 147 incl (W530 × 92 to 219 incl)			
	W10 × 12 to 45 incl (W250 × 17.9 to 67 incl)	W18 × 76 to 119 incl (W460 × 113 to 177 incl)			
	W8 × 10 to 48 incl (W200 × 15.0 to 71 incl)	W16 × 67 to 100 incl (W410 × 100 to 149 incl)			
	W6 × 9 to 25 incl (W150 × 13.5 to 37.1 incl)	W14 × 61 to 132 incl (W360 × 91 to 196 incl)			
	W5 × 16 & 19 (W130 × 23.8 & 28.1)	W12 × 65 to 106 incl (W310 × 97 to 158 incl)			
	W4 × 13 (W100 × 19.3)	W10 × 49 to 112 incl (W250 × 73 to 167 incl)			
		W8 × 58 & 67 (W200 × 86 & 100)			

489

TABLE A *Continued*

Shape Type	Group 1	Group 2	Group 3	Group 4	Group 5
M Shapes	to 37.7 lb/ft, incl (to 56 kg/m, incl)				
S Shapes	to 35 lb/ft, incl (to 52 kg/m, incl)	over 35 lb/ft (over 52 kg/m)			
HP Shapes		to 102 lb/ft, incl (to 152 kg/m, incl)	over 102 lb/ft (over 152 kg/m)		
C Shapes	to 20.7 lb/ft, incl (to 30.8 kg/m, incl)	over 20.7 lb/ft (over 30.8 kg/m)			
MC Shapes	to 28.5 lb/ft, incl (to 42.4 kg/m, incl)	over 28.5 lb/ft (over 42.4 kg/m)			
L Shapes	to ½ in., incl (to 13 mm, incl)	over ½ to ¾ in., incl (over 13 to 19 mm, incl)	over ¾ in. (over 19 mm)		

TABLE B Product Analysis Tolerances

Element	Upper Limit, or Maximum Specified Value, %	Tolerances, %	
		Under Minimum Limit	Over Maximum Limit
Carbon	to 0.15 incl	0.02	0.03
	over 0.15 to 0.40 incl	0.03	0.04
Manganese[c]	to 0.60 incl	0.05	0.06
	over 0.60 to 0.90 incl	0.06	0.08
	over 0.90 to 1.20 incl	0.08	0.10
	over 1.20 to 1.35 incl	0.09	0.11
	over 1.35 to 1.65 incl	0.09	0.12
	over 1.65 to 1.95 incl	0.11	0.14
	over 1.95	0.12	0.16
Phosphorus	to 0.04 incl	. . .	0.010
	over 0.04 to 0.15 incl	. . .	N.A.[a]
Sulfur	to 0.05 incl	. . .	0.010
Silicon	to 0.30 incl	0.02	0.03
	over 0.30 to 0.40 incl	0.05	0.05
	over 0.40 to 2.20 incl	0.06	0.06
Nickel	to 1.00 incl	0.03	0.03
	over 1.00 to 2.00 incl	0.05	0.05
Chromium	to 0.90 incl	0.04	0.04
	over 0.90 to 2.10 incl	0.06	0.06
Molybdenum	to 0.20 incl	0.01	0.01
	over 0.20 to 0.40 incl	0.03	0.03
	over 0.40 to 1.15 incl	0.04	0.04
Copper	0.20 minimum only	0.02	. . .
	to 1.00 incl	0.03	0.03
	over 1.00 to 2.00 incl	0.05	0.05
Titanium	to 0.10 incl	0.01[b]	0.01[b]
Vanadium	to 0.10 incl	0.01[b]	0.01[b]
	over 0.10 to 0.25 incl	0.02	0.02
	minimum only specified	0.01	. . .
Boron	any	N.A.[a]	N.A.[a]
Columbium	to 0.10 incl	0.01[b]	0.01[b]
Zirconium	to 0.15 incl	0.03	0.03
Nitrogen	to 0.030 incl	0.005	0.005

[a] N.A.—Product analysis not applicable.
[b] If the minimum of the range is 0.01 %, the under tolerance is 0.005 %.
[c] Manganese product analyses tolerances for bars and bar size shapes shall be: to 0.90 incl ±0.03; over 0.90 to 2.20 incl ± 0.06.

TABLE C Bend Test Requirements

| Specification | Grade | Ratio of Bend Diameter to Specimen Thickness[a] | | | | | | |
| | | Material Thickness, in. (mm) | | | | | | |
		≤¾ (19.0)	>¾ to 1 (25.4)	>1 to 1½ (38.1)	>1½ to 2 (50.8)	>2 to 3 (76.2)	>3 to 4 (102)	>4
A 36	...	½	1	1½	2½	3	3	3
A 242	...	1	1½	2	2½	3	3	...
A 283	A	flat	flat	½	1	1½	2	2½
	B	flat	flat	¾	1½	2	2½	3
	C	flat	½	1	2	2½	3	3½
	D	½	1	1½	2½	3	3½	4
A 284	A	flat	flat	½	1	1½	2	2½
	B	flat	½	1	1½	2	2½	3
	C	½	1	1½	2	2½	3	3½
	D	½	1	1½	2½	3	3½	4
A 328	...	2	...	...	...	...	...	...
A 441	...	1	1½	2	2½	3	3	...
A 514	all	2	2	3	3	4	4	...
A 529	...	1	...	...	...	...	...	...
A 572	42	1	1½	2	2½	3	3	4[f]
A 514	all	2	2	3	3	4	4	...
A 529	...	1	...	...	...	...	...	...
A 572	42	1	1½	2	2½	3	3	4[f]
	45	1	1½	2	2½[c]	...	...	...
	50	1	1½	2½	3[c]	...	...	...
	55	1½	2	3	3½[c]	...	...	...
	60	2	2½	3	...	...	...	...
	65	2½[e]	3	3½	...	...	...	...
A 573	65	1½	1½	2	...	...	...	...
	70	2	2	2	...	...	...	...
A 588	all	1	1½	2	2½	3	3	3[g]
A 633	all	2	2	2½	2½	3	3	3
A 656	50	[b]	...	...	...	...	...	...
	60	[h]	...	...	...	...	...	...
	70	[i]	...	...	...	...	...	...
	80	[j]	...	...	...	...	...	...
A 678	A	1	2	2	...	...	...	...
	B	2	2	2	2½	2½[d]	...	...
	C	2	3	3	3	...	...	...
A 690	...	2	2	...	...	...	...	...
A 699	all	2	2	...	...	...	...	...
A 709	36	½	1	1½	2½	3	3	3
	50	1	1½	2½	3[c]	...	...	...
	50W	1	1½	2	2½	3	3	3[g]
	100	2	2	3	3	4	4	...
	100W	2	2	3	3	4	4	...
A 710	all	2	2	...	...	...	...	...

[a] The above ratios apply to the bending performance of a test specimen only. This specimen is always taken in the longitudinal direction and usually has some edge preparation. Where plates are to be bent in a fabricating operation more liberal bend radii must be used, particularly if this bend axis is in the unfavorable (longitudinal) direction.
[b] To ¼ in. (6.35 mm): ½; over ¼ to ⅝ in. (15.9 mm): 1.
[c] Applicable to webs of structural shapes.
[d] Over 2 to 2½ (50.8 to 63.5 mm) incl.
[e] ½ in. (13 mm) max specimen thickness.
[f] Over 4 to 6 in. (102 to 152 mm), incl.
[g] Over 4 to 8 in. (102 to 203 mm), incl.
[h] To ¼ in. (6.35 mm): 1; over ¼ to ⅝ in. (15.9 mm): 1½.
[i] To ¼ in. (6.35 mm): 1½; over ¼ to ⅝ in. (15.9 mm): 2.
[j] To ¼ in. (6.35 mm): 2; over ¼ to ⅝ in. (15.9 mm): 2½.

TABLE 1 Permissible Variations in Thickness for Rectangular Carbon, High-Strength Low Alloy, and Alloy-Steel Plates, 15 in. and Under in Thickness When Ordered to Thickness

NOTE 1—Permissible variation under specified thickness, 0.01 in.
NOTE 2—Thickness to be measured at ⅜ to ¾ in. from the longitudinal edge.
NOTE 3—For thickness measured at any location other than that specified in Note 2, the permissible maximum over tolerance shall be increased by 75 %, rounded to the nearest 0.01 in.

Specified Thickness, in.	Tolerance Over Specified Thickness, For Widths Given, in.											
	48 and under	Over 48 to 60, excl	60 to 72, excl	72 to 84, excl	84 to 96, excl	96 to 108, excl	108 to 120, excl	120 to 132, excl	132 to 144, excl	144 to 168, excl	168 to 182, excl	182 and over
To ¼, excl	0.03	0.03	0.03	0.03	0.03	0.03	0.03	0.03	0.04	...	...	...
¼ to ⁵⁄₁₆, excl	0.03	0.03	0.03	0.03	0.03	0.03	0.03	0.04	0.04	...	...	...
⁵⁄₁₆ to ⅜, excl	0.03	0.03	0.03	0.03	0.03	0.03	0.03	0.04	0.04	0.05	...	...
⅜ to ⁷⁄₁₆, excl	0.03	0.03	0.03	0.03	0.03	0.03	0.04	0.04	0.05	0.06	0.06	...
⁷⁄₁₆ to ½, excl	0.03	0.03	0.03	0.03	0.03	0.03	0.04	0.04	0.05	0.06	0.06	...
½ to ⅝, excl	0.03	0.03	0.03	0.03	0.03	0.03	0.04	0.04	0.05	0.06	0.07	...
⅝ to ¾, excl	0.03	0.03	0.03	0.03	0.03	0.04	0.04	0.04	0.05	0.06	0.07	0.07
¾ to 1, excl	0.03	0.03	0.03	0.03	0.04	0.04	0.05	0.05	0.06	0.07	0.08	0.09
1 to 2, excl	0.06	0.06	0.06	0.06	0.06	0.07	0.08	0.10	0.10	0.11	0.13	0.16
2 to 3, excl	0.09	0.09	0.09	0.10	0.10	0.11	0.12	0.13	0.14	0.15	0.15	...
3 to 4, excl	0.11	0.11	0.11	0.11	0.11	0.13	0.14	0.14	0.14	0.15	0.17	...
4 to 6, excl	0.15	0.15	0.15	0.15	0.15	0.15	0.15	0.15	0.15	0.20	0.20	...
6 to 10, excl	0.23	0.24	0.24	0.24	0.24	0.24	0.24	0.24	0.24	0.27	0.28	...
10 to 12, excl	0.29	0.29	0.33	0.33	0.33	0.33	0.33	0.33	0.33	0.33	0.35	...
12 to 15, incl	0.29	0.29	0.35	0.35	0.35	0.35	0.35	0.35	0.35	0.35	0.35	...

TABLE 2 Permissible Variations in Thickness for Rectangular Mill and Universal Mill Plates Over 2 in. in Thickness (Applies to Alloy Steel Specifications Only).

NOTE 1—Tolerance under specified thickness, 0.01 in.
NOTE 2—These tolerances only apply when the thickness is measured ⅜ in. from the longitudinal edges of plates.
NOTE 3—For overweight tolerances which limit the overall thickness of the plate, see Table 1.

Specified Thickness, in.	Variations over Specified Thickness for Widths Given in.					
	To 36, excl	36 to 60, excl	60 to 84, excl	84 to 120, excl	120 to 132, excl	132 and over
Over 2 to 3, excl	¹⁄₁₆	³⁄₃₂	⁷⁄₆₄	⅛	⅛	⁹⁄₆₄
3 to 4, excl	⁵⁄₆₄	³⁄₃₂	⁷⁄₆₄	⅛	⅛	⁹⁄₆₄
4 incl	³⁄₃₂	⅛	⁹⁄₆₄	⁹⁄₆₄	⁵⁄₃₂	¹¹⁄₆₄

TABLE 3 Permissible Variations in Weight for Rectangular Sheared Plates and Universal Mill Plates 612.0 lb/ft² and Under When Ordered to Weight.

NOTE 1—Permissible variations in overweight for lots of circular and sketch plates shall be 1¼ times the amounts in this table.
NOTE 2—Permissible variations in overweight for single plates shall be 1½ times the amounts in this table.
NOTE 3—Permissible variations in overweight for single circular and sketch plates shall be 1% times the amounts in this table.
NOTE 4—The adopted standard density of rolled steel is 490 lb/ft³.

Permissible Variation in Average Weight of Lots[a] for Widths Given in Inches, Expressed in Percentage of the Specified Weights per Square Foot

Specified Weights, lb/ft²	48 and under		Over 48 to 60, excl		60 to 72, excl		72 to 84, excl		84 to 96, excl		96 to 108, excl		108 to 120, excl		120 to 132, excl		132 to 144, excl		144 to 168, excl		168 and over	
	Over	Under	Over	Under	Over	Under	Over	Under	Over	Under	Over	Under	Over	Under	Over	Under	Over	Under	Over	Under	Over	Under
To 10, excl	4.0	3.0	4.5	3.0	5.0	3.0	5.5	3.0	6.0	3.0	7.5	3.0	9.0	3.0	11.0	3.0	13.0	3.0	⋯	⋯	⋯	⋯
10 to 12.5, excl	4.0	3.0	4.5	3.0	4.5	3.0	5.0	3.0	5.5	3.0	6.5	3.0	7.0	3.0	8.0	3.0	9.0	3.0	12.0	3.0	⋯	⋯
12.5 to 15.0, excl	4.0	3.0	4.0	3.0	4.5	3.0	4.5	3.0	5.0	3.0	5.5	3.0	6.0	3.0	7.5	3.0	8.0	3.0	11.0	3.0	⋯	⋯
15 to 17.5, excl	3.5	3.0	3.5	3.0	4.0	3.0	4.5	3.0	4.5	3.0	5.0	3.0	5.5	3.0	6.0	3.0	7.0	3.0	9.0	3.0	10.0	3.0
17.5 to 20, excl	3.5	2.5	3.5	2.5	3.5	3.0	4.0	3.0	4.5	3.0	4.5	3.0	5.0	3.0	5.5	3.0	6.0	3.0	8.0	3.0	9.0	3.0
20 to 25, excl	3.5	2.5	3.5	2.5	3.5	3.0	3.5	3.0	4.0	3.0	4.0	3.0	4.5	3.0	5.0	3.0	5.5	3.0	7.0	3.0	8.0	3.0
25 to 30, excl	3.0	2.5	3.5	2.5	3.5	2.5	3.5	2.5	3.5	3.0	3.5	2.5	4.0	3.0	4.5	3.0	5.0	3.0	6.5	3.0	7.0	3.0
30 to 40, excl	3.0	2.0	3.0	2.0	3.0	2.0	3.0	2.0	3.5	2.0	3.5	2.5	3.5	2.5	4.0	3.0	4.5	3.0	6.0	3.0	7.0	3.0
40 to 81.7, excl	2.5	2.0	3.0	2.0	3.0	2.0	3.0	2.0	3.5	2.0	3.5	2.0	3.5	2.5	3.5	3.0	4.0	3.0	5.5	3.0	6.5	3.0
81.7 to 122.6, excl	2.5	2.0	3.0	2.0	3.0	2.0	3.0	2.0	3.5	2.0	3.5	2.0	3.5	2.5	3.5	3.0	3.5	3.0	4.0	3.0	6.0	3.0
122.6 to 163.4, excl	2.5	1.5	2.5	1.5	2.5	1.5	2.5	1.5	2.5	2.0	2.5	2.0	2.5	2.0	2.5	2.0	2.5	2.0	3.0	2.0	4.5	2.0
163.4 to 245.1, excl	2.5	1.0	2.5	1.0	2.5	1.0	2.5	1.0	2.5	1.0	2.5	1.0	2.5	1.0	2.5	1.0	2.5	1.0	3.0	1.0	3.5	1.0
245.1 to 409.0, excl	2.5	1.0	2.5	1.0	2.5	1.0	2.5	1.0	2.5	1.0	2.5	1.0	2.5	1.0	2.5	1.0	2.5	1.0	2.5	1.0	3.5	1.0
409.0 to 490.1, excl	2.0	1.0	2.0	1.0	2.5	1.0	2.5	1.0	2.5	1.0	2.5	1.0	2.5	1.0	2.5	1.0	2.5	1.0	2.5	1.0	3.0	1.0
490.1 to 613.0, excl	2.0	1.0	2.0	1.0	2.0	1.0	2.0	1.0	2.5	1.0	2.5	1.0	2.5	1.0	2.5	1.0	2.5	1.0	2.5	1.0	2.5	1.0

[a] The term "lot" means all the plates of each tabular width and weight group represented in each shipment.

TABLE 4 Permissible Variations in Width and Length for Sheared Plates 1½ In. and Under in Thickness; Length Only of Universal Mill Plates 2½ In. and Under in Thickness

Specified Dimensions, in.		Variations over Specified Width and Length[a] for Thicknesses, in., and Equivalent Weights, lb/ft², Given							
		To ⅜, excl		⅜ to ⅝, excl		⅝ to 1, excl		1 to 2, incl[b]	
Length	Width	To 15.3, excl		15.3 to 25.5, excl		25.5 to 40.8, excl		40.8 to 81.7, incl	
		Width	Length	Width	Length	Width	Length	Width	Length
To 120, excl	To 60, excl	⅜	½	7/16	⅝	½	¾	⅝	1
	60 to 84, excl	7/16	⅝	½	11/16	⅝	⅞	¾	1
	84 to 108, excl	½	¾	⅝	⅞	¾	1	1	1⅛
	108 and over	⅝	⅞	¾	1	⅞	1⅛	1⅞	1¼
120 to 240, excl	To 60, excl	⅜	¾	½	⅞	⅝	1	¾	1⅛
	60 to 84, excl	½	¾	⅝	⅞	¾	1	⅞	1¼
	84 to 108, excl	9/16	⅞	11/16	15/16	13/16	1⅛	1	1⅜
	108 and over	⅝	1	¾	1⅛	⅞	1¼	1⅛	1⅜
240 to 360, excl	To 60, excl	⅜	1	½	1⅛	⅝	1¼	¾	1½
	60 to 84, excl	½	1	⅝	1⅛	¾	1¼	⅞	1½
	84 to 108, excl	9/16	1	11/16	1⅛	⅞	1⅜	1	1½
	108 and over	11/16	1⅛	⅞	1¼	1	1⅜	1¼	1¾
360 to 480, excl	To 60, excl	7/16	1⅛	½	1¼	⅝	1⅜	¾	1⅝
	60 to 84, excl	½	1¼	⅝	1⅜	¾	1½	⅞	1⅝
	84 to 108, excl	9/16	1¼	¾	1⅜	⅞	1½	1	1⅞
	108 and over	¾	1⅜	⅞	1½	1	1⅝	1¼	1⅞
480 to 600, excl	To 60, excl	7/16	1¼	½	1½	⅝	1⅝	¾	1⅞
	60 to 84, excl	½	1⅜	⅝	1½	¾	1⅝	⅞	1⅞
	84 to 108, excl	⅝	1⅜	¾	1½	⅞	1⅝	1	1⅞
	108 and over	¾	1½	⅞	1⅝	1	1¾	1¼	1⅞
600 to 720, excl	To 60, excl	½	1¾	⅝	1⅞	¾	1⅞	⅞	2¼
	60 to 84, excl	⅝	1¾	¾	1⅞	⅞	1⅞	1	2¼
	84 to 108, excl	⅝	1¾	¾	1⅞	⅞	1⅞	1⅛	2¼
	108 and over	⅞	1¾	1	2	1⅛	2¼	1¼	2½
720 and over	To 60, excl	9/16	2	¾	2⅛	⅞	2¼	1	2¾
	60 to 84, excl	¾	2	⅞	2⅛	1	2¼	1⅛	2¾
	84 to 108, excl	¾	2	⅞	2⅛	1	2¼	1¼	2¾
	108 and over	1	2	1⅛	2⅜	1¼	2½	1⅜	3

[a] Permissible variation under specified width and length, ¼ in.

[b] Permissible variations in length apply also to Universal Mill plates up to 12 in. in width for thicknesses over 2 to 2½ in., incl, except for alloy steel up to 1¾ in. thick.

TABLE 5 Permissible Variations in Width for Mill Edge Plates in Coils and Cut Lengths for Plates Produced on Strip Mills (Not Applicable to Alloy Steel).

Specified Width, in.	Variations over Specified Width, in.[a, b]
To 14, excl	7/16
14 to 17, excl	1/2
17 to 19, excl	9/16
19 to 21, excl	5/8
21 to 24, excl	11/16
24 to 26, excl	13/16
26 to 28, excl	15/16
28 to 35, excl	1 1/8
35 to 50, excl	1 1/4
50 to 60, excl	1 1/2
60 to 65, excl	1 5/8
65 to 70, excl	1 3/4
70 to 80, excl	1 7/8
80 and over	2

[a] No permissible variation under specified width.
[b] These variations do not apply to the uncropped ends of mill-edge plates in coils.

TABLE 7 Permissible Variations in Diameter for Sheared Circular Plates 1 in. and Under in Thickness

Specified Diameters, in.	Permissible Variations over Specified Diameter for Thicknesses Given, in.[a]		
	To 3/8, excl	3/8 to 5/8, excl	5/8 to 1, incl
To 32, excl	1/4	3/8	1/2
32 to 84, excl	5/16	7/16	9/16
84 to 108, excl	3/8	1/2	5/8
108 to 130, excl	7/16	9/16	11/16
130 and over	1/2	5/8	3/4

[a] No permissible variations under specified diameter.

TABLE 6 Permissible Variations in Rolled Width for Universal Mill Plates 15 in. and Under in Thickness

Specified Width, in.	Variations over Specified Width[a] for Thickness, in., or Equivalent Weights, lb/ft,[2] Given					
	To 3/8, excl	3/8 to 5/8, excl	5/8 to 1, excl	1 to 2, incl	Over 2 to 10, incl	Over 10 to 15, incl
	To 15.3, excl	15.3 to 25.5, excl	25.5 to 40.8, excl	40.8 to 81.7, incl	81.7 to 409.0, incl	409.0 to 613.0, incl
Over 8 to 20, excl	1/8	1/8	3/16	1/4	3/8	1/2
20 to 36, excl	3/16	1/4	5/16	3/8	7/16	9/16
36 and over	5/16	3/8	7/16	1/2	9/16	5/8

[a] Permissible variation under specified width, 1/8 in.

TABLE 8 Permissible Variations in Diameter for Gas-Cut Circular Plates (Not Applicable to Alloy Steel).

Specified Diameter, in.	Variations over Specified Diameter for Thicknesses Given, in.[a]					
	to 1, excl	1 to 2, excl	2 to 4, excl	4 to 6, excl	6 to 8, excl	8 to 15, incl
To 32, excl	3/8	3/8	1/2	1/2	5/8	3/4
32 to 84, excl	3/8	1/2	1/2	5/8	3/4	7/8
84 to 108, excl	1/2	9/16	5/8	3/4	7/8	1
108 to 130, excl	1/2	9/16	11/16	7/8	1	1 1/8
130 and over	5/8	3/4	7/8	1	1 1/8	1 1/4

[a] No permissible variation under specified diameter.

TABLE 9 Permissible Variations in Width and Length for Rectangular Plates When Gas Cutting is Specified or Required (Applies to Alloy Steel Specifications Only).

NOTE 1—Plates with universal rolled edges will be gas cut to length only.

Specified Thickness, in.	Variations Over for All Specified Widths or Lengths, in.[a]
To 2, excl	3/4
2 to 4, excl	1
4, incl	1 1/8

[a] These variations may be taken all under or divided over and under, if so specified.

TABLE 10 Permissible Variations in Width and Length for Rectangular Plates When Gas Cutting is Specified or Required (Not Applicable to Alloy Steel).

NOTE 1—Plates with universal rolled edges will be gas cut to length only.

Specified Thickness, in.	Variations Over for All Specified Widths or Lengths, in.[a]
To 2, excl	1/2
2 to 4, excl	5/8
4 to 6, excl	3/4
6 to 8, excl	7/8
8 to 15, incl	1

[a] These variations may be taken all under or divided over and under, if so specified.

TABLE 11 Permissible Variations in Diameter for Gas-Cut Circular Plates (Applies to Alloy Steel Specifications Only).

Specified Diameter, in.	Variations over Specified Diameter for Thicknesses Given, in.[a]					
	to 1, excl	1 to 2, excl	2 to 4, excl	4 to 6, excl	6 to 8, excl	8 to 15, incl
To 32, excl	½	½	¾	¾	1	1
32 to 84, excl	½	⅝	⅞	1	1⅛	1¼
84 to 108, excl	⅝	¾	1	1⅛	1¼	1⅜
108 to 130, incl	⅞	1	1⅛	1¼	1⅜	1½

[a] No permissible variations under specified diameter.

TABLE 12 Permissible Camber[a] for Carbon, Alloy, and High-Strength Low-Alloy Universal Mill Plates and Alloy and High-Strength Low-Alloy Sheared Special-Cut or Gas-Cut Rectangular Plates

Thickness, in.	Specified Weights, lb/ft²	Widths, in.	Camber Tolerances for Thicknesses and Widths Given
To 2, incl	to 81.7, incl	all	⅛ in. × (no. of feet of length/5)
Over 2 to 15, incl	81.7 to 613.0, incl	to 30, incl	3/16 in. × (no. of feet of length/5)
Over 2 to 15, incl	81.7 to 613.0, incl	over 30	¼ in. × (no. of feet of length/5)

[a] Camber as it relates to plates is the horizontal edge curvature in the length, measured over the entire length of the plate in the flat position.

TABLE 13 Permissible Camber for Sheared Plates and Gas-Cut Rectangular Plates, All Thicknesses (Applies to Carbon Steel Only).

Maximum permissible camber, in. =
⅛ in. × (number of feet of length/5)

TABLE 14 Permissible Variations From Flatness for Carbon Steel Rectangular Sheared Plates, Universal Mill Plates, and Circular and Sketch Plates (Applies to Carbon Steel Only).

NOTE 1—When the longer dimension is under 36 in., the permissible variation should not exceed ¼ in. When the longer dimension is from 36 to 72 in., incl, the permissible variation should not exceed 75 % of the tabular amount for the specified width, but in no case less than ¼ in.

NOTE 2—These variations apply to plates which have a specified minimum tensile strength of not more than 60 000 psi (415 MPa) or compatible chemistry or hardness. The limits in the table are increased 50 % for plates specified to a higher minimum tensile strength or compatible chemistry or hardness.

NOTE 3—This table and these notes cover the permissible variations for flatness of circular and sketch plates, based on the maximum dimensions of those plates.

Specified Thickness, in.	Specified Weight, lb/ft²	Permissible Variations from a Flat Surface for Specified Widths, in.[a, b]										
		To 36, excl	36 to 48, excl	48 to 60, excl	60 to 72, excl	72 to 84, excl	84 to 96, excl	96 to 108, excl	108 to 120, excl	120 to 144, excl	144 to 168, excl	168 and Over
To ¼, excl	To 10.2, excl	9/16	¾	15/16	1¼	1⅜	1½	1⅝	1¾	1⅞	...	...
¼ to ⅜, excl	10.2 to 15.3, excl	½	⅝	¾	15/16	1⅛	1¼	1⅜	1½	1⅝	...	...
⅜ to ½, excl	15.3 to 20.4, excl	½	9/16	⅝	⅝	¾	⅞	1	1⅛	1¼	1⅞	2⅛
½ to ¾, excl	20.4 to 30.6, excl	7/16	½	9/16	⅝	⅝	¾	1	1	1⅛	1½	2
¾ to 1, excl	30.6 to 40.8, excl	7/16	½	9/16	⅝	⅝	⅝	¾	⅞	1	1⅜	1¾
1 to 2, excl	40.8 to 81.7, excl	⅜	½	½	9/16	9/16	⅝	⅝	⅝	11/16	1⅛	1½
2 to 4, excl	81.7 to 163.4, excl	5/16	⅜	7/16	½	½	½	½	9/16	⅝	⅞	1⅛
4 to 6, excl	163.4 to 245.1, excl	⅜	7/16	½	½	9/16	9/16	⅝	¾	⅞	⅞	1
6 to 8, excl	245.1 to 326.8, excl	7/16	½	½	⅝	11/16	¾	⅞	⅞	1	1	1
8 to 10, excl	326.8 to 409.0, excl	½	½	⅝	11/16	¾	13/16	⅞	15/16	1	1	1
10 to 12, excl	409.0 to 490.1, excl	½	⅝	¾	13/16	⅞	15/16	1	1	1	1	1
12 to 15, incl	490.1 to 613.0, incl	⅝	¾	13/16	⅞	15/16	1	1	1	1	1	...

[a] *Flatness Variations for Length*—The longer dimension specified is considered the length, and permissible variations in flatness along the length should not exceed the tabular amount for the specified width in plates up to 12 ft in length, or in any 12 ft of longer plates.

[b] *Flatness Variations for Width*—The flatness variations across the width should not exceed the tabular amount for the specified width.

TABLE 15 Permissible Variations From Flatness for High-Strength Low-Alloy and Alloy Steel Rectangular Sheared Plates, Universal Mill Plates, and Circular and Sketch Plates, Hot Rolled or Thermally Treated (Not Applicable to Carbon Steel).

NOTE 1—When the longer dimension is under 36 in., the variation should not exceed 3/16 in. When the larger dimension is from 36 to 72 in. incl, the variation should not exceed 75 % of the tabular amount for the specified width.

NOTE 2—This table and notes cover the tolerances for flatness of circular and sketch plates, based on the maximum dimensions of those plates.

Specified Thickness, in.	Specified Weights, lb/ft²	Flatness Tolerances for Specified Widths, in.[a, b]										
		To 36, excl	36 to 48, excl	48 to 60, excl	60 to 72, excl	72 to 84, excl	84 to 96, excl	96 to 108, excl	108 to 120, excl	120 to 144, excl	144 to 168, excl	168 and Over
To 1/4, excl	To 10.2 excl	13/16	1 1/8	1 3/8	1 7/8	2	2 1/4	2 3/8	2 5/8	2 3/4	...	...
1/4 to 3/8, excl	10.2 to 15.3, excl	3/4	15/16	1 1/8	1 3/8	1 3/4	1 7/8	2	2 1/4	2 3/8	...	...
3/8 to 1/2, excl	15.3 to 20.4, excl	3/4	7/8	15/16	15/16	1 1/8	1 9/16	1 1/2	1 5/8	1 7/8	2 3/4	3 1/8
1/2 to 3/4, excl	20.4 to 30.6, excl	5/8	3/4	13/16	7/8	1	1 1/8	1 1/4	1 3/8	1 5/8	2 1/4	3
3/4 to 1, excl	30.6 to 40.8, excl	5/8	3/4	7/8	7/8	15/16	1	1 1/8	1 9/16	1 1/2	2	2 5/8
1 to 2, excl	40.8 to 81.7, excl	9/16	5/8	3/4	13/16	3/4	3/4	3/4	7/8	1	1 5/8	2 1/4
2 to 4, excl	81.7 to 163.4, excl	1/2	9/16	11/16	3/4	3/4	3/4	15/16	1 1/8	1 1/4	1 1/4	1 5/8
4 to 6, excl	163.4 to 245.1, excl	9/16	11/16	3/4	3/4	7/8	7/8	15/16	1 1/8	1 1/4	1 1/4	1 1/2
6 to 8, excl	245.1 to 326.8, excl	5/8	3/4	3/4	1	1 1/8	1 1/4	1 5/16	1 3/8	1 1/2	1 1/2	1 1/2
8 to 10, excl	326.8 to 409.0, excl	3/4	13/16	15/16	1	1 1/8	1 1/4	1 5/16	1 3/8	1 1/2	1 1/2	1 1/2
10 to 12, excl	409.0 to 490.1, excl	3/4	15/16	1 1/8	1 1/4	1 5/16	1 3/8	1 1/2	1 1/2	1 1/2	1 1/2	1 1/2
12 to 15, incl	490.1 to 613.0, incl	7/8	1	1 3/16	1 9/16	1 3/8	1 1/2	1 1/2	1 1/2	1 1/2	1 1/2	1 1/2

[a] *Flatness Variations for Length*—The longer dimension specified is considered the length, and variations from a flat surface along the length should not exceed the tabular amount for the specified width in plates up to 12 ft in length, or in any 12 ft of longer plates.

[b] *Flatness Variations for Width*—The flatness variation across the width should not exceed the tabular amount for the specified width.

TABLE 16   Permissible Variations in Waviness for Rectangular Plates, Universal Mill Plates, and Circular and Sketch Plates

NOTE—Waviness denotes the maximum deviation of the surface of the plate from a plane parallel to the surface of the point of measurement and contiguous to the surface of the plate at each of the two adjacent wave peaks, when the plate is resting on a flat horizontal surface, as measured in an increment of less than 12 ft of length.

The waviness tolerance is a function of the flatness tolerance as obtained from Table 14 or 15 as appropriate.

Flatness Tolerance, in., from Tables 14 or 15	Waviness Tolerance, in., When Number of Waves in 12 ft is						
	1	2	3	4	5	6	7
5/16	5/16	1/4	3/16	1/8	1/8	1/16	1/16
3/8	3/8	5/16	3/16	3/16	1/8	1/16	1/16
7/16	7/16	5/16	1/4	3/16	1/8	1/8	1/16
1/2	1/2	3/8	5/16	3/16	3/16	1/8	1/16
9/16	9/16	7/16	5/16	1/4	3/16	1/8	1/8
5/8	5/8	1/2	3/8	1/4	3/16	1/8	1/8
11/16	11/16	1/2	3/8	5/16	3/16	3/16	1/8
3/4	3/4	9/16	7/16	5/16	1/4	3/16	1/8
13/16	13/16	5/8	7/16	5/16	1/4	3/16	1/8
7/8	7/8	11/16	1/2	3/8	1/4	3/16	1/8
15/16	15/16	11/16	1/2	3/8	5/16	1/4	3/16
1	1	3/4	9/16	7/16	5/16	1/4	3/16
1 1/8	1 1/8	7/8	5/8	1/2	3/8	1/4	3/16
1 1/4	1 1/4	15/16	11/16	1/2	3/8	5/16	1/4
1 3/8	1 3/8	1 1/16	3/4	9/16	7/16	5/16	1/4
1 1/2	1 1/2	1 1/8	7/8	5/8	1/2	3/8	1/4
1 5/8	1 5/8	1 1/4	15/16	11/16	1/2	3/8	5/16
1 3/4	1 3/4	1 5/16	1	3/4	9/16	7/16	5/16
1 7/8	1 7/8	1 7/16	1 1/16	13/16	9/16	7/16	5/16
2	2	1 1/2	1 1/8	7/8	5/8	1/2	3/8
2 1/8	2 1/8	1 5/8	1 3/16	7/8	11/16	1/2	3/8
2 1/4	2 1/4	1 11/16	1 1/4	15/16	11/16	9/16	3/8
2 3/8	2 3/8	1 13/16	1 5/16	1	3/4	9/16	7/16
2 1/2	2 1/2	1 7/8	1 7/16	1 1/16	13/16	9/16	7/16
2 5/8	2 5/8	2	1 1/2	1 1/8	13/16	5/8	7/16
2 3/4	2 3/4	2 1/16	1 9/16	1 1/8	7/8	5/8	1/2
2 7/8	2 7/8	2 3/16	1 5/8	1 3/16	15/16	11/16	1/2
3	3	2 1/4	1 11/16	1 1/4	15/16	11/16	9/16
3 1/8	3 1/8	2 3/8	1 3/4	1 5/16	1	3/4	9/16

TABLE 17 Permissible Variations in Cross Section for W, S, M, C, and MC Shapes

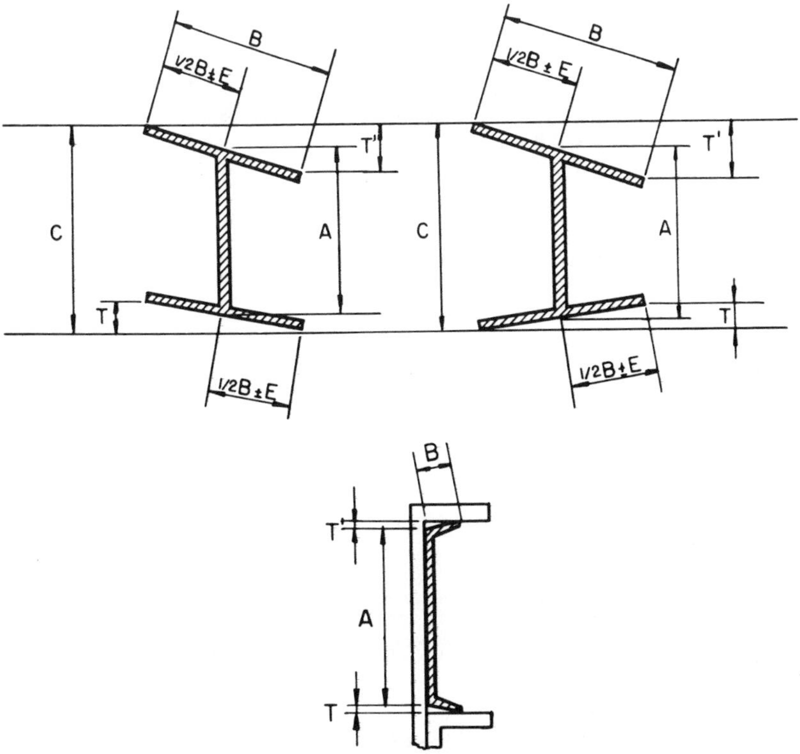

NOTES—*A* is measured at center line of web for S, M, and W shapes; at back of web for C and MC shapes. Measurement is overall for C shapes under 3 in. *B* is measured parallel to flange. *C* is measured parallel to web.

Shape	Section Nominal Sizes in.	*A*, Depth, in.		*B*, Flange Width, in.		$T + T'$[a] Flanges Out-of-Square, max. in.[b]	*E*, Web off Center, max. in.[c]	*C*, Maximum Depth at any Cross Section over Theoretical Depth, in.	Thickness of Web for Thickness Given	
		Over Theoretical	Under Theoretical	Over Theoretical	Under Theoretical				3/16 and under	Over 3/16
W	Up to 12, incl	1/8	1/8	1/4	3/16	1/4	3/16	1/4	...	...
	Over 12	1/8	1/8	1/4	3/16	5/16	3/16	1/4	...	...
S and M	3 to 7, incl	3/32	1/16	1/8	1/8	1/32	...	...	...	...
	Over 7 to 14, incl	1/8	3/32	5/32	5/32	1/32	...	...	...	...
	Over 14 to 24, incl	3/16	1/8	3/16	3/16	1/32	...	...	...	...
C and MC	1½ and under	1/32	1/32	1/32	1/32	1/32	...	...	0.010	0.015
	Over 1½ to 3, incl	1/16	1/16	1/16	1/16	1/32	...	...	0.015	0.020
	3 to 7, incl	3/32	1/16	1/8	1/8	1/32	...	...	...	...
	Over 7 to 14, incl	1/8	3/32	1/8	5/32	1/32	...	...	...	...
	Over 14	3/16	1/8	1/8	3/16	1/32	...	...	...	...

[a] $T + T'$ applies when flanges of channels are toed in or out. For channels 5/8 in. and under in depth, the permissible out-of-square is 3/64 in./in. of depth.
[b] Tolerance is per inch of flange width width for S, M, C, and MC shapes.
[c] Variation of 5/16 in. max for sections over 426 lb/ft.

TABLE 18 Permissible Variations in Cross Section for Angles (L Shapes), Bulb Angles, and Zees

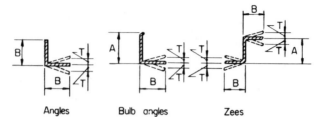

Angles   Bulb angles   Zees

Section	Nominal Size, in.	A, Depth, in.		B, Flange Width or Length of Leg, in.		T, Out of Square per Inch of B, in.	Variations from Thickness for Thicknesses Given, Over and Under, in.		
		Over Theoreti-cal	Under Theoreti-cal	Over Theoreti-cal	Under Theoreti-cal		³⁄₁₆ and under	Over ³⁄₁₆ to ⅜, incl	Over ⅜
Angles"	1 and under	...	...	¹⁄₃₂	¹⁄₃₂	³⁄₁₂₈[b]	0.008	0.010	...
(L Shapes)	Over 1 to 2, incl	...	...	³⁄₆₄	³⁄₆₄	³⁄₁₂₈[b]	0.010	0.010	0.012
	Over 2 to 3, excl	...	...	¹⁄₁₆	¹⁄₁₆	³⁄₁₂₈[b]	0.012	0.015	0.015
	3 to 4, incl	...	...	⅛	³⁄₃₂	³⁄₁₂₈[b]	...	...	...
	Over 4 to 6, incl	...	...	⅛	⅛	³⁄₁₂₈[b]	...	...	...
	Over 6	...	...	³⁄₁₆	⅛	³⁄₁₂₈[b]	...	...	...
Bulb angles	(Depth) 3 to 4, incl	⅛	¹⁄₁₆	⅛	³⁄₃₂	³⁄₁₂₈[b]	...	...	...
	Over 4 to 6, incl	⅛	¹⁄₁₆	⅛	⅛	³⁄₁₂₈[b]	...	...	...
	Over 6	⅛	¹⁄₁₆	³⁄₁₆	⅛	³⁄₁₂₈[b]	...	...	...
Zees	3 to 4, incl	⅛	¹⁄₁₆	⅛	³⁄₃₂	³⁄₁₂₈[b]	...	...	...
	Over 4 to 6, incl	⅛	¹⁄₁₆	⅛	⅛	³⁄₁₂₈[b]	...	...	...

" For unequal leg angles, longer leg determines classification.
[b] ³⁄₁₂₈ in./in. = 1½ deg.

TABLE 19 Permissible Variations in Sectional Dimensions for Rolled Tees

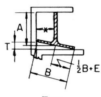

Tees

* Back of square and center line of stem to be parallel when measuring "out-of-square."

Nominal Size," in.	A, Depth,[b] in.		B, Width,[b] in.		T, Out-of-Square per Inch of B, in.	E, Web-off-Cen-ter, max, in.	Stem Out-of-Square,[c] in.	Thickness of Flange, in.		Thickness of Stem, in.	
	Over	Under	Over	Under				Over	Under	Over	Under
1¼ and under	³⁄₆₄	³⁄₆₄	³⁄₆₄	³⁄₆₄	...	...	¹⁄₃₂	0.010	0.010	0.005	0.020
Over 1¼ to 2, incl	¹⁄₁₆	¹⁄₁₆	¹⁄₁₆	¹⁄₁₆	...	...	¹⁄₁₆	0.012	0.012	0.010	0.020
Over 2 to 3, excl	³⁄₃₂	³⁄₃₂	³⁄₃₂	³⁄₃₂	...	...	³⁄₃₂	0.015	0.015	0.015	0.020
3 to 5, incl	³⁄₃₂	¹⁄₁₆	⅛	⅛	¹⁄₃₂	³⁄₃₂	...	...	...	...	...
Over 5 to 7, incl	³⁄₃₂	¹⁄₁₆	⅛	⅛	¹⁄₃₂	⅛	...	...	...	...	...

" The longer member of an unequal tee determines the size for permissible variations.
[b] Measurements for both depth and width are overall.
[c] Stem-out-of-square is the variation from its true position of the center line of stem, measured at the point.

502

TABLE 20 Permissable Variations in Length for S, M, C, MC, L, T, Z, and Bulb Angle Shapes

Nominal Size,[a] in.	Variations from Specified Length for Lengths Given, in.													
	5 to 10 ft, excl		10 to 20 ft, excl		20 to 30 ft, incl		Over 30 to 40 ft, incl		Over 40 to 50 ft, incl		Over 50 to 65 ft, incl		Over 65 ft	
	Over	Under	Over	Under	Over	Under	Over	Under	Over	Under	Over	Under	Over	Under
Under 3	⅝	0	1	0	1½	0	2	0	2½	0	2½	0	...	...
3 and over	½	¼	½	¼	½	¼	¾	¼	1	¼	1⅛	¼	1¼	¼

[a] Greatest cross-sectional dimension.

TABLE 21 Permissible Variations in Ends Out-Of-Square for S, M, C, MC, L, T, Z, and Bulb Angle Shapes

Shapes	Permissible Variations
S, M, C, and MC	¹⁄₆₄ in./in. of depth
L[a]	³⁄₁₂₈ in./in. of leg length or 1½ deg
Bulb angles	³⁄₁₂₈ in./in. of depth or 1½ deg
Rolled Tees[a]	¹⁄₆₄ in./in. of flange or stem
Zees	³⁄₁₂₈ in./in. of sum of both flange lengths

[a] Permissible variations for ends out-of-square are determined on the longer members of the shape.

TABLE 22 Permissible Variations in Straightness for S, M, C, MC, L, T, Z, and Bulb Angle Shapes

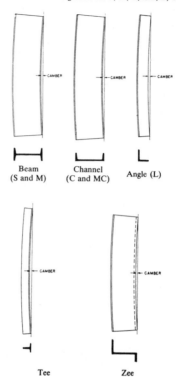

Beam
(S and M)

Channel
(C and MC)

Angle (L)

Tee

Zee

Positions for Measuring Camber of Shapes

Variable	Nominal Size,[a] in.	Permissible Variation, in.
Camber	under 3	¼ in. in any 5 ft, or ¼ × (number of feet of total length/5)
	3 and over	⅛ × (number of feet of total length/5)
Sweep	all	Due to the extreme variations in flexibility of these shapes, straightness tolerances for sweep are subject to negotiations between the manufacturer and the purchaser for the individual sections involved.

[a] Greatest cross-sectional dimension.

TABLE 23 Permissible Variations in Length for W Shapes[a, b]

W Shapes	Variations from Specified Length for Lengths Given, in.			
	30 ft and under		Over 30 ft	
	Over	Under	Over	Under
Beams 24 in. and under in nominal depth	⅜	⅜	⅜ plus ¹⁄₁₆ for each additional 5 ft or fraction thereof	⅜
Beams over 24 in. in nominal depth and all columns	½	½	½ plus ¹⁄₁₆ for each additional 5 ft or fraction thereof	½

[a] When W shapes are used as bearing piles, the length tolerance is plus 5 in. and minus 0 in. This length tolerance also applies to steel sheet piles.
[b] The ends out-of-square tolerance for W shapes shall be ¹⁄₆₄ in./in. of depth, or of flange width if it is greater than the depth.

TABLE 24 Permissible Variations for Length and Ends Out-of-Square, Milled Shapes

Nominal, Depth, in.	Length, ft[a,c]	Milled Both Ends[b]			Milled One-End[b]		
		Length, in.		Maximum End Out-of-Square, in.	Length, in.		Maximum End Out-of-Square, for Milled End, in.
		Over	Under		Over	Under	
6 to 36	6 to 70	1/32	1/32	1/32	1/4	1/4	1/32

[a] Length is measured along center line of web. Measurements are made with the steel and tape at the same temperature.
[b] Ends out-of-square are measured by (a) squaring from the center line of the web and (b) squaring from the center line of the flange. The measured variation from true squareness in either plane may not exceed the total tabular amount.
[c] Length variation and out-of-square variation are additive.

TABLE 25 Permissible Variations in Straightness for W Shapes.

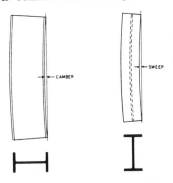

Positions for Measuring Camber and Sweep of W Shapes

	Permissible Variation
Camber and sweep	1/8 in. × (number of feet of total length[a]/10)
When certain sections[b] with a flange width approximately equal to depth are specified on order as columns:	
Lengths of 45 ft and under	1/8 in. × (number of feet of total length/10) but not over 3/8 in.
Lengths over 45 ft	3/8 in. + [1/8 in. × ([number of feet of total length − 45]/10)]

[a] Sections with a flange width less than 6 in., tolerance for sweep = 1/8 in. × (number of feet of total length/5).
[b] Applies only to:
8-in. deep sections 31 lb/ft and heavier,
10-in. deep sections 49 lb/ft and heavier,
12-in. deep sections 65 lb/ft and heavier, and
14-in. deep sections 90 lb/ft and heavier.
If other sections are specified on the order as columns, the tolerance will be subject to negotiation with the manufacturer.

TABLE 26 Permissible Variations in Dimensions for Split Tees and Split Angles (L Shapes)[a]

Specified Depth, in.	Variations from Depth,[b] Over and Under, in.
To 6, excl (beams and channels)	1/8
6 to 16, excl (beams and channels)	3/16
16 to 20, excl (beams and channels)	1/4
20 to 24, excl (beams)	5/16
24 and over (beams)	3/8

[a] The length tolerance for split tees or angles are the same as those applicable to the section from which the tees or angles are split.

[b] The above tolerances for depth of tees or angles include the allowable tolerances in depth for the beams or channels before splitting. Tolerances both for dimensions and straightness, as set up for the beams or channels from which these tees or angles are cut, will apply, except

straightness = 1/8 in. × (length in feet/5)

TABLE 28 Permissible Variations in Sectional Dimensions for Round and Square Bars and Round-Cornered Squares

Specified Size, in.	Variations from Size, in.		Out-of-Round or Out-of-Square, in.[a]
	Over	Under	
To 5/16	0.005	0.005	0.008
Over 5/16 to 7/16, incl	0.006	0.006	0.009
Over 7/16 to 5/8, incl	0.007	0.007	0.010
Over 5/8 to 7/8, incl	0.008	0.008	0.012
Over 7/8 to 1, incl	0.009	0.009	0.013
Over 1 to 1 1/8, incl	0.010	0.010	0.015
Over 1 1/8 to 1 1/4, incl	0.011	0.011	0.016
Over 1 1/4 to 1 3/8, incl	0.012	0.012	0.018
Over 1 3/8 to 1 1/2, incl	0.014	0.014	0.021
Over 1 1/2 to 2, incl	1/64	1/64	0.023
Over 2 to 2 1/2, incl	1/32	0	0.023
Over 2 1/2 to 3 1/2, incl	3/64	0	0.035
Over 3 1/2 to 4 1/2, incl	1/16	0	0.046
Over 4 1/2 to 5 1/2, incl	5/64	0	0.058
Over 5 1/2 to 6 1/2, incl	1/8	0	0.070
Over 6 1/2 to 8 1/4, incl	5/32	0	0.085
Over 8 1/4 to 9 1/2, incl	3/16	0	0.100
Over 9 1/2 to 10, incl	1/4	0	0.120

[a] Out-of-round is the difference between the maximum and minimum diameters of the bar, measured at the same transverse cross section. Out-of-square section is the difference in perpendicular distance between opposite faces, measured at the same transverse cross section.

TABLE 27 Permissible Variations in Sectional Dimensions for Square Edge and Round Edge Flat Bars

Specified Widths, in.	Variations from Thickness, for Thicknesses Given, Over and Under, in.							Variations from Width, in.	
	0.203 to 0.230, excl	0.230 to 1/4, excl	1/4 to 1/2, incl	Over 1/2 to 1, incl	Over 1 to 2, incl	Over 2 to 3, incl	Over 3	Over	Under
To 1, incl	0.007	0.007	0.008	0.010	...	...	...	1/64	1/64
Over 1 to 2, incl	0.007	0.007	0.012	0.015	1/32	...	...	1/32	1/32
Over 2 to 4, incl	0.008	0.008	0.015	0.020	1/32	3/64	3/64	1/16	1/32
Over 4 to 6, incl	0.009	0.009	0.015	0.020	1/32	3/64	3/64	3/32	1/16
Over 6 to 8, incl	[a]	0.015	0.016	0.025	1/32	3/64	1/16	1/8[b]	3/32[b]

[a] Flats over 6 to 8 in., incl, in width are not available as hot-rolled carbon steel bars in thickness under 0.230 in.

[b] For flats over 6 to 8 in., in width, and to 3 in. incl in thickness.

TABLE 29 Permissible Variations in Sectional Dimensions for Hexagons

Specified Sizes Between Opposite Sides, in.	Variations from Size, in. Over	Variations from Size, in. Under	Maximum Difference, Three Measurements, in.[a]
½ and under	0.007	0.007	0.011
Over ½ to 1, incl	0.010	0.010	0.015
Over 1 to 1½, incl	0.021	0.013	0.025
Over 1½ to 2, incl	¹⁄₃₂	¹⁄₆₄	¹⁄₃₂
Over 2 to 2½, incl	³⁄₆₄	¹⁄₆₄	³⁄₆₄
Over 2½ to 3½, incl	¹⁄₁₆	¹⁄₆₄	¹⁄₁₆

[a] Out-of-hexagon section is the greatest difference in distance between any two opposite faces measured at the same transverse cross section.

TABLE 30 Permissible Variations in Straightness for Bars

Maximum Permissible Variation in Straightness, in.[a]

¼ in any 5 ft, or ¼ × (number of feet of total length/5)

[a] Permissible variations in straightness do not apply to hot-rolled bars if any subsequent heating operation has been performed.

TABLE 32 Permissible Variations in Length for Bars Recut Both Ends After Straightening[a, b]

Sizes of Rounds, Squares, Hexagons, Width of Flats and Maximum Dimension of Other Sections, in.	Permissible Variations for Specified Length, in. To 12 ft, incl Over	Permissible Variations for Specified Length, in. To 12 ft, incl Under	Permissible Variations for Specified Length, in. Over 12 ft Over	Permissible Variations for Specified Length, in. Over 12 ft Under
To 3, incl	³⁄₁₆	¹⁄₁₆	¼	¹⁄₁₆
Over 3 to 6, incl	¼	¹⁄₁₆	⅜	¹⁄₁₆
Over 6 to 8, incl	⅜	¹⁄₁₆	½	¹⁄₁₆
Rounds over 8 to 10, incl	½	¹⁄₁₆	⅝	¹⁄₁₆

[a] For flats over 6 to 8 in., incl, in width, and over 3 in. in thickness, consult the producer for length tolerances.

[b] Variations are sometimes required all over or all under the specified length, in which case the sum of the two tolerances applies.

TABLE 31 Permissible Variations in Length for Hot-Cut Steel Bars[a]

Specified Sizes of Rounds, Squares, and Hexagons, in.	Specified Sizes of Flats, in. Thickness	Specified Sizes of Flats, in. Width	Permissible Variations over Specified Length Given in Feet, in. (No Variation Under) 5 to 10 ft. excl	10 to 20 ft. excl	20 to 30 ft. excl	30 to 40 ft. excl	40 to 60 ft. incl
To 1, incl	To 1, incl	To 3, incl	½	¾	1¼	1¾	2¼
Over 1 to 2, incl	Over 1	to 3, incl	⅝	1	1½	2	2½
Over 1 to 2, incl	To 1, incl	Over 3 to 6, incl	⅝	1	1½	2	2½
Over 2 to 5, incl	Over 1	Over 3 to 6, incl	1	1½	1¾	2¼	2¾
Over 5 to 10, incl	...	...	2	2½	2¾	3	3¼
	0.230 to 1, incl	Over 6 to 8, incl	¾	1¼	1¾	3½	4
	Over 1 to 3, incl	Over 6 to 8, incl	1¼	1¾	2	3½	4
Hot Sawing							
2 to 5, incl[b]	1 and over	3 and over	[b]	1½	1¾	2¼	2¾
Over 5 to 10, incl	...	...	[b]	2½	2¾	3	3¼

[a] For flats over 6 to 8 in., incl, in width and over 3 in. in thickness, consult the producer for length tolerances.

[b] Smaller sizes and shorter lengths are not commonly hot sawed.

ANNEX

A1. DIMENSIONS OF STANDARD SHAPE PROFILES

A1.1 Listed herein are dimensions and weight (mass) of some standard shape profiles. While this annex is an integral part of this specification, only the U.S. customary units are to be regarded as standard. Conformance to the SI units listed in this annex for dimensions and mass is not mandatory except when so agreed prior to acceptance of the order by the manufacturer.

ACI Standard

Recommended Practice for Selecting Proportions for Normal and Heavyweight Concrete (ACI 211.1-77)*

Reported by ACI Committee 211
JOHN R. WILSON
Chairman

Edward A. Abdun-Nur
Frederick R. Allen
James E. Bennett, Jr.
Robert A. Burmeister
Alan C. Carter
William A. Cordon
Edwin A. Decker
Donald E. Dixon
Frank G. Erskine
H. P. Fauerby
A. T. Hersey
William W. Hotaling, Jr.
Edward J. Hyland

Paul Klieger
Frank J. Lahm
Gary R. Mass
Richard C. Meininger
Austin H. Morgan, Jr.
J. Neil Mustard
Sandor Popovics
John M. Scanlon, Jr.
George B. Southworth
George W. Washa
Cecil H. Willetts
John C. Wycoff

Describes, with examples, two methods for selecting and adjusting proportions for normal weight concrete. One method is based on an estimated weight of the concrete per unit volume; the other is based on calculations of the absolute volume occupied by the concrete ingredients. The procedures take into consideration the requirements for placeability, consistency, strength, and durability. Example calculations are shown for both methods, including adjustments based on the characteristics of the first trial batch.

The proportioning of heavyweight concrete for such purposes as radiation shielding and bridge counterweight structures is described in an appendix. This appendix uses the absolute volume method which is generally accepted and is more convenient for heavyweight concrete.

---

*Adopted as a standard of the American Concrete Institute in September 1977, to supersede ACI 211.1-74 (Revised 1975), in accordance with the Institute's standardization procedure.

Keywords: adsorption; aggregates; air-entrained concretes; air entrainment, cement content; coarse aggregates; concrete durability; concretes; consistency; durability; exposure; fine aggregates; heavyweight aggregates; heavyweight concretes; mix proportioning; quality control; radiation shielding; slump tests; volume; water-cement ratio; workability.

1. SCOPE

1.1—This recommended practice describes methods for selecting proportions for concrete made with aggregates of normal and high density (as distinguished from lightweight and special high density aggregates) and of workability suitable for usual cast-in-place construction (as distinguished from special mixtures for concrete products manufacture).

1.2—The methods provide a first approximation of proportions intended to be checked by trial batches in the laboratory or field and adjusted, as necessary, to produce the desired characteristics of the concrete.

1.3—U.S. customary units are used in the main body of the text. Adaptation for the metric system is provided in Appendix 1, and demonstrated in an example problem in Appendix 2.

1.4—Test methods mentioned in the text are listed in Appendix 3.

2. INTRODUCTION

2.1—Concrete is composed principally of cement, aggregates, and water. It will contain some amount of entrapped air and may also contain purposely entrained air obtained by use of an admixture or air-entraining cement. Admixtures are also frequently used for other purposes such as to accelerate, retard, improve workability, reduce mixing water requirement, increase strength, or alter other properties of the concrete.

2.2—The selection of concrete proportions involves a balance between reasonable economy and requirements for placeability, strength, durability, density, and appearance. The required characteristics are governed by the use to which the concrete will be put and by conditions expected to be encountered at the time of placement. These are often, but not always, reflected in specifications for the job.

2.3—The ability to tailor concrete properties to job needs reflects technological developments which have taken place, for the most part, since the early 1900s. The use of the water-cement ratio as a tool for estimating strength was recognized about 1918. The remarkable improvement in durability resulting from the entrainment of air was recognized in the early 1940s. These two significant developments in concrete technology have been augmented by extensive research and development in many related areas, including the use of admixtures to counteract possible deficiencies, develop special properties, or achieve economy.* It is beyond the scope of this discussion to review the theories of concrete proportioning which have provided the background and sound technical basis for the relatively simple methods of this recommended practice. More detailed information can be obtained from the list of references.

2.4—Proportions calculated by any method must always be considered subject to revision on the basis of experience with trial batches. Depending on circumstances, the trial mixes may be prepared in a laboratory or, perhaps perferably, as full-size field batches. The latter procedure, when feasible, avoids possible pitfalls of assuming that data from small batches mixed in a laboratory environment will predict performance under field conditions. Trial batch procedures and background testing are described in Appendix 3.

3. BASIC RELATIONSHIP

3.1—Concrete proportions must be selected to provide necessary placeability, strength, durability, and density for the particular application. Well established relationships governing these properties are discussed briefly below.

3.2—*Placeability* (including satisfactory finishing properties) encompasses traits loosely accumulated in the terms ''workability'' and ''consistency.'' For the purpose of this discussion, *workability* is considered to be that property of concrete which determines its capacity to be placed and consolidated properly and to be finished without harmful segregation. It embodies such concepts as moldability, cohesiveness, and compactability. It is affected by the grading, particle shape and proportions of aggregate, the amount of cement, the presence of entrained air, admixtures, and the consistency of the mixture. Procedures in this recommended practice permit these factors to be taken into account to achieve satisfactory placeability economically.

3.3—*Consistency,* loosely defined, is the wetness of the concrete mixture. It is measured in terms of slump—the higher the slump the wetter the mixture—and it affects the ease with which the concrete will flow during placement. It is related to but not synonymous with workability. In properly proportioned concrete, the unit water content required to produce a given slump will depend on several factors. Water requirement increases as aggregates become more angular and rough textured (but this disadvantage may be offset by improvements in other characteristics such as bond to cement paste).

---

*See ACI Committee 212, ''Admixtures for Concrete,'' ACI JOURNAL, *Proceedings* V. 60, No. 11, Nov. 1963, pp. 1525–1534.

Required mixing water decreases as the maximum size of well graded aggregate is increased. It also decreases with the entrainment of air. Mixing water requirement may often be significantly reduced by certain admixtures.

3.4—*Strength.* Strength is an important characteristic of concrete, but other characteristics such as durability, permeability, and wear resistance are often equally or more important. These may be related to strength in a general way but are also affected by factors not significantly associated with strength. For a given set of materials and conditions, concrete strength is determined by the net quantity of water used per unit quantity of cement. The net water content excludes water absorbed by the aggregates. Differences in strength for a given water-cement ratio may result from changes in: maximum size of aggregate; grading, surface texture, shape, strength, and stiffness of aggregate particles; differences in cement types and sources; air content; and the use of admixtures which affect the cement hydration process or develop cementitious properties themselves. To the extent that these effects are predictable in the general sense, they are taken into account in this recommended practice. However, in view of their number and complexity, it should be obvious that accurate predictions of strength must be based on trial batches or experience with the materials to be used.

3.5—*Durability.* Concrete must be able to endure those exposures which may deprive it of its serviceability—freezing and thawing, wetting and drying, heating and cooling, chemicals, deicing agents, and the like. Resistance to some of these may be enhanced by use of special ingredients: low-alkali cement, pozzolans, or selected aggregate to prevent harmful expansion due to the alkali-aggregate reaction which occurs in some areas when concrete is exposed in a moist environment: sulfate resisting cement or pozzolans for concrete exposed to seawater or sulfate-bearing soils; or aggregate free of excessive soft particles where resistance to surface abrasion is required. Use of a low water-cement ratio will prolong the life of concrete by reducing the penetration of aggressive liquids. Resistance to severe weathering, particularly freezing and thawing, and to salts used for ice removal is greatly improved by incorporation of a proper distribution of entrained air. Entrained air should be used in all exposed concrete in climates where freezing occurs.*

3.6—*Density.* For certain applications concrete may be used primarily for its weight characteristic. Examples of applications are counterweights on lift bridges, weights for sinking oil pipelines under water, shielding from radiation, and for insulation from sound. By using special aggregates, placeable concrete of densities as high as 350 lb per cu ft can be obtained—see Appendix 4.

---

*For further details, see ACI Committee 201, "Durability of Concrete in Service," ACI JOURNAL, *Proceedings* V. 59, No. 12, Dec. 1962, pp. 1771–1820.

4. BACKGROUND DATA

4.1—To the extent possible, selection of concrete proportions should be based on text data or experience with the materials actually to be used. Where such background is limited or not available, estimates given in this recommended practice may be employed.

4.2—The following information for available materials will be useful:

4.2.1 Sieve analyses of fine and coarse aggregates

4.2.2 Unit weight of coarse aggregate

4.2.3 Bulk specific gravities and absorptions of aggregates

4.2.4 Mixing water requirements of concrete developed from experience with available aggregates

4.2.5 Relationships between strength and water-cement ratio for available combinations of cement and aggregate

4.3—Estimates from Tables 5.3.3 and 5.3.4, respectively, may be used when the last two items of information are not available. As will be shown, proportions can be estimated without the knowledge of aggregate specific gravity and absorption, Item 4.2.3.

5. PROCEDURE

5.1—The procedure for selection of mix proportions given in this section is applicable to normal weight concrete. Although the same basic data and procedures can be used in proportioning heavyweight concrete, additional information as well as sample computations for this type of concrete are given in Appendix 4.

5.2—Estimating the required batch weights for the concrete involves a sequence of logical, straightforward steps which, in effect, fit the characteristics of the available materials into a mixture suitable for the work. The question of suitability is frequently not left to the individual selecting the proportions. The job specifications may dictate some or all of the following:

5.2.1 Maximum water-cement ratio

5.2.2 Minimum cement content

5.2.3 Air content

5.2.4 Slump

5.2.5 Maximum size of aggregate

5.2.6 Strength

5.2.7 Other requirements relating to such things as strength overdesign, admixtures, and special types of cement or aggregate.

5.3—Regardless of whether the concrete characteristics are prescribed by the specifications or are left to the individual selecting the proportions, establishment of batch weights per cubic yard of concrete can best be accomplished in the following sequence:

5.3.1 *Step 1. Choice of slump.* If slump is not specified, a value appropriate for the work can be selected from Table 5.3.1. The slump ranges shown apply when vibration is used to consolidate the concrete. Mixes of the stiffest consistency that can be placed efficiently should be used.

5.3.2 *Step 2. Choice of maximum size of aggregate.* Large maximum sizes of well graded aggregates have less voids than smaller sizes. Hence, concretes with the larger-sized aggregates require less mortar per unit volume of concrete. Generally, the maximum size of aggregate should be the largest that is economically available and consistent with dimensions of the structure. In no event should the maximum size exceed one-fifth of the narrowest dimension between sides of forms, one-third the depth of slabs, nor three-fourths of the minimum clear spacing between individual reinforcing bars, bundles of bars, or pretensioning strands. These limitations are sometimes waived if workability and methods of consolidation are such that the concrete can be placed without honeycomb or void. When high strength concrete is desired, best results may be obtained with reduced maximum sizes of aggregate since these produce higher strengths at a given water-cement ratio.

5.3.3 *Step 3. Estimation of mixing water and air content.* The quantity of water per unit volume of concrete required to produce a given slump is dependent on the maximum size, particle shape and grading of the aggregates, and on the amount of entrained air. It is not greatly affected by the quantity of cement. Table 5.3.3 provides estimates of required mixing water for concretes made with various maximum sizes of aggregate, with and without air entrainment. Depending on aggregate texture and shape, mixing water requirements may be somewhat above or below the tabulated values, but they are sufficiently accurate for the first estimate. Such differences in water demand are not necessarily reflected in strength since other compensating factors may be involved. For example, a rounded and an angular coarse aggregate, both well and similarly graded and of good quality, can be expected to produce

TABLE 5.3.1—RECOMMENDED SLUMPS FOR VARIOUS TYPES OF CONSTRUCTION

Types of construction	Slump, in.	
	Maximum*	Minimum
Reinforced foundation walls and footings	3	1
Plain footings, caissons, and substructure walls	3	1
Beams and reinforced walls	4	1
Building columns	4	1
Pavements and slabs	3	1
Mass concrete	2	1

*May be increased 1 in. for methods of consolidation other than vibration.

TABLE 5.3.3—APPROXIMATE MIXING WATER AND AIR CONTENT REQUIREMENTS FOR DIFFERENT SLUMPS AND NOMINAL MAXIMUM SIZES OF AGGREGATES*

Slump, in.	Water, lb per cu yd of concrete for indicated nominal maximum sizes of aggregate							
	⅜ in.	½ in.	¾ in.	1 in.	1½ in.	2 in.†	3 in.†	6 in.†
Non-air-entrained concrete								
1 to 2	350	335	315	300	275	260	240	210
3 to 4	385	365	340	325	300	285	265	230
6 to 7	410	385	360	340	315	300	285	—
Approximate amount of entrapped air in non-air-entrained concrete, percent	3	2.5	2	1.5	1	0.5	0.3	0.2
Air-entrained concrete								
1 to 2	305	295	280	270	250	240	225	200
3 to 4	340	325	305	295	275	265	250	220
6 to 7	365	345	325	310	290	280	270	—
Recommended average‡ total air content, percent, for level of exposure:								
Mild exposure	4.5	4.0	3.5	3.0	2.5	2.0	1.5§**	1.0§**
Moderate exposure	6.0	5.5	5.0	4.5	4.5	4.0	3.5§**	3.0§**
Extreme exposure††	7.5	7.0	6.0	6.0	5.5	5.0	4.5§	4.0§

*These quantities of mixing water are for use in computing cement factors for trial batches. They are maxima for reasonably well-shaped angular coarse aggregates graded within limits of accepted specifications.

†The slump values for concrete containing aggregate larger than 1½ in. are based on slump tests made after removal of particles larger than 1½ in. by wet-screening.

‡Additional recommendations for air content and necessary tolerances on air content for control in the field are given in a number of ACI documents, including ACI 201, 345, 318, 301, and 302. ASTM C 94 for ready-mixed concrete also gives air content limits. The requirements in other documents may not always agree exactly, so in proportioning concrete consideration must be given to selecting an air content that will meet the needs of the job and also meet the applicable specifications.

§For concrete containing large aggregates which will be wet-screened over the 1½ in. sieve prior to testing for air content, the percentage of air expected in the 1½ in. minus material should be as tabulated in the 1½ in. column. However, initial proportioning calculations should include the air content as a percent of the whole.

**When using large aggregate in low cement factor concrete, air entrainment need not be detrimental to strength. In most cases mixing water requirement is reduced sufficiently to improve the water-cement ratio and to thus compensate for the strength reducing effect of entrained air on concrete. Generally, therefore, for these large maximum sizes of aggregate, air contents recommended for extreme exposure should be considered even though there may be little or no exposure to moisture and freezing.

††These values are based on the criteria that 9 percent air is needed in the mortar phase of the concrete. If the mortar volume will be substantially different from that determined in this recommended practice, it may be desirable to calculate the needed air content by taking 9 percent of the actual mortar volume.

concrete of about the same compressive strength for the same cement factor in spite of differences in water-cement ratio resulting from the different mixing water requirements. Particle shape per se is not an indicator that an aggregate will be either above or below average in its strength-producing capacity.

Table 5.3.3 indicates the approximate amount of entrapped air to be expected in non-air-entrained concrete in the upper part of the table and shows the recommended average air content for air-entrained concrete in the lower part of the table. If air entrainment is needed or desired, three levels of air content are given for each aggregate size depending on the purpose of the entrained air and the severity of exposure if entrained air is needed for durability:

Mild exposure—When air entrainment is desired for a beneficial effect other than durability, such as to improve workability or cohesion or in low cement factor concrete to improve strength, air contents lower than those needed for durability can be used. This exposure includes indoor or outdoor service in a climate where concrete will not be exposed to freezing or to deicing agents.

Moderate exposure—Service in a climate where freezing is expected but where the concrete will not be continually exposed to moisture or free water for long periods prior to freezing and will not be exposed to deicing agents or other aggressive chemicals. Examples include: exterior beams, columns, walls, girders, or slabs which are not in contact with wet soil and are so located that they will not receive direct application of deicing salts.

Severe exposure—Concrete which is exposed to deicing chemicals or other aggressive agents or where the concrete may become highly saturated by continual contact with moisture or free water prior to freezing. Examples include: pavements, bridge decks, curbs, gutters, sidewalks, canal linings, or exterior water tanks or sumps.

The use of normal amounts of air entrainment in concrete with a specified strength near or about 5000 psi may not be possible due to the fact that each added percent of air lowers the maximum strength obtainable with a given combination of materials.[18] In these cases the exposure to water, deicing salts, and freezing temperatures should be carefully evaluated. If a member is not continually wet and will not be exposed to deicing salts, lower air content values such as those given in Table 5.3.3 for moderate exposure are appropriate even though the concrete is exposed to freezing and thawing temperatures. However, for an exposure condition where the member may be saturated prior to freezing, the use of air entrainment should not be sacrificed for strength.

When trial batches are used to establish strength relationships or verify strength-producing capability of a mixture, the least favorable combination of mixing water and air content should be used. This is, the air content should be the maximum permitted or likely to occur, and the concrete should be gaged to the highest permissible slump. This will avoid developing an overoptimistic estimate of strength on the assumption that average rather than extreme conditions will prevail in the field. For information on air content recommendations, see ACI 201, 301, and 302.

5.3.4 *Step 4. Selection of water-cement ratio.* The required water-cement ratio is determined not only by strength requirements but also by factors such as durability and finishing properties. Since different aggregates and cements generally produce different strengths at the same water-cement ratio, it is highly desirable to have or develop the relationship between strength and water-cement ratio for the materials actually to be used. In the absence of such data, approximate and relatively conservative values for concrete containing Type I portland cement can be taken from Table 5.3.4(a). With typical materials, the tabulated water-cement ratios should produce the strengths shown, based on 28-day tests of specimens cured under standard laboratory conditions. The average strength selected must, of course, exceed the specified strength by a sufficient margin to keep the number of low tests within specified limits.*

For severe conditions of exposure, the water-cement ratio should be kept low even though strength requirements may be met with a higher value. Table 5.3.4(b) gives limiting values.

5.3.5 *Step 5. Calculation of cement content.* The amount of cement per unit volume of concrete is fixed by the determinations made in Steps 3 and 4 above. The required cement is equal to the estimated mixing water content (Step 3) divided by the water-cement ratio (Step 4). If, however, the specification includes a separate minimum limit on cement in addition to requirements

TABLE 5.3.4(a)—RELATIONSHIPS BETWEEN WATER-CEMENT RATIO AND COMPRESSIVE STRENGTH OF CONCRETE

Compressive strength at 28 days, psi*	Water-cement ratio, by weight	
	Non-air-entrained concrete	Air-entrained concrete
6000	0.41	—
5000	0.48	0.40
4000	0.57	0.48
3000	0.68	0.59
2000	0.82	0.74

*Values are estimated average strengths for concrete containing not more than the percentage of air shown in Table 5.3.3. For a constant water-cement ratio, the strength of concrete is reduced as the air content is increased.

Strength is based on 6 x 12 in. cylinders moist-cured 28 days at 73.4 ± 3 F (23 ± 1.7 C) in accordance with Section 9(b) of ASTM C 31 for Making and Curing Concrete Compression and Flexure Test Specimens in the Field.

Relationship assumes maximum size of aggregate about ¾ to 1 in.; for a given source, strength produced for a given water-cement ratio will increase as maximum size of aggregate decreases; see Sections 3.4 and 5.3.2.

*See "Recommended Practice for Evaluation of Compression Test Results of Field Concrete (ACI 214-65)."

TABLE 5.3.4(b)—MAXIMUM PERMISSIBLE WATER-CEMENT RATIOS FOR CONCRETE IN SEVERE EXPOSURES*

Type of structure	Structure wet continuously or frequently and exposed to freezing and thawing†	Structure exposed to sea water or sulfates
Thin sections (railings, curbs, sills, ledges, ornamental work) and sections with less than 1 in. cover over steel	0.45	0.40‡
All other structures	0.50	0.45‡

*Based on report of ACI Committee 201, "Durability of Concrete in Service," previously cited.
†Concrete should also be air-entrained.
‡If sulfate resisting cement (Type II or Type V of ASTM C 150) is used, permissible water-cement ratio may be increased by 0.05.

for strength and durability, the mixture must be based on whichever criterion leads to the larger amount of cement.

The use of pozzolanic or chemical admixtures will affect properties of both the fresh and hardened concrete.*

5.3.6 *Step 6. Estimation of coarse aggregate content.* Aggregates of essentially the same maximum size and grading will produce concrete of satisfactory workability when a given volume of coarse aggregate, on a dry-rodded basis, is used per unit volume of concrete. Appropriate values for this aggregate volume are given in Table 5.3.6. It can be seen that, for equal workability, the volume of coarse aggregate in a unit volume of concrete is dependent only on its maximum size and the fineness modulus of the fine aggregate. Differences in the amount of mortar required for workability with different aggregates, due to differences in particle shape and grading, are compensated for automatically by differences in dry-rodded void content.

The volume of aggregate, in cubic feet, on a dry-rodded basis, for a cubic yard of concrete is equal to the value from Table 5.3.6 multiplied by 27. This volume is converted to dry weight of coarse aggregate required in a cubic yard of concrete by multiplying it by the dry-rodded weight per cubic foot of the coarse aggregate.

5.3.6.1 For more workable concrete, which is sometimes required when placement is by pump or when concrete must be worked around congested reinforcing steel, it may be desirable to reduce the estimated coarse aggregate content determined using Table 5.3.6 by up to 10 percent. However, caution must be exercised to assure that the resulting slump, water-cement ratio, and strength properties of the concrete are consistent with the recommendations in Sections 5.3.1 and 5.3.4 and meet applicable project specification requirements.

*See report of ACI Committee 212 "Admixtures for Concrete," ACI JOURNAL, *Proceedings* V. 60, No. 11, Nov. 1963, pp. 1481-1524.

TABLE 5.3.6—VOLUME OF COARSE AGGREGATE PER UNIT OF VOLUME OF CONCRETE

Maximum size of aggregate, in.	Volume of dry-rodded coarse aggregate* per unit volume of concrete for different fineness moduli of sand			
	2.40	2.60	2.80	3.00
⅜	0.50	0.48	0.46	0.44
½	0.59	0.57	0.55	0.53
¾	0.66	0.64	0.62	0.60
1	0.71	0.69	0.67	0.65
1½	0.75	0.73	0.71	0.69
2	0.78	0.76	0.74	0.72
3	0.82	0.80	0.78	0.76
6	0.87	0.85	0.83	0.81

*Volumes are based on aggregates in dry-rodded condition as described in ASTM C 29 for Unit Weight of Aggregate.
These volumes are selected from empirical relationships to produce concrete with a degree of workability suitable for usual reinforced construction. For less workable concrete such as required for concrete pavement construction they may be increased about 10 percent. For more workable concrete see Section 5.3.6.1.

5.3.7 *Step 7. Estimation of fine aggregate content.* At completion of Step 6, all ingredients of the concrete have been estimated except the fine aggregate. Its quantity is determined by difference. Either of two procedures may be employed: the "weight" method (Section 5.3.7.1) or the "absolute volume" method (Section 5.3.7.2).

5.3.7.1 If the weight of the concrete per unit volume is assumed or can be estimated from experience, the required weight of fine aggregate is simply the difference between the weight of fresh concrete and the total weight of the other ingredients. Often the unit weight of concrete is known with reasonable accuracy from previous experience with the materials. In the absence of such information, Table 5.3.7.1 can be used to make a first estimate. Even if the estimate of concrete weight per cubic yard is rough, mixture proportions will be sufficiently accurate to permit easy adjustment on the basis of trial batches as will be shown in the examples.

If a theoretically exact calculation of fresh concrete weight per cubic yard is desired, the following formula can be used:

$$U = 16.85 \, G_a \, (100 - A) + C(1 - G_a/G_c) - W(G_a - 1) \tag{5-1}$$

where

U = weight of fresh concrete per cubic yard, lb

G_a = weighted average specific gravity of combined fine and coarse aggregate, bulk SSD*

---

*SSD indicates saturated-surface-dry basis used in considering aggregate displacement. The aggregate specific gravity used in calculations must be consistent with the moisture condition assumed in the basic aggregate batch weights—i.e., bulk dry if aggregate weights are stated on a dry basis, and bulk SSD if weights are stated on a saturated-surface-dry basis.

G_c = specific gravity of cement (generally 3.15)

A = air content, percent

W = mixing water requirement, lb per cu yd

C = cement requirement, lb per cub yd

5.3.7.2 A more exact procedure for calculating the required amount of fine aggregate involves the use of volumes displaced by the ingredients. In this case, the total volume displaced by the known ingredients—water, air, cement, and coarse aggregate—is subtracted from the unit volume of concrete to obtain the required volume of fine aggregate. The volume occupied in concrete by any ingredient is equal to its weight divided by the density of that material (the latter being the product of the unit weight of water and the specific gravity of the material).

5.3.8 *Step 8. Adjustments for aggregate moisture.* The aggregate quantities actually to be weighed out for the concrete must allow for moisture in the aggregates. Generally, the aggregates will be moist and their dry weights should be increased by the percentage of water they contain, both absorbed and surface. The mixing water added to the batch must be reduced by an amount equal to the free moisture contributed by the aggregate—i.e., total moisture minus absorption.

5.3.9 *Step 9. Trial batch adjustments.* The calculated mixture proportions should be checked by means of trial batches prepared and tested in accordance with ASTM C 192, "Making and Curing Concrete Compression and Flexure Test Specimens in the Laboratory," or full-sized field batches.

TABLE 5.3.7.I—FIRST ESTIMATE OF WEIGHT OF FRESH CONCRETE

Maximum size of aggregate, in.	First estimate of concrete weight, lb per cu yd*	
	Non-air-entrained concrete	Air-entrained concrete
⅜	3840	3690
½	3890	3760
¾	3960	3840
1	4010	3900
1½	4070	3960
2	4120	4000
3	4160	4040
6	4230	4120

*Values calculated by Eq. (5-1) for concrete of medium richness (550 lb of cement per cu yd) and medium slump with aggregate specific gravity of 2.7. Water requirements based on values for 3 to 4 in. slump in Tables 5.3.3. If desired, the estimated weight may be refined as follows if necessary information is available: for each 10 lb difference in mixing water from the Table 5.3.3. values for 3 to 4 in. slump, correct the weight per cu yd 15 lb in the opposite direction; for each 100 lb difference in cement content from 550 lb, correct the weight per cu yd 15 lb in the same direction; for each 0.1 by which aggregate specific gravity deviates from 2.7, correct the concrete weight 100 lb in the same direction.

Only sufficient water should be used to produce the required slump regardless of the amount assumed in selecting the trial proportions. The concrete should be checked for unit weight and yield (ASTM C 138) and for air content (ASTM C 138, C 173, or C 231). It should also be carefully observed for proper workability, freedom from segregation, and finishing properties. Appropriate adjustments should be made in the proportions for subsequent batches in accordance with the following procedure.

5.3.9.1 Re-estimate the required mixing water per cubic yard of concrete by multiplying the net mixing water content of the trial batch by 27 and dividing the product by the yield of the trial batch in cubic feet. If the slump of the trial batch was not correct, increase or decrease the re-estimated amount of water by 10 lb for each required increase or decrease of 1 in. in slump.

5.3.9.2 If the desired air content (for air-entrained concrete) was not achieved, re-estimate the admixture content required for proper air content and reduce or increase the mixing water content of paragraph 5.3.9.1 by 5 lb for each 1 percent by which the air content is to be increased or decreased from that of the previous trial batch.

5.3.9.3 If estimated weight per cubic yard of fresh concrete is the basis for proportioning, re-estimate that weight by multiplying the unit weight in pounds per cubic foot of the trial batch by 27 and reducing or increasing the result by the anticipated percentage increase or decrease in air content of the adjusted batch from the first trial batch.

5.3.9.4 Calculate new batch weights starting with Step 4 (Paragraph 5.3.4), modifying the volume of coarse aggregate from Table 5.3.6 if necessary to provide proper workability.

6. SAMPLE COMPUTATIONS

6.1—Two example problems will be used to illustrate application of the proportioning procedures. The following conditions are assumed:

6.1.1 Type I non-air-entraining cement will be used and its specific gravity is assumed to be ~~3.15.†~~ 3.15

6.1.2 Coarse and fine aggregates in each case are of satisfactory quality and are graded within limits of generally accepted specifications.‡

6.1.3 The coarse aggregate has a bulk specific gravity of 2.68† and an absorption of 0.5 percent.

6.1.4 The fine aggregate has a bulk specific gravity of 2.64,* an absorption of 0.7 percent, and fineness modulus of 2.8.

---

†The specific gravity values are not used if proportions are selected to provide a weight of concrete assumed to occupy 1 cu yd.

‡Such as the "Specifications for Concrete Aggregates," (ASTM C 33).

*The specific gravity values are not used if proportions are selected to provide a weight of concrete assumed to occupy 1 cu yd.

6.2—*Example 1.* Concrete is required for a portion of a structure which will be below ground level in a location where it will not be exposed to severe weathering or sulfate attack. Structural considerations require it to have an average 28-day compressive strength of 3500 psi.† On the basis of information in Table 5.3.1, as well as previous experience, it is determined that under the conditions of placement to be employed, a slump of 3 to 4 in. should be used and that the available No. 4 to 1½-in. coarse aggregate will be suitable. The dry-rodded weight of coarse aggregate is found to be 100 lb per cu ft. Employing the sequence outlined in Section 5, the quantities of ingredients per cubic yard of concrete are calculated as follows:

6.2.1 *Step 1.* As indicated above, the desired slump is 3 to 4 in.

6.2.2 *Step 2.* The locally available aggregate, graded from No. 4 to 1½ in., has been indicated as suitable.

6.2.3 *Step 3.* Since the structure will not be exposed to severe weathering, non-air-entrained concrete will be used. The approximate amount of mixing water to produce a 3- to 4-in. slump in non-air-entrained concrete with 1½-in. aggregate is found from Table 5.3.3 to be 300 lb per cu yd. Estimated entrapped air is shown as 1 percent.

6.2.4 *Step 4.* From Table 5.3.4(a), the water-cement ratio needed to produce a strength of 3500 psi in non-air-entrained concrete is found to be about 0.62.

6.2.5 *Step 5.* From the information derived in Steps 3 and 4, the required cement content is found to be 300/0.62 = 484 lb per cu yd.

6.2.6 *Step 6.* The quantity of coarse aggregate is estimated from Table 5.3.6. For a fine aggregate having a fineness modulus of 2.8 and a 1½ in. maximum size of coarse aggregate, the table indicates that 0.71 cu ft of coarse aggregate, on a dry-rodded basis, may be used in each cubic foot of concrete. For a cubic yard, therefore, the coarse aggregate will be $27 \times 0.71 = 19.17$ cu ft. Since it weighs 100 lb per cu ft, the dry weight of coarse aggregate is 1917 lb.

6.2.7 *Step 7.* With the quantities of water, cement, and coarse aggregate established, the remaining material comprising the cubic yard of concrete must consist of sand and whatever air will be entrapped. The required sand may be determined on the basis of either weight or absolute volume as shown below:

6.2.7.1 *Weight basis.* From Table 5.3.7.1, the weight of a cubic yard of non-air-entrained concrete made with aggregate having a maximum size of 1½ in. is estimated to be 4070 lb. (For a first trial batch, exact adjustments of

---

†This is not the specified strength used for structural design, but a higher figure expected to be produced on the average. For the method of determining the amount by which average strength should exceed design strength, see "Recommended Practice for Evaluation of Compression Test Results of Field Concrete (ACI 214-65)."

this value for usual differences in slump, cement factor, and aggregate specific gravity are not critical.) Weight already known are:

Water (net mixing)	300 lb
Cement	484 lb
Coarse aggregate	1917 lb (dry)‡
Total	2701 lb

The weight of sand, therefore, is estimated to be

$$4070 - 2701 = 1369 \text{ lb (dry)}‡$$

6.2.7.2 *Absolute volume basis.* With the quantities of cement, water, and coarse aggregate established, and the approximate entrapped air content (as opposed to purposely entrained air) taken from Table 5.3.3, the sand content can be calculated as follows:

$$\text{Volume of water} = \frac{300}{62.4} = 4.81 \text{ cu ft}$$

$$\text{Solid volume of cement} = \frac{484}{3.15 \times 62.4} = 2.46 \text{ cu ft}$$

$$\text{Solid volume of coarse aggregate} = \frac{1917}{2.68 \times 62.4} = 11.46 \text{ cu ft}$$

$$\text{Volume of entrapped air} = 0.01 \times 27 = 0.27 \text{ cu ft}$$

$$\text{Total solid volume of ingredients except sand} = 19.00 \text{ cu ft}$$

$$\text{Solid volume of sand required} = 27 - 19.00 = 8.00 \text{ cu ft}$$

$$\text{Required weight of dry sand} = 8.00 \times 2.64 \times 62.4 = 1318 \text{ lb}$$

6.2.7.3 Batch weights per cubic yard of concrete calculated on the two bases are compared below:

---

‡Aggregate absorption is disregarded since its magnitude is inconsequential in relation to other approximations.

	Based on estimated concrete weight, lb	Based on absolute volume of ingredients, lb
Water (net mixing)	300	300
Cement	484	484
Coarse aggregate (dry)	1917	1917
Sand (dry)	1369	1318

6.2.8 *Step 8*. Tests indicate total moisture of 2 percent in the coarse aggregate and 6 percent in the fine aggregate. If the trial batch proportions based on assumed concrete weight are used, the adjusted aggregate weights become

Coarse aggregate (wet) $= 1917 (1.02) = 1955$ lb
Fine aggregate (wet) $= \cancel{1369} (1.06) = \cancel{1451}$ lb
  $\quad\quad 1318 \quad\quad\quad 1397$ lb

Absorbed water does not become part of the mixing water and must be excluded from the adjustment in added water. Thus, surface water contributed by the coarse aggregate amounts to $2 - 0.5 = 1.5$ percent; by the fine aggregate $6 - 0.7 = 5.3$ percent. The estimated requirement for added water, therefore, becomes

$$\overset{1318}{300 - 1917 (0.015) - \cancel{1369} (0.053)} = 199 \text{ lb}$$

The estimated batch weights for a cubic yard of concrete are:

Water (to be added)	199 lb
Cement	484 lb
Coarse aggregate (wet)	1955 lb
Fine aggregate (wet)	1451 lb

6.2.9 *Step 9*. For the laboratory trial batch, it is found convenient to scale the weights down to produce 0.03 cu yd or 0.81 cu ft of concrete. Although the calculated quantity of water to be added was 5.97 lb, the amount actually used in an effort to obtain the desired 3 to 4 in. slump is 7.00 lb. The batch as mixed therefore, consists of

Water (added)	7.00 lb
Cement	14.52 lb
Coarse aggregate (wet)	58.65 lb
Fine aggregate (wet)	43.53 lb
Total	123.70 lb

The concrete has a measured slump of 2 in. and unit weight of 149.0 lb per cu ft. It is judged to be satisfactory from the standpoint of workability and finishing properties. To provide proper yield and other characteristics for future batches, the following adjustments are made:

6.2.9.1 Since the yield of the trial batch was

$$123.70/149.0 = 0.830 \text{ cu ft}$$

and the mixing water content was 7.00 (added) +0.86 on coarse aggregate +2.18 on fine aggregate = 10.04 lb, the mixing water required for a cubic yard of concrete with the same slump as the trial batch should be

$$\frac{10.04 \times 27}{0.830} = 327 \text{ lb}$$

As indicated in Paragraph 5.3.9.1, this amount must be increased another 15 lb to raise the slump from the measured 2 in. to the desired 3 to 4 in. range, bringing the net mixing water to 342 lb.

6.2.9.2 With the increased mixing water, additional cement will be required to provide the desired water-cement ratio of 0.62. The new cement content becomes

$$342/0.62 = 552 \text{ lb}$$

6.2.9.3 Since workability was found to be satisfactory, the quantity of coarse aggregate per unit volume of concrete will be maintained the same as in the trial batch. The amount of coarse aggregate per cubic yard becomes

$$\frac{58.65}{0.83} \times 27 = 1908 \text{ lb wet}$$

which is

$$\frac{1908}{1.02} = 1871 \text{ lb dry}$$

and

$$1871 (1.005) = 1880 \text{ SSD*}$$

6.2.9.4 The new estimate for the weight of a cubic yard of concrete is $149.0 \times 27 = 4023$ lb. The amount of sand required is, therefore,

$$4023 - (342 + 552 + 1880) = 1249 \text{ lb SSD}$$

---

*Saturated-surface-dry.

or

$$1249/1.007 = 1240 \text{ lb dry}$$

The adjusted basic batch weights per cubic yard of concrete are

Water (net mixing)	342 lb
Cement	552 lb
Coarse aggregate (dry)	1871 lb
Fine aggregate (dry)	1240 lb

6.2.10 Adjustments of proportions determined on an absolute volume basis follow a procedure similar to that just outlined. The steps will be given without detailed explanation:

6.2.10.1 Quantities used in nominal 0.81 cu ft batch are

Water (added)	7.00 lb
Cement	14.52 lb
Coarse aggregate (wet)	58.65 lb
Fine aggregate (wet)	41.91 lb
Total	122.08 lb

Measured slump 2 in.; unit weight 149.0 lb per cu ft; yield 122.08/149.0 = 0.819 cu ft; workability o.k.

6.2.10.2 Re-estimated water for the same slump as trial batch:

$$\frac{27(7.00 + 0.86 + 2.09)}{0.819} = 328 \text{ lb}$$

Mixing water required for slump of 3 to 4 in.:

$$328 + 15 = 343 \text{ lb}$$

6.2.10.3 Adjusted cement content for increased water:

$$343/0.62 = 553 \text{ lb}$$

6.2.10.4 Adjusted coarse aggregate requirement:

$$\frac{58.65}{0.819} \times 27 = 1934 \text{ lb wet}$$

or

$$1934/1.02 = 1896 \text{ lb dry}$$

6.2.10.5 The volume of ingredients other than air in the original trial batch was

Water	$\dfrac{9.95}{62.4}$	$= 0.159$ cu ft
Cement	$\dfrac{14.52}{3.15 \times 62.4}$	$= 0.074$ cu ft
Coarse aggregate	$\dfrac{57.50}{2.68 \times 62.4}$	$= 0.344$ cu ft
Fine aggregate	$\dfrac{39.54}{2.64 \times 62.4}$	$= 0.240$ cu ft
Total		$= 0.817$ cu ft

Since the yield was 0.819 cu ft, the air content was

$$\frac{0.819 - 0.817}{0.819} = 0.2 \text{ percent}$$

With the proportions of all components except fine aggregate established, the determination of adjusted cubic yard batch quantities can be completed as follows:

Volume of water	$= \dfrac{343}{62.4}$	$= 5.50$ cu ft
Volume of cement	$= \dfrac{553}{3.15 \times 62.4}$	$= 2.81$ cu ft
Volume of air	$= 0.002 \times 27$	$= 0.05$ cu ft
Volume of coarse aggregate	$= \dfrac{1896}{2.68 \times 62.4}$	$= 11.34$ cu ft
Total volume exclusive of fine aggregate		$= 19.70$ cu ft
Volume of fine aggregate required	$= 27 - 19.70$	$= 7.30$ cu ft
Weight of fine aggregate (dry basis)	$= 7.30 \times 2.64 \times 62.4$	$= 1203$ lb

The adjusted basic batch weights per cubic yard of concrete, then, are:

Water (net mixing)	343 lb
Cement	553 lb
Coarse aggregate (dry)	1896 lb
Fine aggregate (dry)	1203 lb

These differ only slightly from those given in Paragraph 6.2.9.4 for the method of assumed concrete weight. Further trials or experience might indicate small additional adjustments for either method.

6.3—*Example 2*. Concrete is required for a heavy bridge pier which will be exposed to fresh water in a severe climate. An average 28-day compressive strength of 3000 psi will be required. Placement conditions permit a slump of 1 to 2 in. and the use of large aggregate, but the only economically available coarse aggregate of satisfactory quality is graded from No. 4 to 1 in. and this will be used. Its dry-rodded weight is found to be 95 lb per cu ft. Other characteristics are as indicated in Section 6.1.

The calculations will be shown in skeleton form only. Note that confusion is avoided if all steps of Section 5 are followed even when they appear repetitive of specified requirements.

6.3.1 *Step 1*. The desired slump is 1 to 2 in.

6.3.2 *Step 2*. The locally available aggregate, graded from No. 4 to 1 in., will be used.

6.3.3 *Step 3*. Since the structure will be exposed to severe weathering, air-entrained concrete will be used. The approximate amount of mixing water to produce a 1 to 2-in. slump in air-entrained concrete with 1-in. aggregate is found from Table 5.3.3 to be 270 lb per cu yd. The recommended air content is 5 percent.

6.3.4 *Step 4*. From Table 5.3.4(a), the water-cement ratio needed to produce a strength of 3000 psi in air-entrained concrete is estimated to be about 0.59. However, reference to Table 5.3.4(b) reveals that, for the severe weathering exposure anticipated, the water-cement ratio should not exceed 0.50. This lower figure must govern and will be used in the calculations.

6.3.5 *Step 5*. From the information derived in Steps 3 and 4, the required cement content is found to be 270/0.50 = 540 lb per cu yd.

6.3.6 *Step 6*. The quantity of coarse aggregate is estimated from Table 5.3.6. With a fine aggregate having a fineness modulus of 2.8 and a 1 in. maximum size of coarse aggregate, the table indicates that 0.67 cu ft of coarse aggregate, on a dry-rodded basis, may be used in each cubic foot of concrete. For a cubic yard, therefore, the coarse aggregate will be 27 × 0.67 = 18.09 cu ft. Since it weighs 95 lb per cu ft, the dry weight of coarse aggregate is 18.09 × 95 = 1719 lb.

6.3.7 *Step 7*. With the quantities of water, cement and coarse aggregate established, the remaining material comprising the cubic yard of concrete must consist of sand and air. The required sand may be determined on the basis of either weight or absolute volume as shown below.

6.3.7.1 *Weight basis.* From Table 5.3.7.1, the weight of a cubic yard of air-entrained concrete made with aggregate of 1 in. maximum size is estimated to be 3900 lb. (For a first trial batch, exact adjustments of this value for differences in slump, cement factor, and aggregate specific gravity are not critical.) Weights already known are:

Water (net mixing)	270 lb
Cement	540 lb
Coarse aggregate (dry)	1719 lb
Total	2529 lb

The weight of sand, therefore, is estimated to be

$$3900 - 2529 = 1371 \text{ lb (dry)}$$

6.3.7.2 *Absolute volume basis.* With the quantities of cement, water, air, and coarse aggregate established, the sand content can be calculated as follows:

Volume of water	=	$\dfrac{270}{62.4}$	= 4.33 cu ft
Solid volume of cement	=	$\dfrac{540}{3.15 \times 62.4}$	= 2.75 cu ft
Solid volume of coarse aggregate	=	$\dfrac{1719}{2.68 \times 62.4}$	= 10.28 cu ft
Volume of air	=	0.05×27	= 1.35 cu ft
Total volume of ingredients except sand			= 18.71 cu ft
Solid volume of sand required	=	$27 - 18.71$	= 8.29 cu ft
Required weight of dry sand	=	$8.29 \times 2.64 \times 62.4$	= 1366 lb

6.3.7.3 Batch weights per cubic yard of concrete calculated on the two bases are compared below:

	Based on estimated concrete weight, lb	Based on absolute volume of ingredients, lb
Water (net mixing)	270	270
Cement	540	540
Coarse aggregate (dry)	1719	1719
Sand (dry)	1371	1366

6.3.8. *Step 8.* Tests indicate total moisture of 3 percent in the coarse aggregate and 5 percent in the fine aggregate. If the trial batch proportions based on assumed concrete weight are used, the adjusted aggregate weights become

Coarse aggregate (wet) $= 1719 \,(1.03) = 1771 \text{ lb}$
Fine aggregate (wet) $= 1371 \,(1.05) = 1440 \text{ lb}$

Absorbed water does not become part of the mixing water and must be excluded from the adjustment in added water. Thus, surface water contributed by the coarse aggregate amounts to $3 - 0.5 = 2.5$ percent; by the fine aggregate $5 - 0.7 = 4.3$ percent. The estimated requirement for added water, therefore, becomes

$$270 - 1719 \,(0.025) - 1371 \,(0.043) = 168 \text{ lb}$$

The estimated batch weights for a cubic yard of concrete are:

Water (to be added)	168 lb
Cement	540 lb
Coarse aggregate (wet)	1771 lb
Fine aggregate (wet)	1440 lb
Total	3919 lb

6.3.9 *Step 9.* For the laboratory trial batch, the weights are scaled down to produce 0.03 cu yd or 0.81 cu ft of concrete. Although the calculated quantity of water to be added was 5.04 lb the amount actually used is in an effort to obtain the desired 1 to 2-in. slump is 4.50 lb. The batch as mixed, therefore, consists of

Water (added)	4.50 lb
Cement	16.20 lb
Coarse aggregate (wet)	53.13 lb
Fine aggregate (wet)	43.20 lb
Total	117.03 lb

The concrete has a measured slump of 2 in., unit weight of 141.8 lb per cu ft, and air content of 6.5 percent. It is judged to be slightly oversanded for the easy placement condition involved. To provide proper yield and other characteristics for future batches, the following adjustments are made:

6.3.9.1 Since the yield of the trial batch was

$$117.03/141.8 = 0.825 \text{ cu ft}$$

and the mixing water content was 4.50 (added) + 1.29 on coarse aggregate + 1.77 on fine aggregate = 7.56 lb the mixing water required for a cubic yard of concrete with the same slump as the trial batch should be

$$\frac{7.56 \times 27}{0.825} = 247 \text{ lb}$$

The slump was satisfactory but, since the air content was too high by 1.5 percent, more water will be needed for proper slump when the air content is corrected. As indicated in Paragraph 5.3.9.2, the mixing water should be increased roughly 5 × 1.5 or about 8 lb, bringing the new estimate to 255 lb per cu yd.

6.3.9.2 With the decreased mixing water, less cement will be required to provide the desired water-cement ratio of 0.5. The new cement content becomes

$$255/0.5 = 510 \text{ lb}$$

6.3.9.3 Since the concrete was found to be oversanded, the quantity of coarse aggregate per unit volume will be increased 10 percent, to 0.74, in an effort to correct the condition. The amount of coarse aggregate per cubic yard becomes

$$0.74 \times 27 \times 95 = 1898 \text{ lb dry}$$

or

$$1898 \times 1.03 = 1955 \text{ lb wet}$$

and

$$1898 \times 1.005 = 1907 \text{ lb SSD*}$$

6.3.9.4 The new estimate for the weight of the concrete with 1.5 per-

---

*Saturated-surface-dry.

cent less air is 141.8/0.985 = 144.0 lb per cu ft or 144.0 × 27 = 3888 lb per cu yd. The weight of sand, therefore, is

$$3888 - (255 + 510 + 1907) = 1216 \text{ lb SSD*}$$

or

$$1216/1.007 = 1208 \text{ lb dry}$$

The adjusted basic batch weights per cubic yard of concrete are

Water (net mixing)	255 lb
Cement	510 lb
Coarse aggregate (dry)	1898 lb
Fine aggregate (dry)	1208 lb

Admixture dosage must be reduced to provide the desired air content.

6.3.10 Adjustments of proportions determined on an absolute volume basis would follow the procedure outlined in Paragraph 6.2.10 which will not be repeated for this example.

REFERENCES

1. Fuller, William B., and Thompson, Sanford E., "The Laws of Proportioning Concrete," *Transactions*, ASCE, V. 59, Dec. 1907, pp. 67–143.

2. Abrams, Duff A., "Design of Concrete Mixtures," *Bulletin* No. 1, Structural Materials Research Laboratory, Lewis Institute, Chicago, 1918.

3. Edwards, L. N., "Proportioning the Materials of Mortars and Concretes by Surface Areas of Aggregates," *Proceedings*, ASTM, V. 18, Part 2, 1918, p. 235.

4. Young, R. B., "Some Theoretical Studies on Proportioning Concrete by the Method of Surface Area of Aggregate," *Proceedings*, ASTM, V. 19, Part 2, 1919, p. 444.

5. Talbot, A. N., "A Proposed Method of Estimating the Density and Strength of Concrete and of Proportioning the Materials by Experimental and Analytical Consideration of the Voids in Mortar and Concrete," *Proceedings*, ASTM, V. 21, 1921, p. 940.

6. Weymouth, C. A. G., "A Study of Fine Aggregate in Freshly Mixed Mortars and Concretes," *Proceedings*, ASTM, V. 38, Part 2, 1938, pp. 354–372.

*Saturated-surface-dry.

7. Dunagan, W. M., "The Application of Some of the Newer Concepts to the Design of Concrete Mixes," ACI JOURNAL, *Proceedings* V. 36, No. 6, June 1940, pp. 649-684.

8. Goldbeck, A. T., and Gray, J. E., "A Method of Proportioning Concrete for Strength, Workability, and Durability," *Bulletin* No. 11, National Crushed Stone Association, Dec. 1942, 30 pp. (Revised 1953 and 1956).

9. Swayze, M. A., and Gruenwald, E., "Concrete Mix Design—Modification of Fineness Modulus Method," ACI JOURNAL, *Proceedings* V. 43, No. 7, Mar. 1947, pp. 829-844.

10. Discussion of "Concrete Mix Design—A Modification of the Fineness Modulus Method" by Stanton Walker and Fred F. Bartel, ACI JOURNAL, *Proceedings* V. 43, Part 2, Dec. 1947, pp. 844-1-844-17.

11. Henrie, James O., "Properties of Nuclear Shielding Concrete," ACI JOURNAL, *Proceedings* V. 56, No. 1, July 1959, pp. 37-46.

12. Mather, Katharine, "High Strength, High Density Concrete," ACI JOURNAL, *Proceedings* V. 62, No. 8, Aug. 1965, pp. 951-960.

13. Clendenning, T. G.; Kellam, B.; and MacInnis, C., "Hydrogen Evolution from Ferrophosphorous Aggregate in Portland Cement Concrete," ACI JOURNAL, *Proceedings* V. 65, No. 12, Dec. 1968, pp. 1021-1028.

14. Popovics, Sandor, "Estimating Proportions for Structural Concrete Mixtures," ACI JOURNAL, *Proceedings* V. 65, No. 2, Feb. 1968, pp. 143-150.

15. "Tentative Specification for Aggregates for Radiation-Shielding Concrete," (ASTM C 637), American Society for Testing and Materials, Philadelphia.

16. Davis, H. S., "Aggregates for Radiation Shielding Concrete," *Materials Research and Standards,* V. 7, No. 11, Nov. 1967, pp. 494-501.

17. *Concrete for Nuclear Reactors,* SP-34, American Concrete Institute, Detroit, 1972, 1736 pp.

18. Gaynor, Richard D., "High-Strength Air-Entrained Concrete," *Joint Research Laboratory Publication* No. 17, National Ready Mixed Concrete Association and National Sand and Gravel Association, 1968, 19 pp.

APPENDICES

APPENDIX 1—METRIC SYSTEM ADAPTATION

A1.1—Procedures outlined in this recommended practice have been presented using British (United States customary) units of measurement. The principles are equally applicable in the metric system with proper adaptation of units. This Appendix provides all of the information necessary to apply the proportioning procedure using International SI (metric) measurements. Table A1.1 gives relevant conversion factors. A numerical example is presented in Appendix 2.

A1.2—For convenience of reference, numbering of subsequent paragraphs in this Appendix corresponds to the body of the report except that the designation "A1" is prefixed. All tables have been converted and reproduced. Descriptive portions are included only where use of the metric system

TABLE A1.1—CONVERSION FACTORS, BRITISH TO METRIC UNITS*

Quantity	British (U.S. customary) unit	SI† (Metric) unit	Conversion factor (Ratio: British/SI)
Length	inch (in.)	centimeter (cm)	2.540
	inch (in.)	millimeter (mm)	25.40
Volume	cubic foot (ft³)	cubic meter (m³)	0.02832
	cubic yard (yd³)	cubic meter (m³)	0.7646
Mass	pound (lb)	kilogram (kg)	0.4536
Stress	pounds per square inch (psi)	kilograms force per square centimeter (kgf/cm²)	0.0703
Density	pounds per cubic foot (lb/ft³)	kilograms per cubic meter (kg/m³)	16.02
	pounds per cubic yard (lb/yd³)	kilograms per cubic meter (kg/m³)	0.5933
Temperature	degrees Fahrenheit (F)	degrees Centigrade (C)	‡

*Gives names (and abbreviations) of measurement units in the British (U.S. customary) system as used in the body of this report and in the S.I. (metric) system, along with multipliers for converting the former to the latter. From "ASTM Metric Practice Guide" (2nd Edition, 1966).

†Systéme International d'Unités

‡C = (F − 32)/1.8.

requires a change in a procedure or formula. To the extent practicable, conversions to metric units have been made in such a way that values are realistic in terms of usual practice and significance of numbers. For example, aggregate and sieve sizes in the metric tables are ones commonly used in Europe. Thus, there is not always a precise mathematical correspondence between British and metric values in corresponding tables.

A1.5.2 *Steps in calculating proportions.* Except as discussed below, the methods for arriving at quantities of ingredients for a unit volume of concrete are essentially the same when metric units are employed as when British units are employed. The main difference is that the unit volume of concrete becomes the cubic meter and numerical values must be taken from the proper "A1" table instead of the one referred to in the text.

A1.5.2.1 *Step 1. Choice of slump.* See Table A1.5.2.1.

A1.5.2.2. *Step 2. Choice of maximum size of aggregate.*

A1.5.2.3. *Step 3. Estimation of mixing water and air content.* See Table A1.5.2.3.

A1.5.2.4. *Step 4. Selection of water-cement ratio.* See Table A1.5.2.4.

A1.5.2.5. *Step 5. Calculation of cement content.*

A1.5.2.6 *Step 6. Estimation of coarse aggregate content.* The dry weight of coarse aggregate required for a cubic meter of concrete is equal to the value from Table A1.5.2.6 multiplied by the dry-rodded unit weight of the aggregate in kilograms per cubic meter.

A1.5.2.7 *Step 7. Estimation of fine aggregate content.* In the metric system, the formula for calculation of fresh concrete weight per cubic meter is:

$$U_M = 10G_a(100-A) + C_M(1-G_a/G_c) - W_M(G_a-1)$$

where

$$
\begin{aligned}
U_M &= \text{weight of fresh concrete, kg/m}^3 \\
G_a &= \text{weighted average specific gravity of combined} \\
    &\quad \text{fine and coarse aggregate, bulk, SSD} \\
G_c &= \text{specific gravity of cement (generally 3.15)} \\
A &= \text{air content, percent} \\
W_M &= \text{mixing water requirement, kg/m}^3 \\
C_M &= \text{cement requirement, kg/m}^3
\end{aligned}
$$

A1.5.2.9 *Trial batch adjustments.* The following "rules of thumb" may be used to arrive at closer approximations of unit batch quantities based on results for a trial batch:

A1.5.2.9.1 The estimated mixing water to produce the same slump as the trial batch will be equal to the net amount of mixing water used divided by the yield of the trial batch in m^3. If slump of the trial batch was not correct,

TABLE A1.5.2.1—RECOMMENDED SLUMPS FOR VARIOUS TYPES OF CONSTRUCTION (METRIC)

Types of construction	Slump, cm	
	Maximum*	Minimum
Reinforced foundation walls and footings	8	2
Plain footings, caissons, and substructure walls	8	2
Beams and reinforced walls	10	2
Building columns	10	2
Pavements and slabs	8	2
Heavy mass concrete	8	2

*May be increased 2 cm for methods of consolidation other than vibration.

TABLE A1.5.2.3—APPROXIMATE MIXING WATER REQUIREMENTS FOR DIFFERENT SLUMPS AND MAXIMUM SIZES OF AGGREGATES (METRIC)*

Slump, cm.	Water, kg/m³ of concrete for indicated maximum sizes of aggregate in mm							
	10	12.5	20	25	40	50†	70†	150†
Non-air-entrained concrete								
3 to 5	205	200	185	180	160	155	145	125
8 to 10	225	215	200	195	175	170	160	140
15 to 18	240	230	210	205	185	180	170	—
Approximate amount of entrapped air in non-air-entrained concrete, percent	3	2.5	2	1.5	1	0.5	0.3	0.2
Air-entrained concrete								
3 to 5	180	175	165	160	145	140	135	120
8 to 10	200	190	180	175	160	155	150	135
15 to 18	215	205	190	185	170	165	160	—
Recommended average total air content, percent	8	7	6	5	4.5	4	3.5	3

*These quantities of mixing water are for use in computing cement factors for trial batches. They are maxima for reasonably well-shaped angular coarse aggregates graded within limits of accepted specifications.

†The slump values for concrete containing aggregate larger than 40 mm are based on slump tests after removal of particles larger than 40 mm by wet-screening.

TABLE A1.5.2.4(a)—RELATIONSHIPS BETWEEN WATER-CEMENT RATIO AND COMPRESSIVE STRENGTH OF CONCRETE (METRIC)

Compressive strength at 28 days, kgf/cm²*	Water-cement ratio, by weight	
	Non-air-entrained concrete	Air-entrained concrete
450	0.38	—
400	0.43	—
350	0.48	0.40
300	0.55	0.46
250	0.62	0.53
200	0.70	0.61
150	0.80	0.71

*Values are estimated average strengths for concrete containing not more than the percentage of air shown in Table A1.5.2.3. For a constant water-cement ratio, the strength of concrete is reduced as the air content is increased.

Strength is based on 15 x 30 cm cylinders moist-cured 28 days at 23 ± 1.7 C in accordance with Section 9(b) of ASTM C 31 for Making and Curing Concrete Compression and Flexure Test Specimens in the Field. Cube strengths will be higher by approximately 20 percent.

Relationship assumes maximum size of aggregate about 20 to 30 mm; for a given source, strength produced by a given water-cement ratio will increase as maximum size decreases; see Sections 3.4 and 5.3.2.

TABLE A1.5.2.4(b)—MAXIMUM PERMISSIBLE WATER-CEMENT RATIOS FOR CONCRETE IN SEVERE EXPOSURES (METRIC)*

Type of Structure	Structure wet continuously or frequently and exposed to freezing and thawing†	Structure exposed to sea water or sulfates
Thin sections (railings, curbs, sills, ledges, ornamental work) and sections with less than 3 cm cover over steel	0.45	0.40‡
All other structures	0.50	0.45‡

*Based on the report of ACI Committee 201, "Durability of Concrete in Service," previously cited.

†Concrete should also be air-entrained.

‡If sulfate resisting cement (Type II or Type V of ASTM C 150) is used, permissible water-cement ratio may be increased by 0.05.

TABLE A1.5.2.6—VOLUME OF COARSE AGGREGATE PER UNIT OF VOLUME OF CONCRETE (METRIC)

Maximum size of aggregate, mm	Volume of dry-rodded coarse aggregate* per unit volume of concrete for different fineness moduli† of sand			
	2.40	2.60	2.80	3.00
10	0.50	0.48	0.46	0.44
12.5	0.59	0.57	0.55	0.53
20	0.66	0.64	0.62	0.60
25	0.71	0.69	0.67	0.65
40	0.76	0.74	0.72	0.70
50	0.78	0.76	0.74	0.72
70	0.81	0.79	0.77	0.75
150	0.87	0.85	0.83	0.81

*Volumes are based on aggregates in dry-rodded condition as described in ASTM C 29 for Unit Weight of Aggregate.

These volumes are selected from empirical relationships to produce concrete with a degree of workability suitable for usual reinforced construction. For less workable concrete such as required for concrete pavement construction they may be increased about 10 percent. For more workable concrete, such as may sometimes be required when placement is to be by pumping, they may be reduced up to 10 percent.

†Fineness modulus of sand = sum of ratios (cumulative) retained on sieves with square openings of 0.149, 0.297, 0.595, 1.19, 2.38, and 4.76 mm.

TABLE A1.5.2.7.1—FIRST ESTIMATE OF WEIGHT OF FRESH CONCRETE (METRIC)

Maximum size of aggregate, mm	First estimate of concrete weight, kg/m³*	
	Non-air-entrained concrete	Air-entrained concrete
10	2285	2190
12.5	2315	2235
20	2355	2280
25	2375	2315
40	2420	2355
50	2445	2375
70	2465	2400
150	2505	2435

*Values calculated by Eq. (A1.5.2.7) for concrete of medium richness (330 kg of cement per m³) and medium slump with aggregate specific gravity of 2.7. Water requirements based on values for 8 to 10 cm slump in Table A1.5.2.3. If desired, the estimate of weight may be refined as follows if necessary information is available: for each 5 kg difference in mixing water from the Table A1.5.2.3 values for 8 to 10 cm slump, correct the weight per m³ 8 kg in the opposite direction; for each 20 kg difference in cement content from 330 kg, correct the weight per m³ 3 kg in the same direction; for each 0.1 by which aggregate specific gravity deviates from 2.7, correct the concrete weight 70 kg in the same direction.

increase or decrease the re-estimated water content by 2 kg/m³ of concrete for each increase or decrease of 1 cm in slump desired.

A1.5.2.9.2 To adjust for the effect of incorrect air content in a trial batch of air-entrained concrete on slump, reduce or increase the mixing water content of A1.5.2.9.1 by 3 kg/m³ of concrete for each 1 percent by which the air content is to be increased or decreased from that of the trial batch.

A1.5.2.9.3 The re-estimated unit weight of the fresh concrete for adjustment of trial batch proportions is equal to the unit weight in kg/m³ measured on the trial batch, reduced or increased by the percentage increase or decrease in air content of the adjusted batch from the first trial batch.

APPENDIX 2—EXAMPLE PROBLEM IN METRIC SYSTEM

A2.1—Example 1. Example 1 presented in Section 6.2 will be solved here using metric units of measure. Required average strength will be 250 kgf/cm² with slump of 8 to 10 cm. The coarse aggregate has a maximum size of 40 mm and dry-rodded weight of 1600 kg/m³. As stated in Section 6.1, other properties of the ingredients are: cement—Type I with specific gravity of 3.15; coarse aggregate—bulk specific gravity 2.68 and absorption 0.5 percent; fine aggregate—bulk specific gravity 2.64, absorption 0.7 percent, and fineness modulus 2.8.

A2.2—All steps of Section 5.3 should be followed in sequence to avoid confusion, even though they sometimes merely restate information already given.

A2.2.1 *Step 1.* The slump is required to be 8 to 10 cm.

A2.2.2 *Step 2.* The aggregate to be used has a maximum size of 40 mm.

A2.2.3 *Step 3.* The concrete will be non-air-entrained since the structure is not to be exposed to severe weathering. From Table A1.5.2.3, the estimated mixing water for a slump of 8 to 10 cm in non-air-entrained concrete made with 40-mm aggregate is found to be 175 kg/m³.

A2.2.4 *Step 4.* The water-cement ratio for non-air-entrained concrete with a strength of 250 kgf/cm² is found from Table A1.5.2.4(a) to be 0.62.

A2.2.5 *Step 5.* From the information developed in Steps 3 and 4, the required cement content is found to be 175/0.62 = 282 kg/m³.

A2.2.6 *Step 6.* The quantity of coarse aggregate is estimated from Table A1.5.2.6. For a fine aggregate having a fineness modulus of 2.8 and a 40 mm maximum size of coarse aggregate, the table indicates that 0.72 m³ of coarse aggregate, on a dry-rodded basis, may be used in each cubic meter of concrete. The required dry weight is, therefore, 0.72 × 1600 = 1152 kg.

A2.2.7 *Step 7.* With the quantities of water, cement and coarse aggregate established, the remaining material comprising the cubic meter of concrete must consist of sand and whatever air will be entrapped. The required sand may be determined on the basis of either weight or absolute volume as shown below:

A2.2.7.1 *Weight Basis.* From Table A1.5.2.7.1, the weight of a cubic meter of non-air-entrained concrete made with aggregate having a maximum size of 40 mm is estimated to be 2420 kg. (For a first trial batch, exact adjustments of this value for usual differences in slump, cement factor, and aggregate specific gravity are not critical.) Weights already known are:

Water (net mixing)	175 kg
Cement	282 kg
Coarse aggregate	1152 kg
Total	1609 kg

The weight of sand, therefore, is estimated to be

$$2420 - 1609 = 811 \text{ kg}$$

A2.2.7.2 *Absolute volume basis.* With the quantities of cement, water, and coarse aggregate established, and the approximate entrapped air content (as opposed to purposely entrained air) of 1 percent determined from Table A1.5.2.3, the sand content can be calculated as follows:

Volume of water	$=$	$\dfrac{175}{1000}$	$= 0.175 \text{ m}^3$
Solid volume of cement	$=$	$\dfrac{282}{3.15 \times 1000}$	$= 0.090 \text{ m}^3$
Solid volume of coarse aggregate	$=$	$\dfrac{1152}{2.68 \times 1000}$	$= 0.430 \text{ m}^3$
Volume of entrapped air	$=$	0.01×1.000	$= 0.010 \text{ m}^3$
Total solid volume of ingredients except sand			0.705 m^3
Solid volume of sand required	$=$	$1.000 - 0.705$	$= 0.295 \text{ m}^3$
Required weight of dry sand		$= 0.295 \times 2.64 \times 1000$	$= 779 \text{ kg}$

A2.2.7.3 Batch weights per cubic meter of concrete calculated on the two bases are compared below:

	Based on estimated concrete weight, kg	Based on absolute volume of ingredients, kg
Water (net mixing)	175	175
Cement	282	282
Coarse aggregate (dry)	1152	1152
Sand (dry)	811	779

A2.2.8 *Step 8.* Tests indicate total moisture of 2 percent in the coarse aggregate and 6 percent in the fine aggregate. If the trial batch proportions based on assumed concrete weight are used, the adjusted aggregate weights become

Coarse aggregate (wet)	= 1152(1.02) =	1175 kg
Fine aggregate (wet)	= 811(1.06) =	860 kg

Absorbed water does not become part of the mixing water and must be excluded from the adjustment in added water. Thus, surface water contributed by the coarse aggregate amounts to $2 - 0.5 = 1.5$ percent; by the fine aggregate $6 - 0.7 = 5.3$ percent. The estimated requirement for added water, therefore, becomes

$$175 - 1152(0.015) - 811(0.053) = 115 \text{ kg}$$

The estimated batch weights for a cubic meter of concrete are:

Water (to be added)	115 kg
Cement	282 kg
Coarse aggregate (wet)	1175 kg
Fine aggregate (wet)	860 kg
Total	2432 kg

A2.2.9 *Step 9.* For the laboratory trial batch, it is found convenient to scale the weights down to produce 0.02 m^3 of concrete. Although the calculated quantity of water to be added was 2.30 kg, the amount actually used in an effort to obtain the desired 8 to 10 cm slump is 2.70 kg. The batch as mixed, therefore, consists of

Water (added)	2.70 kg
Cement	5.64 kg
Coarse aggregate (wet)	23.50 kg
Fine aggregate (wet)	17.20 kg
Total	49.04 kg

The concrete has a measured slump of 5 cm and unit weight of 2390 kg/m^3. It is judged to be satisfactory from the standpoint of workability and finishing properties. To provide proper yield and other characteristics for future batches, the following adjustments are made:

A2.2.9.1 Since the yield of the trial batch was

$$49.04/2390 = 0.0205 \text{ m}^3$$

and the mixing water content was 2.70 (added) + 0.34 (on coarse aggregate) + 0.86 (on fine aggregate) = 3.90 kg, the mixing water required for a cubic meter of concrete with the same slump as the trial batch should be

$$\frac{3.90}{0.0205} = 190 \text{ kg}$$

As indicated in A1.5.2.9.1, this amount must be increased another 8 kg to raise the slump from the measured 5 cm to the desired 8 to 10 cm range, bringing the total mixing water to 198 kg.

A2.2.9.2 With the increased mixing water, additional cement will be required to provide the desired water-cement ratio of 0.62. The new cement content becomes

$$198/0.62 = 319 \text{ kg}$$

A2.2.9.3 Since workability was found to be satisfactory, the quantity of coarse aggregate per unit volume of concrete will be maintained the same as in the trial batch. The amount of coarse aggregate per cubic meter becomes

$$\frac{23.50}{0.0205} = 1146 \text{ kg wet}$$

which is

$$\frac{1146}{1.02} \quad 1124 \text{ kg dry}$$

and

$$1124 \times 1.005 = 1130 \text{ kg SSD*}$$

A2.2.9.4 The new estimate for the weight of a cubic meter of concrete is the measured unit weight of 2390 kg/m³. The amount of sand required is, therefore

$$2390 - (198 + 319 + 1130) = 743 \text{ kg SSD}$$

or

$$743/1.007 = 738 \text{ kg dry}$$

The adjusted basic batch weights per cubic meter of concrete are

Water (net mixing)	198 kg
Cement	319 kg
Coarse aggregate (dry)	1124 kg
Fine aggregate (dry)	738 kg

---

*Saturated-surface-dry

542

A2.2.10 Adjustments of proportions determined on an absolute volume basis follow a procedure similar to that just outlined. The steps will be given without detailed explanation:

A2.2.10.1 Quantities used in the nominal 0.02 m³ batch are

Water (added)	2.70 kg
Cement	5.64 kg
Coarse aggregate (wet)	23.50 kg
Fine aggregate (wet)	16.51 kg
Total	48.35 kg

Measured slump 5 cm; unit weight 2390 kg/m³; yield 48.35/2390 = 0.0202 m³; workability o.k.

A2.2.10.2 Re-estimated water for same slump as trial batch:

$$\frac{2.70 + 0.34 + 0.83}{0.0202} = 192 \text{ kg}$$

Mixing water required for slump of 8 to 10 cm:

$$192 + 8 = 200 \text{ kg}$$

A2.2.10.3 Adjusted cement content for increased water:

$$200/0.62 = 323 \text{ kg}$$

A2.2.10.4 Adjusted coarse aggregate requirement:

$$\frac{23.50}{0.0202} = 1163 \text{ kg wet}$$

or

$$1163/1.02 = 1140 \text{ kg dry}$$

A2.2.10.5 The volume of ingredients other than air in the original trial batch was

$$\text{Water} = \frac{3.87}{1000} = 0.0039 \text{ m}^3$$

$$\text{Cement} = \frac{5.64}{3.15 \times 1000} = 0.0018 \text{ m}^3$$

$$\text{Coarse aggregate} = \frac{23.04}{2.68 \times 1000} = 0.0086 \text{ m}^3$$

$$\text{Fine aggregate} = \frac{15.58}{2.64 \times 1000} = 0.0059 \text{ m}^3$$

$$\text{Total} \qquad\qquad\qquad 0.0202 \text{ m}^3$$

Since the yield was also 0.0202 m³, there was no air in the concrete detectable within the precision of the unit weight test and significant figures of the calculations. With the proportions of all components except fine aggregate established, the determination of adjusted cubic yard batch quantities can be completed as follows:

Volume of water $\quad = \quad \dfrac{200}{1000} \quad = 0.200$ m³

Volume of cement $\quad = \quad \dfrac{323}{3.15 \times 1000} \quad = 0.103$ m³

Allowance for volume
of air $\qquad\qquad\qquad\qquad\qquad\quad = 0.000$ m³

Volume of coarse
aggregate $\quad = \quad \dfrac{1140}{2.68 \times 1000} \quad = \underline{0.425\ \text{m}^3}$

Total volume exclusive
of fine aggregate $\qquad\qquad\qquad\quad = 0.728$ m³

Volume of fine
aggregate required $\quad = \quad 1.000 - 0.728 \quad = 0.272$ m³

Weight of fine
aggregate (dry basis) $= 0.272 \times 2.64 \times 1000 \quad = 718$ kg

The adjusted basic batch weights per cubic meter of concrete, then, are:

Water (net mixing)	200 kg
Cement	323 kg
Coarse aggregate (dry)	1140 kg
Fine aggregate (dry)	718 kg

These differ only slightly from those given in Paragraph A2.2.9.4 for the method of assumed concrete weight. Further trials or experience might indicate small additional adjustments for either method.

APPENDIX 3—LABORATORY TESTS

A3.1—Selection of concrete mix proportions can be accomplished effectively from results of laboratory tests which determine basic physical properties of materials to be used, establish relationships between water-cement ratio, air content, cement content, and strength, and which furnish information on the workability characteristics of various combinations of ingredient materials. The extent of investigation desirable for any given job will depend on its size and importance and on the service conditions involved. Details of the laboratory program will also vary, depending on facilities available and on individual preferences.

A3.2—Properties of cement

A3.2.1 Physical and chemical characteristics of cement influence the properties of hardened concrete. However, the only property of cement used directly in computation of concrete mix proportions is specific gravity. The specific gravity of portland cements of the types covered by ASTM C 150 and C 175 may usually be assumed to be 3.15 without introducing appreciable error in mix computations. For other types such as the blended hydraulic cements of ASTM C 595, the specific gravity for use in volume calculations should be determined by test.

A3.2.2. A sample of cement should be obtained from the mill which will supply the job, or preferably from the concrete supplier. The sample should be ample for tests contemplated with a liberal margin for additional tests that might later be considered desirable. Cement samples should be shipped in airtight containers, or at least in moisture-proof packages.

A3.3.—Properties of aggregate

A3.3.1 Sieve analysis, specific gravity, absorption, and moisture content of both fine and coarse aggregate and dry-rodded unit weight of coarse aggregate are physical properties useful for mix computations. Other tests which may be desirable for large or special types of work include petrographic examination and tests for chemical reactivity, soundness, durability, resistance to abrasion, and various deleterious substances. Such tests yield information of value in judging the long-range serviceability of concrete.

A3.3.2 Aggregate gradation as measured by the sieve analysis is a major factor in determining unit water requirement, proportions of coarse aggregate and sand, and cement content for satisfactory workability. Numerous "ideal" aggregate grading curves have been proposed, and these, tempered by practical considerations, have formed the basis for typical sieve analysis requirements in concrete standards. ASTM C 33, "Specification for Concrete Aggregates," provides a selection of sizes and gradings suitable for most concrete. Additional workability realized by use of air-entrainment permits, to some extent, the use of less restrictive aggregate gradations.

A3.3.3 Samples for concrete mix tests should be representative of aggregate available for use in the work. For laboratory tests, the coarse aggregates should be separated into required size fractions and reconstituted at the time of mixing to assure representative grading for the small test batches. Under some conditions, for work of important magnitude, laboratory investigation may involve efforts to overcome grading deficiencies of the available aggregates. Undesirable sand grading may be corrected by: (1) separation of the sand into two or more size fractions and recombining in suitable proportions; (2) increasing or decreasing the quantity of certain sizes to balance the grading; or (3) reducing excess coarse material by grinding or crushing. Undesirable coarse-aggregate gradings may be corrected by: (1) crushing excess coarser fractions; (2) wasting sizes that occur in excess; (3) supplementing deficient sizes from other sources; or (4) a combination of these methods. Whatever grading adjustments are made in the laboratory should be practical and economically justified from the standpoint of job operation. Usually, required aggregate grading should be consistent with that of economically available materials.

A3.4—Trial batch series

A3.4.1 The tabulated relationships in the body of this report may be used to make rough estimates of batch quantities for a trial mix. However, they are too generalized to apply with a high degree of accuracy to a specific set of materials. If facilities are available, therefore, it is advisable to make a series of concrete tests to establish quantitative relationships for the materials to be used. An illustration of such a test program is shown in Table A3.4.1.

A3.4.2 First, a batch of medium cement content and usable consistency is proportioned by the described methods. In preparing Mix No. 1, an amount of water is used which will produce the desired slump even if this differs from the estimated requirement. The fresh concrete is tested for slump and unit weight and observed closely for workability and finishing characteristics. In the example, the yield is too high and the concrete is judged to contain an excess of sand.

A3.4.3 Mix No. 2 is prepared, adjusted to correct the errors in Mix No. 1, and the testing and evaluation repeated. In this case, the desired properties are achieved within close tolerances and cylinders are molded to check the compressive strength. The information derived so far can now be used to select proportions for a series of additional mixes, No. 3 to 6, with cement contents above and below that of Mix No. 2, encompassing the range likely to be needed. Reasonable refinement in these batch weights can be achieved with the help of corrections given in the notes to Table 5.3.7.1.

A3.4.4 Mix No. 2 to 6 provide the background, including the relationship of strength to water-cement ratio for the particular combination of ingredients, needed to select proportions for a range of specified requirements.

A3.4.5 In laboratory tests, it seldom will be found, even by experienced operators, that desired adjustments will develop as smoothly as indicated in Table A3.4.1. Furthermore, it should not be expected that field results will check exactly with laboratory results. An adjustment of the selected trial mix on the job is usually necessary. Closer agreement between laboratory and field will be assured if machine mixing is employed in the laboratory. This is especially desirable if air-entraining agents are used since the type of mixer influences the amount of air entrained. Before mixing the first batch, the laboratory mixer should be "buttered" or the mix "overmortared" as described in ASTM C 192. Similarly, any processing of materials in the laboratory should simulate as closely as practicable corresponding treatment in the field.

A3.4.6 The series of tests illustrated in Table A3.4.1 may be expanded as the size and special requirements of the work warrant. Variables that may require investigation include: alternative aggregate sources, maximum sizes

TABLE A3.4.I—TYPICAL TEST PROGRAM TO ESTABLISH CONCRETE-MAKING PROPERTIES OF LOCAL MATERIALS

Mix No.	Cubic yard batch quantities, lb						Concrete characteristics				
	Cement	Sand	Coarse Aggregate	Water		Total used	Slump, in.	Unit wt., lb per cu ft	Yield, cu ft	28-day Compressive strength, psi	Work-ability
				Estimated	Used						
1	500	1375	1810	325	350	4035	4	147.0	27.45	—	Oversanded
2	500	1250	1875	345	340	3965	3	147.0	26.97	3350	o.k.
3	400	1335	1875	345	345	3955	4.5	145.5	27.18	2130	o.k.
4	450	1290	1875	345	345	3960	4	146.2	27.09	2610	o.k.
5	550	1210	1875	345	345	3980	3	147.5	26.98	3800	o.k.
6	600	1165	1875	345	345	3985	3.5	148.3	26.87	4360	o.k.

and gradings; different types and brands of cement; admixtures; and considerations of concrete durability, volume change, temperature rise, and thermal properties.

A3.5—Test methods

A3.5.1 In conducting laboratory tests to provide information for selecting concrete proportions, the latest revisions of the following methods should be used:

A3.5.1.1 *For tests of ingredients:*

Sampling hydraulic cement—ASTM C 183

Specific gravity of hydraulic cement—ASTM C 188

Sampling stone, slag, gravel, sand, and stone block for use as highway materials—ASTM D 75

Sieve or screen analysis of fine and coarse aggregates—ASTM C 136

Specific gravity and absorption of coarse aggregates—ASTM C 127

Specific gravity and absorption of fine aggregates—ASTM C 128

Surface moisture in fine aggregate—ASTM C 70

Total moisture content of aggregate by drying—ASTM C 566

Unit weight of aggregate—ASTM C 29

Voids in aggregate for concrete—ASTM C 30

Fineness modulus—Terms relating to concrete and concrete aggregates, ASTM C 125

A3.5.1.2 *For tests of concrete:*

Sampling fresh concrete—ASTM C 172

Air content of freshly mixed concrete by the volumetric method—ASTM C 173

Air content of freshly mixed concrete by the pressure method—ASTM C 231

Slump of portland cement concrete—ASTM C 143

Weight per cubic foot, yield, and air content (gravimetric) of concrete—ASTM C 138

Concrete compression and flexure test specimens, making and curing in the laboratory—ASTM C 192

Compressive strength of molded concrete cylinders—ASTM C 39

Flexural strength of concrete (using simple beam with third-point loading)—ASTM C 78

Flexural strength of concrete (using simple beam with center point loading)—ASTM C 293

Splitting tensile strength of molded concrete cylinders—ASTM C 496

A3.6—Mixes for small jobs

A3.6.1 For small jobs where time and personnel are not available to determine proportions in accordance with the recommended procedure, mixes in Table A3.6.1 will usually provide concrete that is amply strong and durable

TABLE A3.6.1—CONCRETE MIXES FOR SMALL JOBS

Procedure: Select the proper maximum size of aggregate (see Section 5.3.2). Use Mix B, adding just enough water to produce a workable consistency. If the concrete appears to be under-sanded, change to Mix A and, if it appears oversanded, change to Mix C.

			Approximate weights of solid ingredients per cu ft of concrete, lb			
Maxi-mum size of aggre-gate, in.	Mix desig-nation	Cement	Sand*		Coarse aggregate	
			Air-entrained concrete†	Concrete without air	Gravel or crushed stone	Iron blast furnace slag
½	A	25	48	51	54	47
	B	25	46	49	56	49
	C	25	44	47	58	51
¾	A	23	45	49	62	54
	B	23	43	47	64	56
	C	23	41	45	66	58
1	A	22	41	45	70	61
	B	22	39	43	72	63
	C	22	37	41	74	65
1½	A	20	41	45	75	65
	B	20	39	43	77	67
	C	20	37	41	79	69
2	A	19	40	45	79	69
	B	19	38	43	81	71
	C	19	36	41	83	72

*Weights are for dry sand. If damp sand is used, increase tabulated weight of sand 2 lb and, if very wet sand is used, 4 lb.

†Air-entrained concrete should be used in all structures which will be exposed to alternate cycles of freezing and thawing. Air-entrainment can be obtained by the use of an air-entraining cement or by adding an air-entraining admixture. If an admixture is used, the amount recommended by the manufacturer will, in most cases, produce the desired air content.

if the amount of water added at the mixer is never large enough to make the concrete overwet. These mixes have been predetermined in conformity with the recommended procedure by assuming conditions applicable to the average small job, and for aggregate of medium specific gravity. Three mixes are given for each maximum size of coarse aggregate. For the selected size of coarse aggregate, Mix B is intended for initial use. If this mix proves to be oversanded, change to Mix C; if it is undersanded, change to Mix A. It should be noted that the mixes listed in the table are based on dry or surface-dry sand. If the sand is moist or wet, make the corrections in batch weight prescribed in the footnote.

A3.6.2 The approximate cement content per cubic foot of concrete listed in the table will be helpful in estimating cement requirements for the job. These requirements are based on concrete that has just enough water in it to permit ready working into forms without objectionable segregation. Concrete should slide, not run, off a shovel.

APPENDIX 4—HEAVYWEIGHT CONCRETE MIX PROPORTIONING

A4.1—Concrete of normal placeability can be proportioned for densities as high as 350 lb per cu ft by using heavy aggregates such as iron ore, barite, or iron shot and iron punchings. Although each of the materials has its own special characteristics, it can be processed to meet the standard requirements for grading, soundness, cleanliness, etc. The acceptability of the aggregate should be made depending upon its intended use. In the case of radiation shielding, determination should be made of trace elements within the material which may become reactive when subjected to radiation. In the selection of materials and proportioning of heavyweight concrete, the data needed and procedures used are similar to that required for normal weight concrete except that the following items should be considered.

A4.1.1—In selecting an aggregate for a specified density, the specific gravity of the fine aggregate should be comparable to that of the coarse aggregate in order to lessen settlement of the coarse aggregate through the mortar matrix. Typical materials used as heavy aggregates include the following:

Material	Description	Specific gravity	Approx. concrete unit wt (lb/cu ft)
Limonite Goethite	Hydrous iron ores	3.4–3.8	180–195
Barite	Barium sulfate	4.0–4.4	205–225
Ilmenite Hematite Magnetite	Iron ores	4.2–4.8	215–240
Iron	Shot, pellets, punchings, etc.	6.5–7.5	310–350

A4.1.2—When the concrete in service is to be exposed to a hot, dry environment, it should be proportioned so that the fresh unit weight is at least 10 lb per cu ft higher than the required dry unit weight.

A4.1.3—When entrained air is required to resist conditions of exposure, allowance must be made for the loss in weight due to the space occupied by the air. To achieve adequate consolidation using high frequency vibrators and close insertion intervals, without the excessive loss of entrained air, plastic concrete should be designed for a high air content to offset this loss during placement.

A4.1.4—Heavyweight concrete is often used for radiation shielding. In this case, the aggregate type and concrete weight should be selected consistent with the type of radiation involved. Generally speaking, the greater the mass the better are the shielding properties against gamma and beta rays. However, neutron attenuation depends more on the specific elements present in the concrete, i.e., hydrogen, carbon, boron, etc.

A4.1.5—Ferrophosphorous and ferrosilicon (heavyweight slags) materials should be used only after thorough scrutiny. Hydrogen evolution in heavyweight concrete containing these aggregates has been known to result in a reaction of a self-limiting nature, producing over 25 times its volume of hydrogen before the reaction ceases.

A4.1.6—In Section 5.3.7 (Step 7) caution must be exercised if the weight method (Section 5.3.7.1) is used to estimate the fine aggregate batch weight. The values in Table 5.3.7.1 must be corrected for overall aggregate specific gravity since the table is based on an average aggregate specific gravity of 2.7. Therefore, it is recommended that the required amount of fine aggregate be determined by the absolute volume procedure (Section 5.3.7.2).

A4.2—*Production and quality control.* The technique and equipment for producing heavyweight concrete are the same as used with normal weight concrete. In the selection of heavyweight materials and combinations thereof for the purposes of proportioning specification concretes, attention must be directed to aggregate effects on placeability, strength, and durability of the concrete. Testing and quality control measures assume greater importance than with normal weight concrete. Control of aggregate grading is essential because of the effect on the placing and consolidating properties of concrete, and on the unit weight of the concrete. In enforcing strict quality control special attention should be paid to the following:

A4.2.1—Prevention ot contamination with normal weight aggregate in stockpiles and conveying equipment.

A4.2.2—Purging of all aggregate handling and batching equipment, premixers and truck mixers, before batching and mixing heavyweight concrete.

A4.2.3—Accuracy and condition of conveying and scale equipment, aggregate storage and concrete batching bins. Due to the greater weight of heavyweight aggregate, the permissible volume batched in a bin is considerably less than the design capacity. For example: a 100 ton aggregate bin designed for 75 cu yd of normal weight aggregate should not be loaded with more than 25 to 55 cu yd for the range of specific gravities shown in Section A4.1.1.

A4.2.4—Condition and loading of mixing equipment. For concrete of a weight range of approximately 4800 to 9500 lb per cu yd, the capacity of a truck mixer, without overloading, is reduced from 20 to 60 percent.

A4.2.5—Accurate aggregate proportioning to maintain w/c ratio. Degradation of some coarse heavyweight aggregates, iron ores in particular, is another production problem which should be carefully controlled. Either the coarse aggregate should be rescreened immediately prior to incorporation into the concrete or adjustments made in the mixture proportions that compensate for the increased percentage of fines in the coarse aggregate, caused by aggregate breakdown during handling. Therefore, caution should be exercised and frequent gradation checks made on stockpiled aggregates.

A4.2.6—Frequent checks of fresh unit weight.

A4.2.7—Design and construction of forms to handle additional weight of concrete.

A4.2.8—Vibrators for consolidation.

A4.3—*Example problem.* Concrete is required for counterweights on a lift bridge not subjected to freezing and thawing conditions. An average 28-day compressive strength of 4500 psi will be required. Placement conditions permit a slump of 2 to 3 in. and a maximum size aggregate of 1 in. The design of the counterweight requires a dry unit weight of 230 lb per cu ft. An investigation of economically available materials has indicated the following:

Cement	—Type I (non-air-entraining)
Fine aggregate	—Specular Hematite
Coarse aggregate	—Ilmenite

The table in Section 4.1.1 indicates that this combination of materials may result in a dry unit weight of 215 to 240 lb per cu ft. The following properties of the aggregates have been obtained from laboratory tests:

	Fine aggregate	Coarse aggregate
Fineness modulus	2.30	—
Specific gravity (Bulk SSD)	4.95	4.61
Absorption (percent)	0.05	0.08
Dry rodded weight	—	165 lb per cu ft
Maximum size	—	1 in.

Employing the sequence outlined in Section 5 of this recommended practice, the quantities of ingredients per cubic yard of concrete are calculated as follows:

A4.3.1 *Step 1.* As indicated above, the desired slump is 2 to 3 in.

A4.3.2 *Step 2.* The available aggregate sources have been indicated as suitable, and the coarse aggregate will be a well-graded and well-shaped crushed ilmenite with a maximum size of 1 in.

A4.3.3 *Step 3.* By interpolation in Table 5.3.3, non-air-entrained concrete with a 2 to 3 in. slump and a 1 in. maximum size aggregate requires a water content of approximately 310 lb per cu yd. The estimated entrapped air is 1.5 percent. (Non-air-entrained concrete will be used because (1) the concrete is not exposed to severe weather, and (2) a high air content could reduce the dry unit weight of the concrete.)

Note: Table 5.3.3 values for water requirement are based on the use of well-shaped crushed coarse aggregates. Void content of compacted dry fine or coarse aggregate can be used as an indicator of angularity. Void contents of compacted 1 in. coarse aggregate of significantly more than 40 percent indicate angular material which will probably require more water than that listed in Table 5.3.3. Conversely rounded aggregates with voids below 35 percent will probably need less water.

A4.3.4 *Step 4.* From Table 5.3.4(a) the water-cement ratio needed to produce a strength of 4500 psi in non-air-entrained concrete is found to be approximately 0.52.

A4.3.5 *Step 5.* From the information derived in Steps 3 and 4, the required cement content is calculated to be 310/0.52 = 596 lb per cu yd.

A4.3.6 *Step 6.* The quantity of coarse aggregate is estimated by extrapolation from Table 5.3.6. For a fine aggregate having a fineness modulus of 2.30 and a 1 in. maximum size aggregate, the table indicates that 0.72 cu ft of coarse aggregate, on a dry-rodded basis, may be used in each cubic foot of concrete. For a cubic yard, therefore, the coarse aggregate will be 27 × 0.72 = 19.44 cu ft. Since the dry-rodded unit weight of the coarse aggregate is 165 lb per cu ft, the dry weight of coarse aggregate to be used in a cubic yard of concrete would be 19.44 × 165 = 3208 lb. The angularity of the coarse aggregate is compensated for in the ACI proportioning method through the use of the dry-rodded unit weight; however, the use of an extremely angular fine aggregate may require a higher proportion of fine aggregate, an increased cement content, or the use of air-entrainment to produce the required workability.

A4.3.7 *Step 7.* For heavyweight concrete, it is recommended that the required fine aggregate be determined on the absolute volume basis. With the quantities of cement, water, air and coarse aggregate established, the sand content can be calculated as follows:

Volume of water	=	$\dfrac{310}{62.4}$	= 4.97 cu ft
Volume of air	=	0.015×27	= 0.40 cu ft
Solid volume of cement	=	$\dfrac{596}{3.15 \times 62.4}$	= 3.03 cu ft
Solid volume of coarse aggregate	=	$\dfrac{3208}{4.61 \times 62.4}$	= 11.15 cu ft
Total volume of all ingredients except sand			= 19.55 cu ft
Solid volume of sand	=	$27 - 19.55$	= 7.45 cu ft
Required weight of sand		$= 7.45 \times 4.95 \times 62.4$	= 2301 lb

A4.3.8 *Step 8.* Tests indicate total moisture of 0.15 percent in the fine aggregate and 0.10 percent in the coarse aggregate; therefore, the adjusted aggregate weights become:

Fine aggregate (wet)	$= 1.0015 \times 2301 = 2304$ lb
Coarse aggregate (wet)	$= 1.0010 \times 3208 = 3211$ lb

Absorbed water does not become part of the mixing water and must be excluded from the adjustment in added water. Thus surface water contributed by the fine aggregate amounts to $0.15 - 0.05 = 0.10$ percent; by the coarse aggregate $0.10 - 0.08 = 0.02$ percent. The estimated requirement for added water, therefore becomes:

$$310 - 2301 (0.001) - 3208 (0.0002) = 307 \text{ lb}$$

A4.3.9 *Step 9.* The resulting estimated proportions by weight of the heavyweight concrete becomes:

Cement	$=\ \ 596$ lb
Fine aggregate (wet)	$= 2304$ lb
Coarse aggregate (wet)	$= 3211$ lb
Water	$=\ \ 307$ lb
Estimated unit wt (fresh)	$= 6418/27 = 237.7$ lb per cu ft

A4.4—The above heavyweight concrete proportioned mixture was actually used for approximately 5060 cu yd. Field adjustments resulted in the following actual batch weights:

Cement	590 lb
Fine aggregate	2310 lb
Coarse aggregate	3220 lb
Water	285 lb (plus a water-reducing agent)

The actual field test results indicated the concrete possessed the following properties:

Unit weight (fresh)	235.7 lb per cu ft
Air content	2.8 percent
Slump	2½ in.
Strength	5000 psi at 28 days

Metric Units and Conversions

BASIC SI UNITS

Length	metre	m	
Mass	kilogram	kg	
	gram	g	(1000 g = 1 kg)
	tonne	t	(1 t = 1000 kg)
Volume	litre	L	(1000 L = 1 m^3)
Force	Newton	N	(9.807 N = 1 kg force)
Pressure	Pascal	Pa	(1 Pa = 1 N/m^2)
Area	hectare	ha	(1 ha = 10 000 m^2)
Time	second	s	

Multiplication Factor	Prefix	Symbol
1 000 000 000 = 10^9	giga	G
1 000 000 = 10^6	mega	M
1 000 = 10^3	kilo	k
0.01 = 10^{-2}	centi	c
0.001 = 10^{-3}	milli	m
0.000 001 = 10^{-6}	micro	μ
0.000 000 001 = 10^{-9}	nano	n
0.000 000 000 001 = 10^{-12}	pico	p

CONVERSION FACTORS (FOR SIGNIFICANT FIGURES)

Length	1 ft = 0.3048 m
	1 in. = 2.540 cm
	1 mi = 1.609 km
Area	1 ft^2 = 0.09290 m^2
	1 in^2 = 6.452 cm^2
	1 acre = 0.4047 ha

Volume	1 gallon (U.S.) = 3.785 L
	1 gallon (Can.) = 4.546 L
	1 in^3 = 16.39 cm^3
	1 ft^3 = 0.02832 m^3
	1 yd^3 = 0.7646 m^3
Mass	1 lb = 0.4536 kg
	1 ton = 0.9072 t
Force	1 lb = 4.448 N
Pressure	1 lb/in^2 = 6.895 kPa
	1 lb/ft^2 = 47.88 Pa
Viscosity	1 poise = 0.1 Pa·s
	1 stoke = 1 cm^2/s
Density	1 lb/ft^3 = 16.02 kg/m^3
Concentration	1 lb/yd^3 = 0.5933 kg/m^3

Approximate Relationships

These conversion factors are suitable for many calculations in soils and materials.

62.4 lb/ft^3 = 1000 kg/m^3 = 1 g/cm^3 (density of water)
1 kg = 2.2 lb
1 m = 3.3 ft
1 m^3 = 1.3 yd^3
1 kg force = 9.8 N
1 km = 0.6 mi
100 kPa = 1 ton/ft^2 (1.04) = 1 kg/cm^2 (1.02)
$\qquad$ = 15 lb/in^2 (14.5 psi) = 1 atmosphere

Index

Y

Z